THE LOES AND WILFORD
POOR LAW INCORPORATION
1765–1826

THE LOES AND WILFORD
POOR LAW INCORPORATION
1765–1826

"A Prison with a Milder Name"

Edited by
JOHN SHAW

General Editor
HARVEY OSBORNE

The Boydell Press

Suffolk Records Society
VOLUME LXII

A Suffolk Records Society publication
First published 2019
The Boydell Press, Woodbridge

ISBN 978-1-78327-382-9

Issued to subscribing members for the year 2018–2019

The Boydell Press is an imprint of Boydell & Brewer Ltd
PO Box 9, Woodbridge, Suffolk IP12 3DF, UK
and of Boydell & Brewer Inc.
668 Mt Hope Avenue, Rochester, NY 14620–2731, USA
website: www.boydellandbrewer.com

The publisher has no responsibility for the continued existence or accuracy of
URLs for external or third-party internet websites referred to in this book, and
does not guarantee that any content on such websites is, or will remain, accurate
or appropriate

A catalogue record for this book is available
from the British Library

This publication is printed on acid-free paper

Printed and bound in Great Britain by
TJ International Ltd, Padstow, Cornwall

CONTENTS

ILLUSTRATIONS, MAPS AND TABLES

PREFACE AND ACKNOWLEDGEMENTS

Almost a century has now elapsed since Sidney and Beatrice Webb's *Statutory Authorities for Special Purposes* offered the first detailed consideration of 'The Incorporated Guardians of the Poor'.[1] The Webbs noted that the incorporations, established between 1696 and 1834 and numbering in all about 125, were created not by general statute but by individual Acts of Parliament, with many of the legal powers formerly vested in individual parishes being transferred to them.[2] Edward Twisleton, an assistant Poor Law commissioner, defined the incorporations' legal status as follows:

> A parish or incorporation of parishes under a Local Act is, in reference to the Poor Laws, a parish or incorporation in which the general law of the land relating to the relief of the poor has been modified by a special Act of Parliament, but in which the general law prevails otherwise than as it is modified by such Act.[3]

The incorporations were given a significant role in the Webbs' chronological framework of Poor Law history:

> It was from these ... authorities that was derived the machinery of administration by committees, for unions of parishes, through salaried officials, with the workhouse in the background, out of which was constructed the Poor Law reform of 1834.[4]

Despite the incorporations' importance, the Webbs acknowledged that they had 'been almost ignored by historians', pledging to return to these 'interesting experiments' in a forthcoming volume on the Poor Laws.[5]

It was these comments by the Webbs that served to pique my interest in the East Anglian incorporations. Nationally, Norfolk and Suffolk had the greatest number of rural incorporations. Norfolk contained six, but it was Suffolk's nine incorporations, covering some 253 parishes, which provided the greatest concentration.[6] Twisleton commented: 'the county of Suffolk presented the singular spectacle of a considerable number of its hundreds being organised for the relief of the poor in a different manner from all other counties in the kingdom'.[7] We are fortunate in that the Ipswich and Lowestoft branches of the Suffolk Record Office contain extensive

---

1   S. and B. Webb, *Statutory Authorities for Special Purposes* (London, 1922). The Incorporated Guardians of the Poor are considered in Chapter 2, pp. 107–51.
2   Webbs, *Statutory Authorities*, p. 107.
3   E. Twisleton, *Report on Local Acts*, Ninth Annual Report of the Poor Law Commissioners (London, 1843), p. 90.
4   Webbs, *Statutory Authorities*, pp. 109, 142.
5   Webbs, *Statutory Authorities*, pp. 108–9. The Webbs did, indeed, revisit the incorporations as part of their three-volume history of the Poor Laws, published between 1927 and 1929, though this offered few fresh insights, as it comprises no more than a *verbatim* copy of the earlier chapter. S. and B. Webb, *English Poor Law History: Part 1 The Old Poor Law* (London, 1927), pp. 101–48.
6   A tenth incorporation, Hartismere, Hoxne and Thredling, obtained Royal Assent, but then failed to raise sufficient capital.
7   Twisleton, *Local Acts*, p. 106.

collections for seven of the Suffolk incorporations. It was these records that formed the core of my doctoral thesis, completed during the 1980s, on the Incorporated Hundreds of East Anglia.[8]

During research into the incorporations, Loes and Wilford's unique position became clear. First, it was one of the earliest to be established in the county (1765) and the only incorporation to be disincorporated (1826). Second, it possessed by far the most comprehensive range of formal organisational documents of any incorporation, not least a complete run of quarterly and weekly minute books. Third, it offered the richest seam of informal miscellaneous supporting documents of any of the incorporations. These documents provide comprehensive background information concerning the establishment and operation of the incorporation, considerable detail of the political machinations that underlay the enacting of the amending Act of 1810 and much evidence concerning the disincorporation process of 1825–26. With their breadth of coverage the documents are a treasure-trove for the social and economic historian of the eighteenth and early nineteenth centuries. For these reasons Loes and Wilford was the obvious choice when deciding which of the incorporations should be the focus of an attempt to transcribe their extant materials. But there is also a fourth reason for selecting Loes and Wilford: it was the incorporation most derided by the Webbs. For the Suffolk incorporations in general, the Webbs opined that there was 'something pathetic in the dismal uniformity' of their operation, leading to their 'uniform failure'. Much of the evidence deployed by the Webbs to support their argument was selected from Loes and Wilford's records. It is hoped, therefore, that the breadth of documents found within this volume will provide a more generous interpretation of Loes and Wilford's operation, illustrating the promoters' philanthropic designs, and so offering a complementary view to the Webbs' earlier work.[9]

In selecting, editing and transcribing the documents for this volume, I have incurred a number of debts. I would like to thank particularly Dr Harvey Osborne, my general editor. Any remaining mistakes are mine. I would also like to thank Mike Durrant for producing the maps and the staff of the Ipswich branch of the Suffolk Record Office for their help and for permission to publish the documents in their custody.

The Suffolk Records Society is grateful to an anonymous donor and to Melton Parish Council for donations towards the cost of printing this volume.

John Shaw
Harwich, December 2018

I dedicate this volume to my wife, Margaret
and our children, Eleanor and Edward.

---

8   J. Shaw, 'The Development of the Local Poor Law Acts 1696–1833, with particular reference to the Incorporated Hundreds of East Anglia', unpublished PhD thesis, University of East Anglia, 1989.
9   Webbs, *Statutory Authorities*, pp. 133–4, 136, 139; Webbs, *Old Poor Law*, pp. 141, 143.

ABBREVIATIONS

BLPES	British Library for Political and Economic Science.
HCPP	House of Commons Parliamentary Papers
HLPP	House of Lords Parliamentary Papers
PSIA(H)	*Proceedings of the Suffolk Institute of Archaeology (and History)*
QMB	Quarterly Minute Book
Shaw, *Thesis*	John Shaw, 'The Development of the Local Poor Law Acts 1696–1833, with particular reference to the Incorporated Hundreds of East Anglia', unpublished PhD, University of East Anglia, 1989
SROI	Suffolk Record Office, Ipswich branch
WMB	Weekly Minute Book

INTRODUCTION

By the late 1770s, Suffolk was unique in the range of approaches it offered to address poverty. By that date considerably less than half the county's parishes remained under sole control of the Elizabethan poor laws (see map 1). The transformation had begun almost a century earlier when in 1702 Sudbury obtained partial autonomy through a local act.[1] The same year witnessed the first of Ipswich's unsuccessful attempts to gain a local act.[2] Bury St Edmunds secured Suffolk's second local act in 1748.[3] The watershed came in 1756, when the twenty-eight parishes of the hundreds of Carlford and Colneis created the first rural incorporation in England.[4] Wishing to emulate their success, a further 193 parishes combined in the years 1764–65 to form the incorporations of Blything, Bosmere and Claydon, Samford, Mutford and Lothingland, Wangford, and Loes and Wilford.[5] A further thirty-two parishes followed in 1778–79, creating the incorporations of Stow and Cosford.[6] The sixty-four parishes of Hartismere, Hoxne and Thredling Hundreds also gained Royal Assent in 1779, but failed to raise sufficient capital to put the Act into effect.[7] These ten incorporations comprised 317 parishes, some 61 per cent of the county's total (see map 2). Later, following the Gilbert Act of 1782, Framlingham and Woodbridge adopted its provisions and became Gilbert Unions. In 1822 Ipswich's twelve parishes revisited the possibility of a union but this also failed to come to fruition.[8] This distinctive Poor Law provision meant that for Suffolk 'it was the incorporation movement of the eighteenth century and not the national reform in the Poor Law Amendment Act of 1834 that made a decisive break with the Elizabethan basis of the Old Poor Law'.[9]

This variation was further emphasised by the geographical distribution of the incorporations, located primarily in the eastern half of the county. This marked difference in provision did not escape contemporaries: George Crabbe's verses contrast those parishes retaining the overseer and poor house, evocatively described in *The Village*, with the superior but impersonal provision of the incorporations' houses of industry, such as that found at Melton, as he described in *The Borough*:[10]

---

[1] Act of Parliament, 1 Anne, Session 1 c. 34.

[2] G. Clarke, *The History and Description of Ipswich* (London, 1830), p. 7.

[3] 21 Geo. 2 c. 21.

[4] 29 Geo. 2 c. 29.

[5] 4 Geo. 3 c. 56 (Blything), 4 Geo. 3 c. 57 (Bosmere and Claydon), 4 Geo. 3 c. 59 (Samford), 4 Geo. 3 c. 89 (Mutford and Lothingland), 4 Geo. 3 c. 91 (Wangford) and 5 Geo. 3 c. 97 (Loes and Wilford).

[6] 18 Geo. 3 c. 35 (Stow) and 19 Geo. 3 c. 30 (Cosford).

[7] 19 Geo. 3 c. 19 (Hartismere, Hoxne and Thredling).

[8] *Suffolk Chronicle*, 8 July 1822, 10 August 1822, 7 September 1822, 5 October 1822 and 6 December 1822.

[9] A. Digby, *Pauper Palaces* (London, 1978), p. 2. Norfolk was the second most densely incorporated county with 184 parishes in five incorporations comprising 26 per cent of the total. Buxton became a Gilbert's Union in 1806. Kings Lynn (1700) and Norwich (1712) were urban incorporations.

[10] George Crabbe was born in 1754 in Aldeburgh where his father served as parish overseer during his childhood. In 1775 he returned to Aldeburgh after training as an apothecary, and he would have seen the parish poor house first hand. During his training at Woodbridge from 1771 to 1775, Crabbe would

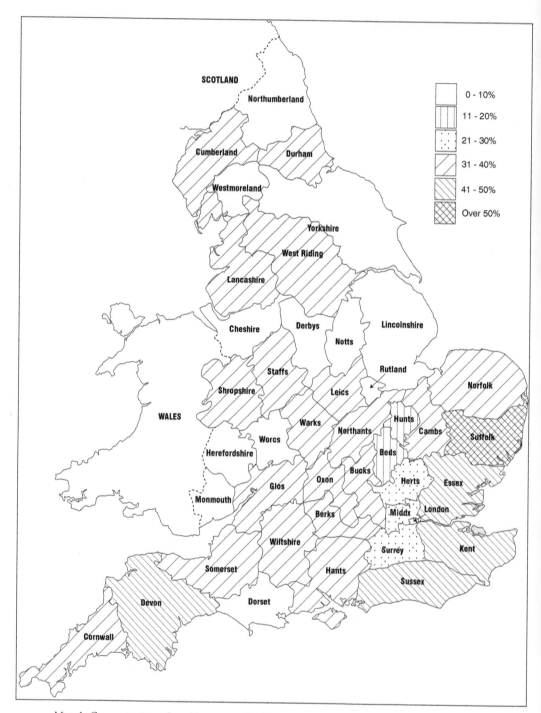

Map 1. Concentration of workhouses in England and Wales by county, 1777

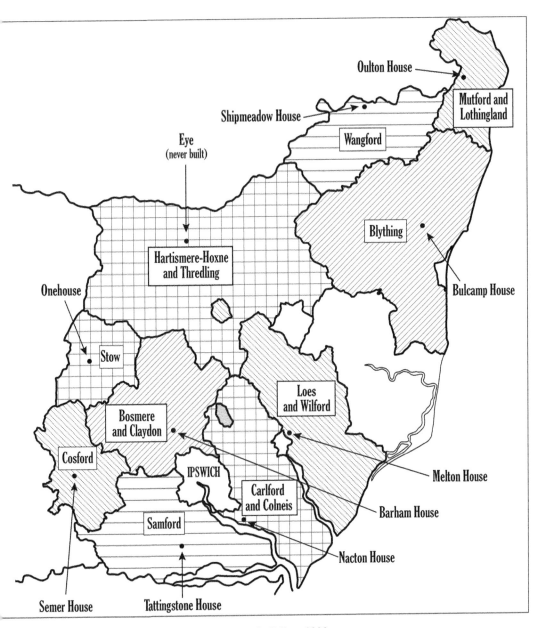

Map 2. The incorporated hundreds of East Suffolk in 1800

The Village

> Theirs is yon House that holds the parish poor,
> Whose walls of mud scarce bear the broken door;
> There, where the putrid vapour, flagging, play,
> And the dull wheel hums doleful through the day; –
> There children dwell who know no parents' care;
> Parents, who know no children's love, dwell there!
> Heart-broken matrons on their joyless bed,
> Forsaken wives, and mothers never wed;
> Dejected widows with unheeded tears,
> And crippled age with more than childhood fears;
> The lame, the blind, and, far the happiest they!
> The moping idiot, and the madman gay.[11]

The Borough

> Your plan I love not; – with a number you
> Have placed your poor, your pitiable few:
> There, in one house, throughout their lives to be,
> The pauper palace which they hate to see:
> That giant building, that high bounding wall,
> Those bare-worn walks, that lofty thund'ring hall,
> That large loud clock, which tolls each dreaded hour,
> Those gates and locks, and all those signs of power;
> It is a prison, with a milder name,
> Which few inhabit without dread or shame.
>
> Be it agreed – the poor who hither come
> Partake of plenty, seldom found at home;
> That airy rooms and decent beds are meant
> To give the poor by day, by night, content ...
> They have no evil in the place to state,
> And dare not say it is the house they hate ...
> I own it grieves me to behold them sent
> From their own homes; 'tis pain, 'tis punishment,
> To leave each scene familiar, every face,
> For a new people and a stranger race ...[12]

Eighteenth-century Poor Law history

Old Poor Law legislation was both voluminous and complex. Some 264 general acts were enacted between 1601 and 1850. What follows is a summary of the legal structure prior to the implementation of the Poor Law Amendment Act of 1834.[13]

---

have heard about the house of industry at Melton. Then, through his relationship with the Elmy family of Beccles, he would no doubt have viewed Wangford's house at Shipmeadow and Blything's house at Bulcamp. His experiences of Aldeburgh's poor house are reflected in *The Village* while his verses in *The Borough* are an amalgam of the various houses of industry that he had observed.

[11] George Crabbe, *The Village* (1783). *The Life and Poetical Works of the Rev. George Crabbe by his Son* (London, 1866), p. 117, lines 228–39.

[12] George Crabbe, *The Borough* (1810), *ibid.*, pp. 233–4, Letter XVIII, The Poor and their Dwellings, lines 109–22, 133–4 and 201–4.

[13] S. King, *Poverty and Welfare in England 1700–1850* (Manchester, 2000), p. 18. The 1834 Act grouped the nation's parishes into unions managed by elected guardians, authorised the building of

At the heart of the Old Poor Law were the Elizabethan statutes of 1597–98 and 1601, the latter referred to as the 43 Eliz. These statutes made the parish the unit for poor relief: out-door relief was to be provided for the impotent poor (the old, the sick and children), work provided for the able-bodied, and punishment administered to those able but unwilling to work. The system was to be supervised by an unpaid, annually elected overseer who was to collect the parish poor rate, levied on property, and distribute it as necessary. Though the 43 Eliz. remained in force for over two hundred years, 'it did so only in the sense in which the first cluster of polyps form the foundation of a coral reef', with subsequent acts tending to supplement rather than replace existing legislation.[14]

The parochialism embedded in this system was strengthened by the Settlement Act of 1662. Labourers moving into a parish to occupy a tenement under the yearly value of £10 could be removed within forty days if the overseer believed they might become chargeable to the parish. After 1697, parishes provided settlement certificates for those inhabitants who wished to move elsewhere, accepting financial responsibility should they become chargeable.

Convinced of the unsuitability of the single parish for poor law administration, the series of local acts, of which the Suffolk incorporations were a part, enabled parishes to offer a variation from the national model.[15] At their most complex, they created a comprehensive welfare system for the parishes involved, and their history can be traced back to the Bristol Corporation of 1696.[16] From the early 1700s schemes for the union of parishes increased in popularity. The 1750s was to be the decisive decade. In 1753, Sir Richard Lloyd, Member of Parliament for Maldon in Essex, submitted a bill to the Commons for the establishment of a 'house of industry' in every rural hundred, with oversight vested in a committee of landowners who would make bye-laws and appoint salaried officers. The bill failed to pass into law.[17]

Suffolk initiatives

In December 1755, Admiral Edward Vernon, Member of Parliament for Ipswich, submitted a petition to the Commons for the incorporation of the parishes in the hundreds of Carlford and Colneis.[18] Vernon was assisted by Sir Richard Lloyd in framing the petition and drafting the bill.[19] The petition regretted 'the great increase of the Poor within the ... hundreds, and the present method of maintaining such poor, and of the want of power to compel those to work who are able, and also of the want of some better method of instructing the children of the poor, enduring them to labour'.[20] It was referred to a Commons' committee in February 1756, where Mileson Edgar, a future director of Nacton House, stated that the poor 'hath

---

a workhouse and prohibited out-door relief to able-bodied paupers.

14 J. Poynter, *Society and Pauperism* (London, 1968), p. 1.
15 Between 1696 (Bristol) and 1833 (Forehoe Amending Act) some 145 initial and 141 amending local acts obtained Royal Assent. Shaw, *Thesis*, pp. 9–10; S. Thompson, 'Population Growth and Corporations of the Poor', pp. 199–200, in C. Briggs (ed.), *Population, Welfare and Economic Change in Britain, 1290–1834* (Woodbridge, 2014).
16 It is important to note that these Acts created *additional* powers and methods rather than *replacing* the existing framework.
17 F. M. Eden, *The State of the Poor* (London, 1797), Volume 1, pp. 318–20.
18 Edward Vernon was M.P. for Ipswich from 1741 until his death in October 1757.
19 Sir Richard Lloyd and Edward Vernon had clashed over the Ipswich seat in 1754. Although Lloyd had been recorder of Ipswich since 1739, he envisaged strong competition from Vernon and so declined the poll in April 1754. Lloyd became member for Totnes in December 1754.
20 HCPP, *Common's Journal*, Volume 27, p. 329, 8 December 1755.

of late years greatly increased; and that the rates are some hundreds of pounds more than formerly', caused by 'the present method of allowing a separate weekly allowance to each poor person; and that if they were brought together, they might be maintained much better and cheaper'.[21] The petition was unopposed, and the bill obtained Royal Assent in April 1756, with the inaugural directors' meeting held in June 1756.[22] The house of industry, located at Nacton, opened its doors in March 1758.[23]

Little interest was expressed in the venture until the early 1760s, when a series of eulogies appeared in the *Gentleman's Magazine*. These were written by the Revd Richard Canning, a Nacton director, according to whom Nacton House had saved local ratepayers £2,093 by 1762.[24] The final letter justified the establishment of the Incorporation:

> The office of overseer is both troublesome and expensive ... and sometimes it falls upon such persons as are not fit to govern anything. As to parish meetings, if the parishioners are numerous they are very mobbish assemblies. At these every contributor to the rate claims an equal importance with the rest; and the vulgar people ... by their rude and abusive language, drive away the better and wiser sort of men. To take the management of the poor out of such hands, and to put them under the government of more discrete and reputable persons, would be a probable means of having them better taken care of.[25]

Nacton's success acted as an impetus to the neighbouring gentry. They believed that the house of industry 'afforded a more comfortable subsistence to the poor, than they would have in their own parishes', whilst 'sufficiently demonstrating the advantage of it to the rich'.[26] They were aware, however, of the labourers' aversion to the institution. In a letter to Canning, Stephen White, a future director of Loes and Wilford, admitted that his attempts to reassure the labourers within his own parish had failed abysmally. He sought Canning's assistance in publishing an article to refute the rumours circulating about Nacton: 'I have been told ... that the poor are imprisoned, and suffocated for want of air ... that all your savings arise from the poor people starving themselves to death rather than go into this sad house ...'.[27]

Five petitions were submitted to the Commons between December 1763 and January 1764. Henry Negus's evidence to the committee reviewing the bills was typical when he stated that 'the poor are of late years considerably increased, and the rates higher than formerly'.[28] More specific was the evidence offered by John Woods, of Blything, and Lott Knight, of Bosmere and Claydon: the former stated that the rates 'had increased about one half in the last ten years', the latter that supporting the poor 'in the last eight years is in many places double to what it was in the eight preceding years'.[29] William Truelove, Carlford and Colneis's treasurer, supported each petition, and 'confirmed the evidence ... in relation to the good

21 HCPP, *Common's Journal*, Volume 27, p. 420, 15 February 1756.
22 HCPP, *Common's Journal*, Volume 27, p. 584, 19 April 1756. See HCPP, *Common's Journal*, Volume 27, p. 531 (17 March 1756), p. 537 (18 March 1756), p. 557 (1 April 1756), p. 565 (5 April 1756) and p. 578 (12 April 1756) for the bill's passage through the Commons.
23 Carlford and Colneis Minute Book, 20, 21, 22 and 23 March 1758. SROI ADA10/A/B/1.
24 BLPES, *Webbs' Collection*, Volume 231.
25 BLPES, *Webbs' Collection*, Volume 231.
26 *East Anglian Magazine*, Volume 15 (1955–56), pp. 597–8.
27 *East Anglian Magazine*, Volume 15 (1955–56), pp. 597–8.
28 HCPP, *Common's Journal*, Volume 29, pp. 754 (8 December 1763), p. 767 (14 December 1763).
29 HCPP, *Common's Journal*, Volume 29, pp. 770–1 (31 January 1764).

effects which have arisen from incorporating these two hundreds'.[30] The bills passed through both Houses unopposed during April 1764.

No single factor has been identified for the concentration of incorporations in eastern Suffolk. Anne Digby has argued that there was a strong economic incentive in these more densely populated hundreds due to the pressure the poor rate exerted on the moderately resourced owners and occupiers. She has also identified the active role played by the resident gentry and clergy in the ventures.[31] The main driving force for Suffolk appears to have been the central role played by Admiral Vernon, with proselytisation occurring through effective example.[32] Vernon was renowned for his single-mindedness. As an M.P. he would have been aware of the proposals of Lloyd, who later assisted with the drafting of the Carlford and Colneis bill. There would have been significant contact between Nacton's directors and the neighbouring gentry through administrative and social functions. It was this social contact, as well as the printed eulogies, that were instrumental in spreading this innovative approach.[33]

Local opposition to the incorporations first appeared in December 1764, when the following letter was reproduced in the *Ipswich Journal*:

> Gentlemen this is to quaint you all conserning the billing of this war hous think to starve the poore theare Stephen Wite Stratford Lews of Barfild Wite of Tatason Loyd Hintlesham but let them tak care of thon selves for farst that is hap on shall theare brans be blown out and that soon as sure as death and faile not and the hous shall not be bilt a toyle for theare shall be 3000 men planted soon as will di att it and pull Wites hous downe.[34]

Suffolk remained peaceful until August 1765. Loes and Wilford's inaugural meeting in July 1765 occurred without incident, but their second meeting, held at the White Hart inn, Wickham Market, on 1 August was far more eventful. The directors had just completed assigning quarterly assessments to the parishes when an armed crowd of some 500 encircled the inn. They forced entry into the meeting, demanded the directors cease their business and turned them out onto the green. Here they were forced to sign a declaration stating that they would not pursue their plans for a house 'and they were informed of the dire consequences that would attend such an action'.[35] Four days later, further disturbances erupted at Nacton and Bulcamp.[36] About 200 people assembled on Nacton Heath. Facing them were magistrates supported by soldiers from the Ipswich garrison. The magistrates warned them of 'the danger and rashness' of their actions and 'the fatal consequences that must attend it'. The Riot Act was read, and the dragoons were deployed. This stirred

---

30 HCPP, *Common's Journal*, Volume 29, pp. 770–1 (31 January 1764).

31 Digby, *Pauper Palaces*, p. 32.

32 This was true also for the expansion of urban incorporations in the early 1700s, which emulated John Cary's lead in establishing the Bristol Corporation, and for the Shropshire incorporations following the example of Isaac Wood at Shrewsbury in 1783.

33 Shaw, *Thesis*, pp. 61–3.

34 *Ipswich Journal*, 22 December 1764.

35 *Ipswich Journal*, 2 August 1765; P. Muskett, *Riotous Assemblies: Popular Disturbances in East Anglia, 1740–1822* (Ely, 1984), p. 14. Two of the Incorporation's documents make reference to the prosecution of one of the rioters' ringleaders, James Woolnough. There are the payment of Jerome Bright's expenses so he could attend Woolnough's trial as a witness (Document 31) and Richard Wood's expenses associated with serving three subpoena on the witnesses, Bright, Rivett and Jeaffreson, as well as his costs for attending the hearing (Document 32).

36 *Ipswich Journal*, 10 August 1765.

the crowd into action and 'they fell upon both horses and men with such arms as they had, peasemakers, tredge stakes, cudgels ... a skirmish ensued, and in five minutes time the affair was over'.[37] Simultaneously, a second group descended on the partially built and unprotected house at Bulcamp. The *Ipswich Journal* describes the crowd's actions: 'a few of them mounted the works and climbed to the top of the poles of the scaffold, waved their hats and huzz'd. In about half an hour there was a much greater number of people, and by ... night the whole building was levelled to the ground ... the damage is computed at £2,000.'[38] The authorities feared more violence and four companies of the 43rd Regiment of Foot were deployed, but this 'picturesque little rebellion' had run its course.[39]

To the rioters it appeared that the gentry were jettisoning their traditional social responsibilities. The gentry, aware of the labourers' belief that the houses were little more than prisons, took steps to dispel their fears. Articles were published in the *Ipswich Journal* to disprove the 'false and unaccountable tales'.[40] While the comfort of the houses described in the articles reveals the directors' philanthropic design, the descriptions also illustrate why the labourers felt that their traditional social rights were being curtailed. The directors couched such loss of liberty in flowing rhetoric: the paupers exchanged their pitiable rags for a well-made uniform, and the eleven-and-a-half hour day was interrupted by regular breaks with wholesome meals. Confinement to the house was dismissed with incredulity: the inmates were, with prior consent, allowed visitors, and they could walk out freely during their leisure time. The directors could not understand why 'some of them do not like milk-broth, and pease-broth but would rather choose meat'. Finally, the rumours that 'persons were whip'd immoderately ... and some actually whip'd to death' were dismissed as groundless. Such punishments as did exist, for the 'obstinate and stubborn', were but of 'the mildest kind'. Disquiet smouldered on into 1766, but there were to be no equivalent disturbances until January 1796.[41]

Historiography

Despite their importance, the Suffolk incorporations have received scant attention. Sidney and Beatrice Webb offered some treatment in the 1920s, with the next significant reference appearing half a century later in Anne Digby's study of the Norfolk poor laws.[42] Thereafter the Suffolk incorporations have only obtained a passing comment in general surveys, with most texts failing even to mention their existence.[43]

---

37 *Ipswich Journal*, 10 August 1765.

38 *Ipswich Journal*, 10 August 1765.

39 P. Muskett, 'A Picturesque Little Rebellion? The Suffolk Workhouses in 1765', *Bulletin for the Society for the Study of Labour History* (1980), pp. 28–30. *Ipswich Journal*, 17 August 1765.

40 *Ipswich Journal*, 31 August 1765, 7 September 1765 and 14 September 1765.

41 Muskett, *Riotous Assemblies*, p. 37. *Ipswich Journal*, 8 February 1766.

42 Webbs, *Old Poor Law*, pp. 125–48. Digby, *Pauper Palaces*, pp. 34–52. There was a brief description provided by Dorothy Marshall in 1926 in *The English Poor in the Eighteenth Century* (London, 1969 reprint), pp. 155–9.

43 For example, King, *Poverty and Welfare*, p. 160, refers to the incorporations in just a few sentences in his review of welfare provision in the south and east. There are four articles and one doctoral thesis focussing on the Suffolk incorporations: H. Fearn, 'The Apprenticing of Pauper Children in the Incorporated Hundreds of Suffolk', *PSIA*, 26 (1953), pp. 85–97; H. Fearn, 'The Financing of the Poor Law Incorporations for the Hundreds of Colneis and Carlford in the County of Suffolk, 1758–1820', *PSIA*, 27 Part 2 (1956), pp. 96–111; M. Lloyd Prichard, 'Early days of the Wangford

The Webbs' critique, which held sway for most of the twentieth century, offered a highly subjective interpretation. The Suffolk incorporations appear to have had their own niche within the Webbs' history of the Poor Laws: 'there is something pathetic in their dismal uniformity', they opined. Given the Webbs' involvement with the Poor Law Royal Commission of 1905–09 their views need to be treated with caution.[44] Their treatment of the Loes and Wilford Incorporation is particularly scathing. In order to support their contention that only 'dissolute and worthless persons' resided in Melton House they quoted selectively from the Incorporation's documents.[45] The Webbs' legacy has had a negative impact on Old Poor Law research, and it is only relatively recently that the administration has been given a more balanced and dispassionate treatment.[46]

The current view is that the Old Poor Law provided a framework which offered relatively responsive relief, supplying comprehensive benefits to individuals.[47] This approach is reflected in the Incorporations' aspirations 'to balance the interests of the poor in a humane system of relief with those of the rate payers in an economical administration', as outlined in Loes and Wilford's preamble:

> Whereas the Poor in the Hundreds of Loes and Wilford, in the County of Suffolk, are very numerous, and are maintained and supported at a great expence by their respective parishes: and whereas the granting of proper powers for the better government and regulation of the poor in the said Hundreds, and providing a place for their general reception, will tend to the more effectual relief and assistance of such as by age, infirmities, or diseases are rendered incapable of supporting themselves by their labour, to the better employment of the able and industrious, to the correction and punishment of the profligate and idle, and to the education of poor children in religion and industry; and thereby the poor, instead of being wholly supported by the publick, may contribute to the support, assistance and relief mutually of each other, and be of some advantage to the community to which they have hitherto been only a heavy and grievous burthen.[48]

Digby has identified the material comfort found within the houses.[49] Their success led not only to glowing accounts by contemporaries, but also to interest from the Poor Law Commission in the early 1830s. Charles Mott, the Assistant Poor Law Commissioner despatched to East Anglia, advised the Poor Law Commission to convert the Suffolk incorporations into unions as swiftly as possible so that the benefits could 'be immediately shown as an example to the country at large.'[50]

Hundred workhouse', *PSIA*, 30 Part 2 (1965), pp. 175–82; J. Shaw, 'The Financing and Construction of the East Anglian Houses of Industry', *PSIAH*, 37 Part 4 (1992), pp. 351–65; Shaw, *Thesis*.

44 J. Kidd, 'Historians or polemicists? How the Webbs wrote their History of the English Poor Laws', *Economic History Review*, 40 (1987), pp. 401–2. The Webbs were the principal authors of the 1909 *Poor Law Minority Report*.

45 Webbs, *Old Poor Law*, p. 144.

46 A. Tomkins, *The Experience of Urban Poverty: Parish, Charity and Credit* (Manchester, 2006), pp. 12–13.

47 King, *Poverty and Welfare*, p. 10; Tomkins, *Experience*, p. 12.

48 Digby, *Pauper Palaces*, p. 36. 5 Geo 3 c. 91. Similar preambles may be found in all the Suffolk local acts.

49 Digby, *Pauper Palaces*, p. 45.

50 Digby, *Pauper Palaces*, p. 52; T. Ruggles, *The History of the Poor* (2 volumes, London, 1793–94), Volume 2, pp. 286–8; A. Young, *General View of the Agriculture of Suffolk* (London, 1804), pp. 272–3.

Documents of the Loes and Wilford Incorporation

The Incorporation's extant documents are referenced as ADA11 and are located at the Ipswich branch of the Suffolk Record Office (SROI). The most important documents can be divided into the following categories:

Reference Number	Details
ADA11/A/A/1/1–33	Bundles of loose papers (letters, memorandum, draft bills, notes of meetings etc.) covering a wide range of topics such as the passage of the 1765 and 1791 Acts as well as papers concerning debates over the 1810 and 1826 Acts; title deeds; account books of Wood and Son; papers relating to the trustees overseeing the disincorporation; resolutions passed at meetings
ADA11/A/B/1/1–7	Complete run of Quarterly Minute Books, 1765–1826
ADA11/A/B/2/1–5	Draft Quarterly Minute Books, 1765–95
ADA11/A/B/3/1–11	Complete run of Weekly Minute Books 1768–1826 and a list from 1795 stating allowances to large families
ADA11/A/C/1–4	Treasurer's Accounts 1781–1826; draft accounts; cash books 1797–1826; various extracts from the Treasurer's Accounts
ADA11/A/G/1–2	Various papers concerned with out-door relief
ADA11/A/K/1–2	Registers of securities and loan agreements
ADA11/A/L/1	Registers of apprentices
ADA11/A/Q/2/1–7	Bundles of papers covering title deeds to Melton House; agreements with the builders etc.
ADA11/C/B/1–5	Admission and discharge ledgers; day books; registers of baptisms and burials
ADA11/C/D/3	Bills and vouchers for repairs, food, clothing and medicines etc.

Space precludes a detailed survey of the Incorporation's history so the following identifies significant themes for the years covered by the individual Quarterly Minute Books (hereafter QMB).

The first Quarterly Minute Book, 1765–84

The first QMB covers the years 1765 to 1784.[51] Written in the clear hand of Richard Wood, the Incorporation's clerk, it measures 25cm by 39cm and contains 340 numbered pages with an index inserted in the front. The volume's final pages contain details of the Incorporation's investors for the years 1766 to 1790. The QMB is supported by four draft QMBs. The first comprises 32 loose pages covering 1 July 1765 to 3 August 1767; the second comprises 36 loose pages covering 1 February 1768 to 1 July 1769; the third, covering September 1769 to September 1775, has 90 loose pages; and the fourth, covering 26 December 1775 through to 28 March 1785, is a softback volume

---

[51] SROI ADA11/A/B/1/1.

measuring 21cm by 32cm.[52] There are three Weekly Minute Books (hereafter WMB) for these years. The first dates from 18 July 1768 to 20 June 1774.[53] This volume measures 25cm by 37cm and, like all the other WMBs, contains a number of inserts. The second measures 25cm by 37cm and covers 5 September 1774 to 19 June 1780, and the third, of a similar size, encompasses 26 September 1780 to 21 June 1790.[54]

Financial records exist for the final three years of this QMB in the first Treasurer's Account Book.[55] This volume measures 21cm by 32cm and runs from Michaelmas 1781 to Michaelmas 1791. It comprises a number of pre-printed double-pages listing parishes and their quarterly assessment, each set interspersed with eight blank pages for hand-written entries. Approximately half the volume has been used. Although subsequent account books are completed using standardised sub-headings, this volume's entries are not classified because they are made on the basis of the date of payment or receipt. Accurate operating figures are missing before Michaelmas 1781, though the QMB offers some financial detail from the Christmas Quarter 1768: outdoor relief; salaries for officers; medicines; and some payments for provisions and fuel. Such figures are incomplete as numerous payments are excluded.

Although the minutes of meetings held to oversee the bill's enactment are no longer extant, various papers allow for the process to be sketched out. The initial meeting, when the petition was drawn up, was in April 1764. Three further meetings were held at which the petition and bill were framed.[56] These were submitted to the Commons in January 1765, and referred to committee.[57] 'To prove the [petition's] allegations', Samuel Kilderbee and William Truelove stated that 'the poor within the several parishes … are greatly increased and maintained at a much greater expence than formerly'. The bill's first and second readings were in February 1765.[58] On 25 March the committee reported that it had found the allegations to be true and the bill, with some minor amendments, was engrossed.[59] The bill's third reading was in late March, passing through to a committee of the Lords in April 1765.[60] It gained Royal Assent on 10 May 1765.[61]

The Incorporation's inaugural meeting was held on 1 July 1765, at the White Hart, Wickham Market. Thirty-one guardians were present and Richard Savage-Nassau was elected chairman.[62] The directors proceeded to fulfil the requirements of the Act: twenty-four directors were elected to oversee the establishment of the Incorporation, John Revett was chosen as treasurer, and Richard Wood senior as clerk. Subsequent

---

52 SROI ADA11/A/B/2/1, ADA11/A/B/2/2, ADA11/A/B/2/3, and ADA11/A/B/2/4. When the draft QMB is compared to the QMB, the vast majority of material found in the former has been transcribed into the QMB. Where this is not the case and the omission is significant, the material has been highlighted in the document section.

53 SROI ADA11/A/B/3/1.

54 SROI ADA11/A/B/3/2 and ADA11/A/B/3/3 respectively.

55 SROI ADA11/A/C/1/1.

56 Document 4.

57 HCPP, *Commons' Journal*, Volume 30, pp. 12–13 (14 January 1765), p. 93 (7 February 1765).

58 HCPP, *Commons' Journal*, Volume 30, p. 155 (18 February 1765) and p. 180 (25 February 1765).

59 HCPP, *Commons' Journal*, Volume 30, pp. 301–2 (25 March 1765).

60 SROI ADA11/A/H/1/1, 23 August 1764, 8 October 1764, and 3 November 1764 for meetings to draft petition and bill; 23 January 1765 and 13 March 1765 for meetings with overseers. SROI ADA11/A/A/1/23 for Kilderbee and Poyntz invoices.

61 HCPP, *Commons' Journal*, Volume 30, p. 417 (10 May 1765). HLPP, *Lord's Journal*, Volume 31, p. 191 (10 May 1765). Documents 1–4.

62 Richard Savage-Nassau had been Member of Parliament for Colchester, 1747–54. He returned to Parliament as Member for Maldon in 1774.

entries reveal this body's tentative steps in establishing the Incorporation. Four areas required immediate attention: the raising of capital; the purchase of land; the planning, building and fitting out of the house; and the admittance of the paupers.

Capital

The Act allowed for up to £10,000 to be borrowed on the security of the poor rates.[63] Interest of 4 per cent was initially offered, but investors only appeared when the rate was increased to 4½ per cent in April 1766. Robert Barthrop of Hollesley invested £1,000, sufficient for immediate needs. Further investment took place in October 1766: £500 from Elizabeth Wythe of Wickham Market, £400 from the Revd Christopher Jeaffreson of Melton and £250 from Anne Growse of Bury St Edmunds.[64]

Land

The Incorporation could purchase up to 50 acres of freehold land.[65] In all, seven sites were considered. In March 1766, Mr Collett's farm in Bromeswell was visited as well as that of a Mr Brograve. By April the search had widened, John Whincopp's property, White Pightle in Melton, and that of William Waller, the Whinney, also in Melton, being considered. A committee was appointed to treat with these as well as with a Mr Skinner of Bredfield and William Negus of Melton. At the next meeting the Revd Christopher Jeaffreson, a director, offered four pieces of his land in Melton, totalling 27 acres, which were purchased at 28 years' valuation, totalling £852 12s.[66]

The house of industry

Requests for plans for a building to house 350 inmates were made in May 1766. The first design, by Matthew Grayston of Woodbridge, was deemed too extensive. John Redgrave, appointed surveyor to the directors, amended Grayston's plans, which were then put out to tender.[67] In July, John Lane's tender of £4,350 was accepted but this was soon withdrawn, so the second highest tender, by Matthew Grayston of Woodbridge and Thomas Fulcher of Debenham for £4,500, was accepted.[68]

Although Fulcher and Grayston's contract is no longer extant, that drafted for John Lane survives and offers details of the payment schedule.[69] The first £1,000 was to be released on the completion of the foundations; £550 when the first-floor joists were laid; £550 when the eves and garret-floor joists were reached; £700 when the house was tiled; £550 when the offices were completed; and the balance following a final survey.[70] Some of the payments to the builders can be traced though the QMB. £500 was paid in January 1767, followed by a second instalment of £500 in March when the drains, cellars and foundations had been completed.

---

[63] This was similar to other Incorporations: Carlford and Colneis £6,000; Mutford and Lothingland, Stow £8,000; Bosmere and Claydon, Samford, Wangford, Cosford £10,000; Blything £15,000; Hartismere, Hoxne and Thredling £25,000. Shaw, *Thesis*, p. 121.

[64] Document 35.

[65] This was similar to other incorporations: Carlford and Colneis 20 acres; Stow 30 acres; Bosmere and Claydon, Samford, Cosford 40 acres; Mutford and Lothingland, Blything, Wangford 50 acres; Hartismere, Hoxne and Thredling 200 acres. Shaw, *Thesis*, pp. 121–3.

[66] Documents 5 and 20.

[67] Documents 9 and 14.

[68] Documents 23 and 24.

[69] Document 22.

[70] SROI ADA11/A/H/1/1.

£700, on completion of the first-floor joists, was remitted in June, £550 for the eves and garret-floor joists in August, and £700 for the tiling in November.[71] In February 1768, £550 was paid following completion of the offices. The builders also took on additional work, for example in February 1768, when an additional £400 was paid for the pest house, coal bing, bog house, and entrance gates. October 1768 saw the final scheduled payment to the builders. One month later the builders were bankrupt, and Daniel Manthorp was contracted to complete the house. Fulcher and Grayston's final invoice of £728 12s. 7¾d. was paid to their assignees in July 1769.

Fitting out the house ran concurrent with construction. Advertisements for tenders to supply furniture and brewing utensils as well as other work were placed in the *Ipswich Journal* during November 1767 and contracts were signed with local tradesmen. The directors progressed to beds, bedding, clothes and linen goods in December. One contract offers some indication as to the expected number of residents: Henry Topple of Alderton, shoemaker, was to provide eighty pairs each of boys' and girls' shoes and sixty pairs each of men's and women's shoes. Then, just before the paupers' admission, contracts were signed for the provision of consumables, revealing something about the inmates' staple diet: beef, butter, cheese, hops, mutton, oatmeal, rice, spices, sugar and wheat.

Admission of paupers

Thomas Tibbs, who was appointed governor in February 1768 at an annual salary of £40, oversaw the final preparations. The paupers' admission was staggered over six days between 11 and 16 July 1768 inclusive, as shown in the table below:[72]

Date	Parish	Total	Date	Parish	Total
11 July 1768	Ash	3	**14 July 1768**	Ash	3
	Capel	2		Hollesley	6
	Kettleburgh	2		Monewden	1
	Marlesford	22		Wickham	9
	Melton	19	**15 July 1768**	Charsfield	5
12 July 1768	Butley	7		Cretingham	1
	Earlsoham	9		Eyke	6
	Letheringham	5		Petistree	1
	Ramsholt	5		Shottisham	4
13 July 1768	Bawdsey	1		Ufford	4
	Bredfield	9	**16 July 1768**	Alderton	2
	Easton	3		Bouldge	11
	Hatcheston	7		Dallingho	11
	Hoo	2		Kenton	7
	Sutton	16		Rendlesham	3

Table 1. Admissions to Melton House of Industry, 11–16 July 1768

---

71 Documents 26 to 28.
72 No inmates were received from Brandeston, Bromeswell, Boyton and Debach even though they were on the schedule. Brandeston's first admission to the house was on 21 November 1768, Bromeswell's on 24 October 1768, Boyton's on 22 January 1769 and Debach's on 17 January 1774.

Age	Male	%	Female	%	Total	%
0–14	66	79	61	60	127	68
15–29	1	1	8	8	9	5
30–44	1	1	17	16	18	10
45–59	2	2	5	5	7	4
60–89	14	17	11	11	25	13
Total	84		102		186	

Table 2. Age and sex distribution of 186 paupers admitted to Melton House, 11–16 July 1768

Table 2 illustrates that the age distribution for Melton matches the traditional pattern for institutional relief: 68 per cent of inmates were aged under fifteen years and 13 per cent were aged over sixty years. There were only two male paupers aged between fifteen and forty-four. This is similar to Nacton's and Bulcamp's admissions: both had 65 per cent aged under fourteen years; Nacton had 18 per cent aged over sixty, Bulcamp 27 per cent.[73] This skewed distribution is supported by other studies which indicate that the house of industry was directed at the young, unmarried mothers, the aged and families 'overburdened' with children.[74]

Themes from the first Quarterly Minute Book

The first QMB charts the Incorporation's early history, and what follows is a commentary on some of the key themes from those years.

Finance

The Incorporation's main source of income was the quarterly parish assessment, fixed at £517 7s. 6¼d. This assessment, plus the paupers' earnings, was expected to meet the house's day-to-day operating costs, repay the investments, and cover outdoor relief. Capital was required for the construction of the house, and the Incorporation's need to offer 4½ per cent has already been mentioned. £2,150 was received during 1766; a further £3,050 in 1767; and another £3,500 before the opening in July 1768. By the end of 1769 a total of £9,200 had been borrowed at 4½ per cent.[75]

At 4½ per cent the interest of £414 per annum equated to almost one fifth of the annual assessments. In an attempt to lessen this particular financial burden, in October 1770 it was decided to reduce the rate offered to 4 per cent, with those who refused to accept the change being threatened with repayment of their investment. Nathaniel Fletcher, for example, who refused to accept 4 per cent for his investment of £2,000, was repaid £1,200 in 1771 and the balance in 1772.[76] Such repayments were met in part from operating income but also through fresh investments at 4 per cent. By the close of 1772, the Incorporation was paying interest of £328 per annum on outstanding capital of £8,200.

---

[73] Shaw, *Thesis*, pp. 292–3.
[74] Tomkins, *Experience*, p. 47.
[75] Document 35.
[76] Document 35.

By early 1782, the directors faced a significant challenge: the executors of the estates of three deceased investors were demanding immediate repayment. The Incorporation had insufficient reserves to meet the demand. So, in July 1782 the directors voted by twenty-nine to three to publish a 'memorial' to 'gentlemen of landed property', urging them to enter into a subscription.[77] The memorialists stated that, even though the debt had been reduced to £6,700, insufficient funds were available to pay the demands of the creditors. They argued that while investors resided outside the incorporation – several came from Ipswich, Bury St Edmunds and Cambridge – they would naturally place their own interests above the good of the hundreds. The solution was for local landowners to invest 'in proportion to their property' either voluntarily or, if necessary, through powers provided by a new act. An act was not required: by June 1783 an additional £1,700 had been invested and the executors' demands met.[78]

Industry

From the outset, inmates were employed in the spinning of wool, with John Stannard contracted to supply the house with wheels and reels.[79] Oversight was provided by the governor, and the industrious inmates were rewarded for their labour, twenty-five receiving 3s. 6d. each in March 1769.[80] Initially John Stocks provided the house with 'wool of different sorts' for spinning until Ray and Oakes of Bury St Edmunds took over.[81] No figures are extant for the manufacture of yarn during these years, though there are references in the QMB to alterations to the spinning rooms.[82] The committee appointed in 1780 to review the accounts of the house identified several weaknesses with the manufactory and recommended that weekly operating accounts should be compiled. As this task was beyond the governor's capabilities, when a schoolmaster was appointed in November 1780 one of his roles was to assist the former with the accounts.[83]

Ray and Oakes continued to supply the house with combed wool until the depression of the early 1780s.[84] In March 1781 their contract was terminated and the Revd Mr Richard Frank's proposal for distributing wool to the out-door poor for spinning was adopted. The finished yarn was then to be sold to a Norwich factor on commission.[85] In May 1781 William Barber of Nayland was appointed packman, receiving 9s. a week and free lodgings. He was to distribute wool to fifteen parishes as well as to the house, making weekly returns of the wool distributed and the yarn collected.[86]

The directors' sudden interest in the manufactory took the governor by surprise, leading to an unexpected discovery. During an inspection in 1781, 233 tops of wool, claimed by the governor, Thomas Tibbs, as his property, were found secreted in

---

77   15 directors and 14 acting guardians for the motion with 2 directors and 1 acting guardian voting against. There is no record of the names attached to the votes.
78   SROI ADA11/A/B/1/1, rear of Quarterly Minute Book. Document 35.
79   SROI ADA11/A/B/1/1, 14 December 1767 and 6 June 1768.
80   SROI ADA11/A/B/1/1, 27 March 1769.
81   SROI ADA11/A/B/1/1, 4 July 1768.
82   For example, SROI ADA11/A/B/1/1, 30 March 1778.
83   SROI ADA11/A/B/1/1, 2 October 1780 and 13 November 1780.
84   J. Fiske, *The Oakes Diaries: Business, Politics and the Family in Bury St Edmunds, 1778–1827,* Suffolk Records Society Volumes 32 and 33 (Woodbridge, 1990–91),Volume 1, p. 38.
85   SROI ADA11/A/B/1/1, 26 March 1781.
86   SROI ADA11/A/B/1/1, 14 May 1781 and 21 May 1781.

the building.[87] A committee found the tops belonged to the Incorporation.[88] Further investigation revealed that Tibbs had sold '500 weight [of wool] at 12 or 13 pence per pound' to an Ipswich wool factor by the name of Maw without the directors' knowledge.[89] Tibbs was fined £120 and summarily dismissed, with John Elliott, the schoolmaster, now fulfilling the role.[90]

The account books extant from 1781 onwards reveal that the wool manufactory continued to underperform, with the outlay to Barber far exceeding the income received from sales. The issue of the wool manufactory was raised at several meetings, and despite the increasing losses it was continued for two more years.[91] The directors finally realised that it was not 'sufficiently answering the intended purpose', and the treasurer was ordered to write to local wool merchants for their terms for supplying the house with combed wool and their best offer for the existing spun tops. The responses were discussed in July 1783, with the decision made in favour of Cumberland and Co.[92] No interest was expressed in the stock of yarn, estimated to be worth almost £1,000, so the best of it was sent to Samuel Williams, a Norwich factor, and a few parcels were retained to be sold locally.[93] When these failed to sell, this stock, too, was sent to Williams.[94] By the close of the first QMB, the directors were awaiting a reply concerning the yarn's sale, and had requested Cumberland and Crosbie to remove all the wool unsuitable for spinning from the house.[95]

Out-door relief

Decisions concerning out-door relief were taken at the weekly committee. The approach straddled two systems: either out-door relief, similar to any parish in England, or admission to the house of industry. One key difference between the Incorporation and neighbouring parishes was the absence of relief in kind: the provision of clothes, furniture, food and fuel, so common under parochial management. The WMBs contain just a handful of references to such provision.[96] The directors even insisted that the house's uniform was relinquished on discharge, so depriving the pauper of a set of clothing.[97]

A second difference was the offer of the house, which operated in three distinct ways: the admission of at least one child when out-door relief was first requested by a family; the admission of whole families, rather than granting out-door relief; and granting out-door relief on a short-term basis, before the threat of admission was

---

[87] SROI ADA11/A/B/1/1, 11 June 1781. Tibbs claimed these as his based on his commission from Ray and Oakes of 4 ounces for every 12 pounds spun.

[88] SROI ADA11/A/B/1/1, 25 June 1781.

[89] SROI ADA11/A/B/1/1, 29 June 1781.

[90] SROI ADA11/A/B/1/1, 1 October 1781. The fine is recorded in the Treasurer's Account Book, SROI ADA11/A/C/1/1/1.

[91] SROI ADA11/A/B/1/1, 25 June 1782.

[92] SROI ADA11/A/B/1/1, 6 July 1783 and 28 July 1783. Despite dining with John Revett at the Stowmarket *White Horse*, James Oakes's efforts to regain the contract were in vain (Fiske, *Oakes Diaries*, Volume 1, p. 39). Oakes lost not only the spinners in the house but those living in the two hundreds.

[93] SROI ADA11/A/B/1/1, 16 October 1783.

[94] SROI ADA11/A/B/1/1, 27 October 1783.

[95] SROI ADA11/A/B/1/1, 11 February 1784 and 25 February 1784.

[96] WMB, 10 October 1768 and 27 March 1769.

[97] WMB, 7 December 1768.

made.[98] For permanently pauperised families, the admission and discharge of their children became an annual cycle.

Not all destitution was treated equally. The elderly and widows fared best under the system. Elderly widows commonly received a pension of from 1s. to 2s. a week for life.[99] Younger widows with children were generally treated equally benevolently, with the allowance varying depending on family size. There are very few references to widowers receiving pensions; the Incorporation's support for the bereaved husband usually ended with the interment of the deceased.[100] The payment for an adult burial remained constant during these years at £1, and that for a child at between 5s. and 10s.[101]

Most pregnant women also fared reasonably well. Support began with the lying in. The decision on the level of allowance had several variables: was the mother unmarried and, if so, how much indemnity could be obtained from the putative father; was it a first pregnancy, or were there other children in the family; and was the father in employment, also in receipt of relief, or had he absconded? Unless there was a medical complication, admission to the house appears to have been reserved primarily for illegitimate births. Home birth was the norm, with the provision of a midwife and nurse(s) and the surgeon being requested only for complications. From 2s. 6d. to 3s. 6d. was the normal weekly relief for lying-in if the family was few in number, with payments of up to 30s. for larger families. Unmarried women were taken before the magistrate to filiate the child, and were threatened with the Bridewell if they refused.[102] The putative father of an illegitimate child was forced to enter into a bond for the indemnification of the Incorporation either in his own name or in the name of two guarantors. The usual sum accepted was between £10 and £20, providing an income for the mother 'so long as the child may live'.

The long-term mentally and physically handicapped also fared well. There are examples in the WMB of blind and lame and of 'lunatik' paupers gaining regular allowances, the sum varying depending on the size of the household, but 2s. a week was not unusual for a single adult.

Children were usually admitted for relatively short spells, while the parent recovered or obtained employment. Those admitted over a longer term were usually put out for hire for a year's duration when of a suitable age. Hiring could occur at any time during the year and was within the remit of the weekly committee, whilst apprenticing occurred at specific times during the year at a quarterly meeting. Children hired or apprenticed were usually issued with a full set of clothing.

Another group were those receiving short-term relief for injury or illness. The range of ailments is quite extensive: reference is made to broken arms, thighs, ribs, wrists, fingers and dislocated shoulders. There is mention of smallpox as well as mortification, dropsy, rheumatism, putrid fever, burns, bruises, strains, ague, thrush, growths in the abdomen, measles and miscarriage. Most of these were dealt with by short-term out-door relief, though admissions to the pest house increased when smallpox was prevalent. Occasionally surgeons received one-off payments, such as

---

98 SROI ADA11/A/B/3/3, 26 March 1770 and 27 November 1775; SROI ADA11/A/B/3/4, 5 December 1777.
99 SROI ADA11/A/B/3/2, 18 July 1768 (1s.), 26 September 1768 (1s. 6d. and 2s.).
100 SROI ADA11/A/B/3/2, 4 September 1769.
101 SROI ADA11/A/B/3/2, 11 December 1769 (5s.).
102 SROI ADA11/A/B/3/2, 20 March 1769.

when Samuel Salmon was paid £2 2s. for setting a compound fracture.[103] Details of out-door relief payments exist from Christmas 1768: during the 1770s out-door relief hovered around £126 per annum, rising to £395 per annum in the depression of the early 1780s, before falling to £288 per annum by 1784.

Comprehensive medical cover was provided from the outset. In June 1768 Samuel Salmon was appointed surgeon to the house at an annual salary of £40. William Henchman was employed as out-surgeon for Loes Hundred and John Syer as out-surgeon for Wilford, both at an annual salary of £25.[104] Within a year this tripartite approach had been superseded by the appointment of a single surgeon at an annual salary of £100.[105] In 1780 medical care was reorganised yet again.[106] This time Salmon was allocated the house (for £40 per annum) as well as fifteen neighbouring parishes (for £45 per annum). Thurston Whimper was allotted eleven parishes (for £33 per annum) and William Henchman seven parishes (for £21 per annum).

Inmate life

Extant documents provide a glimpse of what life was like in the house. On admission the pauper's name, age, place of settlement and of residence were recorded. Their clothes would be exchanged for the house's uniform: shirt, waistcoat, breeches, socks, shoes, coat and a cap or hat for boys and men; shift, gown, petticoat, stockings, shoes, bonnet and stays for girls and women. The uniform removed any vestiges of the paupers' individuality, and also served to stigmatise them whenever they left the house as the Incorporation's initials – LWP – were emblazoned on the items.[107] One room was provided for married couples, with a dozen dormitories being single sex. There was a nursery for the very young, a room for old men and another for old women.

Daily life was regulated by a tolling bell. The day began with the rising bell at either 6 am (in summer) or 7 am (in winter); the inmates rose and dressed in the house uniform. Half-an-hour was allowed for breakfast, usually bread and gruel, served and eaten in silence in the dining hall. Prayers were said by the governor and inmates answered to a roll call. The mid-day break lasted for one hour, the meal usually consisting of beef, dumplings and vegetables. Supper, of bread and cheese, was served when work had finished at 6 pm, and prayers were read again. The paupers were then granted some freedom until bedtime: 8 pm (in winter) and 9 pm (in summer). A full muster parade was held on Sunday followed by attendance at church. Inmates could only leave the grounds with the governor's approval and visitors could enter only with the agreement of the weekly committee.

Although the diet was monotonous, it was far superior to that available in the paupers' homes. Frederick Morton Eden, when visiting Melton House, was informed by the governor that to provide a weekly diet for 280 paupers required the following provisions: 140st. of flour; 25st. of beef; 9st. of cheese; 3½st. of butter; 3st. of salt; 3 pecks of oatmeal; and 6 barrels of beer. In addition 1¼st. of soap and 10lb. of

---

[103] SROI ADA11/A/B/1/1, 29 March 1773.
[104] SROI ADA11/A/B/1/1, 27 June 1768.
[105] SROI ADA11/A/B/1/1, 29 June 1769.
[106] SROI ADA11/A/B/1/1, 28 June 1773 and 26 June 1780.
[107] Frederick Morton Eden, *The State of the Poor* (London, 1797), Volume 2, p. 688.

candles were consumed each week and 90 chaldron of coals over the year.[108] The diet at Melton appears to have compared favourably with other Suffolk houses and the Poor Law Commissioners would identify this 'excess of dietary' as one of the 'chief features in the mismanagement of the Houses'.[109]

The second Quarterly Minute Book, 1784–94

The second QMB covers the period 28 June 1784 to 2 August 1791 and measures 26cm by 38cm.[110] A further QMB was in use following the 1791 amending Act and while that is no longer extant we are fortunate that there is a draft QMB for 1785–95 as well as two WMBs covering the missing years.[111] Up until 1791 both the QMB and the draft QMB have a layout not dissimilar to the first QMB, providing considerable detail about the Incorporation's operation; but from 1791 the style changes dramatically: the minutes become little more than an account of out relief paid to the parishes, lists of miscellaneous bills and salaries paid, with comments concerning the day-to-day management of the house becoming far more intermittent.

The chief event of these years was the passing of the amending Act of 1791.[112] By October 1790 parochial assessments were failing to meet operating costs, so a committee was established to scrutinise the accounts. The committee presented its report in February 1791.

The report began by outlining why the investigation had focussed on the years 1781 to 1790. By 1781 the capital debt had been reduced to £6,200 and the Incorporation's quarterly income and expenditure was balanced. However, the committee identified that for the ten years in question, expenditure had normally exceeded income for each quarter, requiring an additional £3,700 to be borrowed, increasing total indebtedness to £9,900.[113]

The report pulled no punches. First, it identified cases of mismanagement in the purchasing of basic commodities. Second, it raised questions over the directors' ability to utilise effectively the house's deterrent: out-door relief was frequently issued 'without proper discrimination' yet on other occasions whole families were admitted to the house at 'needless expense', rather than 'trifling sums' of out-door relief being offered. Third, the directors were accused of negligence over the apprenticing of children. Children sent to the house were held too long, 'being exposed to the vigorous young women' who were maintained there. Fourth, the directors were criticised for their lax management, their failure to impose fines on their peers for non-attendance, and for failing to keep the overseers in check.

The greatest censure was reserved for the winding up of the manufactory. As mentioned earlier, by 1783 the directors had agreed to cease yarn production, valuing the stock at £1,202. Rather than accept an offer made for this sum, the report describes the convoluted journey to dispose of the stock, resulting in a loss of £150. For the years 1783–88 no employment was offered until the introduction of a

---

108 Eden, *State of the Poor*, Volume 2, pp. 685–6. Beer was provided when there was no broth or gruel served. According to the governor, children could eat 'as much as they liked'.

109 Shaw, *Thesis*, p. 298. The figures are extracted from the Report from Assistant Commissioner James Philip Kay. HCPP 1836, Volume 29, pp. 155–6.

110 SROI ADA11/A/B/1/2 runs until August 1791, thereafter the draft QMB until April 1794.

111 SROI ADA11/A/B/2/5, ADA11/A/B/3/3 and ADA11/A/B/3/4.

112 It gained Royal Assent on 13 May 1791. HCPP, *Commons' Journal*, 13 May 1791.

113 Over the ten years income was £23,893 0s.11½d. and expenditure was £25,355 18s. 7½d.

hemp manufactory in 1788. The report contended that even this venture had been a drain on capital; so 'the sinews of your labour have been ham strung and hocked'.

Similar opprobrium was levelled at other areas of management. The report noted that instead of correcting the profligate and idle, during the winter months the house accepted a great number of 'lazy, notorious and abandoned prostitutes', and the mothers of bastards were placed in charge of the nursery. The aged and infirm were similarly forsaken: the aged languished in their beds; the surgeon seldom visited, leaving nurses to deal with the sick; the same adulterated salve was used for all sorts of sores; many patients were left lying in bed, leading to 'ulcers and gangrene'; and the nursery was severely overcrowded. Finally, the report questioned the propriety of the directors' supplying the house with provisions.

The outcome was inevitable: the directors resolved to petition Parliament for an amending act.[114] Sir John Rous oversaw the bill's progress through the Commons.[115] The petition stated that the Incorporation's capital limit would soon be reached, yet a 'large sum ... was wanted for the immediate repairs, alterations and enlargement' to the buildings.[116] The new Act increased the Incorporation's capital limit to £14,000 and its quarterly assessments by one-third. Many of the amending Act's clauses were punitive: following Tibbs' offence, those committed of embezzlement were to receive a fine triple the value of the fraud; a house of correction was to be built; fines could be imposed on those receiving stolen goods from the house; and fines for non-attending directors were to be increased fivefold.

The first general meeting was held in May 1791. The house surgeon, Samuel Salmon, was forced to tender his resignation; Simon Paternoster was dismissed as treasurer and Richard Wood appointed to this post. Committees were established to review all officeholders, to review the Incorporation's bye-laws and to review the house's linen manufactory.[117] An inventory was taken of all goods; a new medical structure was instigated; Robert Rainbird and his wife were appointed governor and matron; and the quarterly assessments were raised by the one third permitted to £689 16s. 6¼d., where they remained until the close of this QMB.[118]

The third Quarterly Minute Book, 1795–1805

The third QMB covers the period July 1795 to July 1805 and measures 26cm by 38cm.[119] These years are also covered by three WMBs: one until 1798, another from 1798 to 1804 and a third from 1804.[120] There is also a set of additional sheets linked to the increase in out-door relief during the summer months of 1795.[121] Unlike earlier QMBs, most of the entries in this volume are perfunctory and mechanistic; the previous meetings consist of a statement of the rates to be assessed, the out-door relief granted and a list of bills and salaries to be paid; the quarterly meetings, in

---

[114] Document 38.

[115] HCPP, *Commons' Journal*, Volume 46, p. 204 (21 February 1791).

[116] HCPP, *Commons' Journal*, Volume 46, p. 317 (21 March 1791), p. 360 (29 March 1791), p. 369 (31 March 1791) and p. 415 (15 April 1791).

[117] Document 37.

[118] Document 36.

[119] SROI ADA11/A/B/1/3.

[120] SROI ADA11/A/B/3/4–6.

[121] SROI ADA11/A/B/3/11.

turn, are lists of the out-door relief to be granted and only occasionally are other matters mentioned.

These years were a watershed for the Incorporation. 1795 saw the start of wartime inflation, which left the Incorporation's finances in a critical state. In response to high food prices during the Napoleonic Wars, the Incorporation linked out-door allowances to the market price of wheat, with an additional allowance offered once wheat had reached a specified price.

The Act of 1791 had enabled the Incorporation's quarterly assessments to be raised to £689 16s. 6¼d. and they remained at this figure until 1795. Even this level was found insufficient during the summer of 1795, when the directors were forced to obtain an advance of £1,200 secured against future rates. The directors realised that further powers were required and so convened a general meeting in November 1795, where it was agreed to petition Parliament. For the first time in the Incorporation's history there was open dissent, and the final vote was far from unanimous, with twenty-eight votes for the petition and fourteen against. The petition illustrates the issues faced by the Incorporation: the directors, having 'no power or authority ... of raising any further sum', were burdened with a debt of £10,500 on which they were unable to meet the interest charges.

The need for an amendment act was removed when Parliament enacted a General Act in December 1795.[122] This acknowledged the 'very great increase of the price of corn ... and other necessary articles' in recent years as well as the fact that the poor had 'greatly increased in numbers'. Provided the initial parish ratio was maintained, incorporations could increase assessments by any amount. This provision was to remain in force until January 1798 and thereafter the assessment was limited to double the December 1795 figure. The additional financial freedom afforded by the Act is immediately reflected in the accounts: the quarterly assessment increased from £689 16s. 6¼d. for the Christmas Quarter 1795 to £2,069 9s. 6½d. for the Lady Quarter 1796, where it remained until the Michaelmas Quarter 1796.

Frederick Morton Eden's survey of the nation's poor, *The State of the Poor*, published in 1797, offers insight into the impact on allowances. Prior to the crisis Eden noted the following pattern for the out-door relief offered by the Incorporation:[123]

A single man, or single woman, ill; 1s. per week respectively
A man and his wife, both ill; 2s. per week
A man and his wife, with one or more children (the man being ill); 2s. per week, with an addition of 6d. per head for children under 10 years of age, if necessary
A man and his wife with more than two children, (the woman being ill); 1s. per week
A single woman with a bastard child; not an object of relief
A widow woman in health, having only one child; not an object of relief
A man in health, having only three children; not generally to be considered as an object of relief

These allowances changed dramatically in July 1795 when it was noted that 'the price of all the necessaries of life are at present so high that labourers having fami-

---

122 36 Geo. 3 c. 10 (Poor Relief Act, 1795).
123 Eden, *State of the Poor*, Volume 2, p. 687.

lies cannot maintain them at the present price of labour without some relief'. The additional relief offered was:

1s. a week to families with two children under twelve years of age
1s. 6d. to those with three children
2s. to those with four children
3s. to those with five children
4s. to those with six children
and 6s. to those with seven or more children[124]

This scale was to operate until August 1795, though 'if the price of corn be not then reduced' it was to remain in force until that September.[125] Given the expense to the Incorporation, the approach was short-lived, with alternative measures quickly adopted: the overseers were to obtain 'wheat and flour at a reduced price during the high price of bread corn', which they were empowered to sell to the poor at below market rate; and a horse mill was erected to grind flour for use in the house. After the summer of 1795, there are no further references to such allowances although, as in the other incorporations, they must have continued intermittently for a number of years.

The financial impact on the level of allowances was enormous. In 1784, out-door relief stood at £288 per annum, gradually rising to £438 per annum by 1794. The increase of the mid-1790s was startling. In 1795, at £611 per annum, out-door relief was 40 per cent higher than the previous year; in 1796, at £1,167 per annum, over 166 per cent higher. The in-door costs were also higher than in previous years. Graph 1 illustrates the amount spent quarterly on in-door and out-door relief during the years 1796–1802.

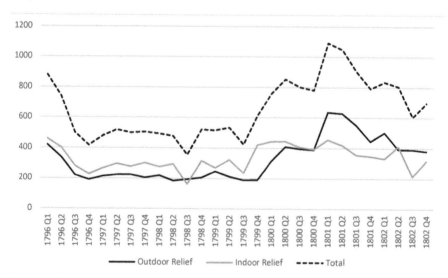

Graph 1. Expenditure on indoor and outdoor relief, 1796–1802

---

124 SROI ADA11/A/B/1/3.

125 Unlike other Suffolk incorporations, where frequent references are made to the adjustment of their allowance scales to reflect the market price of wheat, there is just one reference to a scale for Loes and Wilford.

The income from the house's manufactory offered little to offset these figures. One of the main justifications for incorporating had been to reduce the cost of poor relief through the income generated by setting the in-door poor to work. However, during these years of crisis, income from the manufactory remained disappointingly low, as Table 3 indicates.

Year	Spinning	Hiring out of labourers	Total
1793	£83 9s. 11d.	–	£83 9s. 11d.
1794	£81 1s. 8d.	£37 18s. 9d.	£119 0s. 5d.
1795	£79 3s. 2d.	£27 6s. 7d.	£106 9s. 9d.
1796	£82 11s. 0d.	£30 11s. 0d.	£113 2s. 0d.
1797	£98 6s. 7d.	£40 2s. 11d.	£138 9s. 6d.
1798	£92 8s. 3d.	£11 9s. 4d.	£103 17s. 7d.
1799	£95 19s. 1d.	£28 2s. 9d.	£124 1s. 10d.
1800	£159 13s. 1d.	£60 1s. 9d.	£219 14s. 10d.
1801	£171 19s. 1d.	£66 2s. 10d.	£238 1s. 11d.
1802	£189 7s. 10d.	£7 14s. 3d.	£197 2s. 1d.

Table 3. Income arising from inmates' labour, 1793–1802

Financial pressure led to a further review of the management of the house. In July 1796, nine committees were created to operate in conjunction with the weekly and quarterly meetings. As the directors were to nominate themselves to committees, the outcome should have been anticipated: key committees, such as maintenance, obtained ten volunteers, and that for industry seven; the more mundane, such as law, obtained just one volunteer. Their effectiveness is difficult to judge since, once established, there is no further mention of them in the minute books.

A second development was an interest in schools of industry, to provide pauper children with elementary instruction. Their establishment was first mooted in July 1796 and a committee was established to investigate. Its report led to a series of resolutions: that schools would be beneficial both to the poor 'by increasing their comfort' and to the Incorporation 'by decreasing the heavy burthen of the poor rates'. The committee requested details of the number of children in the parishes aged under twelve. The response stunned the directors: returns indicate that there were about 1,800 children aged under twelve, of which almost 800 were under the age of five. Realising that the expense for 'the education of so large a number of children' was 'much beyond the capability of the corporation', the directors make no further reference to the initiative.

The fourth Quarterly Minute Book, 1805–12

The fourth QMB covers the period 14 October 1805 to 15 October 1812. It measures 26cm by 38cm and is supported by a single WMB for the years 1804–12.[126] The

---

[126] SROI ADA11/A/B/1/4 and ADA11/A/B/3/6.

entries in this volume are largely perfunctory and mechanistic, with one issue dominant: the acrimonious debate concerning the passage of the 1810 amending Act.

The problem lay in the inability of the rating system to respond to the increasing level of relief. By the early 1800s the parochial assessments calculated during the 1760s bore little resemblance to the parishes' true costs to the Incorporation.[127] The rating system's inflexibility had been of concern to some parishes for many years. For example, though Debach's first admission to the house was not until January 1774, during the years 1768–73 the parish had contributed £54 8s. 0d. to the common fund, yet received just £6 17s. 6d. for out-door relief.[128]

The first indication that another amending act was under consideration came in January 1808. Once again, legal action threatened by an investor provided the impetus. A number of meetings were held during 1808–09.[129] Hopes that the amending act would be easily obtained were soon dispelled. The meeting of 8 August was attended by attorneys for the parishes of Sutton and Kenton, who argued for the reassessment of all the parishes. Their request fell on deaf ears and the petition submitted to Parliament retained the original assessments.

Little indication of the significance of the dissent can be ascertained from entries in the QMB but the plethora of extant letters and papers make its seriousness obvious. The dissenting parishes convened their own rival meeting. Here Sutton and Kenton were joined by representatives from Marlesford. These parishes argued that the original averages were distorted due to an outbreak of the smallpox, which led to them paying by 'a quadruple degree' more to the Incorporation than they had received. An alternative method of assessment was suggested. A parish's contribution towards in-door relief should be calculated by dividing the annual cost of the house by the average number of inmates, with this sum being allocated in proportion to the number of paupers each parish had sent to the house. This would be combined with the parish's previous year's out-door relief, providing the parish's total contribution. As this figure would vary from year to year, and recognising that financial stability was required, the dissenters proposed that fresh averages would be calculated 'once in every four years'. This approach, they believed, would create 'a degree of interest in the respective parishes as to the prosperity of the corporation' and force them 'to be more circumspect in the applications they may make to the house for relief'. They also proposed that the debt should be repaid using the new average. The meeting decided to draft a counter-petition and a fund was established to meet costs.

A copy of the above meeting's deliberations is still extant, annotated by a director.[130] The director's irritation is displayed by his derogatory annotations. The value of land and the level of wages were central to the rebuttal. There had been 'scarcely an estate in the two hundreds but what have been bought and sold since the establishment of this corporation'. The price of land reflected the fact that the poor rates were 'finally fixed', with a higher price paid for property in parishes which were 'very moderately assessed to the poor rate'. Likewise, over the years workers had been 'let and hired on the same principal'. Further, the four-yearly computation would be impossible to undertake with any degree of accuracy and would be too

---

[127] The initial assessments were calculated on the average of a parish's poor relief for the seven years Easter 1753 to Easter 1760.

[128] This was based on the average for the seven years 1753–60.

[129] Document 39.

[130] Document 40.

time consuming. The director remarked that the counter-petition would not, as suggested, be for 'the interests of the Hundreds at large' but would be beneficial only 'to a few individuals in three parishes'.

A chasm developed between the parties. The Incorporation's petition was the first to be presented and was referred to a committee chaired by Sir Charles Bunbury.[131] Bunbury, as Member of Parliament for Suffolk from 1761 to 1784 and then 1790 onwards, had helped steer the earlier acts through Parliament and was sympathetic to the Incorporation. He reported to the Commons in January 1810, begging leave to bring in a bill for an amending act. The bill was read a second time in early February.[132] Thereafter matters moved swiftly. In a letter dated 12 February Bunbury warned the directors that the dissenting parishes had also requested his support.[133] Even at this stage compromise was possible. On 14 February, the dissenting parishes submitted a number of amending clauses to the Incorporation's petition and awaited a response.[134] The Incorporation's agent reported that the counter-petition had still to be presented: 'I believe they wait your answer [to the clauses] – of course I shall not disclose your sentiment.'[135] The letter warned the directors that they would be unable to deny the counter-petitioners access to the Incorporation's books should the Commons committee order it.[136] When the counter-petition was finally presented at the end of February the number of dissenting parishes had risen to four: Marlesford, Sutton, Kenton and Charsfield. The petition was assigned to Bunbury's committee.[137]

In early April another counter-petition was laid before the Commons by the parishes of Butley, Eyke, Easton, Ramsholt, Ash, Petistree, Creetingham and Capel: the number of dissenting parishes was now twelve.[138] This petition was also submitted to Bunbury's committee. Bunbury later reported that the committee had heard counsel both for the Incorporation and for the dissenting parishes and as a result had 'gone through the bill' and made 'several amendments thereunto'. These were agreed by the house. The bill was read for a third time before delivery to the Lords, where it was again submitted to committee. The bill was approved without any amendments, gaining Royal Assent on 24 May.[139]

The bill's apparently smooth passage through Parliament fails to do justice to the political machinations that occurred within the hundreds. Shortly after the presentation of the first counter-petition, a detailed defence of the Incorporation's stance was delivered to the Commons committee. It argued that, as the Incorporation offered relief to all the poor legally settled within the hundreds, settlement issues were only pursued for those whose settlement lay elsewhere. However, if assessments were to be calculated on the number of paupers a parish sent to the house then costs associated with intra-hundred settlement disputes would arise. The opposition's proposals would take power away from the directors and place it in the hands of 'a set of

---

[131] HCPP, *Commons' Journal*, Volume 65, p. 9 (25 January 1810). Document 41.

[132] HCPP, *Commons' Journal*, Volume 65, p. 14 (29 January) and p. 34 (5 February 1810).

[133] Document 42.

[134] Document 41.

[135] Document 44.

[136] Document 43.

[137] HCPP, *Commons' Journal*, Volume 65, p. 120 (23 February 1810).

[138] HCPP, *Commons' Journal*, Volume 65, p. 242 (3 April 1810).

[139] HCPP, *Commons' Journal*, Volume 65, p. 287 (16 April 1810), p. 298 (18 April 1810), p. 382 (18 May 1810) and p. 402 (24 May 1810). HLPP, *Lords' Journal*, Volume 47, p. 609 (18 April 1810), p. 634 (9 May 1810), p. 663 (17 May 1810), p. 669 (18 May 1810) and p. 692 (24 May 1810).

illiterate officers'. More importantly, the 'cruelty of the churchwardens and the over-seers would be very severely felt by the poor' prior to the calculation of the new averages because each parish sought to 'screw down the number of poor relieved'. Finally, as only two directors and three acting guardians supported the opposition, it would be morally indefensible that so few 'should have power to overthrow the whole and present system'.[140]

Despite this defence, Bunbury found substance to the opposing petitions and ordered that a wide range of documents be laid before the committee and so be acces-sible to the dissenting parishes.[141] Notes taken at the Commons committee convened for 6 and 7 March 1810 fortunately survive. The case centred on three issues: the ease with which the paupers' parish of settlement could be determined; the impact the assessments had on the price of land and labour rates; and the supposed inequali-ties of the current system of rating. The notes reveal that the majority of witness statements were generalisations with few facts offered. The committee found itself unable to offer judgement and recommended that the parties meet to negotiate a compromise.[142]

A general meeting was arranged for 29 March 1810. Prior to the meeting, the directors offered new proposals to the dissenting parishes. They accepted that the 'rates are in part unequal and disproportionate' and that fresh assessments were required. They also accepted the dissenters' mode of calculation, but suggested ten- rather than four-year averages.[143] For the existing debt, however, the existing aver-ages would remain.[144]

Believing this would assuage their opponents, the directors became overconfi-dent. The general meeting quickly accepted the need for fresh assessments every ten years. Then discussion turned to the method for repaying the debt. The Incorpora-tion argued for retaining the original assessment and the motion was put to the vote. Thirty-three delegates voted to liquidate the debt by the new assessment ratio, with only twenty-six voting against.[145] The Incorporation had been outmanoeuvred.[146] An extant letter reveals that prior to the meeting a letter had been sent to all the aggrieved parishes, 'which was the cause of the [directors] being outnumbered'. A copy sent to the ratepayers of Ufford remains in the Incorporation's papers. The letter makes reference to the forthcoming meeting, where 'certain clauses for the more just and equal regulation' of the rates would be considered as well as the means for paying off the existing debt. The letter continued: sixteen parishes had made an excess contribution of £7,759 to the Incorporation, 'of which the parish of Ufford has paid the sum of £752 14s. 2d.'. In contrast, seventeen other parishes' deficiency of contributions 'amounts to the sum of £8,625 and upwards'. The letter went on to state that 'it must be the interest of the owners and occupiers in the 16 aggrieved parishes to lend their aid towards correcting this very oppressive evil'. It concluded by begging leave 'to press the urgent and indispensable necessity of full attendance, at the time and place proposed'.[147]

---

[140] Document 46.
[141] Document 48.
[142] Documents 49 and 50.
[143] 1 January 1800 to 1 January 1810.
[144] Document 51.
[145] Document 54.
[146] Document 52.
[147] Document 55.

Following their defeat the directors were forced onto the back foot. Their response was to petition the Commons on two occasions, and both documents are still extant. The first refers to a distinction that would later become known as 'open' and 'closed' parishes. The author describes the former as 'favourite parishes' to which the poor flock and attempt to gain a settlement because of the numerous 'good natured gentlemen living therein'. In contrast, they 'flee from [the] parishes' comprised of fewer landowners who can control settlement and 'are less generous'. Under the proposal, should the overburdened parishes be 'visited with any sickness' it would lead to their 'total ruin'.[148] The second document questioned the tactic of sending the letter to sixteen 'supposed aggrieved parishes' and 'not one into the other parishes'. It was 'kept so great a secret' that 'no one of the gentlemen that composed the meeting ... knew of this until they came to the meeting'. The under-hand practices meant that although it was agreed to allow the Commons committee to determine the issue 'after ... part of the meeting were gone' it was clear that 'nothing would satisfy a part of the meeting' unless put to the vote.[149]

The Incorporation was unsuccessful in its bid to amend the bill. The newly calculated ten-year average would be used for repaying the loan as well as covering general running costs. The new average, first computed in August 1810, fixed the assessment for in-door and out-door relief at £5,263 10s. 0d. and that for repaying the loan at £1,507 10s. 0d.

The Incorporation was to have its revenge. In July 1810, the opponents requested that the Incorporation should meet their costs: the request was rejected. Undeterred, William Shuldham wrote explaining how the new average meant that his parish, Marlesford, would be paying £64 a year less and so, by extrapolation, it had paid over £600 too much in the previous ten years. He continued that as 'the contending parties have partly succeeded, and in part failed in their respective objects ... I would recommend a compromise between them' which included the dissenting parishes' costs being met by the Incorporation. The Incorporation declined.[150] The third and final exchange came in 1811, when the directors received a letter arguing that the term 'opponent' was inaccurate, as their action had been for the 'general benefit of the hundreds at large' and their plan 'has since in great measure been adopted'. It suggested that costs would have been substantially lower if 'more amity and less suspicion and jealousy' had been displayed by the Incorporation. The directors' terse response stated that they were 'not authorised to order their treasurer to pay any part of the opposing party's expenses'.[151]

The fifth and sixth Quarterly Minute Books, 1813–18 and 1818–20[152]

The fifth QMB covers the period 4 January 1813 to 9 July 1818. It measures 26cm by 38cm. It is supported by two WMBs, one covering 1812–17 and the other 1817–20. The sixth QMB covers the period 12 October 1818 to 18 October 1820 and measures 26cm by 38cm, with only one-third of the volume used. It is supported by

---

[148] Document 56.
[149] Document 57.
[150] Document 59.
[151] Document 60.
[152] SROI ADA11/A/B/1/5–6.

one WMB, which covers 1817–20.[153] The comments for previous volumes pertain to this and the entries are largely mechanistic in nature.

The seventh Quarterly Minute Book, 1820–26[154]

The seventh and final QMB covers the period 12 October 1820 to 12 October 1826, measures 29cm by 41cm and is supported by two WMBs. The first of these covers 1820–24 and the second 1824–26.[155] New decennial averages were calculated in October 1820, but financial problems soon arose. The directors compared Melton's costs with those of neighbouring incorporations: Blything's house, at Bulcamp, was visited; their accounts examined; and other local acts were reviewed.

In April 1824 the question of a further amending act was raised, because the decennial averages were seen as too unresponsive. It was recommended that the house's expenditure should be subdivided into fixed and variable costs, with fresh averages being calculated every five years, and a petition was also drafted for an amending act.[156]

By October 1824 the situation had changed dramatically.[157] The general meeting convened to finalise the new petition moved on to consider whether 'the existence of the said House does or does not materially and unnecessarily increase the expense of maintaining the poor'. Another committee was convened that was granted full access to the Incorporation's records. Meeting during November 1824, it interrogated documents dating back to 1800, revealing the upward trend in costs: the yearly average for operating costs during 1800–10 was £5,268; for 1810–20 it had risen to £9,326; and for the years 1820–24 it had averaged £10,008. The committee decided to consider a bill for disincorporation.[158]

In January 1825 another committee was established to frame the petition and bill.[159] Meetings were held in each of the parishes during February and March 1825, where 'a great majority of the parishes … consented and agreed to pay a proportion of the expences'.[160] However, not all were happy, and the directors were forced to circulate a pamphlet justifying their decision.[161] Unlike the crisis of 1810 little remains of the opponents' papers.[162] Still extant, however, is the brief submitted by the Incorporation in support of the bill. This document concluded that the 'experience [of incorporating] has proved it to be in every respect radically bad' and it would be 'expedient to return to the old English system of parochial economy with regard to the poor as enacted by the 43 of Eliz'.[163]

---

153 SROI ADA11/A/B/3/8.
154 SROI ADA11/A/B/1/7.
155 SROI ADA11/A/B/3/9–10.
156 Documents 61 and 63.
157 Documents 64 and 65.
158 Document 66.
159 Document 71.
160 Six parishes voted against the proposal: Earl Soham, Easton and Kettleburgh in Loes Hundred and Debach, Ramsholt and Ufford in Wilford Hundred. The vote was close in three of these parishes but in both Ufford and Kettleburgh 28 dissented to the bill and 10 assented; in Ramsholt all 24 voted against the bill. Documents 72–4, 87.
161 Document 75.
162 Document 86.
163 Document 83.

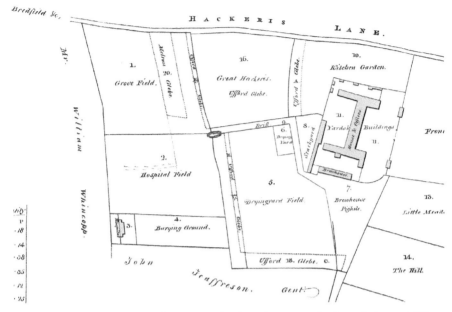

Plate 1. Portion of plan of Melton House, lands and premises, by Isaac Johnson, 1825

The petition was submitted to the Commons in February 1826, and was referred to a committee chaired by Lord John Fitzroy and Sir William Rowley.[164] Leave was granted to bring in a bill, which was laid before the chamber on 15 February.[165] After the bill's second reading, a counter-petition was laid before the chamber.[166] This had little influence as the bill, with minor amendments, was ingrossed on in March, gaining Royal Assent on 22 March 1826.[167] It is worth noting that the sole extant pre-disincorporation plan of Melton House dates from the years covered by this minute book. Isaac Johnson (1753–1835) of Woodbridge surveyed the incorporation's lands on 23 September 1825. His rough workings, sketched on paper (40cm by 32cm), were then reproduced on parchment (60cm by 45cm) in ink and watercolour (plate 1). It contains several tables stating the size of the fields and buildings owned by the incorporation. The plan appears to have been drawn up to facilitate an exchange of land between Ufford rectory and the Incorporation. The land to be exchanged measured 3 acres 2 rods and 38 perches. Ufford rectory was to acquire Grove Field, which lay at the very edge of the Incorporation's extensive site, while the land to be obtained by the Incorporation lay closer to the main buildings. No reference is made to the proposed exchange in either the quarterly or the weekly minute books.[168]

---

164 HCPP, *Commons' Journal*, Volume 81, p. 31 (10 February 1826).

165 HCPP, *Commons' Journal*, Volume 81, p. 40 (14 February 1826) and pp. 49–50 (15 February 1826).

166 HCPP, *Commons' Journal*, Volume 81, p. 80 (20 February 1826) and p. 104 (27 February 1826).

167 HCPP, *Commons' Journal*, Volume 81, p. 122 (3 March 1826), p. 132 (7 March 1826) and p. 163 (22 March 1826). HLPP, *Lords' Journal*, Volume 58, p. 86 (7 March 1826) and p. 93 (22 March 1826).

168 SROI ID407/D/1 (rough sketch) and SROI ID407/D/18 (parchment copy). There is no reference to this survey in John Blatchly's account of Johnson, but similar examples are illustrated therein. As

Plate 2. The front of the Melton Asylum Administration Block, 1908

Post-Disincorporation Documents

The first trustees' meeting was held on 16 October 1826.[169] It agreed that the paupers resident in the house should be discharged as quickly as possible, an inventory of the Incorporation's property drawn up and legal opinion sought over the disposal of the church lands.[170] There were ninety-seven inmates, of whom eighteen were from Ramsholt, the only parish which voted unanimously against disincorporation.[171] It was agreed to return all parish paperwork as soon as possible and John Lewin was appointed to oversee the auction of the Incorporation's possessions. Robert Cana of Woodbridge was commissioned to dispose of Melton House by public auction, and if that failed, George Thompson of Woodbridge would be appointed to dispose of the house through private contract.[172]

At their second meeting, the trustees were approached by a deputation of county magistrates.[173] Led by Ambrose Harbord Steward, a deputy-lieutenant for Suffolk, they hoped to purchase and then convert the house into a lunatic asylum. As no bid had been received by the cut-off date, negotiations opened with the county's representatives. The trustees' initial price of £10,000 was met by a counter-offer of £6,500. This figure was declined, though the trustees' new figure of £8,000 was

---

Blatchly notes (*Isaac Johnson of Woodbridge: Georgian Surveyor and Artist* (Dorchester, 2014), p. 2), land surveys provided nine-tenths of Johnson's income with the other tenth arising from his better known artistic commissions.

[169] Document 93.
[170] Document 94.
[171] Document 95.
[172] Documents 90 and 91.
[173] Document 98.

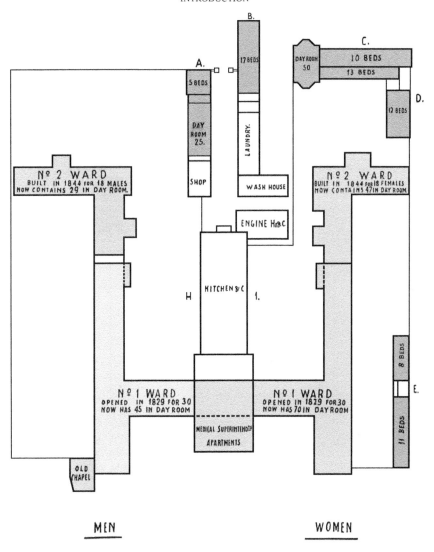

MEN

WOMEN

Plate 3. Ground floor plan of St Audry's Hospital, 1879

seen as acceptable.[174] By the time of the final trustees' meeting on 24 May, £7,568 14s. 3d. remained to be apportioned amongst the parishes in the ratio of the original assessments, a task completed by 24 September 1827.[175]

Melton House reopened in 1829, this time as the Suffolk County Lunatic Asylum (plates 2–5). In 1906 it was redesignated as the Suffolk District Asylum, and it was renamed St Audry's Hospital in 1917. From 1930 until its closure in 1993 it

---

[174] Document 103.
[175] Document 113.

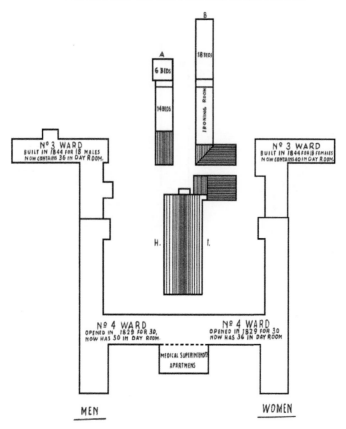

Plate 4. First floor plan of St Audry's Hospital, 1879

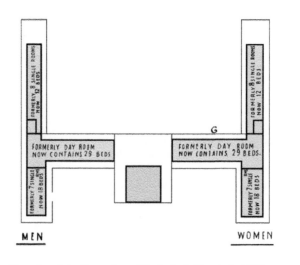

Plate 5. Attic floor plan of St Audry's Hospital, 1879

was known as St Audry's Hospital for Mental Diseases. Parts of the building have now been converted into private residences; the administration block with the main entrance has been a Grade II listed building since 11 June 1985 and the South Entrance Pavilion has been Grade II listed since 14 November 1997.

The Loes and Wilford Local Acts

The Loes and Wilford Incorporation became a legal entity in 1765 when seventeen of the nineteen parishes in Loes Hundred combined with the sixteen parishes of Wilford.[176] Loes, the smaller of the two, covered some 25,143 acres while Wilford covered 31,500 acres (see map 3 and table 4). A body of directors and acting guardians became responsible for poor relief in these hundreds for the next sixty-one years.[177] This governing body, vested with additional powers, operated alongside the traditional structure of overseers and churchwardens. The Act of 1765 was amended by further Acts passed in 1791 and 1810.[178]

Loes			Wilford		
Parish	**Acreage**	**Population**	**Parish**	**Acreage**	**Population**
Brandeston	1,196	287	Alderton	2,600	425
Butley	2,000	250	Bawdsey	2,640	344
(Campsey) Ash	1,814	327	Boulge	545	39
Charsfield	1,290	411	Boyton	1,890	201
Cretingham	1,639	246	Bredfield	1,067	334
Earl Soham	1,945	563	Bromeswell	1,442	143
Easton	1,462	304	Capel	2,000	162
Eyke	2,800	308	Dallingho	1,495	246
Hacheston	1,727	543	Debach	500	117
Hoo	1,164	124	Hollesley	2,600	461
Kenton	1,210	243	Melton	1,408	501
Kettleburgh	1,400	272	Petistree	1,768	241
Letheringham	1,100	138	Ramsholt	1,990	152
Marlesford	1,268	315	Shottisham	1,033	161
Monewden	1,063	157	Sutton	5,789	406
Rendlesham	2,065	216	Ufford	1,555	450
			Wickham Market	1,178	896
Total	**25,143**	**4,700**		**31,500**	**5,279**

Table 4. Parishes of the Loes and Wilford Incorporation with their size and population in 1801

---

[176] 5 Geo. 3 c. 91 (1765).

[177] The term director(s) refers to both director(s) and acting guardian(s) hereafter.

[178] 31 Geo. 3 c. 72 (1791) and 50 Geo. 3 c. 119 (1810).

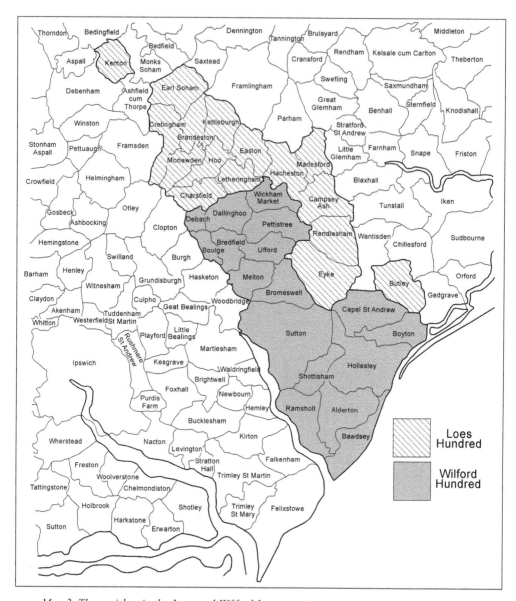

Map 3. The parishes in the Loes and Wilford Incorporation

Powers invested in the 1765 Act	Amendments of 1791 and 1810
Guardians of the poor comprise freeholders rated at £30 per annum, leaseholders rated at £60 per annum, JPs and rectors. To operate as one body politic and corporate in law.	1791. Directors rated at £50 per annum for freeholders.
24 directors to be elected at the first meeting which must be held within three months of gaining Royal Assent.	1791. The initial 24 directors that were to continue to hold office named.
The corporation may borrow up to £10,000.	1791. The corporation may borrow up to £14,000. 1810. The corporation may borrow an additional £5,000.
The corporation may buy up to 50 acres of land.	1791. The corporation may enlarge the house of industry and build a house of correction.
The corporation may bind children as apprentices: males to the age of 21 and females to the age of 18.	1791. No apprenticeship to extend beyond the age of 18.
The corporation may appoint a governor and a clergyman for the house of industry.	1791. A governor, matron, surgeon, clergyman and schoolmaster may be appointed.
A general meeting must be called within three months of the house's completion to fill any vacancies in the body of directors and to elect 36 acting guardians. The meeting is to appoint a treasurer and a clerk.	1791. A security is to be taken from the treasurer when the office is taken up.
The director and acting guardians may make bye-laws, rules and orders for the better government of the poor.	1791. The former bye-laws to remain in force and new ones may be made.
Annual meetings are to be held to elect director and acting guardians, to audit the treasurer's accounts, and to appoint six directors and nine acting guardians for each quarter of the following year.	
General Meetings of the director and acting guardians to be held once a quarter. For non-attendance at a quarterly meeting a director to be fined 20s. and an acting guardian fined 10s.	1791. The fine for non-attendance of a director increased to £5 and for an acting guardian to 50s.
Weekly meetings to held at the house every Monday morning from 10 am.	1791. Fine for the absence of a director from the weekly meeting set at 20s.; for an acting guardian, 10s.

Powers invested in the 1765 Act	Amendments of 1791 and 1810
Each parish's contribution to the annual assessment is to be based on an average of the poor rates raised 1753–60.	1791. May increase the assessments by up to 33 per cent. The assessment may not fall to below that figure until at least 66 per cent of the capital sum borrowed has been repaid. 1810. Assessments divided into two forms: 1. Average ongoing expenses for maintenance of poor to be freshly calculated every ten years and allocated by the average number of poor each parish admits to the house over those years. 2. The original debt is to be paid off based on ratio of the new assessments.
Parish officers not assisting the director and acting guardians may be fined up to £5.	1791. Overseers failing to inform the director and acting guardians of paupers moving into their parish without certificate or of a single woman to be fined 40s. and the costs of maintenance to be met by the parish concerned.
Director and acting guardians may issue settlement certificates and are to receive all existing parish bastardy certificates.	1791. Illegitimate children may not gain a settlement in Melton by being born in the house. All future bastardy certificates to be issued by the director and acting guardians.
Director and acting guardians may set inmates of the house to work on a stock of flax, hemp, wool etc.	1791. The director and acting guardians may contract out the employment of the poor. Idle persons may be punished.
The poor found guilty of profanity to be punished through abatement of diet and distinction of dress.	1791. Punishment increased to solitary confinement, abatement of diet, distinction of dress and diet, or being placed in the stocks for up to 24 hours.
The poor convicted of stealing the corporation's materials may be sent to house of correction and be publicly whi**pped.**	**1791. 20s. to £10 fine** for those convicted of receiving goods stolen from the house of industry.
The industrious poor may be granted rewards from the profits of their industry.	1791. Any poor persons able to support themselves may be discharged. Likewise if they can be supported by family members or friends.
Extraordinary general meetings can be called by ten or more directors and acting guardians rated in excess of £5,000 pa.	

Powers invested in the 1765 Act	Amendments of 1791 and 1810
1826 Act of Disincorporation All the former acts repealed. The trustees for overseeing the disincorporation are named and all the property of the Incorporation is vested in the trustees. The trustees are empowered to collect any debts owing to the corporation and to pay demands from creditors as far as the common funds will allow. The trustees may pull down or sell the existing buildings along with the land and the contents of the property. All monies raised are to be vested in the trustees.	

Table 5. An overview of the 1765 Act of Incorporation set alongside later amendments

Loes and Wilford was disincorporated in 1826, with poor relief reverting to the individual parishes.[179] All paupers resident in the house at the time of its sale were sent to their parish of settlement, and once the house was sold, the proceeds from the sale were reimbursed to the parishes in the same ratio as the original assessments.

Did disincorporation provide the hoped for savings? Graph 2 displays the money expended on maintaining the poor by the Incorporation from 1813 to 1834. In 1825, the final full year before disincorporation, the Incorporation expended £12,771 on maintaining the poor. Although this figure fell by an average of 13 per cent during the following four years, from 1830 onwards expenditure reverted to a figure similar to 1826 and even exceeded it in 1832. Disincorporation offered mixed blessings for the individual parishes too. Seven of the twelve parishes that were so vehemently anti-Incorporation in 1810 gained, at least to some degree, from disincorporation. Charsfield fared best and achieved substantial savings, with expenditure on the poor reducing from £615 in 1825 to £352 in 1833 and £463 in 1834. Other parishes were not so fortunate: Eyke's expenditure rose from £250 to over £400 for the same dates.

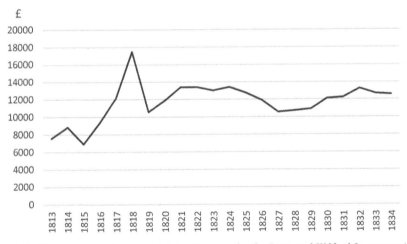

Graph 2. Money expended on maintaining the poor by the Loes and Wilford Incorporation, 1813–34

---

[179] Repealed by 7 Geo. 4 c. 1 (1826). Earlier amendments were 31 Geo. 3 c. 72 (1791) and 50 Geo. 3 c. 119 (1810).

Following the Poor Law Amendment Act of 1834 the thirty-three parishes were allocated either to the Plomesgate Union or to the Woodbridge Union.[180] The former, created on 30 December 1835, consisted of forty parishes and was centred on the purpose-built union workhouse at Wickham Market.[181] The Woodbridge Union, created on 3 October 1835, was centred on Carlford and Colneis' former house of industry at Nacton.[182] The unions remained in operation until 1929, when the Local Government Act of that year transferred their functions to the newly created county councils.[183]

---

[180] 4&5 William IV c. 75.

[181] The following parishes from Loes and Wilford formed part of the Plomesgate Union: Brandeston, Butley, Campsey Ash, Cretingham, Earl Soham, Easton, Eyke, Hacheston, Hoo, Kenton, Kettleburgh, Letheringham, Marlesford, Monewden, Rendlesham and Wickham Market.

[182] The following parishes from Loes and Wilford formed part of the Woodbridge Union: Alderton, Bawdsey, Boulge, Boyton, Bredfield, Bromeswell, Capel, Charsfield, Dallingho, Debach, Hollesley, Melton, Petistree, Ramsholt, Shottisham, Sutton, and Ufford.

[183] 19 Geo. V c. 17.

EDITORIAL NOTES

Emmanuel Le Roy Ladurie once observed that historians are either parachutists or truffle hunters. The first hover far above the landscape of the past looking for general patterns; the second grub about with their noses searching for some minute and precious fact. Each offers a vital perspective on the past and one can often correct the other.[1] Acknowledging that most historians are a complex amalgam of the two, Ladurie's metaphor underpins the editorial decisions taken for this volume, the overriding requirement of which is to provide an accurate portrayal of the archival records associated with the Loes and Wilford Incorporation. This volume will, therefore, cater to the needs of the truffle hunter. But to have transcribed merely a single Quarterly Minute Book (QMB) in its entirety would have failed to do justice to the rich variety of records available and would have neglected to provide the reader with a sense of the Incorporation's rich narrative thread: the parachutist's approach.

In order to reduce the Incorporation's wide array of documents to an assimilable form, decisions have been taken over how to edit the enormous range of material. At the heart of this volume are the seven QMBs which cover the entire history of the Incorporation. Reflecting the directors' initial enthusiasm, the first three QMBs provide considerable information concerning the decisions required to manage the Incorporation. As the years progressed and the directors' fervour waned, the entries became far more mechanistic and repetitive so that the final four QMBs comprise little more than lists of out-door relief granted. In addition, from the outset the QMBs, like any cyclical record book, contain recurring themes, which become almost rhythmic: lists of children apprenticed or hired out; lists of merchants supplying the house; lists of those receiving out-door allowances; lists of paupers admitted into and discharged from the house; lists of salaries paid, and so on. The approach adopted here to deal with this material has been to record the first occurrence of a regular entry but to omit it thereafter. The only exception to this rule is the election of the governing body.

A similar approach has been adopted for the Weekly Minute Books (WMB), as these suffer from the same issue as the QMBs: the first two volumes provide considerable detail as to whom and why out-door relief was granted; the final volumes become a register of names and the amount of relief granted.

Omissions from the Minute Books should be clear to the reader: meetings recorded in the QMB were usually held in December/January, March, June and September/October each year; those recorded in the WMB took place every Monday throughout the year unless they coincided with the Quarterly Meeting. The main omissions from the first three QMBs are listed below.[2]

---

[1]   L. Stone, *The Past and Present Revisited* (London, 1987), p. 8.
[2]   A similar approach was adopted by Jane Fiske in editing *The Oakes Diaries*, where James Oakes' diary was cut by about half (Suffolk Records Society 32, p. 203).

First QMB   March 1771; September, December 1772; December 1773; June,
                       October 1775; March 1776; March 1777
Second QMB December 1785
Third QMB   June, October, December 1797; December 1798; October,
                       December 1799; December 1800; June, October,
                       December 1801; June, October, December 1802;
                       October, December 1803; June, October, December
                       1804
Fourth to Seventh QMB   Only the first full Quarterly Meeting has been tran-
                       scribed.

Finally, the directors' actions are supported by a multitude of extant miscellaneous papers. Where these documents assist understanding they have been included
in the relevant chapter. Documents 1 to 35 relate to the years covered by the first
QMB, documents 36 to 38 to the second QMB, documents 39 to 60 to the fourth
QMB, documents 61 to 88 to the seventh QMB, and documents 89 to 120 to the
post-disincorporation period. In each case an explanatory note is offered to explain
the relevance of a document.

The structure of each chapter follows the same pattern: the QMB, the WMB,
and then reference to any relevant miscellaneous documents. The history of the
Incorporation is charted in the following manner:

Chapter	Quarterly Minute Book	Draft Quarterly Minute Book	Weekly Minute Book
1	1765–84 SROI ADA11/A/B/1/1	1765 SROI ADA11/A/B/2/1 1768–69 SROI ADA11/A/B/2/2 1769–75 SROI ADA11/A/B/2/3 1776–85 SROI ADA11/A/B/2/4	1768–74 SROI ADA11/A/B/3/1 1774–80 SROI ADA11/A/B/3/2 1780–90 SROI ADA11/A/B/3/3
2	1784–91 SROI ADA11/A/B/1/2	1785–95 SROI ADA11/A/B/2/5	1790–98 SROI ADA11/A/B/3/4
3	1795–1805 SROI ADA11/A/B/1/3		1798–1804 SROI ADA11/A/B/3/5
4	1805–12 SROI ADA11/A/B/1/4		1804–12 SROI ADA11/A/B/3/6
5	1813–18 SROI ADA11/A/B/1/5		1812–17 SROI ADA11/A/B/3/7
6	1818–20 SROI ADA11/A/B/1/6		1817–20 SROI ADA11/A/B/3/8
7	1820–26 SROI ADA11/A/B/1/7		1820–24 SROI ADA11/A/B/3/9 1824–26 SROI ADA11/A/B/3/10
8	Papers relating to the disincorporated parishes		

EDITORIAL CONVENTIONS, WEIGHTS,
MEASURES AND MONEY

The following symbols have been used during editing:

< >   for deletions by the editor, usually of material of a repetitive nature or elements of the text detrimental to the overall flow

<6 named Directors>   indicates deletions by the editor with the substance of the deletion included within the chevron

[ ]   editorial insertions or explanations are in italics in square brackets. For example, [*Building Committee*] indicates that entry as being from the directors elected to the Building Committee

\ / editorial insertions of material that was loose in the minute books

Original spelling has been retained where this does not cause confusion. Abbreviated names, dates and places have been transcribed in full.

Avoirdupois weight

16 drams	=	1 ounce (oz.)
16 ounces	=	1 pound (lb.)
14 pounds	=	1 stone (st.)
28 pounds	=	1 quarter (qtr)
4 quarters	=	1 hundredweight (cwt)
20 hundredweights	=	1 ton (approximately equivalent to 1,016 kilograms)

Wool weight

7 pounds	=	1 clove
2 cloves	=	1 stone
2 stone	=	1 tod
60 tods	=	1 wey
2 wey	=	1 sack
12 sacks	=	1 last
240 pounds	=	1 pack

Liquid measure (ale and beer)

4 gills	=	1 pint (pt)
2 pints	=	1 quart (qt)
4 quarts	=	1 gallon (gal.) (approximately equal to 4.5 litres)
9 gallons	=	1 firkin
2 firkins	=	1 kilderkin
2 kilderkins	=	1 barrel
1½ barrels	=	1 hogshead
2 hogsheads	=	1 butt
1 butt	=	1 tun

Dry measure

2 pints	=	1 quart
4 quarts	=	1 gallon
2 gallons	=	1 peck
4 pecks	=	1 bushel
4 bushels	=	1 comb
8 bushels	=	1 quarter
5 quarters	=	1 load
2 loads	=	1 last

Long measure

12 inches (in.)	=	1 foot (ft)
3 feet	=	1 yard (yd)
5½ yards	=	1 rod, pole or perch
4 rods	=	1 chain
10 chains	=	1 furlong
8 furlongs	=	1 mile

Square measure

144 square inches	=	1 square foot
9 square feet	=	1 square yard
30¼ square yards	=	1 square rod
40 square rods	=	1 rood
4 roods	=	1 acre
1 acre	=	4,840 square yards

Money

2 farthings (¼d.)	=	1 halfpenny (½d.)
2 halfpennies	=	1 penny (1d.)
12 pennies	=	1 shilling (1s. or 1/-)
20 shillings	=	1 pound (£ or L)
21 shillings	=	1 guinea (1gn.)

GLOSSARY

Ale stool: trestle or X-stand for barrels
Apron: cloth or leather garment worn down the front for work and to protect other clothing
Architrave: elements of a door or window surround
Barrel: unit of capacity, a barrel of beer being 34 gallons
Bayse: thickish woollen cloth with short nap
Blewen: powder with mild bleaching property made of ultramarine, bicarbonate of soda and glucose
Boiler: hanging pot or cauldron for boiling
Bolster: long stuffed pillow, usually the width of the bed
Bolting mill: a chest fitted with a sieve for sifting flour
Bombazine: a twilled or corded material made from a mixture of silk and worsted or sometimes cotton and worsted
Broadcloth: originally black cloth for garments, 54 inches wide
Bunching block: heavy wooden stock or table on which to strike, thump or pound hemp or flax to bruise the flesh prior to retting (*q.v.*)
Bushel: a dry measure for grain containing 8 gallons
Butt: a large cask for beer containing one 108 gallons
Chaise: a light open carriage for one or more people
Chaldon: a measure of coal equivalent to 36 heaped bushels or 25½ hundredweight
Chamber pot: small earthenware pot for night-time urination
Chandler: a candle supplier
Cistern: a large container for liquid, of wood, pewter, lead or other materials
Cloth: a measure of wool
Clove: a measure of wool equivalent to 7 pounds
Comb/Coombe: a measure of capacity equalling 4 bushels
Copper: large vessel of copper hanging on chains over a fire, or fixed in a masonry stand with a fire underneath, used for heating water, boiling clothes, brewing etc.
Damask: fabric of linen and worsted
Fearnought: thick woollen cloth
Firkin: a cask whose capacity varied with its use: for butter 56 pounds, for beer 9 gallons
Gallipot: pot for ointment, usually of glazed earthenware
Garret: room on the top floor of the building, or in the roof space
Gridiron: iron grid, sometimes with legs and handle, for cooking in front of an open hearth
Guinea: £1 1s. 0d., the modern equivalent being £1 5p
Gyle vat: vessel containing wort fermenting during the process of brewing
Harrateen: stiff linen furnishing fabric, imitating damask
Heifer: young cow before it has calved
Hogshead: a measure of beer containing 54 gallons

Keeler: wide, shallow wooden tub or bowl used for cooling liquids like milk and also for purposes such as washing

Kersey: coarse cloth woven from long wool

Kneading trough: shallow trough for kneading dough for bread, usually standing on four legs

Lady Day: 25 March, an annual quarter day

Mash tub: large wooden vat containing the mash (malt plus hot water)

Mudscuppet: shovel with concave blade for digging out waterlogged ditches

Peck: a measure of capacity equal to one quarter of a bushel or two gallons of dry goods

Pewter: silvery grey alloy of tin and lead, the main metal for tableware

Plaister: plaster

Retting: use of micro-organisms and moisture on hemp to dissolve or rot away much of the cellular tissues surrounding the fibre bundles, and so facilitating separation of the fibre from the stem

Scantlings: dimensions, particularly cross-section of timber

Scuppet: a narrow shovel with edges turned up for turning malt or shovelling corn

Serge: woollen fabric used for furnishing and clothing

Sorts: wool that has been sorted and graded

Tick: case or covering for a pillow, mattress etc.; or linen cloth for bed linen

Tod: a unit of weight of wool equal to 28 pounds

Wool top: balls of wool from which the short fibres have been removed in the process of combing

THE DOCUMENTS

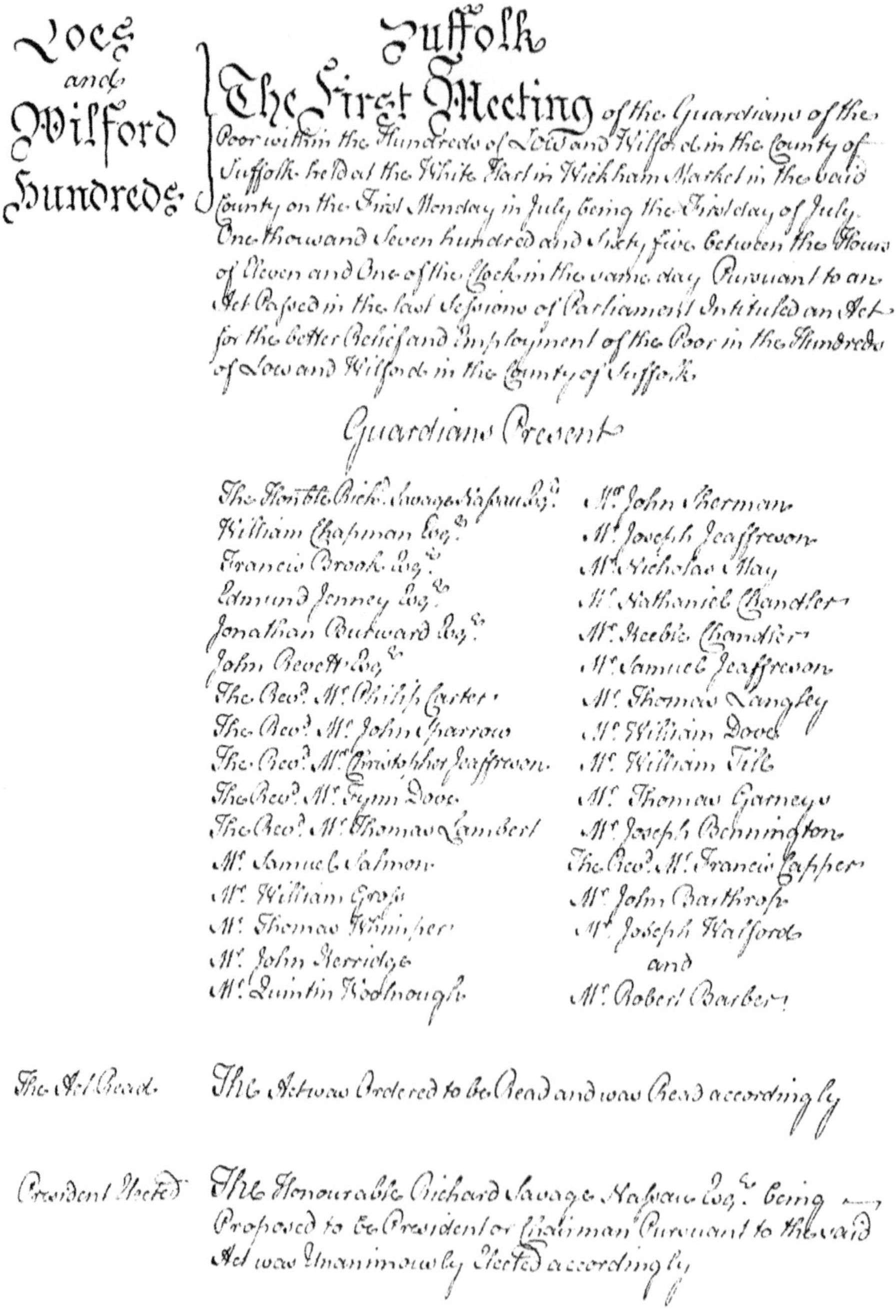

Loes and Wilford Hundreds

Suffolk

The First Meeting of the Guardians of the Poor within the Hundreds of Loes and Wilford in the County of Suffolk held at the White Hart in Wickham Market in the said County on the First Monday in July being the First day of July One thousand Seven hundred and Sixty five Between the Hours of Eleven and One of the Clock in the same day Pursuant to an Act Passed in the last Sessions of Parliament Intituled an Act for the better Relief and Employment of the Poor in the Hundreds of Loes and Wilford in the County of Suffolk.

Guardians Present

The Hon.ble Rich.d Savage Nassau Esq.r
William Chapman Esq.r
Francis Brook Esq.r
Edmund Jenney Esq.r
Jonathan Burward Esq.r
John Revett Esq.r
The Rev.d M.r Philip Carter
The Rev.d M.r John Garrow
The Rev.d M.r Christopher Jeaffreson
The Rev.d M.r Dynn Dove
The Rev.d M.r Thomas Lambert
M.r Samuel Salmon
M.r William Gross
M.r Thomas Whimper
M.r John Berridge
M.r Quintin Rodbrough

M.r John Sherman
M.r Joseph Jeaffreson
M.r Nicholas May
M.r Nathaniel Chandler
M.r Keeble Chandler
M.r Samuel Jeaffreson
M.r Thomas Langley
M.r William Dove
M.r William Tile
M.r Thomas Garney
M.r Joseph Bennington
The Rev.d M.r Francis Capper
M.r John Barthrop
M.r Joseph Walford
and
M.r Robert Barber

The Act Read. The Act was Ordered to be Read and was Read accordingly

President Elected The Honourable Richard Savage Nassau Esq.r being Proposed to be President or Chairman Pursuant to the said Act was Unanimously Elected accordingly

Plate 6. Minutes of the inaugural Quarterly Meeting held 1 July 1765

FIRST QUARTERLY MINUTE BOOK
1 July 1765–4 March 1784[1]

1 July 1765[2]

The first meeting of the Guardians of the Poor within the Hundreds of Loes and Wilford in the county of Suffolk, held at the White Hart in Wickham Market, on the first Monday in July, between the hours of eleven and one of the clock in the same day, pursuant to an Act passed in the last sessions of Parliament intituled An Act for the Better Relief and Employment of the Poor in the Hundreds of Loes and Wilford in the county of Suffolk.

Guardians Present

The Hon'ble Richard Savage Nassau Esq.	Mr John Sherman
William Chapman Esq.	Mr Joseph Jeaffreson
Francis Brook Esq.	Mr Nicholas May
Edmund Jenney Esq.	Mr Nathaniel Chandler
Jonathan Burward Esq.	Mr Keeble Chandler
John Revett Esq.	Mr Samuel Jeaffreson
The Revd Mr Philip Carter	Mr Thomas Langley
The Revd Mr John Sparrow	Mr William Dove
The Revd Mr Christopher Jeaffreson	Mr William Till
The Revd Mr Fynn Dove	Mr Thomas Garneys
The Revd Mr Thomas Lambert	Mr Joseph Bennington
Mr Samuel Salmon	The Revd Mr Francis Capper
Mr William Gross	Mr John Barthrop
Mr Thomas Whimper	Mr Joseph Walford
Mr John Kerridge	and
Mr Quintin Woolnough	Mr Robert Barber

The Act was ordered to be read and was read accordingly.

The Honourable Richard Savage Nassau Esq., being proposed to be President or Chairman pursuant to the said Act, was unanimously elected accordingly.

The following persons were unanimously elected by ballott, Directors of the Poor within the Hundreds of Loes and Wilford pursuant to the said Act.[3]

The Hon'ble Richard Savage Nassau Esq.	The Revd Mr Thomas Lambert
William Chapman Esq.	Mr Thomas Whimper
John Revett Esq.	Mr Joseph Jeaffreson
Jonathan Burward Esq.	Mr Thomas Gooding
Edmund Jenney Esq.	Mr Joseph Bennington

---

1   SROI ADA11/A/B/1/1. See Plate 1.
2   The date of this inaugural meeting was specified in the Act of Incorporation.
3   The Act required twenty-four directors to be elected to oversee the establishment of the Incorporation, to be replaced by a body of directors and acting guardians once the Incorporation was operational. Such directors were to be 'twenty-four of the most able and discreet of the Guardians'.

3

William Negus Esq.
Francis Brook Esq.
The Revd Mr Francis Capper
The Revd Mr Fynn Dove
The Revd Mr Eden Howard
The Revd Mr Philip Carter
The Revd Mr Christopher Jeaffreson

Mr Quintin Woolnough
The Revd Mr John Sparrow
Mr Joseph Walford
Mr William Woods
Mr John Bates
Mr Samuel Salmon
Mr John Sherman

John Revett Esq., being proposed to be Treasurer to the said Guardians pursuant to the said Act, was ballotted for and unanimously elected accordingly, and his salary appointed to be six pounds six shillings a year.[4]

Richard Wood, being proposed to be Clerk to the said Guardians pursuant to the said Act, was ballotted for and unanimously elected accordingly, and his salary appointed to be ten pounds and ten shillings a year.[5]

Ordered that the Treasurer procure a seal with a proper device for the Corporation.[6]

Ordered that proper books be provided by the Clerk.

Ordered that the Directors do meet ◇ at the White Hart in Wickham Market, in order to settle the proportions each of the parishes in the said Hundreds are to pay. And the officers of each parish are ordered to meet the Directors in the afternoon of the same day and place, to receive their books and are required to bring an account of the number of poor in each of their respective parishes.

1 August 1765[7]

At this meeting the proportions each of the several and respective parishes within the said Hundreds are to be assessed on a medium pursuant to the Act for incorporating the said Hundreds were settled in the following manner viz:[8]

	£	s.	d.		£	s.	d.
Ash	102	12	8	Alderton	59	15	1
Brandeston	66	16	11½	Bawdsey	44	6	0
Butley	65	5	3½	Boulge	28	18	7½
Charsfield *£93 16s. 1d.*	94	2	5¾	Bredfield	73	17	9
Creetingham *£80 2s. 3d.*	80	3	7½	Bromeswell	27	16	9
Dallingho	56	0	8½	Boyton *£10 2s. 5¾d.*	9	15	8¼
Earl Soham	80	8	4	Capell	39	11	4½
Easton	94	5	8½	Debach *£9 1s. 3½d.*	9	13	10½

---

4   The Act of Incorporation states the treasurer should be a 'proper and substantial person'.

5   The Act of Incorporation states the clerk should be a 'sufficient person'. The firm of Wood and Son were the Incorporation's legal representatives for its entire history. Richard Wood (1727–1806) established the firm in Woodbridge. He was the senior partner and his eldest son, also Richard (1756–86), the junior partner. Following Richard Wood junior's death, his place was taken by his younger brother John (1766–1856). John Wood became the senior partner on the death of his father in 1806. John Wood senior's son, John Wood junior (1795–1858), joined the firm as junior partner in 1815.

6   The Incorporation was a legal entity – it could sue and be sued. The seal was designed at a cost of 3s., and cost six guineas to manufacture. See below, miscellaneous document 2, p. 121.

7   Those present at this and subsequent meetings are omitted from future entries. Attendance hereafter only listed for the Annual Meetings.

8   The parochial assessment was to be based on an average for the seven years from Easter Day 1753 to Easter Day 1760 inclusive. The amount in italics is the amended figure following appeal.

Parish	£	s	d	Parish	£	s	d
Eyke	51	2	8¼	Hollesly	92	15	0
Hatcheston	71	9	7	Melton	73	10	9¼
Hoo *£24 9s. 0d.*	25	1	9½	Petistree	63	18	7¾
Kettleburgh	53	14	0	Ramsholt	63	12	3¾
Kenton	83	4	1½	Sutton	146	17	6¼
Letheringham	32	15	6	Shottisham	25	15	9
Monewden	15	15	10¼	Ufford *£94 19s. 4¾d.*	98	1	7½
Marlesford	97	10	6¼	Wickham Market	108	9	1
Rendlesham	36	12	8		966	15	10¼
	1,107	2	6		3	8	0¼
	1	0	6¾		963	7	10¼
	1,106	1	11¼		1,106	1	11¼
				Annual Income	2,069	8	9¼

4 November 1765

Ordered that the sum of four hundred pounds be borrowed on the credit of this Corporation at the interest of four pounds per cent per annum.[9]

Ordered that the next meeting of Directors be advertized that appeals at that meeting will be heard of such parishes who think themselves aggrieved by the assessment made upon them. And it is ordered that notice be forthwith sent to each parish within the said Hundreds of sums assessed.[10]

13 January 1766

It is ordered on the appeals being this day heard of the several parishes following, that the yearly assessment of the said several parishes following shall be assessed at the following sums, that is to say: the parish of Boyton at the yearly sum £10 2s. 5¾d., the parish of Charsfield £93 16s. 1d., the parish of Debach £9 1s. 3½d., the parish of Hoo £24 9s. 0d., the parish of Ufford £94 19s. 4¾d., and the parish of Creetingham £80 2s. 3d.[11]

Ordered that the next meeting of the Directors be advertized <> that proposals will then be received by the Directors from any person that hath a parcel of land to dispose of in a convenient part of either of the said Hundreds not exceeding fifty acres nor less than twenty acres, and to be purchased for the use of the Directors and Guardians of the Poor within the said Hundreds.[12]

3 March 1766

Ordered that the Clerk do make an inquiry against the next meeting whether there is a piece of freehold land in Bromeswell, near to Mr Collett's farm, sufficient to build a House upon for the use of the poor of the said Hundreds. And that inquiry

---

9   The Act of Incorporation allowed the directors to borrow any sum up to £10,000.

10 Overseers and churchwardens were instructed to attend the meeting on 1 July 1765 and leave their account books for the years 1753 to 1760 with the directors. The directors could keep the books for up to forty days. If no book was offered then the directors could assess that parish at their discretion.

11 The parish officers had the right to appeal. Appeals led to a reduction for the parishes of Charsfield, Creetingham, Debach, Hoo and Ufford and an increase for Boyton. These changes are shown in italics in the entry for 1 August 1765.

12 The Act of Incorporation specified a maximum of 50 acres. Such land was to be located in an area 'which [the directors] think most fit and convenient for the situation of an house for the reception and employment of the poor'. It was to be purchased in fee simple, and was to have no impact on the assessment levied for the parish in which it was situated.

be likewise made of Mr Kilderbee about Mr Brograve's estate in the occupation of John Steggall of Wickham Market in order to purchase.

Ordered that the next meeting of the Directors be advertized <> that the sum of four hundred pounds will then be wanted to be borrowed on the credit of the said Corporation in shares of one hundred pounds each.[13]

14 April 1766

Ordered that the Clerk do apply for one thousand pounds, at four pounds and ten shillings per cent per annum against the next meeting, and that it be mentioned in the next advertizement that such a sum is wanted at that interest.[14]

Ordered that the Clerk do apply to Mr John Whincopp to know if he will dispose of White Pightle in Melton, and any other lands adjourning and the price, and likewise to apply to Mr William Waller to know if he will dispose of the Whinney Hill in Melton or other lands adjourning, and the price. And if they will either of them dispose of the above lands to desire their attendance at the next meeting.

Ordered that the Clerk do apply to William Chapman Esq. to know if he will enfranchise Mr Anthony Collett's farm in Bromeswell, and if he will then to apply to the heirs at law of Mr Chapman's estate to know if they will join and to report their answers at the next meeting.

Ordered that at the next meeting <> proposals will be received for the purchase of land not exceeding fifty acres.

28 April 1766

Ordered that <8 named directors>[15] be a Committee appointed to inspect Mr Wallers, Mr Whincopps, and Mr Skinners lands.[16] And to meet at the Coach and Horses, in Melton, on Friday next to treat with either of them for the purchase of either or any part of their lands for the use of the Corporation as they shall think proper.

Ordered that two hundred particulars be imediately got printed by the Clerk as this day settled, and four of them be sent to the officers of each parish within the said Hundreds, and the rest to be divided amongst the Directors to be distributed by them as they shall think proper.

The sum of six hundred pounds being this day borrowed of Robert Barthrop of Hollesly, in the said county, Gent. for six months at the rate of four pounds and ten shillings per cent per annum. It is ordered the same be imediately paid into the hands of John Revett Esq., the Treasurer, for the use of the said Corporation.

Ordered that the Treasurer do pay Mr Samuel Kilderbee, the Solicitor, his bill for obtaining the Act, and Mr Richard Wood his bill as Clerk to the Committee for settling the Act.

---

13 There had been no response to the request for funding made on 4 November 1765.
14 After the failure to raise capital at 4 per cent, the interest rate was increased to 4½ per cent.
15 The names of members of the various committees are omitted from subsequent entries.
16 The Act of Incorporation specified a committee of seven to purchase of the land and oversee the building of the house of industry.

2 May 1766[17]

At a meeting of the Committee appointed to treat for the purchase of lands for the use of the Corporation of the Directors and Guardians of the Poor within the said Hundreds held at the Coach and Horses in Melton within the Hundred of Wilford.

The Committee, having looked over Mr Whincopps land, do not approve either of situation or price. The Committee do agree that Skinners land in Bredfield be agreeable to be purchased for the use of the Corporation at the price of £330, being 30 years purchase if the Directors approve of it. The Committee having looked over a messuage and lands belonging to William Negus Esq., in Melton, do agree that the same is agreeable to be purchased for the use of the said Corporation at the price of £550, being 25 years purchase if the Directors approve of it.

12 May 1766

The Committee appointed ◇ having reported at this meeting that Mr Waller will not dispose of his land, that Mr Whincopps land is very improper, that Mr Skinners land, together with some land belonging to William Negus Esq., in Melton, within the Hundred of Wilford, is agreeable, if approved of by the Directors. And the Revd Mr Christopher Jeaffreson having now proposed to sell some lands in Melton, aforesaid, for the use of the Corporation. It is ordered that <7 named directors> be a Committee appointed to look over the said land belonging to Mr Jeaffreson and to report the quality and situation thereof immediately to the Directors present.[18]

The above Committee, having reported to the Directors that the Revd Mr Jeaffresons land in Melton, aforesaid is of a good quality, and of a proper situation for the purchasing for the use of the Corporation. And the Directors having treated with Mr Jeaffreson for the same. It is ordered that four pieces belonging to Mr Jeaffreson in Melton, aforesaid, containing about twenty seven acres, be purchased of Mr Jeaffreson for the use of the Corporation on the following terms viz: that the land be measured hedge, ditch and row, to be set at one guinea an acre, and to be paid for out at the rate of twenty eight years purchase. The timber to be valued as to the quantity by two indifferent persons, one to be chosen by the Directors and the other by Mr Jeaffreson, and to be paid for at the rate of three pounds and ten shillings a load. The pollards (except such as stand in the rows and banks, which are included in the purchase) to be likewise valued by two indifferent persons as aforesaid, and to be paid for as they shall value them. The land to be conveyed on or before the tenth day of October next at the expense of the Directors, and the Directors to receive the rents and profits from that time. The Directors to have liberty to go on to the lands imediately to erect their buildings or otherwise, paying Mr Jeaffreson such damages as shall be done to his corn as two indifferent persons shall value it at. And Mr Jeaffreson to make good his title or otherwise at his expence.

Ordered that the timber and pollards upon Mr Jeaffresons lands be valued by Anthony Matthews and Daniel Manthrop in the presence of Francis Brooke Esq. And that such of them be immediately felled by the direction of Mr Brooke and Mr Jeaffreson as shall be thought fit. That the top wood and bark be disposed of for the use of the Corporation at their discretion. And that the land be measured by John Johnson and Simon Paternoster for both parties.

---

17 The entry for 2 May 1766 is in the draft QMB, SROI ADA11/A/B/2/1, and has not been transferred to the QMB.

18 The Revd Mr Christopher Jeaffreson was a director of the Incorporation. The land appears to have been inspected while the other directors continued with the meeting.

The sum of four hundred pounds being this day borrowed of Robert Barthrop of Hollesly in the said county, Gent., for six months at the interest of four pounds and ten shillings per cent per annum. ◇ NB. Five indentures were accordingly signed by the Directors present at two hundred pounds each as a security for the above four hundred pounds and the former six hundred pounds advanced by the said Robert Barthrop at the last meeting, which said indentures bear date and commence from the twenty eighth day of April last.

Ordered that the next meeting be advertized ◇ that plans will then be received for the building a Poor House for the said Hundreds to contain 350 persons. And that such person whose plan shall be approved of will be paid five guineas for the same.

26 May 1766

Francis Brooke Esq. at this meeting reported that the timber and pollards upon Mr Jeaffresons lands have been carefully valued by Anthony Matthews and Daniel Manthrop, and that the timber amounts to forty pounds and twelve shillings, and the pollards to thirty two pounds and twelve shillings, the whole to seventy three pounds and four shillings. The measurement of Mr Jeaffresons land by John Johnson and Simon Paternoster being likewise produced, amounts to twenty nine acres exclusive of Ufford Glebe, Melton Glebe, and Mr Edwards's land which are intermixed and which Mr Jeaffreson is to make good. It is ordered that the conveyances be prepared for the said land. And that Mr Jeaffreson be paid for the timber as above, and for the land according to the quantity as measured agreeable to the agreement made by the Directors and Mr Jeaffreson at the last meeting.

Ordered that Francis Brooke Esq. do pay Mr Matthews for his trouble in measuring the timber, and Mr Manthrop for his trouble in ordering the timber to be felled, and the top wood and bark to be disposed of. And that Mr Brooke do bring in the account for the same as soon as conveniently he can.

Ordered that Mr Wood, the Clerk, do prepare an abstract of Mr Jeaffresons title to the above lands, and likewise a draft of the conveyance from Mr Jeaffreson to himself as a Trustee for the Guardians and Directors. And that the same be laid before Humphry Rant Esq. for his approbation on behalf of the Corporation.

Ordered that the Treasurer do pay Mr Simon Paternoster ten shillings and six pence for measuring Mr Jeaffresons land on behalf of the Corporation.

Ordered that the Treasurer do pay Mr Kilderbee six pounds nineteen shillings and six pence for the Corporation Seal, and that the rest of Mr Kilderbee's bill be referred to another meeting.

Ordered that <9 named directors> or any five of them, be a Committee ◇ to settle the plan of Matthew Grayston, approved of this day for a building. And to settle the particulars on such plan in order for estimates.

Ordered that the Treasurer do pay one guinea for the expenses of the persons that this day delivered in their plans.

Ordered that the next meeting ◇ estimates will be received for a building for a House of the Poor according to the plan and particulars which will be left in the hands of Mr Richard Wood, the Clerk, on <5 June> for inspection.[19]

---

[19] The Act specified that the directors had two years in which to build the house of industry.

3 June 1766[20]

A Meeting of the Committee appointed to settle a plan and particulars for a building held at the White Hart in Wickham Market.

The above Committee having again surveyed the plan of Matthew Grayston do find that the building agreeable to that plan will not only be attended with too great an expence but will likewise be too extensive for the purpose required and after consulting the person who was appointed to meet the Committee on this occasion have discovered several objections of consequence to the principal part of the building. The Committee have therefore thought proper to order the deferring the advertisement for estimates till they can have the sentiments of the Directors at the next meeting.

Mr Lane and Mr Aldis produced to the Committee two plans for a building which they were ordered to bring again at the next meeting of the Directors together with particulars and scantlings of each in order that no delay may be given to this business. And they likewise ordered that Mr Redgrave be desired to meet the Directors at the said Meeting to give his advice with regard to the plans and particulars in order that estimates may be imediately delivered in. And that this advertisement be altered that estimates cannot be received at the next meeting the plan not being as yet approved of.

16 June 1766

At this meeting Mr Lane, Mr Aldis, and Mr Grayston produced other plans. And Mr Redgrave, being likewise present, the Directors did therefore, with his assistance, approve of the plan delivered at this meeting by Mr Grayston, with the alterations as proposed by Mr Redgrave. It is ordered that Mr Grayston do alter his plan as proposed by Mr Redgrave, and make particulars of the scantlings thereupon to be approved of by Mr Redgrave. That the plan and particulars should be left with the Clerk, for inspection and that a proper quantity of the particulars be got printed by the Clerk. That at the next meeting ◇ estimates will be received for a building according to the said plan and particulars. And that no estimate will be received after that time.

Ordered that the Treasurer do pay Mr Matthew Grayston five guineas for his plan being approved of.

Ordered that the Clerk do make an inquiry for evidence against James Woolnough, and proceed against him at the next assizes at the expence of the Corporation for a riot and misdemeanour committed against the Directors on the first day of August last.

7 July 1766

Ordered that the Treasurer do pay the Revd Mr Christopher Jeaffreson the sum of seven pounds seven shillings and nine pence for hay seeds and clover and laying the land.

Order that the Treasurer do pay Mr Richard Wood, the Clerk, his bill of thirty three pounds nineteen shillings and ten pence for advertizements, stamps, salary etc.

Mr John Lane, having delivered in his estimate of four thousand three hundred and fifty pounds for building a House of Industry for the said Hundreds, being the

---

20 The entry for 3 June 1766 is in the draft QMB, SROI ADA11/A/B/2/1, and has not been transferred to the QMB.

least sum offered. Ordered that articles be prepared between the Guardians and Directors and the said John Lane for the building the same accordingly.

Ordered that the Treasurer do pay Mr Matthew Grayston the sum of ten guineas for his trouble in settling the plan, elevations, sections, and particulars for the said building.

Ordered that the Treasurer do pay Mr Thomas Aldis two guineas for his trouble in making a plan and attending the Directors by their order.

Ordered that the Treasurer be paid six guineas for his salary due the first day of July instant.

Ordered that Mr Quintin Woolnough and Mr Joseph Bennington do look over and value the barley growing on Mr Jeaffresons land whereon the House is to be built. That the same may be cut down imediately and report it at the next meeting.

Ordered that the next meeting ◇ execute articles. And that a Committee of seven of the Directors do meet ◇ and go to the land and set out the building.

14 July 1766

Mr Woolnough and Mr Bennington reported at the meeting that they had looked over and valued the barley on Mr Jeaffresons land. And that they had valued it at eighty comb, the price to be ascertained at a medium of the market price of barley between Michaelmas and Christmas. And Mr Jeaffreson to allow eight pounds out of the same.

Ordered that Mr Jeaffreson be paid for the same accordingly.

Ordered that Mr Jeaffreson be paid twenty shillings for damage done to his wheat by carting, as estimated by Mr Woolnough and Mr Bennington.

Ordered that the next meeting ◇ execute articles between the Directors and John Lane. And that he be acquainted with the same and to appoint an inspector.

22 July 1766

Mr John Redgrave, being proposed by Francis Brooke Esq., and this day agreed upon to be Surveyor and Inspector of the building of the House of Industry intended to be erected at Melton.[21] It is ordered that the said John Redgrave do attend at the said building once a week at least, to inspect the same until it is completed. And that he be paid half a guinea a time for such his attendance and if he finds it necessary to attend oftener, that he be paid for the same accordingly. And that he enter in a book every attendance and what he shall do at that time. And to acquaint the Committee to be appointed to superintend the said building from time to time of the days of his attendance or of any other business as shall be necessary concerning the said building.

Mr John Lane, having refused to enter into articles for building the House of Industry or being any further concerned in the same, and Mr Matthew Grayston, on behalf of himself and Thomas Fulcher, having this day agreed to build the said House for the sum of four thousand and five hundred pounds, together with the timber now felled on the said premises. Ordered that articles be prepared between the Guardians and Directors and the said Matthew Grayston and Thomas Fulcher for the building the same accordingly.[22]

---

[21] John Redgrave acted as surveyor for several Suffolk incorporations. He was also overseeing the building of Bulcamp House for Blything Incorporation by this date.

[22] Thomas Fulcher of Debenham and Matthew Grayston of Woodbridge built several houses of industry. Their partnership began with the house of industry at Bulcamp (Blything). Fulcher's plans for the

Ordered that the Treasurer do pay Mr John Redgrave four guineas for his trouble in attending the Directors, settling the plan and particulars, and staking out the ground for the building.

Ordered that the next meeting <> execute articles.

29 July 1766

This day the articles being executed between the Guardians and Directors and Matthew Grayston and Thomas Fulcher for the building of the House of Industry for the said Hundreds. It is ordered that <16 named directors> or any seven of them be a Committee appointed to superintend the said building.[23]

Ordered that the Treasurer do pay Jerome Bright his bill for attending the assizes to give evidence against James Woolnough.

Ordered that the next meeting <> borrow twelve hundred pounds for the use of the Corporation.

13 October 1766

Ordered that the Treasurer do pay Mr Samuel Kilderbee the sum of ten pounds and seventeen shillings for interest on the money advanced by him to the clerk of the House of Commons.

Ordered that the sum of eight hundred and fifty two pounds and twelve shillings be paid by the Treasurer to the Revd Mr Christopher Jeaffreson for the purchase of the land according to the agreement made at a former meeting.[24]

The sum of five hundred pounds was this day borrowed of Elizabeth Wythe of Wickham Market in the county of Suffolk, spinster, at the interest of £4 10s. per cent per annum and four hundred pounds of Christopher Jeaffreson of Melton in the said county, Clerk, at the like interest and for which nine several securitys were given at £100 each payable in six months. The sum of two hundred and fifty pounds was likewise this day borrowed of Ann Growse of Bury St Edmunds in the said county, spinster, for which two several securitys were given at £100 and £150 payable in six months.[25]

Ordered that the Clerk do write to Mr John Lane and inform him that if he will make the Directors satisfaction at the next meeting for the barley that was cut by his order, that they will accept it and discharge him of all other damages. But if he refuses this offer then that the Directors will prosecute him for that and all other damages sustained by his not performing his agreement.

---

house were accepted by John Redgrave. Fulcher then tendered £7,045 17s. and Grayston £7,847 13s. 5d. The directors ordered Redgrave to amend the plans to make the building less expensive, which he did, estimating the new build at £6,841 16s. 6d. Fulcher tendered £7,199 8s. and Grayston £7,193. The directors decided to award the contract to both of them if Redgrave's lower figure was accepted, which it duly was. Redgrave was also Wangford's surveyor, and here Fulcher and Grayston's tender of £4,664 was accepted even though it had been underbid by Harris and Fish at £4,060. Although Grayston went into bankruptcy during the building of Melton House for £4,500, Fulcher went on to win the contract for building Stow's house at Onehouse for £5,434 6s.

23 The contract specifies when payments would be made: £1,000 when drains, cellars and foundations were completed; £550 for laying the first-floor joists; £550 when the eves were reached; £700 when tiled in; £550 when offices were completed; and the balance when all site work was finished.

24 Jeaffreson was paid £852 12s. for his 29 acres. Only a few incorporations appear to have purchased land offered following an advertisement: Wangford's directors paid £784 11s. for 44 acres at Shipmeadow, and Samford's directors paid £550 for 52 acres at Tattingstone. Colonel Wollaston, Stow's chairman, sold 22 acres for £598; John Rous, Blything's chairman, sold 25 acres for £236.

25 Subsequent entries concerning investments have been omitted.

12 January 1767

Ordered that the Treasurer do pay Mr Matthew Grayston and John Fulcher the builders <> the sum of five hundred pounds as a part of one thousand pounds which will be due to them for the first payment when they have compleated the drains and buildings to the water tables.

Ordered that Mr Matthew Grayston do provide a proper box to retain the papers and writings belonging to the Corporation.

Mr John Lane, having been wrote to by the Clerk agreeable to the order of the last meeting, he accordingly appeared at this and the Directors present consented to release him of all other damages on payment of the sum of thirty pounds for the barley agreeable to the order of the last meeting, which sum he refused to pay. It is therefore ordered that the said John Lane do pay the said sum of thirty pounds to the Treasurer on or before the next meeting and on non-payment thereof to be referred to the order of the Directors that shall be then present.

2 March 1767

Mr John Lane, having wrote to the Clerk that he would pay thirty pounds according to the order of the last meeting at any time when he should be drawn upon for the same. Ordered that the Treasurer do draw upon him for the same and give a discharge for the use of the Incorporation.

Ordered that the Treasurer do pay Matthew Grayston and John Fulcher <> the sum of five hundred pounds, being the remainder the sum of one thousand pounds due to them for their first payment for the building, the drains and buildings being compleated to the water tables.

11 May 1767

Ordered that the Treasurer do pay the Revd Mr Christopher Jeaffreson the sum of thirty six pounds for the barley as valued.

Ordered that the Treasurer do pay Mr Matthew Grayston, for self and partner, the sum of two hundred pounds in part of the sum of seven hundred pounds which will be due to them for the second payment for the building when the first floor of joists are laid.

Ordered that the Clerk do write to Mr Redgrave, the Surveyor, for his directions about the pumps, and on receipt of his answers to give directions to Mr Grayston the builder accordingly.

8 June 1767

Ordered that the lead pumps be continued, and that copper barrels be added to each of the pumps for the suckers to work in. It being an addition of one guinea to each pump, which is ordered to be paid to the builders over and above the contract.

Ordered that the Treasurer do pay Grayston and Fulcher, the builders, the sum of five hundred pounds <> being the remainder of the sum of seven hundred pounds, the second payment due to them when the first floor of joists are laid, which the surveyor has certifyed will be compleated by that time.

Ordered that the Boghouses be set farther backward than in the plan, that the filth may be conveyed into bings and not to run through the drains as designed in the plan. And that the additional expense be considered to the builders.

3 August 1767

Ordered that the Treasurer do pay Mr Richard Wood, the Clerk, his bill of sixty three pounds fifteen shillings and four pence.

Ordered that the Treasurer do pay Messrs. Grayston and Fulcher, the builders, the sum of five hundred and fifty pounds, being the third payment, the building being compleated to the eves.

This day, three securitys of one hundred pounds each, made to Elizabeth Wythe were transferred to Susanna White of Cambridge, spinster, and entred with the Clerk pursuant to the statute.[26]

Ordered that Francis Brooke Esq. do cause the turnips belonging to the Corporation to be twice well howed, and to be allowed six shillings and three pence an acre for both howings.

Ordered that Matthew Grayston do build a book case with yellow deal without a pediment, agreeable to the plan now delivered in, at the price seven pounds and seven shillings. And he to be paid for it when the same shall be completed.

Ordered that Matthew Grayston do finish and compleat the inside of the Chapple agreeable to the plan now delivered in, at the price of forty pounds. And he to be paid for it when the same shall be compleated.

2 November 1767

Ordered that the Treasurer do pay Messrs. Grayston and Fulcher, the builders, the sum of seven hundred pounds, being the fourth payment, the main building being tiled in.

Ordered and agreed that Matthew Grayston do erect, build, compleat and finish a Pest House, Bog House, and Coal Bing on the Corporation land in Melton, according to the plan delivered by Mr John Redgrave, for the sum of three hundred and sixty eight pounds and five shillings. For the well with a wooden pump for the said House, the sum of twenty eight pounds, and for the gates posts and irons to the same the sum of three pounds and fifteen shillings in the whole the sum of four hundred pounds, which is to be paid to the said Matthew Grayston when the whole shall be compleated and finished with the approbation of the said John Redgrave.

Ordered that at the next meeting ◇ estimates and proposals will then be received for providing the House of Industry with household furniture and brewing utensils for the said House as braziers work, tin work, pewterers work, coopers work, cast iron, wrought iron and carpenters work according to the dimensions, particulars and design which is left in the hands of Mr Richard Wood, Clerk to the Directors.

14 December 1767

Ordered that Matthew Grayston do compleat and fit up the Brew House ◇ according to the dimensions and scantlings this day signed by him at the price of one hundred pounds.

Ordered that John Smith, brazier, do compleat, finish and supply the said House of Industry with braziers work and tin work agreeable to the proposals and prices fixed on and signed by him this day.

Ordered that John Welton, dish turner, do compleat, finish and supply ◇ turners work agreeable to the goods, proposals and prices fixed on and signed by him this day.

---

[26] Similar entries concerning the transfer of securities are omitted.

Ordered that John Rogers, cooper, do compleat, finish and supply ⬦ coopers work agreeable to the goods, proposals and prices fixed on and signed by him this day.

Ordered that John Stannard, chair maker, do compleat, finish and supply ⬦ chairs, wheels, and reels agreeable to the quantity and prices fixed on and signed by him this day.

Ordered that Matthew Grayston do compleat, finish and supply ⬦ household furniture for the Governors apartments, also wrought iron, cast iron and carpenters work for the finishing the said House agreeable to the quantity, proposals and prices fixed on and signed by him this day.

Ordered that the inscription agreed on at the meeting be fixed on the piedemont over the Chapple door of the said House. And also another inscription agreed on at this meeting be fixed over the chimney at both ends of the great dining room by Matthew Grayston as soon as conveniently maybe.

Ordered that proposals with patterns will be received from such person or persons as shall be willing to offer the same for the providing of beds, bedding, cloaths and linnen for the poor of the House of Industry for the said Hundreds.[27]

1 February 1768

Ordered that Matthew Grayston ⬦ do render and white wash the innard brick walls of the main building wings, and Pest House for the sum of sixty five pounds. But in case the measurements of the same shall not amount to the money when surveyed, then the said Matthew Grayston to allow five pence a yard for such deficiency, and not to be allowed any more than the said sum of sixty five pounds if it should come to more.[28]

Thomas Tibbs of Ipswich, yeoman, being at this meeting approved of for a Governor of the House of Industry for the said Hundreds. Ordered that he go into the said House and enter upon his office at Lady Day next, and to continue in the same until the General Meeting of the Directors and Guardians.[29]

Ordered and agreed that Francis Brooke Esq., have the two pieces of land belonging to the Corporation called the Six Acres and Orphan Close, containing in the whole twelve acres, for one year from Michaelmas last at the rent of twelve guineas. And Orphan Close for one year longer from Michaelmas next at six guineas rent. To lay the Six Acre piece next spring, and Orphan Close the spring following, in a husband like manner with six sacks of hay seeds and three pounds of Dutch clover seed to an acre, and to be ploughed four clean earths and two baulking earths and harrowing in proportion.

Ordered that Thomas Whiting of Woodbridge, draper, do provide the Corporation with the following goods for cloathing of the poor of the House of Industry for the said Hundreds that is to say plain Yorkshire cloth, half thick Kersey, Padua serge, bays, Lancashire linnen, Russia linnen, check handkerchiefs, checks, hessens, Lancashire sheeting, fearnoughts, West Country ticks, blankets, breeches, feathers and hats. To be delivered ⬦ made and unmade, on or before <20 June>. To be paid

---

[27] The majority of contracts for fitting out Melton went to local tradesman. The same was true for the other houses of industry. Melton's directors would spend approximately £1,244 on fitting out the house. Blything's expended £2,414, Samford's, £1,385 and Carlford and Colneis' £855.

[28] All the houses of industry were modified during their building. For Melton this added approximately £1,300 to the overall cost. At Blything alterations added over £4,000 to the contract price.

[29] Thomas Tibbs would remain governor until June 1781.

for the same according to the several bills of parcells to be produced by him, being allowed a commission of five pounds per cent on the whole amount for his judgement, trouble and carriage providing the same.

Ordered that Henry Topple of Alderton, shoemaker, do provide the Corporation with shoes for men, women and children to be delivered <> on or before <25 June> according to the patterns and proposals approved of and delivered at this meeting. [*60 mens, 60 womens, 80 boys, 80 girls*][30]

Ordered that John Ablitt of Ipswich, stay maker, do provide the Corporation with leather stays for women and girls, to be delivered <> on or before <25 June> according to the patterns and proposals approved of and delivered at this meeting. [*80 womens, 60 girls*][31]

Ordered that the Treasurer do pay Messrs. Grayston and Fulcher, the builders, the sum of five hundred and fifty pounds being the fifth payment the offices to the buildings being erected and finished.

29 February 1768

Ordered that Mr Thomas Whiting do provide over and above the order at the last meeting roll towells at fourteen pence each, womens caps at six pence halfpenny each, girls caps at five pence halfpenny each, mens caps at six pence each, and boys caps at five pence each for the use of the Corporation.

Ordered that Matthew Grayston, the builder, be paid by the Treasurer the sum of four hundred pounds for the erecting and building a pest house for the Corporation,<> the same being completed, as reported by Mr Redgrave.

Ordered that Matthew Grayston do provide two large wainscott tables for the Committee Room, occasionally to join together, and to procure a proper bell for the cupula belonging to the House of Industry.[32]

11 April 1768

Ordered that the partition be taken down between two rooms at the end of the Great Chamber adjoining to the Governors apartment. That the door be stopt up into the said Great Chamber, and another made into the Governors apartment. That a fire place be made into the said room, and that shelves be affixed therein for laying the cloaths and bedding and other materials as a store room.[33]

Ordered that Mr Thomas Whiting do provide necessary table and bed linnen for the Governor agreeable to the provision made at the other Houses.

6 June 1768

Ordered that the Treasurer do pay John Ablitt his bill of twenty six pounds ten shillings and six pence for leather stays <> agreeable to his contract.

Ordered that the Treasurer do pay Mr Thomas Whiting the sum of five Hundred pounds in part of his contract for cloathing and bedding.

Ordered that the Treasurer do pay Mr John Welton his bill of fourteen pounds seventeen shillings and six pence for turners ware <> agreeable to his contract.

---

[30] SROI ADA1/A/B/2/2. This information was not transcribed to the QMB.

[31] SROI ADA1/A/B/2/2. This information was not transcribed to the QMB.

[32] The committee chamber was fitted out with a bookcase, two square wainscot tables, a large deal committee table and thirty oak chairs.

[33] The oversight of clothing and bed linen was a major issue for all the incorporations.

24 June 1768[34]

Ordered that the Treasurer do pay Mr John Smith, brazier, his bill of one hundred and thirty five pounds for brazier's goods, agreeable to his contract and for other necessarys for the House of Industry.

Ordered that the Treasurer do pay Mr Thomas Whiting the further sum of four hundred and seventy one pounds nineteen shillings and two pence in full for his contract for cloathing and bedding for the said House.

Ordered that the Treasurer do pay Mr John Rogers his bill of fifty six pounds ten shillings and six pence for coopers work, agreeable to his contract for the House of Industry.

Ordered that the Treasurer do pay Mr Joseph Thompson his bill of ten pounds nine shillings and four pence for malt, malt combs and hops for the said House.

Ordered that the Treasurer do pay Mr Henry Topple his bill of forty one pounds and six shillings for shoes, agreeable to his contract for the said House.

Ordered that the Treasurer do pay Mr John Stannard his bill of twenty pounds and nineteen shillings for chairs, wheels and reels, agreeable to his contract for the said House.

Ordered that the Treasurer do pay Mr Thomas Tibbs, the Governor, his bill of twelve pounds and twelve shillings for necessarys for the said House, and the sum of twenty three pounds and thirteen shillings for his salary and board to Midsummer 1768.

Ordered that the Treasurer do pay Mr Matthew Grayston, the builder, five hundred pounds in part of his last payment for his contract for the building and finishing the House of Industry.

Ordered that the Treasurer be paid his salary of six pounds and six shillings to the first July 1768.

27 June 1768[35]

Directors Present

The Hon'ble Richd Savage Nassau Esq.	The Revd Mr John Sparrow
Jonathan Burward Esq.	Mr Thomas Whimper
Francis Brooke Esq.	Mr Thomas Goodwin
John Revett Esq.	Mr John Bates
Mr John Sherman	Mr Quintin Woolnough
The Revd Mr Philip Carter	Mr Samuel Salmon
The Revd Mr Christopher Jeaffreson	Mr Joseph Bennington

Guardians Present

Mr John Whimper	Mr Henry Garrod
Mr Robert Sheming	Mr William Athow
Mr Thomas Page	Mr Jonathan Simpson
Mr William Waller	Mr Thomas Chandler
Mr Francis Rush	Mr George Lamb

---

34 This is the first example of a Previous Meeting. These were held a few days before the Quarterly Meeting for the perusal and approval of tradesmen's bills, to review the out-door allowances paid and agree the officers' salaries. Due to their repetitive nature subsequent previous meetings are omitted unless there is a point of note.

35 The first Annual Meeting after the House was completed. At this meeting spaces within the body of directors caused by those dying, removing or refusing to act were to be filled by ballot and thirty-six acting guardians were to be elected.

Mr Jeptha Waller

Mr Stephen Vertue

Mr John Woods

Mr William Dove

Mr Nathaniel Barthorp

Mr Thomas Taylor

Mr Stephen Blomfield

Mr Daniel Raydon

Mr Ralph Hall

Mr Thredkell

New Directors

Mr Martin Harsant of Earl Soham

The Revd Mr William Cooperthwaite

Mr John Sheppard of Monewden

Mr Robert Shemming of Rendlesham

Mr John Whimper of Alderton

and

Mr William Dove of Capell

Mr John Baldry of Alderton

were balloted for Directors to fill up the vacancies of such of the directors as are dead and refuse to act and were duly elected.

The following persons were ballotted for Acting Guardians to the House of Industry and were unanimously elected.

In Loes Hundred		In Wilford Hundred	
Ash	Mr William Crisp	Alderton	Mr John Barthorp
Brandeston	Mr John Pitcher		Mr John Moor
	Mr Edward Adams	Bawdsey	Mr John Harper
Butley	Mr Thomas Chandler	Bredfield	Mr Thomas Page
Charsfield	Mr Thomas Cole	Boyton	Mr Robert Barber
Creetingham	Mr Thomas Smith	Hollesly	Mr Thomas Trusson
Dallingho	Mr Stephen Blomfield		Mr Thomas Hendy
	Mr Ralph Hall	Melton	Mr James Woods
Earl Soham	Mr Samuel Barber		Mr George Linsted
	Mr John Scotchmer	Petistree	Mr John Jeaffreson
Easton	Mr Edmund Boyns	Ramsholt	Mr Thomas Saunders
Eyke	Mr William Gross	Sutton	Mr John Growse
Hatcheston	Mr Nathaniel Barthrop		Mr William Waller
Hoo	Mr William Till		Mr Francis Rush
Kettleburgh	Mr Thomas Langley	Shottisham	Mr Jeptha Waller
Kenton	Mr Thomas Garneys		Mr John Woods
Letheringham	Mr Richard Brook	Wickham Mkt	Mr Stephen Vertue
Marlesford	Mr Philip Moore		Mr Simon Paternoster

John Revett Esq., being proposed as Treasurer, was duly elected at his former salary.

The Revd Mr George Jones Palmer, being proposed to be Chaplain to the House of Industry, was duly elected, and his salary fixed at thirty five pounds a year.

Mr Thomas Tibbs, being proposed to be Governor to the said House, was duly elected, and his salary fixed at forty pounds a year.

Mr Samuel Salmon was ballotted to be Surgeon to the said House, and was duly elected, and his salary fixed at forty pounds a year.

Mr William Henchman was proposed and elected Out Surgeon for the Hundred of Loes, at the salary of twenty five pounds a year. And Mr John Syer was proposed and elected to be Out Surgeon for the Hundred of Wilford, at the like salary of twenty five pounds a year, and Mr Syer to be allowed extraordinary on account of the small pox being in Boyton and Hollesly.

Ordered that notices be sent to the several parishes within the said Hundreds to bring in their poor to the House of Industry in manner following:

Monday   July 11 1768   Kettleburgh, Capell, Brandeston

Bromeswell, Marlesford, Melton

Tuesday	12	Boyton, Letheringham, Ramsholt Butley and Earl Soham
Wednesday	13	Hatcheston, Hoo, Bredfield Sutton, Bawdsey and Easton
Thursday	14	Wickham Market, Hollesly, Ash Debach and Monewden
Friday	15	Eyke, Shottisham, Ufford Charsfield, Creetingham, Petistree
Saturday	16	Rendlesham, Dallingho, Alderton Boulge and Kenton

Ordered that the Governor do provide all proper necessarys for the House of Industry for the reception of the poor until further orders.

Mr Richard Wood was re-elected Clerk, and his salary fixed at twenty pounds a year.

Ordered that a meeting of the Directors and Acting Guardians <> for receiving of malt hops, wheat etc. for the remainder of the quarter until Michaelmas next and for coals for the years consumption.

The following persons were appointed Directors and Acting Guardians for the first quarter from Midsummer to Michaelmas.[36]

Directors	Guardians	
The Hon'ble Mr Nassau	1st Month	Mr Thomas Saunders
Jonathon Burward Esq.	Mr George Linsted	3rd Month
John Revett Esq.	Mr James Woods	Mr Thomas Smith
Edmund Jenney Esq.	Mr Thomas Trusson	Mr Ralph Hall
The Revd Mr Sparrow	2nd Month	Mr Francis Rush
Mr Thomas Whimper	Mr Edmund Boyns	Mr William Crisp

The following persons were appointed Directors and Acting Guardians for the second quarter from Michaelmas to Christmas.

Directors	Guardians	
William Negus Esq.	1st Month	Mr William Waller
Mr John Bates	Mr Thomas Cole	Mr John Moor
The Revd Mr Carter	Mr Richard Brook	3rd Month
Mr Thomas Goodwin	Mr John Jeaffreson	Mr Philip Moor
Mr Martin Harsant	2nd Month	Mr John Harper
Mr John Sheppard	Mr Thomas Page	Mr Thomas Garneys

The following persons were appointed Directors and Acting Guardians for the third quarter from Christmas to Lady Day.

Directors	Guardians	
Francis Brooke Esq.	1st Month	Mr John Pitcher
Mr Quintin Woolnough	Mr John Scotchmer	Mr John Woods
Mr Joseph Bennington	Mr Simon Paternoster	3rd Month
Mr William Dove	Mr Robert Barber	Mr Stephen Vertue
The Revd Mr Howard	2nd Month	Mr Stephen Blomfield
The Revd Mr Cooperthwaite	Mr William Till	Mr Jeptha Waller

---

[36] The Act of Incorporation specified that fifteen directors and acting guardians, of which six had to be directors, should be nominated for each quarter of the succeeding year. They could also divide themselves into committees of five to act for each month within that quarter. Any three of those five, one to be a director, were to meet at the House every Monday morning.

The following persons were appointed Directors and Acting Guardians for the fourth quarter from Lady Day to Midsummer.

Directors	Guardians	
The Revd Mr Jeaffreson	1st Month	Mr Samuel Barber
Mr John Whimper	Mr Thomas Langley	Mr William Gross
Mr John Baldry	Mr Thomas Chandler	3rd Month
Mr Robert Sheming	Mr Thomas Hendry	Mr Edward Adams
Mr Samuel Salmon	2nd Month	Mr John Barthorp
Mr Joseph Walford	Mr Nathaniel Barthorp	Mr John Growse

4 July 1768

Ordered that Mr John Stocks do provide the House of Industry with necessary wool of different sorts for spinning for this quarter from Midsummer to Michaelmas.[37]

11 July 1768

Ordered that Mr John Stow do provide twenty comb of wheat agreeable to the Sample No 1, at twenty nine shillings per comb, to be delivered at the House of Industry. And that Mr Henry Hall and Mr Robert Barrell do grind and dress the same, at eighteen pence per comb.

Ordered that Matthew Grayston do immediately provide a bolting mill for dressing the corn for the said House.

Ordered that Mr Henry Hall do provide ten of the best five bushell sacks, and to be marked Loes and Wilford for the said House.

Ordered that Mr Thomas Gross and Daniel Packard do provide the said House with allens coals, or such as they now have, to be delivered at the said House at £1 2s. 6d. per chaldron, free of all charges, for this year's consumption to Midsummer next agreeable to their proposals.

Ordered that Mr Nathaniel Barthorp do provide the said House with malt for this quarter, agreeable to the sample, at 16s. per comb to be delivered at the said House at ten comb a time.

Ordered that Mr Thomas Hicks do provide the said House with fine oatmeal for this quarter, at 5s. 4d. a bushel, to be delivered at the said House.

Ordered that Mr Henry Churchyard and Mr Jonathan Churchyard do provide the said House this quarter with good beef and mutton. The beef at 30s. per hundred, and the mutton at 3½d. per pound.

Ordered that Mr Benjamin Baldry do provide the said House this quarter, with a pockett of hops agreeable to the sample at £5 12s. 0d. per hundred, candles at seven shillings per dozen, soap at £2 16s. 0d. per hundred, hair brooms at 16s. and 18s. per dozen, flagg brooms at 4s. 6d. per dozen, mops at 9s. and 12s. per dozen, and Lancashire cheese at 33s. per hundred.[38]

Ordered that Mr William Penning do provide the said House this quarter, with rice at 17s. per hundred, blewen at 15d. per pound, sugar at £2 8s. 0d. per hundred, Poland starch at 6d. per pound, and plumbs at 3s. 6d. per stone.

---

[37] By the Act of Incorporation, the directors were to 'provide a convenient stock of flax, hemp, wool, cotton, thread, iron, stone, wood, leather, or other materials, for the employment of the poor'.

[38] No menu appears to be extant for Loes and Wilford, but the weekly diet would have been similar to other Suffolk houses as mentioned in the introduction.

Ordered that Mr Samuel Barber do provide the said House this quarter, with firkin butter at 28s. per firkin.

Ordered that Mr Richard Wood, the Clerk, do give directions for a surplice for the clergyman, a church prayer book and Bible, a best French pewter flagon, a cup and two plates for the Chapple, and a cushion and trimmings for the pulpit and desk.

Ordered that a parcell of wood be had of Mr Joseph Walford at fourteen shillings a load, and that Mr Thomas Taylor do deliver the same at the House of Industry, at five shillings a load.

11 July 1768–16 July 1768[39]

Parish	Date	Name	Age	Discharged	Dead
Ash	July 11th	Thomas Branson	6	14 Oct. 1769	
		James Branson	5		11 June 1769
		John Branson	10	10 Sept. 1770	
Capell	July 11th	Elizabeth Woolnough	24		4 Jan. 1771
		Rebekah Woolnough	15	26 July 1770	
Kettleburgh	July 11th	Lionel Emerson	86		19 Sept. 1768
		Christian Emerson	82		20 July 1769
Marlesford	July 11th	Mary Levell	72		19 July 1769
		Sarah Green	32		8 June 1769
		Mary Riches	31		
		Martha Riches	12	1 Oct. 1770	
		Susana Riches	10	1 Oct. 1770	
		Benjamin Riches	9	9 July 1770	
		Jane Riches	7	9 July 1770	
		David Riches	5	28 June 1777	
		Iona Riches	1		20 Aug. 1768
		Sarah Daman	54		20 Oct. 1768
		Samuel Daman	66		26 April 1769
		Susan Moore	33		12 Feb. 1770
		Philip Moore	6		23 Jan. 1774
		Susan Moore	7	12 June 1769	
		Mary Moore	3		18 April 1770
		Lydia Moore	1		20 May 1770
		Sarah West	29	4 Oct. 1775	
		Elizabeth West	5		10 Feb. 1770
		John West	2		12 Sept. 1768
		Elizabeth Bloomfield	41	29 July 1771	
		Chapman Bloomfield	5	29 July 1771	
		William Bloomfield	1	29 July 1771	
Melton	July 11th	Elizabeth Hadman	14	2 April 1770	
		Mary Hadman	13		17 Oct. 1768
		Susan Hadman	10		9 Sept. 1768
		Richard Hadman	9	10 April 1769	

---

[39] SROI ADA11/C/B/1/1. Admission of the paupers to the house of industry has been inserted at this point to provide a sense of continuity in the establishment of the House.

		Hannah Durrant	14	8 Oct. 1770	
		Lydia Durrant	7		18 April 1769
		Joseph Durant	4	4 Aug. 1774	
		Matthew Noble	10	15 Feb. 1769	
		Mary Noble	9	15 Feb. 1769	
		Thomas Noble	8	28 June 1778	
		Susan Lumly	30		
		Philip Fink	11	8 May 1769	
		Elizabeth Fink	12	15 May 1769	
		John Fink	6	15 May 1769	
		Charles Fink	4	6 Sept. 1768	
		Thomas Green	40		11 Aug. 1769
		John James	11	1 Jan. 1770	
		Samuel Ringe	13	10 April 1774	
		Mary Brewer	18	2 Aug. 1770	
Butley	July 12th	Hazel Bloomfield	18	25 July 1768	
		Rose Green	60	2 July 1769	
		James Lettuce	7		3 June 1771
		Richard Wright	9	10 Nov. 1771	
		Mary Dowsing	10	29 Oct. 1770	
		John Dowsing	6	29 Oct. 1770	
		Joseph Cortnal	80		27 July 1769
Earl Soham	July 12th	Mary Warner	30		
		Edmund Warner	12	21 Aug. 1769	
		Anthony Warner	7		
		Birch Warner	2		17 Nov. 1769
		Elizabeth Capon	44		14 Oct. 1769
		John Capon	8		25 Jan. 1771
		Sarah Woolner	11	5 March 1770	
		Susan Woolner	6		
		Elizabeth Hemson	70		22 March 1771
Letheringham	July 12th	Lydia Hewett	40	30 Nov. 1772	
		Joseph Hewett	2	4 Oct. 1778	
		Robert Hewett	4		29 June 1777
		Lydia Hewett	5	30 Nov. 1772	
		James Hewett	1		9 June 1769
Ramsholt	July 12th	John Weston	49		30 April 1775
		Mary Johnson	9		22 July 1769
		Elizabeth Johnson	7		16 July 1769
		Benjamin Lewis	9	20 Oct. 1772	
		John Lewis	8		
Bawdsey	July 13th	Elizabeth Rockett	79		12 April 1771
Bredfield	July 13th	James Underwood	3	10 Nov. 1776	
		Easter Pyman	7		
		Jamima Pyman	9		
		Rachel Dun	17		15 May 1769
		Lydia Watling	26	17 Oct. 1768	
		Henry Watling	2		18 June 1769
		Elizabeth Kerridge	8	15 Nov. 1770	
		Mary Wellam	38	30 April 1770	

Parish	Date	Name	Age		
		Samuel Punchard	65		10 April 1772
Easton	July 13th	Mary Salley	44		1 Aug. 1774
		Mary Clark	85		11 Aug. 1769
		Joseph Watts	11	2 Aug. 1770	
Hatcheston	July 13th	Robert Persons	77		4 Dec. 1770
		Matha Hood	30		28 June 1786
		Margaret Hood	4	29 Sept. 1771	
		John Hood	7		
		Mary Hood	1		6 Sept. 1768
		Edward Skinner	18	4 Aug. 1776	
		Elizabeth Scrutton	8	29 Sept. 1777	
Hoo	July 13th	Mary Whitman	40	22 Jan. 1769	
		Ann Whitman	2		7 Sept. 1768
Sutton	July 13th	William Reeve	56		17 Aug. 1769
		Sarah Rick	35	28 June 1777	
		Samuel Rick	12	14 Nov. 1768	
		Robert Rick	10	10 May 1772	
		John Rick	8	12 Aug. 1774	
		James Rick	5		10 Dec. 1773
		Ruth Rick	2	11 June 1776	
		Mary Pain	10	4 Sept. 1773	
		Sarah Pain	8		2 Jan. 74
		Isaac Pain	11	9 Oct. 1769	
		Sarah Rotton	8		8 Sept. 1769
		William Elder	12	10 Oct. 1769	
		Robert Pettitt	14		26 Sept. 1768
		Deborah Spawl	14	2 July 1770	
		Thomas Spawl	12	21 May 1770	
		Benjamin Spawl	11	10 Nov. 1771	
Ash	July 14th	Susannah Gibson	11		9 Oct. 1774
		John Gibson	6		4 June 1773
		Joseph Gibson	4	19 June 1770	
Hollesly	July 14th	Thomas Shimmings	65		6 Nov. 1773
		Charles Flury	6		25 Aug. 1769
		Amy Flury	7		
		Mary Button	5	30 April 1770	
		Hannah Page	11	13 April 1772	
		Susan Whitmoor	9		23 Sept. 1770
Monewden	July 14th	John Curtis	77		26 June 1769
Wickham	July 14th	Edward Wright	80		1 Jan. 1775
		Elizabeth Wright	49		4 July 1769
		James Clamp	80		11 July 1769
		Ann Lee	39	2 July 1770	
		George Lee	3	2 July 1770	
		Mary Lee	5	2 July 1770	
		Sarah Lee	10	2 July 1770	
		Mary Milden	70		18 May 1769
		Mary Howard	6		
Charsfield	July 15th	George Clarke	70		23 July 1770
		Susan Pilkinton	45		

		Robert Luecock	6	26 March 1770	
		Ann Luecock	4	26 March 1770	
		Hannah Luecock	7	12 Sept. 1768	
Creetingham	July 15th	Ann Emerson	40	10 April 1769	
Eyke	July 15th	Mary Phesant	70		
		Plesance Thrower	9	8 Aug. 1768	
		John Thrower	8		
		Francs Clarke	10		7 Sept. 1769
		Elizabeth Clarke	7		21 June 1769
		Sarah Clarke	8	8 May 1769	
Petistree	July 15th	Susan Gross	60	10 May 1770	
Shottisham	July 15th	Isabel Page	26	30 April 1770	
		Elizabeth Page	1		1 April 1770
		Susan Page	14	2 April 1770	
		Joseph Page	14		7 June 1775
Ufford	July 15th	Mary Ox	78		6 Sept. 1769
		Ann Bishop	82		2 Sept. 1769
		James Holmes	78		18 Sept. 1769
		Daniel Wilson	14	16 Oct. 1769	
Alderton	July 16th	Hannah Crisp	72	4 May 1771	
		James Crisp	6	1 Nov. 1773	
Boulge	July 16th	John Topple	7	1 Aug. 1768	
		Robert Topple	6	*do*	
		Mary Topple	8	*do*	
		Sarah Topple	5	*do*	
		William Topple	4	*do*	
		Henry Topple	1	*do*	
		Sarah Topple	40	*do*	
		Robert William	11		5 May 1772
		Robert Lockwood	8		10 March 1771
		Thomas Lockwood	7		24 Dec. 1770
		Martha Lockwood	5		2 Feb. 1771
Dallingho	July 16th	Susan Mingy	45	17 June 1771	
		Mary Mingy	5	17 June 1771	
		Sary Mingy	1		26 Sept. 1769
		Ann Wayman	45		26 Aug. 1768
		Daniel Wayman	5	4 Oct. 1776	
		James Wayman	4		10 Feb. 1771
		Hannah Wayman	8	10 March 1769	
		Edward Candler	68		19 Nov. 1774
		William Rattle	7	8 Aug. 1768	
		Sarah Rattle	12	8 Aug. 1768	
		Susan Rattle	6	8 Aug. 1768	
Kenton	July 16th	John Legatt	4	23 April 1770	
		William Legatt	1		16 June 1769
		Elizabeth Legatt	37	2 July 1769	
		Alec Wayman	64		12 July 1769
		Jamima Long	4		4 June 1772
		James Long	10	2 Aug. 1770	
		Judeth Long	6	3 Aug. 1772	

Rendlesham	July 16th	Abegail Brown	19	7 July 1775
		Lydia Brown	9	7 July 1775
		William Brown	5	7 July 1775

26 September 1768

Ordered that the following bills be allowed and paid by the Treasurer.

	£	s.	d.
Mr Salmons bill for attending to take in the poor of.	3	7	0
Mr Brookes bill for mending the road of.	1	0	0
Mr Hicks bill for oatmeal.	1	1	4
Mr Walfords bill for wood.	11	18	0
Mr Baldrys bill for shop goods.	46	11	9
Mr Barbers bill for butter and a cow.	15	16	0
Mr Stannards bill for chairs etc .	6	18	6
Mr Stows bill for wheat.	29	0	0
do for wheat and pease.	12	0	0
Mr Tunmers bill for a cart.	6	7	0
Mr Birds Bill for irons for *do.*	5	19	0
Mr Mayhews bill for a clock etc.	5	14	6
Mr Coles bill for flour.	21	0	9
Mr Toples bill for shoes and mending.	2	16	9
Mr Whitings bill for cloathing etc.	119	16	0
Mr Halls for grinding for meal.	9	17	3
Mr Walfords bill for sacks.	1	5	6
Mr Barrells bill for grinding.	1	1	9
Mr Pennings bill for shop goods.	17	11	2
Mr Woods bill for church Bible prayer book and salary.	11	17	8
Mr Churchyards bill for meat.	22	12	10
Mr Barthorps bill for malt and wheat.	52	12	6
Mr Hingstons bill for journeys and on account of the small pox at Boyton.	1	3	0
Mr Chandlers bill on account of small pox at Butley.	3	16	6
	411	4	9

3 October 1768

	£	s.	d.
The Governors bill for sundries.	97	9	6½
do his quarters salary to Michaelmas 1768.	10	0	0
Mr Syers bill on account of the small pox.	22	17	9
do his quarters salary .	6	5	0
The overseers of Boyton on account of the small pox.	15	6	1
The Overseers of Hollesly *do.*	13	19	10
Mr Hinchman his quarters salary.	6	5	0
Mr Salmon his quarters salary.	10	0	0
The Revd Mr Palmer *do.*	8	15	0
The Treasurer *do.*	1	11	6
The Revd Mr Lambert one year's tythes.	4	0	0
	196	9	8½

Ordered that Robert Woolnough of Sutton, labourer, and Sarah his wife, and Rebecca seven years of age, John of six years, and Alithea of two years their children, have a certificate granted to the parish of Snape.

Ordered that William Crosbe of Hollesly, miller, Hannah his wife and their infant child named William of the age of one year or thereabouts have a certificate granted to the parish of Dedham in the county of Essex.

The Revd Mr Samuel Hingston was ballotted for to be a Director in the room of the Revd Mr Cooperthwaite, who lives out of the Hundreds, and was duly elected.

Ordered that Mr Henry and Jonathan Churchyard do provide the House of Industry this quarter with good beef and mutton. Beef at 28s. per hundred and mutton at 3½d. per pound to be delivered at the said House.

Ordered that Mr Nathaniel Barthorp do provide the House with good malt for this quarter at 14s. a comb to be delivered at the said House.

Ordered that Mr Thomas Hicks do provide the House with oatmeal for this quarter at 5s. 4d. per bushell to be delivered at the said House.

Ordered that the Treasurer do pay Mr Matthew Grayston five hundred pounds, on account.

Ordered that Henry Topple do provide the House with shoes according to sample at the following prices: first size at 3s. 10d., second size at 3s. 8d., and third size at 3s. 6d. per pair.

Ordered that Mr Benjamin Baldry do provide the House with candles at 7s. per dozen, soap at 56s. per hundred, Lancashire cheese at 33s. 6d. per hundred, and chamber oyl at 3s. 6d. per gallon for this quarter.

Ordered that Mr James Woodard do provide the House with sugar at 44s. per hundred, lump sugar at 7d. per pound, ginger at 10d. per pound, starch at 54s. per hundred, bluen at 15d. per pound, black pepper at 15d. per pound, nutmegs at 9s. 6d. per pound, cinnamon at 18s., mace at 21s., cloves at 14s. stone, brimstone at 3d., common tea at 3s., rice at 18s. 6d. per hundred, mops, brooms and brushes at the usual prices for this quarter.

21 November 1768

Ordered that Francis Brooke Esq. be desired to provide a proper person to have the Coal Bing removed, to have the Spinning Ward parted off, to have two close stools for the two Long Wards, to have some yeast trays made, to have the Stable and Cow House finished and to have a door to the back of the Mill House. And to be paid for them as Mr Redgraves, the Surveyor, shall value them.

Ordered that Mr Redgrave, the Surveyor, and Mr Tibbs, the Governor, do look over Mr Grayston, the builders, account and report it to the next Quarterly Meeting.

23 December 1768

Ordered that no more be allowed the officers of any parish than four shillings a day and night, for a man and horse going after the business of the Corporation.

26 December 1768

Mr John Syer, one of the Out Surgeons, being removed out of the Hundreds, and Mr William Goodwin of Woodbridge, surgeon, offering himself to be Out Surgeon in his room. Ordered that Mr Goodwin by appointed Out Surgeon in Mr Syer's room for the next half year, at the like salary Mr Syer was to receive.

Nicholas Smith and Richard Newman, Overseers of the parish of Hatcheston, being duly summoned according to the Act of Parliament for incorporating the said

Hundreds, for neglect of duty. And they being fully charged with the same are ordered to be fined one shilling each for their said neglect which they paid to the Treasurer accordingly.

Ordered that Mr Redgrave, the Surveyor, do contract with Mr Daniel Manthrop for the compleating and finishing and making the deficiencys good in the buildings agreeable to Graystons contract.

Ordered that Philemon Ayton of Rendlesham, schoolmaster, Ann his wife and Obadiah their child have a certificate granted to the parish of Dennington.

Ordered that Thomas Moore of Ufford, carpenter, Mary his wife and Mary their child have a certificate granted to the parish of Walton.

Ordered that John Reeve of Ash, carpenter, Sarah his wife and Ann and Sarah their children have a certificate granted to the parish of St Marys in Bury St Edmunds

Ordered that Daniel Sawyer of Earl Soham, labourer, Ann his wife and Daniel, James and Elizabeth their children have a certificate granted to the parish of Saxmundham.

Ordered that Robert Spalding of Kettleburgh, labourer, Elizabeth his wife and Robert their child have a certificate granted to the parish of Framlingham.

Ordered that John Lay of Kettleburgh, labourer, Mary his wife and John, Mary and Thomas their children have a certificate granted to the parish of Framlingham.

27 March 1769

Ordered that the Clerk do write to Mr Redgrave, the Surveyor, to fix a day to attend the Committee for Superintending the Building at the House of Industry in order to settle the deficiencys in Matthew Grayston's contract. And that the Clerk do write to the Building Committee appointed <> for that purpose to attend.

It being agreed between the Directors and Guardians and Francis Brooke Esq., the Revd Mr Palmer, Rector, and Mr William Woods, on behalf of themselves and the rest of the inhabitants of the parish of Ufford, that the inhabitants of Ufford shall make a good road through Mill Lane to the House of Industry. And it is ordered that the Governor do inform all persons coming to the said House from Ufford and those parts that they are to go in that road only.

Ordered that all the accounts in regard to the House be laid before the Weekly Committee every week, both in regard to the expences of the House and in regard to the Governor separately. And that the Governor do receive nothing into the House for consumption without a bill of the same. And that the Governor do provide a book and enter those several bills.

Ordered that 25 of the poor in the said House be allowed 3s. 6d. a piece for their industry, and that the Governor do affix up their several names in the said House.

1 May 1769 [*Building Committee*][40]

The following estimate being made by Mr John Redgrave and Mr Thomas Aldis for repairing and making good the cornish and eves of the House of industry in Melton to wit

	£	s.	d.
To cover the cornish with lead one foot wide six pound to the foot.	58	17	0
To boarding for lead and making good the tiling.	12	12	0
	71	9	0

---

[40] For editorial purposes, abbreviated titles of the relevant committee are included but their membership is omitted.

Ordered that Mr Thomas Aldis do perform the above work in a workman like manner at the above price. And that the assignees of Mathew Grayston do allow thirty five pounds towards the same.

26 June 1769

Directors	Present	Guardians
The Hon'ble R S Nassau		Mr Robert Sheming
Francis Brooke Esq.		Mr James Woods
Jonathan Burward Esq.		Mr Richard Brooks
Edmund Jenney Esq.		Mr Edmund Boyns
William Negus Esq.		Mr Edward Adams
John Revett Esq.		Mr Thomas Chandler
The Revd Mr Philip Carter		Mr John Barthorp
The Revd Mr John Sparrow		Mr Nathaniel Barthorp
The Revd Mr Samuel Hingeston		and
Mr Joseph Walford		Mr Thomas Garneys
Mr Samuel Salmon		
Mr Martin Harsant		
Mr Thomas Whimper		

The following persons were duly elected Directors and Acting Guardians for the year ensuing and were appointed to act on the Committee the several times herein after mentioned:

Directors		1st Quarter	Guardians
July	Edmund Jenney Esq.		Mr George Linsted
	Mr Thomas Whimper		Mr Thomas Garneys
			Mr Richard Brooke Jun.
Aug.	The Revd Mr Carter		Mr William Damant
	The Revd Mr Howard		Mr George Lord
			Mr Thomas Saunders
Sept.	The Hon'ble Mr Nassau		Mr Thomas Smith
	Jonathan Burward Esq.		Mr William Athow
			Mr George Lamb
Oct.	John Revett Esq.	2nd Quarter	Mr Thomas Cole
	The Revd Mr Sparrow		Mr Richard Brooke Sen.
			Mr John Jeaffreson
Nov.	William Negus Esq.		Mr Thomas Page
	Mr Anthony Collett		Mr William Waller
			Mr John Moore
Dec.	Mr John Bates		Mr Thomas Crisp Sen.
	Mr John Sheppard		Mr John Harper
			Mr James Woods
Jan.	Francis Brooke Esq.	3rd Quarter	Mr John Scotchmer
	Mr Q. Woolnough		Mr Simon Paternoster
			Mr Robert Barber
Feb.	Mr Joseph Bennington		Mr Thomas Mann
	Mr William Dove		Mr Stephen Gale
			Mr John Woods
Mar.	The Revd Mr Hingeston		Mr Southwell Golding
	Mr Martin Harsant		Mr Stephen Blomfield
			Mr Jeptha Waller

Apl.	Mr John Whimper	4th Quarter	Mr Thomas Chandler

Apl.   Mr John Whimper   4th Quarter   Mr Thomas Chandler
        Mr John Baldry   Mr John Wase
                                              Mr Thomas Hendry
May   Mr Robert Sheming   Mr Nathaniel Barthorp
        Mr Samuel Salmon   Mr Samuel Barber
                                              Mr James Gooding
June   The Revd Mr Jeaffreson   Mr Edward Adams
        Mr Joseph Walford   Mr John Barthorp
                                              Mr Thomas Ablitt

Ordered that 25 of the poor in the House of Industry be allowed £3 2s. 6d. for their industry, to be distributed at the discretion of the Governor, and that he do affix up their several names in the said House.

Ordered that the Clerk do get the Rules and Orders for the Poor in the said House printed and afterwards affixed up in the House.

Ordered that John Revett Esq. be continued Treasurer, The Revd Mr Palmer, Chaplain, Mr Richard Wood, Clerk, and Mr Thomas Tibbs, Governor, at their usual salarys.

Ordered that Mr Samuel Salmon be appointed Surgeon for the out and in patients for the two Hundreds for one year at the salary of one hundred pounds.

Ordered that a General Meeting of the Directors Superintending the Building be held <> in order to settle the deficiencys in Graystons contract.

1 July 1769 [*Building Committee*]

Deductions made by the surveyors <> for work not done nor finished according to the contract.

	£	s.	d.
To 85 Feet of drains at ¼.	5	13	4
To lower the earth in Back Court.	5	11	0
To repair the tileing.	0	15	0
Deduct for the casements.	40	0	0
Tileing.	35	0	0
Bell overcharged.	1	13	4
Lye leech and rollers.	0	4	6
Linnen carts.	0	10	0
Sundries.	0	3	3
To two ewsers.	0	8	0
Overcharged rendring the walls.	5	2	6
do for lead.	0	9	0
Ceiling joist.	16	1	10
Stone caps.	0	11	3
Steps to the doors.	0	18	6
Curbs to cellar windows.	0	7	2
Linnen shed.	3	0	0
do not put up.	36	17	0
Hogs houses.	1	10	0
Cow house and stables.	1	0	0
For the half rounds.	1	10	0
For bricks.	4	0	0
For larths.	10	10	0

Lattice.	4	4	0
Lump paving.	0	6	8
Gutter bricks.	0	11	4
Bog house door cases.	0	2	0
For the oven.	1	8	0
	178	7	10

Ordered that the Treasurer do pay the assignees of Matthew Grayston, a bankrupt, the sum of £728 12s. 7¾d. in full of all demands on the Directors and Guardians of the House of Industry for the said Hundreds – errors excepted.

2 October 1769

Ordered that it be referred to the Weekly Committee to treat with any persons for the placing out of any of the children apprentices according to the said Act.

Mr Matthews and Mr Garrett's bill for surveying the House against the builder £2 2s. 0d.

Ordered that in case the Treasurer shall be obliged to advance any sum or sums of money over and above the balance now in his hands, that he shall be allowed lawfull interest for the same together with other such reasonable allowance as he shall sustain on account of advancing the same until he shall be repaid the sum or sums so advanced.[41]

1 January 1770

It being ballotted for whether the appeal between the parish of Rendlesham and the parish of Wantisden concerning the removal of Samuel Pettit and wife should be prosecuted. Ordered that it should be prosecuted.

26 March 1770

Ordered that the Governor do provide the House of Industry with beef and mutton for this quarter in the best manner he can.

25 June 1770

Directors	Present	Guardians
The Hon'ble Mr Nassau		Mr Richard Brook Sen.
Jonathan Burward Esq.		Mr Simon Paternoster
The Revd Mr Philip Carter		Mr Thomas Gale
The Revd Mr Eden Howard		Mr Jeptha Waller
The Revd Mr John Sparrow		Mr Edward Adams
The Revd Mr Christopher Jeaffreson		Mr Thomas Ablitt
The Revd Mr Hingeston		Mr Thomas Page
Mr Joseph Bennington		Mr John Scotchmer
Mr Samuel Salmon		Mr William Waller
Mr Thomas Whimper		Mr James Woods
		Mr Thomas Mann
		Mr Nathaniel Barthrop
		Mr John Woods

The following persons were duly elected Directors and Acting Guardians ◇:

---

[41] The need for the treasurer to loan the Incorporation various sums became a regular feature of the Quarterly Accounts. He was paid interest on this sum at the same rate received by the investors.

	Directors	1st Quarter	Guardians
July	Mr Edmund Jenney Esq.		Mr George Linsted
	Mr Thomas Whimper		Mr Richard Brook Jun.
			Mr Thomas Garneys
Aug.	The Revd Mr Carter		Mr Edmund Boyns
	The Revd Mr Howard		Mr Thomas Saunders
			Mr George Lord Jun.
Sept.	The Hon'ble Mr Nassau		Mr Edmund Tye
	Jonathan Burward Esq.		Mr John Syred
			Mr Ralph Cotton
Oct.	John Revett Esq.	2nd Quarter	Mr Joseph Kersey
	The Revd Mr Sparrow		Mr Richard Brook Sen.
			Mr John Jeaffreson
Nov.	William Negus Esq.		Mr Thomas Page
	Mr Anthony Collett		Mr William Waller
			Mr John Moor
Dec.	John Sheppard Esq.		Mr Thomas Glanfield
	Mr John Bates		Mr John Harper
			Mr Joseph Thompson
Jan.	Francis Brooke Esq.	3rd Quarter	Mr John Scotchmer
	Mr Q. Woolnough		Mr Simon Paternoster
			Mr Robert Barber
Feb.	Mr Joseph Bennington		Mr Thomas Mann
	Mr William Dove		Mr Stephen Gale
			Mr John Woods
Mar.	The Revd Mr Hingeston		Mr Russell Chilton
	Mr Martin Harsant		Mr Nicholas May/Mr John Levett
			Mr Jeptha Waller
Apl.	Mr John Whimper	4th Quarter	Mr Thomas Chandler
	Mr John Baldry		Mr Robert Kerridge/
			Mr Thomas Langley
			Mr Stephen Vertue
May	Mr Robert Sheming		Mr Nathaniel Barthrop
	Mr Samuel Salmon		Mr Samuel Barber
			Mr James Gooding
June	The Revd Mr Jeaffreson		Mr Edward Adams
	Mr John Barthrop		Mr William Harris
			Mr Thomas Ablitt

Ordered that Thomas Thursby, a poor person of the parish of Charsfield, be allowed fifty shillings towards placing one of his children in the Hospital at Ipswich, and that the same be paid to Humphry Rant Esq. by the Governor.

Ordered that the Governor be allowed and paid by the Treasurer, twenty one pounds for his extraordinary trouble during the small pox being in the House of Industry.

Ordered that ten pieces of plain cloth for coats, ten pieces of half thick sets for women's coats, six pieces of bays, twenty pieces of three quarter hemp, two pieces of Russia, two dozen of handkerchiefs, one piece of check, twenty pieces of hessen, two pieces of Irish for caps, one piece of lawn for borders, buttons, tapes, threads, laces and pins be supplyed by Mr Thomas Whiting for the use of the House of Industry according to the samples and prices.

Ordered ten pieces of Padua serge be supplyed by Mr Metcalf according to the sample and price for the use of the said House.

1 October 1770

Ordered that the Treasurer do pay off one hundred pounds principal money to William Fletcher Esq., and one hundred pounds principal money to Miss Elizabeth Gooding.

Ordered that Joseph Watts, a poor child of the parish of Easton, in the House of Industry, be apprenticed to Samuel Leeds of the parish of Saint Matthews, in the Borough of Ipswich, in the county of Suffolk, brush maker, for seven years from the twenty third day of July last past and the common seal of the Corporation was this day affixed to one part of the indentures accordingly.

Ordered that James Long, a poor child of the parish of Easton, in the House of Industry, be apprenticed to Robert Brown of the parish of Saint Clement, in the Borough of Ipswich, in the County of Suffolk, mariner, for seven years from the twenty ninth day of July last past and the common seal of the Corporation was this day affixed to one part of the indentures accordingly.

Ordered that Edmund Minter, a poor child of the parish of Kettleburgh, in the House of Industry, be apprenticed to Robert Brown of the parish of Saint Clement, in the Borough of Ipswich, in the county of Suffolk, mariner, for seven years from the twenty ninth day of July last past and the common seal of the Corporation was this day affixed to one part of the indentures accordingly.

Ordered that the Clerk do write to two of the several persons who have advanced money to the Corporation as they stand in rotation to have two hundred pounds principal money paid off at Christmas next, and to write to the rest of the persons to know whether they would take 4 per cent for the remainder of the moneys advanced by them to the said Corporation.

31 December 1770

Ordered that the Clerk do write to Mr John Redgrave, the Surveyor, to attend the next Quarterly Meeting in regard to his bill as the Directors and Guardians think that he did not do his duty in regard to his contract.

1 July 1771

Directors	Present	Guardians
The Hon'ble Mr Nassau		Mr Simon Paternoster
Jonathan Burward Esq.		Mr Edward Adams
Francis Brooke Esq.		Mr Edmund Tye
John Revett Esq.		Mr Thomas Mann
The Revd Mr Philip Carter		Mr Thomas Page
The Revd Mr Eden Howard		and
The Revd Mr Chris Jeaffreson		Mr Stephen Vertue
The Revd Mr John Sparrow		
The Revd Mr Hingeston		
Mr Thomas Whimper		
Mr Samuel Salmon		
Mr Joseph Bennington		

The following persons were duly elected Directors and Acting Guardians ◇:

31

	Directors	1st Quarter	Guardian
July	Edmund Jenney Esq.		Mr James Woods
	Mr Thomas Whimper		Mr Daniel Hart
			Mr Thomas Crisp
Aug.	The Revd Mr Carter		Mr Edmund Boyns
	The Revd Mr Howard		Mr George Lord Jun.
			Mr Thomas Saunders
Sept.	The Hon'ble Mr Nassau		Mr John Aldus
	Jonathan Burward Esq.		Mr Stephen Blomfield
			Mr Ralph Cotton
Oct.	John Revett Esq.	2nd Quarter	Mr Joseph Kersey
	The Revd Mr Sparrow		Mr Richard Brook Sen.
			Mr John Jeaffreson
Nov.	William Negus Esq.		Mr Thomas Page
	Mr Anthony Collett		Mr William Waller
			Mr William Upson
Dec.	John Sheppard Esq.		Mr Thomas Glanfield
	Mr Samuel Barber		Mr Philip Whincopp
			Mr Joseph Thompson
Jan.	Francis Brooke Esq.	3rd Quarter	Mr Benjamin Baldry
	Mr Q. Woolnough		Mr Simon Paternoster
			Mr Robert Barber
Feb.	Mr Joseph Bennington		Mr Thomas Mann
	Mr William Dove		Mr John Pitcher
			Mr John Woods
Mar.	The Revd Mr Hingeston		Mr Russell Chilton
	Mr Martin Harsant		Mr John Levett
			Mr Jeptha Waller
Apl.	Mr John Whimper	4th Quarter	Mr Thomas Chandler
	Mr John Baldry		Mr William Smith
			Mr Philip Richbell
May	Mr Nathaniel Barthrop		Mr David Samson
	Mr Samuel Salmon		Mr William Ashford
			Mr James Gooding
June	The Revd Mr Jeaffreson		Mr Edward Adams
	Mr John Barthrop		Mr William Harris
			Mr Thomas Ablitt

Ordered that the Committee for the months of August or September be impowered to contract for coals for the year's consumption for the House of Industry.

Ordered that the Clerk do give notice to Nathaniel Fletcher Esq. to pay him off £200 as soon as he pleases this quarter.

Ordered that the Treasurer do pay the Governor three pounds, allowed by the Directors and Guardians out of the profits of the work, for his diligence and fidelity pursuant to this Act for Incorporation the said Hundreds to this day.

Ordered that the Governor do pay Robert Baxter, the Chapple Clerk, twenty shillings as his salary for last year attending and that the salary of twenty shillings be paid to him annually so long as he shall be continued clerk.

30 September 1771

The sum of three hundred pounds was this day borrowed of William Parmenter of Playford in the County of Suffolk, Gent., in three different shares of one hundred pounds each at the interest of four pounds per cent per annum in order to pay off the same sum of three hundred pounds to Nathaniel Fletcher Esq. being at the interest of four pounds and ten shillings per cent per annum, he not being willing to assign. Ordered that the said sum of three hundred pounds be paid to the Treasurer in order to pay off the same as aforesaid.[42]

Ordered that the Governor do pay thirty shillings towards the cloathing of Daniel Murdock, a poor boy now placed out as servant to Mr Henry Kemp.

Ordered that John Dallinger, a poor child of the parish of Ufford, now in the House of Industry, be apprenticed to the Governor for seven years from this day, to learn the trade of Cordwainer, and the common seal of the Corporation was this day affixed to one part of the indenture accordingly.

30 December 1771

Ordered that the Clerk do sign an order to the parish of Little Glenham acknowledging Francis Robinson of Marlesford, labourer, Catherine, his wife, Robert, of the age of eight years, Ann of the age of seven years, Francis of the age of three years, and William of the age of twenty weeks, their children, to belong to the parish of Marlesford. And that the Directors and Guardians will be answerable for all the expences that the said Francis Robinson, his wife and family may be to the said parish of Little Glenham until Michaelmas next.[43]

Ordered that the Governor do make an alteration of a passage to the Dining Room in the said House, and have the bell sold and a new one provided in the best manner he can.

30 March 1772

Ordered that Mr John King do sign an advertisement to be inserted in the Ipswich paper one week, acknowledging his fault and begging pardon of the Directors and Guardians for falsely aspersing them and pay the expences of the witnesses and of this advertisement.[44]

Ordered that the Governor do provide two hundred of soap from London and two hundred of soap from Crawleys of Ipswich for the use of the House of Industry.

29 June 1772

Directors	Present	Guardians
The Hon'ble Mr Nassau		Mr Simon Paternoster
Jonathan Burward Esq.		and
William Negus Esq.		Mr Thomas Ablitt
John Revett Esq.		
Anthony Collett Esq.		

---

[42] Fresh capital provided at 4 per cent was used to pay off investors receiving 4½ per cent. Subsequent similar entries are omitted.

[43] Settlement issues were only partially addressed by the creation of the Incorporation. Internally, legal expenses concerning settlement were reduced as relief was offered to paupers settled in any of the thirty-three parishes. A pauper moving out of the Incorporation would be granted a settlement certificate by the Incorporation rather than the individual parish.

[44] King had made accusations about the treatment of the inmates in the House.

The Revd Mr John Sparrow
The Revd Mr Christopher Jeaffreson
Mr Thomas Whimper
Mr Samuel Barber
Mr William Dove
Mr Samuel Salmon

Ordered that the Treasurer do pay the Governor the sum of one hundred and fifty pounds for the use of the current quarter.

The following persons were duly elected Directors and Acting ◇:

	Directors	1st Quarter	Guardians
July	Edmund Jenney Esq.		Mr Henry Hall
	Mr Thomas Whimper		Mr Samuel Hart
			Mr Thomas Crisp
Aug.	The Revd Mr Carter		Mr Robert Plant
	The Revd Mr Howard		Mr John King
			Mr William Smith
Sept.	The Hon'ble Mr Nassau		Mr Thomas Moss
	Jonathan Burward Esq.		Mr Stephen Blomfield
			Mr George Lamb
Oct.	John Revett Esq.	2nd Quarter	Mr Joseph Kersey
	The Revd Mr Sparrow		Mr Benjamin Cooper
			Mr Southwell Golding
Nov.	William Negus Esq.		Mr John Dennington
	Anthony Collett Esq.		Mr William Waller
			Mr William Upson
Dec.	The Revd Mr Jeaffreson		Mr Thomas Glanfield
	The Revd Mr William Clubbe		Mr Searles Syer
			Mr Francis Betts
Jan.	Francis Brooke Esq.	3rd Quarter	Mr Benjamin Baldry
	Mr Q. Woolnough		Mr Simon Paternoster
			Mr Robert Barber
Feb.	Mr Joseph Bennington		Mr Thomas Mann
	Mr William Dove		Mr John Pitcher
			Mr John Woods
Mar.	The Revd Mr Hingeston		Mr Russell Chilton
	Mr Martin Harsant		Mr John Levett
			Mr Jeptha Waller
Apl.	Mr John Whimper	4th Quarter	Mr Thomas Chandler
	Mr John Baldry		Mr Thomas Saunders
			Mr John Kemp
May	Mr Nathaniel Barthrop		Mr David Sampson
	Mr Samuel Salmon		Mr William Ashford
			Mr James Gooding
June	Mr Samuel Barber		Mr Robert Harvey
	Mr John Barthrop		Mr William Harris
			Mr Thomas Ablitt

29 March 1773

Ordered that the Governor do pay Mr William Dove of Capell two pounds and two shillings towards the Surgeons bill for curing a compound fracture of Robert

Boons, a poor boy living with the said Mr Dove, the said Robert Boon not being capable of paying the Surgeon himself, but this is to be considered as a matter of favour and not to be made a president of.

Ordered that Mr Wood, the Clerk, do prosecute an appeal against an order of John Dade Esq. and Francis Capper, Clerk, two of His Majesty's Justices of the Peace, for the removal of Robert Nainton and Elizabeth, his wife, from the parish of Framlingham to the parish of Ufford.

Mr John Grout, Overseer of Kettleburgh, having raised a false report of Thomas Peters, a poor child of the same parish lately discharged from the House of Industry, having been ill-treated in the said House, being back beaten and belly beaten. Ordered that the said John Grout do sign a writing retracting the said report and that the same was false and without foundation which he signed accordingly.[45]

28 June 1773

Directors	Present	Guardians
Jonathan Burward Esq.		Mr Simon Paternoster
Francis Brooke Esq.		Mr Thomas Ablitt
The Revd Mr Jeaffreson		Mr John Kemp
The Revd Mr Sparrow		Mr Southwell Golding
The Revd Mr Howard		Mr Thomas Chandler
The Revd Mr Philip Carter		Mr Robert Barber
Mr Thomas Whimper		Mr Benjamin Cooper
Mr Samuel Barber		and
Mr Samuel Salmon		Mr Stephen Vertue
Mr John Barthorp		
Mr Martin Harsant		
Mr Nathaniel Barthorp		

The following persons were duly elected Directors and Acting Guardians◇:

	Directors	1st Quarter	Guardians
July	Edmund Jenney Esq.		Mr Henry Hall
	Mr Thomas Whimper		Mr William Whitman
			Mr John Bigsby
Aug.	The Revd Mr Carter		Mr Stephen Catchpole
	The Revd Mr Howard		Mr John King
			Mr William Smith
Sept.	The Hon'ble Mr Nassau		Mr Edward Keer
	Jonathan Burward Esq.		Mr Stephen Blomfield
			Mr George Lamb
Oct.	John Revett Esq.	2nd Quarter	Mr Joseph Kersey
	The Revd Mr Sparrow		Mr Benjamin Cooper
			Mr Southwell Golding
Nov.	Anthony Collett Esq.		Mr John Dennington
	Mr Simon Paternoster		Mr William Waller
			Mr William Upson
Dec.	The Revd Mr Jeaffreson		Mr Benjamin Barthorp

---

[45] Rumours were common concerning the ill treatment of inmates. There is only one example in the minute books where the governor is reprimanded for using excessive force against a recalcitrant inmate.

	The Revd Mr Clubbe		Mr Searles Syer
			Mr James Woods
Jan.	Francis Brooke Esq.	3rd Quarter	Mr Thomas Kindred
	Mr Q. Woolnough		Mr Stephen Vertue
			Mr Robert Barber
Feb.	Mr Joseph Bennington		Mr Nathaniel Fuller
	Mr William Dove		Mr John Pitcher
			Mr John Woods
Mar.	The Revd Mr Hingeston		Mr Samuel Buck
	Mr Martin Harsant		Mr John Gross
			Mr Jeptha Waller
Apl.	Mr John Whimper	4th Quarter	Mr Thomas Chandler
	Mr John Baldry		Mr Thomas Saunders
			Mr John Kemp
May	Mr Nathaniel Barthorp		Mr Francis Hayle
	Mr Samuel Salmon		Mr William Ashford
			Mr James Gooding
June	Mr Samuel Barber		Mr Robert Harvey
	Mr John Barthorp		Mr Philip Whincopp
			Mr Thomas Ablitt

It being moved that Mr Samuel Salmon should be removed from his office as Surgeon to the House of Industry, and ballot being demanded, a ballot was accordingly taken. And it was ordered that Mr Samuel Salmon be continued as Surgeon to the said House at his usual salary.[46]

I, John Edwards of Dennington, in the County of Suffolk, Gent., do hereby agree to sell and convey unto the Guardians of the Poor within the Hundreds of Loes and Wilford in the said county a certain piece of land in Melton, in the same county, intermixed with the lands belonging to the said Guardians, at the price of fifteen guineas to be paid to me on executing the conveyances thereof which are to be made at the end of the said Guardians on or before Michaelmas day next. As witness my hand John Edwards.

Ordered that the Clerk do pay off one security of the late William Negus Esq. of one hundred pounds there being a sufficient balance in the Treasurers hands to pay the same.

14 October 1773

Ordered that Simon Paternoster of Wickham Market, Schoolmaster, be appointed Treasurer in the room of John Revett Esq., deceased, at the salary of ten guineas a year.

Ordered that John Revett of Brandeston Esq. be appointed Director in the room of John Revett Esq., his father, deceased, and to act on the Committee for this present month of October.

28 March 1774

Ordered that in case any person shall be permitted to send their servant having the small pox into the Pest House belonging to the House of Industry, then that

---

[46] There are only a few instances minuted where such votes of confidence took place. Salmon would be removed from his post following the internal report of 1791.

such person shall pay to the Directors and Guardians for the use of the Corporation four guineas for the first month, and five shillings a week for every other or further week continuance.

27 June 1774

Directors	Present	Guardians
The Hon'ble Mr Nassau		Mr William Smyth
Jonathan Burward Esq.		and
Francis Brooke Esq.		Mr Francis Hayle
John Revett Esq.		
The Revd Mr John Sparrow		
The Revd Mr Christopher Jeaffreson		
Mr Samuel Barber		
Mr John Barthrop		
Mr Thomas Whimper		
Mr Simon Paternoster		
Mr Samuel Salmon		

The following persons were duly elected Directors and Acting Guardians ⬦:

	Directors	1st Quarter	Guardians
July	Edmund Jenney Esq.		Mr Henry Hall
	Mr Thomas Whimper		Mr William Whitman
			Mr John Bigsby
Aug.	The Revd Mr Carter		Mr Edmund Boyns
	The Revd Mr Howard		Mr John King
			Mr Joseph Howell
Sept.	The Hon'ble Mr Nassau		Mr Edward Keer
	Jonathan Burward Esq.		Mr Ralph Hall
			Mr George Baker
Oct.	John Revett Esq.	2nd Quarter	Mr Joseph Kersey
	The Revd Mr Sparrow		Mr Benjamin Cooper
			Mr John Loyns
Nov.	Mr Anthony Collett Esq.		Mr John Dennington
	Mr Simon Paternoster		Mr William Waller
			Mr Samuel Thompson
Dec.	Francis Brooke Esq.		Mr Benjamin Barthrop
	The Revd Mr Jeaffreson		Mr Richard Syer
			Mr James Woods
Jan.	The Revd Mr Purvis	3rd Quarter	Mr Thomas Kindred
	Mr Quintin Woolnough		Mr Stephen Vertue
			Mr William Miller
Feb.	Mr Joseph Bennington		Mr Nathaniel Fuller
	Mr William Dove		Mr James Aldhouse
			Mr John Woods
Mar.	The Revd Mr Hingeston		Mr Samuel Buck
	Mr Martin Harsant		Mr Thomas Sheming
			Mr Richard Cole
Apl.	Mr John Whimper	4th Quarter	Mr Thomas Chandler
	Mr John Baldry		Mr Thomas Saunders
			Mr John Kemp

May	Mr Nathaniel Barthrop		Mr Francis Hayle
	Mr Samuel Salmon		Mr William Ashford
			Mr James Gooding
June	Mr Samuel Barber		Mr Robert Harvey
	Mr John Barthrop		Mr William Harris
			Mr Thomas Ablitt

Ordered that the Treasurer do pay Mrs Tibbs, the Governess, five guineas, the usual gratuity for her care and trouble.

3 October 1774

Ordered that the Clerk do write to the Churchwardens and Overseers of the several parishes that have children in the said House capable of being put out apprentice. That they do provide masters for them against the next Quarterly Meeting, otherwise that the Directors and Guardians will place them out to such persons in their parishes as they shall think proper.

26 December 1774

Ordered that John Smith of Woodbridge, brazier, do provide a new brewing copper for the House of Industry to contain four barrells more than the present one. That he do take the present copper, being decayed, and do allow for the same 11d. per lb. and that he be paid for the new copper 15d. per lb. according to the weight.

27 March 1775

Ordered that the Treasurer do pay off £200 to Robert Scholding and John Barthrop executors of Robert Barthrop deceased being at £4 10s. per cent, the Treasurer having the same in hand.

26 June 1775

Directors	Present	Guardians
The Hon'ble Mr Nassau		Mr Robert Harvey
Francis Brooke Esq.		
Jonathan Burward Esq.		
John Revett Esq.		
The Revd Mr Philp Carter		
The Revd Mr John Sparrow		
Mr Thomas Whimper		
Mr John Barthrop		
Mr Samuel Barber		
Mr Nathaniel Barthrop		
Mr Samuel Salmon		
Mr Simon Paternoster		
Mr Joseph Bennington		

The following persons were duly elected Directors and Acting Guardians ⬦:

	Directors	1st Quarter	Guardians
July	Edmund Jenney Esq.		Mr Francis Betts
	Mr Thomas Whimper		Mr Samuel Darby
			Mr John Bigsby
Aug.	The Revd Mr Carter		Mr Robert Plant
	The Revd Mr Howard		Mr John Girling
			Mr Thomas Langley

Sept.	The Hon'ble Mr Nassau		Mr Edward Keer
	Jonathan Burward Esq.		Mr Ralph Hall
			Mr George Baker
Oct.	John Revett Esq.	2nd Quarter	Mr Thomas Cole
	The Revd Mr Sparrow		Mr Joseph Bennington Jun.
			Mr Southwell Golding
Nov.	Anthony Collett Esq.		Mr Thomas Cole
	Mr Simon Paternoster		Mr William Waller
			Mr Samuel Thompson
Dec.	Francis Brooke Esq.		Mr Benjamin Barthrop
	The Revd Mr Jeaffreson		Mr Nathaniel Elliott
			Mr James Woods
Jan.	The Revd Mr Purvis	3rd Quarter	Mr George Lord
	Mr Quintin Woolnough		Mr Stephen Vertue
			Mr William Miller
Feb.	Mr Joseph Bennington		Mr Thomas Mann
	Mr Benjamin Cooper		Mr John Garrett
			Mr John Woods
March	The Revd Mr Hingeston		Mr Samuel Bucke
	Mr Martin Harsant		Mr Thomas Sheming
			Mr Richard Cole
Apl.	Mr John Whimper	4th Quarter	Mr Thomas Chandler
	Mr John Baldry		Mr Thomas Saunders
			Mr John Kemp
May	Mr Nathaniel Barthrop		Mr Joseph Burrell
	Mr Samuel Salmon		Mr William Ashford
			Mr James Gooding
June	Mr Samuel Barber		Mr Robert Harvey
	Mr John Barthrop		Mr William Harris
			Mr Thomas Ablitt

Ordered that no certificate be granted upon any account whatsoever to any person belonging to any parish within the said Hundreds into any Corporation town.

Ordered that the Clerk do have a quantity of advertisements to be printed, and sent to the Officers of the several parishes within the said Hundreds, to inform them that they are not to send to the Surgeons for any pauper until they have informed themselves of the necessity and the illness of such pauper. And not to require such Surgeon to attend but by writing under their hands, and not to desire such Surgeon to attend in cases of midwifery except too difficult for a woman midwife.

1 January 1776

Ordered that no person that shall be brought to the House of Industry with any distemper or disordered in their senses (unless it is certain they have had the small pox) be sent to the Pest House on any account whatever.

25 June 1776

Directors	Present	Guardians
The Hon'ble Mr Nassau		Mr William Ashford
Francis Brooke Esq.		and
Jonathan Burward Esq.		Mr Samuel Bucke
John Revett Esq.		

The Revd Mr Jeaffreson
Mr John Barthrop
Mr Samuel Barber
Mr Samuel Salmon
Mr Simon Paternoster
Mr John Whimper

The following persons were duly elected Directors and Acting Guardians ◇:

	Directors	1st Quarter	Guardians
July	Edmund Jenney Esq.		Mr Ralph Randall
	Jonathan Burward Esq.		Mr Thomas Garneys
			Mr Stephen Catchpole
Aug.	The Revd Mr Cole		Mr John Bigsby
	The Revd Mr Howard		Mr John Scotchmer Sen.
			Mr William Smith
Sept.	The Hon'ble Mr Nassau		Mr Edward Keer
	Mr John Tovell		Mr Thomas Taylor
			Mr George Baker
Oct.	John Revett Esq.	2nd Quarter	Mr William Cole
	The Revd Mr Sparrow		Mr Joseph Bennington Jun.
			Mr John Loyns
Nov.	Anthony Collett Esq.		Mr John Dennington
	Mr Simon Paternoster		Mr William Waller
			Mr Samuel Thompson
Dec.	Francis Brooke Esq.		Mr Benjamin Barthrop
	The Revd Mr Jeaffreson		Mr John Trusson
			Mr James Woods
Jan.	The Revd Mr Purvis	3rd Quarter	Mr George Lord
	Quin. Woolnough		Mr Joseph Rust
			Mr Nathaniel Fuller
Feb.	John Sheppard Esq.		Mr William Miller
	Mr Benjamin Cooper		Mr John Garrett
			Mr John Woods
Mar.	The Revd Mr Hingeston		Mr Samuel Bucke
	Mr Martin Harsant		Mr Thomas Sheming
			Mr Jeptha Waller
Apl.	Mr John Whimper	4th Quarter	Mr Thomas Chandler
	Mr John Baldry		Mr Thomas Saunders
			Mr John Kemp
May	Mr Nathaniel Barthrop		Mr Joseph Burrell Jun.
	Mr Samuel Salmon		Mr William Ashford
			Mr Richard Syer
June	Mr Samuel Barber		Mr Robert Harvey
	Mr John Barthrop		Mr William Harris
			Mr Thomas Ablitt

Ordered that every application that shall be made to the Weekly Committee be entered in the Committee Book whether allowed or disallowed.

Ordered that no poor persons dying in any of the incorporated parishes, (who shall not at the time of their death be paupers actually receiving relief), shall be buried by the Overseers in the parish where they die at the expence of the Corporation. But in those cases where any poor person not receiving relief shall die, not leaving sufficient to defray the expence of his burial, and application shall be made to the Overseers by the relations of the deceased, the Overseers, if satisfyed of the truth of the case, shall give notice to the Governor of the House of Industry who is to provide a shroud and coffin, and send for the corpse and cause it to be interred in the cemetery belonging to the said House. But this order is not to extend to unknown poor persons casually dying within the said Hundreds. But such are to be buried in the parish where they die, and that no sum exceeding one pound be allowed for burial in any case. And that this order be printed and sent to every parish in the said Hundreds.

30 September 1776

Ordered that the Clerk do write to the Overseers of Great Thornham to request they will not imediately remove Timothy Denny and family as the Directors and Guardians acknowledge them to belong to the parish of Earl Soham in the Hundred of Loes, and that Denny waits only at Thornham until he can get a house in the Hundreds.

Ordered that the Treasurer do pay the Overseers of Wickham Market their bill of £1 12s. 0d. for the burial of Robert Berry, a person killed by accident in the said parish, and that the Clerk do write to Mr Robert Button of Dennington, his master, to pay the Clerk the said £1 12s. 0d. so much being due from him to the said Robert Berry for wages.

Ordered that the Clerk do write to the Overseers of Hollesly for payment of the last two quarters assessments due to the Corporation which they have neglected to pay.[47]

30 December 1776

Ordered that the Treasurer do pay Mr Thurston Whimper one pound eleven shillings and six pence, his bill for attending Thomas Fuller a pauper at Melton having broke his leg and arm.

30 June 1777

Directors	Present	Guardians[48]
The Hon'ble Mr Nassau		
Francis Brooke Esq.		
The Revd Mr Jeaffreson		
The Revd Mr John Sparrow		
The Revd Mr Samuel Hingeston		
The Revd Mr Denny Cole		
Mr John Barthrop		
Mr Nathaniel Barthrop		
Mr Samuel Salmon		
Mr Simon Paternoster		

The following persons were duly elected Directors and Acting Guardians ◇:

	Directors	1st Quarter	Guardians
July	Edmund Jenney Esq.		Mr Ralph Randall

---

[47] Late payment of the quarterly assessments was surprisingly infrequent.

[48] There were no guardians present at this meeting.

	Jonathan Burward Esq.		Mr Thomas Garneys
			Mr Stephen Catchpole
Aug.	The Revd Mr Cole		Mr Francis Hayle
	The Revd Mr Howard		Mr John Scotchmer Jun.
			Mr John Wase
Sept.	The Hon Mr Nassau		Mr Samuel Farrer
	John Tovell Esq.		Mr Thomas Taylor
			Mr Ralph Cotton
Oct.	The Revd Mr Sparrow	2nd Quarter	Mr William Cole
	Mr Nathaniel Barthrop		Mr Joseph Bennington
			Mr John Jeaffreson
Nov.	Francis Brooke Esq.		Mr John Dennington
	Anthony Collett Esq.		Mr Thomas Whimper
			Mr Samuel Thompson
Dec.	Mr Simon Paternoster		Mr Benjamin Barthrop
	Mr William Waller		Mr Whimper Bradley
			Mr James Woods
Jan.	The Revd Mr Purvis	3rd Quarter	Mr George Lord
	The Revd Mr Richard Frank		Mr Joseph Rust
			Mr Thomas Mann
Feb.	Mr Quin. Woolnough		Mr William Miller
	Mr Benjamin Cooper		Mr Edward Adams
			Mr John Woods
March	The Revd Mr Hingeston		Mr Samuel Bucke
	Mr Martin Harsant		Mr John Levett
			Mr Jeptha Waller
Apl.	Mr John Whimper	4th Quarter	Mr Thomas Chandler
	Mr John Baldry		Mr Thomas Saunders
			Mr Richard Syer
May	Mr Samuel Salmon		Mr Joseph Burrell
	John Revett Esq.		Mr William Ashford
			Mr Stephen Vertue
June	Mr Samuel Barber		Mr Robert Harvey
	Mr John Barthrop		Mr William Harris
			Mr Thomas Ablitt

30 September 1777

Ordered that Mr Richard Wood, the Clerk, do commence actions against James Skeet and Richard Brooke on their bond for maintenance of a bastard child born of the body of Sarah Prew of Ufford.

29 December 1777

Ordered that the Governor do bring in a list of such boys and girls in the House of Industry and of the parishes they severally belong to as are fit for service or apprenticeship at the next Quarterly Meeting. That the Directors and Guardians then present may give such orders and directions for placing them out as they shall think proper.

30 March 1778

Ordered that the Governor do pay five pounds to James Freeman of Framlingham, Cordwainer, as a consideration for binding Samuel Ringe, a poor lame boy of Easton, apprentice to him for three years from <10 October 1777> and the indentures to be at an equal expence.

The list of boys and girls now in the House of Industry that are fit for service or apprenticeship being this day produced <>. It is ordered that notice be given by the Clerk to the Overseers of the respective parishes within the said Hundreds of Loes and Wilford to attend, and to deliver to the Directors and Acting Guardians of the Poor within the said Hundreds as shall be present at the next general Quarterly Meeting <> a list of all persons within their respective parishes who are liable by law to take parish apprentices. That if the several parishes cannot agree among themselves to take such children, the Directors and Guardians have come to a determined resolution to place out such boys and girls to such person or persons of the said several parishes as shall by law be compelled to take them.

It being thought that the Spinning Rooms now used in the House of Industry do not admit of sufficient air for the preservation of the health of the children working therein. It is ordered that <7 named directors> be a Committee appointed to attend at the said House, together with such other Directors and Guardians as shall think proper, to inspect the said rooms, and give such directions for the altering and improving the said rooms as they shall think proper.

1 April 1778 [*Committee reviewing the Spinning Room*]

On viewing and inspecting the Spinning Rooms in the House of Industry <>. Ordered that the partition between the spinning rooms be taken down from end to end within five foot of the floor, and that supporters be erected at each beam. That the bond timber to be laid on to the wall be ten inches wide and four inches thick of redwood deal. That the supporters be also of fir and of nine inches square. That the old casements be taken away, and two small casements be made at the top of each window in lieu thereof. That the two upper panels of the door at the end of the Spinning Room on to the Chapple Gallery be taken out, and two small iron bars be affixed in each panel. That Daniel Manthorp of Ufford, carpenter, Thomas Symonds of Shottisham, bricklayer, Thomas Garrett of Ufford aforesaid, blacksmith, and Lawrence Newson of Wickham Market, glazier, do make the above alterations, and that the said Daniel Manthorp do attend the above Committee on <8 April> at the said House of Industry.

8 April 1778 [*Committee reviewing the Spinning Room*]

Ordered that Mr Daniel Manthorp do the carpenters work in the Spinning Rooms of the House of Industry according to the estimate delivered by him this day. That the alteration of the door at the end of the Spinning Room on the Chapple Gallery be postponed for the present.

That when the Spinning Rooms are finished they be white washed and that chains be fixed to the casements in the Spinning Rooms to prevent their being broke against the wall.

29 June 1778

Directors	Present	Guardians
The Hon'ble Mr Nassau		Mr Stephen Vertue
Francis Brooke Esq.		and
John Tovell Esq.		Mr William Harris

John Rivett Esq.
The Revd Mr Frank
Mr John Barthrop
Mr Samuel Barber
Mr Martin Harsant
Mr Samuel Salmon
Mr Simon Paternoster
Mr John Whimper
The following persons were duly elected Directors and Acting Guardians ◇:

	Directors	1st Quarter	Guardians
July	Edmund Jenny Esq.		Mr Ralph Randall
	The Revd Mr Jeaffreson		Mr James Seaman
			Mr Stephen Catchpole
Aug.	The Revd Mr Cole		Mr Francis Hayle
	The Revd Mr Howard		Mr John Scotchmer Jun.
			Mr William Smith
Sept.	The Hon'ble Mr Nassau		Mr Samuel Farrer
	John Tovell Esq.		Mr John Cooper
			Mr Ralph Cotton
Oct.	The Revd Mr Fowler	2nd Quarter	Mr William Cole
	Mr Nathaniel Barthrop		Mr Joseph Bennington
			Mr John Jeaffreson
Nov.	Francis Brooke Esq.		Mr John Dennington
	Anthony Collett Esq.		Mr John Bull
			Mr Samuel Thompson
Dec.	The Revd Mr Purvis		Mr Benjamin Barthrop
			Mr Whimper Bradley
			Mr Thomas Stammers
Jan.	Mr Simon Paternoster	3rd Quarter	Mr William Smith
	Mr William Waller		Mr Joseph Rust
			Mr Richard Harris
Feb.	The Revd Mr Hingeston		Mr William Miller
	Mr William Goodwin		Mr James Aldhous
			Mr John Woods
Mar.	Mr Samuel Salmon		Mr Samuel Bucke
	Mr Benjamin Cooper		Mr Richard Cole
			Mr William Heffer
Apl.	Mr John Whimper	4th Quarter	Mr Thomas Chandler
	Mr John Baldry		Mr Thomas Sanders
			Mr Richard Syer
May	John Rivett Esq.		Mr Joseph Burrell
	Mr Q. Woolnough		Mr John Hayward
			Mr Benjamin Gale
June	Mr Samuel Barber		Mr Robert Harvey
	Mr John Barthrop		Mr William Harris
			Mr Thomas Ablitt

William Harris and Philip Whincopp, Overseers of the parish of Bawdsey, being duly summoned according to the Act of Parliament for Incorporating the said Hundreds for neglect of duty, and they being fully charged with the same are ordered to be fined ten shillings and six pence together with the Clerks charges for summons etc. for such their neglect, which they paid accordingly.

Ordered that the Overseers of every parish within the said Hundreds that shall be summoned for the future for neglect of duty and shall be convicted thereof shall be fined not less than forty shillings. And that the Clerk do in the next advertizement for the Previous and Quarterly Meeting insert that such Overseers as shall neglect their payments or any other part of their duty will be proceeded against for such their neglect according to the Act for Incorporating the said Hundreds.

Ordered that Mr Wood, the Clerk, do prosecute John Welton, late Overseer of Earl Soham, at the next Quarter Sessions by indictment of his threatening to pull down the House of Industry, but if an indictment will not lay then to commence an action against him at common law for the same or otherwise to proceed against him as he shall be advised.

Ordered that the Governor do hire a proper man into the House of Industry for brewing and other services, not exceeding the wages of eight pounds a year. And also that he do provide a schoolmistress to teach the children to read, sew and knit at the wages of three pounds a year.

5 October 1778

Ordered that no certificates shall be granted to any person from this Corporation, unless the person requesting the same shall produce an examination taken before one of his Majesty's Justices of the Peace showing that he belongs to one of the parishes within the said Hundreds.[49]

Ordered that James Cooke, a poor boy of the parish of Earl Soham, now in the said House be let to Mr Robert Hayward, of the same parish, for a year from this day.

Ordered that Hannah Cooke, a poor girl of the same parish of Earl Soham, now in the said House be let to Mr John Scotchmer Junior, of the same parish, for a year from this day.

Ordered that Elizabeth Cooke, a poor girl of the same parish of Earl Soham, now in the said House be let to Mr John Scotchmer Junior, of the same parish, for a year from this day.

Ordered that the Clerk do summons John Felgate, Overseer of Kettleburgh ◇ to show cause why he has refused to obey the orders of the Directors and Guardians and neglecting to do his duty, particularly in neglecting to go after and take Robert Clarke according to the Justices Warrant for that purpose being charged with being the father of the bastard child born of the body of Christian Skutt of Kettleburgh.

\We the Directors and Acting Guardians of the Poor within the Hundreds of Loes and Wilford in the County of Suffolk whose names are hereunto set do by virtue of an Act of Parliament ◇ summon you John Felgate Overseer of the Poor in the parish of Kettleburgh ◇ to appear at the next General Quarterly Meeting ◇ to shew cause why the several penaltys incurred by you for disobeying their orders and

---

49 A person acquired a settlement in a parish by serving an apprenticeship there, by being hired for a year, by holding local office, by paying local taxes, or by renting or owning local property. Women acquired their husband's settlements on marriage and legitimate children inherited the rights of their parents.

neglecting and refusing to do your duty should not be levied upon you in pursuance of the sad Act. <signatures>/[50]

28 December 1778

Ordered that the Surgeon do deliver in an account every Monday to the Committee of the state of all out paupers under his or the Out Surgeons care.

It being represented to the Directors and Guardians at this meeting that there was not sufficient care and attendance taken of the infant children in the Nursery in the House of Industry in Melton. Ordered that a Committee of seven Directors <7 named directors> or a majority of them, do meet at the said House of Industry <> to superintend the same and make such orders and regulations as they shall think proper. It is likewise ordered that the above said Committee, do at the same time inspect the tileing of the said House of Industry being very much out of repair, and make such orders and regulations for repairing the same as they shall think proper.

Ordered that the Clerk do summons the Overseers of Eyke to appear at the next Quarterly Meeting to show cause why they have refused to obey the orders of the Directors and Guardians, particularly in not paying the Quarterly Assessment for the said parish of Eyke.

31 December 1778 [*Committee for the care of children in the Nursery*]

On viewing and inspecting the tiling of the House of Industry, <> ordered that all the garret windows on the north side of the North Wing of the said House, (except the window into the present Lodging Room for the poor in the said House), also the two garret windows on the hip ends of the east front, the two garret windows on the south side of the South Wing over the Governors Apartments, and all the garret windows on the north side of the South Wing over the Kitchen, Backhouse and Outhouses be taken down and the tiling made good as soon as conveniently may be and the season of the year will permit, the time to be fixed at a future meeting of the Directors. It is also ordered that Edward Fletcher of Wickham Market, brick-layer, Daniel Manthorp the younger of Ufford, carpenter, and Lawrence Newson of Wickham Market aforesaid, plumber and glazier, do attend such of the above Committee, and shall be present at the next Previous Meeting <> in order to take-down one of the windows of the north side of the North Wing of the said House. To inspect and make an estimate of the expences of taking down the windows and making the tiling good. Also to make an estimate of the expences of taking down, repairing and leading the tops and sides of the remaining garret windows in the said House and also of the repairing the tiling of the said House.

After having viewed and inspected the care and attendance taken of the infant children in the Nursery <> it is ordered that the following examinations be taken viz.

Elizabeth Noller, the nurse having the care of the infants in the said Nursery, saith that she has under her care five small children above a year old, and two about two years old, one of them at her own breast. That the children have always had everything necessary for their maintenance and support, and every care and attendance taken of them as she can wish or desire for persons in such a situation of life.[51]

---

[50] Note inserted in WMB, SROI ADA11/A/B/3/2, referring to the QMB entry for 5 October 1778.

[51] Elizabeth Noller from Charsfield had been admitted into the House on 24 November 1777 aged twenty-four. Her daughter, Elizabeth, was aged seven. SROI ADA11/C/B/3/1.

Mary Wright, the schoolmistress, saith she has under her care thirteen children in the School. Has seen the white bread and believes it of general use for infants and sick people. Has a child in the Nursery, has the liberty of seeing and looking after her child when she please, and that her child is as well taken care of as she wishes for persons in such a situation of life.[52]

Rachael Turtle saith she has three children, two in the Spinning Rooms and one in the Nursery, has full liberty to look after her children, one of which she has at the breast, and is fully satisfied with the care taken of them, they having such white bread and milk as hath been produced to the Committee here present.[53]

Fanny Pipe has three Children in the School Room in the said House, has buried two, one of which, about a year and three quarters old, was taken ill soon after she came into the House with a cancer in its mouth, continued very Ill for near five weeks. She was with it for some days before its death. The other infant, about six weeks old, appeared to be very well except its growing thin and pale, but died by her side in bed in the night. She puts her three children to bed and takes them up and dresses them herself every morning, and when she lay in had every necessary care taken of her that she could desire.

It appearing to us the Committee by the above examinations, that every care and attendance has been taken of the children in the said House. That the reports that have been spread in the neighbourhood of the neglect of the infants in the Nursery have been misrepresented, and it appearing that it is entirely without foundation. Ordered that the thanks of this Committee be given to the Governor and Governess of the said House for their care and attention to the paupers in the said House.

22 March 1779

Messrs. Fletcher, Manthrop and Newson, having this day taken down the window on the north side of the North Wing of the House of Industry agreeable to the order of the last meeting, and the Committee for that purpose having inspected the same, ordered that Newson do new lead the sides and bottom of one of the windows against Monday next, and then to take his further orders. And that the fourteen windows ordered to be taken down ◇ be imediately taken down by Manthrop and Fletcher and the tiling made good by them.

29 March 1779

Ordered that Wayman Bardwell, a certificate person from the parish of Creetingham to Sco Ruston in the county of Norfolk, having six small children be allowed eighteen pence a week from Michaelmas last old stile towards their maintenance to this day and to be continued to further orders. And that the Clerk do write to the officers of Sco Ruston that the Directors and Guardians have ordered the same and to be continued to be paid half yearly until further orders.[54]

Samuel Rowe, Overseer of the poor of the parish of Eyke, being duly summoned according to the Act of Parliament for incorporating the said Hundreds, for neglect

---

52 Mary Wright from Charsfield had been admitted into the House on 6 October 1777 aged thirty. SROI ADA11/C/B/3/1.

53 Rachel Turtle from Hacheston was admitted into the House on 16 June 1777, aged forty-four. She had two children, William aged seven and George aged six. SROI ADA11/C/B/3/1.

54 Relief was permitted to those who had moved out of the hundreds during these early years of the Incorporation. As outdoor relief increased during the 1790s then such families were increasingly brought into the house of industry.

of duty in not making his quarterly payment. And on his appearing this day and not making a proper excuse for the same, is ordered to be fined forty shillings for such his neglect.

Ordered that the Clerk do summons the Overseers of the several parishes of Rendlesham and Boyton to appear at the next Quarterly Meeting to show cause why they have refused to obey the orders of the Directors and Guardians, particularly in not paying their Quarterly Assessment for the said several parishes.

29 March 1779 [*Committee to review the tiling of the House*]

Ordered that Mr Newson, the glazier, (as proposed by him), do take the old lead from the garret windows intended to be taken down at the House of Industry, agreeable to the former order for that purpose, and new lead the remainder of them according to one already done (viz.) – the cheeks to be five feet six inches long and twelve inches broad, the apron five feet long and twelve inches wide, to be cast lead of six pound to the foot and, and to paint the sides twice over of a lead colour at fifteen shillings per window. And it is further ordered that the Governor do procure four chaldron of lime for the purpose of new tiling the north side of the Governors Apartment in the said House and repairing other parts of the said House. And that Francis Brooke Esq. be desired to send ten thousand plain tiles, and five hundred ridge tile for the use of the said House as soon as conveniently may be.

\Rec'd March 30 1779 of Mr Sam Rowe overseer if Eyke, forty shillings for a fine set upon him by the Directors and Guardians of the Hundreds of Loes and Wilford for disobeying their order and neglecting to pay the Qtly assessment due to them from the said parish. I say received for the use of the Directors and Guardians. Rd. Wood. £2.0.0./[55]

28 June 1779

Directors Present	Guardians
The Hon'ble Mr Nassau	Mr Richard Syer
John Brand Esq.	
Francis Brooke Esq.	
John Tovell Esq.	
John Rivett Esq.	
The Revd Mr Frank	
The Revd Mr Jeaffreson	
The Revd Mr Fowller	
The Revd Mr Purvis	
The Revd Mr Cole	
Mr Samuel Barber	
Mr John Barthorp	
Mr John Whimper	
Mr Quintin Woolnough	
Mr Samuel Salmon	
Mr Simon Paternoster	

The following persons were duly elected Directors and Acting Guardians ◇:

Directors	1ˢᵗ Quarter	Guardians

---

[55] Note inserted within SROI ADA11/A/B2/4.

July	Edmund Jenney Esq.		Mr Joseph Oldham
	The Revd Christopher Jeaffreson		Mr James Seaman
			Mr John Ralph
Aug.	The Revd Denny Cole		Mr Francis Hayle
	The Revd Eden Howard		Mr John Scotchmer Jun.
			Mr William Smith
Sept	The Hon'ble Mr Nassau		Mr Edmund Tye
	John Tovell Esq.		Mr John Cooper
			Mr William Eastaugh
Oct.	The Revd Richard Fowller	2nd Quarter	Mr William Cole
	Mr Nathaniel Barthrop		Mr Joseph Bennington
			Mr John Jeaffreson
Nov.	Francis Brooke Esq.		Mr Thomas Crisp
	Anthony Collett Esq.		Mr George Payne
			Mr Samuel Thompson
Dec.	The Revd Thomas Purvis		Mr Benjamin Barthrop
	The Revd Richard Frank		Mr Whimper Bradley
			Mr William Wase
Jan.	Mr Simon Paternoster	3rd Quarter	Mr William Smith
	Mr William Waller		Mr Joseph Rust
			Mr Richard Harris
Feb.	John Brand Esq.		Mr William Miller
	Mr Samuel Salmon		Mr James Aldhouse
			Mr Jeptha Waller
Mar.	The Revd Sam. Hingeston		Mr Warner Litsenburgh
	Mr Benjamin Cooper		Mr Samuel Lawrence
			Mr William Heffer
Apl.	Mr John Whimper	4th Quarter	Mr Thomas Chandler
	Mr John Baldry		Mr Thomas Sanders
			Mr Richard Syer
May	John Revett Esq.		Mr William Whimper
	Mr Q. Woolnough		Mr Robert Hayward
			Mr Benjamin Gale
June	Mr Samuel Barber		Mr Robert Harvey
	Mr John Barthorp		Mr Thomas Ablitt
			Mr John Rivers

Mr John Levett Overseer of the poor of the parish of Rendlesham being duly summoned according to the Act of Parliament for Incorporating the said Hundreds for neglect of duty in not making his quarterly payment and appearing this day and making a reasonable excuse to the satisfaction of the Directors is discharged from any fine.

Mr William Miller Overseer of the poor of the parish of Boyton being duly summoned according to the Act of Parliament for Incorporating the said Hundreds for neglect of duty in not making his quarterly payment and appearing this day and making a reasonable excuse to the satisfaction of the Directors is discharged from any fine.

The fine of forty shillings set on Samuel Rowe, Overseer of the poor of the parish of Eyke, at the last Quarterly Meeting, and since paid, being now considered. It is ordered to be returned to the said Samuel Rowe.

Ordered that the Governor do cloathe Jeffery Boone, a poor blind person of the parish of Monewden, at the expence of the Corporation as follows viz. with 3 shirts, 2 pair of stockings, a pair of shoes, a coat, a waistcoat, a pair of breeches, a hat, and a neck cloth, when ordered by the Hon'ble Mr Nassau or John Revett Esq.

4 October 1779

At a Quarterly Meeting held <29 December 1777> it was ordered that the Governor should bring in a list of such boys and girls in the House of Industry and of the parishes that they severally belonged to as were fit for service or apprenticeship at the next Quarterly Meeting. It is now ordered that the Governor shall deliver in such a list at the meeting previous to every Annual Meeting, and that the Clerk shall, at the said Previous Meeting, send notices to the Overseers of such parish as the children in the said list shall belong to. That the parishioners are desired to agree among themselves to take such child or children. And if the parishioners cannot agree among themselves who shall take them, the Overseers of that parish are to be required to bring or send a list at the said next Annual Meeting of such persons in their parish who are liable to take parish apprentices, that such child or children may be apprenticed as the said Act directs.

Ordered that the Governor, at every Quarterly Meeting, do deliver in a state of the poor in the House of Industry, containing the names, ages and parishes to which they severally belong, entered at or since or were in the said House at the Previous Quarterly Meeting, together with the particular infirmities any of them may labour under, and also any other matter or matters concerning them which he may think necessary to be laid before the Directors and Acting Guardians then present.

Ordered that Mary Mingay a poor girl apprenticed to Thomas Mann of Dallingho farmer (upon the complaint of the said Thomas Mann for her abusing and disobeying his orders) be discharged from her said apprenticeship by two of His Majesty's Justices of the Peace for this county and sent to the House of Industry.

Ordered that the Clerk do give notice to the Overseers of the several parishes in the said Hundreds of Loes and Wilford, requiring them when they bring or send any poor person belonging to their parish to be received into the House of Industry, to bring or send with them a certificate of the age of such poor person from the parish register of the parish wherein such poor person was born.

Ordered that a Committee <7 named directors> or a majority of them, do attend at the House of Industry <> for the purpose of stating a case for councell's opinion respecting the Act of Parliament relative to the maintenance of the familys of substitutes serving in the Suffolk Militia, and that the said Directors do order such case as they shall approve of to be laid before such councell as they shall think proper.[56]

11 October 1779 [*Committee concerning Militia Men*]

Ordered That the Clerk do state a case to the following effect.

---

[56] A General Militia Meeting was held once a year, when the justices of the peace and at least one deputy lieutenant received lists of men eligible to serve in the Militia. The county quota was then apportioned among the hundreds in proportion to the number of men liable to serve in each. The hundred quotas were apportioned among the parishes and a ballot was held to choose those men who were to serve for each. The chosen men were given at least seven days' notice at their homes of the next subdivision meeting in three weeks' time, at which they were to appear. Substitutes, approved by the deputy lieutenants, could be paid for and some men took out insurance against being chosen. Funds were set up to provide substitutes for poor married men to prevent their families becoming chargeable (Fiske, *Oakes Diaries*, Volume 1, p. 214).

By an Act of the 2nd Geo 3rd Ca 20 Sec 31st it is enacted that if any militia man *etc vide* the Act.

By an Act of <1765> the Hundreds of Loes and Wilford in the county of Suffolk were incorporated for the better relief and employment of the poor in the said Hundreds. And at the time of putting the said Act in execution, when the quota of every parish in the said Hundreds was fixed for them to pay to the Corporation, all moneys raised and paid by every parish to the Treasurer of the (called Marshalsea Money) were deducted by the Directors out of the whole account of the Overseers before such quota was fixed.

By an Act of the 18th George 3rd it is enacted that one half of the allowance made to the familys of substitutes, hired man or volunteers serving in the Militia, when embodied and called out into actual service, and ordered to march becoming charge-able to the parishes to which they belong, shall be reimbursed to the Overseers of such parish by the Treasurer of the county in which such parish shall be.

By an Act of the 19th Geo 3rd it is enacted that in case any substitute serving in the Militia whose family may become chargeable to his parish shall not serve for the parish where his family shall dwell, the Justice who makes order for relief may direct the Overseers of the parish for which he shall serve to reimburse the money paid to them.

NB. As the Marshalsea Money (paid to the Treasurer of the county) was deducted out of the payments of every parish to the said Incorporated Hundreds there is no fund in the said Corporation for payment of relief to the militia man's familys. And if the incorporated parishes now pay relief to the militia men's familys they will not be more burthened than any other parish not incorporated, as the Marshalsea Money was deducted out of their several payments to the Corporation.

Whether on the circumstances of this case (after perusing the several Acts) is the incorporated parish to which such militia man belongs obliged to pay the mainte-nance of such militia man's family themselves over and above their quota paid to the Corporation or is such maintenance to come out of the common stock of the Corporation.

25 October 1779 [*Committee concerning Militia Men*]

The Committee having perused and settled the case, do order that the Clerk do lay the same before S. LeBlanc Esq. for his opinion thereon.

27 December 1779

The Governor not being able at this meeting to make a return agreeable to the order of the last Quarterly Meeting. Ordered that the Governor do make a return at the next Quarterly Meeting in the best manner he can, to be approved of by the Directors and Guardians then present. And that the plan of such return being proposed by the Revd Mr Frank be left with the Governor for the approbation of the Directors and Guardians against the next Quarterly Meeting.

27 March 1780

Ordered and the Revd Mr Frank is requested to provide two ledger books, prop-erly ruled, for the purpose of the Governor making a quarterly return of the state of the paupers in the House of Industry agreeable to the order of the last Quarterly Meeting.

Ordered that the Treasurer do pay Mr Richard Wood Junior of Melton, ten pounds for his care and trouble in making an index to the Rules and Orders for the better government of the poor in the said Hundreds from the first institution of this Corporation.

Ordered that the councell's opinion on the case respecting the maintenance of the familys of substitutes serving in the Militia be entered among the records of the Corporation. Which is entered accordingly and is as follows:

On perusal of the several Acts of Parliament above referred to, I am of opinion that the incorporated parish to which such militia man belongs or for which he serves, is obliged to pay for the maintenance of his family over and above their quota paid to the Corporation, and that the same is not to come out of the common stock of the Incorporation.

The Incorporating Act of the Hundreds of Loes and Wilford was made expressly for the purpose of providing a place for the general reception of the poor and finding them employment there, in a better and less expensive manner than the single parishes were able to do. And the clause of the Act directing the assessments to be made says expressly for providing for the poor to be employed or relieved in such House or Houses so that I conceive that the Guardians have nothing to do with the maintenance of such persons as are not liable to be sent to their House. And the proviso in the Militia Act 19 G 3 seems to say expressly that the families of such militia men are not to be considered as parish poor.

Besides which, I think the clause of the Incorporating Act, p.14, as applying directly to this case when it is considered that before the passing of the Act the payment of money for the support of the families of the militia men was, by a former Militia Act, viz. 2 Geo 3, directed to be made out of the rates for the relief of the poor. Add to this the circumstance of the Marshalsea Money having been deducted at the time the quota was fixed for each parish which takes away all pretence of complaint of hardship or inequality on any of the incorporated parishes. S. Leblanc, Inner Temple. 17 Nov 1779.

26 June 1780

Directors	Present	Guardians
Francis Brooke Esq.		Mr Francis Hayle
John Brand Esq.		Mr John Cooper
John Revett Esq.		Mr Thomas Chandler
The Revd Mr Frank		Mr Joseph Oldham
The Revd Mr Jeaffreson		and
The Revd Mr Purvis		Mr Thomas Crisp
The Revd Mr Fowller		
The Revd Mr Hingeston		
Mr John Whimper		
Mr Samuel Barber		
Mr John Barthorp		
Mr Samuel Salmon		
Mr Simon Paternoster		

The following persons were duly elected Directors and Acting Guardians ◇:

	Directors	1st Quarter	Guardians
July	Edmund Jenney Esq.		Mr James Oldham
	The Revd Mr Jeaffreson		Mr James Seaman
			Mr John Ralph
Aug.	The Revd Mr Cole		Mr John Scotchmer Jun.
	The Revd Mr Howard		Mr William Smith

52

			Mr Joseph Burrell Jun.
Sept.	Wm Henry Nassau Esq.		Mr Thomas Smith
	John Tovell Esq.		Mr John Cooper
			Mr John Steptoe
Oct.	The Revd Mr Fowller	2nd Quarter	Mr Thomas Whimper
	Mr Nathaniel Barthrop		Mr Joseph Bennington
			Mr William Cole
Nov.	Francis Brooke Esq.		Mr Thomas Crisp
	Anthony Collett Esq.		Mr Samuel Thompson
			Mr George Payne
Dec.	The Revd Mr Purvis		Mr Benjamin Barthropp
	The Revd Mr Frank		Mr Robert Linsted
			Mr William Wase
Jan.	Mr Simon Paternoster	3rd Quarter	Mr George Lord
	Mr William Waller		Mr Joseph Rust
			Mr Richard Harris
Feb.	John Brand Esq.		Mr Jeptha Waller
	Mr Samuel Salmon		Mr Nathaniel Bennington
			Mr James Aldhous
March	The Revd Mr Hingeston		Mr William Ablett
	Mr Benjamin Cooper		Mr Samuel Lawrence Jun.
			Mr James Grout
Apl.	Mr John Whimper	4th Quarter	Mr Thomas Chandler
	Mr John Baldry		Mr Thomas Sanders
			Mr Richard Syer
May	John Revett Esq.		Mr Francis Hayle
	Mr Q. Woolnough		Mr Samuel Lancaster Jun.
			Mr Benjamin Gale
June	Mr Samuel Barber		Mr Henry Woods
	Mr John Barthorp		Mr Thomas Ablitt
			Mr Robert Adams

Joseph Bennington and Thomas Chandler, Overseers of the Poor of the parish of Butley, being duly summoned according to the Act of Parliament for incorporating the said Hundreds for neglect of duty in not paying the assessment for the said parish of Butley on the day ordered for payment thereof. And they having this day appeared in pursuance of the said summons. It appears that the said Thomas Chandler is the only acting Overseer and as such hath neglected to pay the said assessment. Ordered that he the said Thomas Chandler be fined fifty shillings for such his neglect.

Ordered that Mr Samuel Salmon be continued Surgeon to the House of Industry at the salary of forty pounds a year, and do attend the paupers in the several parishes of Ash, Charsfield, Dallingho, Easton, Hatcheston, Letheringham, Marlesford, Rendlesham, Boulge, Bredfield, Debach, Melton, Petistree, Ufford, and Wickham Market at the further salary of forty five pounds a year. That Mr Thurston Whimper, Surgeon, do attend the paupers in the several parishes of Butley, Eyke, Alderton, Bawdsey, Bromeswell, Boyton, Capell, Hollesly, Ramsholt, Sutton, and Shottisham at the salary of thirty three pounds a year. And that Mr William Henchman, Surgeon, do attend the several parishes of Brandeston, Creetingham, Earl Soham, Hoo, Kettleburgh, Kenton, and Monewden, at the salary of twenty one pounds a year.

Ordered that the several Surgeons this day appointed do, from time to time, deliver an account in writing of the state of the several paupers they attend to such paupers or their familys in order that such account may be produced to the Weekly Committee on the Monday following in case application shall be made for the relief of such paupers.

Ordered that the Clerk do get a number of instructions to Overseers, as settled this day and hereafter mentioned, printed and distributed to the Overseers of the several parishes within the said Hundreds at Easter, yearly, being the time of their appointment to the said office as follows:

Whereas great inconveniences to the poor and frequent impositions upon the Corporation have happened within the Incorporated Hundreds of Loes and Wilford by the negligence or ignorance of the Overseers of the Poor of the respective parishes within the hundreds aforesaid, to prevent such inconveniencies and impositions in future.

Ordered that the following directions and instructions be printed and annually distributed to the Overseers of the Poor of the respective parishes within the said hundreds, as well that they may not plead ignorance, as that they may be assured that every neglect of their duty will be punished with the utmost severity of the law.

First, by the Act of Incorporation ◇ it is enacted that the Churchwardens, Overseers ◇ within the said Hundreds, shall from time to time and at all times hereafter, aid and assist the said Guardians, Directors and Acting Guardian, to the best of their power, and shall at all times obey their warrants and reasonable orders relative to the execution of this Act. And in case any Churchwarden or Overseer ◇ shall refuse or neglect to raise and levy the sums so assessed upon his respective parish ◇ or to pay at the time and place appointed the monies so collected and levied, or to obey any such warrants or orders, every such Churchwarden, Overseer ◇ so neglecting or refusing, shall be summoned by writing under the hands of any three Directors or Acting Guardians, to appear ◇ so summoned, shall neglect or refuse to appear at such general Quarterly Meeting, or appearing, he or any of them shall not sufficiently excuse or justify him or themselves, but shall in the judgment of the major part of the said Directors and Acting Guardians assembled ◇ be adjudged guilty of disobeying such warrant ◇ that then and in every such case all and every person and persons so adjudged guilty as aforesaid, shall forfeit and pay for every such offence any sum not exceeding five pounds, to be levied by distress and sale of the offenders goods, by warrant under the hand and seal of any one Justice of the Peace for the said county of Suffolk. And such forfeitures shall be paid to the Treasurer of the said Guardians and added by him to the common stock for the use of the poor.

But if any such Churchwarden, Overseer ◇ so offending and convicted as aforesaid, shall think himself aggrieved, that then it shall and may be lawfull for such respective officer to appeal to the next Quarter Sessions ◇ against the judgment of the said Quarterly Meeting and the Justices of the Peace for the said county at the said Sessions so assembled, shall and may hear and determine such appeal, and may mitigate or set aside such penalties in such manner as they shall think proper, and the judgment of such justices at such Quarter Sessions shall be final, without any other appeal and such justices shall and may on every such appeal, and in all other cases of the appeal to them made, award such costs to the person or persons who to them shall appear to be aggrieved as to them shall seem meet.

As the duty of an Overseer is founded on upon principles of humanity to the poor and justice to the Corporation, the Directors and Acting Guardians at their Annual Meeting assembled do require every Overseer whenever a pauper makes application to him for relief, whether in sickness or otherwise, to visit such pauper and inquire minutely into the state of his or her circumstances and family and at no time to make application to the Committee for relief for such pauper unless the case should appear to be such as he would of himself have granted relief in case his parish had not been Incorporated. At the same time he must remember that he will subject himself to the penalties of the above recited clause whenever he neglects or refuses to apply to the Committee upon proper and necessary occasions in person or by writing under his hand.

Whenever an order is issued from a Justice of the Peace directing an Overseer to make an allowance to a pauper or to shew cause at any time appointed why such order should not be complied with it is the duty of an Overseer to wait upon such Justice at the time appointed and then and there shew cause against such order if any just one can be alleged.

Whenever the assistance of the Surgeon is applyed for the Overseer is required to visit the pauper and inform himself of the real state of the pauper as to necessity and sickness and if he finds the case requires it he is then to apply to the Surgeon in person or by writing under his hand otherwise the Surgeon will not be obliged to attend.

In cases of midwifery the Overseers are not to require the attendance of the Surgeon except only where the pauper has been attended by a woman midwife who had declared that in her opinion the assistance of a man midwife is necessary.

The Surgeon is not engaged to attend any poor persons but such as are resident in one of the incorporated parishes nor is he engaged to attend any sick person that shall at that time be an hired servant. If therefore any Overseer shall call in the Surgeon to anyone not within these rules such Overseer will himself be liable to pay the Surgeon his demand as the Committee will not allow it in the Overseers accounts.

No sum exceeding one pound will be allowed for the expences of burial of paupers in any case whatever.

Ordered that a Committee <10 named directors> or any five of them do meet at the House of Industry <> for the purpose of examining inspecting and inquiring what servants are indispensably necessary to do the work of the House of Industry and to make such order therein as they shall think proper.

7 July 1780 [*Committee into what servants are indispensable*]

Ordered that the Governor do hire two men as labourers and to have their dinners in the House of Industry until Michaelmas next at six shillings a week each his hired servant having left him. And that he do get two women as Nurses for the Pesthouse and the Nursery until Michaelmas next in the best manner he can. And that the said Committee do adjourn <17 July 1780> for the purposes of inspecting and examining the accounts of the expences of maintaining the poor in the said House.

17 July 1780 [*Committee to inspect the accounts*]

On examining the accounts of the expences of maintaining the poor in the House of Industry which accounts not appearing satisfactory to the Committee there appearing to be expended nearly as much wheat, meat and other articles in the said House at this time as when there were near one hundred more paupers in the said House. Ordered that the Committee do adjourn <until 29 September> for further examining into the accounts. And it is requested the gentlemen of this Committee or some of them do make such inquirys at other Houses of Industry relating to the expences of maintaining of paupers in their Houses as they shall think proper and report their enquirys to the Committee at the said next meeting.

29 August 1780 [*Committee for inspecting the tiling of the outhouses*]

Ordered that the Governor do give notice to Mr Theophilus Blansbury of Woodbridge, bricklayer, to repair the tiling on the North Side of the Granary and Brewhouse, the Washhouse belonging to the Sick Ward, and the Necessary Houses belonging to the said House of Industry, and to strip off the old tile where necessary. Also to repair the tiling of the Coalhouse, Hogstys, Coach Houses, and Sheds, and to go about the work as soon as possible. And it is ordered that Mr Thomas Crisp, of Melton, do deliver in at the said House what necessary tiles and Mr Thomas Brewster, of Woodbridge, such quantity of lime as will be wanting for that purpose.

29 September 1780 [*Committee to inspect the accounts*]

1st Resolved that is the opinion of this Committee that from Midsummer 1779 to Midsummer 1780 the number of paupers maintained in the House of Industry have been fewer than usual but that the quantities of meat, flour and cheese consumed within that time have been greater. Resolved that there must have been some great abuse or mismanagement and it is necessary that the same should be strictly inquired into.

2nd Resolved that it appears to this Committee that the allowance of wine for the Committee and to the Governor for his expences at market are unnecessary and improper and that it be recommended to the Quarterly Meeting to discontinue them for the future.

3rd Resolved that it is the opinion of this Committee that it would be for the advantage of this Corporation to have the wheat bought by commission and that it be recommended to the Quarterly Meeting to order the same accordingly.

4th Resolved that it will be for the advantage for the Corporation to buy the cheese and hops by contract.

5th Resolved that the money given to the industrious poor should be given by the Directors and Acting Guardians upon the recommendation of the Governor and Governess and not as has been usual by the Governor himself.

6th Resolved that the decrease in paupers in the House is owing to the immense increase in allowances to the out poor and that the increase is above double what it used to be.

7th Resolved that in consequence of the decrease of the poor within the House the profits arising from the spinning has in proportion decreased.

8th Resolved that all extraordinary and unnecessary out allowances are in direct opposition to the institution of this Corporation and that it be recommended to the Quarterly Meeting to order the Clerk to read on the first Weekly Committee day in every month an order requesting the gentlemen of the Committee to be very cautious in making the same.

9th Resolved that it be recommended to the Quarterly Meeting to order the Governor to deliver in to the Weekly Committee an account of the number of paupers in the House of Industry, the quantities of provisions received and expended, and the amount of the work done in the preceding week. That it be signed and allowed by such Weekly Committee.

10th It having appeared to this Committee upon an examination of Robert Bloss, the contractor for the last quarter to serve the House with beef and mutton, that the accounts delivered into the House do not exactly agree with the account in his Day

Book and that he does sometimes send in meat of an higher price and that he is obliged to make up the difference by deducting from the beef. Resolved that such transaction is an imposition upon the Corporation and an injury to the poor in the House.

2 October 1780
Ordered that no pauper be relieved by an out allowance (unless in cases of urgent necessity) untill the Surgeon has visited the pauper and reported the necessity of their having relief to the next Weekly Committee.

Ordered <> that Philip Riches of Woodbridge, merchant, do procure such wheat as will be wanting for the use of the House of Industry at a commission of 3d. per comb.

Ordered that Francis Brooke Esq. is requested to procure a book ready ruled agreeable to the plan he has this day produced <> and that the same be regularly kept by the Governor of the said House and be delivered by him to the Weekly Committee to be by them allowed and signed.

Ordered that a Committee <9 named directors> or any 5 of them or such other Directors as are agreeable to attend do meet at the House of Industry <on 6 October> for the purpose of inspecting into what servants are indispensably necessary and wanting in the said House and to make such order therein as they shall think proper. And that they be continued a Committee to adjourn to what time or times they shall think proper during this quarter and on any other business as may occur.

Ordered that the said Francis Brooke Esq. is further requested to procure another book ready ruled agreeable to the plan he has this day produced as an annual state of payments, receipts on account of this Corporation to be returned annually at midsummer.

Resolved that the resolutions entred into by the Special Committee <29 September 1780> were founded on facts, highly proper and are this day unanimously agreed to.

6 October 1780 [*Committee into what servants are indispensable*]
Ordered that the Clerk do advertize in the Ipswich Journal for a person as a Schoolmaster to live in the House (if a single man the more agreeable) to teach the children in the House to read and assist the Governor in keeping accounts and making the weekly and other returns of the state of the said House and to deliver in their terms to the Governor which terms are to be by him produced to this Committee at the next meeting.

Also a Taylor to live in the said House to apply as above.

Also a man servant to work in the garden, assist in brewing and other work necessary to be done in the said House to apply as above.

25 October 1780 [*Committee into what servants are indispensable*]
<Adjourned to 13 November 1780>

13 November 1780 [*Committee into what servants are indispensable*]
Ordered that Mr John Elliott of Ufford be appointed Schoolmaster and House Clerk at the salary of sixteen pounds a year who is to teach the children to read and write in a room fixed upon for that purpose. To attend the Governor when anything is brought into the House or expended there. To weigh and measure the same and to keep the weekly accounts of the House agreeable to the plan agreed upon by the Directors and Acting Guardians. That he have board, washing and lodging in the

House. That he dine with the Governor and have a bedroom appropriated to himself alone. That he be considered as a servant of the Incorporation and that all complaints from him or against him be made to the Weekly Committee.

Ordered that Francis Brooke Esq. do give directions for the altering the School masters apartments agreeable to the plan this day agreed upon.

26 December 1780

Ordered that the Treasurer do pay Mr Peter Stoughton of Windham in Norfolk five guineas towards his expences in applying for and obtaining an Act of Parliament for obviating doubts respecting poor apprentices and for ascertaining the settlement of bastard children born in the House of Industry.[57]

Ordered that out of the next savings arising from the income of the Corporation the Treasurer do pay off three securitys of one hundred pounds each and the interest due thereon to the executors of Mr Jane Whimper deceased.

29 January 1781 [*Committee enquiring into a housekeeper and matron*]

Ordered that the Governor do provide a person imediately for Housekeeper of the House of Industry untill the next Quarterly Meeting and then that she be continued or rejected and such other order be made concerning the same as shall then be thought proper.

The small pox being now in the said House of Industry ordered that Mr Salmon the surgeon do inoculate such of the poor in the said House as have not had it that shall voluntarily desire it.

26 March 1781

Proposed by the Revd Mr Frank that the Directors and Guardians do supply the House of Industry and the several parishes within the Incorporated Hundred with wool ready Combed and pounded fit for spinning and sell their yarn by commission by which means they will be enabled to increase the wages of spinning and derive an advantage to the Corporation. The same being unanimously agreed to. Ordered that <15 names> or any three of them, be a Committee <> to consider of and give such directions for the supplying the said House and parishes with wool and taking in and disposing of the same in such manner as they shall think proper.

Ordered that John Elliott, the Schoolmaster to the House, be allowed eight shillings a quarter over and above his salary for tea and sugar, and that he be allowed the use of household linnen by the said House.

Ann Proctor, the person provided by the Governor as a Matron to the House of Industry, being approved of. Ordered that she be continued Matron to the said House until Midsummer next and to be paid by the Governor out of his salary.

The Revd Mr Hingeston, having proposed that the moneys that are now out at interest due from the Corporation being at 4 per cent should be advanced to 5 per cent was ballotted for and the proposition rejected.

There being a vacancy for a Director in the room of Mr Quintin Woolnough and the Revd Mr Gunning being proposed by the Revd Mr Frank and George Nassau

---

[57] Illegitimate children born in the house of industry acquired the settlement of the parents' parish rather than that of Melton.

being proposed by John Revett Esq., were ballotted for and Mr Nassau was duly elected a Director to act in the month of May next.[58]

14 May 1781 [*Wool committee*]

Ordered that William Barber of Nayland, in the county of Suffolk, Woolcomber, (being recommended by John Roche of the city of Norwich, manufacturer) be and is hereby appointed Packman to the Corporation in order to distribute the wool provided by the Corporation to the House of Industry and to the following parishes viz; Brandeston, Butley, Charsfield, Earl Soham, Eyke, Easton, Marlesford, Alderton, Bredfield, Boyton, Hollesly, Melton, Shottisham, Ufford, and Wickham Market and to take in the same.

That he make a proper return every week of the wool distributed and taken in to the House Clerk that he may make a proper return to the Weekly Committee. That the said William Barber be allowed for his trouble and care therein nine shillings a week, a horse, board, washing and lodging. That he dine with the Governor and breakfast and sup in his own apartment which is to be provided for him in the room under the Committee Room.

Ordered that the Governor do get the said room cleaned and white washed a proper bed and bedding and other conveniences fixed up in the same for the use of the said William Barber.

21 May 1781 [*Wool committee*]

Ordered that William Barber, the Packman, do deliver the wool for spinning to the House of Industry and the several parishes and persons following:

Parishes	Persons
Butley	Dowsing
Brandeston	Bedwell
Charsfield	Burwood
Earl Soham	Crowe
Eyke	Funnell
Easton	Barthrop
Marlesford	Knights
Alderton	Sawyer
Bredfield	Oxborough
Boyton	Bird
Hollesly	Reeve
Melton	Oldham
Shottisham	Bedingfield
Ufford	Johnson
Wickham Market	Woodard

That he this week go to the several persons to advise them of the wool coming to them and to begin to deliver out the wool on Monday next and if any of them refuse taking in the wool then to deliver it to such person in the same parish as he shall be advised will take it in.

Ordered that William Barber, the Packman, do go to Mr Oldham, of Melton, and request him to provide him with brown roll for his packs, scales and weights,

---

[58] One of the few examples of more than one person standing for a vacant directorship.

books, paper, pens and ink and what other things that Barber shall want to carry on the spinning business.

11 June 1781 [*Wool committee*]

Ordered that the Treasurer do pay imediately to William Barber, the Packman, the sum of twenty pounds in order to pay the spinners and which the said William Barber is to place to his account.

There being 233 tops of wool now in the House of Industry which the Governor claims as his property, it being as he says four ounces in twelve pounds allowed him by Ray and Oaks which he has saved to the above quantity. Ordered that the same be reported and enquired into at the next Quarterly Meeting.

25 June 1781

Directors	Present	Guardians
George Nassau Esq.		Mr Robert Adams
Francis Brooke Esq.		Mr Benjamin Gall
John Revett Esq.		Mr George Lord
Edmund Jenney Esq.		and
John Brand Esq.		Mr Robert Linsted
John Tovell Esq.		
The Revd Mr Jeaffreson		
The Revd Mr Purvis		
The Revd Mr Fowller		
The Revd Mr Cole		
The Revd Mr Hingeston		
Mr Samuel Barber		
Mr John Barthorp		
Mr John Whimper		
Mr John Baldry		
Mr Samuel Salmon		
Mr Simon Paternoster		

The following persons were duly elected Directors and Acting Guardians ◇:

	Directors		Guardians
		1st Quarter	
July	Edmund Jenney Esq.		Mr James Woods
	The Revd Mr Jeaffreson		Mr James Seaman
			Mr Stephen Catchpole
Aug.	The Revd Mr Cole		Mr William Whimper
	The Revd Mr Gunning		Mr William Smyth
			Mr John Scotchmer Jun.
Sept.	William Henry Nassau Esq.		Mr Thomas Smith
	John Tovell Esq.		Mr John Cooper
			Mr Henry Edwards
Oct.	The Revd Mr Fowller	2nd Quarter	Mr Thomas Whimper
	Mr Nathaniel Barthrop		Mr John Osborne
			Mr William Cole
Nov.	Francis Brooke Esq.		Mr Thomas Crisp
	Anthony Collett Esq.		Mr Samuel Thompson
			Mr John Cole
Dec.	The Revd Mr Purvis		Mr John Dennington
	The Revd Mr Frank		Mr Benjamin Barthrop

			Mr Robert Linsted
Jan.	Mr Simon Paternoster	3rd Quarter	Mr Nathaniel Keeble
			Chandler
	Mr William Waller		Mr Joseph Rust
			Mr Nathaniel Fuller
Feb.	Mr John Brand Esq.		Mr Jeptha Waller
	Mr Samuel Salmon		Mr Nathaniel Bennington
			Mr James Aldhous
Mar.	The Revd Mr Hingeston		Mr Nathaniel Steptoe
	Mr Benjamin Cooper		Mr Samuel Lawrence
			Mr William Ablett
Apl.	Mr John Whimper	4th Quarter	Mr Thomas Chandler
	Mr John Baldry		Mr Francis Hayle
			Mr Richard Syer
May	George Nassau Esq.		Mr William Upson
	John Revett Esq.		Mr Samuel Lancaster Jun.
			Mr John Kemp
June	Mr Samuel Barber		Mr Thomas Ablitt
	Mr John Barthorp		Mr Robert Adams
			Mr Henry Woods

In pursuance of the order of the last Special Meeting ◇ the tops of wool claimed by the Governor as his property was at this meeting unanimously declared to be the property of the Corporation.

Ordered that the Directors and Guardians ◇ do meet in the House of Industry at Melton <29 June> to inquire into the Governors conduct and for other purposes relating to the Corporation.

29 June 1781 [*Governor's conduct committee*]

On Mr Thomas Tibbs, the Governor, being examined touching the tops of wool found in the House of Industry, and unanimously declared and agreed at the last Annual Meeting to be the property of the Corporation and being maturely considered. The Committee present do confirm the said agreement at the said Meeting, that the said tops are the property of the said Corporation and further that all tops before sold by the Governor and not accounted for were also the property of the Corporation and must be accounted for by the Governor, it being reported to the said Committee, by Mr Jonathan Beaumont, that the Governor, about four or five years ago, sold to Mr Maw, of Ipswich, about 500 weight at twelve or thirteen pence per pound at one time.

Mr Thomas Tibbs, the Governor, being in the opinion of the Committee sufficiently charged with imbezzling and misapplying the monies, goods and chattels belonging to the Corporation and of disobeying the orders of the Directors and Guardians and it being ballotted for was unanimously agreed and ordered that the said Thomas Tibbs be discharged from his said office of Governor to the House of Industry and he is discharged accordingly. And it is further ordered that he be proceeded against for such imbezzling and misapplying of the monies, goods and chattels of the said Corporation according to the Act of Parliament for incorporating the said Hundreds.

Ordered that John Elliott, the Schoolmaster and House Clerk, do take upon himself the care of the House of Industry during the vacancy of a Governor or until it shall be otherwise ordered.

30 July 1781 [*Governor's conduct committee*]

Thomas Tibbs, the late Governor of the House of industry, being proceeded against before the Revd Mr Carthew and the Revd Mr Capper, two of his Majesty's Justices of the Peace for the county of Suffolk. It was recommended by the said Justices for the Guardians to accept of the sum of one hundred and twenty pounds from the said Thomas Tibbs in lieu of all penaltys occasioned by his imbezzling and misapplying of the goods and chattels of the Corporation which the said Guardians agreed to accept and which said sum of one hundred and twenty pounds has been paid by the said Thomas Tibbs (by Mr Bartholomew Long his attorney) to Richard Wood, the Clerk, which hath been paid over by him to the Treasurer and on payment thereof all further prosecutions were to cease and Mr Tibbs was to take all the goods at the House of Industry his property only.

Mr Tibbs appearing this day before the said Directors and Guardians and making a claim of several household goods, plate china, household linnen, wearing apparel, port wine, grape wine and other made wines, pickle jars, garden nets, flowers and shrubs in pots only, poultry and a pig his property.

Ordered that the several goods and things so claimed be delivered to the said Thomas Tibbs under the inspection of John Elliott, the House Clerk, but nothing else but what is so claimed.

Ordered that Mr Elliott, the House Clerk, do imediately after the delivery of the goods and effects to Mr Tibbs claimed by him as his property make a just inventory of all the goods and effects belonging to the Corporation to be entred in a book to be procured for that purpose.

28 August 1781 [*Governor's conduct committee*]

Ordered that Mr Wood, the Clerk, do cause an advertisement to be inserted in the Ipswich Journal for a Governor and Matron to the House of Industry being single persons agreeable to the advertisement settled at this meeting and for such persons as were desirous of being Governor and Matron to deliver in their proposals at the next Previous Meeting to be held at the House of Industry.

1 October 1781

John Elliott, being proposed as Governor to the House of Industry, was ballotted for and duly elected untill Midsummer next at the salary of thirty pounds a year and Catherine Maltward, being proposed as Matron to the said House, was ballotted for and duly elected until Midsummer next, at the salary of fifteen pounds a year with the allowance of tea and sugar at the rate of one pound of 8s. tea each quarter.

Ordered and a meeting of the Directors and Guardians is appointed to be held <13 November 1781> for the purpose of inspecting into and revising the rules, orders and regulations of the said House and for making such other orders as shall be thought proper and that the same be advertized by the Clerk two weeks in the Ipswich Journal previous thereto.

Ordered that the Treasurer do borrow two hundred pounds at £5 per cent per annum for the use of the Corporation between this time and Christmas next.

13 November 1781 [*Committee established to review the rules and orders*]

Ordered that the consideration of the rules, orders and regulations intended to be settled and agreed upon at this meeting be adjourned <> the Directors present not choosing to enter on the said business there being so few present.

31 December 1781

Ordered that the Clerk do lay the case (concerning the payment of principal and interest due from the Corporation) as settled at this meeting before Mr Graham for his opinion.

Ordered that the sum of three hundred pounds be borrowed of Mr Thomas Mulliner, on a promissory note to be signed by the Directors and Guardians present at the interest of 5 per cent payable which was signed accordingly.

Ordered that when the Packman receives wool from the comber that he finds not so good as ought to be that he report it to the next Weekly Committee and the said Committee are requested to order it to be returned.

Ordered and a Committee of seventeen Directors (whereof five of the said Directors to be a Committee) are requested to attend at the House of Industry in Melton on <17 January 1782> for the purpose of inspecting into and revising the rules and orders of this Corporation. That the Clerk do write to such of the above mentioned Directors as are absent from this meeting to request their attendance at the said meeting and that they do adjourn for the purposes aforesaid from time to time untill the next Quarterly Meeting as they shall think proper.

17 January 1782 [*Committee established to review the rules and orders*]

Ordered that the Clerk do transcribe the several Rules and Orders as are agreed on at this Meeting and leave the same in the Committee Room for the inspection of the Directors and Guardians until the next Quarterly Meeting. That the Directors and Guardians be requested to peruse them and make such alterations as they shall think proper and that this Committee be adjourned and is hereby adjourned to <24 January 1782>. And that the Clerk do write to the several Directors of this Committee not present to acquaint of the said adjournment and request their attendance.

24 January 1782 [*Committee established to review the rules and orders*]

Ordered that the settling of the Rules and Orders produced this day be deferred to a publick meeting of the Directors and Guardians now agreed and ordered to be held on <14 March 1782>. And that the Clerk do advertise the same in the Ipswich Journal.

14 March 1782 [*Committee established to review the rules and orders*]

The Rules and Regulations this day proposed for the better Government of the Poor within the said Hundreds having been revised, regulated and settled are unanimously agreed to and recommended to the next General Quarterly Meeting to be confirmed.

26 March 1782

Ordered that Edmund Keeble of Melton, Norwich carrier, do carry the wool spun in the House of Industry to Norwich to be taken from the said House at five shillings a pack agreeable to his proposals.

Several of the creditors of the Corporation, having applied to be paid their securitys or to be paid interest at the rate of 5 per cent. Councell's opinion having been taken on the same. Ordered that all persons to whom securitys are due from the Corporation be paid from this time interest at the rate of 5 per cent.

Messrs. Ray and Oakes, not having prosecuted Thomas Tibbs, the late Governor, for imbezzling yarn, nor making it appear that the 233 tops now in the House of Industry are their property. Ordered that the order made at the last Annual Meeting

◇ concerning their being the property of the Corporation be confirmed and that the said tops be now spun in the House of Industry for the benefit of the Corporation.

Ordered that <6 named directors> or any three of them be a Committee to meet at the House of Industry ◇ in order to inspect into and make an inquiry concerning certificates being missing out of the lockers at the said House. And also to inquire concerning the books of the state of the House not being made up and to give such directions therein as they shall think proper and that the said Committee do adjourn from time to time for the purposes aforesaid as they shall see proper.

The Rules Orders and Regulations for the Better Government of the Poor within the said Hundreds as settled at the last General Meeting having been this day read are unanimously approved and confirmed. And it is recommended to the Directors and Acting Guardians strictly and invariably to adhere to and be guided by them. And it is further ordered that they be fairly copied and laid on the table every Weekly Committee day for the inspection and direction of the Directors and Acting Guardians there attending until the next Annual Meeting.

1 April 1782 [*Special meeting into missing certificates*]

Ordered that Mr Simon Paternoster do enter up the house books for the two last quarters at the expence of the Corporation and that the Governor do after the same are so entred and settled continue to keep them entred for the future he having undertaken so to do. And it is required and he is expected to do the same.

Ordered that Mr Daniel Manthorp Junior do attend Francis Brooke Esq. and Mr Richard Wood, the Clerk, in order to take such directions for securing the lockers in the Committee Room at the said House in such manner as they shall direct.

23 May 1782

The Directors having this day met for consulting upon the raising money on the security of the Corporation for discharging and satisfying the claims of several persons who have demanded their debts due from the Corporation but there being only five Directors present. Ordered that this Meeting be adjourned <10 June 1782>. And that the Clerk do write to all the Directors and Guardians requesting them to attend on the above business.

10 June 1782

<17 named directors and 15 named acting guardians>

We the Directors and Guardians present having consulted upon a method to be adopted for satisfying the demands for money due from this Corporation and having by ballott (29 for and 3 against) agreed that a Memorial shall be drawn up for an application to be made to the gentlemen of landed property in the said Hundreds for entering into a subscription for raising money on the security of the Corporation to discharge the debt thereon. Do order and appoint a Special Committee to meet at the House of Industry on <13 June> to draw up and settle a Memorial ◇ for the purpose of raising money for the above purposes.

13 June 1782

Ordered that the Clerk do procure three quire of printed copys of the Memorial as this day settled and some of them to be distributed to the principal proprietors of estates within the said Hundreds agreeable to a list produced this day for that purpose.

25 June 1782

Directors   Present
George Nassau Esq.   The Revd Mr Richard Fowller
Francis Brooke Esq.   The Revd Mr Denny Cole
John Revett Esq.   Mr John Whimper
John Tovell Esq.   Mr John Barthorp
The Revd Mr Richard Frank   Mr Samuel Barber
The Revd Mr Christopher Jeaffreson   Mr Samuel Salmon
The Revd Mr Thomas Purvis   Mr Simon Paternoster

The following persons were duly elected Directors and Acting Guardians ◇:

	Directors	1st Quarter	Guardians
July	Edmund Jenney Esq.		Mr Thomas Stammers
	The Revd Mr Jeaffreson		Mr Thomas Garneys
			Mr Stephen Catchpole
Aug.	The Revd Mr Cole		Mr William Whimper
	The Revd Mr Gunning		Mr William Smith
			Mr John Scotchmer Jun.
Sept.	Earl of Rochford		Mr Thomas Smyth
	John Tovell Esq.		Mr John Cooper
			Mr Henry Edwards
Oct.	George Nassau Esq.	2nd Quarter	Mr Thomas Whimper
	The Revd Mr Fowller		Mr Joseph Bennington
			Mr William Cole
Nov.	Francis Brooke Esq.		Mr Thomas Edwards
	Anthony Collettt Esq.		Mr Samuel Thompson
			Mr George Payne
Dec.	The Revd Mr Purvis		Mr William Whincopp
	The Revd Mr Frank		Mr Benjamin Barthrop
			Mr Robert Vertue
Jan.	Mr William Waller	3rd Quarter	Mr John Gross
	Mr Nathaniel Barthrop		Mr Joseph Rust
			Mr Andrew Blake
Feb.	John Brand Esq.		Mr John Welham
	Mr James Lynn		Mr Nathaniel Bennington
			Mr James Aldhous
Mar.	The Revd Mr Hingeston		Mr Nathaniel Steptoe
	Mr Benjamin Cooper		Mr Samuel Lawrence
			Mr Samuel Jeaffreson
Apl.	Mr John Whimper	4th Quarter	Mr Thomas Chandler
	Mr John Baldry		Mr Francis Hayle
			Mr Richard Syer
May	John Revett Esq.		Mr William Upson
	The Revd Mr Williams		Mr Benjamin Baldry
			Mr John Kemp
June	Mr Samuel Barber		Mr Thomas Ablitt
	Mr John Barthorp		Mr Robert Adams
			Mr Henry Wood

On several arguments being made by the Directors present concerning the wool trade. The question being put whether the trade should be carried on or given up was balloted for and declared to be carried on.

Ordered and a Committee of four Directors is appointed to meet from time to time and have the management of the wool trade in the said House and Hundreds.

Ordered and a Committee is appointed to meet from time to time as they shall think proper at the House of Industry to inspect and examine the accounts of the Corporation and report the same to the following Quarterly Meetings, the said Committee to consist of <7 named directors> or any three of them who appoint their first meeting to be held at the said House on <1 July>.

1 July 1782 [*Committee to review the accounts*]

Ordered that the vouchers of accounts from Midsummer (1777) to Midsummer (1782) be delivered to the above Committee viz. one year's vouchers to each Director to be examined against the next meeting.

Memorial 1 July 1782

To the proprietors of land within the Incorporated Hundreds of Loes and Wilford. The Memorial of the Directors and Acting Guardians of the Poor within the Hundreds.

Sheweth,

That the said Hundreds, by an Act passed in <1765> the Directors and Acting Guardians did borrow of divers persons, sums of money to the amount of £9,200; that £2,500, part of the said debt has been discharged by your Memorialists, and that there now remains undischarged the sum of £6,700, including the capital in their trade, which amounts to £500 and upwards, and to which their stock is fully equal; and that the said debt is divided into the several sums, and due to the several persons, as appear in the Schedule annexed. That many urgent and pressing calls to a considerable amount have been made, and many more are expected to be made upon your Memorialists, from several creditors, for their respective debts, and that some of the claimants have been threatened with all the vengeance of the law, in case several legacies, and other just matters due from them to other people, are not paid, and which cannot be done unless they can obtain the payment of their claims upon the Corporation.

That notwithstanding the power granted by the said recited Act, and the securities bearing and interest of £5 per cent regularly paid, and even a premium of £5 per cent having been offered, neither the said claimants or the Treasurer of the Corporation have been able to obtain a transfer or assignment for any one of them.

That your Memorialists, at a general meeting on <10 June> did take the premises into consideration; and it became a matter of great concern to them to find, that it was absolutely out of their power to satisfy the just demands of the said claimants, who on that account must, and are suffering many and great inconveniences; and it is to be feared that they will be advised, and must have recourse to Chancery, for the recovery of their respective debts, that if that should be the case, not only a great discredit, but a very heavy burthen of expense must necessarily fall upon the Corporation.

And this Memorial further sheweth – that the Directors and Acting Guardians have attended most minutely to the economical expenditure of the income intrusted to their care; but that notwithstanding all their diligence, such has been the unhappy state of the poor of the said hundreds, within a few years last past, that they have had great difficulties in supporting the heavy burthen necessarily brought upon the said Corporation, as will appear on the one hand, from the increased numbers in the House of Industry, from the large allowances made to the out poor on account of illness and from your Memorialists having been obliged to raise their interest from

66

£4 to £5 per cent; on the other hand, from the great decrease of the Norwich yarn trade, the only manufactory carried on in the said House, bearing so low a price, the earnings of the poor amount to but a trifle: from all these considerations it is not to be wondered at, that your Memorialists cannot save, but how they contrive to avoid running further into debt.

That you Memorialists having it very much at heart to save the credit and promote the interest of a most excellent and useful institution, which, under its present circumstances, respecting its debt, is in the greatest danger of being totally ruined, have applied themselves to think of a remedy, which may not only answer the purpose of stopping the present, but preventing the increasing future inconveniences of the like nature, for as long as the creditors of the corporation have a power of calling in and enforcing the payment of the principal, it will be impossible for your Memorialists to carry into execution the good purposes of the said recited Act. And it appearing to your Memorialists, that whilst the present description of creditors remain unconnected, (as they are with its interests) it is not to be expected but that they will prefer their own to that of the Corporation; and therefore any means which may be devised to satisfy the present claimants only, is a proclamation of the evil, and an additional trouble and concern to your Memorialists. And it further appearing to your Memorialists that it is but just and equitable, that whosoever are to reap the advantages which may arise, and which in the present have arisen from the said institution, ought also to bear their proportionable share of inconvenience, if any such should accrue.

That your Memorialists ◇ did agree, (at the aforesaid meeting, upon a division of 15 Directors and 14 Guardians for, and 2 Directors and 1 Guardian against the question), that an application should be made to the several gentlemen of landed property within the said Hundreds, not doubting but they would readily see the propriety of, and cheerfully join in the following proposition, which is not less founded in equity than efficient to the purpose designed; viz.

"That every person who has property in the Hundreds, should each, in proportion to that property, which it is supposed will amount to about thirty pounds per cent on one years income, voluntarily, or if hereafter thought necessary, under a new Act of Parliament for the purpose to be obtained, raise a sum of money as a loan, to pay off the present set of creditors, and that the money so raised should bear an interest of £5 per cent per annum till the whole shall be paid off".

An event not unreasonable to be hoped for, if it be considered, that notwithstanding the said House of Industry has been inhabited only fourteen years, of which the last seven have been attended with various circumstances of distress to the poor, and consequently burthen to the Corporation, your Memorialists have nevertheless paid off nearly one-third of their original debt, (viz. £2,500 discharged and £500 in stock). And further, that from the united exertions of the whole empire, and the inclinations which his Majestys ministers have expressed, the blessing of peace may not be far distant.[59]

Your Memorialists therefore, trusting to your generosity and the equity of the proposition, have a well-founded hope that you will honour it with your approbation and support, or if it should appear objectionable, that you will either assist your Memorialists by removing such objections, or by proposing some other plan, by

---

[59] American Revolutionary War, 1775–83.

which your own interests, which are closely connected with those of the institution, may be supported, and the institution itself preserved from ruin.

Your Memorialists request the favour of an answer as soon as may be convenient.

By order of the aforesaid meeting

Melton, 1 July 1782   R. Wood, Clerk

THE SCHEDULE to which the MEMORIAL refers

Account of the Corporation debt:

£

Borrowed	13,400
Paid	7,200
Due of original Debt	6,200
Borrowed since, for trade	500
1782 now due	£6,700

To whom due:

	£		£
William Parmenter	500	Brought forward	5,000
Dorothy Sherman	150	Philip Catt	500
Sarah Watling	200	Southwell Golding	600
Ann Revett	400	Samuel Hingeston	100
Elizabeth Wood (dead)	350	Joseph Rust	100
Nathaniel Randall	200	Jenney Braham	1,800
Elizabeth Creighton	200	Daniel Copland	100
Mary Pipe	100	James Hacon	100
John Syred (dead)	300	Thomas Mulliner	300
Christopher Jeaffreson	200	Southwell Golding	200
Jane Whimper (dead)	300		£6,700
Carried forward	£5,000		

30 September 1782

Ordered that the following paupers now in the House of Industry be apprenticed to the several persons in the several parishes and for the number of years hereunder specified to commence on <10 October> and that the Clerk do prepare Indentures accordingly.[60]

The parishes they belong to	Names and ages	To whom apprenticed and number of years
Butley	Margaret Spalding 14 yrs.	William Brill of Butley Farmer 5 yrs.
Boyton	John Fuller 12 yrs.	William Miller of Boyton Farmer 5 yrs.
Charsfield	William Lucock 13 yrs.	William Cole of Charsfield Farmer 5 yrs.
Creetingham	William Bardwell 13 yrs.	Edmund Tye of Creetingham Farmer 5 yrs.

---

[60] Subsequent similar entries omitted.

do	Elizabeth Bardwell 15 yrs.	Thomas Smyth of Creetingham Farmer 3 yrs.
Dallingho	William Wright 12 yrs.	Thomas Wright, House of Ind. Cordwainer 7 yrs.
Easton	Elizabeth Crosby 12 yrs.	Samuel Vertue of Easton Farmer 5 yrs.
Eyke	Richard Boon 12 yrs.	Anthony Collett Esq. of Eyke 5 yrs.
Hacheston	Elizabeth Sawer 14 yrs.	Stephen Fuller of Hacheston Farmer 3yrs
do	William Turtle 12 yrs.	William Heffer of Hacheston Farmer 5 yrs.
Hoo	Edmund Markham 15 yrs.	James Scolding of Hoo Farmer 5 yrs.
Hollesly	William Barrell 16 yrs.	John Trusson of Hollesly Farmer 3 yrs.
Kettleburgh	Jane Minter 15 yrs.	John Wright of Kettleburgh Farmer 2 yrs.
Marlesford	Robert Stanton 14 yrs.	Thomas Smith of Wickham Market Farmer 5 yrs.
Sutton	George Brown 12 yrs.	William Waller of Sutton Farmer 5 yrs.
do	Isaac Giles 13 yrs.	Philip Rush of Sutton Farmer 5 yrs.
Ufford	Sarah Bennett 16 yrs.	Francis Brooke of Ufford Esq. 1 yr.

Ordered that the Clerk do write to the above persons to acquaint them of the above apprentices to be put to them and request their attendance on <14 October> to sign indentures and accept the apprentices.

Ordered that the Committee appointed at the last Annual Meeting for examining the accounts of the Corporation be continued for the like purposes.

Mrs Christian Brightwell, being with several others to be Matron to the House of Industry for the said Hundred in the room of Catherine Maltward, late Matron deceased, was balloted for and duly elected at the salary of fourteen pounds a year with the allowance of tea and sugar at the rate one pound of eight shilling tea per quarter.

30 December 1782

Ordered that the Governor do pay Elizabeth Haws, Nurse in the Pesthouse, one guinea, to Rachael Turtle, Nurse in the Sick Wards, one guinea, to Eunice Crane, Nurse in the Nursery, half a guinea, and to Elizabeth Welham, Judith Pizzey, and Sarah Wright, realers in the said House, five shillings each as gratuity for their particular care and trouble.

31 March 1783

John Revett Esq., having moved that the Bye Law No 1 relating to apprentices be repealed and being seconded by Mr William Whimper was ballotted for being nineteen for the repeal and six against it upon which it was accordingly repealed.

Ordered that the Clerk do advertise that from five hundred pounds to one thousand pounds is wanted to be borrowed at 5 per cent on the credit of the Corporation.

Protests of five of the Directors requested to be entered on the repeal and the new order relating to apprentices.[61]

"John Revett Esq. having moved that the Bye Law No 1 relating to apprentices be repealed and being seconded by Mr William Whimper was ballotted for being 19 for the repeal and six against it upon which it was accordingly repealed"

Dissentient:

First because the Bye Law proposed to be repealed appears to us to be founded in law, justice and equity – In law because it is agreeable to the Act of Incorporation and the 43rd of Queen Eliz – In justice to the children who are the objects of it and whose interest we are bound by every tie of honour and humanity to promote – And in equity to the persons to whom such children are liable by law to be apprenticed their burthen being lightened as much as is consistent with the interests of the Corporation and the just rights of the children.

Secondly, because the said Bye Law had been fully canvassed – 1st in a Committee appointed for the especial purpose of revising, correcting and amending the Bye Laws. 2nd in a General Committee called <> for the particular purpose of discussing the intended alteration and amendments of the Bye Laws. 3rd at a General Quarterly Meeting it was again proposed and discussed and then with many others was approved, confirmed and ordered to be considered from the next Annual Meeting as the rule of law by which the Directors and Acting Guardians were to be governed. At each of these meetings all were invited and many who are supposed to be interested in it were present and upon debate it was reduced to its present form with their consent and approbation.

Thirdly, because no proofs were given of injury or inconvenience having arisen from it nor any arguments adduced for its repeal but what seemed to us to be founded solely in the interests of certain persons who are by law liable to take parish apprentices.

Revd Frank, Francis Brooke, Joseph Gunning, Samuel Hingeston and Denny Cole.

"That notices be given by the Clerk to several parishes against every previous Meeting of the number of paupers in their respective parishes fit to be placed out to service or apprenticeship that they may agree between themselves to take such children to service at any Weekly Committee meeting and if they do not agree among themselves that they will be apprenticed at the Lady or Michaelmas Quarterly Meetings from their ages of eleven years"

Dissentient

First, because of the above order the children may be detained in the House of Industry longer than is necessary and be thereby deprived of their just right to be apprenticed out as soon as they are of a fit age.

Secondly, because the keeping of the children longer in the House of Industry than is necessary is injurious to their health and renders them of less service to the persons to whose lot they may fall.

Thirdly, because it is contrary to the interest of the Corporation and unbecoming us as Trustees of the publick estate to keep boys and girls in the House of Industry at a great expence after they have arrived at an age fit to be apprenticed out.

---

61 Insertion in the Minute Book after the meeting.

Revd Frank, Francis Brooke, Joseph Gunning, Samuel Hingeston and Denny Cole.

30 June 1783

Directors	Present	Guardians
The Revd Mr Williams	Mr Thomas Ablitt	Mr William Cole
John Revett Esq.	Mr William Whimper	Mr Nathaniel Steptoe
Francis Brooke Esq.	Mr Samuel Lawrence	Mr George Payne
Edmund Jenney Esq.	Mr Stephen Hayle	Mr John Cooper
John Tovell Esq.	Mr James Aldhouse	Mr Benjamin Barthrop
The Revd Mr Jeaffreson	Mr Robert Adams	Mr William Whincopp
The Revd Mr Gunning	Mr John Gross	Mr John Kemp
The Revd Mr Hingeston	Mr Samuel Jeaffreson	Mr Thomas Stammers
The Revd Mr Frank	Mr Thomas Smyth	Mr William Smith
The Revd Mr Purvis	Mr Henry Edwards	Mr Thomas Whimper
The Revd Mr Fowller	Mr John Welham	Mr Stephen Catchpole
The Revd Mr Cole	Mr Nathaniel Bennington	Mr Robert Vertue
Mr James Lynn	Mr Samuel Thompson	and
Mr Samuel Barber	Mr Andrew Blake	Mr John Scotchmer
Mr John Barthorp		
Mr William Waller		
Mr John Whimper		

The following persons were duly elected Directors and Acting Guardians<>:

	Directors		Guardians
		1st Quarter	
July	Edmund Jenney Esq.		Mr Thomas Stammers
	The Revd Mr Jeaffreson		Mr James Seaman
			Mr Stephen Catchpole
Aug.	The Revd Mr Cole		Mr William Whimper
	The Revd Mr Gunning		Mr John Felgate
			Mr John Scotchmer Junior
Sept.	Earl of Rochford		Mr Richard Ashford
	John Tovell Esq.		Mr John Cooper
			Mr Henry Edwards
Oct.	George Nassau Esq.	2nd Quarter	Mr Thomas Whimper
	The Revd Mr Fowller		Mr John Weeding
			Mr William Cole
Nov.	Francis Brooke Esq.		Mr Thomas Edwards
	Anthony Collett Esq.		Mr James Catchpole
			Mr George Payne
Dec.	The Revd Mr Purvis		Mr William Whincopp
	The Revd Mr Frank		Mr Thomas Crisp
			Mr Robert Vertue
Jan.	Mr William Waller	3rd Quarter	Mr John Gross
	Mr Nathaniel Barthrop		Mr Philip Dikes
			Mr Andrew Blake
Feb.	John Brand Esq.		Mr John Welham
	Mr James Lynn		Mr Nathaniel Bennington
			Mr James Aldhous
Mar.	The Revd Mr Hingeston		Mr Nathaniel Steptoe

	Mr Benjamin Cooper		Mr Nathaniel Keeble
			Chandler
			Mr Samuel Jeaffreson
Apl.	Mr John Whimper	4th Quarter	Mr John Stopher
	Mr John Baldry		Mr Francis Hayle
			Mt Richard Syer
May	John Revett Esq.		Mr William Upson
	The Revd Mr Williams		Mr John Jeaffreson
			Mr Thomas Hicks
June	Mr Samuel Barber		Mr Thomas Ablitt
	Mr John Barthorp		Mr Robert Adams
			Mr William Pipe

Ordered that the Tenth Order under the Head Committee Directors etc. of the Rules and Orders of the Corporation setting forth that Directors and Guardians were not eligible to serve the House of Industry with any commodity whatever being thought injurious to the said Corporation is unanimously repealed.

John Revett Esq., moving that the part of the Law No 2 under the Head of Committee Directors etc. concerning the seconding any question be repealed and being seconded by Mr Stephen Hayle, was ballotted for and repealed 30 being for the repeal and 10 against it.

John Revett Esq., moving that the wool trade now carried on in the Hundreds be given up and no longer carried on was ballotted for 28 being for giving up and 3 for carrying it on. Ordered that the trade be given up.

Order that the Clerk do advertise a meeting at the House of Industry on <28 July> and to write to Mr James Oakes, wool merchant at Bury, and two other wool merchants, to know upon what terms they will supply the said House with wool and what they will give for the present stock of yarn.

6 July 1783[62]

Gentlemen

The Directors of the House of Industry at Melton finding the wool trade they entered into two years ago not sufficiently answering the intended purpose mean to decline carrying it on. The Directors have ordered me to write to be informed whether you will supply the House with wool for spinning agreeable to the original plan and upon what terms and what you will give for the present stock of yarn,

Your immediate answer will oblige the Directors.

Sir, your obedient servant.   R. W.

Messrs. Ray & Oakes,   Messrs. Cumberland & Co.,
Wool merchants, Bury.   Wool merchant, Bury.
Messrs. Blomfield,   Messrs. Harmer & Barnard,
Wool merchants at Nayland.   Wool merchant, Bury.
Mr John Roach,
Wool merchant, Norwich.

---

[62] SROI ADA11/A/B/2/4. The entries for 6 and 28 July 1783 were not transferred from the draft QMB.

28 July 1783

Several proposals having this day been produced from Messrs. Ray & Co., Messrs. Harmer & Co., Messrs. Cumberland & Co., wool merchants for supplying the House of Industry with combed wool for spinning in the said House on the former plan (the wool trade having been given up) and having heard the several partys and on ballott for Cumberland & Co., 9 for 5 against, for Harland & Co., 8 for 6 against, and Ray & Co., 5 for 9 against. Ordered that Messrs. Cumberland & Co. do supply the said House with combed wool for spinning agreeable to their proposals this day delivered.

30 September 1783

Ordered that Mr Wood, the Clerk, do prosecute and appeal to the order of Temple Chevalier, Clerk, and John Dade Esq., two of his Majestys Justices of the Peace, for the removal of James Gardiner, Mary, his wife, and Charlotte, their daughter, from the parish of Saxtead, to the parish of Hacheston as to the merits.

Ordered that Mr Wood, the Clerk, do procure one hundred Acts of Parliament for incorporating these Hundreds.

Ordered that the Clerk do advertise a General Meeting of the Directors and Guardians on <16 October> at the House of Industry. And that he do imediately write to Messrs. Cumberland and Crosbie for an answer to Mr Revetts letter concerning the prices of all the several sorts of yarn. And that they will imediately order some wool to the House of Industry for the spinners.

John Revett Esq., proposing that the persons in the several parishes within the said Hundreds that hire paupers out of the House of Industry shall be exempt from the taking a parish apprentice during that year in which such pauper is hired out of the said House it being ballotted for was allowed and declared to pass as a bye law of this Corporation.

16 October 1783

Ordered that the stock of yarn now in the House of Industry be bundled and sent imediately to Samuel Williams a factor at Norwich, to be disposed of by him to the best advantage as soon as possible, allowing him his usual commission for so doing. And that the said factor do send an account and remit the money arising from the sale thereof to Mr Simon Paternoster, the Treasurer of the said Hundreds. And that the clerk do write to Messrs Cumberland and Co to acquaint them of the above. (about 800 bundles worth near £1,000).

Ordered that the clerk do advertise that the stock of wool in the House of Industry consisting of the following parcells viz. 2pk. 10sc. 3lb. of 2s. bombazine wool, 2pk. 3sc. 0lb. of 2s. oil'd wool, 3pk. 0sc. 12lb. of 18d. wool, and 3pk. 1sc. 4lb. of wool. In all 11pk. 2sc. 19lb. will be sold on <27 October> and the three following Mondays where the Packman will attend. The parcells to be sold each sort in one lot, being four lots, the prices proposed by the buyers to be approved of or rejected by the Directors and Guardians then attending. And that the clerk do write to Messrs. Cumberland and Co. to request them to send a weekly account (for the four next weeks) of the market prices of the above sorts to enable the Directors to dispose of the same to the best advantage.

Ordered that the Treasurer do pay Mr John Roach, wool factor at Norwich, £109 15s. 0d. being the balance of his account for wool sent to the House of Industry. And that the clerk do write to Mr Roach to acquaint him that the money will be remitted to him in a week.

Ordered that the Governor do apply to the Magistrates at their next sitting at Woodbridge for summoning Henry Sheming and Robert Pooley the fathers of four poor children in the House of Industry to appear before them to show cause why they do not maintain their familys being enabled that they may be.

Ordered that the Governor do in the next brewing of beer for use of the House of Industry make trial of two comb and a half of oats to seven comb and a half of malt it being thought to make pleasant beer, and afterwards report the quality and utility of it to the Directors and Guardians. The Governor to apply to Mr Philip Riches of Woodbridge to procure five comb of the best oats for the above purpose.

27 October 1783

No person appearing this day to purchase any parts of the wool in the House of Industry. Ordered that the poor in the said House be imediately set to spinning the different sorts of wool under the inspection of William Barber, the late Packman.

Ordered that the yarn in the House be sent to Mr Samuel Williams, yarn factor in Norwich, for sale as he shall direct as to quantity and sorts and to be allowed the usual commission no factor having been fixed on before.

3 November 1783

Ordered that Robert Pooley of Bawdsey, (appearing this day on summons), do pay to the Overseers of Alderton two shillings and sixpence a week for and towards the maintenance of Robert and Amy Pooley, his children, until further orders to be accounted for to the Corporation.

Ordered that the Clerk do write to the Special Committee for managing the wool trade, to request they will send or deliver such part of the accounts and vouchers relating to the wool trade as are in their possession, to the Directors and Guardians as shall be present at a General Meeting to be held at the said House <> as conclusive accounts of that trade cannot properly be made out without them.

Ordered that the Governor do provide such additional package for the purpose of sending the yarn to market as William Barber, the late Packman, shall think necessary.

17 November 1783

Francis Brooke Esq., and the Revd Mr Frank, <> producing an account of receipts and disbursements of money on account of the spinning, being the only account remaining in the hands of the Special Committee on the Wool Trade. Ordered and it is referred to the next Quarterly Meeting for their determination as to any further inquiry to be made respecting the accounts or whether any further account of the said trade shall be made out.

Ordered that William Barber, the late Packman, do continue to send the yarn to Norwich market as fast as possible till all be sent that the same may be imediately sold and that an account may be sent to the said William Barber of such sale as soon after as possible.

29 December 1783

Resolved that the Act of Incorporation, having provided always that at all Quarterly Meetings the major part assembled <> shall give their assent to all orders. It is necessary that the Directors and Acting Guardians should ballot separately and their specific number taken in order to ascertain whether the question to be determined be legally assented to or not.

Ordered that William Whimper of Bredfield, maltster, do supply the House of Industry with malt unground for this quarter at 23s. per comb.

Ordered that John Lankester of Woodbridge, tallow chandler, do supply the said House for this quarter with candles at six shillings and three pence per dozen.

Ordered that John Gosling of Woodbridge, butcher, do supply the said House for the quarter with good steer beef and weather mutton at 30s. per hundred.

Ordered that Joseph Oldham of Melton, grocer, do supply the said House for this quarter with sugar, blue starch, soap, caraway seeds, mops etc. according to samples and prices delivered this day.

Ordered that Thomas Stammers of Melton, miller, do supply the said House with thirds flour at 34s. per sack for this quarter.

Ordered that a Committee of the whole House of Directors and Acting Guardians, whereof <8 named directors> or five of them, to be of the said Committee, do attend at the House of Industry <> to inspect the working rooms, lodging rooms and nurserys in the said House, being too enclosed and unhealthy for the poor, and make such alterations as they shall think necessary and on such other business as shall come before them.

Ordered that every proposition that shall in future be made by any Director or Acting Guardian of the said Hundreds, shall be made at one Quarterly Meeting and ballotted for at the following Quarterly Meeting. Such intended Bye Law or alteration to be entred in a book for the inspection of the Directors and Acting Guardians between the day of the proposition being made and the day of the ballot.

Proposed by Francis Brooke Esq., that the bye laws be revised and settled against the next Quarterly Meeting and, if then approved of, to be printed for the use of the Directors and Guardians.

Matthew Kindred, butcher, and James Sawer, taylor, of Alderton being on ballott of last quarterly meeting each to take an apprentice and it appearing that they are not eligible to take parish apprentices on account of their poverty ordered and they are discharged there from the parish to be given notice again of such paupers being fit for apprenticeship at Lady next.

7 January 1784 [*Committee to inspect the rooms*]

The Directors and Guardians present, having on view of the Working Rooms, Nurserys and other rooms in the House of Industry, do find that some alterations are necessary to be made. Do order that the old men be removed from the room they now sit in in the North Wing of the said House and placed in the room that used to be appropriated for the overseers coming on business to the Weekly Committee, and the room the old men leave, to be appropriated for the use of sick children, they being now kept in the Nursery with well children, and it is further ordered that the Governor do apply to Mr Packard of Woodbridge, brazier, to make six ventulators of eight inches diameter imediately, and place them in the end and centre windows of the two Spinning Rooms, there not being sufficient air for the number of paupers employed there.

Ordered that John Plumbly, (having this day refused before the Directors present to work in the Spinning Rooms), be punished by distinction in diet to have bread and water only on the two next meat days of the paupers in the said House and that the Governor do report his conduct to the next Weekly Committee.

Ordered that the Clerk do write to Messrs. Cumberland and Crosby to know what they will give for the bombazine and oiled wool now in the said House as it cannot be spun there and if they won't purchase it to inform of the market prices and value of them and whether they can dispose of them.

4 February 1784

On account of there being no more than three directors and one guardian present at this meeting no business could be proceeded upon.

11 February 1784

It is agreed and ordered that Messrs. Cumberland & Crosbies proposals for buying the remaining stock of the bombazine and oiled wool that cannot be spun in the said House be accepted being at the rate of twenty pounds a pack for the bombazine and eighteen pounds a pack for the oiled wool. Ordered that the Clerk do write to them of the above and to take the wool away imediately.

25 February 1784

Ordered that the Clerk do write to Mr Williams, the yarn factor at Norwich, for answers to the particular questions required of him in a letter of the 11th instant his answer of the 6 instant not being satisfactory.

Ordered that Mr Daniel Manthorp do take down the lodging rooms intended for married persons now in the Spinning Room and that Mr Packard do put three ventilators in the windows of each side the said room and one ventilator in each of the two Nursery and School Room.

4 March 1784

On account of there being no more than two Directors present no business could be proceeded upon.

The first Weekly Minute Book,
18 July 1768–20 June 1774[63]

18 July 1768[64]

Present

The Revd Mr Sparrow	Mr James Woods
John Revett Esq.	Mr Thomas Trusson
	Mr George Linsted

Ordered that Mr Thomas Whiting do provide twill for fifty pairs of small breeches for children.[65]

Ordered that a small cart and horse be provided.

Ordered that Jonathan Churchyard do provide two good cows imediately for the House and ten pigs.

Ordered that the Governor do provide two comb of good boiling pease.

Ordered that John Syed, of Petistree, be allowed eight shillings having dislocated his shoulder bone to be paid by the Overseer.

Ordered that Mr Grayston do provide six small forms for children and carry on the common share of the right wing 56 foot.

Ordered that the Governor do provide a taylor in the House to alter the childrens cloaths. To get a small jack for the kitchen, some patterns for the women, two gallons of raisin wine for the sick, six nursing chairs, six little chairs and one dozen common wooden chairs.

Ordered that Frances Warren of Wickham Market, be allowed five shillings for this week being ill and incapable of being removed to be paid by the Overseer.

Ordered that Elizabeth Stork and James Riches of Eyke, be allowed one shilling a week each to be paid by the Overseer untill further notice.

Ordered that Mary Buckenham and her son Thomas Buckenham of Bredfield, an idiot and she old and infirm, be allowed two shillings and six pence a week to be paid by the Overseer untill further orders.

Ordered that Susan Gibson of Ash, be allowed one shilling a week having two small children to be paid by the Overseers untill further orders.

Ordered that William Kemp and Mary his wife of Ash, be allowed one shilling a week each being bed rid to be paid by the Overseers untill further orders.

Ordered that Grace Knights of Dallingho, be allowed one shilling a week being old and infirm to be paid by the Overseers untill further orders.

Ordered that Mary Neech of Sutton, be allowed one shilling a week being ill and incapable of being removed to be paid by the Overseers untill further orders.

---

[63] SROI ADA11/A/B/3/1.

[64] The first weekly meeting from each WMB is wholly transcribed. Extracts from subsequent meetings focus on the various forms of out-relief offered and any key points or issues. Full attendance at a weekly meeting would have been two directors and three acting guardians.

[65] Major purchases were made at the quarterly meeting, with smaller ones at the weekly meeting.

Ordered that Mary Harvey of Ufford, be allowed eighteen pence a week having three small children to be paid by the Overseers untill further orders.

Ordered that the Treasurer do pay Mr Tibbs, the Governor, thirty pounds on account.

25 July 1768

Ordered that Robert Birch and his wife of Rendlesham, be allowed two shillings a week <> he being a mad man.

Ordered that Robert Bury of Wickham Market be allowed three shillings a week having nine children.

Ordered that Ann Knights of Ash, be allowed two shillings a week having four small children.

Ordered that the Treasurer do pay Benjamin Jacob six pounds and six shillings for a cow.

1 August 1768

Ordered that the Governor do receive Hannah Lucock into the House, daughter of Hannah Lucock of the parish of Charsfield.

I, Thomas Smith of Boulge, farmer, do agree to hire of the Directors and Guardians John Topple a poor boy belonging to the House of Industry untill Michaelmas 1769 and to cloath him at the end of the term in such manner as he now receives him as witness by my hand Thomas Smith. 2 shirts, a coat, waistcoat, breeches, shoes and stocks, hat & cap.

Ordered that Nathaniel Gray of Ash be allowed <> eleven shillings a week for last week and this he being very ill and having six children.

8 August 1768

Ordered that the Governor do receive Robert Lockwood of Boulge into the House of Industry.

Ordered that the Governor do receive Susan Birch of Sutton into the said House of Industry.

Ordered that the Governor do receive Mary Lockwood and Mary her daughter of Boulge into the said House.

Ordered that Jonathan Churchyard do provide six more pigs for the use of the said House.

Ordered that the Governor do provide a brand with Loes and Wilford for marking, do provide a dozen knives and forks for the use of the kitchen, a large copper boiler for the kitchen with a cock and a barber to shave the poor once a week.

I, Anthony Hunt of Parham, thatcher, do agree to take Pleasance Thrower a poor child belonging to the parish of Eyke from the House of Industry as cloathed by the said House and do agree that she shall not be any ways further chargeable to the said House as witness my hand.

Witness Richard Wood The mark of Anthony Hunt X

2 shifts, a gown, petticoats, shoes, stockings, cap & hat.

15 August 1768

Ordered that the Treasurer do pay Mr Thomas Taylor the sum of four pounds and five shillings for carriage of seventeen loads of wood.

Ordered that the Overseers of Bredfield do inquire into the circumstances of Mary Bacon a poor person of their parish now taken with the small pox and allow her such relief as they shall think necessary and report what they have done to the next Weekly Committee.

Ordered that the Governor do provide a saddle and bridle and gears for the horse and cart.

22 August 1768

Ordered that Mary Bacon a poor person of Bredfield, be allowed ⬦ forty shillings for last week and this she being ill with the small pox.

Ordered that the Governor do provide five comb of wheat.

Ordered that John Smith of Monewden, be allowed four shillings for this week he being ill of a mortification and not capable of being removed.

29 August 1768

Ordered that Mary Bacon a poor person of Bredfield, be allowed ⬦ ten shillings and six pence for this week she being very ill with the small pox.

Ordered that Mr Thomas Tibbs, the Governor, do demand and receive the debts, goods and effects of Ann Wayman, a poor person in the House of Industry.

Ordered that Mr Wood, the Clerk, do provide a proper register book for births and burials.

\Whereas James Partridge of Easton, labourer, is charged with being the father of a male bastard child born of the body of Sarah Reeve of Marlesford, single woman, which is likely to be chargeable to the Corporation of the Hundreds of Loes and Wilford. And whereas I, Edmund Boyns of Easton, aforesaid, farmer, have agreed with the Directors and Guardians acting for the said Hundreds to pay to the said Directors and Guardians on the <29 September 1768> the sum of ten pounds and on the <29 September 1771> the further sum of five pounds in case the said bastard child then be living in full discharge of all maintenance that the said James Partridge shall at any time hereafter be charged with on account of this said child. Witness my hand <29 August 1768> Edmund Boyns. witness Richard Wood./[66]

5 September 1768

Ordered that the Overseers of Ufford be allowed five shillings which they expended on Martha, the wife of Thomas Robinson, a poor person of the same parish who is since dead.

Ordered that the Governor do receive Sarah Curtis and Mary Bacon, poor persons of the parish of Bredfield, into the House of Industry.

Ordered that Matthew Grayston to make proper hogs troughs and two field gates and hang them.

Ordered that the Governor do provide a proper cinder screen and twenty small spinning wheels.

12 September 1768

Ordered that Hannah Lucock of the parish of Charsfield, be delivered to her mother with her shoes and stockings – being chiefly worn out in the said House.

---

[66] Note inserted in SROI ADA11/A/B/3/1.

Ordered that the Governor do provide a pepper mill, to order the door to be removed, to have a bell hanged, to have the back walls raised with the bricks from the dirt holes, to provide five comb of wheat and one comb of pease and some onions and to have the garden ground plowed up.

26 September 1768

Ordered that the Overseers of Hatcheston be allowed their bill of £3 14s. 0d. for maintenance of Elizabeth Hudson and seven other poor persons of the same parish.

Ordered that Mr Salmon do inquire concerning John Woodard and Robert Leech poor persons of the parish of Hoo, having the small pox and to order as he shall think proper.

Ordered that the Overseers of the parish of Earl Soham do allow the Widow London two shillings a week, Sarah Coats one shilling a week, and the Widow Savage eighteen pence a week until further orders.

10 October 1768

Ordered that the Governor do receive William Kemp, Mary Pollock and Mary Branson, poor persons of the parish of Ash, into the House.

Ordered that Mary, the wife of William Kemp of Ash, be allowed one shilling a week she being bedrid.

Ordered that Mary Bacon a poor person from Bredfield, now in the said House be discharged and to leave all her cloaths belonging to the said House.

Ordered that John Tout of the parish of Hoo, be allowed a coat and a pair of breeches.

Ordered that the Governor do apply to a Justice of the Peace for warrants for the apprehending of Robert Hewett of Letheringham, and John Hawkins of Earl Soham, for running away and leaving their familys chargeable.

Ordered that the Governor do receive Jonathan Walker, William Spall, Susan Chenery and Mary Chenery, poor persons of the parish of Sutton into the said House.

17 October 1768

Catherine Plant, being sent to the House of Industry <> by a Director from the parish of Kettleburgh, being then in labour, ordered that the Governor do continue her in the said House.

Ordered that the Governor do receive Mary Peak, widow, Mary Markham, widow, Ann Lebbell, single woman, Catherine Partridge, single woman, poor persons of the parish of Marlesford into the said House.

Ordered that William Cook of the parish of Butley, be allowed seven shillings for last week and this being lame and not capable of being removed and having a wife and four small children.

Ordered that Lydia Watling a poor person in the said House, be permitted to go out of the said House having let herself as a servant to Mr George Mully of Ipswich, and she is to allow six pence a week to the House towards the maintenance of her child now in the said House, and she to have the cloaths – 2 shifts a gown petticoats, 2 pair of stockings, a pair of shoes a check apron mantle a pair of stays & 2 caps.

Ordered that the Governor do allow Sarah Topple of Boulge, some old things that were brought to the House with the poor persons.

Ordered that Richard Lettice of the parish of Butley, be allowed <> two shillings for this week being ill of an ague & fever.

Ordered that the Governor be allowed for ten comb of wheat bought the week before last and that he do provide wheat, pease, two acres of turnips of Mr Brooke, milk and cloth of Mr Whiting for coats.

31 October 1768

Ordered that the Overseers of the parish of Hollesly do allow Bone, his wife and two children, three pounds thirteen shillings and six pence and expences for victuals for them at Woodbridge in their way to Lancashire where they belong.

Ordered that the Overseers of Kettleburgh do allow John Minter five shillings for this week, being very ill of a fever and thrush and not capable of being removed and having a wife and four children.

Ordered that the Governor do receive John Chenery, Lydia his wife and Frances their child, poor persons of the parish of Sutton in to the said House.

Ordered that the Overseers of Shottisham allow Mary Syer, widow, a poor person with three small children, incapable of getting their living, two shillings a week untill the next Quarterly Meeting.

Ordered that the Treasurer do pay Mr Thomas Tibbs, the Governor, eighty pounds on account.

Ordered that the Governor do provide two pieces of cloth for coats and waiscoats of Mr Baldry according to the pattern No 2 at 1s. 10d. per yard.

7 November 1768

Ordered that Deborah Ling, a poor child belonging to the parish of Ash now in the House of Industry, be delivered to her parents with the cloaths she came in with.

Ordered that the Governor do provide 100 earthen chamber pots for the use of the said House.

14 November 1768

Ordered that the application of the Overseers of Melton for the bringing into the House or relieving of Mary the wife of James Fisher by order of Thomas Carthew, Clerk, one of His Majesty's Justices of the Peace be referred to the next meeting and that she continue on the said Justices order untill then.

Ordered that Thomas Mills of Stowmarket late of Wickham Market, glover, do pay the Treasurer eighteen shillings for thirty six weeks pay due this day for the maintenance of Mary Howard a bastard child now in the said House of which he was adjudged the father.

Ordered that the Governor do make an information before one of His Majesty's Justices of the Peace against Robert Welham, a poor boy in the House for breaking of windows and committing other breaches of the peace in the said House.

21 November 1768

Ordered that the Governor do receive Mary, the wife of James Fisher and four small children, accidental poor in the parish of Melton, into the said House and the Clerk do make enquiry after the father who is run away.

Ordered that the Treasurer do pay Mr Fisk, Constable of St Osyths in Essex, one pound eleven shillings and six pence for removing of John Watts.

Ordered that Philip Burch do pay to the Treasurer ten pounds, according to his agreement for the maintenance of a female bastard child born of the body of Mary Robinson of Sutton.

28 November 1768

Ordered that the Clerk do provide Burns Justice for the use of the Corporation.[67]

Ordered that the Governor do provide three load of wood of Mr Negus in the best manner he can.

5 December 1768

Ordered that the Overseers of Sutton do appeal to the order of removal of Elizabeth Woolnough, single woman, from the parish of Walpole to the said parish of Sutton, and that the Clerk do prosecute such appeal.

Ordered that the Governor do receive the above Elizabeth Woolnough into the House.

12 December 1768

Order that the Clerk do send Graystons policy to be renewed, and that it be referred to the Previous Meeting to consider on what sum to insure.

Ordered that the Overseers of Kettleburgh do allow John Cook, a poor person of the said parish, two shillings for part of last week and four shillings for this having fractured his arm and not capable of removing, and having a wife and four small children.

Ordered that the Governor do inquire after John Watling, a driver supposed to be in the Middlesex Militia and, if found, to get a warrant for the apprehending him for running away from his wife and child and leaving them chargeable to the House.

Ordered that the Overseers of Easton do allow Thomas Rogers, a poor boy of the said parish, two shillings and six pence a week for two weeks being very much burnt and not capable of being removed.

Ordered that the Overseers of Creetingham do allow the wife of Stephen Osborn of the same parish, five shillings which he allowed by order of a Justice of the Peace, she being in her labour and not capable of being removed, and to allow two shillings and six pence for this week.

26 December 1768

Ordered that Mary Fisher, a poor person in the said House, be taken by the Governor to the next Justices sitting at Woodbridge to be examined touching her settlement.

Ordered that the Overseers of Creetingham do appeal to the order of removal of Stephen Osborn and Lydia his wife from the parish of Otley to the parish of Creetingham, and the Clerk do prosecute such appeal.

Ordered that the Overseers of Eyke do allow John Wightman for Sarah Fuller widow, a poor person of the said parish, one shilling a week for her life.

2 January 1769

Ordered that William Sawyer, a poor boy of Hatcheston, be apprenticed to Mr Simon Paternoster of Wickham Market for 5 years from 26 December last, and to be allowed by the Corporation 50s. a year for cloathing and to leave him at the end of his term as he receives him and the House to allow a Surgeon and Apothecary if wanted.

---

[67] Richard Burn (1709–85) published *Justice of the Peace and Parish Officer* in 1755. This was for many years the standard authority on the law relating to justices of the peace.

Ordered that the Governor do advertize the several persons run away from their wives and familys and left a charge to this House of Industry.

9 January 1769
Ordered that the Governor do purchase two cows for the use of the House that have calved.

16 January 1769
Ordered that the Governor do pay £11 15s. 6d. for the premium and policy for the House being £11 6s. 0d. a year for an insurance of £6,000. No. 265060. And that the Governor do pay the sum of £11 6s. 0d. on the 25 December in every year.

Ordered that the Governor do get orders of removal for James Fishers wife and family, to Wymondham in Norfolk, the place of his settlement, agreeable to his examination taken by Lord Orwell, the 20 July 1761.

Ordered that the Overseers of Melton do take Margaret Noble before a Justice of Peace to be examined touching her marriage with Matthew Noble and the places of birth of her children Matthew, Thomas and Mary.

Ordered that Henry Topple do send a person into the House to mend shoes.

23 January 1769
Ordered that the Overseers of Dedham be paid £4 19s. 8d. for their expences allowed by a Justice of Peace for the maintenance of Samuel Brown, a certificate person from the parish of Kettleburgh lying ill of the small pox and that Mr Woolnough be so kind as to order the payment.

Ordered that William Maplestone be allowed a penny a person for shaving the head and faces belonging to the said House.

Ordered that the Governor do provide some necessary fire irons, some hay, and straw.

6 February 1769
Ordered that the Overseers of Hollesly do allow Eleanor Charity, a poor person of the same parish, two shillings and six pence for this week, and four weeks being ill of a mortification and not capable of being removed.

Ordered that the Governor do allow two shillings towards the expences of taking Patience Ward, a poor child belonging to Ash, back to Ipswich.

13 February 1769
Ordered that that the Governor do take Mary Noble, a poor child in the House of Industry, a bastard born in the parish of Woodbridge, to the Overseers of the same parish and if they will not accept her on her mother's examination then to get orders of removal.

Ordered that the Governor do receive Elizabeth, the wife of Thomas Woolnough, removed by order from Blythburgh to Hatcheston.

Ordered that the Governor do get the pieces of land adjoining to the House of Industry plowed one earth by Mr Brook if he thinks proper to do it, if not by any other person in the cheapest manner he can. And that he do get a new door and frame to the oven and to be allowed for the old one as agreed for.

Ordered that the Clerk do take Counsels opinion concerning the settlement of Thomas Woolnough and wife, removed by order from Blythburgh to Hatcheston.

27 February 1769

Ordered that the Overseers of Sutton do allow Mary, the wife of William Spall, a poor person now lying in and having two children, twelve shillings for this week for midwife and other expences, and five shillings for next week not capable of being removed.

Ordered that the Governor do purchase a parcell of wood of Mr Brook for use of the oven.

6 March 1769

Ordered that the Governor do receive Margaret, a female bastard child born of the body of Margaret Middleton of the parish of Marlesford, of which William Newson is charged to be father, and that the said Margaret Middleton do allow six pence a week towards the maintenance of the said child.

Ordered that the Overseers of Sutton do allow Mary, the wife of William Spall, a poor person of the same parish, two shillings and sixpence for this week she now lying in.

Ordered that the Governor do take Elizabeth Fuller, a poor person in the said House, before a Justice of the Peace to be dealt with according to the law for running away from the said House with the cloaths of the Corporation without leave and inticeing another to go with her.

20 March 1769

Ordered that the Overseers of Easton do take Mary Stannard before a Justice of Peace to filiate the child of which she is now pregnant, and if she will not do it, then to have her committed to the Bridewell.[68]

27 March 1769

Ordered that the Overseers of Charsfield do allow William Lancaster, a poor person of the same parish, ten shillings for a bed and blanket.

Ordered that William Knights, a poor child in the said House, be discharged from the House and be delivered to his mother.

Ordered that the Overseers of Sutton do allow William Sawer, a poor person of the same parish, three shillings for this week, he having a violent disorder in his arm and not capable of working, and having a wife and two small children.

Ordered that the Overseers of Melton do allow John Avis, a poor person of the same parish, thirty shillings for removing his goods from Sotterly to Melton.

Ordered that the Overseers of Hoo do allow Murdock of the same parish nineteen shillings and six pence for 13 weeks past, and to allow eighteen pence a week for this quarter she being blind.

---

[68] Under an Act of 1733 the overseer could present any unmarried woman he believed to be pregnant before a justice of the peace (who was often a director in the hundreds) to swear, on threat of imprisonment, as to the putative father's identity. A warrant was then issued for his arrest. Once detained the putative father was brought before the justices where two courses of action were open to him: he could admit to being the father and either marry the woman or consent to a bond of indemnity; or deny the charge and enter into a recognisance to appear at the next Quarter Sessions. Here the justices could impose an affiliation order on him should they deem it necessary. The bond of indemnity was usually accompanied by the payment of a surety which the Incorporation could draw on to cover the child's maintenance. The surety was normally between £10 and £20. Other bonds were accepted without a surety but these were supported by two or three bondsmen, usually relatives, who would pay for the child's maintenance if the putative father defaulted.

10 April 1769

Ordered that the Governor do provide a load of hay for the cows, a bier for the dead, three firkins of butter, and a pillion.

17 April 1769

Ordered that the Overseers of Creetingham do provide a being for Stephen Osborn and wife, either in their parish or in some parish within the Hundreds, as no certificate will be granted to labouring men out of the Hundreds.

24 April 1769

Ordered that the Overseers of Marlesford do allow Ann Chapman, a poor person of the same parish, eighteen pence a week she being a cripple. And I, William Bailey of Swefling, farmer, do agree to take and maintain the said Ann Chapman for the said eighteen pence a week during her life, without any further trouble or expence to the Corporation, in case Ann Bailey her mother and my wife shall so long live as witness my hand.

The mark of William Bailey. X   Witness Richard Wood.

Ordered that the Overseers of Petistree do allow Elizabeth Smith, now in her labour, from time to time such sums as they in their discretion shall think fit not exceeding forty shillings.

1 May 1769

Ordered that the Overseers of Easton do allow the Widow Rogers, a poor person of the same parish, the sum of twenty shillings for the burial of her husband.

8 May 1769

Ordered that the Overseers of the parish of Charsfield do allow Mary Wade, a poor person of the same parish, thirty shillings for a month for her lying in.

Ordered that the Overseers of Wickham Market are required to allow John Marriott fifteen shillings for his expences in removing his goods, which he is to return again to the Directors and Guardians at Michaelmas next.

\Rec'd May 8th 1769 of the Guardians of the Poor within the Hundreds of Loes and Wilford, the sum of fifteen shillings which I promise to pay to the said Guardians or their order at Michaelmas next as witness my hand. The mark of John Marriott X Witness Richard Wood./[69]

15 May 1769

Ordered that the Overseers of the parish of Butley do allow William Caley, a poor person, six shillings for this week and next, he having broke one of his ribs.

22 May 1769

Ordered that the Governor do receive William Dallinger, Ann his wife, and John, James, William and Susanna their children, poor persons of the parish of Ufford, into the House of Industry.

Ordered that the Overseers of the parish of Wickham Market do allow Bezaliel Hart, a poor person of the same parish, two shillings a week for two weeks now having the rheumatism.

---

[69] Note inserted in SROI ADA11/A/B/3/1.

85

10 July 1769

Ordered that the Overseers of Kenton do allow Edward Buckingham, a poor person ⬦ seven shillings and six pence being ill and having a sore under his arm.

The small pox being very much in the House of Industry, ordered by the consent of the Directors and Guardians for this Quarter, that all that choose to be inoculated that are in the said House be inoculated imediately by the Surgeon of the said House. And that such children as are in the said House and whose parents are not with them be not inoculated till their parents consent are obtained, and that the Governor do imediately apply to the parents for such consent.[70]

17 July 1769

Ordered that the Overseers of Rendlesham do allow Mary, the wife of Samuel Hart, two shillings for this week and two shillings for next week, her husband having run away and left her with two small children.

24 July 1769

Whereas Samuel Newson, of Easton, labourer, has been charged before Thomas Carthew, Clerk, with being the father of a female bastard child born of the body of Esther Battell, of Melton, spinster. Ordered and agreed by the Directors and Guardians present and John Ralph of Easton, aforesaid, farmer, that in consideration of the payment of sixteen pounds now paid down, and of all other charges and expences concerning the said child to this time, that the said Samuel Newson shall be fully discharged from all charges and expences concerning the said bastard child from this time. This same was paid to Francis Brooke Esq. for the use of the Treasurer.

31 July 1769

Ordered that James Skinner, son of Francis Skinner, a certificate man from the parish of Butley to Woodbridge, be received into the House of Industry having the small pox, and if it should appear that he does not belong to the Incorporated Hundreds then the expences to be born by the parish of Woodbridge as undertaken by the parish officers of Woodbridge.

7 August 1769

Ordered that the Overseers of Bredfield do allow Mary Buckenham and Thomas Buckenham her son, he being an idiot and she old and infirm, two shillings and six pence a week for four weeks.

Ordered that the Overseers of Dallingho do allow Grace Knights, she being old and infirm, one shilling a week for four weeks.

Ordered that the Clerk do send an acknowledgement to the parish of Bradfield St. George, acknowledging Elizabeth Barnock, of the age of seven years, to belong to the Corporation, and that they will be ready to receive the said child if she should become chargeable to the said parish, and which acknowledgement was signed by the Clerk accordingly.

Ordered that the Overseers of Kettleburgh do allow Samuel Webb and wife, poor persons, seven shillings for two weeks, he continuing ill and not capable of being removed and having five small children.

---

[70] At this date the inoculation would have been through the insertion of a small quantity of smallpox matter into a vein.

14 August 1769

Ordered that the Overseers of Creetingham do allow Samuel Harvey and wife, poor persons of the same parish, ten shillings for two weeks, she now lying in and not capable of being removed and having eight small children, four of the children being infants.

I, John Moor of Alderton in the County of Suffolk, farmer, do agree to hire Isaac Pain (a poor boy belonging to the parish of Sutton now in the House of Industry) of the Directors and Guardians thereof for one year from Michaelmas next and to cloath the said boy at the end of the term in such manner as I now receive him.

(2 shirts, coat & wainscot breeches a pair of shoes 2 pair of stockings & a hat).

And it is agreed by the Directors and Guardians that if the above Isaac Pain does not behave well then that the said Mr John Moor shall return him to the said House and take another boy in his room.

\Mr William Sawer[71]

I desire you will deliver the following goods belonging to me and which you have acknowledged to have in your custody to Mr Thomas Tibbs and his receipt shall be your discharge. That is to say one bed with brown curtains, a large chest of drawers, a large corner cupboard, one boiler, a small brewing tub, one killer, coal irons, half a dozen pewter plates, one pewter dish, two tables, half a dozen chairs, a grid iron, one brass candlestick, a large spit, a box iron and heaters, a stool, some shelves and one vessel. As witness my hand this 14th day of August 1769.

Melton, April 4 1770

Mr Sawer

Unless you imediately deliver up the goods of Mr Pallant that you have in your custody and which the Governor of the House of Industry gave you an account of together with the sum of £8 18s. 6d., which you and Mrs Sawer received off Mrs Pallant, I have orders from the Directors and Guardians to sue you for the same without further notice.   Richard Wood/

4 September 1769

Ordered that the Governor do receive Robert Parsons and his wife and four children, and the wife of Edward Fox the elder, poor persons of the parish of Melton, into the Pest House, they having the small pox.

Ordered that the Overseers of Melton do allow Edward Fox the elder, a poor person of the same parish, two shillings for this week.

9 October 1769

Ordered that Sarah Sawer, a poor child now in the House of Industry, be discharged and delivered to her grandmother, and that the said be allowed three pence a week with the said child.

6 November 1769

Ordered that Hannah Scarlet, an infant now with Robert Maulden of Charsfield, be allowed two shillings a week for four weeks, to be deducted out of the sum of three guineas now in the hands of the said Robert Maulden, and which arose out of the effects of William Scarlet, the father of the said infant.

---

71   Note inserted in SROI ADA11/A/B/3/1.

Ordered that the Governor do receive Ann and Elizabeth Scarlet, two poor children belonging to the parish of Alderton, into the said House.

Ordered that the Overseers of Ufford do allow the Widow Walsingham eighteen pence a week for four weeks, and the Widow Harvey one shilling a week for four weeks.

11 December 1769

Ordered that the Overseers of Melton do allow Thomas Cooper, a poor person of the same parish, five shillings towards the burial of his child.

Ordered that Susan Swenecroft, a poor girl now in the House of Industry, be put in the dungeon and kept with only bread and water for twenty four hours on account of her destroying and making away with the wool belonging to the House of Industry.

28 January 1770

Ordered that the Overseers of Ufford do allow Thomas Eldridge, a poor person, two shillings and sixpence for this week, he being very ill and not capable of being removed and having a large family, and do bury the Widow Walsingham at the usual allowance of 20s.

Ordered that the Governor do inquire after George Lees, a pensioner late belonging to the 1st Dragoon Guards Regiment, and endeavour to have him apprehended for running away from his wife and family now in the House. And also apprehend Mary Stannard and Robert Haughton for running away from the House with the cloaths of the Corporation.

Ordered that Mr Thomas Crisp do plow the garden piece twice for ten shillings and six pence, and harrow it at 3s. a time and 12s. for fetching two loads of straw.

5 February 1770

Ordered that the Overseers of Hatcheston, or the Governor, do go imediately to Rickinghall Superior and examine into the certificate of Mary the widow of Martin Bales with her two daughters, and if they find they belong to Hatcheston and they can't do without relief to dispose of their effects and bring them in to the House of Industry.

Ordered that the Governor do get the work done to the Hog Stye and put out the ditching for the garden.

19 February 1770

Order that the Governor do pay Mr John Woods forty shillings for him to allow Lydia Coates, of Sutton, such sums from time to time as he shall think proper till the whole is expended for her maintenance and lying in.

Ordered that Mr Wood, the Clerk, do prosecute an appeal on the behalf of the Corporation to an order of removal of John Leman and Robert Buxton, clerks of Henry Baldry, Amy his wife and Ann their child from the parish of Blythburgh to the parish of Hollesly.

6 March 1770

Ordered that the Overseers of Hatcheston do pay Catherine Sawer five shillings and nine pence for 23 weeks allowance of 3d. for Sarah Sawer and 3d. a week for the future.

12 March 1770

Ordered that the Overseers of Melton do allow William Headman, a poor person of the same parish, five shillings for this week, he being very ill of the fever and having a very bad leg.

Ordered that Ann Briten do pay the Governor five shillings and sixpence for 11 weeks allowance of Ann Briten, her child now in the House of Industry, at six pence a week to this day, and that the said Ann Britten, the child, be discharged from the said House and delivered to her mother.

26 March 1770

Ordered that the Overseers of Easton do allow Thomas Cooke five shillings on account of his wife lying in and wanting assistance.

Ordered that the Governor do receive Mary Baxter and Joseph Baxter, two poor children of the parish of Kettleburgh, into the House of Industry.

9 April 1770

Ordered that the Governor do provide 26 sacks of hay seeds and nine pounds of Dutch clover seeds to lay the wheat piece, and that Mr Brooke do order the same to be sown and harrowed.

Ordered that the Overseers of Ufford do allow Ann Parker ten shillings on account of her lying in and 20s. for the burial of her husband.

30 April 1770

Ordered that the Overseers of Hatcheston do take up John Eagle by virtue of a warrant now in hand for beggatting Ann Kindred with child, and if they will be married (their banns being out and asked) for the Overseers to pay the expences of their marriage.

Ordered that the Overseers of Ufford do dispose of the goods of Susan Gibson deceased, a poor person of the same parish, and account for the same to the Directors and Guardians of the Hundreds and that they do also allow Ann Parker, widow, ten shillings on account of her lying in.

Ordered that the sum of ten pounds that day paid by William Ashford for Thomas Taylor, on account of the said Thomas Taylor being charged with being the father of a male bastard child lately born of the body of Mary Dale of Earl Soham, single woman. Ordered that the Overseers of Earl Soham do allow Mary Dale, a poor person of the same parish, with her infant bastard child, one shilling a week for three weeks in case the said child shall so live.

Ordered that the Governor do receive Charles Pyot, Sarah his wife, and Phebe their daughter, poor persons of the parish of Earl Soham, into the said House.

Ordered that John Chenery, Lydia his wife, Mary and Susan their children, poor persons of the parish of Sutton now in the House of Industry, be discharged from the said House.

7 May 1770

The Committee having agreed with William Sawer of Sudborn to take of him two guineas in full for all monies and goods due from him to the Widow Pallant, a poor person belonging to the parish of Melton, now in the House of Industry, which sum of two guineas is received by the Governor.

18 June 1770

Ordered that the Overseers of Sutton do allow Elizabeth Ox, widow, three shillings on account of John Ox, her husband, lying dead and leaving her with three small children, and twenty shillings for his burial.

23 July 1770

Ordered that the Overseers of Creetingham do allow Mary Peck, with her infant bastard child, one shilling a week for two weeks unless George Fuller, the father of the said child, do pay the same.

Ordered that the Overseers of Earl Soham do allow Mary Dale, with her infant bastard child, one shilling a week for three months in case the said child shall so long live.

30 July 1770

Ordered that the Overseers of Kenton do pay to the Overseer of Debenham three shillings, being paid by him to Ann Long and her two children, certificate persons in pursuance of an order of one of His Majesty's Justices of the Peace.

6 August 1770

Ordered that the Overseers of Brandeston do inquire and get Joshua Nunn of Horham the arrears of his allowances of nine pence a week, and the continuance of the payment thereof to Catherine Sawer, for the maintenance of Sarah Sawer, a bastard child in pursuance of his bond.

13 August 1770

Ordered that the Governor do receive John Turner and Elizabeth his wife, poor persons of the parish of Ramsholt, John Legg and her son of the parish of Kenton, and Ann Woolnough of the parish of Wickham Market into the House of Industry.

20 August 1770

Ordered that the Governor do get the windows of the House of Industry repaired and mended.

Ordered that the Governor do pay the industrious poor in the House of Industry £3 2s. 6d., the usual allowance.

27 August 1770

Ordered that at the next Quarterly Meeting Mr Tibbs, the Governor of the House of Industry, do bring in an account of the millers bringing home short weight, the times when and what quantity each time, and to bring proof of the millers selling corn belonging to the Corporation.

Ordered that the Governor do pay to Thomas Eldridge five shillings and three pence for a quarter rent due from the Widow Gibson at Michaelmas next, and to place it to his account, she being buried by the Corporation and they having taken her effects.

Ordered that the Governor do pay Rebecca Woolmer, servant to Lord Archibald Hamilton, sixteen shillings to buy her cloathing.

Ordered that the Governor do provide one stone and a half of plumbs instead of suet for this week.

3 September 1770

Ordered that the Overseers of Easton do allow Robert Clarke, a poor person, six shillings he continuing ill, and if he makes any further application then that the Governor do receive the said Robert Clarke into the House of Industry.

10 September 1770

Ordered that Mr Wood, the Clerk, do prosecute an appeal on the behalf of the Corporation to an order of removal of Miles Wallis Esq. and Peter Clarke, Gent., for the removal of William Pissey and Mary his wife and William their son, from the parish of Saint Clement in the Borough of Ipswich to the parish of Campsey Ash.

Ordered that the Governor do apply for a warrant and apprehend William Pissey for not staying in the parish of Campsey Ash, where he was removed by order from the parish of St Clement in Ipswich.

24 September 1770

Ordered that the Governor do provide a chest of drawers in the best manner he can.

15 October 1770

Ordered that the Governor do pay Mary Levers three pounds and three shillings for her last year's services in the said House.

29 October 1770

I promise to pay Mr Tibbs, Governor of the House of Industry at Melton, the sum of three shillings per week for the use of the Directors and Guardians of the said House until all expences are paid for the keeping of my child in the said House. As witnessed by my hand the mark of Anthony Cole X witness John Johnson.

Ordered a certificate be granted to the parish of Woodbridge with Anthony Cole and Martha, his wife, at the next Quarterly Meeting.

5 November 1770

Ordered that Robert Bird be wrote to for to pay the sum of £1 1s. 0d., to make up the deficiency of the cloaths of Ann Syer when she was returned from her service.

Ordered that a note be given by the Clerk to the parish of St Nicholas in Ipswich acknowledging George Cullum to be a parishioner of the parish of Melton and that he will be allowed a certificate at the next Quarterly Meeting.

Ordered that the Governor do receive Edmund Warner, belonging to Earl Soham (passed from Norwich to Earl Soham as a rogue and vagabond), in the said House and that he be confined with a clog.

12 November 1770

Ordered that the Governor do receive William, Susanna and Jemma Reeve, poor children of the parish of Easton, into the House of Industry.

19 November 1770

Ordered that the Governor do receive Thomas Rackham, a male bastard child born of the body of Elizabeth Rackham of Melton, into the House of Industry, and Elizabeth Rackham to pay one shilling a week to the Directors and Guardians towards the maintenance, but in case the child shall not be brought in then the Directors do agree to continue the allowance of one shilling a week for this month.

3 December 1770

Application being made from the parish of St Margarets in Ipswich, on account of Francis Emerson and four small children, certificate persons from the parish of Brandeston, having the small pox in the said parish of St Margaret's. Ordered that the Governor do go to Ipswich and see whether there be any certificate, and if there is to treat for their being taken care of in the best manner he can.

Ordered that Joshua Nunn do pay to the Overseers of Brandeston for the use of the Directors and Guardians, £3 5s. 3d. for the maintenance of Sarah Sawer, a bastard child at 9d. a week to Christmas next.

10 December 1770

Ordered the Governor to pay to the administrators of Samuel Simpson deceased, the sum of 17s. due to the said deceased.

Ordered that the Overseers of Wickham Market do pay to Bezaliel Hart, a poor lame man of the said parish, ten shillings towards buying a quantity of lemons nuts etc he promising to pay the same back again at the next Quarterly Meeting.

14 January 1770

Ordered that the Overseers of Boulge be allowed ten shillings which they have disbursed to John Topple, his wife and family, poor persons of the same parish, in pursuance of an order of Thomas Carthew, Clerk, one of His Majesties Justice of Peace.

21 January 1771

Ordered that the Overseers of Boulge be repaid three shillings which they had disbursed to John Topple and family, on account of his wife lying in, and that the Overseer do allow the said John Topple, three shillings this week and three shillings for next week on account thereof.

28 January 1770

Ordered that the Overseers of Rendlesham do allow Henry Mays two shillings and six pence for this week, his having broke his arm and otherwise bruised.

11 February 1770

Ordered that the Overseers of Ufford do allow the wife of Henry Benham five shillings on account of her lying in, and her husband being lately recovered from an illness.

Ordered that the Overseers do allow Benjamin Walsingham three shillings on account of his wife's lying in, and having three small children and he not capable of getting work.

18 February 1771

Ordered that the Governor do take Daniel Grayston, a poor boy belonging to the parish of Charsfield now in the House of Industry, to the Clerk of the Cheque at Harwich and enter him on board a man of war.

Ordered that the Overseers of Alderton be allowed for the maintenance of Mary Clarke for the last weeks, and for her burial, she being now dead and to dispose of what cloaths she me have and account for the same.

Ordered that the Overseers of Melton do allow Robert Bloss, a poor person being ill of the measles, two shillings and sixpence a week for two weeks.

Francis Brooke Esq. having taken Daniel Murdock, a poor boy, out of the House at Michaelmas last and not being able to keep him any longer. Ordered that Mr Brooke do pay the Governor seven shillings and six pence for the time the said boy has been with him.

Ordered that the Overseers of Boulge do allow Thomas Topple, a poor person, seven shillings on account of his wife's lying in and having 5 small children, and to allow him two shillings and six pence for this week, and two shillings and six pence for next week.

Ordered that the Overseers of Kettleburgh be allowed seven shillings which they have paid to Thomas Coates, a poor person on account of his wife's lying in and being lame himself, and having three small children and three shillings for this week.

25 February 1771

Ordered that the Governor do apply to a Justice of the Peace for a warrant against Charles Pyett, for running away from the House of Industry with the cloths of the Corporation, and to be proceeded against according to the Act of Parliament for incorporating the said Hundreds.

4 March 1771

Ordered that the Overseers of Earl Soham do allow Sarah Savage, a poor ancient woman belonging to the said parish, two shillings a week for three weeks she continuing ill.

11 March 1771

\As Robert Bicker is in actual possession of the estate in Bredfield in right of his wife, he has most certainly by residing upon it, gained a settlement in Bredfield equally as if he had the absolute fee in himself. It is therefore referred to the Gentlemen of the Committee to enquire into Bicker's circumstances and to order him relief as they think proper.
Thomas Carthew/[72]

Ordered that the Governor do receive Robert Bicker, a poor person of the parish of Bredfield, into the House of Industry. And ordered that Thomas Whiskin, tenant to the said Robert Bicker, do pay the growing rent to the Directors and Guardians for premisses he occupys in Bredfield, towards the maintenance of the said Robert Bicker, and I, the said Thomas Whiskin, do hereby agree to the above.

18 March 1771

Ordered that the Governor do allow Susanna Dallinger, a poor person of Ufford now lying in at Norwich, from time to time as he shall see occasion not exceeding one pound eleven shillings and six pence.

25 March 1771

Ordered that William Dallinger, the shoemaker in the House, be allowed an addition of six pence a week to shoe the poor in the house.

---

[72] Note inserted in SROI ADA11/A/B/3/1.

1 April 1771

Ordered that the Overseers of Charsfield do allow the Widow Fisher and family, having the small pox, three shillings a week for this week and next.

13 May 1771

Ordered that the Overseers of Easton do demand the cloaths and linnen of Mary White, a poor person now in the House of Industry, of Samuel Vertue and William Wright, with whom the same were left, and after recovery thereof to deliver them to the Governor. (3 long gowns, 2 short gowns, 3 petticoats, 5 shifts and a new piece of cloth, 4 pair stockings one pair of shoes 2 caps, 2 coloured handkerchiefs 3 white handkerchiefs).

10 June 1771

Ordered that John Fink, a poor boy now in the House of Industry belonging to the parish of Melton, be discharged from the said House in order to go upon likeing to Robert Sherington, glover and breeches maker, at Blythburgh.

17 June 1771

\An account of Mrs Pallant's wearing apparel taken the 17th June 1771. A chest containing 1 cotton gown, 2 stuff gowns, 1 cotton bed gown, a body of a black stuff gown, 1 black silk cloak, 1 silk bonnett, 1 black calamanco tufted petticoat, 1 scarlet cardinal, 1 light cloth cloak, sheets, 6 towells, 1 table cloth, 2 pair stays, 2 pillow biers, 5 shifts, 3 white aprons, 2 coloured aprons, 1 white handkerchief, 2 coloured handkerchiefs, 3 petticoats, old shift sleeves stockings and trifles/[73]

Ordered that the Governor do dispose of such of the wearing apparel belonging to the widow Pallant, now deceased, as he shall think proper and to keep the rest of the things for the use of the House, and to account for the same and to be allowed what he has paid out for her. And further ordered that she be carried to Marlesford, being her last request, to be buried by her husband, and the Governor to give an account of the expences thereof.

24 June 1771

Ordered that the Overseers of Hatcheston do allow John Keeble, a poor person of the same parish, three shillings a week for the two former weeks he having put out his collar bone.

\We the Directors and Acting Guardians whose names are here unto set do by virtue of an Act of Parliament <> summon John Woolnough, Overseer of the Poor of the parish of Hatcheston <> to appear at the next General Quarterly Meeting on <1July> to answer the charge <> for neglecting and refusing to do your duty/[74]

22 July 1771

Ordered that the Governor do confine Edmund Warner, a boy belonging to the House of Industry, in the dungeon all Wednesday next only on bread and water, on account of his disorderly behaviour and running away from the House.[75]

---

[73] Note inserted in SROI ADA11/A/B/3/1.

[74] Note inserted in SROI ADA11/A/B/3/1.

[75] The standard punishment meted out appears to have been to set the paupers in the house's stocks during meal times, placed on a diet of bread and water, or be set in the stocks with a note around

Ordered that the Governor do take Bridget Heffer before a Justice of the Peace to be dealt with according to law for having a bastard child and having charged a wrong person with being the father.

Ordered that the Clerk do take £500 of Mr William Parmenter of Playford and to allow him 4 per cent from the time of taking it in order to pay off security for that sum at £4 10s. per cent as soon as possible.

12 August 1771

Ordered that Daniel Manthorp do affix up a square pump in the Brewhouse for three guineas, and that the Governor do dispose of the lead pump to be taken up where this is to be fixed in the best manner he can.

Ordered that the Overseer of Ash do go to Orford and agree with the Overseers in the best manner they can for the maintenance of Dorothy and [   ] Lyon poor persons of the same parish of Ash, certificated persons to Orford they being ill and not capable of being removed and to report what they do to the next committee.

Ordered that Mr John Stow do provide the House of Industry with mount moor coals for this year's consumption at 25s. per chaldron to be delivered to the said House agreeable to his proposals.

19 August 1771

The Overseers of Ash having been to Orford according to order and having reported to this Committee that Mr Randall had agreed to see after Dorothy and [ ] Lyon and to manage in the best manner he can. Ordered that the Overseers of Ash do pay Mr Randall what is reasonable for their maintenance and looking after them.

9 September 1771

Ordered that the Governor do allow Thomas Thursby, a poor person belonging to the parish of Charsfield now living in Ipswich, his wife now lying in and having five small children five shillings.

Ordered that the Governor do receive Bridget Heffer, widow, a poor person of the parish of Hollesly having the small pox in to the Pest House belonging to the House of Industry.

Ordered that Benjamin Thurston do pay the Governor for the use of the Corporation, eighteen pence a week from this day towards the maintenance of his wife now in the House of Industry, otherwise to be proceeded against for running away and not maintaining her.

7 October 1771

Ordered that the Governor do allow Philip Pratt, a poor person of the parish of Hollesly, now in the parish of Benhall, five shillings for this week he continuing ill.

Ordered that the Governor do allow Robert Michelson, the taylor to the House of Industry, one pound eleven shillings and six pence for his trouble and care instructing Edward Stimmer, a poor boy in the said House, in the trade.

their neck explaining their misdemeanour. Another common approach was the use of a separate table at meal times with a board explaining why they were there.

21 October 1771

Ordered that the Governor do receive Philip Pratt and Rebecca his wife, Mary, Sarah and Elizabeth their children, poor persons of the parish of Hollesly, in to the House of Industry.

4 November 1771

Ordered that the Governor do receive Margery Smith, a poor person of the parish of Earl Soham into the House of Industry, she being moved by a vagrant pass from the parish of St Margaret's, Westminster to Earl Soham, aforesaid.

30 December 1771

Mr George Ansell, having informed the Committee that Elizabeth Lankester of the parish of Bredfield, single woman hath lately been delivered of a female bastard child in the said parish of Bredfield which is likely to become chargeable to the Corporation, and not being willing that the father of the said bastard child should be known, hath agreed with the said Committee and the said Committee doth agree (the lying in having been paid for) to accept of twenty guineas in full discharge for all charges that shall accrue on account of the said bastard child, which said sum of twenty guineas hath been paid the Treasurer accordingly to be placed to the credit of the Corporation.

10 February 1772

Ordered that the Governor do receive Joseph and James Page, two poor children of the parish of Shottisham, into the said House. Ordered that the Overseers of Shottisham do allow John Page, being ill and having 3 small children, three shillings for this week and three shillings for next week.

Ordered that the Governor do apply for a licence and get John Capon of Benhall, now in Bridewell, and Sarah Nichols of Hatcheston married.

17 February 1772

Ordered that the Governor do provide 100 earthen chamber pots for the use of the said House.

15 June 1772

Ordered that the Overseers of Eyke do allow Richard Boone, a poor person being ill and having three small children, two shillings for this week, and Thomas Arnold, having broke his rib, two shillings for this week

6 July 1772

Ordered that the Overseers of Easton do allow the wife of Richard Crosby, he having gone away and left four small children, two shillings for this week.

17 August 1772

Ordered that the Overseers of Bredfield do allow the wife of John Thompson, having lately miscarried and being very ill, two shillings and six pence for last week and two shillings and six pence for this week.

12 October 1772

Ordered that the Governor do receive Letitia Lambert, a poor person belonging to the parish of Melton into the House her father to allow one shilling six pence a week for her maintenance.

Ordered that the Governor do receive Mary Crosby, Dorothy, William, Jacob and Elizabeth her children belonging to the parish of Easton, Lydia Capon and Thomas Cook poor children of the same parish into the said House

Ordered that the Governor do receive Sarah Martin, Henry and John her children, poor persons of the parish of Wickham Market, into the said House, and her husband to allow three shillings a week to be paid every month from <10 October>.

19 October 1772

Ordered that the Overseers of Marlesford do allow Edward Giles, his daughter being big with child and just ready to lye in, twenty shillings and after she is delivered of such child or children as she is now pregnant with as an allowance for her months lying in.

Ordered that the Governor do pay Mr Andrew Baldry, Overseer of St Margaret in Ipswich, one pound and one shilling ordered by a Justice of the Peace for the relief of Thomas Thursby and family lying ill of the small pox.

21 December 1772

Ordered that the Governor do receive Edmund Wilson, a poor person belonging to the parish of Boulge, provided that on his examination before a Justice of Peace he belongs to the said parish into the said House.

4 January 1773

Ordered that the Overseers of the parish of Creetingham do imediately apprehend William Wells, and Thomas Wells of Framlingham, labourers, pursuant to the warrant of Francis Capper Clerk one of His Majestys Justices of the Peace, dated in January and March 1771, being charged with being the father of two bastard children born of the bodys of Mary Smith and Mary Gates, which said children have been chargeable to the said House and if there shall be any neglect in the said Overseers then that said Overseers be summoned to appear at the next General Quarterly Meeting to answer such neglect.

18 January 1773

Ordered that the Overseers of Charsfield do allow the wife of James Crane, and her two children being ill and her husband being ill of the small pox in the House of Industry two shillings for this week and two shillings for the next.

25 January 1773

Ordered that the Overseers of Wickham Market do allow Joseph Green, an accidental poor continuing ill, four shillings a week for 4 weeks.

15 February 1773

Ordered that the Overseers of Shottisham do allow John Page, a poor person being ill of the dropsy, two shillings for this week and two shillings for the next.

1 March 1773

Ordered that the Overseers of Wickham Market do allow Joseph Green, an accidental poor continuing ill, four shillings a week for this month

15 March 1773

Ordered that the Clerk do send an order to discharge John Green now in Bridewell, being charged with being the father of a bastard child born of the body of Elizabeth Smith of Wickham Market, and that the officers of Wickham Market do apply for an order of bastardy against the said John Green.

\5 April 1773

Money disbursed for the poor of the parish of Easton by me Moses Crisp, Overseer of the aforesaid parish

	£	s.	d.
Paid for a coffin for Jonathan Reeve	0	8	6
Paid for winding and laying forth	0	6	0
Paid to the sexton for ringing the bell and diging the grave	0	3	0
Beer to the bearers	0	2	0
The affidavet	0	0	6
Paid to Robert Bayleys wife by order of Doctor Salmon	0	2	6
	1	2	6/[76]

12 April 1773

Ordered that the Overseers of Hatcheston do allow James Noys and family six shillings for this week, Walter Holmes and family seven shillings for this week, they being ill of the small pox, and John Gooding three shillings and six pence for this week to attend on both families.

19 April 1773

Ordered that the Overseers of Hatcheston do allow James Noys and family six shillings for this week, and Walter Holmes and family seven shillings for this week, they being ill of the small pox, and John Gooding three shillings and six pence for this week to attend on both families, and Nurse Leggatt two shillings and six pence.

26 April 1773

Ordered that the Governor do receive John Gooch, a servant boy of Mr Dewel's of Bredfield, into the pest house having the small pox, Mr Dewel having promised to pay expences.

7 May 1773

Ordered that Philip Pratt, Rebecca his wife, and Elizabeth and Sarah their children, poor persons of the parish of Hollesly now in the House of Industry, be discharged from the said House, and that the Governor do allow the said Philip Pratt five shillings to assist him in removing his goods from the said House.

---

[76] Note inserted in SROI ADA11/A/B/3/1.

12 July 1773
Ordered that the Governor do pay James Huggins, Keeper of Woodbridge Bridewell, three shillings for his trouble in going to Monewden and Earl Soham with William Garbold.

19 July 1773
Ordered that Sigh Crisp, a poor person in the House of Industry, be punished for disorderly behaviour by abatement of diet and distinction of dress at the discretion of the Governor.

23 August 1773
Ordered that the Overseers of Hatcheston do allow Ann Eagle, a poor person having broke her wrist, two shillings for this week.

30 August 1773
Ordered that the Governor do receive Ann Eagle, a poor person belonging to the parish of Hatcheston, having strained her wrist into the House.
Ordered that the Overseers of Letheringham do allow John Scotchman, his wife now lying in and one of his children having his thigh broke, and having seven small children, four shillings for this week.

2 November 1773
Ordered that the Overseers of Hatcheston do allow John Salmon one pound two shillings and six pence for expences and burial of William Pyett, a poor person belonging to Earl Soham, taken ill in the road at Hatcheston and dying at the house of the said John Salmon.

9 November 1773
Ordered that the Governor do receive Elizabeth Eldridge, let to Mr Mann of Dallingho the 8th instant, on account of her being ill at the time of her being hired, and Mr Mann agreeing to take another girl out of the House. (Took Sarah Keeble instead).

10 January 1774
Ordered that the Governor do pay the officers of St Margarets parish, Ipswich £5 15s. 2½d., for expences relieving Thomas Thursby, wife and family, poor people belonging to the parish of Charsfield, burying him and bringing his wife and children to the House of Industry.
Ordered that the Governor do receive the widow Thursby and Katherine, Dorothy and Elizabeth and Frederick her children, poor people belonging to the parish of Charsfield removed by order from the parish of St Margarett Ipswich to Charsfield into the House of Industry.

17 January 1774
Ordered that the Governor do allow John Ward, a poor person belonging to the parish of Boyton now living in the parish of Little Oakley in Essex under a certificate, and having a wife and six small children and his wife big with the seventh, ten shillings and six pence.

24 January 1774

Ordered that the Governor do pay William Turtle a poor person of the parish of Hatcheston, removed by Order from Holton, one guinea which he hath agreed shall be paid out of his pension of Chelsea Hospital.

7 February 1774

Ordered that Mr John Youngman, Overseer of Butley, do apprehend or cause to be apprehended Edward Lewis, labourer, now or late of the parish of Shottisham, by vertue of a warrant of Philp Carter, Clerk, one of His Majestys Justices of the Peace charged with the getting of Elizabeth Harlock of Butley with child.

28 February 1774

Ordered that the Governor do pay the Overseer of Heveningham two shillings and six pence allowed William Levett, a certificated person from Petistree to Heveningham last week, three shillings for the officers journey, and fifteen shillings and six pence for William Levett, his wife and family, being very ill for three weeks making together the sum of one Guinea.

4 April 1774

Ordered that the Overseers of Sutton do inquire into the circumstances of Martha Giles and whether she is capable of maintaining her child, and also to inquire what was the reason the allowance of one shilling a week was taken off from being allowed about three quarters since and to report it to the Committee on Monday next.

20 June 1774

Ordered that the Overseers of Boulge do allow Thomas Topple, his wife and four small children being ill, two shillings for this week.

\Boulge June 27th 1774

Gentlemen this is to acquaint you that the family of Thomas Topple has all had the masels and the woman is very bad now and is not likely to get her strength of sum time for she was dangerously bad with it thare was she and fower of her children down with it to gether therefor no dout but that you will consider sumthing of a lowance for them as your men of grate sperits to alow such a family two shillings wen between seven and eight pound was paid in the same day I must tel you if you had no grater benifit of it han the love has you wont have the spirit you have. George Smith Churchwarden.

I, George Smith of Boulge in the county of Suffolk, farmer, do own and acknowledge myself to be in fault in having aspersed the characters of the Gentlemen of the Committee by letter and do hereby beg parson for the same as witness my hand the fourth day of July 1774/[77]

\Gentlemen, upon an application from the Overseer of Cretingham, I issued a warrant for the apprehending of Robert Jay the reputed father of a bastard child on the body of Ann Cooke, He left the country and would probably never have returned again had not Mr List of Framsden interfered who is answerable for the appearance

---

[77] Note inserted in SROI ADA11/A/B/3/1.

of the young man. When the woman has been delivered a month when all charges are to be paid. Robert Jay is a youth under twenty and the woman is near forty years of age of most infamous life and character so that it would have been ruin if he had been persuaded to marry her, this method was then taken as the next likely way to save him, if the house will take the woman forty shillings will be paid for the lying in but if that is objected to some other method must be found out by Jay and his surety.

I am your humble servant Francis Capper/[78]

---

[78] Note inserted in SROI ADA11/A/B/3/1.

The second Weekly Minute Book,
5 September 1774–17 June 1780[79]

5 September 1774

Directors	Guardians
Jonathan Burward Esq.	Mr Ralph Hall
The Hon'ble Mr Nassau	Mr George Baker
	Mr Edward Keer

Ordered that the Overseers of Dallingho do allow Robert Walton, a poor person, twenty shillings towards the burial of his wife.

Ordered that the Overseers of Easton do allow John Boon, continuing very ill, three shillings for this week and three shillings for next week.

Ordered that the Overseers of Kenton do allow James Driver, a poor person in the same parish, ten shillings and six pence on account of his being ill and having lately buried a child and his wife now lying in.

Ordered that the Clerk do write to the several persons in rotation whose moneys are at £4 10s. per cent to know if they will accept of £4 per cent, or otherwise they will be paid off their principal and interest within three months.

12 September 1774

January 9 1775   I, Elizabeth Fosdick of Easton in the County of Suffolk, do agree to hire (Rose Good) Lydia Brown a poor girl belonging to the parish of (Ufford) Rendlesham, now in the House of Industry of the Directors and Guardians of the said Hundreds untill Michaelmas next and from thence for one year untill Michaelmas 1775. And I do promise to pay the said Directors and Guardians at Michaelmas 1775 twenty shillings for her wages as witness my hand.

         The mark X of Elizabeth Fosdick.

         Witness R. Wood Jun.[80]

Ordered that the Overseers of Petistree do allow Robert Glanfield, his wife being ill and having four small children, two shillings and six pence a week for three weeks.

Ordered that the Overseers of Ufford do allow John Garnage, a poor person being ill and having a wife and two children, one shilling a week for three weeks.

Ordered that the Overseers of Kettleburgh do allow John Kent, his wife being very ill and having five small children, one shilling and six pence for last week and three shillings a week for two weeks.

---

[79] SROI ADA11/A/B/3/2.
[80] Rose Good was returned for Lydia Brown. The reason is not stated.

3 October 1774

Ordered that the Overseers of Ufford so allow Ann Warner, a poor idiot child, two shillings a week, and the Widow Rolton having four small children, eighteen pence a week for this quarter in case the children shall so long live.

Ordered that the Overseers of Kenton do allow Thomas Pettit, a poor person having broke his leg, four shillings and six pence a week.

Ordered that the Overseers of Ufford do allow John Garnage a poor old person being ill, one shilling a week for this month.

10 October 1774

Ordered that Henry Martin, a poor child now in the House of Industry belonging to the parish of Wickham Market, be discharged and delivered to his aunt.

17 October 1774

Ordered that the Overseers of Ufford do allow the Widow Hearn, having seven small children, eighteen pence a week for three weeks.

31 October 1774

Ordered that the Overseers of Easton do allow John Boon, a poor person continuing ill, three shillings for this week, and in case he wants any further assistance to be brought to the House of Industry.

7 November 1774

Ordered that the Overseers of Hollesly do allow two pounds towards the burial of Thomas and Mary Skeet, poor persons belonging to the parish of Alderton, and fifteen shillings for the expence of the jury on the inquest, and twenty shillings towards the burial of Mary Cosby, a poor person.

28 November 1774

Ordered that the Governor do receive Mary Berry, a poor person removed by order from Baddingham to Brandeston, into the House of Industry.

19 December 1774

Ordered that the Overseers of Eyke do allow Margaret Harris five shillings for nursing and cooking for the Widow Hudson.

26 December 1774

Ordered that the Overseers of Melton do allow the Widow Wilby, a poor certificate person from the parish of Dickleburgh in Norfolk, three shillings a week untill further notice.

Ordered that the Overseers of Earl Soham do allow John Hall, a poor person he and his two children having had the small pox thirty shillings towards his expences.

9 January 1775

Ordered that the Governor do receive John Burward, Elizabeth his wife, Susanna, Elizabeth, Priscilla, Phebe, John and Deborah their children, poor persons removed by order from the parish of Playford to the parish of Melton into the House of Industry. Also Ann Britton, a poor child belonging to the said parish of Melton, into the said House.

Ordered that the Overseers of Charsfield do allow Robert Hurnard, his wife being very ill, two shillings a week for two weeks, and Benjamin Reed two shillings and six pence towards the burial of his infant child.

Ordered that the Governor do receive William and John Spalding, poor children belonging to the parish of Earl Soham, into the House of Industry.

Ordered that the Governor do allow George Head, a poor person of the parish of Boulge, having three small children ill, eighteen pence a week for three weeks, and Robert Lucock, a poor person of the parish of Charsfield being very ill and having a wife and five children, three shillings a week for three weeks.

16 January 1775

Ordered that the Governor do allow Mrs Cooper five shillings for laying the wife of [   ] Topple in bed, a poor person of the parish of Boulge.

Ordered that the Overseers of Dallingho do allow the wife of [   ] Topple, a poor person of the parish of Boulge, she now lying in and having 5 small children, two shillings and six pence a week for two weeks and two shillings for last week.

The Overseers of Sutton are required to allow Mary Todd, she continuing ill, nine shillings for this week, she being alone person, delirious and not capable of being removed.

The Governor is required to receive Robert and Ann Lucock, poor children of the parish of Charsfield, into the House of Industry.

Ordered that the Governor do receive William Gunnold, a poor boy of the parish of Boyton, into the said House.

Ordered that the Overseers of Hatcheston do allow twenty shillings towards the burial of Elizabeth Hail.

23 January 1775

The Governor is required to receive George Pitt, the son of Uriah Pitt of the parish of Sutton into the Pest House, having the small pox for whose nursing and care the said Uriah Pitt has promised to pay four guineas.

Ordered that the Governor do pay the Overseers of Saxmundham one pound eleven shillings and sixpence expended by him on Francis Burrell, a poor child belonging to the parish of Eyke.

Ordered that the Overseers of Wickham Market do allow twenty shillings towards the burial of Joseph Lee.

Ordered that the Overseers of Petistree do allow Thomas Leech, his wife being ill and having seven small children, five shillings for this week.

Ordered that the Governor do pay sixteen shillings and seven pence for the burial of a child of George Head, a poor person belonging to the parish of Boulge.

30 January 1775

The Overseers of Kettleburgh are required to allow Benjamin Baxter, his wife continuing ill two shillings for this week and two shillings for next week.

Ordered that the Overseers of Eyke do allow Richard Booth, a poor person of this parish, his wife being ill and having five small children, two shillings and six pence a week for two weeks.

Ordered that the Overseers of Creetingham do allow Wayman Bardwell a certificate from the said parish to Sco Ruston in Norfolk, his wife being ill and having four small children, one guineas.

13 February 1775

Ordered that John Burwood, his wife and family removed by order of two Justices from the parish of Playford to the parish of Melton, now in the House of Industry, be discharged from the said House.

20 February 1775

Ordered that the Overseers of Boulge do allow George Kidd six shillings and six pence towards the burial of his infant child.

6 March 1775

Ordered that the Overseers of Wickham Market do allow Elizabeth Brown, a poor old infirm person continuing very ill, eighteen pence a week for three weeks over and above the one shilling a week already allowed her, and Deborah Lingwood continuing ill, eighteen pence for this week.

17 April 1775

Ordered that the Overseers of Letheringham do allow towards the burial of John Lyon and [   ] Scotchmer, six shillings towards the burial of his child, and William Woodard ten shillings towards the burial of his daughter aged 16 years.

24 April 1775

Ordered that the Overseers of Boyton do allow John Ward, a poor person of the same parish, a certificate person to the parish of Little Oakley in Essex, being there very ill and having five small children, ten shillings and six pence.

26 June 1775

Ordered that the Overseers of Easton do allow Sarah Edgar, a poor old infirm person, one shilling a week, and Frances Hunt and Mary Woodard with their infant bastard children, one shilling a week each for this quarter in case they so long live.

Ordered that the Overseers of Kenton do allow Jonathan Good, having dislocated his shoulder, two shillings a week for three weeks.

Ordered that the Governor do pay one shilling a week towards the maintenance of the Widow Thursbys children now in Ipswich, belonging to the parish of Charsfield.

31 July 1775

Ordered that the Overseers of Rendlesham do allow Jeremiah Moulton, being blind, two shillings and six pence for last week and two shillings and six pence for this week.

Ordered that the Clerk do certify to the Governor of the London Hospital, that Stephen Manlove the younger is an inhabitant legally settled in the parish of Melton in order that he may be admitted as a patient in the said hospital for the cure of his fits.

21 August 1775

Ordered that Mr Wood the Clerk do commence an action against John Smith, John Warner and Henry Smith on their bond dated 8th April 1767 made to George Alexander, Churchwarden, and William Ashford, Overseer of Earl Soham, in the penal sum of £50 conditioned for indemnifying the said Churchwarden and Overseer and parishioners on account of a female bastard child born of the body of Ann Welton.

27 November 1775

Ordered that the Governor do receive John Mallett, Anna his wife, and John, Mary, Henry, Elizabeth and Thomas their children, poor persons belonging to the parish of Hatcheston into the said House.

18 December 1775

Ordered that John Mallett, Anna his wife, Elizabeth and Thomas their children, poor persons belonging to the parish of Hatcheston, be discharged from the said House and that the Overseers do allow them five shillings.

26 December 1775

Ordered that the Overseers of Creetingham do allow John Aldhouse, his wife being ill and disordered in her senses, two shillings for this week.

22 January 1776

Ordered that the Governor do receive Thomas Fairweather and Elizabeth, his wife of Brandeston (removed by Order from Manningtree in Essex), into the House of Industry.

29 January 1776

Ordered that the Overseers of Sutton do allow the wife of John Mills being ill having two children and her husband in the Bridewell two shillings a week for three weeks.

11 March 1776

Ordered that the Governor do receive Frances Lewis, a poor person removed by order from Rochford in Essex to Brandeston, in to the House of Industry.

22 April 1776

Ordered that the Governor do pay £9 9s. 0d. to the Overseers of Rochford in Essex for the removal of Frances Lewis, a certificate person from Rochford to Brandeston.

13 May 1776

Ordered that the remaining sum of five pounds agreed by Thomas Caley to be paid for a male bastard child born of the body of Mary Stebbing of Capel, of which Thomas Ashland was charged to be the father, be paid to the Governor, the former £10 and £5 being before paid to the Governor for the use of the Corporation, in full for all charges attending the said bastard child.

1 July 1776

Application being made to relieve Samuel Noller and wife, poor old persons of the parish of Charsfield. It is ordered that they be brought into the House.

Francis Sawyer, a poor person of the parish of Dallingho, having applied again for further relief it is ordered (he and his wife getting better), that they send two of their children into the House.

15 July 1776

Application being made by the Overseers of Earl Soham for an allowance of one shilling a week for the maintenance of a child of the Widow Alexander, deceased. Ordered that the child be brought into the House and an allowance be made. And the Overseers do allow twenty shillings towards the burial of the said Widow Alexander.

Application being made to take John Mallett, a poor boy belonging to the parish of Marlesford now in the House of Industry, to go to his father, ordered that he do not go to his father but that if his father can get a place for him and the master will apply to the Committee they will let him.

Ordered that the Overseers of Hatcheston do allow Daniel Hudson, a poor person of the said parish being ill, two shillings a week for two weeks, and if any further assistance is wanting that he be taken into the House.

29 July 1776

Ordered that John Goldsbury of Woodbridge, merchant, do supply the House of Industry with 80 chaldron of the best Washington main coals at £1 6s. 9d. per chaldron (21 chaldron to the score), 40 chaldron to be laid in at the said House on or before the 10th October next, and the remainder on or before the 5th April next. One half of which to be paid for at Christmas and the remainder at Midsummer next.

19 August 1776

Application being made by the wife of William Cockerell of Eyke, now lying in and being very ill, but the Overseer not knowing her particular case. Ordered that he do inquire into their circumstances and report them to the committee next week.

26 August 1776

Ordered that the Overseers of Eyke do allow Edward Kettle being ill, and having a wife and five small children, four shillings for this week, and William Cockerell his wife now lying in and being very ill, three shillings for last week and three shillings for this.

2 September 1776

Ordered that the Overseers of Eyke do allow William Cockerell his wife continuing ill, two shillings for this week and two shillings for next, and do allow Edward Kettle continuing ill four shillings for this week.

9 September 1776

Ordered that the Overseers of Eyke do allow Edward Kettle continuing ill, four shillings for this week.

23 September 1776

Application being made to relieve Abraham Alexander, his wife lying in and having two small children, it is ordered that one of his children be brought into the House of Industry.

14 October 1776

The Overseers of Marlesford applying for the burial of the wife of Richard Amis but not having received relief could not be allowed agreeable to the Order of the Annual Meeting.

Ordered that the Overseers of Earl Soham do allow James Kemp, being ill from a fall and having seven small children, five shillings a week for two weeks, and in case he wants any further relief to send some of his children to the House of Industry.

28 October 1776

Ordered that the Governor do go to Bawdsey to take an account of the effects of Thomas Fuller (now a pauper at Melton) belonging to the said parish of Bawdsey, having broke his arm and leg and report it to the next Weekly Committee.

24 March 1777

Ordered that the Overseers of Bawdsey be allowed seven shillings and six pence towards relieving and removing Edward Cornish, a poor infirm person from Bawdsey to Stowmarket.

28 July 1777

Ordered that John Keable and Sarah his wife, now in the House of Industry belonging to the parish of Hatcheston, be discharged from the said House and the Governor do allow the wife a shift of cloaths in consideration of her being servant in the House for upwards of nine years.

Application being made by William Read, a poor person of the parish of Alderton to be discharged from the House of Industry, and it appearing that he has not behaved well and not likely able to maintain himself out of the House. Ordered that he be not discharged but continue in the said House untill further orders.

15 December 1777

Ordered that the Overseers of Brandeston do allow Jeffrey Boon, his wife now lying in and having five small children, five shillings for two weeks, and if they want any further assistance some of the eldest children to be brought into the House.

23 February 1778

Ordered that the Overseers of Hollesly do allow Edward Fox continuing lame, two shillings and six pence a week for this week and next, and if he require any further assistance the Overseer is ordered attend the Committee to report the case.

16 March 1778

Ordered that the Overseers of Kettleburgh do allow William Page, a certificate man to Ashfield, ten shillings towards the burial of his infant child and two shillings and six pence a week for two weeks, his wife and another child being very ill.

Ordered that the Overseers of Hatcheston do allow the Widow Eagle, two shillings for this week, and to be brought into the House next week, and Francis Sawer being ill, two shillings for this week, and if he wants any further assistance to send one of his children into the said House.

23 March 1778

Ordered that the Overseers of Kettleburgh do allow William Page seven shillings and ten pence for the remainder of the expences for the burial of his infant child.
Burying Page of 7 yrs. Kettleburgh

| A coffin | 6s. | |
| 2 yds of bay | 2s. | 4d. |

Laying forth	2s.	6d.
Expence of burial	4s.	0d.
	14s.	10d.
Cakes and ale	3s.	0d.
	17s.	10d.

It being ordered last week that John Bowes, a poor person belonging to Wickham Market being ill, should be brought into the House. He was received and it is now ordered that on his own consent be discharged from the said House.

13 April 1778
Ordered that the Overseers of Eyke do allow Thomas Studd being ill, two shillings and six pence for this week, and in case he is capable of being removed to be brought to the House, and also do allow Richard Boon being ill and having five small children, three shillings for this week, and in case he wants any further assistance to send some of his children to the House.

Ordered that the Overseers of Earl Soham do allow Edward Barker being ill and having 6 children, four shillings for last week, three shillings for this week, and three shillings for next, and in case he wants any further assistance to send some of his children to the said House.

18 May 1778
Ordered that the Overseers of Wickham Market do allow Susan Finch and her four children (her husband having left her), eighteen pence a week until the next Quarterly Meeting.

Ordered that the Overseers of Melton do allow Elizabeth Fink now lying in, four shillings for last week, five shillings for this week, and five shillings for the midwife and five shillings for the burial of the child.

25 May 1778
Application being made to relieve the family of Joshua Johnson, a certificate man from Earl Soham to St Margarets in Ipswich, he being gone out a substitute in the Militia, it is ordered that the Governor do get his wife and family removed to the House of Industry in the best manner he can.

Application being made for inoculating the wife and five children of John Potkins, three children of Edward Buckenham, the wife and five children of George Worlidge, the wife of William Bird, the wife and two children of William Long certificate persons from Kenton to Debenham (the parish of Debenham having agreed to inoculate the poor in the said parish), ordered that Mr Salmon the Surgeon do go to Debenham to view and see the state and condition of the several familys belonging to the said parish of Kenton and report it to the next Weekly Committee.

1 June 1778
Ordered that the Overseers of Kenton do allow Buckenhams wife and three children having the small pox, seven shillings for last week, and seven shillings for this week, and seven shillings for next week, and George Worlidge and six children he being ill and the children having the small pox, eight shillings for this week and eight shillings for next.

8 June 1778

Ordered that Elizabeth, Robert, Thomas and Mary Johnson-Waterman, poor children now in the House of Industry belonging to the parish of Marlesford, be discharged and delivered to Robert Waterman, their grandfather who now lives in Horham, their father and mother being lately dead. And that the Overseers of Marlesford do allow the said Robert Waterman four shillings a week for three weeks, being till the next Quarterly Meeting.

15 June 1778

Ordered that the Overseers of Kenton do allow Buckenhams wife and family continuing ill of the small pox, five shillings for this week, George Worlidge and family continuing ill of the same, four shillings for last week and seven shillings for this week, the wife and two children of William Long being ill of the same, six shillings for the two last weeks and three shillings for this week, and John Potkin his wife and six children being ill of the same seven shillings for this week.

22 June 1778

Ordered that the Overseers of Kenton do allow Buckenhams wife and family continuing ill of the small pox, three shillings for this week and ten shillings and six pence for the nurse and George Worlidge wife and family continuing ill of the same five shillings for this week.

6 July 1778

Ordered that the Overseers of Kenton do allow Edward Buckenham two shillings and six pence for last week, his wife then being very ill and twenty shillings towards her burial she being since dead.

\Gentleman.   It is a metter of consequence or the Directors of the House of Industry to consider how to act with respect to the wives of substitutes – you will find they will all apply for relief without exception whereby a heavy expence will accrue to the corporation if they are all relieved with money. I would therefore beg leave to recommend it to the Directors to call a meeting on purpose and to come to a resolution whether or not to relieve out of the house for there is no doubt but you can insist upon the persons wanting relief to coming into the house in this case as well as others. As I shall have reported applications in this matter I wish you would instruct me as to what resolutions you may come to, that I may act accordingly.   J Carthew/[81]

24 August 1778

Ordered that Mr Richard Wood, the Clerk, do take counsels opinion on the case of Jeffrey Boon and his family, removed by order from Monewden to Woodbridge, it appearing (since the above removal) that the said parish of Monewden in the year 1776 granted the said Jeffery Boon a certificate to Stoke Ash and that the said Jeffery Boon be summoned to attend the next Quarterly Meeting.

7 September 1778

Ordered that the Clerk do give a note to the parish of Little Bealings acknowledging Simon Allen of Melton, brick maker, Sarah his wife, and John and Simon

---

[81] Note inserted in SROI ADA11/A/B/3/2.

their children, to be inhabitants legally belonging to the parish of Melton in the Hundred of Wilford (he having before had a certificate from Melton to Kesgrave).

21 September 1778
Ordered that the Overseers of Kettleburgh do sue after Robert Clarke according to the directions given them, they having a warrant against him for a bastard child or they will be proceeded against for neglect of duty.

26 October 1778
Application being made for the burial of the wife of William Hurst of Brandeston, but she not having received any relief out of the House it could not be allowed as it would have been contrary to the order of the 25th June 1776. Ordered that it be referred to the next Quarterly Meeting.

2 November 1778
Ordered that the Clerk do commence an action against Edmund Cottingham Hayward on his bond to the Guardians for the maintenance of a bastard child born of the body of Mary Creasy of Earl Soham for neglecting to maintain the said child. Money paid.

9 November 1778
Ordered that the Overseers of Sutton do allow the Widow Brown now lying in and having five small children, five shillings for last week, five shillings for this week and five shillings for next, and if she wants any further assistance she and her family to be brought into the House.

16 November 1778
Ordered that the Overseers of Melton do allow the Widow Parsons, twenty shillings towards the burial of her husband, and two shillings for this week having two children and one of them ill, and if she requires any further assistance for her two children to come into the House.

14 December 1778
Ordered that the Governor do receive John Hearn, a poor boy belonging to the parish of Easton into the House of Industry, and that the Overseers be allowed one shilling which they allowed the said John Hearn towards his maintenance last week, and they are required to allow Sarah Bolter, a poor blind person, two shillings for this week, and if she require any further assistance to be brought into the House.

18 January 1779
The Overseers of Melton being applyed to for relief of the wife of George Jay and three children certificate persons from Melton to Duxford in Cambridgeshire where they now are. Ordered that the Clerk do write to the Overseers of Duxford and acquaint them the family cannot be relieved at that distance but that they must be sent home.

12 April 1779
Ordered that the Governor do allow Ann, the wife of William Dallinger, belonging to the parish of Ufford (the said William Dallinger being a substitute in the Suffolk Militia) 2s. 4d. per week for the maintenance of her and one child from the tenth day

of October last (being the time of her fist application to the Directors and Guardians for relief) to this day being 26 weeks (£3 0s. 8d.), one half of which you are required to charge to the said Directors and Guardians and the other half to the Treasurer of the said County – agreeable to an Act of Parliament made in the 15th year of his present Majestys reign – and you are further required to continue to pay the said Ann Dallinger the said allowance of 2s. 4d. per week untill further orders or untill the said William Dallinger, her husband, shall be discharged from the service of his Majesty to be charged as before mentioned.

3 May 1779

\We the Directors of the Hundreds of Loes and Wilford in the County of Suffolk do recommend to the Weekly Committee Francis Foreman, a poor person belonging to the parish of Bromeswell, being old and infirm and incapable of maintaining himself as a proper object of charity, and do request that the Committee will order him an allowance of one shilling a week untill the next Quarterly Meeting, as witness our hands this 28th day of April 1779 <5 signatures>./[82]

Ordered that the Overseers of Bromeswell do allow Francis Foreman, being old and infirm, one shilling a week for this month in case he so long live.

17 May 1779

Ordered that the Governor do pay Richard Sheldrake, a certificate person from Kenton to Woodbridge continuing ill, three shillings for this week, and pay Mr Newson, the Surgeons bill, of thirteen shillings for attending him.

24 May 1779

Ordered that the Overseers of Wickham Market do allow William Cole, his wife continuing ill, five shillings, John Mallett his wife being ill, three shillings for last week, five shillings for the midwife, and two shillings and sixpence for this week, and if he requires any further assistance to send two of his children into the House, and James Sayer continuing ill, two shillings and six pence a week for this week and next, and John Reeve his wife continuing ill, two shillings for this week, and if he requires any further assistance to send two of his children into the House.

19 July 1779

\Sir,   Ipswich July the 13th '79
Dame Pilkington who belong to yr Hundrd is admitted to Mr Tooleys Foundation and as there is a room vacant I would put her in but the rule of the charity is to deliver in a certificate from where she belong. She is much distress as such it would be very kind of you to procure her one otherways she may loose the chance.
Thomas Nuthall/[83]

Ordered that the Clerk do give an order to the parish of St Margarets in Ipswich acknowledging Dorothy Pilkinton widow to belong to Bredfield.

15 November 1779

Ordered that the Governor do go to Framlingham and see whether there is a certificate for Robert Burroughs from Sutton being ill, and if so and if the man is

---

[82] Note inserted in SROI ADA11/A/B/3/2.
[83] Note inserted in SROI ADA11/A/B/3/2.

likely to get well soon to order three shillings a week for a fortnight more being allowed two weeks, and if he is not likely to get well to order the man and his wife into the House of Industry, and in the meantime that the Clerk do write to the Overseer of Framlingham to allow Burroughs three shillings for last week and three shillings for this week.

10 January 1780

Ordered that the Overseers of Capel do allow Margaret Fletcher being ill of a paralytic disorder, three shillings for last week, two shillings for this and two shillings for next, and the Widow Lough being ill and having four small children, three shillings for this week and three shillings for next.

17 April 1780

Ordered that Samuel Block wife and family from Charsfield having recovered of the small pox, and Block declaring that he has been well treated, be discharged from the House.

5 June 1780

Ordered that the Clerk do summon Mr Thomas Chandler of Butley to appear at the next Annual Meeting and bring evidence of a complaint made by him to the Justices at Woodbridge <> that the paupers in the said parish of Butley are not attended by a Surgeon in their illness that they are suffered to lay and die like dogs in a ditch and nobody goes near them to assist them in their distress or that he will be prosecuted and to write to Dr. Whimper to attend the said meeting on the above complaint.

The third Weekly Minute Book,
26 June 1780–16 February 1784[84]

26 June 1780

A Quarterly and Weekly Committee Meeting held at the White Hart <>
Present

Directors	Guardians
Francis Brooke Esq.	Mr Francis Hayle
The Revd Mr Frank	Mr John Cooper
The Revd Mr Jeaffreson	Mr Joseph Oldham
Mr John Whimper	Mr Thomas Chandler
The Revd Mr Fowller	Mr Thomas Crisp
The Revd Mr Purvis	
The Revd Mr Hingeston	
The Revd Mr Coles	
Mr Samuel Barber	
Mr John Barthorp	
Mr Samuel Salmon	
Mr Simon Paternoster	
John Revett Esq.	

Ordered that the Overseers of Ash do allow Robert Dawkins being infirm, Hannah Newson being bed rid, one shilling a week for each for this Qtr. in case they so long live.

Ordered that the Overseers of Brandeston do allow Susan Jeffrys with her infant bastard child, one shilling a week for this Qtr. in case the child so long live, and twenty shillings towards the burial of Stephen Watts, and John Spink his wife being ill, two shillings a week for two weeks.

Ordered that the Overseers of Butley do allow Sarah Crosby with her infant bastard child, and the Widow Ratcliff being infirm, one shilling a week each for this quarter in case they so long live and William Cook being ill, two shillings a week for two weeks.

Ordered that the Overseers of Bawdsey do allow Jane Sevenscraft with her two infant bastard children, two shillings and six pence a week for this quarter in case they so long live.

Ordered that the Overseers of Bredfield do allow Elizabeth Lankester with her infant bastard child, one shilling a week for this Quarter in case the child so long live.

Ordered that the Overseers of Capel do allow Mary Stebbing with her infant bastard child, one shilling a week for this quarter in case the child so long live.

---

84 SROI ADA11/A/B/3/3. Extracts taken from the third WMB run up to the closing date of the first QMB, March 1784. Entries after this date can be found in the chapter relating to the second QMB.

Ordered that the Overseers of Charsfield do allow Jeremiah Leggatt being old and infirm, and Mary Davy with her infant child, one shilling a week each for this Quarter in case they so long live.

Ordered that the Overseers of Creetingham do allow Thomas Bulmer being infirm and crazy, and his son being an ideot, and the wife of John Aldis being bedrid, one shilling a week each for this quarter in case they so long live.

Ordered that the Overseers of Earl Soham do allow Jeremiah Smith and his wife being old and infirm, two shillings a week for this quarter.

Ordered that the Overseers of Easton do allow Phoebe Girling, and the Widow Benham being ill, the Widow Wright having three small children, Frances Hurst, Mary Woodard and Jane Fricker Tyler with their infant bastard children, one shilling a week each for this Quarter <> the Widow Wright continuing ill, two shillings for this week over and above the aforesaid order.

Ordered that the Overseers of Eyke do allow Thomas Studd and his wife being ill, two shillings a week for this Quarter

Ordered that the Overseers of Kettleburgh do allow Mary Mann with her two infant bastard children, two shillings a week for this quarter.

Ordered that the Overseers of Kenton do allow Elizabeth Chenery a poor ideot child, one shilling a week for this Quarter.

Ordered that the Overseers of Letheringham do allow Ann Lyon with her infant bastard child, one shilling a week for this quarter.

Ordered that the Overseers of Monewden do allow the wife of Jeffry Boon with his five children, three shillings a week for this Quarter.

Ordered that the Overseers of Marlesford do allow Ann Chapman a poor bedrid person, eighteen pence a week, the wife of Thomas Burrell, the Widow Partridge, the Widow Knight being ill, and Mary Giles with her infant bastard child, one shilling a week each for this Quarter.

Ordered that the Overseers of Melton do allow Benjamin Johnson and Philip Sherwood being old and infirm, and Jane Crow with her infant bastard child, one shilling a week for this Quarter.

Ordered that the Overseers of Petistree do allow John Johnson, his wife and sister all being very old and infirm and ill, three shillings a week, Lionel Bradstreet and his wife also infirm, two shillings a week, Mary Barnard and Elizabeth Levett also infirm, Ann her daughter, Elizabeth Simpson being lame, Sarah Brown and Amy Lock with their infant bastard children, one shilling a week each for this Quarter.

Ordered that the Overseers of Sutton do allow Sarah Levis with her infant bastard child, one shilling a week for this Quarter.

Ordered that the Overseers of Ufford do allow the Widow Manning having three small children, and Sarah Prew and Elizabeth Fairs with their infant bastard children, one shilling a week each for this Quarter.

Ordered that the Overseers of Wickham Market do allow the wife of Thomas Finch with her four children (her husband having run away), two shillings and six pence a week, Robert Birch a crazy man, two shillings a week, Susanna Clarke with her two children, Mary Luff and Elizabeth Wright with their infant bastard children, one shilling a week each for this Quarter.

Ordered that the Overseers of Dallingho are required to allow Robert Hewitt being blind and bedrid, eighteen pence a week for this Quarter <> and Robert Clarke, twenty shillings towards the burial of his wife.

Ordered that the Overseers of Kenton do allow Thomas Clodd being ill, three shillings for this week over and above the former order and as soon as he and his wife can be removed to be brought to the House of Industry, and John Collins twenty shillings towards the burial of his wife.

Ordered that the Overseers of Hatcheston do allow the Widow Eagle being ill, two shillings for this week.

Ordered that the Overseers of Rendlesham do allow Esther Smith being an ideot, one shilling a week for this Quarter.

Ordered that the Treasurer do pay William Newstead of [   ] with Elizabeth Waterman a poor child about the age of eight years and an half belonging to Marlesford, one shilling a week for this Quarter.

Ordered that the Clerk do write to the Overseers of Sco Ruston in Norfolk that Wayman Bardwell and his family will not be granted a certificate or allowed a quarterly allowance, and if they can't subsist without any allowance to be removed to the House of Industry.

Ordered that the Overseers of Wickham Market do allow Thomas Grimwood twenty shillings towards the burial of his son, and to pay the Constables bill of £2 4s. 6d. for going after Thomas Finch.

Ordered that the Governor do allow Richard Sheldrake continuing lame, three shillings for this week.

Ordered that the Overseers of Butley do allow John Russell being lame, two shillings a week for two weeks, and Elizabeth Ellis having a sore breast, two shillings a week for two weeks.

\September 25th 1780

The goods of Mr Stiverson.

	£	s.	d.
2 old chairs	0	1	0
A table	0	1	0
A old cupboard	0	1	6
3 old coal bars and a hale	0	0	10
A old flock bed	0	9	0
4 old pucturs	0	0	4
	0	13	8/[85]

14 May 1781

Ordered that on Mr Jeptha Wallers being satisfied that Anthony Reed, a poor boy belonging to the parish of Shottisham now in the House of Industry can get employment, that on a note being sent by Mr Waller that the Governor do discharge the said Anthony Reed.

20 August 1781

Ordered that the Overseers of Hatcheston do allow James Garrod being ill of a fever and having 6 small children, 3s. for this week, Thomas Farrow and his wife being ill of a fever and having one child, two shillings and six pence for this week, and application being made for the relief of the wife of Hugh Reed being ill but his earnings being large the Committee did not think him an object of relief.

---

[85] Note inserted in SROI ADA11/A/B/3/3.

10 September 1781

Ordered that William Kettle of Butley (having recovered from a fever) his wife and three children, and the widow Ellis and her 2 daughters, Mary and Elizabeth, (a relation having promised to take care of Mary) now in the House of Industry be discharged from the said House.

22 October 1781

Ordered that the Governor do receive John Holmes, Thomas Holmes and William Holmes, and Charlotte Keable poor chidren of the parish of Hatcheston into the said House, and that the Governor do on Wednesday next apply to the Justices for orders to remove John Holmes to his place of settlement.

19 November 1781

Ordered that the Overseers of Dallingho do allow Sarah the wife of Samuel Keable he not being returned yet, 3s. a week for two weeks, and Richard Tyler 5s. in order to enable him to get to his wife and family at Norwich.

\A catelage of the goods belongin to John Wyard as follows
First a blue coat
A skerlet waiscoat
A pair of buck skin bretches
Two great coats and a frock
Two check aprons and a pair of stockings
Two silk hankerchiefs
Three wite hankerchiefs
A wite apron and two wollon shifts
One iresh shift and 2 undercoats
One outside coat and bonnet and cloake
A brass tea kittel
One silver tea spoon
A black trunk
In cash due six pounds sixteen shillings and six pence./[86]

17 February 1783

Application being made for relief for the wife of John Lyon being ill and having three children, but the man having constant work in husbandry. Relief is not thought necessary and likewise for John Amis being ill with the rheumatism ordered to be brought to the House.

7 July 1783

In pursuance of an order of the last Annual Meeting, Sarah Cottingham widow and Extrix of John Cottingham deceased, paid six guineas in full for the further maintenance of a male bastard child born of the body of Mary Creasy of Earl Soham for which a bond was given, which was delivered up agreeable to the said order and which said 6 guineas was paid to the Governor to be placed to the credit of the Corporation.

Ordered that the Overseers of Dallingho to go to Dovercourt and dispose of the effects of James Squire deceased, a certificate person belonging to the said parish,

---

[86] Note inserted in SROI ADA11/A/B/3/3.

117

and bring the wife and family to the House of Industry at the expense of the Corporation.

Ordered that the Overseers of Dallingho do pay twenty shillings towards the burial of James Squire a certificate man to Dovercourt, twenty two shillings for the doctor and nurses, and three shillings a week to the widow for this month.

15 September 1783

Mr Edward Mayer and Mr William Jones (who gave security for maintenance of a male bastard child born of the body of Lydia Moor of Bredfield 7th January 1781) going to leave the county, have proposed to pay £20 down on condition of the security being given up. Ordered and agreed that the said sum of £20 be accepted in full for the maintenance of the child from this time and that the bond be delivered up. <paid 22 September 1783.>

9 February 1784

It having appeared that the Governor hath corrected Samuel Holmes, a boy in the said House, in too severe a manner for not doing his stinted work, and the Governor thought reprehensible by this Committee hath been reprimanded accordingly and cautioned not to correct in the said House so severely in future.

16 February 1784

Hacheston. John Eagle having 6 children (without work abroad) 4s. last week, John Paxman being ill and having wife and 5 children, 4s. this week, James Noys (without work) and having wife and 5 children 4s. last week and 4s. this, and James Garrod being ill and having wife and 4 children, 4s. a week for last week and this, William Cook (without work) wife and 4 children 4s., John Knappit (without work), 4s. last week.

Miscellaneous documents linked to the passing
of the Act of Incorporation

1. Richard Wood's expenses associated with the initial public meetings
28 April 1766[87]

Loes & Wilford Hundreds 1764   Dr to Richard Wood as Committee Clerk

	£	s.	d.
August 23ᵈ Attending the meeting of the Gents. at Wickham Market to consider about obtaining an Act for the Relief of the Poor within the Hundreds of Loes and Wilford when the Petition was signed and the Committee appointed for settling the Heads of a Bill and making a list of the Committee.	1	1	0
Paid expences.	0	4	0
Making fair copy of list of Committee for Mr Kilderbee.	0	1	0
Oct. 8ᵗʰ Attending a meeting of the Committee at Wickham Market and taking down the Heads of a Bill.	1	1	0
Paid expences.	0	4	0
Drawing advertizement for another meeting of the Committee and fair copy for the printer.	0	2	6
Nov. 3d Attending a meeting of the Committee at Wickham Market when the Bill was read over and alterations made.	1	1	0
Paid expences.	0	4	0
Letters and messenger to the Overseers of Earl Soham, Brandeston, Easton, Kettleburgh, Monewden, Shottisham, and Bawdsey to meet Mr Kilderbee with their books to see the increase for the last 5 or 6 years.	0	14	0

---

[87] Richard Wood's bill for settling the Act of Incorporation. This document is useful for outlining the timeline for the obtaining of the Act. The Local Acts were introduced into the Commons. The process was: Petition submitted to bring forward a bill; First Reading, where no vote is taken; Second Reading, where general principles are discussed and voted on before passing to Committee Stage; Committee Stage, clauses of the bill examined in detail and suggested amendments offered; amendments considered at the Report Stage; Third Reading sees a debate and vote on the final text. The bill is then passed to the House of Lords where an almost identical process is followed. The (amended) bill is then passed to the House of Commons for scrutiny before processing for Royal Assent. This particular invoice relates to the meetings that took place in formulating the bill, obtaining Poor Rate assessments from the various parishes and then circulating the Act once the Royal Assent had been obtained. SROI ADA11/A/H/1/1.

1765

Jany. 23	Attending Mr Kilderbee and the Overseers of the above parishes at Woodbridge all day, examining their books and taking an account several years back to see the increase of the Poor's Rates.	1	1	0
	Letters and messenger to the Overseers of Earl Soham, Bawdsey, Boyton, Petistree, Marlesford, Ufford, Alderton, and Letheringham to meet Mr Kilderbee again with their books to see the increase of their rates.	0	16	0
Mar. 13th	Attending Mr Kilderbee, Mr Truelove and the Overseers of the above parishes at Woodbridge examining their books and taking an account several years back to see the increase of the Poor's Rates.	1	1	0
	Paid for the carriage of Acts.	0	0	6
	Distributing the several Acts to the Gents.	1	1	0
	Postage of letters.	0	5	0
	Drawing advertizement for the first meeting pursuant to the Act.	0	1	6
	Attending the Hon'ble Mr Nassau at Easton to know if he approved of it.	0	10	6
	Fair copy for the printer.	0	1	0
	Paid the printer.	0	12	0
	Drawing notice to serve on the officers of each parish within the Hundreds pursuant to the Act.	0	2	6
	34 fair copys to serve.	1	14	0
	Attending the Guardians at Wickham Market to get same signed.	0	10	6
	Service on the Overseers of 34 parishes at their houses.	1	14	0
		14	3	0

Received April 28th 1766 of John Rivett Esq. Treasurer the above contents.
£14. 3s. 0d.   Richard Wood

2. Fees and expenses incurred by N. Poyntz, the Incorporation's parliamentary agent

4 May 1765[88]

Session 1765

An account of fees and expenses upon passing the Act of Parliament for the better relief and employment of the poor in the Hundreds of Loes and Wilford in the county of Suffolk.

---

[88] James Kilderbee's payments to Poyntz for the passing of the Act of Incorporation. This document is useful in outlining the various stages to the bill's passage through Parliament. SROI ADA11/A/A/1/23.

	£	s.	d.
Paid for reading the Petition and order of reference.		15	4
For copies for said Committee.	10	0	
Paid Committee fees on the petition.	2	19	8
Settling the report title of the Bill and copy.		6	8
Paid for entering the report in the Journal and order for said Bill.	1	3	4
For printing settling and blanking said Bill.	5	5	0
Fair copy.	3	6	0
do for printer.	3	6	0
Fair copy for the House.	3	6	0
Drawing the brief of said Bill.	1	1	0
Fair copy for the Speaker.	5	0	
Paid Great Fees on Second Reading of the Bill.	28	0	0
For copies for said Committee.	10	0	
For filling up printed Bill with the amended words for the Members of the Committee.	4	1	0
For examining and settling the report.		13	4
Paid committee fees on the Bill.	6	4	0
For a Bill filled up complete for the Ingrossing clerk.		12	0
do for the printer.		12	0
For examining the Ingrossed Act and proof act from the press with the draft Bill and amendments.	1	1	0
Paid for Ingrossing the Act.	32	10	0
Paid Housekeepers and Messengers fees.	3	6	0
Paid door keepers for delivering the Bills.	1	1	0
At the House of Lords			
Paid Great fees on Second Reading of the Bill.	54	0	0
Paid for the order of the Committee.	1	1	0
Paid for swearing witnesses.		4	0
Paid committee clerks fees.	4	4	0
Paid yeoman ushers fees.	1	1	0
Paid door keepers fees.	4	4	0
Coach hire, letters, porters and other small expences and gratuities to servants of both Houses	1	15	6
Paid for printing the Bill and Acts for both House of Parliament to send into the country.	20	9	6
For my trouble in passing the Act through both Houses of Parliament.	21	0	0
	208	13	4
Rec'd off Mr Kilderbee.	160	0	0
Remains due	48	13	4

Rec'd May 4th 1765 of Mr Kilderbee the contents in full. N. Poyntz

3. Cost of designing and manufacturing the Incorporation's seal

The Hundreds of Wilford & Loes[89]

1765		£	s.	d.
Dec. Paid for a design for a seal for the Hundred.		0	3	0
Paid for the seal.		6	6	0
Paid carriage.		0	7	0
Letters and postage about it.		0	3	6
The money paid the clerk of the House of Commons being in all £208 13s. 4d. upon which a profit arises to the Solicitor of the Bill. The Solicitor hopes he is intitled to interest for the same from the time of payment till the money was raised viz.				
Paid him on the 24th Aug 1765 £160. Interest thereof from that time to 24th April 1766.		8	0	0
The like to the 16th May 1766 when the money was received.		0	9	6
Paid clerk of the House in full the 4th May 1765 £48 13s. 4d. interest thereof for one year.		2	8	6
		17	17	6

4. Fees and expenses incurred by N. Poyntz, the Incorporation's parliamentary agent[90]

16 May 1766

The Hundreds of Wilford & Loes

1764		£	s.	d.
Apl. 23	Attending a meeting this day to come to resolutions concerning incorporating the Hundreds for better maintaining and providing for the Poor .	1	1	0
	Drawing resolution and fair copy.		3	6
	Dr and Ingrossing Petition to Parliament for the above purposes.		5	0
	Parchment.		1	0
	Letters to Lord Maynard, Mr Holt and Sir Charles Bunbury to acquaint them of being named of the Committee and also Lord Orwell.		10	6
	Dr advertisement of meeting for 8th Oct. and attended printers.		1	6
	Paid advertising twice.		7	0
Oct. 8th	Attended meeting at Wickham Market and taking down the Heads of a Bill etc.	1	11	6
	Perusing several acts of Parliament in order to draw Bill.	1	1	0

---

89 SROI ADA11/A/A/1/23. James Kilderbee's bill for settling the Act of Incorporation.
90 SROI ADA11/A/A/1/23.

		£	s	d
	Drawing Bill.	5	5	0
	Fair copy.	1	12	0
Nov. 3rd	Attended at Wickham Market, examining same and making alterations out two days.	2	2	0
	Chaise hire etc.	1	1	0
	Two fair copies of Draft Bill as settled one for Agent and one for myself.	3	4	0
	Paid Agent perusing Bill and examining same.		6	8
	Fair copy for Sir Charles Bunbury.	1	12	0
	The like for Mr Holt.	1	12	0
	The like of Petition.		2	0
	The like of exemption.		1	0
	Fair copy of Bill for the press.	1	12	0
1765				
Jan. 7th	Agents attending Mr Holt with Bill and Petition in Pall Mall.		6	8
	The like Sir Charles Bunbury, Whitehall.		6	8
Jan.14th	Attending the House when petition referred to a Committee.		13	4
Jan 23rd	Journey to Woodbridge to meet the Overseers of several parishes with Mr Truelove to examine the Poor rates in order to make proof of the allegations in the Petition.	1	1	0
	Chaise hire etc.		7	0
	Paid expenses of Overseers etc.	1	1	6
Jan 25th	Agent attending Mr Holt to appoint the Committee.		6	8
Feb. 4th	The like.		6	8
	Journey to London on the 2nd to attend the Committee of the House of Commons to prove the allegations in the Petition and a hearing and proving same, attending, correcting the press to prevent errors in the printed copies out from home necessarily on this occasion 13 days.	13	13	0
	expences at 7s. 6d. a day.	4	17	6
	Horse hire.	1	12	6
	Lodgings.	1	0	0
	Paid Mr Truelove for his journey to London and and attending to prove the utility of the scheme.	5	5	0
	Agent attending the Committee.	6	8	0
	Agents attending & examining printing Bill.	6	8	0
	Agents attending the First Reading and getting a copy of the general poor bill.	6	8	0
Mar. 13th	Journey to Woodbridge with Mr Truelove to make further searches as to the increasing expences of the poor to lay before the Lords which was advised to be necessary.	1	1	0
	Expenses of Mr Truelove and self and officers who attended.	14	0	0
April	Journey to London to attend the House of Lords			

to prove the allegations in the Petition and finish the business out necessarily 12 days.		12	12	0
Expences at 7s 6d per day.		4	10	0
Lodgings.		1	0	0
Paid Mr Truelove for his journey and attending.		5	5	0
Coach hire and expenses for Mr Truelove & self up & down.		3	12	6
Paid carriage of Acts of Parliament and postage thereof.			7	6
Porters and coach hire in town both times.			6	9
Letters and postages.			6	6
July 1st	Journey to Wickham to attend the first meeting after the Bill had passed self and clerk attending same.	1	11	6
	Chaise hire and expences.		16	6
July 2nd	Paid advertising.	4	0	0
		87	15	11
Paid Mr Poyntz as by his bill.		208	13	4
		296	9	3
Deduct fair copy of bill charged by mistake for the printer.		1	12	0
		294	17	3

Rec'd this 16 May 1766 of John Revett Esq. Treasurer of the contents above in full James Kilderbee.

Documents associated with the building
of the house of industry

Preparation and purchase of the site, documents 5–21

5. Simon Paternoster's bill for measuring the site[91]

27 May 1766

Rec'd. of John Revett Esq. by the order of the Directors of the Poor of the Hundreds of Loes and Wilford the sum of ten shillings and sixpence for measuring the lands purchased by the said Directors of the Reverend Mr Jeaffreson.

By me Simon Paternoster.

6. Robert Lust's charges for peeling two loads of bark on the site[92]

30 May 1766

The account of peeling of two loads of bark apon the lands late belonging to the Revd Mr Jeferson of Melton.

May 30. To 5 days work of 5 men at 1s. 6d. each.	£1	17s. 6d.
To two men 3 days and a ½ the same.	£0	10s. 6d.
	£2	8s. 0d.

Received in full contence.   Robert Lust.

7. Robert Clarke's charges for felling timber on the site[93]

2 June 1766

Acount of the time of felling the timber oaks apon the lands late belonging to the Revd Mr Jeferson of Melton.

To 6 days of Robert Clarke at 2s. 0d. per day.	0	12s. 0d.
To 5 days and a half of John Gilingham.	0	11s. 0d.
	1	3s. 0d.

Received the contents in full as above by me Robt. X Clarke.

8. John Hearn's charges for removing the felled timber from the site[94]

3 June 1766

Recd. of Daniel Manthorp the sum of eleven shillings and three pence in full for making six loads and three quarter of wood apon the lands late belonging to the Revd Mr Jefreson of Melton.

---

91 SROI ADA11/A/H/1/1.
92 SROI ADA11/A/H/1/1. The bark, once removed, would have been sold separate from the timber.
93 SROI ADA11/A/H/1/1.
94 SROI ADA11/A/H/1/1.

Rec'd by me John Hearn.   X his mark.

9. Payment to Matthew Grayston for his building plan[95]

3 June 1766

Of John Rivett Esq. Treasurer for the Hundreds of Loes and Wilford the sum of five pounds and five shillings for a plan approved of by the Directors for a Poor House for the said Hundreds.   Matthew Grayston.

10. Anthony Matthew's charges for valuing trees on the site[96]

5 June 1766

Received of Francis Brook Esq. by the hands of Daniel Manthorp the sum of ten shillings and six pence for valuaring a parcel of tress apon the lands that late belonged to the Reverend Mr Jeafffreson by me.   Anthony Matthew.

11. Daniel Manthorp's receipt for sale of bark from the site[97]

21 June 1766

Paid Daniel Manthorp the sum of four pounds for bark on account of the trustees of the general workhouse. Benj. Evans.

12. Daniel Manthorp's charge for inspecting the bark peelers[98]

4 July 1766

Of Fran. Brooke the sum of fifteen shillings in full for my trouble of inspecting the bark peelers and selling said wood for the Directors of Hs of Loes & Wilford. by me   Daniel Manthorp.

13. Costs involved with the Act of Incorporation[99]

5 July 1766
Mr Wood
1766   To Creighton & Jackson Deb[t]

Advertisement notice to persons willing to sell a parcel of land for use of the Directors of the Poor in the Hundreds of Loes and Wilford Feb. 22 March.	0	7	0
Do Meeting of Directors of the Poor in the Hundreds of Loes and W at the White Hart Wickham. March 29 April 5. 12 Letter 1ᵈ.	0	10	7
Do Meeting of Directors of the Poor in the Hundreds of Loes and W at White Hart Wickham to purchase land etc. April 19: 26, May 10.	0	7	0
Printing 200 blank bonds for money borrowed by the Directors of the Poor Loes & W Hundreds whole sheets with endorsement on fine writing Demy.	1	1	0

---

95 SROI ADA11/A/H/1/1.
96 SROI ADA11/A/H/1/1.
97 SROI ADA11/A/H/1/1.
98 SROI ADA11/A/H/1/1.
99 SROI ADA11/A/H/1/1.

	£	s.	d.
Do 200 broadsides particulars of management in the Poor House in the Hundred of Loes and W. Fools Cap.	0	15	0
Advertisement meeting of Directors of the Poor Hundreds of Loes and W at White Hart Wickham. May 3: 10.	0	7	0
Do Meeting of Directors of the Poor Hundreds of Loes and W at White Hart Wickham to receive plans for Poor House. May 17: 24.	0	7	0
Do Meeting of Directors of the Poor Hundreds of Loes and W at White Hart Wickham to receive proposals and estimates for Poor House. May 31 June 7.	0	7	0
Do Meeting of Directors of the Poor in Hundreds of Loes and W to consider further of a plan for House of Industry. June 7:14.	0	7	0
Do Meeting of Directors of the Poor in Hundreds of Loes and Wilford at White Hart Wickham to receive estimates for Poor House. June 21: 28.	0	7	0
Printing 50 particulars for building a House of Industry fools cap folio pica letter.	1	4	0
	5	19	7

July 5 1766. received the contents in full for partner and self.   Wm. Jackson.

14. Matthew Grayston's charges for revised plans of the house of industry[100]

7 July 1766

Rec'd. of John Revett Esq. Treasurer for these Hundreds of Loes and Wilford the sum of ten pounds and ten shillings for my trouble in settling the plan elevation section and particulars for a building for the said Hundreds.
Matthew Grayston.

15. Thomas Aldis' bill for attending directors over the plans for the house of industry[101]

7 July 1766

Rec'd. of John Rivett Esq. Treasurer for the Hundreds of Loes & Wilford the sum of two pounds and two shillings for my trouble attending the Directors.   Thos. Alldis.

16. Payment to Revd Christopher Jeaffreson for crops on the land[102]

7 July 1766

	£	s.	d.
36 sacks of hayseeds.	4	10	
Fetching from Mr Jenneys.		7	6
Expences.		1	
Harrowing and rolling.		8	6
Clover 5 pockets & ½.	1	14	4½
Sowing clover.		2	1½

---

[100] SROI ADA11/A/H/1/1.
[101] SROI ADA11/A/H/1/1.
[102] SROI ADA11/A/H/1/1.

Sowing hayseed.   4   3
                                         7   7   9
Rec'd. of Mr Revett the contents of this bill.   by me C Jeaffreson.

17. Money received of Francis Brooke for wood and bark[103]

8 July 1766

The Directors of the House of Loes & Wilford 1766. Dr to F Brooke.

June 5th pd Mr Matthews. 0 10 6	Recd of Mr Evans for	
	Two loads of bark. 4 0 0	
To 5¾ days work to R. Clarke		
& John Gilingham for felling		
of the timbers. 1 3 0	Recd of do for the peelings	
	of the bark. 1 16 0	
Pd J. Hearne for making six		
loads & ¾ of wood. 0 11 3	Recd by six and half loads	
	of wood at 12s per load. 3 18 0	
Paid Lust for peeling of barks 2 8 0		
Paid Danl Manthorp for		
his trouble etc. 0 15 0	9 14 0	
Gave to sd fellers and	5 12 9	
bark peelers. 0 5 0	remains due to directors. 4 1 3	
5 12 9		

18. Richard Wood's expenses associated with planning the House of Industry[104]

14 July 1766

The Directors of the Poor within the Hundreds of Loes & Wilford.
1766   Dr to Richd Wood.

	£	s.	d.
Paid the printer advertizeing meeting for the Overseers			
to receive their books.	0	7	0
Paid *do* advertizeing meeting for the 4th Nov.	0	10	9
Service of notices of the sums assessed on the several			
Churchwardens and Overseers of the several parishes in			
the Hundreds.	1	14	0
Paid printer advertizeing meeting for appeals.	0	7	0
May 1st Journey to Ipswich to order the printing the securitys and			
getting the same stampt and to order the printing the particulars			
of the Management of the House, horse hire & expences.	1	1	0
12th Five securitys signed by the Directors to Mr Barthrop			
for £1,000 at £200 each.	0	12	6
Five counterparts signed by Mr Barthrop.	0	12	6
Paid Mr John Shave for two books for Treasurer & Clerk	1	6	0
Paid Mr Jackson the printer his bills for advertizements			

---

103 SROI ADA11/A/H/1/1.
104 SROI ADA11/A/H/1/1.

and printing securitys & particulars etc.	5	19	7
Paid Mr Walford for stamps to securitys.	7	12	0
Paid expences at the several meetings.	2	1	6
Clerks salary due the 1st July 1766.	10	10	0
Letters and carriage of parcells.	0	5	0
	32	18	10

July 7th To my trouble in attending and having the builders all the last week at my House taking off the plan and sections.

1	1	0
33	19	10

Rec'd. July 14th 1766 of John Rivett Esq. Treasurer for the Hundreds of Loes and Wilford the above contents.   Richard Wood.

19. Revd Christopher Jeaffreson's payment for timber and pollards[105]

14 July 1766

Rec'd. of Mr John Revett the sum of seventy three pounds and five shillings in full for timber and pollards sold to the Directors of the Poor of the Hundreds of Loes and Wilford.

14 July 1766.   By me C Jeaffreson.

20. Extracts from Abstract of Title Deeds relating to certain lands and hereditaments in the parish of Melton or Ufford purchased by and conveyed to the use of the guardians of the poor within the hundreds of Loes and Wilford, 1766[106]

25 November 1766

By indentures of lease and release the lease made between Christopher Jeaffreson of Melton, Clerk, and Mary his wife, of the one part and Richard Wood of Melton, Gentleman, of the other part and the Guardians of the Poor within the Hundreds of Loes and Wilford.

It is witnessed that in consideration of the sum of £852 12s. to the said Christopher Jeaffreson and Mary his wife paid by the Guardians.

All these four several pieces or parcels of arable land situate lying and being in Melton or Ufford.

Assigns whereof the first is called the Six Acre Piece and buts on the next mentioned piece of land in part and a piece of Ufford glebe land in part East on the lands of John Whincopp, Gentleman, West on Hackeris Land North on a piece of land called Walnut Tree Close belonging to Richard Gater South and contains by estimate seven acres two roods and twenty two perches.

The second piece is called the Three Acre Piece and buts upon the next mentioned called the Road Close East on the before mentioned piece West on Ufford Glebe land North and on Walnut Tree Close aforesaid South and contains by estimation four acres and one rood.

The third piece is called the Road Close and buts on the lands of Francis Brooke Esquire in part and the lands of Jonathan Burward Esquire in part East on the before

---

mentioned Three Acre piece in part and Ufford Glebe land aforesaid in part West on Hackeris Lane aforesaid North and on Orphan Close next mentioned South and contains by estimation nine acres three roods and twenty four perches.

And the fourth piece is called Orphan Close and buts on the lands of the said Jonathan Burward as well as East as South on the Road Close aforesaid North and on Walnut Tree Close aforesaid West and contains by estimation seven acres one rood and seventeen perches.

To hold the said four pieces of land thereby released unto said Richard Wood and his heirs. To the only use of the said Guardians of the Poor within the Hundreds of Loes and Wilford.

21. Extracts from Abstract of Title Deeds relating to certain lands and hereditaments in the parish of Melton or Ufford purchased by and conveyed to the use of the guardians of the poor within the hundreds of Loes and Wilford, 1773[107]

15 December 1773

By indentures of feoffment between John Edwards of Dennington Gent., of the first part and Richard Wood of Melton Gent., of the second part and the Guardians of the Poor of the third part.

In consideration of the sum of £15 15s. the said John Edwards did give grant bargain sell alien infeoff <> all that piece of land lying in Melton containing by estimation half an acre more or less abutting on a piece of land of the said Guardians whereon the House of Industry is erected towards the East West and North and on another piece of land of the said Guardians towards the South and late in the tenure or occupation of the said John Edwards and Thomas Crisp their under tenants or assigns.

The contract with the builders

22. Articles of Agreement with John Lane for constructing the House of Industry[108]

22 July 1766

Articles of agreement indented made concluded and fully agreed upon the [   ] day of [   ] in the year of Our lord <1766> between the Guardians and Directors of the Poor within the Hundreds of Loes and Wilford in the county of Suffolk of the one part and John Lane of Ipswich in the said county of Suffolk carpenter of the other part as follows.

First the said John Lane doth for himself his heirs executors and administrators covenant promise and agree to and with the said Guardians and Directors and their successors by these presents that he the said John Lane his executors administrators workmen agents or assigns shall and will at his their some or one of their own proper costs and charges on or before the Tenth day of October which will be in the year of Our Lord <1767> level the ground and also build erect compleat and finish

---

[107] SROI ADA11/A/A/1/24.

[108] SROI ADA11/A/H/1/1. These articles were never put into effect. Matthew Grayston and Thomas Fulcher's articles are no longer extant. See also 29 July 1766.

or cause to be built erected compleated and finished for the said Guardians and Directors in a neat substantial and workmanlike manner and according to the best rules of workmanship and architecture and with the best materials of the sorts and scantlings mentioned and described in and by the proposals and particulars to these presents annexed a new house or houses other buildings and offices thereto upon a certain piece of land lately purchased for that purpose lying and being in Melton in the said county according to the forms dimensions and descriptions mentioned and described in the plan elevation and sections thereof lately made and agreed upon by the said Guardians and Directors and the said John Lane and in the said proposals and particulars hereto annexed. And shall and will do execute and perform or cause to be done executed and performed all the work contained mentioned and set down in the said proposals and particulars annexed and according to the plan elevations and sections hereby referred to which proposals particulars and plans are signed by [   ] of the said Directors which were present at the execution hereof and the said John Lane.

And that he the said John Lane his executors or administrators shall and will compleat and finish all the said buildings and turn the key thereof or cause to be compleated and finished and the key turned of the said buildings and ntiles according to the dimensions proportions and forms mentioned and agreed to and according to the intent and true meaning of these presents and of the partys hereto and of the said plan elevations and sections hereby referred to and the said proposals particulars and descriptions hereunto annexed on or before the said tenth day of October which will be in the year of Our Lord one thousand seven hundred and sixty seven.

And that the said John Lane his executors or administrators shall not nor will make use of work upon or put into the said building any materials of any sort or kind whatsoever until the surveyor or inspector appointed or to be appointed by the said Guardians and Directors to examine the materials and inspect the execution of the aforesaid works or the committee to be appointed to superintend the said building shall have approved thereof and consented thereto. And shall not nor will do or cause to be done any brick work belonging to any part of the said buildings after the [ ] day of October and before the [ ] day of February next without the licence and consent of such surveyor or inspector or the said committee to be appointed to superintend the said buildings under his or their hands for that purpose first had and obtained.

And the said Guardians and Directors in consideration of the premises do for themselves and their successors covenant grant and agree and with the said John Lane his executors and administrators by these presents that they the said Guardians and Directors or their successors shall and will well and truly pay and cause to be paid to the said John Lane his executors or administrators for the said buildings workmanship and materials the sum of four thousand three hundred and fifty pounds in the proportions and at the times following that is to say the sum of one thousand pounds part thereof when the drains, cellars and foundations of the main buildings wings and offices shall be made raised or built to the water tables. The sum of five hundred and fifty pounds more when the first floor of joists of the same building shall be laid on. The sum of five hundred and fifty pounds more when the said buildings shall be raised or built up to the eves and garrett floor of joists laid. The sum of seven hundred pounds more when all the said last mentioned buildings shall be tiled in. The sum of five hundred and fifty pounds more when the offices to the said buildings shall be erected and finished. And the remaining sum of one thousand pounds when all the buildings and works shall be compleated finished surveyed and measured.

And it is hereby further covenanted concluded and agreed upon by and between the said partys to these presents that in case the said Guardians and Directors or their successors shall at any time hereafter during the time of building the said premises be minded to alter anything in the design or draft thereof by adding thereto or diminishing therefrom that such addition or alteration shall not be esteemed a variation or departure from the said agreement so as to vacate or set aside the same but that it shall be lawful for the said Guardians and Directors or their successors so to do only paying or allowing such reasonable price or making such abatements deductions or allowances for such alterations as shall be agreed upon between the said partys to these presents or do the same shall be valued and estimated at by two persons of sufficient skill and understanding of the value of buildings to be agreed upon between the said Guardians and Directors and the said John Lane for that purpose.

And also that he the said John Lane his executors and administrators shall and will at his and their own proper costs and charges when and as soon as conveniently can be after the first floor of joists of the main building and wings shall be laid on cause or procure all the said buildings intended to be erected as aforesaid to be well and sufficiently insured from fire in some or one of the publick offices of insurance for the said sum of four thousand three hundred and fifty pounds and keep and continue the same so insured until the said buildings shall be compleated finished surveyed and measured as aforesaid.

23. Performance bond of Thomas Fulcher and Matthew Grayston[109]

29 July 1766

Know all when by these presents that *we Matthew Grayston of Woodbridge in the county of Suffolk carpenter, Thomas Fulcher of Debenham in the said county, carpenter, John Grayston of Woodbridge aforesaid carpenter and [   ] are* held and firmly bound to *the Guardians and Directors of the Poor within the Hundreds of Loes and Wilford in the said county of Suffolk in the sum of nine thousand pounds* of good and lawfull money of Great Britain to be paid to the said *Guardians and Directors* or *their* certain attorney successors or assigns for which payment to be well and faithfully made. *We* bind *ourselves and each of us by himself for the whole and every part thereof and the* heirs executors and administrators of *us and each of us* firmly by these presents sealed with our seal dated the *twenty ninth* day of *July* in the *sixth* year of the reign of our sovereign Lord *George the third* by the Grace of God of Great Britain France and Ireland King defender of the faith and in the year of Our Lord One Thousand Seven Hundred *and Sixty Six*

The condition of this obligation is such that if the above bounden *Matthew Grayston and Thomas Fulcher their* heirs executors administrators or assigns do well and truly observe perform fulfill accomplish pay and keep all and singular the covenants grants articles clauses provisions payments conditions and agreements whatsoever which on the part and behalf of the said *Matthew Grayston and Thomas Fulcher their* executors administrators assigns are or ought to be observed performed fulfilled accomplished paid and kept comprised or mentioned in *certain articles of agreement* bearing date with these presents and made or expressed to be made between *the said Guardians and Directors of the poor within the Hundreds*

---

[109] SROI ADA11/A/H/1/1. The words in italics were completed by hand on a pre-printed form.

of Loes and Wilford in the county of Suffolk of the one part and the said Matthew Grayston of Woodbridge in the said county of Suffolk carpenter and Thomas Fulcher of Debenham in the said county carpenter of the other part in all things according to the true intent and meaning of the same then this present obligation to be void and of none effect or use to be and remain in full force power and virtue.

Sealed and delivered being first duly stamped (the several erasures and interlineations being first made) by the above Matthew Grayston, Thomas Fulcher and John Grayston in the presence of Charles Long Jun., Dudley Long.
Signed Matthew Grayston.   Thomas Fulcher.   John Grayston.

24. Letter to John Lane from the directors offering release from his contract[110]

4 December 1766

Melton Dec. 4 1766

Mr Lane
At the last meeting of the Directors of the Poor for the Hundreds of Loes and Wilford it was ordered that I should acquaint you that if you will make them satisfaction at the next meeting which is to be held on Monday the twelfth day of January next at the White Hart in Wickham Market for the damage sustained by the cutting the barley according to your order that they will then discharge you of all other damages. But if you refuse this offer then that they will prosecute you not only for that but for all other damages sustained by the non-performance of your agreement with the utmost severity of the law of which you will please to take notice from.
Your Hon'ble servant.   Richard Wood.

25. Letter concerning the builders' request for an advance payment of £500[111]

12 January 1767

Wickham Market, January 12 1767.

Sir
Mr Grayston the builder of the House of Industry for the Hundreds of Loes & Wilford having this day applied to us for the payment of five hundred pounds as a part of the thousand pounds due to him and partner for the first payment which would have been payable this day if it had not been for the frost. And he has agreed that if we will advance him this sum he will not demand the other £500 until the 2nd March which we have agreed for our next meeting. And as it will be an indulgence to the builders have agreed & do order that you pay Matthew Grayston and Thomas Fulcher the sum of five hundred pounds as a part of their first payment which will be due to them from the Directors when they have compleated the drains and buildings to the water tables. We are, Sir,
John Rivett Esq.   <7 named directors>

---

[110] SROI ADA11/A/B/2/4.
[111] SROI ADA11/A/H/1/1.

26. Payment of Grayston's earlier request for an advance of £500[112]

13 January 1767

Recd. of Mr Revett the sum of five hundred pounds proficient to the within written order.

By me Matthew Grayston.

27. Second instalment to Grayston and Fulcher[113]

2 March 1767

Recd. of John Revett Esq. Treasurer for the Hundreds of Loes and Wilford by the payment of Mr Richard Wood the sum of five hundred pounds being the remaining part of one thousand pounds due to me and Thomas Fulcher my partner for the first payment for the building of the House of Industry for the said Hundreds.

I say received for the use of self and partner Thomas Fulcher.   Matthew Grayston.

28. Initial payment of second instalment to Grayston and Fulcher[114]

11 May 1767

Recd. of John Revett Esq. Treasurer of the Hundreds of Loes & Wilford the sum of two hundred pounds in part of the sum of seven hundred pounds which will be due for the second payment for the building of the House of Industry for the said Hundreds when the floor joists shall be laid.

By me Matthew Grayston.

29. Proposals for preparing the garden belonging to Melton house of industry[115]

6 June 1768

For the better improving the land I think the whole ought first to be sanded which cannot be done for less than 8s. per rod square at one load per rod and the same to be taken out of the pitt on the premises.

Leveling plowing and harrowing the ground at 3d. per rod square.

Digging or trenching the same at 6d. per rod square.

The walks:

If gravel at 6d. per yard square.   Sand 2 per yard.

Turf 2½ per yard.   Hayseeds at 1½ per yard.

Edging at 2 per yard.

If turf'd the Guardians to provide a proper place to cut the turf off.

June 6 1768.   John Blowers

---

[112] SROI ADA11/A/H/1/1.

[113] SROI ADA11/A/H/1/1.

[114] SROI ADA11/A/H/1/1.

[115] SROI ADA11/A/B/2/4.

30. Proposals for alterations to Melton house of industry[116]

8 April 1778

An estimate of the carpenter work and stuf as to be don at the House of Industry in Molton as follows a fir plate to be laid onto the potition wall betwin the spinning rooms to be 10 inch by 4 inchs square and five fir posts 4 feet long each to be 9 inchs square for to support the dormans upon the plate the wholl to be planed and fixed up for the sum of three pounds by me Daniel Manthorp Junr.

Legal matters

31. Jerome Bright's expenses associated with the prosecution of James Woolnough, one of the demonstrators against the building of the house of industry during the summer of 1765[117]

29 July 1766

A bill of expences laid out by Jerome Bright in going to attending at and coming from Bury Summer Assizes 1766 in the trial of the King against James Woolnough.

		£	s.	d.
Expences	At Ipswich.	0	0	8
	At Stow Market.	0	1	6
	At Bury.	0	8	0
	At Woolpit.	0	0	8
	At Stow Market.	0	1	6
	At Ipswich.	0	1	6
	Horse hire.	0	7	6
	3 days time.	0	6	0
		1	6	6

Rec'd July 29 1766 of John Rivett Esq. Treasurer the above contents by me. Jerome Bright.

32. Richard Wood's bill for various legal expenses[118]

3 August 1767

The Directors of the poor within the Hundreds of Loes & Wilford

1766	Dr to Richard Wood.	£	s.	d.
The King				
Agst.	Attending Mr Carthew for examination.	0	6	8
Woolnough.	Three subpoena tickets.	0	3	0
	Service on Mr Rivett.	0	3	4
	Service on Jerome Bright.	0	3	4
	Gave him therewith.	0	2	6
	Service on Mr Jeaffreson.	0	3	4
	Paid Mr Carthews clerk for recognizances.	0	8	0

---

[116] SROI ADA11/A/B/2/4.
[117] SROI ADA11/A/H/1/1.
[118] SROI ADA11/A/H/1/1.

	Attending, examining witnesses in order to prepare brief.	0	6	8
	Drawing brief.	0	6	8
	Fair copy for Councell.	0	6	8
	Fair copy of examination to annex to brief.	0	3	4
	To Mr Rant with brief.	1	1	0
	To his clerk.	0	2	6
	Attending him.	0	3	4
	Attending clerk of assize to proffer and settle the indictment.	0	6	8
	Paid him for subpoena indictment recogn etc.	3	1	8
	Paid cryer swearing witnesses.	0	1	0
	Paid for chaise for Mr Jeaffreson.	2	8	0
	Paid expences.	2	2	0
July 24 25 26 & 27	Journey and attending the Assizes being out four days.	4	4	0
	Drawing articles between the Directors and Mr John Lane for the building.	0	10	0
	Ingrossing two parts.	1	0	0
	Paper and duty.	0	5	6
	Ingrossing the particulars three large sheets.	1	10	0
	Paper and duty.	0	8	3
	Covenant bond and duty.	0	6	8
	Mr Lane refusing to execute articles making special bond from Matthew Grayston to the Directors to execute articles, paper & duty.	0	10	6
	Altering the articles for the building between Messrs Grayston and Fulcher and the Directors.	0	6	8
	Ingrossing two parts.	1	0	0
	Paper and duty.	0	5	6
	Perusing the title deeds and making long abstract of Mr Jeaffresons title to the estate purchased by the Directors.	1	1	0
	Fair copy for Mr Rant.	0	10	6
	Drawing conveyance by lease & release from Mr Jeaffreson and wife to Mr Wood Trustee for the Guardians.	1	1	0
	To Mr Rant to peruse and settle abstract and draft of conveyance.	2	2	0
Aug 16th	Journey to Ipswich and attending Mr Rant with same horse hire and expences.	1	1	0
	Five securitys to Mrs Wythe for £500 and five counterparts.	1	5	0
	Four securitys to Mr Jeaffreson for £400 and four counterparts.	1	0	0
	Two securitys to Mrs Ann Growse for £250 and two counterparts.	0	10	0
	Drawing bargain and sale to be inrolled from Mr Jeaffreson and wife to Mr Wood			

Trustee for the Guardians.	1	1	0
Ingrossing lease and release.	1	5	0
Parchment and duty.	0	7	6
Ingrossing bargain and sale to be inrolled.	1	1	0
Parchment and Duty.	0	4	0
Attending executing the above writings.	0	6	8
Attending Mr and Mrs Jeaffreson to Mr Tye at Woodbridge to acknowledge bargain and sale before him as a Master in Chancery.	0	6	8
Paid him.	0	7	6
Paid stamping bargain and sale.	0	5	0
Attending the Stamp Office for that purpose.	0	6	8
Paid inrolling.	1	7	10
Attending several times for that purpose.	0	13	4
Carriage and porterage of Bargain and Sale to and from London.	0	4	0
Four securitys to Mr Wm White for £400 and four counterparts.	1	0	0
The like to Mrs Eliz Growse for £450.	1	0	0
Two securitys to Mrs Ann Growse for £200 and two counterparts.	0	10	0
One security to Mr Jas. Sherwood for £100 and one counterpart.	0	5	0
Paid Mr Jackson the printer his bill.	2	2	5
Paid Mr Walford for stamps for securitys.	7	10	0
Paid expences at the several meetings.	1	18	6
Clerks salary due the 1st July 1767.	10	10	0
Letters and messengers.	0	6	0
	63	15	4

Rec'd. Augst 3d 1767 of John Revett Esq.
Treasurer the above contents.   Richard Wood.

33. Richard Wood's charges for legal expenses[119]

23 June 1768
The Directors of the Poor within the Hundreds of Loes & Wilford.
1767   Dr to Richd Wood.

		£	s.	d.
Augst 3d	Three securitys to Mrs Eliz. Johnson for £300 and three counterparts.	0	15	0
	Two securitys to Mrs Mary White for £200 and two counterparts.	0	10	0
	One security to The Revd Mr Chris Jeffreson for £100 and one counterpart.	0	5	0
Novr 2d	Seven securitys to Mrs Ann Browne for £700 and seven counterparts.	1	15	0
	Three securitys to Mrs Frances White for £300			

---

119 SROI ADA11/A/H/1/1.

	and three counterparts.	0	15	0
	One security to Mrs Ann Growse for £100 and one counterpart.	0	5	0
	One security to Mr John Sherman for £100 and one counterpart.	0	5	0
Dec[r] 14th	One security to Mr Joseph Simonds for £100 and one counterpart.	0	5	0
	Paid Mr Jackson the printer for advertizements to the 12th Dec.	0	17	7
1768				
Feb[ry] 1st	One security to the Revd Mr John Sparrow for £100 and one counterpart.	0	5	0
	One security to Mr Ralph Randall for £100 and one counterpart.	0	5	0
	Paid Mr Brewer attending to approve of the patterns produced at this meeting for cloathing the poor by order of the Directors.	1	1	0
	Paid his expences.	0	3	6
29th	Six securitys to Mrs Elizabeth Gooding for £600 and six counterparts.	1	10	0
	One security to the Revd Mr James Sherwood for £100 and one counterpart.	0	5	0
Apr[l.] 11th	Twenty securitys to Nathaniel Fletcher Esq. for £2,000 and twenty counterparts.	5	0	0
	One security to Mrs Mary White for £100 and one counterpart.	0	5	0
June 6th	Five securitys to Mr Philip Catt for £500 and five counterparts.	1	5	0
	Paid Mr Jackson the printer his bill.	4	4	4
	Paid Mr Walford for stamps for securitys.	7	10	0
	Paid my expences at the several meetings.	1	8	6
	Paid for wax for sealing securitys.	0	4	0
	Letters, messengers and parcells.	0	7	6
	Clerks salary due 1st July 1768.	10	10	0
	Rec'd. June 23[d] 1768 of John Revett Esq.	39	16	5
	Treasurer the above contents.　　　Richd Wood.			

34. Richard Wood's bill for legal expenses[120]

24 March 1769[121]

The Directors and Acting Guardians of the Poor within the Hundreds of Loes & Wilford.

---

[120] SROI ADA11/A/H/1/1.

[121] This invoice highlights the substantial sums of money that could be expended on settlement cases. Snell mentions that settlement cases could be very costly, citing that they often rose to over £20 a case, with the average cost rising considerably between 1760 and 1810. The three examples here came to £9 15s. 2d (Elizabeth Woolnough), £5 10s. 8d. (Stephen and Lydia Osbourn) and £2 18s. 2d. (Thomas Woolnough). K. Snell, *Parish and Belonging: Community, Identity and Welfare in England and Wales, 1700–1950* (Cambridge, 2006), p. 66.

		£	s.	d.
1768	Dr. to R Wood.			
Dec 26th	Expences attendg the Genl Quarterly Meeting.	0	5	6

1768 Dr. to R Wood.
Dec 26th Expences attendg the Genl Quarterly Meeting. 0 5 6
1769

The inhabitants of Sutton appellts and the inhabitants of Walpole
respondts

	£	s.	d.
Attending, taking instructions for and appeal to the order of removal of Elizabeth Woolnough by order of the Directors and Acting Guardians.	0	6	8
Notice of appeal and two fair copys for the officers to sign .	0	5	0
Attending twice at Sutton to examine witnesses in order to prepare brief.	0	13	4
Attending the pauper and Samuel Garrod, examining them.	0	6	8
Letter and postage to and from Mr Chambers at Norwich to retain him for the Appellnts.	0	3	4
Paid him retaining fee.	1	1	0
Three subpoena tickets.	0	3	0
Service on Henry Garrod Thomas Chevason and Samuel Garrod.	0	10	0
Gave Samuel Garrod same.	0	2	6
Letters and postage to and from the Justices Clerk with copy of examination and paid him.	0	3	4
Drawing brief.	0	6	8
Fair copy for Councell.	0	3	4
Copy of examination to annex to brief.	0	1	0
To Mr Chambers with brief.	1	1	0
To his clerk.	0	1	0
Attending him.	0	3	4
1769 Paid Clerk of the Peace for order etc.	0	17	0
Jan. 8 9th Journey to Beccles to try the appeal out			
&10th three days horse hire and expences.	4	4	0

The inhabitants of Creetingham appellts and the inhabitants of Otley
Respondts

	£	s.	d.
Attending, taking instructions for appeal to the order of removal of Stephen Orsbourn and Lydia his wife by order of the Directors and Acting Guardians.	0	6	8
Notice of appeal and two fair copys for the officers to sign.	0	5	0
Service of same on the Officer at Otley.	0	6	8
Paid for copy of examination.	0	1	0
Letter and postage to and from Mr Rant to retain him for the appellnts.	0	3	4
Paid him retaining fee.	1	1	0
Attending examining the pauper in order to prepare brief.	0	6	8
Drawing brief.	0	6	8
Fair copy for Councell.	0	3	4
Copy of examination to annex to brief.	0	1	0
To Mr Rant with brief.	1	1	0

To his clerk.	0	1	0
Attending him.	0	3	4
Paid witness attending to prove service of notice of appeal.	0	2	0
Jany 11th Attending Qtr. Sessions at Woodbridge when the respondnts moved for a respite for want of Councell which was granted.	0	10	6
Paid Clerk of the Peace auditing Treasurers Accts.	0	10	6
Drawing case by order of the Weekly Committee for Mr Rants opinion concerning the settlement of Thomas Woolnough removed by order from Blythburgh to Hatcheston.	0	3	4
Fair copy for Mr Rant.	0	3	4
Paid him therewith.	1	1	0
Attending him with and for the same.	0	10	6
Paid the printer advertiseing Qtly Meeting.	0	11	6
Paid for letters and parcells.	0	2	6
Paid for paper and wax.	0	2	6
One quarters salary to Lady 1769.	5	0	0
	24	2	0

Rec'd March 24 1769 of John Revett Esq.   The above contents Richard Wood.

Investment in the Incorporation

35. An account of the money borrowed by the directors from April 1766 as well as the repayments made from 3 October 1770. The account closes on 12 June 1783.[122]

Date of securitys	To whom made	at what part of the rates	for securing what sum
April 28th 1766	Robert Barthrop of Hollesly, Gent.	one 50th part	200.0.0
do	do	do	200.0.0
do	do	do	200.0.0
do	do	do	200.0.0
do	do	do	200.0.0
Oct. 13th 1766	Eliabeth Wycth of Wickham Market, spinster.	one 100th part	100.0.0
do	do	do	100.0.0
do	do	do	100.0.0
do	do	do	100.0.0
do	do	do	100.0.0
do	Christopher Jeaffreson of Melton, Clerk.	do	100.0.0
do	do	do	100.0.0
do	do	do	100.0.0
do	do	do	100.0.0

---

[122] SROI ADA11/A/B/1/1, a table located in the final pages of the QMB.

do	Ann Growse of Bury St Edmunds, spinster.	one 75th part	150.0.0
do	*do*	one 100th part	100.0.0
March 2nd 1767	William White of Bury St Edmunds, Gent.	*do*	100.0.0
do	*do*	*do*	100.0.0
do	*do*	*do*	100.0.0
do	*do*	*do*	100.0.0
do	Elizabeth Growse of Sutton, spinster.	one 75th part	150.0.0
do	*do*	one 100th part	100.0.0
do	*do*	*do*	100.0.0
do	*do*	*do*	100.0.0
do	Ann Growse of Bury St Edmunds, spinster.	*do*	100.0.0
do	*do*	*do*	100.0.0
do	James Sherwood of Stonham Aspall, clerk.	*do*	100.0.0
August 3rd 1767	Elizabeth Johnson of Wickham Market, spinster.	*do*	100.0.0
do	*do*	*do*	100.0.0
do	*do*	*do*	100.0.0
do	Mary White of the town of Cambridge, spinster.	*do*	100.0.0
do	*do*	*do*	100.0.0
do	Christopher Jeaffreson of Melton, clerk.	*do*	100.0.0
Nov. 2nd 1767	Anne Browne of Ipswich, Spinster.	one 100th part	100.0.0
do	*do*	*do*	100.0.0
do	*do*	*do*	100.0.0
do	*do*	*do*	100.0.0
do	*do*	*do*	100.0.0
do	*do*	*do*	100.0.0
do	*do*	*do*	100.0.0
do	Frances White of the town of Cambridge, spinster	*do*	100.0.0
do	*do*	*do*	100.0.0
do	*do*	*do*	100.0.0
do	Ann Growse of Bury St Edmunds, spinster.	*do*	100.0.0
do	John Sherman of Melton, Gent.	*do*	100.0.0
Dec. 14th 1767	Joseph Simonds, Gent.	*do*	100.0.0
Feb. 7th 1768	John Sparrow of Kettleburgh, clerk.	*do*	100.0.0
do	Ralph Randall of Melton, collar maker.	*do*	100.0.0
Feb. 29th 1768	Elizabeth Gooding of Bawdsey, spinster.	*do*	100.0.0

do	*do*	*do*	100.0.0
do	*do*	*do*	100.0.0
do	*do*	*do*	100.0.0
do	*do*	*do*	100.0.0
do	*do*	*do*	100.0.0
do	James Sherwood of Stonham Aspall, clerk.	*do*	100.0.0
April 11th 1768	Mary White of Cambridge, spinster.	*do*	100.0.0
do	Nathaniel Fletcher of Ipswich Esq.	*do*	100.0.0
do	*do*	*do*	100.0.0
do	*do*	*do*	100.0.0
do	*do*	*do*	100.0.0
do	*do*	*do*	100.0.0
do	*do*	*do*	100.0.0
do	*do*	*do*	100.0.0
do	*do*	*do*	100.0.0
do	*do*	*do*	100.0.0
do	*do*	*do*	100.0.0
do	*do*	*do*	100.0.0
do	*do*	*do*	100.0.0
do	*do*	*do*	100.0.0
do	*do*	*do*	100.0.0
do	*do*	*do*	100.0.0
April 11th 1768	Nathaniel Fletcher of Ipswich Esq.	one 100th part	100.0.0
do	*do*	*do*	100.0.0
do	*do*	*do*	100.0.0
do	*do*	*do*	100.0.0
do	*do*	*do*	100.0.0
June 6th 1768	Philip Catt of Easton, Gent.	*do*	100.0.0
do	*do*	*do*	100.0.0
do	*do*	*do*	100.0.0
do	*do*	*do*	100.0.0
do	*do*	*do*	100.0.0
March 29th 1769	Jonathan Burward of Woodbridge, Esq.	*do*	100.0.0
do	*do*	*do*	100.0.0
do	*do*	*do*	100.0.0
do	*do*	*do*	100.0.0
do	*do*	*do*	100.0.0
Oct. 3rd 1770	paid to Elizabeth Gooding.	one security of	100.0.0
Oct. 5th 1770	paid to Nathaniel Fletcher.	*do*	100.0.0
July 9th 1771	*do*	*do*	100.0.0
do	*do*	*do*	100.0.0
Oct. 11th 1771	*do*	*do*	100.0.0
do	*do*	*do*	100.0.0
do	*do*	*do*	100.0.0
do	*do*	*do*	100.0.0

do	*do*	*do*	100.0.0
do	*do*	*do*	100.0.0
do	*do*	*do*	100.0.0
do	*do*	*do*	100.0.0
do	*do*	*do*	100.0.0
Sept. 30th 1771	William Parmenter of Playford, Gent.	one 100th part	100.0.0
do	*do*	one 100th part	100.0.0
do	*do*	one 100th part	100.0.0
Dec. 30th 1771	Hannah Chapman of Easton, Spinster.	one 100th part	100.0.0
Dec. 30th 1771	Southwell Golding of Petistree, Farmer.	one 100th part	100.0.0
do	*do*	*do*	100.0.0
do	*do*	*do*	100.0.0
do	*do*	*do*	100.0.0
Jan. 11th 1772	paid to Nathaniel Fletcher.	one security of	100.0.0
do	*do*	*do*	100.0.0
April 11th 1772	*do*	*do*	100.0.0
do	*do*	*do*	100.0.0
do	*do*	*do*	100.0.0
do	*do*	*do*	100.0.0
do	*do*	*do*	100.0.0
do	*do*	*do*	100.0.0
March 30th 1772	John Harper of Hasketon, Farmer.	one 100th part	100.0.0
do	*do*	*do*	100.0.0
do	Elizabeth Bates of Wickham Market, spinster.	*do*	100.0.0
do	Elizabeth Ellis of Tunstal, widow.	*do*	100.0.0
do	Mary Dawkins of Woodbridge, widow.	*do*	100.0.0
do	John Sparrow of Kettleburgh, clerk.	*do*	100.0.0
April 13th 1772	Paid to Christopher Jeafferson.	one security of	100.0.0
	do		100.0.0
Dec. 21st 1772	*do*		100.0.0
March 24th 1773	Paid to Robert Scolding extor of Robt Barthrop Esq.		200.0.0
March 29th 1773	W. Negus of Melton Esq.	one 100th part	100.0.0
do	Ann Bates of Wickham Market, widow.	*do*	100.0.0
June 30th 1773	paid to extors Wm Negus Esq. L. Growse.	one security	100.0.0
Dec. 27th 1773	paid to extors Mrs Hannah Chapman.	one security	100.0.0
do	The Honble Richd Savage Nassau.	one 100th part	100.0.0

March 28th 1774	Paid to the Revd Mr John Sparrow.	one security	100.0.0
Sept. 17th 1774	Paid to Ralph Randall.	one security	100.0.0
Oct. 5th 1774	Paid to Eliz Brill late Gooding	do	100.0.0
do	do	do	100.0.0
do	do	do	100.0.0
Oct. 12th 1774	Paid to Extors of Robt Barthrop.	one security	200.0.0
do	do	do	200.0.0
Oct. 13th 1774	Paid to Christopher Jeaffreson.	one security	100.0.0
Nov. 12th 1774	Paid to Susanna White. (late Eliz Wycth).	do	100.0.0
do	do	do	100.0.0
do	do	do	100.0.0
Nov. 12th 1774	Paid to Ann Gibbs (late Brown).	one security	100.0.0
Dec. 6th 1774	Paid to Mary Gee (late White).	do	100.0.0
do	Paid to Eliz Lany. (late Wm White's).	do	100.0.0
do	Paid to Ann Gibbs (late Brown).	one security	100.0.0
Oct. 10th 1774	Jenney Braham of Campsey Ash spinster.	one 100th part	100.0.0
do	do	do	100.0.0
do	do	do	100.0.0
do	do	do	100.0.0
do	do	do	100.0.0
do	do	do	100.0.0
do	do	do	100.0.0
do	do	do	100.0.0
do	do	do	100.0.0
do	do	do	100.0.0
do	do	do	100.0.0
do	do	do	100.0.0
do	do	do	100.0.0
do	do	do	100.0.0
do	do	do	100.0.0
do	do	do	100.0.0
Nov. 12th 1774	Daniel Copland of Yoxford clerk & Legria Brown of Beccles.	do	100.0.0
April 28th 1775	Paid to the exetors of Robt Barthrop.	one security	200.0.0
Oct. 10th 1775	do	do	200.0.0
do	Paid to Mrs Mary Lany (late Jeaffresons).	one security	100.0.0
do	Paid to Miss Eliz Lany (late Wm Whites).	do	100.0.0

do	Paid to do (late Ann Growse).	two securitys	200.0.0	
do	Paid to Eliz Doyley. (late Eiz Bates).	one scurity	100.0.0	
do	Jenney Braham of Campsey Ash spinster.	one 100th part		100.0.0
do	*do*	*do*		100.0.0
do	*do*	*do*		100.0.0
do	Southwell Goulding of Petistree farmer.	*do*		100.0.0
do	*do*	*do*		100.0.0
do	Mary Kemp of Brandeston spinster.	*do*		100.0.0
do	*do*	*do*		100.0.0
March 25th 1776	Ann Revett of Wickham Market Spinster.	*do*		100.0.0
April 9th 1776	Paid to Mrs Frances White.	two securitys	200.0.0	
April 26th 1776	Paid to John Sherman Esq.	one security	100.0.0	
Feb. 3rd 1777	Paid to the Revd Mr Gee (late Mary Whites).	*do*	100.0.0	
June 30th 1777	Paid to Mr John Gross (late Eliz Goodings).	*do*	100.0.0	
Oct 30th 1777	Paid to Mrs Mary Dawkins.	one security	100.0.0	
Feb 2nd 1778	Paid to Mr Brand of Jon Burward Esq.	two securitys *do*	200.0.0	
March 27th 1778	paid to Miss Mary Kemp.	one security	100.0.0	
Oct 2nd 1777	paid to Mr Robt Scholding (late Eliz Johnsons).	*do*	100.0.0	
April 9th 1778	James Haran of Tunstal Yeoman.	one 100th part		100.0.0
April 18th 1778	Paid to Mr Brand of Jon Burward Esq.	one security	100.0.0	
July 4th 1778	Paid to Mr Brand of Jon Burward Esq.	one security	100.0.0	
Oct. 7th 1778	Paid to Mr Brand of Jon Burward Esq.	one security	100.0.0	
Dec. 28th 1778	Paid the Hon Mr Nassau	one security	100.0.0	
March 27th 1779	Paid to Mr Salmon extor of Eliz Ellis	one security	100.0.0	
March 27th 1780	Paid to Mrs Ann Bates late Wm Negus	one security	100.0.0	
October 1780	Paid to Mr Newcomen one security late Eliz Johnson.		100.0.0	
Dec 1780	*do*		100.0.0	
Jan. 22 1783	William Jennens of Acton Esq.	one 100th part		100.0.0
Jan. 22 1783	*do*	*do*		100.0.0
Jan. 22 1783	*do*	*do*		100.0.0
Jan. 22 1783	*do*	*do*		100.0.0
Jan. 22 1783	*do*	*do*		100.0.0

Jan. 27th 1783	Paid to the exetors of Mrs Jane Whimper.	3 securitys	300.0.0
do	Paid to the Extors of Mr John Syed.	2 securitys	200.0.0
May 26th 1783	Jonathan Dains of Falkenham Gent.	one 100th part	100.0.0
do	*do*	*do*	100.0.0
do	*do*	*do*	100.0.0
do	*do*	*do*	100.0.0
do	*do*	*do*	100.0.0
do	*do*	*do*	100.0.0
do	*do*	*do*	100.0.0
do	*do*	*do*	100.0.0
June 11th 1783	Rebecca Kersey of Framsden widow.	*do*	100.0.0
do	*do*	*do*	100.0.0
June 29th 1783	Southwell Goulding of Petistree Gent.	*do*	100.0.0
do	*do*	*do*	100.0.0
June 12th 1783	Paid to Joseph Rust one security Late Ann Bates.		100.0.0

Extract from the First Treasurer's Account Book, 1781–91[123]

An assessment made by the Directors and Acting Guardians within the Hundreds of Loes and Wilford, in the county of Suffolk, upon every parish within the said Hundreds, pursuant to an Act of Parliament made in the fifth year of the reign of his Majesty King George the Third, intitled, "An Act for the Better Relief and Employment of the Poor in the Hundreds of Loes and Wilford in the County of Suffolk." Parishes in Loes Hundred:

	Per Quarter				Per Quarter		
	£	s.	d.		£	s.	d.
Ash	25	13	2	Brought forward	*172*	*12*	*8¼*
Brandeston	16	14	3	Hacheston	17	17	4½
Butley	16	16	4	Hoo	6	2	3
Charsfield	23	9	0¼	Kettleburgh	13	8	6
Creetingham	20	0	6¼	Kenton	20	16	6½
Dallingho	14	0	2¼	Letheringham	8	3	10½
Earl Soham	20	2	1	Monewden	3	18	11½
Easton	23	11	5¼	Marlesford	24	7	7¼
Eyke	12	15	8	Rendlesham	9	3	2
	172	*12*	*8½*		276	10	6½

Parishes in Wilford Hundred:

Per Quarter   Per Quarter

---

[123] SROI ADA11/A/C/1/1/1.

	£	s.	d.		£	s.	d.
Alderton	14	18	9¼	Brought forward	96	11	1½
Bawdsey	11	1	6	Melton	18	7	8¼
Boulge	7	4	8	Petistree	15	9	8
Bredfield	18	9	5¼	Ramsholt	15	18	1
Bromeswell	6	19	2¼	Sutton	36	14	4½
Boyton	2	10	7½	Shottisham	6	8	11¼
Capell	9	17	10¼	Ufford	23	14	10¼
Debach	2	5	4	Wickham Market	27	2	3¼
Hollesly	23	3	9	Wilford	240	17	0
carried forward	96	11	1½	Loes	276	10	6¼
				Total	517	7	6¼

The Directors and Guardians of the Poor of the Hundreds of Loes and Wilford.

Dr.

To Simon Paternoster Treasurer.

1781		£	s.	d.
1 June 25	To cash paid the Revd Mr Jeaffreson for 33 comb of wheat, 25cb. thereof at 25s. 6d. per cb. and the other 8cb. at 23s. per cb.	41	1	6
	To *do* paid Francis Brooke Esq. for 29Cb. of wheat 25s. 6d. per cb.	39	19	6
	To *do* paid Ash allowance for last quarter.	2	19	0
June 29	To *do* paid to Mr Wood to get a draft of Mr Riches, to be sent to Mr Roach wool and yarn factor.	175	0	0
July 2	To *do* paid by order to Ann Proctor the late Matron for her journey and expences from and to London.	5	5	0
July 3	To *do* paid to the Packman on account.	20	0	0
July 7	To *do* paid Mr Catt for ½ a year's interest of £500 due to the 6 June last.	10	0	0
July 11	To *do* paid the Clerk of the Peace for auditing the accounts and expences at the Qtly Meeting and Qtr. Sessions.	1	1	0
	To *do* for procuring £200 of Mr Goulding for the use of the Corporation making the security, journies, horsehire and expences.	1	1	0
July 16	To *do* paid to the Packman on acct.	30	0	0
July 18	To *do* paid to Mr Creighton for ½ a year's interest of £200 due the 28 Feb. and the 2 of Mar. last.	4	0	0
July 26	To *do* paid to the Packman on account.	30	0	0
July 30	To *do* paid John Baker for wood to the House of Industry.	25	10	0
Aug. 4	To *do* paid Francis Brooke for 12cb. of wheat at 25s. 6d.	15	6	0
Aug. 7	To *do* paid Mr Salmon's bill for 17 pigs etc.	6	9	0
Aug. 20	To *do* paid the Packman on account.	30	0	0
Sept. 3	To *do* paid to the House Clerk as by Voucher.	39	16	10¼
Sept. 10	To *do* paid the Packman on account.	30	0	0
	To *do* paid to Mrs Pipe for 2 years interest of £100 due the 3 August last.	8	0	0

	To a journey, horsehire, and expences to borrow the two last mentioned sums, as I had none in hand nor any of my own by me. Interest etc.	0	5	0
Sept. 24	To Ash allowance.	2	16	0
	To Brandeston *do.*	2	6	2
	To Butley *do.*	7	16	4
	To Charsfield *do.*	1	14	0
	To Creetingham *do.*	9	8	6
	To Dallingho *do.*	3	10	0
	To Earl Soham *do.*	2	11	0
	To Easton *do.*	5	7	6
	To Eyke *do.*	1	11	0
	To Hatcheston *do.*	4	13	0
	To Hoo *do.*	0	7	6
	To Kenton *do.*	2	2	0
	To Monewden *do.*	1	12	0
	To Marlesford *do.*	8	7	0
	To Rendlesham *do.*	0	14	0
	To Kettleburgh *do.*	1	5	0
	To Alderton *do.*	2	0	0
	To Bawdsey *do.*	2	7	6
	To Boulge *do.*	1	6	6
	To Bredfield *do*	2	17	0
	To Bromeswell *do.*	3	7	0
	To Boyton *do.*	0	2	6
	To Capell *do.*	2	19	3
	To Debach *do.*	0	9	0
	To Hollesly *do.*	1	5	0
	To Melton *do.*	7	5	0
	To Petistree *do.*	4	15	0
	To Ramsholt *do.*	0	4	0
	To Sutton *do.*	2	13	0
	To Ufford *do.*	6	8	6
	To Wickham *do.*	8	4	6
	To Mr Gosling's bill.	51	19	2
	To Mr Cronie's bill.	38	14	1½
	To Mr Gross's bill.	18	15	0
	To Thomas Wright's bill.	2	0	0
	To Edward Fletcher's bill.	0	13	4
	To Thomas Perrimen's bill.	4	4	0
	To Daniel Manthorp's bill.	1	1	0
	To Thomas Hicks's bill.	2	13	4
	To Mr Brewster's bill.	4	9	3
	To Mr Lankester's bill.	5	3	8
	To Mr Newson's bill.	3	14	1½
	To Mr Collett's bill.	0	7	10
	To Mr Oldham's bill.	18	19	4½
	To Mr Randall's bill.	2	1	6
	To Mr Hurwood's bill.	0	18	0
	To Mr Garrett's bill.	1	5	2

To Mr Wood's bill & salary.	16	14	6
To Thomas Turtel's bill.	2	13	3
To Mr John Barthorp's bill for malt.	18	15	0
To Mr Riches bill for buying 163 comb of wheat at 3d. per comb.	2	0	9
To Dr. Newson's bill for medicines & attendance on Robert Wilson of Kesgrave.	0	12	6
Paid the Packman on account.	10	10	0
and for 18 weeks wages at 9s. per week up to the day.	8	2	0
To Mr Whimper's bill and salary for this quarter.	8	16	6
To Mr Hinchman's Receipt for a Qtr. Salary.	5	5	0
To Mr Salmon's *do* for *do.*	21	5	0
The House Clerk's whole disbursements £77 14s. 5½d. in part of which he had as in above £39 16s. 10¼d.	37	17	7¼
To the Chaplain's salary for this Quarter.	8	15	0
To the Treasurer's do, postage and letters.	2	15	0
	915	19	7
Balance in the Treasurer's hands at Mich. 1781.	102	12	6

Per contra.

		Crs.		
		£	s.	d.
	By balance in the hands of the Treasurer at Midsummer 1781.	123	15	8¼
June 25	By cash received of the overseer of Ash for last quarter which should have been paid at the Previous Meeting.	25	13	2
June 29	By Rec. of Mr Goulding which was this day borrowed of him at a Special Committee of the whole Corporation held at the House of Industry on note at 5 per cent.	200	0	0
July 26	By *do* recd for a fine set upon Mr Tibbs for embezzling wool etc.	120	0	0
Aug. 7	By *do* recd of Mr Moore for the last payment for Amy Locke's bastard child by Wm. Levett.	5	0	0

Sep 24	Rec'd of the House Clerk which he rec'd of Robert Robinson of Marlesford on account					
	of a note for a bastard.	£15	0s.	0d.		
	of Holmes for two calves.	£1	2s.	0d.		
	for eggs.	£0	1s.	3d.		
	of Mr Tibbs a balance on Wyard's acct.	£3	16s.	2½d.		
	of Edmund Stannard on acct of a note for a bastard.	£4	0s.	0d.		
	of Harland towards his wife and childrens maintenance.	0	6s.	0d.		
	of *do* for *do.*	0	4s.	0d.		
	of Mr Perriman for 2 strikes of bran.	0	0s.	6d.		
	of Wm Copping for 33 strikes of *do.*	0	8s.	3d.		
	of Mr Salmon for 30 *do.*	0	7s.	6d.		
	of Mr Crisp for 120 *do.*	£1	10s.	0d.	26	15	8½

By cash rec'd of the several parishes.		517	7	6¼
		1,018	12	1

149

SECOND QUARTERLY MINUTE BOOK
28 June 1784–2 August 1791/April 1795[1]

28 June 1784

Directors	Present	Guardians
John Revett Esq. President	Mr William Whincopp	Mr N. K. Chandler
The Revd Mr Hingeston	Mr James Catchpole	Mr James Aldous
The Revd Mr Cole	Mr Nathaniel Steptoe	Mr Samuel Jeaffreson
Mr Samuel Barber	Mr Thomas Stammers	Mr John Felgate
Mr John Barthorp	Mr John Cooper	Mr Andrew Blake
Mr Francis Hayle	Mr Thomas Whimper	Mr James Pipe
Mr Nathaniel Barthrop	Mr William Whimper	Mr Robert Adams
Mr John Levett		

The following persons were duly elected Directors and Acting Guardians for the year ensuing:

	Directors	1st Quarter	Guardians
July	The Revd Mr Jeaffreson		Mr Thomas Darby
	Mr Francis Hayle		Mr William Cotton
			Mr James Catchpole
August	The Revd Mr Cole		Mr John Catt
	The Revd Mr Gunning		Mr Jeremiah Wase
			Mr John Scotchmer
Sept.	Earl of Rochford		Mr Thomas Moss
	John Tovell Esq.		Mr John Cooper
			Mr Henry Edwards
Oct.	Mr John Levett	2nd Quarter	Mr Thomas Whimper
	Mr William Whimper		Mr John Weeding
			Mr Joseph Kersey
Nov.	Francis Brooke Esq.		Mr Thomas Simpson
	Anthony Collett Esq.		Mr James Woods
			Mr John Waller
Dec.	The Revd Mr Purvis		Mr Benjamin Cooper
	The Revd Mr Frank		Mr Thomas Crisp
			Mr Robert Vertue
Jan.	Mr William Waller	3rd Quarter	Mr John Gross
	Mr Nathaniel Barthrop		Mr Philip Dikes
			Mr Nathaniel Fuller
Feb.	John Brand Esq.		Mr John Welham
	Mr James Lynn		Mr Nathaniel Bennington
			Mr James Aldous

---

[1] Entries in SROI ADA11/A/B/1/2, the second QMB, end on 2 August 1791. Subsequent entries are taken from the draft QMB, SROI ADA11/A/B/2/5, until April 1795.

Mar.	The Revd Mr Hingeston		Mr Nathaniel Steptoe
	Mr Benjamin Cooper		Mr Nathaniel Keeble
			Chandler
			Mr Samuel Jeaffreson
April	Mr John Whimper	4th Quarter	Mr John Stopher
	Mr John Baldry		Mr James Smith
			Mr Richard Syer
May	John Revett Esq.		Mr Henry Topple
	The Revd Mr Williams		Mr John Jeaffreson
			Mr Thomas Hicks
June	Mr Samuel Barber		Mr Thomas Ablitt
	Mr John Barthorp		Mr John Pitcher
			Mr James Pipe

Ordered that Mr Simon Paternoster be continued Treasurer, the Revd Mr Palmer Chaplain, Mr Richard Wood Clerk, Mr Samuel Salmon, Mr Thurston Whimper, and Mr William Henchman, Surgeons, Mr John Elliott, Governor, and Mrs Christian Brightwell, Matron for the year ensuing at their usual salarys.

Thomas Fox of Shottisham, butcher, having refused to accept Keeble Cook, a pauper ordered at last Quarterly Meeting to be apprenticed to him from Lady Day last. Ordered that the indentures be allowed by two Justices and tendered with the said pauper to the said Thomas Fox, and in case of refusal to sign the counterpart of the indenture and accept the apprentice that he be proceeded against for the recovery of the penalty that will be incurred by such refusal.

Proposed by Mr John Barthorp that the buying of flour is not so advantageous to the Corporation as buying of wheat. Ordered that the same be considered and ballotted for at the next Quarterly Meeting.

Proposed by John Revett Esq., that the following order be argued at the next Quarterly Meeting, and if approved of be entered as a bye law viz.

That no person whatsoever, being of age to account for himself or herself, shall be received into the House of Industry unless he or she produce to the Weekly Committee an examination taken in writing by a Magistrate to prove that the last place of his or her legal settlement is within the Hundreds of Loes and Wilford. That no children or infants shall be received into the said House until the examination of the father, if living and residing with his family, shall be taken by a Magistrate and produced to the Weekly Committee by the Overseer of the Poor of the parish where such poor child or children shall reside. If the father of such poor child or children be dead or not to be found, the examination of the mother shall be taken and produced to the Weekly Committee, or the examination of such better evidence as can be procured by the said Overseer of every parish within the said Hundreds respectively. That all examinations respecting the last place of legal settlement of such paupers as shall be received into the said House shall be filed by the Governor, and registered by him in a book to be kept for that purpose. The above regulation is not intended to prevent, nor does it prevent, Directors and Acting Guardians from sending paupers into the said House who shall be afflicted with the Small Pox or other pestilential disease or with broken limb or being maimed or afflicted with other sudden accidental complaints.

4 October 1784

The order respecting the examinations to be taken of paupers to be received into the House of Industry proposed by John Revett Esq. at the last Quarterly Meeting is this day agreed to confirmed, and ordered to be taken and observed as a rule and bye law of this Corporation.

Ordered that the proposal made by Mr John Barthorp a Director at the last Quarterly Meeting for buying wheat instead of flour be deferred to and considered of at the next Quarterly Meeting.

27 December 1784

Ordered that the Clerk do prosecute an appeal to an order of William Truelove and John Spooner, two Justices, for the removal of Mary Alexander widow of Jonas Alexander and Mary, Jonas, William and James their children from the parish of Saint Nicholas in Ipswich to the parish of Campsey Ash.

28 March 1785

The case of John Thompson of Bredfield, sawyer, having been argued and considered, and it appearing that it would be very injurious to the Corporation, as well as to him, to refuse granting him a certificate (although into a Corporation town) he having made it appear that his average earnings are 16s. a week and that he could not procure such work in the Incorporated Hundreds. Ordered that the said John Thompson, Susan his wife and six children to wit Charlotte aged eleven years, Frances aged ten years, John aged eight years, Alice Ann aged seven years, James aged one year, and Nancy aged three months have a certificate to the parish of St. Nicholas in Harwich, in the County of Essex.

Ordered that Thomas Fox of Shottisham butcher, be indicted at the next Quarter Sessions for beating and ill-treating Keeble Cooke his apprentice bound by the Directors and Guardians, and that the clerk do proceed against him thereon as he shall see proper or be advised at the expense of the Corporation.

Ordered that the proposals made by Mr John Barthorp, for buying wheat instead of flour, be deferred and considered at the next Quarterly Meeting.

Proposed by John Revett Esq. that the children in the House of Industry shall not be apprenticed or let to service until they have been six months in the said House. To be argued at the next Quarterly Meeting.

27 June 1785

Directors Present	Guardians
Mr John Revett Esq. President	Mr John Cooper
The Revd Mr Cole	Mr Nathaniel Steptoe
The Revd Mr Hingeston	Mr William Cotton
Mr Samuel Barber	Mr William Whimper
Mr John Barthorp	Mr Richard Wilkinson
Mr John Whimper	and
Mr Francis Hayle	Mr Thomas Whimper

Ordered that the Clerk do lay a case before Mr Le Blanc for his opinion whether the Directors and Guardians can, under the Corporation Act, apprentice any children for any term or number of years less than to the age of twenty one years.

Ordered that the Weekly Committee do buy wheat in the best manner they can for use in the House of Industry for this quarter. That the Governor do get it ground in the best manner he can, and that he do procure flour for the said House until the wheat can be ground.

Ordered that the yarn in the hands of Mr Williams belonging to the Corporation be imediately sold.

Ordered that the sum of seven hundred pounds be borrowed for the use of the Corporation in order to pay Mr Simon Paternoster the Treasurer the same, being advanced by him for the use of the Corporation and that the Clerk do prepare proper assignments accordingly.

The following persons were duly elected Directors and Acting Guardians:

	Directors	1st Quarter	Guardians
July	The Revd Mr Jeaffreson		Mr Thomas Garneys
	Mr Francis Hayle		Mr John Ralph
			Mr James Catchpole
Aug.	The Revd Mr Gunning		Mr William Heffer
	Mr Richard Wilkinson		Mr Jeremiah Wase
			Mr Martin Harsant Junior
Sept.	Earl of Rochford		Mr John Aldous
	John Tovell Esq.		Mr John Cooper
			Mr Henry Edwards
Oct.	Mr John Levett	2nd Quarter	Mr Thomas Whimper
	Mr William Whimper		Mr John Weeding
			Mr William Cole
Nov.	Francis Brooke Esq.		Mr Thomas Edwards
	Mr Thomas Ablitt		Mr James Woods
			Mr John Waller
Dec.	The Revd Mr Frank		Mr Stephen Vertue
	The Revd Mr Purvis		Mr Thomas Crisp
			Mr Robert Vertue
Jan.	Mr William Waller	3rd Quarter	Mr John Gross
	Mr Nathaniel Barthrop		Mr Philip Dikes
			Mr Richard Harris
Feb.	John Brand Esq.		Mr John Welham
	Mr James Lynn		Mr Nathaniel Bennington
			Mr James Aldous
Mar.	The Revd Mr Hingeston		Mr Nathaniel Steptoe
	Mr Benjamin Cooper		Mr Nathaniel Keeble Chandler
			Mr Samuel Jeaffreson
Apl.	Mr John Whimper	4th Quarter	Mr John Stopher
	Mr John Baldry		Mr John Barthrop
			Mr Fredescant Wade
May	John Revett Esq.		Mr Henry Topple
	The Revd Mr Williams		Mr John Jeaffreson
			Mr Thomas Butcher
June	Mr Samuel Barber		Mr Thomas Wood
	Mr John Barthorp		Mr John Pitcher
			Mr John Felgate

3 October 1785

Proposed by John Revett Esq., that the method of putting out poor children apprentice from the said House be considered at the next Quarterly Meeting.

Proposed by John Revett Esq., that a consideration be allowed to Mr Henchman, the out surgeon, for his extraordinary care and trouble with the several persons in Creetingham having putrid fevers, and that the same be considered at the next Quarterly Meeting.

Ordered that the Clerk do procure a book for the registration of all securities given and money paid for maintenance of bastard children born in the said Hundred.

Ordered that Mr Francis Hayle do supply the said House imediately with 25 comb of old wheat at 24s. per comb, and Mr Nathaniel Smith 15 comb of new wheat at 20s. per comb according to samples to be delivered at the said House, and the Governor is ordered to mix the old and the new wheat before it goes to mill.

27 March 1786

Proposed by Mr James Lynn and ordered that in the advertisement to be inserted in the Ipswich Journal of the next Annual Meeting, it be requested that all the Directors and Guardians will attend the next previous Meeting for the purpose of calling over and examining the paupers in the House of Industry in order to discharge such of them as may appear capable of supporting themselves.

26 June 1786

Directors	Present	Guardians
John Revett Esq. President	Mr William Whimper	Mr John Felgate
The Revd Mr Hingeston	Mr Francis Hayle	Mr Nathaniel Steptoe
The Revd Mr Williams	Mr Richard Wilkinson	Mr Fredescant Wade
Mr James Lynn	Mr John Whimper	Mr Thomas Wood
Mr John Barthorp	and	and
Mr Samuel Barber	Mr Nathaniel Barthrop	Mr James Pitcher

The following persons were duly elected Directors and Acting Guardians:

	Directors	1st Quarter	Guardians
July	The Revd Mr Jeaffreson		Mr Thomas Garneys
	Mr Francis Hayle		Mr Stephen Catchpole
			Mr James Catchpole
Aug.	The Revd Mr Gunning		Mr John Catt
	Mr Richard Wilkinson		Mr Jeremiah Wase
			Mr Martin Harsant Junior
Sept.	The Earl of Rochford		Mr John Aldhouse
	John Tovell Esq.		Mr Samuel Thompson
			Mr Henry Edwards
Oct.	Mr John Levett	2nd Quarter	Mr William Stearn
	Mr William Whimper		Mr John Weeding
			Mr William Cole
Nov.	Francis Brooke Esq.		Mr Thomas Edwards
	Mr Thomas Ablitt		Mr James Woods
			Mr George Payne
Dec.	The Revd Mr Purvis		Mr Stephen Vertue
	Mr Nathaniel Barthrop		Mr Thomas Crisp
			Mr Whimper Bradley
Jan.	Mr William Waller	3rd Quarter	Mr Thomas Crisp
	Mr John Barthorp		Mr Philip Dikes
			Mr Richard Harris
Feb.	John Brand Esq.		Mr John [ ]
	Mr James Lynn		Mr Nathaniel Bennington
			Mr James Aldhouse

Mar.	The Revd Mr Hingeston		Mr Nathaniel Steptoe
	Mr Benjamin Cooper		Mr George Lord
			Mr Samuel Jeaffreson
Apl.	Mr John Whimper	4th Quarter	Mr John Stopher
	Mr John Baldrey		Mr William Button
			Mr Fredescant Wade
May	John Revett Esq.		Mr Henry Topple
	The Revd Mr Williams		Mr John Jeaffreson
			Mr Joseph Rust
June	Mr Samuel Barber		Mr Thomas Wood
	Mr John Barthorp		Mr James Pitcher
			Mr John Felgate

The proposal made by John Revett Esq., for allowing a compensation to Mr William Henchman out surgeon for his extraordinary care and trouble in attending the paupers of Creetingham in July and August last with putrid fevers hath this day been considered and argued, and it is ordered upon a ballot nine to seven that he be allowed a compensation of ten guineas to be paid by the Treasurer.

The proposal made by John Revett Esq., that the method of putting out poor children apprentices should be considered, hath this day been considered and argued. It is ordered that the penaltys that shall at any time hereafter be paid to the Treasurer for refusing to accept an apprentice, conformable to the laws now in being, be appropriated to and for the placing out such apprentice so refused to some other person of some trade or calling at the discretion and order of the Directors and Acting Guardians assembled at any Quarterly Meeting.

The proposal made by John Revett Esq., <> respecting the regulation of the salary and fees of the Surgeons and Clerk to the Corporation hath this day been considered and argued and it is ordered that the same be further considered at a future Quarterly Meeting.

13 July 1786

At this meeting the paupers in the House of Industry were called over and examined and several were ordered to be discharged as will appear at the next Weekly Committee Meeting.

2 October 1786

As the resignation of several gentlemen Directors has taken place at this Meeting and it is stated by some of the Directors present that the cause of such resignations was a belief that on a former matter of business undue influence was practised to obtain votes in order to determine the question. The Directors and Guardians present are of opinion that such a step is highly improper and injurious to the interests of the Corporation. The Revd Mr Williams therefore moves, and is seconded by the Revd Mr Hingston, that the several resignations shall not be accepted by the Meeting but postponed, conceiving that such motion will obviate their several objections and that they be applied to by the Clerk to acquaint them with this motion, and to request they will withdraw their several resignations and continue in the Direction. The motion being ballotted for was carried 14 to one.

Ordered that John Keable of Bredfield Overseer be summoned <> for neglect of duty in not apprehending Robert Holmes for a bastard child of Sarah Moss.

26 December 1786

Daniel Johnston, William Barlow, Charles Jefferson and Gerrard Jacob being proposed for Governor of the House of Industry in the room of John Elliott deceased, were ballotted for and Daniel Johnston was declared duly elected at the salary of thirty five pounds a year.

Ordered that the Clerk do write to Mr Roach of Norwich to give an account of the yarn sent to him by the Corporation.

Ordered that Mr Richard Clarke be paid by the Treasurer the Governor's quarter's salary to this day and that he also be paid three guineas for his trouble in attendance and making up the late Governor's books and in assisting the new Governor.

Ordered and agreed that William Barber do take the twelve pounds of yarn and twenty four pounds of wool now in the House of Industry for his own for the trouble he has had in the wool business.

26 March 1787

Ordered that a proper room be appropriated in the House of Industry for a School Room, and that Mrs Ellis be at present appointed school mistress to teach the children to read and learn the Church catechism. That a small party be instructed first and from time to time others at the discretion of the Governor, and that she be allowed for her trouble such sum as the Directors and Acting Guardians shall think proper.

25 June 1787

Directors Present		Guardians
Mr John Revett Esq. President		Mr Thomas Wood
The Revd Mr Hingeston		Mr Samuel Thompson
Mr Samuel Barber		and
Mr John Barthorp		Mr James Catchpole
Mr Francis Hayle		
Mr William Whimper		
Mr Richard Wilkinson		

The following persons were duly elected Directors and Acting Guardians:

	Directors	1st Quarter	Guardians
July	Mr Samuel Jeaffreson		Mr Abell Ashford
	Mr Francis Hayle		Mr Stephen Catchpole
			Mr Samuel Hart
Aug.	Mr Samuel Thompson		Mr John Catt
	Mr Richard Wilkinson		Mr Jeremiah Wase
			Mr Martin Harsant Junior
Sept.	The Revd Mr William Browne		Mr Thomas Moss
	Mr Edward Keer		Mr Thomas Thredkell
			Mr Henry Edwards
Oct.	Mr John Levett	2nd Quarter	Mr William Stearn
	Mr William Whimper		Mr John Weeding
			Mr William Cole
Nov.	Mr Samuel Salmon		Mr Thomas Edwards
	Mr Thomas Ablitt		Mr James Woods
			Mr George Payne
Dec.	Mr James Catchpole		Mr Thomas Hicks
	Mr Nathaniel Barthrop		Mr Thomas Crisp

			Mr Whimper Bready
Jan.	Mr William Waller	3rd Quarter	Mr Thomas Crisp
	Mr Thomas Wood		Mr Philip Dikes
			Mr Andrew Blake
Feb.	Mr Benjamin Baldry		Mr William Crowe
	Mr James Lynn		Mr Nathaniel Bennington
			Mr James Aldhouse
Mar.	The Revd Mr Hingeston		Mr Nathaniel Steptoe
	Mr Benjamin Cooper		Mr George Lord
			Mr Simon Loyns
Apl.	Mr John Whimper	4th Quarter	Mr John Stopher
	Mr John Mabson		Mr William Button
			Mr Francis Betts
May	John Revett Esq.		Mr Henry Topple
	Mr Thomas Stammers		Mr Thomas Rose
			Mr Joseph Rust
June	Mr Samuel Barber		Mr Robert Baldwin
	Mr John Barthorp		Mr Isaac Bonner
			Mr John Felgate

Ordered that Mr William Salmon be appointed Surgeon to the House of Industry for the year ensuing at the salary of forty pounds, and that he do attend the out paupers in the several parishes of Ash, Charsfield, Dallingho, Easton, Hacheston, Letheringham, Marlesford, Rendlesham, Boulge, Bredfield, Debach, Melton, Petistree, Ufford, and Wickham Market for the year ensuing at the salary of fifty shillings for each parish.

Ordered that Mr Thurston Whimper and Mr William Henchman be continued Out Surgeons for the several parishes they now attend for this quarter at their usual salarys, and that they be requested to attend the next Quarterly Meeting.

Proposed by Mr John Revett Esq., that the Governor shall not receive any pauper into the House of Industry by order of any Directors or Guardians between the Weekly Committee unless on orders of removal or in cases of the small pox, broken limbs or any epidemical distemper, and in these cases not without a certificate from a surgeon.

1 October 1787

Ordered that an agreement be entered into between the Guardians and John Bradey of Hollesly, yeoman and Nathaniel Elliott of London, carpenter for the said John Bradey and Nathaniel Elliott to sell the effects of Hannah Elliott, now a lunatick confined to the House of Industry in Melton, which effects and notes amount to the sum of [   ] as well as the rents and profits of the cottages belonging to the said Hannah Elliott, and for them the said John Bradey and Nathaniel Elliott to pay the said Guardians 3s. 6d. a week for her maintenance so long as she shall continue in the said House of Industry and her effects will extend to pay.

Ordered that Mr Thurston Whimper and Mr William Henchman be continued Out Surgeons for the several parishes they now attend for this quarter at their usual salarys and that their salarys be taken into further consideration at the next Quarterly Meeting.

31 December 1787

Ordered that Sarah Keeble be indicted at the Quarter Sessions at Woodbridge for assaulting Mary Cooke one of the reelers in the House of Industry.

14 January 1788

The matter of spinning wool in the House of Industry being taken into consideration. Ordered that the Governor do provide some wool for two shilling work, to be spun in one room with two reelers, and that the Governor do keep an account to see whether it will answer and whether the earnings will be more or less than the present earnings of the common wool now spun, and that the rest of the House be continued spinning the usual wool.

Ordered that 420 tops of wool now in the House of Industry be disposed of by the Governor to Messrs. Cumberland and Crosbie, and to receive the money for the same and to carry it to the accounts of the Corporation.

31 March 1788

Ordered that Samuel Pratt and William Flory of Sutton, labourers, be advertised for running away and leaving their wives and familys a charge to the Corporation, with a reward of one guinea each and all reasonable expences.

Proposed by Mr William Whimper, that when any paupers are to be received into the House that they shall not be received unless they come with the recommendation as well of the Churchwarden and Overseer and not of the Overseers only (except by order of a Magistrate) the same to be argued at the next Annual Meeting.

30 June 1788

	Directors	Present	Guardians
	John Revett Esq.		Mr Samuel Jeaffreson
	The Revd Mr Hingeston		Mr Thomas Wood
	Mr Samuel Salmon		Mr Benjamin Baldry
	Mr Francis Hayle		Mr Samuel Thompson
	Mr Samuel Barber		and
	Mr John Barthorp		Mr William Whimper

The following persons were duly elected Directors and Acting Guardians:

	Directors	1st Quarter	Guardians
July	Mr Samuel Jeaffreson		Mr Abell Ashford
	Mr Francis Hayle		Mr Stephen Catchpole
			Mr John Harsant
Aug.	Mr Samuel Thompson		Mr John Catt
	Mr Benjamin Baldry		Mr Jeremiah Wase
			Mr Martin Harsant Junior
Sept.	The Revd Mr William Browne		Mr Thomas Moss
	Mr Edward Keer		Mr Joseph Kersey
			Mr Henry Edwards
Oct.	Mr John Levett	2nd Quarter	Mr Joseph Rust
	Mr William Whimper		Mr John Weeding
			Mr William Cole
Nov.	Mr Samuel Salmon		Mr Thomas Edwards
	Mr Thomas Ablitt		Mr James Woods
			Mr George Payne
Dec.	Mr James Catchpole		Mr Robert Crane

	Mr Nathaniel Barthrop		Mr Thomas Crisp
			Mr Whimper Bready
Jan.	Mr William Waller	3rd Quarter	Mr Thomas Crisp
	Mr Thomas Wood		Mr Philip Dikes
			Mr Andrew Blake
Feb.	Mr Richard Wilkinson		Mr John Sutton
			Mr Nathaniel Bennington
			Mr James Aldhous
Mar.	The Revd Mr Hingeston		Mr Nathaniel Steptoe
	Mr Benjamin Cooper		Mr Nathaniel Keeble
			Chandler
			Mr William Neeve
Apl.	Mr John Whimper	4th Quarter	Mr John Waller
	Mr John Mabson		Mr Stephen Vertue
			Mr Edmund Barber
May	John Revett Esq.		Mr Thomas Waller
	Mr Thomas Stammers		Mr Thomas Rose
			Mr William Stearn
June	Mr Samuel Barber		Mr William Smith
	Mr John Barthorp		Mr Isaac Bonner
			Mr John Felgate

The spinning business now going very bad, proposed by Mr Revett that it be taken into consideration whether the poor in the House cannot be employed for the benefit of the Corporation in some other way and that it be argued at the next Quarterly Meeting.

Ordered that the Governor do provide and have a different table for the idle and disorderly poor in the dining room distinct from the rest of the poor, with a board to be painted over the table explaining the meaning of such distinction.

Ordered that the Governor do go with Mary Simonds to Joseph Rust and insist on his taking her as his apprentice, and if he refuses to accept her then that the Clerk do commence an action against him on the covenant of the indenture.

Ordered that Mr Girling and Mr Bennington do pay three guineas for each of their servants sent to the Pest House with the small pox instead of four pounds, and that any person sending a servant to the Pest House for the future shall pay three guineas each out of which the surgeon to be paid one guinea.

30 September 1788

Thomas Gross, Overseer of the parish of Bromeswell, being summoned to appear this day ◇ for disobeying an order of the Directors and Guardians ◇ by stopping part of the payment ordered to be paid for Robert Cranes child of the said parish of Bromeswell, having but one hand and the said Thomas Gross this day appearing, and on hearing all partys the said Thomas Gross was adjudged guilty of the said misdemeanour and fined the sum of twenty shillings which is ordered to be paid to the Treasurer and it is ordered that the Clerk do cause the same to be inserted in the Ipswich Journal.

Ordered that Samuel Reeve of Wingfield, weaver, do provide thirty stone of hemp in the best manner he can. That Mr James Catchpole do provide six wheels and reels for spinning the said hemp, and that the said Samuel Reeve do attend the House of Industry and instruct the paupers in spinning and to be paid for his trouble in a reasonable way.

29 December 1788

The spinning of hemp being began in the House of Industry agreeable to the order of the last Quarterly Meeting. Ordered that the same be continued under and subject to such alterations and regulations as shall be considered upon at the next Quarterly Meeting, and such other alterations as shall be thought proper for the employment of the poor.

Ordered that Mr James Catchpole do look at some hemp belonging to John Avis of Melton, and if he thinks it proper for the House, to inform Mr Revett of it that he may order Samuel Reeve the weaver to attend a Committee to be held at the said House, which is to be advertised by the clerk two weeks, and that the Governor do in the meantime provide six bunching blocks or troughs for bunching of hemp in the said House and that the Governor do order six more wheels for spinning of hemp.

Ordered that that the Surgeon of the House of Industry do make a return every week to the Weekly Committee of the several sick or disordered persons in the said House and Pest house, to be entered in a book to be provided by the Governor for that purpose.

16 January 1788 [*Committee to review hemp business*]

Ordered that Daniel Manthorp of Ufford, carpenter, do make two bunching blocks or troughs for bunching of hemp in the House of Industry.

Ordered that Daniel Manthorp do make a nine inch brick partition between the taylors and shoemakers rooms in order to part the room for the purpose of bunching of hemp and to hang a door out of the Long Ward into the said bunching room.

Ordered that John Avis of Melton do supply the House of Industry with forty stone of hemp of the best sort at six shillings and three pence per stone and five or six stone of the common sort of hemp at three shillings and six pence per stone.

Ordered that Samuel Reeve do procure a person to come to the House of Industry in order to bunch and weave hemp and to teach the paupers in the House of Industry to bunch and weave hemp and that he procure a loom for weaving.

30 March 1789

The spinning of hemp having been used in the House of Industry, ordered that the same be continued under and subject to such alterations and regulations as shall be considered at the next Annual Meeting.

29 June 1789

Directors	Present	Guardians
John Revett Esq.	Mr Thomas Stammers	Mr John Felgate
The Revd Mr Hingeston	Mr Samul Salmon	and
The Revd Mr Reynolds	Mr Samuel Barber	Mr Robert Crane
Mr John Barthorp	Mr William Whimper	
Mr Benjamin Baldry	Mr Francis Hayle	

The following persons were duly elected Directors and Acting Guardians ▽:

	Directors	1st Quarter	Guardians
July	Mr Samuel Jeaffreson		Mr Abell Ashford
	Mr Francis Hayle		Mr Stephen Catchpole
			Mr John Harsant
Aug.	Mr Samuel Thompson		Mr Nathaniel Barthrop Junior
	Mr Benjamin Baldry		Mr Timothy Smith
			Mr Robert Ashford

Sept.	The Revd Robert Reynolds		Mr Samuel Farrow
	Mr Edward Keer		Mr Joseph Kersey
			Mr Henry Edwards
Oct.	Mr John Levett	2nd Quarter	Mr Joseph Rust
	Mr William Whimper		Mr John Weeding
			Mr Thomas Thredkell
Nov.	Mr Samuel Salmon		Mr Thomas Edwards
	Mr Thomas Ablitt		Mr James Woods
			Mr George Payne
Dec.	Mr James Catchpole		Mr Robert Crane
	Mr Nathaniel Barthrop		Mr William Button
			Mr Whimper Bready
Jan.	Mr William Waller	3rd Quarter	Mr Thomas Crisp
	Mr Thomas Wood		Mr Philip Dikes
			Mr Andrew Blake Junior
Feb.	The Revd William Brown		Mr John Sutton
	Mr Richard Wilkinson		Mr Nathaniel Bennington
			Mr James Aldhous
Mar.	The Revd Mr Hingeston		Mr James Smith
	Mr Benjamin Cooper		Mr Nathaniel Keeble Chandler
			Mr William Neeve
Apl.	Mr John Whimper	4th Quarter	Mr John Stopher
	Mr John Mabson		Mr John Kemp
			Mr Edmund Barber
May	John Revett Esq.		Mr Thomas Waller
	Mr John Barthorp		Mr Thomas Rose
			Mr John Ralph
June	Mr John Ayton		Mr John Grout
	Mr Thomas Stammers		Mr Isaac Bonner
			Mr John Felgate

Ordered that Lydia Gray and Susanna Yeldhall, two poor children in the House of Industry, (for whom the penaltys have been paid the Guardians for not taken them apprentice), be apprenticed to William Jepson of Yarmouth, sailcloth weaver, the said Lydia Gray for the term of four years, and the said Susanna Yeldhall for the term of three years, and the said William Jepson to be allowed a premium of four pounds with each child and that the remaining part of the penaltys paid to the said Guardians for them be left in the hands of the Guardians for the benefit of the said children at the expiration of their apprenticeships, and that the character of the said William Jepson be inquired into and approved of by the Guardians before the said children are apprenticed.

5 October 1789

Inquiry having been made of the character of William Jepson to whom Lydia Gray and Susanna Yeldhall were ordered to be apprenticed, and his character not being approved of, ordered that the said two children be not apprenticed to him but remain in the House of Industry to be apprenticed to some other persons.

28 December 1789

Ordered that Robert Crane of Wickham Market, hosier, do supply the said House for this quarter with four thread two penny yarn at 22d. per pound, knit stockings of the same at 3s. 2d. per pound, and wheel spun yarn 18d. per pound.

Ordered that the paupers in the House for the future be provided with yellow stockings.

Proposed that the Governor do make of his wheat in dressing only two sorts and the bran, and that on the meat days he institute bread and potatoes with the meat instead of dumplings.

29 March 1790

Ordered that the Governor do make complaint before a Magistrate against John Whiting for running away and leaving his wife and family a charge to the Corporation, and get him apprehended for the same.

Ordered that the clerk do advertise in the Ipswich Journal that several sums of money are wanted to be borrowed on undeniable security at the interest of £4 10s. per cent, to inquire of Mr Simon Paternoster of Wickham Market in order if possible to reduce the interest of the monies due from the Corporation it being now at the interest of five pounds per cent.

Proposed by Mr William Waller that it be taken into consideration at the next Annual Meeting to have a General Meeting of all the Guardians within the said Hundreds in order for an application to Parliament for a new act for the Incorporated Hundreds.

28 June 1790

Directors	Present	Guardians
John Revett Esq.		Mr John Ralph
The Revd Robert Reynolds		Mr John Grout
Mr John Barthorp		Mr John Felgate
Mr Benjamin Baldrey		Mr Robert Crane
Mr John Ayton		
Mr James Catchpole		
Mr Thomas Stammers		
Mr Samuel Salmon		
Mr William Waller		

The following persons were duly elected Directors and Acting Guardians:

	Directors	1st Quarter	Guardians
July	Mr Francis Hayle		Mr Thomas Garneys
			Mr Stephen Catchpole
			Mr John Harsant
Aug.	Mr Samuel Thompson		Mr Nathaniel Barthrop
	Mr Benjamin Baldry		Mr Timothy Smyth
			Mr Robert Ashford
Sept.	The Revd Robert Reynolds		Mr Samuel Farrow
	Mr Edward Keer		Mr William Cole
			Mr Henry Edwards
Oct.	Mr John Levett	2nd Quarter	Mr Joseph Rust
	Mr William Whimper		Mr John Weeding
			Mr Thomas Thredkell
Nov.	Mr Samuel Salmon		Mr Daniel Manthorp

	Mr Thomas Ablitt		Mr James Wood
			Mr George Payne
Dec.	Mr James Catchpole		Mr Robert Crane
			Mr William Button
			Mr John Bready
Jan.	Mr William Waller	3rd Quarter	Mr Thomas Crisp
	Mr Thomas Wood		Mr Philip Dikes
			Mr Andrew Blake Junior
Feb.	Mr Richard Wilkinson		Mr John Sutton
			Mr William Miller
			Mr James Aldhous
Mar.	The Revd Samuel Hingeston		Mr Samuel Gross
	Mr Benjamin Cooper		Mr Nathaniel Keeble Chandler
			Mr William Neeve
Apl.	Mr John Whimper	4th Quarter	Mr John Waller
	Mr John Mabson		Mr Stephen Vertue
			Mr Robert Bennington
May	Mr John Revett Esq.		Mr Thomas Waller
	Mr John Barthorp		Mr Isaac Churchyard
			Mr John Ralph
June	Mr John Ayton		Mr Jeremiah Wase
	Mr Thomas Stammers		Mr Joseph Jeaffreson
			Mr Corry Cavell

Ordered that the Clerk do state a case and take Counsels opinion upon whether Mr John Carter is liable to take an apprentice for his farm in Alderton, not living there and that the parish of Alderton bear half the expense.

Ordered that the Clerk do apply to the several persons who have money on security of the Corporation to know whether they will accept the interest of 4½ per cent, and report their answers at the next Quarterly Meeting.

Ordered that the Treasurer do pay Thomas Grimwood 30s. towards the expense of inoculating himself and family.

Ordered that the expediency of calling a General Meeting of the Guardians for the purpose of applying to Parliament for a new Act be taken into consideration at the next Quarterly Meeting.

Ordered that the Treasurer do place in the bank of Messrs. Alexander and Cornwell eight hundred pounds at the interest of two pounds and ten shillings per cent per annum untill Michaelmas next.

Ordered that the cushion in the Chapel be new covered.

4 October 1790

Ordered and resolved unanimously ◇ that if any Director or Acting Guardian shall be absent (at any Weekly Committee Meeting for which they are appointed to attend), shall forfeit the several penalties inflicted by the Incorporated Act for such absence, and that the same shall be recovered according to the said Act and that the clerk do write to the several Directors and Acting Guardians informing them of this order and resolution.

It appearing to this Meeting that the present assessments on the several parishes in the said Hundreds are inadequate to the expences necessary for the maintenance of the poor it is therefore resolved that the following advertisement be inserted in the Ipswich Journal:

All the Guardians of the Poor within the said Hundreds of Loes and Wilford are particularly requested to attend at the House of Industry at Melton on <14 December 1790> to take into consideration whether another application to Parliament can by any means be avoided.

Ordered the above be advertised in the three next Ipswich Journals.

14 December 1790

Proposed by the Revd Samuel Henley, that a Committee be founded to look over and examine the Treasurers, Clerks, and Governors accounts and to take into consideration the present state of the Corporation. And the question being put was unanimously carried and the following gentlemen appointed to attend on a Committee <8 named directors> and any five of those gentlemen attending to form a Committee which said Committee is ordered to be left open for all or any of the Guardians within the said Hundreds. And it is also ordered and agreed that the above Committee do and shall attend at the House of Industry in Melton < > for the purposes aforesaid. The thanks of this meeting was unanimously given to the Earl of Rochford, the Chairman.

18 December 1790 [*Committee for reviewing the accounts*][2]

The Treasurers Books and Accounts were this day examined and looked over but not being able to get through them.

Ordered and agreed that the Committee be adjourned for the purpose aforesaid.

27 December 1790

Ordered that John Doyley, wife and three children certificate persons to Nacton may be inoculated there at five shillings and three pence each agreeable to what is allowed by this corporation.

Ordered that the Treasurer do draw upon Messrs. Alexander and Cornwell for two hundred pounds, and for any further sum that may be necessary.

Ordered that a Committee of the Directors do apply to the Committee of Inquiry to know when they will be able to make their report on examining the accounts of the House etc., and the said Directors to meet at the House of Industry <> to receive their answer. And that the Directors do call a meeting of all the Guardians within the said Hundreds by publick advertisement to receive from the said Directors the Report of the Committee of Inquiry, and to determine upon the propriety of an application to Parliament for a new Act and for such other purposes as may appear necessary.

6 January 1791 [*Committee enquiring of the committee for reviewing accounts*][3]

The Committee of Directors this day applied to the Committee of Inquiry for their Report who informed them that they were not at present prepared to make it.

---

[2] This committee met and adjourned on 23 December 1790, 28 December 1790, 30 December 1790, 4 January 1791, 6 January 1791, 8 January 1791, 1 February 1791 and 8 February 1791.
[3] This committee met and adjourned on 17 January 1791, 31 January 1791 and 7 February 1791.

10 January 1791 [*Committee for reviewing the accounts*]

Ordered that the following advertisement be inserted in the Ipswich Journal and Bury and Norwich Post <> and that the clerk do procure printed letters with copies of the advertisement to be sent to all the non-resident proprietors in the said Hundreds.

"A General Meeting of the Owners and Occupiers of lands within the Hundreds of Loes and Wilford in the county of Suffolk and also the creditors of the said Corporation are requested to meet at the Sessions Hall in the town of Woodbridge on <15 February> to receive from the Committee appointed to Examine the actual state of the said Corporation their Reports and to consider the measures proper to be taken thereon".

14 February 1791 [*Committee for reviewing the accounts*]

The Committee proceeded on the above business and unanimously agreed to the following Report and adjourned this meeting to <15 February> instant at the Sessions Hall in the town of Woodbridge for the purpose of presenting it to the General Meeting there to be held, and that the same be accordingly presented by the Revd Samuel Henley.

The Report

A General Meeting of the Owners and Occupiers of lands in the incorporated Hundreds of Loes and Wilford having been convened <> for the purpose of considering "whether another application to Parliament can by any means be avoided" but no documents having been prepared by the persons who called that meeting <> save only a draft of a Bill for a new Act of Parliament, which that very Meeting had been convened to preclude. A motion was made, and unanimously passed, that a Committee should be appointed, "for inquiring into the actual state of the said Corporation". In conformity with this appointment, after having availed ourselves of every source of information that could be obtained from the books and papers of the Corporation, the testimony of those whom it was expedient to examine, and from our own personal inspection; we of the Committee so appointed, whose names are underwritten, do now present our Report: promising only that, in executing the trust to us committed, we have proceeded with as much dispatch as was compatible with the numberless perplexities we have had to unravel, and the desire of rendering justice to those who are now responsible for the execution of their trust, as well as to you who have a right to a faithful account.

In preparing the Report it was thought necessary to go back no farther than midsummer 1781, because the original debt of £9,200 was then reduced to £6,200, and since has been accumulating to the enormous amount of £9,900. Struck at this discovery, we descended to particulars, and accordingly attempted to ascertain by what means this increase had been incurred, and whether the resources of the Corporation could affect its discharge. This at once led us to the two great articles of income and disbursements. The article of income we divided under the heads of determinate and incidental, the former consisting of the settled rates contributed by the several parishes; the latter arising from circumstances contingent. Both making, from the period assigned, the gross sum of £23,893 0s. 11½d., a sum, however, which falls short of the disbursement for the same period, taken under the heads of ordinary and fortuitous expences, no less than £1,462 17s. 8d. exclusive of all the money borrowed, which appears to be £3,700.

So great a defalcation made it necessary to examine how this excess had accrued, and whether, in the chief articles of expenditure, there had been a correspondent increase of consumption, or of price. But having collected with this view the numbers of paupers in these respective years, and turned to the article of provisions, we found that accounts of the Corporation so intricate and confused, that nothing certain could be deduced, more than that in two of those years which came under our notice, though the price of meat in the one was less than in the other, and no change made in the food of the poor, yet the expence of this article in the cheap year exceeded that in the dear year one; no less than 7s. on 13s., all but a halfpenny. And though, as to bread, flour, and malt, we cannot be so exact, yet a similar excess is apparent on each. Hence your Committee cannot but infer both mismanagement and abuse

From provisions we then proceeded to cloathing; but here we met with no better success, for, from the piecemeal manner of buying the materials, and the confusion of the accounts as stated above, it was not possible to obtain precise information

Fuel in the next place engaged our attention. As this consisted of both coals and wood, we began with collecting the expence of the coals. But when we flattered ourselves that this account was compleat, a circumstance occurred to correct that mistake, for, after having drawn out the statement of the books, we learnt that, notwithstanding the quantity there was 70 chaldrons, yet more than 90 were consumed in the year 1786. It is therefore possible that, though the books do not shew it, other years have experienced an equal excess, especially as about that quantity appears to have been spent when the limited number was contracted for no longer.

The consumption of wood is equally uncertain. It may however be observed, that more of this article seems to have been bought in the year when the consumption of coals was the greatest than in any other, and that this was the year of distinguished abuse.

Perceiving the result of our inquiries into these and other collateral matters thus rendered abortive, and yet knowing that other institutions of a like kind had been nearly, if not quite discharged from their debt, we thought it incumbent to seek, what could have here caused so contrary an effect? The chief guides to direct us in such a research were – a consideration of the main objects for which your institution was founded; what provisions the Act of Incorporation and bye-laws had made to attain them; and how both had been administered for attaining their end?

As to the intent for which the Corporation was formed, that is expressed in the title of the Act ◇. That upon you this burthen, instead of being diminished, is increased, you already have but too fully perceived; and that it must be aggravated still further, you will very shortly experience. Nor is it the most tolerable part of your grievance, that powers adapted to accomplish and confided to obtain the best of purposes, should through ignorance, negligence and worse, have been desperately perverted and abused.

For though it appear, in the first instance, that our House was designed, in the words of the Act, "for the general reception of the poor", yet this is evidently ◇. Most of those who apply for relief are forced in to it, or else refused the assistance they need; for hence the poor are either deprived of that aid to which they have an indisputable claim; or else the House is burthened with a needless expense, since it often happens that, from the refusal of a trifling allowance for a short time out of the House, where one person is disabled, the support of a family is entailed upon it. This then is one cause which has materially enhanced the original debt; and to this be it added, that, where out allowances have been granted, they have in general often been bestowed without proper discrimination, and even with great partiality.

Another evil ⬦ is the practice of hiring out children by the year, instead of apprenticing; for ⬦ the state of the House will shew that there are at present many both boys and girls, some grown to be women, encumbrances in it, who ought to have been long ago provided for out of it.

But those unfortunate children who from time to time go back to the House are not its only unnecessary burthens, for there now are a number of vigorous young women ⬦ improperly detained in it, and for no reason we can find unless to keep up the breed.

And as these three are instances in which the income of the Corporation has been certainly squandered, so two others may be mentioned of similar effect. The one refers to such expences as have needlessly been occasioned by those who, abandoning their families, have thrown them entirely on the public, and accordingly are maintained in one instance out of the House, and in others in it, without any exertion to take up such vagrants, and by that means get free from the charge.

The other case pointed at ⬦ is in itself of a contrary kind. Of this one example will suffice. A parish belonging to this Incorporation, being likely to become chargeable with a bastard, through neglect in not apprehending the father, after quietly letting him for some time abscond, thought it behoved them to seek his retreat. The man, a common chaise driver, was found at Rochester, and brought to Woodbridge from London in chaises, at the expence of £13 wanting but 2d. But though the overseers bill was refused by the magistrates, and the Quarterly Meeting, yet when a Director resident in the parish came to preside at a Weekly Committee, the same bill was produced and allowed, in consequence of which, as £20 had been given in security, £13 of your money was paid to take £7 with the douceur of a child.

Another article of injury to the funds of your House arises from the assumption of a power to mitigate fines, where the law is positive and admits of no mitigation. An instance you have in the case of a late overseer, who not only stopped an allowance to a young woman with one arm, for the purpose of paying himself a debt owed by her father, but charged journies for her money from Bromeswell to the House: the Committee abated the half of the fine.

That your Directors and Acting Guardians might be excited to their duty, the Act of Incorporation hath imposed certain penalties for non-attendance upon it; whence if the House were not benefitted by their presence, it at least might be by their fines. But notwithstanding these are expressly directed "to be levied and recovered by distress and sale of goods and chattels, and paid to the Treasurer, and added by him to the common stock for the use of the poor", no fine of the sort hath ever been paid, though the whole of their amount is a considerable sum.

And as forfeitures of this kind have never been collected, so those of another have been unlawfully applied; for notwithstanding the 3rd bye law hath enjoined, "that no money shall at any time be given with an apprentice", children are not only apprenticed, but, by public advertisement, with money. Of this you have an example in the instance of Elizabeth Gall, with whom all of the ten pounds which had been paid for refusing her by one master, was given with her to another saving two shillings. Nor is this practice contrary to the bye law alone, for your Act of Incorporation had previously appointed that "all fines and forfeitures shall be paid to the Treasurer for the use of the House, and not to the apprentices separated from it".

Another matter of injury to the Corporation, and which we are sorry our duty should compel us to notice (because it formerly occasion dissention) is the winding up of the business of the wool. But to remove all idea of being warped by partiality, those of your Committee only, who then were strangers to the County, and unknown to all parties concerned, take thus much of this Report on themselves. And whilst they think it but an act of justice to declare, after the maturest deliberation, that, in their judgement, the project of that business was founded in wisdom; and, if persisted in, must have produced the most beneficial effects; they advert to it now no further than to shew, that those who had an interest in maintaining the contrary, wilfully abused the property of their trust, to furnish out proofs in support of their cause. This, the statement which follows will clearly evince.

It being determined, at the Annual Meeting in 1783, to relinquish the spinning of wool, a valuation was taken of the stock upon hand which appears to have stood as under:

	£	s.	d.
Wool.	239	15	9
delivered to spinners out of the House.	183	18	0
to spinners in the House.	6	10	0
yarn, not bundled.	181	14	4½
ready for market.	454	8	0
to which add:			
expence of spinning the wool delivered out.	130	14	0
of wool spun in the House.	4	19	0
	1,201	19	1½

This, Roach, the factor employed, offered to purchase; but his offer having been rejected at the next Quarterly Meeting, and as spinning the wool on hand had been continued in the interim, a fresh account was taken in October, as follows:

	£	s.	d.
Wool	222	12	10
delivered to the spinners out of the House.	13	9	0
to spinners in the House.	2	17	0
yarn not bundled.	19	13	7
ready for market.	953	3	0
	1,211	15	5

This estimate being made, and Roach, the original factor, discarded, one Williams, "a man in Norwich, of small trade", and unknown to the principal manufacturers, was sought out, as the properest person to dispose of the yarn. To him it was consigned, but after two years, and a considerable part remaining unsold, Barber, the packman, was sent, money being wanted, to sell the stock, or change the factor. In the hands, however, of Williams it was let to remain, who, after getting off a few more parcells, in the February following closed his account. At this time, 50 bundles of yarn were still in undisposed of. For these he proffered the sum of £60 and his proffer was immediately taken. Besides the yarn, however, thus bought and disposed of by him, there was more laid in the House, which, had it been sold when it ought, would have, by the packman's valuation, brought £25 2s. 0d., but, after having been devoted for six whole years to spiders and moths, he thought "it would do very well if it fetched £12 12s. 0d.". As no other person could be found to treat for it, Roach was now solicited to take it on sale. Necessity was urgent, and he remitted for it, at once, £13 13s. 0d.

The gross receipts of the sales were as follow:

	£	s.	d.

of the stock of wool in the House, part was

	£	s.	d.
bought by Cumberland and Crosbie for the sum of.	96	13	10
yarn sold by Williams (on commission).	1,031	17	6
bought by Williams.	60	0	0
remitted by Roach for damaged yarn.	13	13	0
	1,202	4	4

But as the residue of the wool, after the sale to Cumberland and Crosbie, was spun up, and included in the yarn consigned to Williams, the expence of spinning which was £97 10s. 0d. should not only be deducted from the gross receipts, but also the following sums:

	£	s.	d.
discounted on the bills of Cumberland and Crosbie.	0	11	0
discount paid by Williams on bills sent.	1	15	4
ditto to negotiate his bills.	12	8	2
stamps and postage.	0	7	0
Williams commission.	23	7	0
deductions made by him for bitten yarn.	2	16	8
the difference between £25 2s. 0d. and £13 13s.0d. on account of the damage sustained by the yarn sent to Roach.	11	9	0
wool to the packman, which he sold for.	152	14	2
The net receipts of the House will then be reduced to.	£1,049	10	2

Hence it is evident that the clear produce of the wool and yarn fell short of the valuation made in October 1783 not less than £162. 5s. 3d. But if it be recollected, that on giving up the business, Roach offered, upon indisputable security, for the yarn and wool, at that time unspun, the sum, more or less of £1,200 ⬦ it will appear that the rejection of his offer occasioned a loss to the Corporation of £150. 9s. 10d. over and above the loss of interest, whilst the stock lay spoiling; and let it not be forgotten, that after a period of almost nine years, the account is not closed.

Upon what motive the offer of Roach was spurned at, you will judge when you hear that the packman (two years after the business had been relinquished, being dispatched to Norwich, on the spur of necessity, for the purpose of selling the yarn, or again changing the factor) was positively ordered at the Annual Meeting "upon no account to have any dealings with Roach", who, however, seeing him by accident again offered "a good price", would have bought the yarn right out, paid on the spot £100, and the rest of the money in the course of the month.

To shew a thorough congruity of conduct, both Williams and the packman were paid off, one in yarn, and the other in wool, without crediting for either the account of the trade, or valuing the wool which the packman received.

From the statement there given, ⬦ there will not be a doubt but that every contrivance was caught at which a left handed wisdom could devise, to cast an odium, at whatever injury to the Corporation, upon those gentlemen, who introduced the business of spinning; and who, had that business been suffered to proceed, would have precluded the irksome occasion of this days meeting, by the discharge of that debt which had been previously incurred; and the prevention of that increase, which in the hands of their opponents hath brought your Corporation to its bankrupt condition.

Having thus perceived that in several particulars your property had been perverted, diminished and abused, we then went on to inquire, whether it is most obvious resource had been properly directed. For, as the Act of Incorporation designed "the poor instead of being wholly supported by the public, should contribute to the assistance and relief mutually of each other" it became necessary to examine: how their labour had been applied; and, what had been the produce? To this we were the rather incited because we had observed in the last "Returns to Parliament from the Houses of Industry in divers parts of England" a case precisely in point with our own; the same materials, wool and hemp, being the objects of labour in that House and in this. As in the example before us the earnings of the able paupers, at the rate of 2½d. per day each, and 300 days in the year, exceeded above a fourth of the expenditure of the whole House for provisions, cloathing and fuel, we were induced to look for a proportional account. Instead of this, however, we found that from midsummer 1783, the time when the wool trade was given up, till Michaelmas 1788, when the manufacture of hemp was adopted ◇ no determinate object of labour was assigned. And since that time ◇ sufficient evidence comes forward to shew, that from Michaelmas 1788 to the present hour, the hemp business has been so conducted as to have been the reverse of advantageous, even at the exorbitant value set upon the cloth. Nor is this the whole, for it is admitted by the Governor ◇ that the large stock of cloth at present on hand, is in itself of an unsaleable nature, from its having been made of unwhitened thread. Thus, then, as in closing the wool trade, the work of your House was more than thrown away, the yarn producing less than was bidden for the wool; so in your hemp still worse is the case, the best of your manufacture applying to no use.

In this way have the sinews of your labour been ham strung and hocked; and fatally hath that important purpose been defeated; for which, as its name implies, your very building was reared; and which the Act of Incorporation provided as "a place for the better employment of the able and industrious".

Whether it hath contributed more effectually to the next aim in view, "the correction and punishment of the profligate and idle" your Committee leave you to infer from the few facts they proceed to relate. It has, they find, been long a practice to receive into your House at the approach of winter, a number of lazy, notorious and abandoned prostitutes, who, tainted with the foulest of diseases, resort thither for cure; and when the season of summer advances, then quit their retreat. At their admissions the Corporation provides them with cloaths, and these when they depart they always take off, often leaving as a pledge an unaffiliated child; and this all with impunity. Instead of being kept apart, and fed on the meanest viands, and compelled to a severer species of toil, the most profligate of they are permitted in habits of familiar intercourse, and even to board and to bed, not only with each other, but with others of better character, and especially the young.

It is also found that the mothers of bastards are promoted to privileged stations, and appointed to superintend the junior part of your House; to accomplish, no doubt, that intent of your Corporation which looked forward "to the education of poor children in industry and religion". Consistent with this design, and for the purposes of disseminating through the community with these qualities that of honesty also, the present school mistress of your House ◇ is notoriously infamous – the wife of a transported convict, and a partaker in his guilt, though not in his punishment. Thus, according to the motto on your seal, are children trained up in the way they should go.

One other purpose of your existence we now must revert to ◇ for "providing a place for the more effectual relief and assistance of such, by age, infirmities or diseases, are rendered incapable of supporting themselves".

What kind of solace to the aged your mansion affords may be guessed, when you hear that many of this description sought an asylum from its comforts in the infection of your pest house.

170

Of the infirm and diseased we report a few instances from our own personal inspection. The first which claims your attention is ◇ there is not one in the Governors recollection of a sore leg in your House of any person of either sex, or of any age, having ever been healed. Though by the 3rd bye law relating to the surgeons it is required that "every person, whether sick or apparently in health, shall be examined by the surgeon, and that he shall give directions to the Governor as to the diet of every such pauper". This is so far from being done, that, on the contrary, the sick are left, as to diet, without the surgeons adverting to their specific complaints. Their wounds are chiefly dressed by the nurse and her helpers; by the surgeon scarcely ever. The dressing consist of a salve and balsam from a gallipot, which is kept in reserve for all kinds of sores. Some are given up by the surgeons as incurable; others, when applying for relief, are told by him, "I cannot make the old young", and one who has an ailment, which the surgeon has not noticed for more than five years, though often requesting assistance, hath never been able to obtain it.

A disease, originating in filth, by which many children are infected, the sight of several pitch plaisters which an old man was preparing, next drew our attention. These were, by the surgeon directed, to be applied to those afflicted with the scald head; and such were the apprehensions of a girl ◇ from the remembrance of her former sufferings, that she lay, writhing and shrieking, in convulsive agonies, whilst two men and three women were scarce able to hold her. From the remonstrance which we made ◇ we flattered ourselves that this horrid plaister had been banished for ever; but, to our great regret, we yesterday saw that, in spite of all remonstrance, it still keeps it hold.

A wretched woman, one of the abandoned character before mentioned, was found some weeks since by your Committee, a dreadful sufferer she had formerly been a martyr to venereal infection, but since has had a child, which has sometime been dead. About a month after her delivery she was seized with an excruciating pain in her knee, accompanied by a tumour. This the surgeon pronounced the white swelling, and talked of severing the limb; the swelling, however, has often shifted its place, and is now fixed in her ankle and foot. Never, perhaps, was there seen a more ghastly spectacle, emaciated to a skeleton, and her eyes starting with agony. She has thus languished for three months, confined to her bed. Her back is little else but ulcers and gangrene. Yet though she has been suffering thus long, and the surgeon has declared himself unable to relieve her, he has never applied to the Committee on her case; nor ever proposed to call in assistance.

To these many other instances might be adduced; but we shall only add, on the subject of the surgeon, that, notwithstanding the laws of the House requires him "on the 1st and 2nd Monday in every month to deliver in to the Weekly Committee an account in writing signed by himself of the state of the sick paupers in the House and in the Pest house" no such return appears to have been made since August 1787, nor was that even signed.

From the out surgeons, by another bye law, the like account is required; but in all our searches, not one hath occurred.

In going through the House the first time we saw five or six dogs in the dining room and kitchen; two or three were hounds of a neighbouring hunt, and one a pointer belonging to the surgeon. In the midst of dinner, the hall was smeared with their odour. In the spinning room where the boys work, it was observed by us that they all had a squalid appearance, and that every one of them was more or less ragged. The girls were rather in a better plight.

171

The nursery was certainly much overcrowded, and in two of the bed rooms the air was so noxious as greatly to affect the respiration of us all.

Having thus gone through the House we closely interrogated the Governor on the various parts of his duty, and in justice to him, we should add that his answers were direct and pertinent, whether they tended to criminate or commend. One of them, however, greatly surprised us, which was that of the ten bye laws prescribing his duty, he was totally unacquainted with all but the last, and that accidentally came to his knowledge, he being waiting in the room at the time it was made.

In preparing thus much of our Report, as there appeared to be such negligence, misconduct and abuse in almost every department, your Committee thought they should ill discharge their duty did they not proceed till they came to the source. With this view they turned to the state of the direction, and the manner in which business had been managed. Here they perceived, in the first place, that notwithstanding the Act of Incorporation requires all vacancies to be filled at each Quarterly Meeting after they respectively happen – there are at this time three, two of them about a year's standing, and the third of more than two years and half.

That, although the injunction of the Act had not in this point been complied with, there have been, within the limits of our inquiry, not fewer than 45 instances, in which, from the non-attendance of a sufficient number, those who were present, urged by necessity to act as a committee, have consequently acted illegally.

That the office of Acting Guardian hath been scandalously delegated, the person chosen to discharge it being so far from equal to its duties that he could not sign his name to the accounts he admitted, nor read even what he allowed.

That, by not adhering to the first rule for regulating of the Weekly Committees, much confusion hath inevitably arisen. That the penalties incurred, alluded to before, have never been levied as the Act of Parliament requires.

That the 4th bye law, which determines the assignment of apprentices "by ballot" thus referring to the decision of chance what should ever be the result of discretion and judgement is fraught with essential inconveniences, and ought never to have been made. By this extraordinary mode of assigning apprentices, three girls in one parish were severally affixed upon a taylor, a wheelwright and a blacksmith.

That the 6th bye law, which requires "every Director and Acting Guardian, on some one day in the course of his month, to visit the House and scrutinize every part of its economy, offering himself to hear all grievances for the purpose of redressing them, and for other purposes of the highest importance both of the welfare of the Corporation and of those who are the objects of their care" – hath in no one instance been complied with.

That the 9th bye law, declaring that "no servant or officer of the Corporation shall be eligible as a Director or Guardian" hath been collusively evaded in the instance of the surgeon.

That the abolition of the bye law, No. 10, which "prohibited any Director or Acting Guardian from supplying the House with any commodity" hath opened a door to gross imposition.

That the order which was proposed and declared to be a bye law of your Corporation for exempting those who hire children out of the House from the burthen of a parish apprentice, is not only, as before mentioned, the cause of great and unnecessary expence, but is also pregnant with gross inhumanity to the children, with future evil to the Corporation, and with manifest partiality and injustice to those by whom apprentices are taken; and further, that as it was not only made to repeal a bye law agreeable to the Act of Incorporation, but is also inconsistent with the 43rd of Elizabeth, it ought on all these accounts to be exploded as pernicious and absurd.

That the Order Book of the Proceedings of the Directors and Acting Guardians almost everywhere swarms with similar absurdities.

That, preparatory to the making of contracts, sufficient care is not taken to procure proposals on the best terms for the Corporation, and that, at the last Quarterly Meeting, a contract was made for supplying the House with the most expensive kinds of spice.

That, in borrowing money, it has been a customary practice to give bonds which incur interest a considerable time before the money is received.

That at the time the Corporation has been and still is paying interest at the rate of 4½ and 5 per cent for no less a sum that £9,900, the last borrowed sum of £800 was suffered for some time to lie idle; and whilst interest for the whole debt is going on at the rates above mentioned, the residue of £555 is making no more than 2½ per cent, and so must for some time remain.

That, through the poverty brought upon the Corporation, relief, acknowledged to be necessary, has been repeatedly withholden.

That repairs, which ought to long since to have been made, are most destructively increased, and the whole of your House is hastening to ruin.

It would have been a far more pleasant employment to have reported, had there been any ground, that a further application to Parliament might be needless; but it must now we think be evident to all, that without it, the debt of the Corporation can never be discharged.

Samuel Henley, Francis Brooke, William Whitby, Jacob Whitbread, Richard Frank, Joseph Gunning, Edmund Jenney.

15 February 1791

A General Meeting of the owners and occupiers of lands in the said Hundreds ◇ and also the creditors of the said Corporation held at the Sessions Hall in the town of Woodbridge ◇ for the purpose of receiving from the Committee appointed to examine into the actual state of the said Corporation their Report and to consider the measures proper to be taken thereupon.

The Revd Francis Capper, chairman.

The Report of the Committee of Enquiry was received and agreed by this meeting that 500 of the same be imediately printed.

Resolved unanimously that it is the opinion of this Meeting that an application to Parliament is not only unavoidable but necessary to be immediately made.

Resolved unanimously that as no time must be lost in applying to Parliament a Committee be appointed consisting of the same gentlemen who have brought the Report together with <additional 5 names> to prepare and forward a Bill to Parliament for the purpose of obtaining an Act. That any seven of them be a Committee and that the committee be open to any of the Guardians who shall choose to attend.

Resolved unanimously that the following petition be received sealed with the Corporation Seal forwarded to the Members of the County and that they be desired to present it to the honorable House of Commons.

To the Honourable the Commons of Great Britain in Parliament assembled.

The humble petition of the Guardians of the Poor within the Hundreds of Loes and Wilford in the County of Suffolk.

Sheweth,

That an Act of Parliament was passed <> whereby your petitioners were author-ized to erect and fit up certain buildings for the reception and employment of the poor and to borrow money to defray the expence thereof and also to make certain rates or assessments upon the inhabitants for paying the interest of the money so to be borrowed and for defraying the expence attending the management support and maintenance of the poor and divers other powers and authorities were given to your petitioners for carrying the purposes of the said Act into execution.

That in pursuance of the powers and authorities aforesaid your petitioners have caused several buildings to be erected and fitted up and have borrowed a consider-able sum of money upon the credit of the said rates or assessments which has been applied in defraying the expence of erecting and fitting up the said buildings and in the support and maintenance of the poor.

That your petitioners have not a power under the said Act of borrowing more than one hundred pounds over and above what is already borrowed and that a larger sum is wanted for the immediate necessary repairs alterations or enlargement of the aforesaid buildings and that the money arising by the said rates or assessments is found insufficient for the support and maintenance of the poor <> and that the said Act is in other respects ineffectual for the purposes thereby intended and unless the said rates or assessments are increased and some amendments made to the said Act, the poor <> cannot be properly maintained and supported and the said buildings sufficiently repaired, altered or enlarged nor the money borrowed be paid off and discharged.

Your petitioners therefore humbly pray that leave may be given to bring in a Bill for effecting the several purposes before mentioned by such ways and means and in such manner as this honourable house shall think proper.

Given under the common seal of our Corporation <15 February 1791>.

Resolved unanimously that the thanks of the Meeting be presented to the Gentlemen of the Committee of enquiry for their trouble in preparing their report.

Resolved unanimously that the thanks of this meeting be presented to the Chairman.

17 February 1791 [*Committee to obtain an Act of Parliament*][4]

The Committee proceeded on the above business and adjourned this meeting.

11 March 1791 [*Committee to obtain an Act of Parliament*]

The Committee <> went through the several clauses of the new bill and having approved of the same it is unanimously requested that the Revd Richard Frank do use his best endeavours to get the same passed both Houses of Parliament as soon as possible.

28 March 1791

Ordered that the Clerk do write to the Overseer of Charsfield to inform them that the Directors and Guardians request they will give a note to the Overseers of Clopton acknowledging Henry Collins a poor child aged 13 years (his father being dead) to belong to their parish if they are certain he belongs to them.

---

[4]   This committee also met on 24 February 1791.

24 May 1791

The first meeting of the Guardians of the Poor within the Hundreds of Loes and Wilford in the county of Suffolk at the House of Industry in Melton <> in pursuance of an Act of Parliament intitled an Act for the Better Relief and Employment of the Poor within the Hundreds of Loes and Wilford in the County of Suffolk <> for the purpose of choosing twenty four Acting Guardians of the Poor <> together with the twenty four Directors named and appointed in the said Act will have full power and authority to carry the purposes aforesaid into execution.

Present

Richard Frank clerk	Samuel Hingeston clerk
Francis Brooke Esq.	John Ayton Gent.
Jacob Whitbread Esq.	William Waller Gent.
Edmund Jenney Esq.	Samuel Fontenelle Gent.
William Whitby Esq.	Thomas Simpson Gent.
Francis Capper clerk	Richard Wilkinson Gent.
Samuel Kilderbee Sen. Esq.	Martin Harsant Gent.
Robert Trotman Esq.	John Whimper Gent.
Jacob Chilton clerk	Burwell Edwards Gent.
Joseph Gunning clerk	Robert Ashford Gent.
Samuel Kilderbee Junior clerk	John Black clerk
Robert Reynolds clerk	John Woolnough Gent.

The Act was ordered to be read and was read accordingly.

The Revd Richard Frank being proposed to be chairman <> was unanimously elected accordingly.

The Directors present delivered in their several qualifications to the Chairman in pursuance of the said Act.

The following persons were unanimously elected Acting Guardians pursuant to the said Act.

Mr John Woolnough	Mr John Garrett
Mr Benjamin Cooper	Mr Samuel Collett
Mr William Neeve	Mr Benjamin Cooper
Mr John Weeding	Mr Peter Kersey
Mr Corry Cavell	Mr Thomas Thredkell
Mr John Sutton	Mr John Cooper
Mr John Paine	Mr James Aldhous
Mr Thomas Garneys	Mr James Woods
Mr Thomas Waller	Mr Thomas Butcher
Mr Thomas Rose	Mr William Heffer
Mr Robert Linsted	Mr Robert Crane
Mr Thomas Crisp	Mr Thomas Smith

Ordered that the clerk do write to the Treasurer and desire his attendance with his books.

Ordered that the note of Messrs. Cornwell and Co for the sum of £558 3s. 0d. be paid to Robert Trotman Esq. for the use of the Corporation and that Mr Trotman be requested to accept the same.

26 May 1791

Directors	Present	Guardians
Revd Richard Frank Chairman		Mr John Woolnough
Francis Brooke Esq.		Mr Benjamin Cooper

Jacob Whitbread Esq.
Edmund Jenney Esq.
William Whitby Esq.
Samuel Kilderbee Senior Esq.
Robert Trotman Esq.
Revd Jacob Chilton
Revd Joseph Gunning
Revd Samuel Kilderbee Junior
Revd Robert Reynolds
Revd Samuel Hingeston
Mr John Ayton
Mr William Waller
Mr Samuel Fontenelle
Mr Thomas Simpson
Mr Burwell Edwards
Mr Robert Ashford
Mr John Whimper

Mr William Neeve
Mr Thomas Garneys
Mr Thomas Rose
Mr John Garrett
Mr Peter Kersey
Mr Thomas Thredkell
Mr John Cooper
Mr James Aldhous
Mr James Woods
Mr Thomas Butcher
Mr Robert Crane
Mr Thomas Smith
Mr John Sutton
Mr John Paine
Mr Robert Linsted
Mr John Weeding
Mr Corry Cavell
Mr Samuel Collett
Mr Thomas Waller
Mr William Heffer

Twenty two of the Acting Guardians present delivered in their several qualifications to the Chairman in pursuance of the Incorporated Act.

At this meeting Robert Trotman Esq. paid to the Directors and Guardians the sum of £558 3s. 0d. which he received of Messrs. Cornwell and Co., being the residue of the principal and interest of the sum of £800 0s. 0d. mentioned in the late Treasurers Account.

Ordered that the sum of £200 19s. 10d. be paid to the Revd Richard Frank being so much expenditure by him in obtaining the present Act of Parliament ◇ and the remaining sum of £357 3s. 2d. is ordered into the hands of Mr Richard Wood.

	Directors	1st Quarter	Guardians
June	Mr Samuel Fontenelle		Mr John Garrett
	Mr John Ayton		Mr Corry Cavell
July	Robert Trotman Esq.		Mr Samuel Collett
	Francis Brooke Esq.		Mr Thomas Garneys
Aug.	Revd Joseph Gunning		Mr James Woods
	Revd William Brown		Mr Robert Crane Senior
Sept.	Edmund Jenney Esq.	2nd Quarter	Mr John Cooper
	Revd Francis Capper		Mr Thomas Waller
Oct.	Revd Robert Reynolds		Mr John Weeding
	Mr Burwell Edwards		Mr Thomas Thredkell
Nov.	Mr William Waller		Mr William Neeve
	Mr Robert Ashford		Mr Thomas Smythe
Dec.	Revd Richard Frank	3rd Quarter	Mr Peter Kersey
	William Whitby Esq.		Mr James Aldhous
Jan.	Revd Samuel Kilderbee		Mr John Woolnough
	Mr Martin Harsant		Mr Benjamin Cooper B
Feb.	Jacob Whitbread Esq.		Mr Benjamin Cooper L
	Revd Samuel Hingeston		Mr Thomas Rose
Mar.	Mr Thomas Simpson	4th Quarter	Mr John Sutton
	Mr John Whimper		Mr William Heffer

Apl.	Revd Jacob Chilton	Mr Robert Linsted
	Mr Richard Wilkinson	Mr Thomas Butcher
May	Samuel Kilderbee Esq.	Mr Thomas Crisp
	Peter Maber Esq.	Mr John Paine

Ordered that the thanks of the Directors and Acting Guardians be given to the Revd Richard Frank for his great care and assiduity and the trouble he took in procuring the present Act of Incorporation.

Ordered at this meeting <> that Simon Paternoster, the Treasurer under the late Act, attend at this House <> to settle his accounts, he having sent an excuse of illness for his non-attendance on this day and that a copy of this order be served upon him by the clerk of the meetings.

Ordered that the Directors and Acting Guardians be appointed to act on the Committee at the House of Industry in Melton for the following several months hereafter mentioned,

Whereas no officers under the late Act of Incorporation remain to be officers under the present Act, therefore it is ordered <> that such persons as were officers under the late Act <> shall and may continue in office until they are respectively confirmed in the same or others are chosen in their rooms and notice is directed to be given that an election of such officers will take place on the eleventh day of July next,

Ordered that the nine following persons <9 named directors> or any five of them be a Committee to meet at the House of Industry for those who may apply for officers belonging to the Corporation and to submit the same to the consideration of the Directors and Acting Guardians at a meeting to be held on Monday next at the said House of Industry for their approbation.

Ordered that <5 named directors> or any three of them be a Committee to inspect the present bye laws and to make such alterations additions and amendments as they shall think necessary and to report the same at the next general Quarterly Meeting. And that the same persons be a Committee to inspect the repairs necessary to be done to the buildings belonging to the Corporation and to report the same also at the next General Quarterly Meeting and that they be impowered to call in such persons to their assistance as they shall think proper.

30 May 1791

Complaint having been this day made against Mr William Salmon surgeon for neglect of duty in not properly attending the paupers in the House, and Mr Salmon this day attending and not having justified himself against the said complaint but requested to resign the office of surgeon to the House and to the paupers in the several parishes of Ash, Charsfield, Dallingho, Easton, Hacheston, Letheringham, Marlesford, Rendlesham, Boulge, Bredfield, Debach, Melton, Petistree, Ufford and Wickham Market. His resignation is accepted and the Treasurer is ordered to pay William Salmon the proportion of his salary to this day. And Mr James Lynn, being proposed to be surgeon in his room until the next Quarterly Meeting, is unanimously approved and requested to attend accordingly.

Ordered that an inventory be taken of the furniture goods and articles of every kind belonging to the Corporation now in the House of Industry in Melton in the offices or on the premises thereto belonging, and that Mr Read of Woodbridge do assist the Governor in taking such inventory and that the same be delivered to Mr Richard Wood, who is desired to deliver it and also a schedule of all books papers and writings in his possession belonging to the said Corporation as soon as may be.

The Quarterly Meeting being a day of great and multifarious business ordered that the Committee appointed to revise and examine the bye laws do make their report on <24 June> and not at the next Quarterly Meeting.

Ordered that a Committee <5 names> be appointed to examine the present state of the linnen manufacture and report their opinion upon that at the next Quarterly Meeting.

It being the duty of the Directors and Acting Guardians to be careful and economical in the expenditure of the money intrusted to their charge, the Committee appointed to frame a summary of the duty respectively required of the several officers of the Corporation were unanimously of opinion that the offices of Governor and clerk were not only compatible with each other but that a great saving would arise to the Corporation if they were united. It was therefore moved that <> the said offices <> should be united. It being only an act of justice to Mr Richard Wood the present acting Clerk to declare that during the time which he has served that office now about thirty years he hath conducted himself with propriety and respect to the Directors and Acting Guardians and with zeal and attention to the several duties of his office. Therefore the thanks of this meeting are unanimously voted to him and the Directors and Acting Guardians as a proof of the good opinion they entertain of him do appoint him their solicitor in all law business in which the Corporation may be engaged.

Ordered that the advertisement as now altered for the officers' proposals be inserted in the Ipswich and Bury papers untill the 23rd June next and twice in the Morning Post and Morning Herald. Ordered that this meeting be adjourned.

24 June 1791

It being certified that the Committee appointed to revise and examine the bye laws are not prepared to make their report ordered that the report be made at the next Meeting.

Ordered that Mr Beedon the carpenter and Mr Baker the bricklayer do deliver in their estimates and plans of the repairs and alterations of the buildings to the Directors and Acting Guardians.

7 July 1791

Report of the Committee appointed to inquire into the state of the hempen manufactory carried out on in the House of Industry.

This Committee have examined the stock in hand both of the yarn and wove goods <> and perceiving a very considerable difference in the quality of the woven goods. On inquiry find that one loom in the House and one in Ufford are all that have been employed in weaving the same. And though from yarn of the same or nearly the quality, the goods wove at the Ufford loom bear no comparison in point of goodness to those wove in the House <> and this Committee are given to understand that the prices set against those pieces may be obtained in the state they now are <> whilst many of the remaining pieces being of inferior quality would hardly be saleable either in the present or whited state. This Committee are of the opinion that exposing such to sale would injure the credit of the manufactory should the same be continued in the House and do recommend to the General Meeting that the said inferior goods may be reserved for the use of the said House.

This Committee is informed it is usual in manufactories of this kind for the yarn to be whited previous to its being wove which has not been the practice here, and as there is a considerable quantity of yarn in hand, it is recommended by this

Committee to the General Meeting that the said yarn may be whited before wove by persons whose business it is as the process is attended with difficulty and cannot so well be effected in the House.

P. Maber, John Whimper, J. Woolnough.

Ordered that no more yarn be sent to William List to weave, and that the yarn for the future be whited before it is wove, and that the cloth <> be immediately disposed of at the prices mentioned in the said account and that the remainder be made use of in the said House.

The proposals of Mr Lynn, Mr Whimper and Mr James Lynn as surgeons to the House and two districts. The proposals of Mr Denney and Mr Whincopp as resident surgeons. Also the proposals of Mr Riches as Treasurer also the proposal of Daniel Johnston and Christian Brightwell as Governor Clerk and Matron also of William Hatton and wife as Governor and Matron and of Robert Rainbird and wife as Governor Clerk and Matron were this day received.

11 July 1791

No person having offered for Treasurer, Mr Richard Wood is appointed to that office for this quarter and Jacob Whitbread and Mr Samuel Kilderbee engage to be security for his faithful performance of his office.

Robert Rainbird is duly elected into the office of Governor and Clerk, and Ann his wife into the office of Matron in the room of Daniel Johnston and Christian Brightwell which offices they undertake at the salary of fifty pounds a year.

This meeting is of opinion that a resident surgeon and apothecary be elected to take care of all the poor within the Hundreds except those of the parishes of Kenton, Earl Soham, Creetingham, Brandeston, and Kettleburgh and that a surgeon and apothecary be elected for those parishes.

At the meeting Mr William Whincopp is elected resident surgeon and apothecary at the salary of eighty five pounds a year to be found washing lodging fire and candles to board with the Governor and Matron and to have an apartment to himself. To find his own horses but to be allowed hay, grass and straw for any number not exceeding two to be restricted from all other business medicines to be found by the Corporation, to attend the sick as well in the House as in all the parishes within the Hundreds (except those of Kenton, Earl Soham, Creetingham, Brandeston, and Kettleburgh) but to attend such midwifery cases only where a man is necessary. To find his own tea sugar and wine (except wine for medicines) to attend all committees and report the state of his patients. Three months' notice required of both parties on quitting.

At this meeting Mr William Henchman is elected surgeon and apothecary for the parishes of Kenton, Earl Soham, Creetingham Brandeston, and Kettleburgh and to be allowed three pounds a year for the care of each parish.

At the meeting the Revd George Jones Palmer is re-elected chaplain to the House of Industry from this time to midsummer next at his usual salary.

At this meeting it is ordered and agreed that the rates of the several parishes within the Hundreds be raised one third on the present payments.

At this meeting it is ordered that the Clerk do write to the several creditors of the Corporation to know whether they will accept 4½ per cent if not they will be paid their principal as soon as money can be obtained for that purpose.

The Directors and Acting Guardians are requested to meet <> to receive the Report of the Committee for Framing Bye Laws for the Maintenance of Good Order and Regulation of the Poor within the Hundreds and to consider of the necessary repairs of the House.

Ordered that the Clerk do write to the Churchwardens and Overseers of Butley to inform them that as the payment due from their parish was not paid on the last day of payment that they do imediately pay the same to the Treasurer if not the parish will be reassessed for payment thereof.

Ordered that <5 named directors> be a committee to fit up and furnish the surgeons apartment in the House of Industry.

19 July 1791

Ordered that the Governor do send the hemp yarn to Mr Mann of Sibton to be whitened agreeable to proposals.

2 August 1791

This day the bye laws were gone through with and were ordered to be prepared for printing and when printed to be delivered to the Directors and Acting Guardians in order for their approbation at the next Quarterly Meeting.

Ordered that the alterations in the sick wards and the nursery stair case leading to the Committee Room and the garret over the Committee Room be executed by William Baker and William Beeden according to the plan delivered in and at the rates specified in their estimates for work and labour. That all materials and the carriage thereof to be found by the Corporation yet nevertheless their work, when done, to be submitted to inspection and valuation. And it is further ordered that the floors of the nurserys which are to be converted into sick wards and the floors of the spinning rooms be taken up and laid with fir. That the tiling over the other part of the House and out buildings be repaired where absolutely necessary. That a brick wall be built from the North Wing of the House to the Garden Wall and that the water from the eaves of the North Wing be thrown from the House. That a copy of this order be given to the workmen and that they do immediately go about and that <7 named directors> or any five of them be a Committee to put this order in execution <>.

17 October 1791[5]

No Treasurer being elected it is requested that William Whitby and Jacob Whitbread Esqs. and Richard Frank, clerk, take into their charge the money of the Corporation and to receive such further sums as may be paid in and to make such disbursements as shall be ordered by the Corporation until such time as a Treasurer shall be elected.

Ordered that Mr Johnston, the late Governor, be paid one guinea, as a gratuity and Mrs Brightwell, the late Matron, 10s. 6d. as a gratuity for their trouble in assisting the present Governor and Matron.

Ordered that Richard Newman and his wife be appointed schoolmaster and schoolmistress to the House at the salary of £20 a year.

Ordered that the surgeon do procure a warm bath for the use of the paupers in the said House.

Ordered that lamps be used in the said House instead of candles which are now used.

---

5   The following entries are taken from SROI ADA11/A/B/2/5.

Ordered that the Governor do procure two looms for the use of the hemp business in the said House.

Whereas at a meeting held on the 2nd August 1791 <7 named directors> were empowered to put in execution an order touching certain repairs and alterations proposed to be made to the house. But which order by reason of certain circumstances which have since happened has not been executed. And whereas at this season of the year it will be improper to attend to the generality of the said order <> it is at this meeting ordered that the said committee to direct and order such repairs and alterations in and about the house as they in their discretion shall think proper to be done at this season of the year.

Whereas at is found inconvenient to attend to a general discussion of certain printed rules and regulations proposed as a code of bye laws for the good rule, order and government of the house. Therefore it is resolved that such rules and regulations be considered as binding until the next annual meeting and no longer except in respect to certificates which this meeting have determined to grant within the Corporation.

9 January 1792

At this meeting two proposals were offered for the apprentices out poor children one by the Revd Mr Franks and the other by Mr Ayton and both of them having been debated and put to the vote the former was carried against the latter only one voice dissenting.

It is therefore ordered that the proposal offered by Mr Franks be adopted, and that the same be entered amongst the orders of this meeting. And the same one be therefore entered accordingly that is to say,

Apprentices

In apportioning apprentices the following Table and Rules are proposed as most agreeable to the Rule of Law and the principles of equity.

Occupying		who should have						
Every person occupying per annum	£300	6	1	3	6	10	15	21
And every person occupying	£250	5	2	5	9	14	20	
	£200	4	4	8	13	19		
	£150	3	7	12	18			
	£100	2	11	17				
	£50	1	16					

That then every person occupying under £50 and above ten or any sum between £50 and £100 should have one each beginning with the highest.

Then every tradesman (if judged capable) should take one each being appointed as best to that trade. That in all cases when more than one child is to be apprenticed to any parish the eldest child shall be first appointed and so on to the youngest. That care be taken (if possible) that two girls be not apprenticed to the same person immediately following each other.

NB that no child be apprenticed who has not had the smallpox.

Ordered that the burying ground be enlarged and that the Bishop of the Diocese be humbly requested to consecrate a sufficient spot for that purpose.

At this meeting John Carthew gentleman is chosen by a majority of voices to be Treasurer of this Incorporation at the annual salary of £10 he making no other charge whatever in respect to the execution of the office and that the said John Carthew together with Peter Maber, Gent. and Thomas Carthew, clerk, enter into a bond in the penal sum of £1,500 for the due and faithful execution of the said office which is to commence from this day.

12 April 1792

Directors	Present	Guardians
Francis Brooke Esq.		Mr Heffer
Revd Mr Frank		John Woolnough
Mr Whitby		
Revd Kilderbee		
Revd Chilton		
Revd Browne		
Thomas Simpson		
Martin Harsant		
Revd Reynolds		
Revd Gunning		
Mr Edwards		
Mr William Waller		
Mr John Whimper		

The following persons were duly elected Directors and Acting Guardians:

	Directors		Guardians
	Directors	1st Quarter	Guardians
April	Revd Hingeston		Mr Robert Linsted
	Mr Richard Wilkinson		Mr T. Butcher
May	Samuel Kilderbee Esq.		Mr Peter Sparks
	Peter Mabor Esq.		Mr Nathaniel Fuller
June	Mr Samuel Fontenelle		Mr John Felgate
	Mr John Ayton		Mr John Waller
July	Robert Trotman Esq.	2nd Quarter	Mr Thomas Garneys
	Francis Brook Esq.		Mr S. Collet
Aug.	Revd Gunning		Mr Gross
	Revd Browne		Mr Mabson
Sept.	Edmund Jenney Esq.		Mr J. Cooper
	Revd Francis Capper		Mr Blake
Oct.	Revd Reynolds	3rd Quarter	Mr Weeding
	Mr Burwell Edwards		Mr Cooke
Nov.	Mr William Waller		Mr Neeve
	Mr Robert Ashford		Mr Harvey
Dec.	Revd Richard Frank		Mr Kersey
	William Whitby Esq.		Mr John Aldhouse
Jan.	Revd Samuel Kilderbee	4th Quarter	Mr Woolnough
	Mr Martin Harsant		Mr B. Cooper
Feb.	Jacob Whitbread Esq.		Mr Stud
	Revd Jacob Chilton		Mr Catchpole
Mar.	Mr Thomas Simpson		Mr Heffer
	Mr John Whimper		Mr Wasp

8 March 1793

Ordered that Messrs. Wood the solicitors do prosecute Francis Mullinger and Thomas Rade (labourers) at the expense of the aforesaid Corporation for assembling together with the intent to pull down the House of Industry in Melton.

7 April 1793

	Directors	Present	Guardians
	Revd Frank		Mr Woolnough
	J. Whitbread Esq.		Mr R. Linsted
	Revd Kilderbee		Mr J. Waller
	Revd Chilton		Mr W. Neeve
	Revd Reynolds		Mr Studd
	Revd Hingeston		
	Edmund Jenney Esq.		
	Mr Thomas Simpson		
	Revd Browne		
	Robert Trotman Esq.		

The following persons were duly elected Directors and Acting Guardians:

	Directors	1st Quarter	Guardians
Apl.	Revd Chilton		Mr John Linsted
	Mr R. Wilkinson		Mr Thomas Butcher
May	Chaloner Arcedeckne Esq.		Mr Peter Spark
	Peter Maber Esq.		Mr Nathaniel Fuller
June	Mr Samuel Fontenelle		Mr Brewer
	Mr Ayton		Mr John Waller
July	Robert Trotman Esq.	2nd Quarter	Mr Thomas Garneys
	Francis Brook Esq.		Mr Samuel Collet
Aug.	Revd Joseph Gunning		Mr William Schreiber
	Revd Browne		Mr Gross
Sept.	Edmund Jenney Esq.		Mr Edward Man
	Revd Francis Capper		Mr Andrew Blake
Oct.	Revd Hingeston	3rd Quarter	Mr Chandler
	Mr Burwell Edwards		Mr Timothy Smith
Nov.	Mr William Waller		Mr William Neeve
	Mr Robert Ashford		Mr Rust
Dec.	Revd Frank		Captain Hilcoat
	John Syer MD.		Mr Joseph Jeaffreson
Jan.	Revd Samuel Kilderbee	4th Quarter	Mr J. Woolnough
	Mr Martin Harsant		Mr Catt
Feb.	Jacob Whitbread Esq.		Mr Studd
	Revd Robert Reynolds		Mr Bulmer
Mar.	Mr Thomas Simpson		Mr Button
	Mr John Whimper		Mr Stebing Gross

Ordered 1st that no certificate be granted unless the person applying for one fully satisfy the Committee that he or she belong to one of the incorporated parishes.

2nd that no certificate be granted in any case into any Corporation town nor to any place exceeding the distance of 20 miles from the parish to which the person applying for it belongs.

3rd that it appears to this Committee that there is a deficiency of labourers in agriculture no certificate be granted to labourers in that line out of the Hundreds unless it be such as cannot get habitations within the Hundreds and then only to parishes immediately adjoining the parish to which the person applying for the certificate belong.

4th that all certificate persons brought home because they have become chargeable to the place certified to be carried to and examined before a justice of the peace.

A copy of this should be inserted into every Overseers books.

5 April 1794

Directors	Present	Guardians
F. Brooke Esq.		Mr Stebing Gross
Revd Frank		Mr J. Woolnough
Edmund Jenney Esq.		Mr J. Studd
Revd Gunning		Mr W. Neeve
J. Whitbread Esq.		Mr William Schreiber
Revd Browne		Mr S. Collett
Mr S. Fontenelle		
J. Syer M.D.		
Revd Chilton		
Mr Thomas Simpson		
Revd Kilderbee		
Mr William Waller		
Mr Richard Wilkinson		

The following persons were duly elected Directors and Acting Guardians <>:

	Directors		Guardians
	Directors	1st Quarter	Guardians
Apl.	Revd Chilton		Mr John Trusson
	Mr Richard Wilkinson		Mr Nathaniel Barthorp
May	Peter Maber Esq.		Mr Andrew Blake
	Francis Brooke Esq.		Mr Thomas Smith
June	Mr Simon Fontenelle		Mr Jonathan Weeding
	Mr John Ayton		Mr Jonathan Waller
July	Robert Trotman Esq.	2nd Quarter	Mr Thomas Garneys
	Chaloner Arcedeckne		Mr Samuel Collett
Aug.	Revd Gunning		Mr Schreiber
	Revd William Browne		Mr Samuel Gross
Sept.	Edmund Jenney Esq.		Mr Burnett
	Revd Capper		Mr William Cooper
Oct.	Revd Hingeston	3rd Quarter	Mr Balls
	Mr Burwell Edwards		Mr Wase
Nov.	Mr William Waller		Mr William Cook
	Mr Robert Ashford		Mr Stephen Catchpole
Dec.	John Syer M.D.		Mr J. Jeaffreson
	Revd Franks		Captain Hilcoat
Jan.	Revd Kilderbee	4th Quarter	Mr J. Woolnough
	Mr Martin Harsant		Mr Corry Cavel
Feb.	J. Whitbread Esq.		Mr Studd
	Revd Reynolds		Mr Bulmer
Mar.	Mr Thomas Simpson		Mr James Aldhouse
	Mr John Whimper		Mr Stebing Gross

Ordered that Mr Wood the Trustee of the Corporated Estate be directed to present in the name of the Guardians of the Poor <> a petition <>as are used on such occasion to the Right Revd Father in God, Charles, Bishop of Norwich, requesting him that he will be pleased to consecrate the chapple and burial ground belonging to the said Guardians and farther that the said trustee be empowered to make such grant <> as may be deemed necessary.

9 April 1795

	Directors	Present	Guardians
	Revd Frank		Mr John Woolnough
	J. Whitbread Esq.		Mr John Trusson
	Mr S. Fontenelle		Mr Stebing Gross
	Revd Reynolds		Mr Schreiber
	F. Brook Esq.		Mr Stud
	Mr T. Simpson		
	Revd Kilderbee		Directors
	J. Syer M.D.		Mr J. Whimper
	Mr R. Wilkinson		
	Mr M. Harsant		
	Revd Chilton		
	Revd Hingeston		

The following persons were duly elected Directors and Acting Guardians:

	Directors		Guardians
	Directors	1st Quarter	Guardians
Apl.	Revd Chilton		Mr John Trusson
	Mr Richard Wilkinson		Mr Edward Keer
May	Francis Brooke Esq.		Mr Andrew Blake
	Peter Maber Esq.		Mr William Page
June	Mr Samuel Fontenelle		Mr William Heffer
	Mr John Ayton		Mr Thomas Threadkell
July	Robert Trotman Esq.	2nd Quarter	Mr Thomas Garneys
	Chaloner Arcedeckne Esq		Mr Samuel Collett
Aug.	Revd Joseph Gunning		William Schreiber Esq.
	Revd William Browne		Mr Samuel Gross
Sept.	Edmund Jenney Esq.		Mr William Cooper
	Revd Francis Capper		Mr Jonathan Asher
Oct.	Revd Hingeston	3rd Quarter	Mr Thomas Woodward
	Mr Burwell Edwards		Mr Thomas Peck
Nov.	Mr William Waller		Mr John Pitcher
	Mr Robert Ashford		Mr Peter Kersey
Dec.	Revd Frank		Captain Hilcoat
	John Syer M.D.		Mr John Jefferson
Jan.	Revd Samuel Kilderbee	4th Quarter	Mr John Catchpole
	Mr Martin Harsant		Mr John Woolnough
Feb.	Revd Robert Reynolds		Mr Studd
	J. Whitbread Esq.		Mr Isaac Baker
Mar.	Mr Thomas Simpson		Mr Stebing Gross
	Mr John Whimper		Mr Jeptha Waller

The third Weekly Minute Book,
29 March 1784–7 June 1790[6]

29 March 1784

Directors	Present	Guardians
The Revd Mr Hingeston		Mr N. K. Chandler
		Mr Nathaniel Steptoe

Ordered that the Overseers of the following parishes do allow as under:

Ash: Isaac Betts for his daughter being troubled with fits, Widow Dawkins being infirm, Hannah Ling and Ann Curtis with their infant bastard children, 1s. a week each for this Qtr. in case they so long live.

Bredfield: Widow Button having 3 children 1s. a week for this Qtr.

Bromeswell: Susan Cordy being infirm and Robert Crane's child having but one hand 1s. a week each for this Qtr.

Creetingham: Thomas Bulmer being an ideot and the wife of Abraham Browning being bedrid 2s. a week each. Elizabeth Day with her infant bastard child 1s. a week, and Martha and Hannah Jennings poor children 9d. a week each for this Qtr.

Easton: Ann Lyon with her infant bastard child 1s. a week for this Qtr.

Eyke: Widow Studd being infirm 1s. a week for this Qtr.

Kettleburgh: Mary Mann with her infant bastard child 1s. a week for this Qtr.

Kenton: Elizabeth Chenery being an ideot 1s. a week for this Qtr.

Marlesford: John Burrell's wife being bedrid 2s. a week, Francis Blaxhall's wife being blind, widow Frost being infirm, Priscilla Girling and Sarah Bickers with their infant bastard children 1s. a week for this Qtr.

Melton: Benjamin Johnson being infirm and Elizabeth Fairs with her infant bastard child 1s. a week each for this Qtr.

Monewden: Jeffry Boon being blind and having a wife and 4 children 2s. a week for this Qtr.

Petistree: Amy Lock and Elizabeth Warner with their infant bastard children 1s. a week each for this Qtr.

Ramsholt: Widow Nunn having 4 children 2s. 6d a week for this Qtr.

Rendlesham: Esther Smith being an ideot 1s. a week for this Qtr.

Ufford: Widow Manning having 2 children 1s. a week for this Qtr.

Wickham Market: The wife of Thomas Finch with 3 children 2s. a week, Widow Mapleston being a lunatick 1s. a week for this Qtr. and John Spink his wife continuing ill 2s. 6d. for this week.

Eyke: Robert Lock and his wife continuing ill 2s. for this week.

Debach: Robert Atkins his wife being ill and having 5 children 2s. for this week.

Butley: William Garrod continuing ill 2s. 6d. a week for two weeks.

---

[6] SROI ADA11/A/B/3/3. Earlier entries from the third WMB can be found in the chapter relating to the first QMB.

Debach: Widow Marjoram (of Wickham) being infirm 1s. a week for this Qtr. in case she lives, Richard Marjoram of Charsfield undertaking that she shall be no further expence to the Corporation in illness or death.

Charsfield: Ann Borrett with her infant bastard child 1s. a week for this Qtr. and to write to William Foreman of Capell to pay the above allowance or that another action will be commenced against him. Mary Mann with 2 children 10s. for 5 weeks allowance ordered by F. Brooke Esq. and 1s. a week for this Qtr.

Kenton: Elizabeth Barker being very ill 2s. 6d. a week for two weeks.

Easton: Widow Boon continuing ill 2s. a week for 2 weeks.

Alderton: Widow Harvey being ill 2s. a week for 2 weeks and William Willis having but one arm and having a wife and 3 children 1s. a week for the Qtr.

Bawdsey: the wife of John Whiting (he being in Bridewell) 1s. 6d. a week for 2 weeks.

Bredfield: Widow Tricker continuing ill 1s. a week for two weeks.

Hacheston: Widow Pretty having 2 small children 1s. a week for this Qtr.

Ufford: Henry Benham continuing lame 3s. this week., William Cressy his wife being ill and having 4 children 2s. a week for 3 weeks, Widow Parker continuing ill 2s. for this week, and Jonathan Catchpole continuing lame 2s. for this week.

Creetingham: 20s. towards the burial of Mary Johnson an old person.

Dallingho: Robert Battle, his wife lying in and having 4 children 2s. 6d.

I Sarah Bowers of Ash widow do agree to hire Diana Bailey a poor girl of the said parish now in the House of Industry (aged 14 years) of the Directors and Guardians for one year from this day and I do promise to pay the said Guardians one guinea for her wages but if she be cloathed at the expiration of their service in the same manner she is cloathed out of the said House the said Sarah Bowers may retain her wages for such her cloathing. As witness my hand   the mark of Sarah Bowers.
    Witness. Richard Wood Junior.

I Jacob Pawsey of Ash farmer do agree to hire Maria Grayston a poor girl of the said parish now in the House of Industry (aged 15 years) of the Directors and Guardians for one year from this day and I do promise to pay the said Guardians one guinea for her wages but if she be cloathed at the expiration of their service in the same manner she is cloathed out of the said House the said Jacob Pawsey may retain her wages for such her cloathing. As witness my hand   Jacob Pawsey.
    Witness. Richard Wood Junior.

Marlesford: John Bird being lame 2s. for this week, and the Widow Read having 3 children ill 2s. a week for 4 weeks.

Boyton: Ann Pannifer with her infant bastard child 1s. a week for this Qtr.

Hollesly: Robert Mullinger and wife continuing ill 3s. 2d. above the former order and widow Damant and Mary Lamb very ill 6s. ordered by Mr Barthorp last week. Widow Damant 2s 6d. a week for 2 weeks and Mary Wife of John Lamb 3s. a week for two weeks.

I William Whitman of Kenton farmer do agree to hire Edward Kemp a poor boy of the said parish now in the House of Industry aged 14½ years of the Directors and Guardians for one year from this day and I do promise to pay the said Guardians one pound and five shillings for his wages but if he be cloathed at the expiration of the service in the same manner he is cloathed out of the said House the said

187

William Whitman may retain his wages for such his cloathing. As witness my hand William Whitman.

Witness. Richard Wood Junior.

7 February 1785

\Mr Gosling

The Committee at the House of Industry at Melton had this day a complaint made against you for sending last week to the House very bad beef not agreeable to your contract which the Committee this day examined and found to be so therefore ordered me to acquaint you therewith and that they shall insist on your sending right good steer beef according to your contract or they shall compel you thereto and they request you will attend them on Monday next at the House about eleven o'clock in the forenoon. Signed R Wood./[7]

28 February 1785

It appearing to this Committee that John Thompson, sawyer, (who with his wife and six children are removed from St. Nicholas in Harwich to Bredfield) is a very industrious man of good character has constant employment and can earn 6s. a week one week with another and belongs to a Society Club. And it likewise appearing that he must be supported at the expense of the Corporation being unable to procure that kind of work to enable him to support his family in the Hundreds. Ordered that the Clerk do give a note to the said parish of St Nicholas acknowledging them to belong to Bredfield. And that the said Jonathan Thompson do attend the next Quarterly Meeting (with such note) that it may be considered whether a certificate shall be granted or not.

John Thompson wife and 6 children being without work 3s. for last week.

7 March 1785

The officers of the parish of St Nicholas Harwich refusing to accept the note given last week (per order) unless the Corporation will indemnify them for all expences that may accrue on account of John Thompson's family. Ordered that the Clerk do give a note to indemnify them until the next Quarterly Meeting when he is ordered to attend with the note.

The said John Thompson being out of employ and having a wife and 6 children 7s. for last week and this.

18 April 1785

Ordered that Keeble Cook apprenticed to Thomas Fox butcher for three years from <5 April 1784> be assigned over to William Storey of Alderton, brick maker, for the remainder of the term and that the Clerk do prepare assignments accordingly.

9 May 1785

Wickham Market: Widow Smith being ill (a tumour in her breast going to be extirpated) 3s. 6d. for this week.

---

7   Note inserted in SROI ADA11/A/B/3/3.

30 May 1785

Wickham Market: the Governor to allow the wife of Roger Branch with 7 children, he having left them, 6s. for this week, she undertaking to endeavour to find and invite him to return, the Committee promising that if he returns again he shall not be punished.

13 June 1785

Creetingham: James Jay being very ill and having a wife and 2 children 2s. for last week and 3s. for this week.

4 July 1785

Creetingham: the Widow Jay and child being ill of a putrid fever 8s. for last week including a nurse and being obliged to have a nurse 5s. 6d. a week for this week inclusive of wine and nurse.

11 July 1785

Creetingham: for the burial of the Widow Jays child of a putrid fever 18s. for additional wine and maintenance by order of the surgeon 7s 6d. for last week the widow Jay continuing very ill and being obliged to have 2 nurses 1s. a day for their support this week and such wine as the surgeon thinks necessary and the nurses 6d. a day each for this week for their trouble in case the Widow Jay lives.

Creetingham: William Peck, turned off by his master Captain Wetherall on account of a sore on his thigh, received in to the House of Industry and ordered that the Clerk do write to Mr Wetherall to know the cause of discharging him.

25 July 1785

Wickham Market: Roger Branch having got himself and son into constant work at Bury ordered that the Governor do allow him 4s. 6d. he being at that expence over and above his former allowance.

James Fiske a pauper in the House being guilty of running away from the Pest House and going to his parish and endangering them with the Small Pox and returning again to the House is ordered to be punished with having only bread and water on the next meat day.

15 August 1785

Creetingham: Robert Jay continuing ill of putrid fever £3 8s. 10½d. for wine and provisions for last week as by bill delivered and it is ordered that 6 bottles of wine be provided and such provisions as will appear to Mr Henchman to be necessary for them for this week.

Alderton: Henry Smith (aged 7 years) received into the House and Sarah Smith (aged 9 years) discharged and delivered to her mother to be cured of the scald head.

22 August 1785

Creetingham: Robert Jay and family not yet well of putrid fever £2 2s. 9d. for last week's expenses and 7s. for this weeks and Mary Earl the nurse and an infant child of Jay being ill with the same fever 3 bottles of wine and such necessarys as Mr Henchman will think proper for this week.

29 August 1785

Creetingham: Jay's child, Mary Earl and Martha Hollis continuing ill of putrid fever £2 6s. 11½d. for last week's expences as by bill and such necessarys as Mr Henchman will think proper for this week.

5 September 1785

Creetingham: Jay's child, Martha Hollis and Mary Earl continuing ill of the putrid fever £2 2s. 2d. for last week's expenses as by bill and 20s. for the burial of Mary Earl.

12 September 1785

Creetingham: Martha Hollis and Jays child continuing ill of putrid fever £1 8s. 3d. for last week's expenses as by bill and for Martha Hollis continuing ill 4s. 6d. a week for two weeks and for Jays child 1s. 6d. a week for two weeks and Robert Jay 1s. a week for two weeks.

26 September 1785

Creetingham: Daniel Jay an orphan (aged 7 years) 1s. 6d. for this week.

3 October 1785

Creetingham: on 15 August last a deduction of £2 7s. 0d. was made as then appearing an over charge for the attendance of a physician on the paupers then ill of a putrid fever. On further inquiry it appears to have been ordered by Mr Henchman as necessary. Ordered that it be paid by the Overseer.

2 December 1785

\Disbursements for James Martin.

	£	s.	d.
To a pair of breeches	0	4	6
To a pair of shoos	0	5	0
To a hat	0	2	3
To 2 wastcoats	0	10	6
To 6 yards of cloth and making 2 shirts	0	7	6
To 2 pairs stockings	0	4	8
To a pair of bufkins	0	1	0
To a slop and makeing	0	2	0
To shoos mending	0	3	0
	2	0	5

Richard Wilkinson./[8]

6 February 1786

Agreed of the Committee to accept of James Hamblin of Kirton labourer £17 10s. 0d. in full for all charges and expences attending the birth and maintenance of such bastard child or children as Elizabeth Spall of Creetingham single woman is now pregnant with and shall be delivered of which was paid to the Governor for the use of the Corporation.

---

8   Note inserted in SROI ADA11/A/B/3/3.

William Knappit and Simon Spalding paupers in the House were ordered by the above Committee to have only bread and water on the next two meat days for going away from the House one whole day without the leave of the Committee or the Governor.

15 May 1786
William Keable a poor boy (let to Mr George Osborn 21 February 1785) being lame in his knee, received into the House of Industry, the said George Osborn agreeing to hire William Holmes (of Hatcheston) now in the House of Industry in his place, until Michaelmas next or until the said William Keable is recovered of his lameness if he should recover before Michaelmas next.

22 May 1786
Ordered that the Governor doth advance to Roger Branch (a certificate person from Wickham Market to Woodbridge) having a wife and 7 children the sum of thirty shillings to enable him to pay his rent and support his family on his promise of returning three shillings a month until the whole is repaid to the Governor.

23 October 1786
Ash: Jonathan Shepard Esq. paid the penalty of £10 for not taking Sarah Pizzey an apprentice. Revd Mr Kilderbee paid the penalty of £10 for not taking Lydia Gray an apprentice. Nb. the money was paid to the Governor.

30 October 1786
Rendlesham: To be allowed for Samuel Baskett an accidental pauper in the parish now removed to the House having been very ill for a fortnight not removable and attended by a nurse 20s.

5 February 1787
\Gentlemen
This is to certify that Sarah, widow of the late Francis Skinner who died at your House of Industry do belong to the parish of Butley they having a certificate from that parish to Woodbridge in the year 1766 and that the said Sarah have been since her husband's death supported by her son and daughter in Woodbridge.
John Dowsing Woodbridge, January 22nd 1787.[9]
Butley: Sarah Skinner widow received into the House being old and infirm.

\Mr Hunt
You have made a distress of the goods of James Burrows in Sutton have done it in an illegal manner and in particular in removing the goods to Tunstall and having given no account of what has been done with them on account of which he has applyed to a Magistrate who has ordered him 5s. a week which must be paid by the Directors and Guardians. I am therefore ordered by the Directors and Guardians to inform you that unless you imediately make satisfaction for the illegality of the distress you will compell them to take up the matter on behalf of the man and to commence an action against you on account of the same.

---

9   Note inserted in SROI ADA11/A/B/3/3.

I am RW. Melton. August 6th 1787./[10]

\Holbrook August 4th 1786
   To the Directors of Melton House of Industry.
Gentlemen
   A misfortune having happened in our parish to a poor man one John Deal who was killed by a fall from a cart when loading of hay the 25th of June and upon enquiring find a certificate was given from the parish of Bawdsey to this parish the 24th Dec. 1757 by John Jeffreson and Hez Harper. I am referd to you the expenses attending his burial the inquest etc. and which if you will be kind enough to order the payment of to Mr Thos. Shave on the Key at Ipswich it will save the expence of a journey to Melton or Bawdsey and will oblige your humble servant William Daniel Overseer in Holbrook.

Horse and man to the Coroner at Ipswich		2s.	6d.
To the constable swearing a jury		2s.	6d.
Expence attending the inquest		8s.	6d.
To 2 women laying him out and putting him in a coffin etc,		10s.	4d.
Paid for coffin		14s.	
Expenses in carrying him to church		4s.	6d.
Clark and sexton 4s. minister fee 1s 3d		5s.	3d.
	£2	2s.	7d.
Pd for 5yds of bayze & affidavit		5s.	6d.
	£2	8s.	1d.

Melton Aug 15th 1786.
Mr Daniel
   Your letter respecting the expences of burial etc. of John Deal has been laid before the Committee of Directors at Melton House of Industry who know of no such certificate as you mention and before they order payment of such a Bill which does not appear very moderate (10s. 4d. for laying a man out) they expect to be satisfied of such certificate existing, whether the man left any and what family and what goods and effects towards payment of those expenses neither do the Directors conceive that they have anything to do with the expenses of inquest constable etc. RW./[11]

16 March 1789

\26 March 1787. Ordered that John Newson of Hatcheston labourer have a certificate to Walpole in consideration of his having constant work at Sir Gerard Vannecks and Mr Hinton Sir Gerard's steward having undertaken to Mr Hayle that he shall not be unreasonably chargeable to the said Hundreds.

Sir
   The wife of John Newson a labouring man that resides here by certificate from your corporation is at this time very ill and in the opinion of the surgeon that attends her not likely to survive her present affliction she stands in need of the constant

---

[10]   Note inserted in SROI ADA11/A/B/3/3.
[11]   Notes inserted in SROI ADA11/A/B/3/3.

attendance of a nurse and has done for some time which is an expence much too heavy for the man to bear and therefore he has been under the necessity of requiring some relief which he has had to the amount of half a crown only at present but I think he cannot shift with less than three shillings a week during her confinement which I must desire your authority to give him and likewise to satisfy the apothecary if Newson himself should not be able to do it.

Walpole Apl. 8 1788.   Samuel Baddeley.

Sir

The wife of Newson is departed and in that state for it to be necessary not to delay her interment till a letter could arrive from you. I therefore ordered the sum usual with us to be allowed for the burial of her which is eighteen shillings to which you are to add five shillings assistance given before her death and I assure you considering her long and expensive affliction the man has shifted well. There is nothing but the apothecarys demand to pay which I shall direct will be done.

Apl. 17 1788. Samuel Baddeley, Walpole.

The certificate is from Hatcheston signed by Mr Brooke and Mr Carthew.

Sir   Melton April 14th 1788.

I communicated the contents of your letter concerning John Newson, a certificate person to your parish, this day to the Committee at our House of Industry who ordered me to inform you that if he is a certificate person from our Corporation you will please to allow his three shillings a week as long as you think it necessary (if but for a short time) and it shall be paid with the 2s. 6d. you have already allowed but hope you will be as frugal as if it was for your own corporation and when his wife is got better you will please to let me know the whole, and it will be orderou will please to let me know the date of the certificate from what parish and who signed it.

RW./[12]

---

[12] Notes inserted in SROI ADA11/A/B/3/3.

The fourth Weekly Minute Book,
28 June 1790–3 October 1791[13]

28 June 1790

A Quarterly and Weekly Committee Meeting held at the White Hart in Wickham Market

Directors	Present	Guardians
Mr Ayton		Mr Jonathan Ralph
Mr Stammers		Mr Gooch

Ordered that the Overseers of the following parishes do allow as under:

Ash: Widow Dawkins being infirm and William Girling being lame 1s. a week each and Mary Newson with her two infant bastard children two shillings a week for the Qtr.

Brandeston: Widow Spink, Hannah Cooper (residing at Bealings) being infirm 1s. a week each and Mary Chaplin with 2 children 2s. a week for this Qtr.

Bawdsey: Widow Heffer being old sixpence a week for this Qtr.

Boyton: Hannah Kettle with the infant bastard child of Amy her daughter 6d. a week for this Qtr.

Bredfield: Widow Fox with 3 children and Widow of Robert Button with 3 child. 1s. 6d. a week each, Eliz. Bickers being blind, Widow of Ezekiel Button with 2 child, Widow Randall of Woodbridge being old (but to be no further charge) and [ ] Banyard being blind 1s. a week each and the wife of John Whiting with her child her husband being run away 6d. a week for this Qtr. Benj. Bradstray and his wife being old and infirm 2s. a week for this Qtr. in case they so long live.

Butley: Widow Goldsmith with 4 small children 3s. a week and the Widow Woolno' infirm 9d. a week for this Qtr. Widow Fletcher 9d. a week for this Qtr.

Capell: Robert Mays widower with 4 children 1s. 6d. a week and Benjamin Russell being old 6d. a week for this Qtr.

Charsfield: Mary Malden with a lame hand 1s. a week, Mary Crane with her two infant bastard child, Mary Davie with her 2 infant bastard child and Mary Nunn with 3 children. 1s. 6d. a week each. James Fulcher with the infant bastard child of Sarah his daughter and Eliz. Knott with her infant bastard child 6d. a week each for this Qtr.

Creetingham: Thomas Bulmer an ideot 2s. a week, Eliz. Spall with her infant bastard child 1s. a week and Mary Spall with her infant bastard child 1s. 3d. a week for this Qtr.

Dallingho: Widow Squire a certificate person to Dovercourt having 3 children 1s. 6d. a week for this Qtr.

Earl Soham: Mary Bowers with her infant bastard child and the Widow Peck being old 6d. a week each for this Qtr.. Widow Scott and Widow Bowler 1s. a week for this Qtr.

---

13   SROI ADA11/A/B/3/4.

Easton: Widow Lyon of Letheringham, Widow Gall, Widow Plant and James Brinkley all being old and infirm and Lydia Clayton with her infant bastard child 1s. a week each for this Qtr. John Corbold being ill 2s. 6d. a week for 2 weeks.

Eyke: Sarah Adams with her infant bastard child 1s. 6d. a week, Jeremiah Cullum with the infant lame child of William Smith, Jeremiah Ward of Iken and Mary Whitby being old and infirm 1s. a week each, Widow Taylor with 4 small children. 2s. a week. Joseph Boon being bedrid 2s. a week for this Qtr.

Hacheston: Widow Lingwood and Henry Grayston being old and infirm 1s. a week each and the wife of Thomas Bennett having 2 children and he run away 3s. a week for this Qtr. in case he does not return. No 3 of Bennett's children in the House Samuel Brooks 1s. a week for this Qtr. Francis Hill do be admitted into the House.

Hoo: Widow Fryatt being old and infirm 6d. a week for this Qtr.

Kenton: Elizabeth Chenery an ideot 1s. a week, Widow Herring infirm 6d. a week and Stephen Welton being old and infirm 1s. a week for this Qtr. John Potkin being lame 2s. 6d, a week for 2 weeks.

Kettleburgh: John Lay being infirm 1s. a week for this Qtr. Sarah Cressey with her infant bastard child 9d. a week for this Qtr. And 9s. 9d. omitted last Qtr.

Letheringham: Sarah Scotchmer with her infant bastard child 1s. a week for this Qtr.

Monewden: Jeffrey Boon being blind and having a wife and two children 2s. a week for this Qtr.

Marlesford: Widow Eade with 2 children, John Burrell being old and infirm and Sarah Bickers with her infant bastard child 1s. a week each, and Henry Aldred with a lame child 6d. a week for this Qtr.

Melton: Widow Simpson, Widow Crow, Widow Hadman, Widow Bilby Senr, Widow Pierson, John Burrow and Nathaniel Squire all being old and infirm 1s. a week each and Sarah Smith with 2 children belonging to Letheringham 1s. 6d. a week for this Qtr. Widow Bilby 18d. a week for two weeks above her Qtly order. Widow Brand 6d a week for this Qtr.

Ramsholt: Widow Nunn with 2 children 1s. 6d. a week and Alice Allen with her infant bastard child 1s. a week for this Quarter.

Rendlesham: Esther Smith an ideot 1s. a week for this Quarter. Robert Read himself and wife being ill 3s. a week for 2 weeks.

Sutton: Widow Flory with 2 small children 1s. 6d. a week, Widow Woolno' of Snape being old and infirm 1s. a week each and Widow [ ] with 4 small child, 2s. 6d. a week for this Qtr. Widow Hudson 2s. a week for this week and next.

Wickham: Widow Plant, Widow Edwards, Widow Luffe, and Widow Leggatt all old and infirm, Mary Mapleston a lunatick 1s. a week each and Widow Goodwin with 1 child 9d. a week for this Qtr. and Eliz Hunt 1s. a week for this Qtr. Nathaniel Collett 1s. for this week.

Bromeswell: Peter Blundell his wife being ill 1s. for this week.

Alderton: Widow Leach with her three children 1s. 6d. a week for this Quarter.

Hollesley: Widow Day with 5 small children 2s. 6d. a week for this Qtr.

Debach: John Wade 2s. 6d. for this week.

Bouldge: Thomas Topple 1s. a week for this Quarter.

Ufford: Deborah Robinson 1s. a week for this Qtr.

28 February 1791

Bawdsey: 27s. 6d. towards the burial of a person unknown washed up and the jury.

Hatcheston: Sarah Hill being turned out of door by her father received in to the House.

8 August 1791

Ordered that the Governor do procure half a gross of dinning bowls and two pudding cups and a dozen small tooth combs, a carving knife and fork, three pieces of camblet stuff and three pieces of drab cloth being absolutely wanted for the present cloathing of the paupers in the House as no contract was made at the last Quarterly Meeting.

3 October 1791

Capel	Susan Warner	aged 19	discharged being able to maintain herself.
Brandeston	Martha Flatt	aged 24	discharged for *do.*
Wickham Mkt.	Robert Frost	aged 9	discharged his father to support him having no other children.
Brandeston	Ann Tricker	aged 18	discharged being able to maintain herself.
Kettleburgh	Susan Lyon	aged 33	discharged and support her child.
	Susan Lyon	aged 3	the above child.
Monewden	Mary Keeble	aged 33	Mary Keeble to return home to her husband
	William Keeble	aged 7	and the children supported and
	Mary Ann Keeble	aged 2	maintained by him.
	Samuel Keeble	aged 1	
Marlesford	Mary Bird	aged 33	
	Francis Bird	aged 2	
	Ann Bird	aged 3	
	John Bird	aged 1	
Bredfield	Mary Brown	aged 8	to be maintained by her mother.
Ramsholt	Elizabeth Fletcher	aged 13	rec'd into the House.
	John Fletcher	aged 11	*do.*

Miscellaneous documents

36. Inventory of the House of Industry, 24 June 1791[14]

Mill House
Sack cart
3 brooms, scoop
3 scuppets, 2 ladder
Scales and beam, iron
4 half C.
1 Qtr.
2 stone
2 half *do*
6½ lead
1¼ brass
Fan, bushel, rake
Hutch, 2 firkins
Flour mill & 4 cloths
23 sacks 3 bushel
5 bean sacks
9 flour *do*   £11   11s.   6d.
Swill house & Styes
4 pails, tub, trough
Jet, scuppet, fork
Hand barrow
Hogs trough
Engine
3 hogs troughs   £2   0s.   0d.
Neat House
3 wheel barrows
2 stools, 2 shackles   £1   1s.   6d.
Brewhouse
Pair pail slings
Stools, steps & kings
2 scuppets
Fire fork, hoe
2 troughs
Hop skep
3 rudders
Brewing copper & furnace
Pump, mash vat
Under beck

---

14   SROI ADA11/A/H/1/1.

Coolers etc.
Burhg vat   £40   18s.   0d.

Tool house
Saw, 3 skeps, iron crow
3 hatchets, 2 beetles
9 iron wedges
4 hooks, 5 scuppets
Spade, muck fork
3 mattocks, & pick
6 hoes, 4 weeding hoes
2 scythes, sheers
2 cutting knives
13 forks
14 rakes
3 flails, dock shave
2 lime sacks
Large auger, muck fork   £4   1s.   6d.

Carpenter's Shop
Bench
Pitch, kettle, & ladle
Stool, x cut saw
Level
Boards   £1   15s.   0d.

Old Women's Room
4 bedsteads
7 beds & bolsters
8 blankets
4 coverlids
Stool, 2 chairs
Coal hod
Stove
Fender, sifter, poker
Table
7 chamber pots
Coal hod, broom   £13   0s.   6d.

Committee Chamber
Stove grate
Fender
Firepan, poker, tongs
2 square wainscot tables
6 stained matted chairs
30 oak chairs
Deal table
15 hat pins
Stove in room adjoining   £7   9s.   0d.

Garden
Spade, 2 trowels, hoe
Saw, hammer
Garden sheers & rake
Wire sieve & sundries

Water pot, skeps & dibble
1 @ 3 light frame
1 @ 2 light frame
Single light frame
Seat
Garden shears
Wood roll
Wheel barrow
2 *do*
Hand *do*
Cinder screen
Grindstone
Shears
Wire sieve iron *do*
Scythe 3 spades
Scaval, edging knife
2 forks, 5 hoes, 4 rakes
Dibble engine
4 firkins, bud mill
Reel & line   £7   0s.   3d.

Inner yards

Hogs trough
4 cow bins
18 staved ladder
28 *do*
Wool frame
Sawing horse
Stone water trough
4 casks pullies   £3   3s.   9d.

Cellars

46 casks
37 barrels
Gile vat
2 funnels, cork box
Skep, tilders
2 yeast tubs
½ barrel & tub
10 yeast trays   £34   11s.   0d.

Pest house

25 bedsteads
15 beds
11 bolsters
10 pair blankets
10 coverlets
6 chairs
3 tables
2 saucepans
2 wash tubs
Copper & irons
2 dolls

2 pails   £35   3s.   6d.

Little wash house in the yard
3 pails
Stool
Linen horse
Keeler
Small copper
Iron to copper   £1   15s. 0d.

Old men's room
Stove
4 forms
2 hods   £0   15s. 6d.

School and Huckling room
Stove, sifter, fender
6 stools, chair
Coal hod
2 pails, keeler
Hickling room
Stove   £1   5s.   0d.

Taylor's and shoemakers
Stove
Fender, sifter, poker
6 chairs, stool
2 tables
2 coal hods & pail
Shop board
4 shoemakers' seats with tools
Cutting table
40 lasts
Mail pillion & girths   £3   9s.   6d.

In stores and apparel	£	s.	d.
133 tops of wool	7	15	2
14 pr. leather stays	3	12	6
4 new stuff gowns	1	0	0
7 half thick petticoats	1	8	0
1 Woolsey *do*		3	0
8 serge & baize *do*	1	0	0
9 aprons	7	0	
23 jackets	2	12	6
15 mantles	1	2	6
16 yards hemp		15	0
9 yards worsted		9	0
10lb. worsted hose	1	12	6
32lb. shoe leather	1	17	2
Dressed *do*	1	2	0
Wax rosin *do*		3	0
45 yds. duffle cloth	3	8	9
14 yds. *do*	1	4	6
3 yards plain		6	0

21 half thick	1	8	0
24 yds. York	2	2	0
8 boys new coats	2	8	0
1 mans *do*		8	6
9½ yds. twill		16	7½
26 wt. roll	1	4	4½
6 *do* hessg		5	6
30 yds. wt. roll	1	8	4½
7 dozen metal buttons			
13 gross *do*		12	0
7 dozen metal buttons			
1 gross 5½ doz .		3	3
6 pr. twill boys breeches		9	0
2 pr. drab *do*		3	0
5 pr. stay tape		1	3
3 doz. spindles		1	9
21 yds. hemp	1	3	7½
16 *do*		16	0
6lb. 2d. worsted		11	0
14 score handkerchiefs		11	11
28 half *do*		16	8
14 *do*		8	6
12 *do*		7	0
24 yds. ¾ ck.	1	3	0
11 yds. baize		11	5½
13 serge		15	2
4 yds. Russia		2	8
19 *do* hasenewf	1	1	4½
3 *do*		4	0
Shoe heels		15	0
0-2-14 soap	1	17	6
50 women's caps			
22 girls' *do*	1	16	0
21 girls' shifts			
21 *do*	4	14	0
18 boys' shirts	1	16	0
13 mens *do*	2	12	0
8 womens shifts	1	4	0
24 shirts & shifts old	1	4	0
26 pr. new shoes	3	18	0
2 burying cloths		12	0
26 mantles	1	19	0
2 doz. ½ patterns	1	5	0
10lb. threads	1	5	0
6 pieces filleting		6	0
4 ps. tape		2	4
Ps. quality		2	0
11 gross shirt buttons		3	8
6 pr. scizzers		1	6
8 combs		2	6

14 doz. laces		10	6
Odd needles & threads		5	0
Pins & thimbles		2	0
Bluing starch, seeds & spices		3	6
40 pr. sheets hemp	18	0	0
83 pr. old	16	12	0
26 table cloths	2	12	0
5 small *do*		3	9
2 dresser *do*		10	0
10 hand towels		5	0
8 round		8	0
12 towels		9	0
10 napkins		8	0
2 Chapple cloths		10	0
4 table cloths		12	0
7 pr. sheets, 2 pr. cases	3	10	0
7 doz. candles	2	9	0
6st. salt		10	4
9st. butter	3	15	0
42st. cheese	4	18	0
40st. pork	9	0	0
17 comb meal	21	5	0
50st. flour	4	7	6
18 barrel beer	7	4	0
16st. 9lb. beef	3	14	11
	178	7	1

Apparel in wearing	£	s.	d.
155 women's shifts	19	7	6
120 girls	12	0	0
104 boys shirts	10	8	0
109 mens *do*	16	6	0
114 caps	1	18	0
115 handks	1	18	4
70 jackets	5	5	0
38 ch. aprons	2	17	0
28 *do* frocks	2	16	0
248 mantles	12	8	0
40 worsted coats	5	0	0
79 under *do*	5	18	6
79 stays	7	18	0
79 stockings			
120 *do* boys	14	19	0
40 *do* mens	2	0	0
20 hats womens		10	0
79 womens shoes	5	18	6
109 boys & girls *do*	5	9	0
33 mens	3	6	0
33 jackets	4	2	6
33 breeches	4	2	6

49 boys jackets	7	7	0
49 breeches	3	13	6
	163	14	4

Chappel

Communion table
Cloth to *do*
do to desk
do to pulpit
3 cushions
Curtain & rod
24 seats, 3 mats
8 hassocks
Bible, & prayer book

Surplice	£9	11s.	6d.

Yards & fields

	£	s.	d.
Quantity muck	20	0	0
Hay on stacks	68	0	0
Faggot wood	3	12	0
Round *do*	9	0	0
Chickens coop			
Dogs kennel		5	0
11 hogs	17	12	0
2 sows	3	10	0
10 shoats	11	10	0
6 cows, calf	43	12	0

Fields

3 acres wheat	24	0	0
14.1.22 grass	30	0	0

Melton House of Industry

Contents of inventory
Manufactured hemp

cloth for sale	30	3	4
do for use of the house	62	15	11¾
Hemp yarn, hemp &			
Utensils in trade	82	14	0
Total hemp manufactory	175	13	3¾

Utensils, furniture, stores apparel

Garret No. 1	2	12	3
Committee garret	1	14	6
Spinning rooms	14	3	0
Nursery garret	23	16	6
Womens *do*	48	3	6
Mens *do*	45	10	0
Married *do*	32	2	0
Chamber No. 1	2	13	7

do No. 2	3	15	0
do No. 3	4	18	6
do No. 4	3	5	0
do No. 5	2	0	0
do No. 6	2	16	6
do No. 7	2	10	0
do No. 8		10	0
do No. 9		10	0
do No. 10	2	0	0
Yarn room		5	0
Wards	48	15	4
Dead room	2	5	0
Stair case and Passage	4	10	0
Great nursery	9	18	6
Little *do*	5	18	3
Little bed room	4	13	6
Matron's chamber	12	16	6
Governor's *do*	6	11	6
Parlour *do*	7	13	0
Governor's room	6	4	6
Great parlour	1	15	6
Pantry	2	7	6
Study	1	0	6
Larder	7	4	6
Kitchen	21	3	0
Dining room	13	13	0
Cooking *do*	9	11	6
Baking office	3	2	9
Bread room	1	5	0
Dairy	4	8	6
Little wash house	6	0	6
Great *do*	17	17	3
Mill House	11	11	6
Swill house	2	0	0
Neat *do*	1	1	6
Brewing *do*	40	18	0
Tool House	4	1	6
Carpenters shop	1	15	0
Old women's room	13	0	6
Committee chamber	7	9	0
Garden	7	0	3
Inner Yard	3	3	9
Cellars	34	11	6
Pest house	35	3	6
Little wash house in the back yard	1	15	0
Old mens room		15	6
School, or Hicklers room	1	5	0
Taylors & shoemakers	3	9	6
Stores & apparel	178	7	1

Apparel in wear	163	14	4
Chappel	9	11	6
Yards, fields etc.	231	1	0
Furniture, utensils etc.	1,143	15	10
Hemp manufactory etc.	175	13	3¾
Total amount £	1,319	9	1¾
June 24 1791.	Augustine Read.		

37. Extracts from 'Rules and Orders for Regulating the Meetings and Proceedings of the Directors and Acting Guardians of the Poor, and for the better governing, regulating, and employing the Poor of the Hundreds of Loes and Wilford ...'[15]

Preface

It must be evident to everyone who is conversant in public business, that without the establishment of general rules, it can neither be conducted with facility, rectitude, nor even with consistency. When no such rules exist, the same case will at different times be variously determined, as either the contracted, or enlarged views, of different understandings shall regulate the decision, or the mutable humours, caprices, or passions of mankind shall mislead the judgement. Under such circumstances, every question, (however often it may have been determined before) will at the times of meeting to transact business be agitated anew, with all the violence of controversy, and all the obstinacy of error. This will naturally be the result from transacting public business in general, but will more particularly flow from institutions, which are found under the appellation of Houses of Industry, since from their very nature, and the Acts of Parliament framed for their better regulation, persons dissimilar in their understandings, and perhaps in their views, must necessarily meet together. But when general laws are once established by the skill or the ability of the first promoters of an institution, the public is in no danger of losing at any future time, any of the advantages which a former zeal has promised, or a past vigilance had procured. For, should that zeal hereafter abate, or that vigilance relax, the institution by means of its general rules, remains like a machine, which having its springs of motion within itself, will, with but an ordinary attention, and only common application, go on to perform without interruption, its accustomed functions and to produce without variation its usual benefits. Nothing can therefore be more unjust than the common objection to the Houses of Industry, and similar institutions, that however well they may be administered at first, they will at length fall into neglect. For do but establish general rules, and the objection is at once obviated.

These are the observations, and words of an ingenious writer, not less remarkable for his acuteness in reasoning, than his attention to the subject in question. And since we may fairly collect for the improvement for our own institution, whatever rule or observation we may think most conducive to that end, there is no reason why we should reject either the matter, or the mode of his reasoning.

The following bye laws, or general rules are such as are either suggested by experience, or such of which reason foreseeing the utility, – experience has since evinced the necessity.

---

[15] SROI ADA11/A/A/2/1.

If in any case they are broken through, or left open to private opinion, there is great danger of their total annihilation. We trust however that this will only be done in cases of the most extreme necessity: it was therefore with great wisdom ordained that in one instance alone, in rule the second, under the article of allowances out of the House, the expression occurs, "excepting those of urgent necessity" in great tenderness to the poor, setting aside – the usual determination.

May then the great success which has attended the institution of other Houses of Industry be extended to that of Loes and Wilford, and gentlemen then it do dishonour to adapt regulations which a vigilant attention to the public good has suggested, as founded in wisdom, and which experience has approved.

Committees

That exclusive of the committees appointed by the incorporating act, the two following standing committees be appointed.

1. A Committee of Religion and Morality

That this committee shall consist of all the clergy in the direction, and that to them be referred the direction of the education and instruction of the poor within the House, and also the appointment and superintendence of the religious duties, respectively to be performed by the Chaplain, Governor, School Master, and Mistress. That this committee be empowered to meet for the above purposes as often as they may think proper, but it is recommended to meet not less than twice within each quarter of a year, that any two be sufficient to transact business, and that their proceedings be entered into a book, and reported at every quarterly meeting.

2. A Committee of Guardianship of Apprentices

That this committee shall consist of the twenty-four directors. The object of it is to inquire, and it is recommended to them frequently to inquire into the conduct and behaviour of all masters and mistresses towards such apprentices as have been put out to them by the authority of the incorporating act, and to make their report in writing at every quarterly meeting. This is indeed, what the duty of every member of the corporation should incline him to, and what humanity requires at his hands; that it may therefore be more easily and carried into effect, it is proposed that the following division of districts and directors be adopted, viz.

Districts	Directors
Alderton	Frank
Bawdsey	Trotman
Ramsholt	Whimper
Sutton	Gunning
Shottisham	Maber
Rendlesham	Waller
	Edwards
Hollesley	
Boyton	Hingeston
Capell	Fontenelle
Butley	
Bromeswell	

Ufford	Brooke
Melton	Simpson
Eyke	Chilton
Petistree	
Wickham	
Ash	Whitbread
Marlesford	Kilderbee Jun.
Hacheston	Wilkinson
Easton	
Kettleburgh	Kilderbee Sen.
Letheringham	Browne
Brandeston	
Creetingham	Harsant
Monewden	Ashford
Hoo	
Earl Soham	Capper
Kenton	Ayton
Bouldge	
Debach	Jenney
Charsfield	Whitby
Bredfield	Reynolds
Dallingho	

38. Richard Wood's bill associated with legal expenses[16]

21 December 1789

Richard Wood's bill for legal expenses.

1789   The Directors and Guardians within the Hundreds of Loes & Wilford
          To Richd Wood Dr
          Butley appellants and St. Matthew, Ipswich, respondents.

	£	s.	d.
On receivg letter from Mr Luddon Clk to Mr Powell, Collector of Excise acquainting me that James Brock (whose wife and childn were removed by order from St. Matthews to Butley) paid to the Land Tax in the parish of Tattingstone two years advising with the Committee whether should appeal to the Order when was desired to commence & prosecute the same.	0	6	8
Sept. 29 Drawing notice of appeal and two fair copies to serve	0	6	8
Journey to Butley attending on the Churchwardens and Overseers Signing the above notices.	0	13	4
30 My son's journey to Ipswich serving notice of appeal on			

---

16   SROI ADA11/A/H/1.

the Churchwardens of St Matthews in Ipswich, horse hire and Expences.		1	1	0
Paid Clerk of the Peace for the subpoena.			2	6
Letters & postage to & from him with same inclosed.			3	6
Two spa tickets.			2	0

Oct. 3rd Journey to Ipswich serving subpoena on Mr John Milner
to Produce on the trial the Land Tax duplicated for the
parish of Tattingstone & on Mr John Luddon, Mr Powell's
clerk to attend at the Qtr. Sessions and

give evidence on the trial, horse hire and expences.		1	1	0
Paid Mr Milner with Spa.			2	6
Paid Mr Luddon with *do.*			2	6
Attending the pauper Mrs Brock at the House, examining her to several matters in order to prepare brief.			6	8
Drawing brief.			6	8
Fair copy thereof for Council.			6	8
Copy of examination to annex to brief.			1	0
To Mr Hay with brief.		2	2	0
To his clerk.			2	6
Attending him.			6	8

9th Journey and attending Quarter Sessions at Ipswich as
solicitor on hearing the appeal etc. (when appeal was

allowed with Common Costs) horse hire and expences.		1	11	6

My son's journey to the Sessions at Ipswich to prove
notice of Appeal and serving subpoenas etc. horse hire

and expences.		1	1	0
Paid Clerk of the Peace fees in court.			19	0
Paid Mr Milner attending on the tryal with the duplicates of the Land Tax for Tattingstone.			8	6
Paid Mr Luddon for searching the Excise Books and attending on the tryal to prove Brocks paying the Land Tax in Tattingstone.			10	6
Received costs by order of court.	£2	0s.	0d.	

16th Writing several times to Mr Roach of Norwich for an
account of Yarn rece'd by him from the House but co'd
get no answer and afterwds writing by order of Quarterly
Meeting that if he did not send an acct he would have an

action comenced against him for same, when he remitted.			6	8

A draft of 12 guineas to me in part which I paid into the
hands of the Treasurer.

18th Writing to him again by order for an account of the

balance.			3	4

Paid the printer omitted to be charged in the last two
quarters bills for advertising Previous and Quarterly
Meetings came to 4/- more on account of the new duty

which I omitted to charge.			4	0

Oct. 20 Writing to Mr Peter Clarke of Ipswich by order of the
Committee for a copy of examination of Thos Holden
breeches maker who was removed by Orders from Orford

to Hollesly .			3	4

Paid for same and postage.		1	5
Dec. 10 Journey to Orford by order of Committee making inquiries and examining Poor's Rate concerning Thos. Holden's removal from Orford to Hollesly but could not find that he was rated or that he had gained any settlement there, hores hire and expences.		15	0
Paid Loder for a new Weekly Committee book.	1	1	0
Paid for pens ink paper and was for this quarter.		3	6
Letters and parcels		2	6
Quarters salary to Christmas 1789	5	0	0
	21	6	9
Costs rec'd by order of court on above appeal.	2	0	0
	19	6	9

Allowed James Catchpole.   Dec. 21st 1789 by cash. R.W.

Extract from the Second Treasurer's Account Book, 1792–1802[17]

Mr John Carthew in account with the Directors and Acting Guardians of the Poor in the Hundreds of Loes and Wilford in Suffolk.

		£	s.	d.
Dr.				
To a balance received of Messrs Whitbread Whitley and Frank.		55	4	10

To rates from the parishes of:

Parish	£	s.	d.		£	s.	d.
Ash	34	4	2½				
Brandeston	22	5	8				
Butley	21	15	1½				
Charsfield	31	5	4¼				
Cretingham	26	14	1				
Dallingho	18	13	7				
Earl Soham	36	16	1¼				
Easton	31	8	7				
Eyke	17	0	10½				
Hacheston	25	16	6				
Hoo	8	3	0				
Kenton	27	14	8½				
Kettleburgh	17	18	0				
Letheringham	10	18	6				
Marlesford	32	10	2				
Monewden	5	5	3¼				
Rendlesham	12	4	2½				
Alderton	19	18	4¼				
Bawdsey	14	15	4				
Boulge	9	12	10½				
Boyton	3	7	6				
Bredfield	24	12	7				
Bromeswell	9	5	7				
Capell	13	3	9½				
Debach	3	0	5¼				
Hollesley	30	18	4				
Melton	24	10	3				
Petistree	21	6	2½				
Ramsholt	21	4	1¼				
Shottisham	8	11	11				
Sutton	48	19	2				
Ufford	31	13	1½				
Wickham Market	36	3	0¼		689	16	6¼

---

[17] SROI ADA11/A/C/1/1/2.

27th June	To cash received of Mr Rainbird for Quarters Earnings.				24	7	3
	To cash received of Mr Rainbird for the parish of Wyverstone.				2	10	0
	To cash received of Mr Rainbird on account of Samuel Alexander.				0	12	0
					772	10	7¼

Cr
1792

No 1

April 16th	By cash to Mr Rainbird.	50	0	0			
May 14th	By cash paid to *do.*	60	0	0	155	0	0
June 12th	By cash paid to *do.*	45	0	0			
No. 2	Out allowances paid to the Overseers of the several parishes						
	Ash	1	9	6			
	Brandeston	3	19	6			
	Butley	1	19	0			
	Charsfield	5	1	9			
	Dallingho	1	3	0			
	Easton	2	11	0			
	Eyke	5	17	0			
	Hacheston	4	18	0			
	Hoo	1	14	0			
	Kenton	3	7	6			
	Letheringham	0	16	0			
	Marlesford	3	13	0			
	Monewden	1	16	6			
	Alderton	1	13	0			
	Boyton	0	13	0			
	Bredfield	5	1	6			
	Bromeswell	2	8	0			
	Capel	0	10	0			
	Hollesley	3	12	0			
	Petistree	1	2	0			
	Sutton	4	8	6			
	Shottisham	1	3	0			
	Ramsholt	0	12	0			
	Debach	0	4	0			
	Ufford	6	13	6			
	Wickham Market	4	18	6	76	3	3
No. 3	Bills of Repairs						
No. 1	Manthorp and Fulcher	23	19	0			
2	Beedon carpenter	13	16	0			
3	Manthorp for bricks	20	18	0			
4	Fletcher bricklayer	41	15	0			
5	Benham for carting	3	3	6			
6	Allen glazier	19	7	3			
7	Collett for nails etc.	21	4	3			
8	Garrett blacksmith	8	1	0			

9 Jesup for lime and coals	14	2	0	166	6	0

No. 4. Miscellaneous bills

No. 1 Parker butcher	61	3	9			
2 Braggs for grocery	6	14	0			
3 Oldham for grocery drapery	47	13	9½			
4 Osborne miller	4	0	0			
5 Hicks for oatmeal	1	16	0			
6 London for malt	21	9	0			
7 Edwards tanner	14	7	3			
8 Packard brazier	1	11	6			
9 Askettle for mending spinning wheels	0	13	0			
10 Barret for seal	5	12	0			
11 Loder printer	9	2	0			
12 Hubbard for ploughing	8	19	0			
13 Whincopp a Qtr. Salary	21	5	0			
do for dugs etc.	1	0	0½			
14 Revd Black Qtrs. salary and stamps.	8	15	2			
15 Newman and wife *do*	5	0	2			
Treasurers Quarters salary	2	10	0			
Stamps for receipts	0	2	0			
16 Hinchman yrs. salary	15	0	0	236	13	8

No. 5 An account of interest paid this Qtr. due 5th July upon the following securities.

Security No. 3 Mrs S Watling ½yrs interest on £100 at 4%	2	0	0
4 Mrs Syred *do* on £100 @ *do*	2	0	0
5 Revd D Copland *do* on £100 @ *do*	2	0	0
6 Mrs N Brooke *do* on £150 @ *do*	3	0	0
8 Mr Robert Seaman *do* on £200 @ *do*	4	0	0
	13	0	0
	746	2	11
Brought over.	772	10	7¼
	746	2	11
Balance.	26	7	8¼[18]

1st August 1792

Seen and allowed by us. R. Frank.　　　　Francis Brooke.

---

[18] Interestingly this quarterly account was inaccurate. The expenditure totalled £647 2s. 1d. rather than £746 2s. 11d., an error in the Incorporation's favour of £99. The error does not appear to have been corrected in later entries.

THIRD QUARTERLY MINUTE BOOK
6 July 1795–11 July 1805[1]

9 July 1795

Directors	present	Guardians
Revd Dr Franks		Mr Joseph Jeaffreson
P. Maber Esq.		Mr S. Collett
Revd R. Reynolds		Mr John Woolnough
Edmund Jenny Esq.		Mr J. Waller
Revd William Browne		Mr T. Threadkell
Revd Samuel Hingeston		Mr T. Garneys
J. Syer M.D.		Mr William Page
Revd J. Gunning		Mr Aldhous
J. Whitbread		
Mr R. Ashford		

Ordered that the rate for the ensuing Quarter be made the same as the last and that the out allowances and bills having been first examined at the Previous Meeting be forthwith paid by the Treasurer.

Ordered that the following children be apprenticed to their respective parishes:

Butley	Eliz Ellis	aged 16 yrs.	to Mr T. Ablett
	Mary [*deleted*]	aged 16 yrs.	to Mr Gross *sent to her parents*
Bredfield	Mary Catchpole	aged 13 yrs.	to John Dannington
Boulge	John Fairs	aged 11¼ yrs.	to Conrad Short
Bromeswell	Samuel Dammant	aged 11 yrs.	to Stebing Gross Eyke
Brandeston	Sophia Potkins	aged 14¾ yrs.	to Mr Revett
Charsfield	Robert Malden	aged 12¼ yrs.	to William Cooke
Debach	Abraham Garnham	aged 12 yrs.	to James Cork
Easton	William King	aged 11 yrs.	to Moses Crisp
Hatcheston	Elizabeth Ellis	aged 14 yrs.	to Chaloner Arcedeckne
Kenton	John Sheldrake	aged 11 yrs.	to William Whitman
Melton	Mary Clow	aged 11¾ yrs.	to Benjamin Cooper
Monewden	William Keeble	aged 11 yrs.	to Joseph Bulmer
Marlesford	Sarah Bird	aged 16 yrs.	to occupier of [ ] farm
do	Sarah Aldred	aged 13 yrs.	to John Crisp
do	Mary Riches	aged 12¾ yrs.	to James Smith
do	William Eley	aged 12 yrs.	to Richard Wilkinson
do	Robert Eley	aged 11 yrs.	to Widow Skeet
Wick. Mkt.	William Brereton	aged 13 yrs.	to Philip Dykes

Ordered that William More be permitted to assign over his late apprentice John Parsons to William Finch.

---

1   SROI ADA11/A/B/1/3.

Ordered that the Overseers of the following parishes do allow as here in after mentioned for the ensuing Quarter (13 weeks):

Hasketon — James Gardner's children ordered in to the House Jas aged 11, Robert aged 7 and Maryah aged 5yrs

Parish	Name	Weekly		Quarterly		
		s.	d.	£.	s.	d.
Ash	Wd. Woolnough infirm	1	0		13	
	do Wilson do	1	0		13	
	Hannah Kemp	1	0		13	
Brandeston	Wd. Barker with 4 child.	2	0	1	6	0
	do Emerson	1	0		13	
Butley	do Woolnough	1	0		13	
	do Garrod 3 child.	1	6		19	6
	do Crosby 4 child.	2	0	1	6	0
	do Hubbard	1	0		13	
	do Scarlett	1	0		13	
	Ruth Hubbard for Goldsmiths child ordered into the House					
Charsfield	Wd. Malden	1	0		13	
	do Fulcher	1	0		13	
	do Abbot	1	0		13	
	do Mallett 1 child		6		6	6
	Eliz. Carter infirm		9		9	9
	Wd. Wartis do	1	0		13	
	Sarah Gross with B. Child (£20 pd to House)	1	6		19	6
Creetingham	Thomas Bulmer an idiot	2	0	1	6	0
	Elizth Spall with B. Child now Simpson	1	0		13	
	Mary Spall	1	0		13	
	Wd. Peck infirm Wd. Prattle Wd. Moss each	1	0		13	
Dallingho	Stephen Gaymer & wife	2	0	1	6	0
	Wd. Norman	1	0		13	
Earl Soham	Wd. Clarke with 5 child.	3	0	1	19	0
	do Lambert	1	0		13	
	do Salvage	1	0		13	
	do Scott	1	0		13	
	H. Fellingham	1	0		13	
	R. Lanhams blind child	1	0		13	
Easton	Wd. Lyon	1	0		13	
	do Plant	1	0		13	
	S. Capon infirm	1	0		13	
Eyke	J. Booth	2	0	1	6	0
	J. Minter	1	0		13	
	John Culham with child	1	0		13	
	H. Buckenham	1	0		13	
	Wd. Prow	1	0		13	
	Wd. Arnold	1	0		13	

Parish	Name					
	do Pollard	1	6		19	6
Hacheston	Hannah Bennett with 4 child.	2	0	1	6	0
	Letitia Fairs with 3 *do*	1	6		19	6
	H. Graystone	1	0		13	
	Wd. Lingwood	1	0		13	
Hoo	Wd. Fogat	1	0		13	
	Sarah King	1	0		13	
Kettleburgh	Wd. Crisp	1	0		13	
Kenton	Elizth Ginery	1	0		13	
	James Garnham	1	6		19	6
Letheringham	Mary Blaxhall	1	0		13	
Monewden	John Bloss	1	0		13	
Marlesford	Sarah Wilson	1	0		13	
Rendlesham	Esther Smith	1	0		13	
Alderton	Wd. Mealing	1	0		13	
Bawdsey	*do* Savil	1	0		13	
	Wd. Buss	1	0		13	
Boulge	*do* Topell	1	0		13	
	John Crane and wife	2	0	1	6	0
Bredfield	Samuel Brundish lame & 5 child.	2	0	1	6	0
	Wd. Randal	1	0		13	
	do E Button	1	0		13	
	do Button	0	6		6	6
	E. Banyard	1	0		13	
	Wd. Wrights (deceased) children	2	0	1	6	0
Bromeswell	Wd. Brundle	1	0		13	
	John Leach	1	0		13	
Boyton	Wd. Pettit	1	0		13	
	do Ashkettle	0	6		6	6
Debach	Infant child of Susan Curtis	1	0		13	
	Robt Allen & wife	1	0		13	
	Wd. Day with 3 child, 1 infirm 2 under 10ys.	1	0		13	
Melton	Wd. Hadman & an idiot child	2	0	1	6	0
	do Flurry	1	0		13	
	do Crow	1	0		13	
	do Fuller	1	0		13	
	James Wilson	1	0		13	
Petistree	James Jackson	1	0		13	
Shottisham	Thos Smith with his wife & 2 child.	1	6		19	6
Ufford	Wd. Wavers	1	0		13	
	do Blumfield	1	0		13	
	do Davis	1	0		13	
	do Hearn	1	0		13	
	George Davis with is brothers 2 child.	1	0		13	
	John Lamb infirm	1	0		13	
	The wife of Henry Banham	1	0		13	
W. Mkt.	Margret Good with B. Child	1	0		13	
	Mary Maplestone	1	0		13	
	Stephen Spink blind & lame	1	0		13	

Elizth Smith with B.B. child.

father absconded   1   0   13

Ordered that a General Meeting of the Directors and Acting Guardians be holden at the House of Industry <> on Special Business <> to be advertised in the Ipswich Journal.

Resolved that it appears to this Committee that the price of all the necessaries of life are at present so high that labourers having families cannot maintain them at the present price of labour without some relief, and therefore it is ordered that it be and it is hereby recommended to the several Weekly Committees to grant relief under the following regulation, independent of sickness infirmities or other casualties (viz.) to every family where there are more than

	child	under 12 years of age
if	9 children	/
	8 "	/
	7 "	6/-
	6 "	4/-
	5 "	3/-
	4 "	2/-
	3 "	1/6
	2 "	1/-

That this regulation be continued to the 19th August and if the price of corn be not then reduced it be further continued to the 7th of September 1795.

30 July 1795

Resolved that it is incumbent upon this Corporation <> to relieve their real distress and that on account of the present great scarcity of bread corn every necessary assistance should be afforded them.

That we approve the plan proposed at the last Quarterly Meeting and the method in which it has been carried on and that it be recommended to the Committee to pursue the same till <7 September> or longer if they shall see fit increasing or decreasing the allowance as flour rises or falls in price.

Resolved that it is necessary to borrow £1,200 for the use of the Corporation.

Resolved that a Committee be appointed to inspect the accounts and report at the next Quarterly Meeting their sentiments whether any and what retrenchments can be made. <5 named directors>.

27 October 1795

That it is the opinion of this meeting that an application ought to be immediately made to Parliament to raise the rates, and that a meeting of the owners and occupiers of lands in the said Hundreds <> be held and that notice be given in the Ipswich and Bury papers that such a meeting will be held on <10 November> at the Shire Hall in Woodbridge.

Ordered that on meat days the family have potatoes instead of bread and dumplings.

7 November 1795

The reports of the several overseers were read at the meeting respecting providing for labourers as it appeared to the meeting that the parishes in general will find them wheat or flour at a reduced price during the high price of bread corn.

10 November 1795

Jacob Whitbread Esq. Chairman

At this meeting a motion being made for the immediately sending a petition to Parliament for raising the rates or assessments it was put to the vote when it was carried by a majority of 14.

For the sending of the petition   28

For not sending the petition   14

Resolved that the following petition be received, sealed with the Corporation seal and forwarded to the Members of the County and that they be desired to present it to the Honourable House of Commons. And it is particularly requested that the Revd Doctor Franks do deliver the said Petition to the Members.

To the Honourable the Commons of Great Britain in the Parliament assembled.

The humble petition of the Guardians of the Poor within the Hundreds of Loes and Wilford in the County of Suffolk.

Sheweth,

That an Act of Parliament was passed in <1791> for the relief and employment of the poor within the said Hundreds whereby your petitioners were authorised to make certain rates or assessments for certain purposes there in mentioned.

That the money arising by the said rates or assessments is found insufficient for the support of the poor and the other purposes thereby intended and that your petitioners have no power or authority under the said Act of raising any further sum or sums of money than is or are now raised by their present rates or assessments.

That on account of the grate increase in number of the poor and other unavoidable expence your petitioners have incurred a debt of £10,500 for the support and maintenance of the poor which debt they are unable to repay nor can they support or maintain the poor or pay the interest of the money already borrowed or which may be borrowed under the authority of the said Act or pay off and discharge any part of this debt unless a power be given to your petitioners to increase the said rates or assessments.

Your petitioners therefore humbly pray that leave may be given to bring in a bill for effecting the purpose before mentioned by such ways and means and in such manner as the honourable House shall think proper.

Given under the common seal of our Corporation this [   ] day of [   ] in the year <1795>.

Moved and agreed to that the Petition now presented be written fair on parchment and that the Common Seal of the Corporation be thereto annexed in the presence of <>.

9 January 1796

Ordered that the rate for the ensuing quarter be made in the following manner viz. in a triplicate manner (by virtue of the present Act) which is three times the sum previous rates.

Ordered that a Committee of the following gentlemen <5 named directors> be appointed for the taking in to their consideration the erecting of a mill for the use of the House to cut the corn expended in the said House, and that Mr Woolnough is here requested to lend his horse mill to try the experiment.

Ordered that the following advertisement be inserted in the Ipswich Journal:

Melton House of Industry. Wanted a resident baker for the said House who must have a good character and is desired to send proposals to the Governor of the said House.

5 April 1796

Directors	Present	Guardians
Revd Franks D.D.		William Schreiber Esq.
Revd J. Gunning		Mr John Woolnough
Revd William Browne		Capt. Hilcoat
Mr Burwell Edwards		Mr W. Page
Edmund Jenny Esq.		Mr R. Ashford
Revd Jacob Chilton		
Revd S. Kilderbee		
Jacob Whitbread Esq.		
John Syer M.D.		

The following persons were duly elected Directors and Acting Guardians◇:

	Directors	Guardians
May	Francis Brook Esq.	A. Blake
	Peter Maber Esq.	W. Page
June	Mr S. Fontenelle	Mr W. Walker
	Mr John Ayton	William Cook
July	Robert Trotman Esq.	William Whiteman
	Chaloner Arcedeckne Esq.	S. Collett
Aug.	Revd J. Gunning	W. Schreiber
	Revd W. Brown	S. Gross
Sept.	E. Jenny Esq.	Mr William Cooper
	Revd F. Capper	Mr Waller
Oct.	Revd S. Hingston	Mr Beeding
	Mr B. Edwards	J. Crisp
Nov.	Mr Wm Waller	R. Harvey
	Mr R. Ashford	Bulman
Dec.	Revd R. Frank D.D.	Capt. Hilcoat
	J. Syer M.D.	Stow Baldrey
Jan.	Revd S. Kilderbee	J. Woolnough
	Mr Harsant	James Roast
Feb.	J. Whitbread Esq.	J. Studd
	Revd R. Reynolds	J. Cooper
March	Mr J. Simpson	Rath. Randle
	Mr J. Whimper	J. Waller
Apl.	Revd J. Chilton	J. Trusson
	Mr R. Wilkinson	Edward Keer

7 April 1796

Ordered that the erecting of a mill and contracting for the building the same be referred to the Committee appointed last quarter for that purpose.

Ordered that 5 per cent per annum be paid for the several sums of money borrowed commencing Lady Day 1796.

Ordered that the usual advertisement for a resident surgeon for the House of Industry be inserted in the Ipswich London and Bury Post 3 weeks immediately after the Quarterly Meeting.

2 July 1796

Resolved that business of this Corporation cannot be carried on with so great advantage to the Hundreds as with so much propriety ease and satisfaction to the Directors and Acting Guardians as by Committees who will voluntarily undertake the several branches of it.

Resolved that Committees be appointed for the following purposes:
1   Religion and Morality
2   Industry
3   Maintenance
4   Clothing
5   Medicines
6   Building and Repairs
7   Finance
8   Law
9   Guardianship of apprentices after put out as approved by second bye law

Resolved that it is expedient that the Committees meet as often as they may severally think fit but not less than once a quarter and that their proceedings be entered into a book and produced at every Quarterly Meeting to be then and there considered that every Director and Acting Guardian should have a right to attend any Committee but not to vote.

We whose names are herewith subscribed do approve of the above resolution and resolve that we will each of us act as respectively to the best of our judgements carry the same into effect by becoming members of the several committees to which we have subscribed our names:

Committee of Religion and Morality <6 names>
Committee of Industry <7 names>
Committee of Maintenance <10 names>
Committee of Clothing and Bedding <5 names>
Committee of Physic <2 names>
Committee of Finance <6 names>
Committee of Buildings and Repairs <4 names>
Committee of Law <5 names>

Ordered that the further consideration of establishing Schools of Industry within the Hundreds be referred to the Committee of Industry and that they be desired to make a report thereon to a General Meeting to be held on <27 September>.

13 October 1796

Ordered that the rate for the ensuing quarter be made in the following manner viz double the old rate and that the out allowances and bills be forthwith paid by the Treasurer.

Ordered the following amendment be inserted in the bye laws (viz.) after the words from Michaelmas to Lady Day next the words "and to continue till 4 in the afternoon from Michaelmas to Lady Day and from Lady to Michaelmas till six in the afternoon, meal times excepted. And the hours of work shall be as follows, from the 10th of October to the 5th of April meet in the morning at 8 part at 12, in the afternoon meet at two and part at seven, from the 5th of April to the 10th of October in the morning meet at six part at 8 meet at 9 part at twelve in the afternoon meet at two part at 7 and that at such times as candle is necessary the spinning wheel be set by and all hands employed at knitting".

Ordered that the following rewards be given

Teachers to read	2 at	5s. each
Reelers	at	5s. each
Assistants	2 at	2s. 6d. each

And that the other servants within the House be rewarded in the following manner
Class the 1st 3s.   Class the 2nd 2s.   Class the 3rd 1s.

3 November 1796

Ordered that the Report of the Committee appointed at the last General Meeting be received.

Ordered that it be entered upon the books of the Corporation and that the advertisement with the plans and proposals be printed and circulated as soon as possible and that Dr Frank be requested to give the necessary order and directions for the same.

Ordered that a copy be sent to the officiating ministers and the overseers of the poor that the overseers be ordered to call a parish meeting as soon as may be to take the same into consideration and report the result thereof to Dr Frank.

Report

At a General Meeting of the Directors and Acting Guardians held at the House of Industry at Melton this day the following resolutions were proposed and unanimously adopted.

First.

That it is the opinion of this meeting that the establishing of a school of industry in the several parishes in these Hundreds would be rightly beneficial to the poor by the increasing their comfort and of grate public advantage as the means of promoting industry and decreasing the heavy burthen of the poor rates.

Secondly.

That we the Directors and Acting Guardians will in our corporate and individual capacities to the best of our power and judgement promote the same.

Thirdly.

That a Committee be appointed for the purpose of considering and digesting the best means of execution so desirable a project, and that the Committee be desired to form an estimate of the probable expence and report their sentiments to a General Meeting to be called for that purpose.

Fourthly.

That the Committee consist of <11 named directors> and any of the Directors and Acting Guardians who may choose to attend.

In consequence of the above resolutions the Committee met at the Crown Inn Woodbridge on <12 October> and having taken the same into their most serious consideration, directed that a return should be made by the overseers of each parish containing (in a form prescribed) the surnames, christian names and ages of the parents and also the number of their children under 12 years of age with the respective age of each child. And having talked over many other preliminary matters the Committee adjourned <> to receive the returns of the overseers.

R. Frank, Chairman.

On Monday the Committee met again and received the returns from the overseers but as they did not appear quite correct the Committee could not with that precision they wished ascertain an exact account. Numbers may be estimated at or about 1,800 children under 12 years of age, of which there may be about 800 under five years of age, and at or about 1,000 between the ages of 5 and 12 inclusive. The expence of establishing schools of industry sufficient for the education of so large a number of children, and the forming a fund for rewards for the industrious and deserving appeared to the Committee much beyond the ability of the Corporation.

The annexed plan and proposals with the advertisement prefixed were therefore proposed, and have been read unanimously approved and ordered to be made a part of the Report of the Committee, and the chairman was requested and consented to move at the General Meeting that the same be printed and circulated as soon as possible. It was then agreed that a General Meeting to receive the report of the Committee should be held at the House of Industry on <3 November> and the Governor was ordered to write to each of the Directors and Acting Guardians as were not present or to whom notice was not undertaken to be given. The meeting then adjourned to <3 November> to receive and sign the proceedings.

R. Frank, Chairman.

The Committee having received the report approve thereof and do direct the Chairman to present it for the approbation of the General Meeting to be held this day. <12 names follow>.

We whose names are underwritten do approve this report and the plan and proposals annexed <11 names>.

5 April 1797

Directors	Present	Guardians
Revd Dr Frank		Mr S. Baldrey
Revd Wm Kett		Mr W. Page
J. Syer M.D.		Mr S. Collett
Revd J. Chilton		Mr J. Woolnough
Revd S. Kilderbee		Mr S. Gross
E. Jenny Esq.		Mr J. Waller
Revd R. Reynolds		
P. Maber Esq.		
Mr R. Wilkinson		
Revd S. Hingston		

The following persons were duly elected Directors and Acting Guardians <>:

	Directors	Guardians
May	Francis Brooke Esq.	Mr A. Blake
	Peter Maber Esq.	Mr S. Gross
June	Revd William Kett	Mr T. Walker
	Mr W. W. Page	Mr W. Coole
July	Robt Trotman Esq.	Mr T. Garneys
	Chal. Arcedeckne Esq.	Mr S. Collett
Aug.	Revd Jos. Gunning	Mr Neave
	Revd W. Brown	Mr Cooper
Sept.	Ed. Jenny Esq.	Mr W. Cooper
	Revd Fr. Capper	Mr J. Mabson
Oct.	Revd Sam. Hingeston	Mr Wase
	Mr B. Edwards	Mr T. Crisp

Nov.	Mr Wm Waller	Mr Jeaffreson
	Mr R. Ashford	Mr P. Kersey
Dec.	Revd R. Franks D.D.	Mr Aldhouse
	T. Syer M.D.	Mr J. Baldrey
Jan.	Revd S. Kilderbee	Mr J. Woolnough
	Mr M. Harsant	Mr N. Barthorp
Feb.	J. Whitbread Esq.	Mr J. A. Studd
	Revd R. Reynolds	Mr Wilson
Mar.	Mr T. Simpson	Mr R. Randall
	Mr J. Whimper	Mr J. Waller
Apl.	Revd J. Chilton	Mr Stopher
	Mr R. Wilkinson	Mr Butcher

5 April 1798

	Directors	Present	Guardians
	Revd Dr Frank		Mr Samuel Collett
	F. Brook Esq.		Mr J. Waller
	E. Jenny Esq.		Mr R. Randall
	William Page Esq.		Mr Stow Baldrey
	Revd Samuel Kilderbee		Mr Wase
	Revd William Kett		
	Mr T. Simpson		

The following persons were duly elected Directors and Acting Guardians:

	Directors	Guardians
May	F. Brook Esq.	Mr A. Blake
	J. Pitches Esq.	Mr J. Waller
June	Revd Mr Kett	Mr W. Heffer
	Mr W. W. Page	Mr S. Thompson
July	Robert Trotman Esq.	John Catchpole
	Chaloner Arcedeckne Esq.	Mr S. Collett
Aug.	Revd Joseph Gunning	Mr Neave
	Revd Wm. Brown	Mr S. Gross
Sept.	Revd F. Capper	Mr W. Cooper
	E. Jenny Esq.	Mr F. Hayle
Oct.	Revd S. Hingeston	Mr Wase
	Mr B. Edwards	Mr T. Crisp
Nov.	Mr William Waller	Mr R. Adams
	Mr R. Ashford	Mr H. Carter
Dec.	Revd R. Frank D.D.	Mr J. Cooper
	John Syer M.D.	Mr T. S. Baldrey
Jan.	Revd S. Kilderbee	Mr J. Woolnough
	Revd John Clark	Mr Dove
Feb.	Revd R. Reynolds	Mr J. A. Studd
	J. Whitbread Esq.	Mr N. Fuller
Mar.	Mr Thomas Simpson	Mr R. Randall
	Mr John Whimper	Mr J. Waller
Apl.	Revd J. Chilton	Mr J. Waller
	Mr R. Wilkinson	Mr Thomas Butcher

5 July 1798

Ordered that the Governor do make complaint to the Magistrates that no Committees were held at the House of Industry at Melton on the <16 April, 28 May, 4 June> in order that the several and respective defaulters may be summoned to shew cause why the penalty or penalties incurred by the statute in that case made and provided should not be inflicted upon them.

11 October 1798

Ordered that the Governor do make complaint to the Magistrates that no Committee was held at the House of Industry at Melton on <8 October> in order that the several and respective defaulters may be summoned to shew cause why the penalty or penalties incurred by the statute in that case made and provided should not be inflicted upon them.

Ordered that an allowance be made towards cloathing poor children, as circumstances may appear not exceeding ten and sixpence on their parents producing a certificate from the master who hire them for a year.

11 April 1799

	Directors	Present	Guardians
	Revd Dr Frank		Mr R. Randall
	Revd Mr Kett		Mr J. Cooper
	Revd Mr Browne		Mr Stebbing Gross
	Revd Mr Chilton		Mr H. Carter
	Edmund Jenny Esq.		Mr J. Woolnough
	Mr Bur. Edwards		Mr T. Waller
	John Syer M.D.		
	William Page Esq.		

The following persons were duly elected Directors and Acting Guardians <>:

	Directors	Guardians
May	Francis Brook Esq.	Mr Andrew Blake
	John Pytches Esq.	Mr Thomas Waller
June	Revd William Kett	Mr Walker
	Wm Page Esq.	Mr Walford
July	Robert Trotman Esq.	Mr Henry Capper
	Chaloner Arcedeckne	Mr Samuel Collett
Aug.	Revd Joseph Gunning	Mr Stephen Vertue
	Revd William Browne	Mr William Burnett
Sept.	Edmund Jenny Esq.	Mr William Cooper
	Revd Francis Capper	Mr Mabson
Oct.	Revd S. Hingeston	Mr Warren
	Mr Burwell Edwards	Mr Crisp
Nov.	Mr William Waller	Mr William Cooper
	Mr Robt Ashford	Mr Robert Cutting
Dec.	Revd Richard Frank	Mr Jefferson
	John Syer M.D.	Mr J. S. Baldrey
Jan.	Revd S. Kilderbee	Mr John Woolnough
	Revd Joseph Clark	Mr Pitts
Feb.	Jacob Whitbread Esq.	Mr J. A. Studd
	Revd R. Reynolds	Mr Samuel Gross
Mar.	Mr Thomas Simpson	Mr R. Randall

	John Whimper	Mr Jeptha Waller
Apl.	Revd Jacob Chilton	Mr J. Waller
	Mr R. Wilkinson	Mr Butcher

11 July 1799

When applications for the relief of a pauper is made to any Committee and the Committee think it expedient to receive into the House apart of the children of such pauper the children between the ages of 5 and 10 should be selected.

As soon as the children in the House are able to knit a pair of stockings and spin 3d. per day (and if female sew) such children shall be discharged and sent home to their parents unless the parents be deemed on account of infirmities incapable of maintaining them. To each child so discharged shall be given a set of knitting needles and a spinning wheel.

10 April 1800

Directors	Present	Guardians
Edmund Jenny Esq.		Mr R. Randall
W. W. Page Esq.		Mr J. Waller
John Syer M.D.		Mr S. Gross
Mr William Waller		Mr S. Collett
Mr T. Simpson		Mr J. Woolnough
Revd I. Clarke		Mr Jon. Waller

The following persons were duly elected Directors and Acting Guardians:

	Directors	Guardians
May	T. Pytches Esq.	Mr W. Neeve
	Mr Jeptha Waller	Mr Thomas Waller
June	Revd William Kett	Mr W. Coole
	W. W. Page Esq.	Mr Barthorp
July	Robert Trotman Esq.	Mr James Aldhouse
	Chaloner Arcedeckne Esq.	Mr Samuel Collett
Aug.	Revd Joseph Gunning	Mr S. Vertue
	Revd William Browne	Mr John Cooper
Sept.	Edmund Jenney Esq.	Mr Samuel Thompson
	Revd Francis Capper	Mr Mabson
Oct.	Revd Samuel Hingeston	Mr J. Wase
	Mr Burwell Edwards	Mr Thomas Crisp
Nov.	Mr William Waller	Mr Thomas Thredkell
	Mr Robert Ashford	Mr Robert Cutting
Dec.	Revd R. Frank D.D.	Mr Jeaffreson
	John Syer M.D.	Mr J. S. Baldrey
Jan.	Revd Samuel Kilderbee	Mr John Woolnough
	Revd Isaac Clarke	Mr Cater
Feb.	Revd Robert Reynolds	Mr J. A. Studd
	Mr Samuel Gross	Mr Stebbing Gross
Mar.	Mr Thomas Simpson	Mr Ralph Randall
	Mr John Whimper	Mr Steggall
Apl.	Revd Jacob Chilton	Mr John Waller
	Mr R. Wilkinson	Mr Samuel Brewer

10 July 1800

Ordered that Mr Ralph Randall be appointed inspector of our House of Industry with a salary of thirty pounds a year and that an allowance of five guineas be made to him for his trouble in that department up to the date of this meeting.

That Daniel Johnston and Elizabeth his wife be appointed Governor and Matron with a salary of fifty pounds per annum.

16 October 1800

Ordered that Mary Booth the present dairy woman (being very neat and diligent in her business) have a gratuity of five shillings paid her by the Governor as an inducement and encouragement to her future good behaviour.

9 April 1801

Directors	Present	Guardians
Revd Jacob Chilton		Mr Ralph Randall
Revd William Browne		Mr Stebbing Gross
Mr Thomas Simpson		Mr John Woolnough
Mr Jeptha Waller		Mr Samuel Collett
Mr Richard Wilkinson		Mr Thomas Crisp
Mr Samuel Gross		Mr John Waller
Edmund Jenney Esq.		
Revd Robert Reynolds		
Mr Burwell Edwards		
William Woods Page Esq.		
Revd Isaac Clarke		
John Pytches Esq.		

The following persons were duly elected Directors and Acting Guardians ◇:

	Directors	Guardians
May	John Pytches Esq.	Mr Thomas Waller
	Mr Jeptha Waller	Mr John Wilson
June	Revd William Kett	Mr Moses Crisp
	Mr Jeremiah Wase	Mr John Randall
July	Robert Trotman Esq.	Mr John Button
	Chaloner Arcedeckne Esq.	Mr Nathaniel Gross
Aug.	William Woods Page Esq.	Mr William Moor
	Revd William Browne	Mr William Neeve
Sept.	Edmund Jenney Esq.	Mr John Mabson
	Revd Francis Capper	Mr William Cooper
Oct.	Revd Samuel Hingeston	Mr Thomas Crisp
	Mr Burwell Edwards	Mr Joseph Oldham
Nov.	Mr William Waller	Mr Thomas Threadkell
	Mr Robert Ashford	Mr John Felgate
Dec.	John Syer M.D.	Mr J. S. Baldrey
	Mr John Barthropp	Mr Robert Adams
Jan.	Revd Isaac Clarke	Mr John Woolnough
	Revd Charles Brooke	Mr John Carter
Feb.	Jacob Whitbread Esq.	Mr Stebbing Gross
	Mr Samuel Gross	Mr Jonathan A. Studd
Mar.	Mr Thomas Simpson	Mr Ralph Randall

	Mr John Whimper	Mr Robert Vertue
Apl.	Revd Jacob Chilton	Mr Samuel Brewer
	Mr Richard Wilkinson	Mr John Waller

Resolved that an increase of salary be made to the present surgeons in manner following viz. Mr Lynn as House Surgeon sixty pounds per annum instead of the former salary of thirty five pounds; and £6 for each parish he now attends for the corporation. Also that Mr Harsant and Mr Bellman have six pounds each for the several parishes they attend instead of the former salary of £4 10s. for each parish.

8 April 1802

Directors	Present	Guardians
Revd William Browne		Mr Ralph Randall
Jacob Whitbread Esq.		Mr William Neeve
Mr Samuel Gross		Mr John Woolnough
John Syer M.D.		Mr Thomas Threadkell
Revd Jacob Chilton		Mr Nathaniel Gross
Mr Jeremiah Wase		Mr John Waller
Mr Richard Wilkinson		
Mr Thomas Simpson		
W. W. Page Esq.		
Mr Jeptha Waller		

The following persons were duly elected Directors and Acting Guardians ◇:

	Directors	Guardians
May	John Pytches Esq.	Mr Thomas Waller
	Mr Jeptha Waller	Mr John Wilson
June	Revd William Kett	Mr John Catchpole
	Mr Jeremiah Wase	Mr John Randall
July	Robert Trotman Esq.	Mr John Button
	Mr William Henchman	Mr Nathaniel Gross
Aug.	William Woods Page Esq.	Mr William Neeve
	Revd William Browne	Mr Stephen Vertue
Sept.	John Syer M.D.	Mr John Mabson
	Revd Francis Capper	Mr James Catchpole
Oct.	Revd Samuel Hingeston	Mr Thomas Crisp
	Mr Burwell Edwards	Mr Benj. Cooper
Nov.	Mr William Waller	Mr William Catling
	Mr Robert Ashford	Mr Robert Cutting
Dec.	Mr Philip Dikes	Mr J. S. Baldrey
	Mr John Barthropp	Mr John Pitcher
Jan.	Revd Isaac Clarke	Mr John Woolnough
	Revd Charles Brooke	Mr William Pitts
Feb.	Jacob Whitbread Esq.	Mr George Bates
	Mr Samuel Gross	Mr Jonathan Abbott Studd
Mar.	Mr Thomas Simpson	Mr Ralph Randall
	Mr John Whimper	Mr Richard Dove
Apl.	Revd Jacob Chilton	Mr Thomas Warren
	Mr Richard Wilkinson	Mr Thomas Ablett

7 April 1803

Directors	Present	Guardians
Revd Charles Brooke		Mr Ralph Randall
John Syer M.D.		Mr John Woolnough
Revd Wm Browne		Mr John Waller
J. Whitbread Esq.		Mr George Bates
W. W. Page Esq.		
Mr Jeptha Waller		

The following persons were duly elected Directors and Acting Guardians:

	Directors	Guardians
May	John Pytches Esq.	Mr Thomas Waller
	Mr Jeptha Waller	Mr John Waller
June	Revd William Kett	Mr John Woolnough
	Mr Jeremiah Wase	Mr Robert Barthropp
July	Robert Trotman Esq.	Mr John Button
	William Henchman Gent.	Mr Nathaniel Gross
Aug.	William Woods Page Esq.	Mr William Neeve
	Revd William Browne	Mr Stephen Vertue
Sept.	John Syer M.D.	Mr John Mabson
	Revd Francis Capper	Mr William Cooper
Oct.	Revd Samuel Hingeston	Mr Thomas Crisp
	Mr Henry Edwards	Mr Samuel Thompson
Nov.	Edmund Jenney Esq.	Mr William Cole
	Mr Robert Ashford	Mr John Felgate
Dec.	Mr John Barthropp	Mr William Bunnett
	Mr Philip Dikes	Mr Joseph Jeaffreson
Jan.	Revd Isaac Clarke	Mr John Randall
	Revd Charles Brooke	Mr John Bright
Feb.	Jacob Whitbread Esq.	Mr Joseph Stammers
	Mr Samuel Gross	Mr George Bates
Mar.	Mr Thomas Simpson	Mr Ralph Randall
	Mr John Whimper	Mr Richard Ashford
Apl.	Revd Jacob Chilton	Mr James Garrett
	Colonel White	Mr J. S. Baldrey

Ordered that as it appears to this meeting the Overseer of Letheringham was guilty of great neglect in not attending the last Quarter Sessions and by such neglect the reputed father of the B.B. Child of Phillis Mann was released from his recognizance and freed from all expences attending the lying in of the said Phillis Mann and the sustenance of her child to the great damage of the Corporation. The said overseer be fined fifty five shillings and that the expences in bringing up the said Phillis Mann's child shall be defrayed by the parish of Letheringham and not by the Corporation at large.

Ordered that as the Overseer of Marlesford was guilty of great neglect in not apprehending the reputed father of the B.B. child of Susan Farrer whereby the said child has been chargeable to this Corporation. The expence of bringing up the said B.B. child shall be defrayed by the parish of Marlesford and not by the Corporation at large.

Resolved that it is the opinion of this meeting that every labourer who has a wife within the incorporated parishes should be considered a pauper, and when requiring medical assistance should be attended by the surgeon on the surgeon's being requested so to do by the overseer of the parish in which such pauper resides.

7 July 1803

Resolved that as Mr Orford late overseer of Marlesford has this day appeared and cleared himself from the charge of neglect made against him for not apprehending the reputed father of the B.B. child of Susan Farrer – the order at the last Quarterly Meeting be rescinded.

12 April 1804

Directors	Present	Guardians
Revd William Browne		Mr J. S. Baldrey
J. Syer M.D.		Mr John Waller
Revd Jacob Chilton		Mr John Woolnough
Mr Samuel Gross		
Mr Henry Edwards		
Jacob Whitbread Esq.		
W. W. Page Esq.		
Revd William Kett		
Revd Charles Brooke		
Revd George Turner		
Edmund Jenney Esq.		
Mr Jeptha Waller		

The following persons were duly elected Directors and Acting Guardians:

	Directors	Guardians
May	Revd George Turner	Mr Thomas Waller
	Mr Jeptha Waller	Mr Covey Cavell
June	Edmund Jenney Esq.	Mr John Woolnough
	Mr Jeremiah Wase	Mr Thomas Garneys
July	Robert Trotman Esq.	Mr John Button
	Mr William Henchman	Mr Nathaniel Gross
Aug.	William Woods Page Esq.	Mr William Neeve
	Revd William Browne	Mr John Sherwood
Sept.	John Syer M.D.	Mr Joshua Mabson
	Revd Francis Capper	Mr James Catchpole
Oct.	Revd Samuel Hingeston	Mr Thomas Crisp
	Mr Henry Edwards	Mr John Catchpole
Nov.	Revd William Kett	Mr Thomas Kersey
	Mr Robert Ashford	Mr John Waller
Dec.	Mr John Barthropp	Mr Thomas Baldwin
	Mr Philip Dikes	Mr William Burnett
Jan.	Revd Isaac Clarke	Mr William Catling
	Revd Charles Brooke	Mr William Kitson
Feb.	Jacob Whitbread Esq.	Mr J. A. Studd
	Mr Samuel Gross	Mr George Bates
Mar.	Mr Thomas Simpson	Mr Benjamin Cooper
	Thomas Pytches Esq.	Mr Samuel Farrer
Apl.	Revd Jacob Chilton	Mr James Garnett
	John White Esq.	Mr John Stow Baldrey

11 April 1805

	Directors	Present	Guardians
	Mr Samuel Gross		Mr James Garnett
	Revd George Turner		Mr John Waller
	Revd Jacob Chilton		
	John Syer M.D.		
	Mr William Henchman		
	Mr Robert Ashford		
	Mr Jeremiah Wase		
	Jacob Whitehead Esq.		
	Mr Jeptha Waller		
	Mr Henry Edwards		
	Revd Charles Brooke		
	Mr Thomas Waller		

The following persons were duly elected Directors and Acting Guardians◇:

	Directors	Guardians
May	Revd George Turner	Mr Thomas Walker
	Mr Jeptha Waller	Mr Benjamin Colchester
June	Edmund Jenney Esq.	Mr John Woolnough
	Mr Jeremiah Wase	Mr William Bumpstead
July	Robert Trotman Esq.	Mr William Garrett
	Mr William Henchman	Mr Nathaniel Gross
Aug.	Revd William Browne	Mr Samuel Brewer
		Mr John Sherwood
Sept.	John Syer M.D.	Mr John Cutting
	Revd Francis Capper	Mr William Cooper
Oct.	Revd Samuel Hingeston	Mr Edwards Crisp
	Mr Henry Edwards	Mr Joseph Jeaffreson
Nov.	Revd William Kett	Mr Thomas Kersey
	Mr Robert Ashford	Mr John Waller
Dec.	Mr Thomas Waller	Mr Thomas Baldwin
	Mr Philip Dikes	Mr John Wilson
Jan.	Revd Isaac Clarke	Mr William Cook
	Revd Charles Brooke	Mr William Kitson
Feb.	Jacob Whitbread Esq.	Mr James Clubbe
	Mr Samuel Gross	Mr George Bates
Mar.	Mr Thomas Simpson	Mr Benjamin Cooper
	Thomas Pytches Esq.	Mr James Aldhous
Apl.	Revd Jacob Chilton	Mr James Garnett
	Colonel White	Mr John Stow Baldrey

At a meeting of the Committee appointed to be held this day to enquire into the transactions for which William Holmes is committed to Ipswich Gaol it appears to us that the conduct of the Matron has been highly proper and it is resolved that the Governor do in future communicate to the Weekly Committee any infringement of the good order of the House.

Ordered that Mr John Wood, our solicitor, be instructed to prosecute William Holmes a pauper belonging to the parish of Hacheston for a rape committed on the body of Matilda Kent a poor child now in our House of Industry, and also that he prosecute the said William Holmes for the same being committed on the body of Sophia Woolnough a poor child also in the said House.

Resolved that it is the opinion of this Meeting that overseers are not entitled to any remuneration from the Corporation for their loss of time in executing orders of the different Committees or Quarterly Meetings but that the parish for which they respectively act shall pay them for such loss of time.

Resolved that the following gentlemen be appointed a Committee to enquire into the conduct of the Governor and Matron respecting the transactions for which William Holmes late a pauper in the House is committed to Ipswich Gaol. <9 named directors>.

The fourth Weekly Minute Book,
6 July 1795–8 October 1798[2]

6 July 1795

Ordered that the overseers of the following parishes do allow as under:

		No. of weeks	Allowed per week	Total
Earl Soham	the wife of Wm Loades continuing bedrid	4	1s.	4s.
Creetingham	John Swan of the sd. parish resident at Framsden having 5 children 3 under 10 yrs. of age	1	2s.	2s.
Marlesford	Thomas Crarr sick has 3 children under 10 yrs.	1	2s. 6d.	2s. 6d.
Ufford	Thomas Clow continuing sick for last week and	2	2s.	4s.
Hollesly	Lionel Andrews continuing lame	2	1s.	2s.
	Wm Wyard sick 4 children under 10 yrs. of age	1	4s.	4s.
Melton	Samuel Blomfield continuing sick	4	3s. 6d.	14s.
	Joseph Wilson old and infirm	1	1s.	1s.
Bredfield	Burial of Wd. Wright			20s.
Dallingo	Mary Nichols sick, for last week and this John Wicks sick 6 child 5 of them	1	1s.	2s.
	under 10 yrs.	1	4s.	4s.
Wickham	Samuel Corballs wife and daughter sick	1	1s. 6d.	1s. 6d.
	R. Hunnard out of employ	1	1s.	1s.
	John Burgesses wife sick has 3 child. under 10 yrs.	1	1s.	1s.
Kenton	the wife of Jonathan Church being brought to bed and having 5 children under 10 yrs.	2	2s.	4s.
	Mary Root and child ordered into the House			
Hollesly	Wm. Disbury discharged			

---

2   SROI ADA11/A/B/3/4.

The fifth Weekly Minute Book,
15 October 1798–19 March 1804[3]

15 October 1798

Ordered that the Overseers of the parishes allow as following:

Butley	Robert Johnson sick, has a wife and 3 children	2 wks at 3s.	0	6	0
Melton	Wd. Howse sick the week last past and this week at 1s.		0	2	0
Hoo	James Sawyer *do* 6 children under 10 yrs.	2 wks at 6s.	0	12	0
Bawdsey	Thomas Denny lame this and 2 to come	3 wks at 4s.	0	12	0
	Elizabeth Burrows	2 wks at 1s.	0	2	0
Ufford	Robt. Blomfield 3 to come and 1 last past	4 wks at 1s. 6d.	0	6	0
Earl Soham	Wd. Bowler *do*	4 wks at 1s.	0	4	0
	John Kerridge	3 wks at 1s.	0	3	0
Eyke	Enoch Barham	3 wks at 4s.	0	12	0
Hollesly	John Miller	2 wks at 4s. 6d.	0	9	0
	Wm. Birch 1 last past & to come	3 wks at 1s. 6d.	0	4	6
Shottisham	John Welham	2 wks at 4s. 6d.	0	9	0
Petistree	John Pettit	3 wks at 1s.	0	3	0
	John Perriman	3 wks at 1s.	0	3	0
	Jeffry Curtis	3 wks at 5s.	0	15	0
Brandeston	Thomas Cranes 1 last past and 2 to come	3 wks at 2s.	0	6	0
Boyton	John Toppells wife blind 1 last past and 4 to come	5 wks at 1s.	0	5	0
	George Cutler	4 wks at 1s.	0	4	0
Marlesford	Thomas Kent	3 wks at 5s.	0	15	0
	John Sheppard	2 wks at 1s.	0	2	0
	do by order of Directors for last week		0	9	0
Wick.	Harts wife continuing sick 3s for last week and 2 to come 3s.		0	9	0
	Hearns wife *do* 1s. 6d. *do* 1s. 6d.		0	4	6
	Director's order 2s. wine 1s. 6d.		0	3	6
Hatcheston	Ann Meechum	4 wks at 2s. 6d.	0	10	0
	Hannah Gibson	3 wks at 1s.	0	3	0
Boulge	Daniel Parish admitted in last week from Alderton discharged from the House at the request of his father				

---

3   SROI ADA11/A/B/3/5.

Alderton	three pints of wine to Wd. Hill	0	5	3
	for the burial of Wd. Hill	1	0	0
		9	8	9

Ordered that the Treasurer do pay to R. Rainbird the sum of one
hundred pounds for the use of the House of Industry.

100	0	0
109	8	9

Directors	Guardians
Robert Reynolds for Mr. Hingeston	Thomas Crisp
B. Edwards	Joseph Wase

The sixth Weekly Minute Book,
2 April 1804 – 11 July 1805[4]

2 April 1804

Ordered that the Overseers do allow as under:

Parish	Name	Amount	Period	£	s	d
Petistree	Widow Simpson	1s. for	1 week			
	porter for do by order of					
	Mr Harsant	8s. 9d.		0	9	9
Bredfield	Widow Henley	6d.	2 weeks			
	Francis Adams	2s.	2 weeks	0	5	0
	Samuel Brundish	3s.	2 weeks			
	Widow Jaques	6d.	2 weeks	0	7	0
	Widow Catchpole	6d.	2 weeks			
	Widow Allen	6d.	2 weeks	0	2	0
	William Dewell	3s.	2 weeks			
	Mary Rands	1s.	2 weeks	0	8	0
Bromeswell	Robert Austin & wife	1s.	1 week	0	1	0
Hacheston	William Aldridge	2s.	2 weeks			
	Charles Mann	2s.	2 weeks	0	8	0
	Francis Sawyers wife residing					
	at Snape 2s.6d.		2 weeks	0	5	0
	Porter (14 pints) for Charles					
	Mann by order of Mr Harsant			0	2	11
Marlesford	Thomas Martins	2s.	2 weeks			
	Robert Curtis	2s.	1 week	0	6	0
	Widow Clarkson	6d.	2 weeks			
	Elizabeth Downing	1s.	1 week	0	2	0
Boyton	Francis Ashkettle	4s.	1 week	0	4	0
Charsfield	Henry Rattle	2s.	1 week			
	John Wythe's wife	3s. 6d.	1 week	0	5	6
	Joseph Leech	4s.	1 week			
	Elizabeth Aldridge	1s.	1 week	0	5	0
	John Wythe's wife a pint of wine by					
	order of Mr Harsant			0	2	0
Melton	Mary Button	1s.	1 week			
	Richard Booth's wife	2s.	1 week	0	3	0
	George Barrell's wife	3s.	1 week			
	Widow Hawes	1s.	1 week	0	4	0
	Joseph Wilson	5s.	1 week			
	Widow Flory	1s. 6d.	1 week	0	6	6
	Widow Cockerell	6d.	1 week	0	0	6

---

[4] SROI ADA11/A/B/3/6 entries extracted until 11 July 1805.

Dallingho	Stephen Goymer	1s.	1 week			
	Widow Cooper	2s.	1 week	0	3	0
	James Mann	2s.	1 week			
	Samuel Smith's wife	2s.	1 week	0	4	0
Alderton	John Lyon	2s.	1 week			
	Widow Andrews	1s.	1 week	0	3	0
	Widow Good	2s.	1 week	0	2	0
	Richard Whiting aged 56 being ill to be received in to the House					
Creetingham	James Alexander	2s.	1 week			
	John Swann	2s.	1 week	0	4	0
	Abraham Simpson	2s.	1 week	0	2	0
Ash	Deborah Skinner	1s. 3d.	1 week			
	Widow Robinson	1s. 6d.	1 week	0	2	9
	M. A. Downing	1s.	1 week			
	Thos. Holmes' wife	1s.	1 week	0	2	0
Melton	Ordered that Miles Chilton of Woodbridge do pay 2s. per week towards the support of his two children now in the House of Industry					
Kenton	John Bennett	1s.	1 week			
	Rose Good	1s.	1 week	0	2	0
	Frans. Mullinger's wife	1s.	1 week			
	Mary Thompson	6d.	1 week	0	1	6
	Jon. Allen's wife	7s.	1 week			
	Samuel Rope's wife	1s.	1 week	0	8	0
	Sarah Moon	1s.	1 week			
	Abrm. Osborn's child	1s.	1 week	0	2	0
	Robt. Mullinger's child	1s.	1 week	0	1	0
Hollesley	Elizabeth Gunnell	1s.	1 week			
	Joseph Wyard to be rec'd. into the House Thos. Thornton towards clothing his son, to the sea			1	0	0
	Henry Andrews	2s.	1 week	0	2	0
Eyke	John Jackson's son	3s.	1 week			
	John Keeble's wife	2s. 6d.	1 week	0	5	6
Ufford	Susan Powling	1s.	1 week			
	Samuel Bloomfield	5s.	1 week	0	6	0
	Widow Manning	1s.	1 week			
	Stephen Ashkettle	2s.	1 week	0	3	0
	Will. Upson's wife	2s.	1 week			
	Widow Flegg	6d.	1 week	0	2	6
	John Croft	2s.	1 week			
	Harvey	4s.	1 week	0	6	0
Sutton	John Precious	2s.	1 week			
	Benjamin Levis	4s.	1 week	0	6	0
	Widow Gooch	1s.	1 week	0	1	0
Shottisham	Thomas Symonds	2s.	1 week	0	2	0
			Total	8	18	5

Directors	Guardians
Jacob Chilton	James Garrett
John White	J. S. Baldrey

Extract from the Third Treasurer's Account Book, 1803–16[5]

Mr John Wood (Treasurer) in Account with the Directors and Guardians of the Poor within the Hundreds of Loes and Wilford, Suffolk.

Dr. Christmas Quarter 1802

Nov. 9	To balance received of Mr John Carthew the late Treasurer due to the Directors as appears by his account	153	0	4¼
	To a Quarters Rate from the several parishes as appears by the assessment	1,034	8	9¼
Dec. 29	To 2 game convictions rec'd of Dr Frank & Mr Bolton 50s. each	5	0	0
1803	To 2 *do*	5	0	0
Janry 4	To cash rec'd of the Governor on acct of Bastardy	2	6	0
	do on acct of penalties	20	0	0
	do on acct of wool spinning	42	12	8
	do (farm) for hay	45	5	3
	do (farm) for 2 calves	5	18	2
	do (farm) for pork suet	1	15	6
	Brought forward	1,315	6	8½
	Brought up from the other side	1,296	6	4
	Balance due to the Directors	19	0	4½

1802Cr.

Dec. 22	By cash paid the Governor as per order	200	0	0
1803				
Jan. 12	By cash paid the Governor as per order	100	0	0

Out allowances paid as under

Loes Hundred	£	s.	d.	Wilford Hundred	£	s.	d.
Ash	11	12	0	Alderton	11	2	2
Brandeston	13	1	6	Bawdsey	10	17	0
Butley	9	6	6	Boulge	13	2	10½
Charsfield	7	2	0	Boyton	0	0	0
Creetingham	19	6	6	Bredfield	19	0	1½
Dallingho	12	6	0	Bromeswell	10	3	0
Earl Soham	14	0	6	Capell	2	5	6
Easton	14	18	0	Debach	3	0	0
Eyke	14	5	0	Hollesly	16	2	6
Hacheston	19	15	0	Melton	18	8	0
Hoo	4	17	6	Petistree	5	9	6

---

[5]   SROI ADA11/A/C/1/1/3.

Kenton	14	8	6	Ramsholt	1	1	6
Kettleburgh	11	16	0	Shottisham	7	14	0
Letheringham	5	11	6	Sutton	17	19	8
Monewden	6	6	0	Ufford	15	18	0
Marlesford	17	12	6	W Market	26	19	2
Rendlesham	4	18	6		179	3	0
	201	3	6		201	3	6
					380	6	6

Repairs

No. 1	Manthorp builders (including Fulcher's)	36	16	5
No. 2	Silver ironmonger	5	4	7
No. 3	Messrs Fletchers bricklayers	3	1	6
No. 4	Allen plumber	12	9	1
No. 5	Collins millwright	14	7	1
No. 6	Baxter locksmith	4	10	4
No. 7	Garrett blacksmith	5	1	2
		81	10	2

Surgeons etc.

No. 1	Reckett for wine & spirits for sick	9	2	6
No. 2	Riches for Geneva for *do*	7	16	0
No. 3	Messrs. Lynn's salary and bill	40	19	0
No. 4	Mr Harsant *do*	18	1	6
		75	19	0

Miscellaneous

No. 1	Leggatt hozier	8	2	0
No. 2	Studd coal merchant	38	0	0
No. 3	Turner brazier	0	7	0
No. 4	Edwards tanner	20	19	7
No. 5	Braggs drapery	17	14	6
No. 6	Messrs. Gross grocers	21	1	0
No. 7	Messrs. Gross drapers	41	1	5
No. 8	Licence hemp weaver	18	5	4
No. 9	Haken potash maker	2	5	6
No. 10	Oldham drapery	27	4	1
No. 11	Whincopp malster	23	14	0
No. 12	Governor salary	10	0	0
No. 13	Matron salary	5	0	0
No. 14	Loder stationer	3	9	9
No. 15	*do* bill	1	8	10
No. 16	Keer for cheese	62	8	6
No. 17	Revd J Black salary	8	15	0
No. 18	Russell attny order of Sessions	2	0	0
No. 19	Treasurers salary	5	0	0
No. 20	stamps for receipts	0	9	2
		317	5	8

Securities	Interest paid this quarter			
No. 3	Mrs Sarah Watling half a year on £100 due 5th Jan.	2	10	0
No. 4	Mr Ralph Randall (late Syred) *do* on *do*	2	10	0

No. 5	The Exers. of D. Copland dec'd *do* on *do*	2	10	0
No. 6	Mrs Sarah Maber (late Brooke) *do* on £150 *do*	3	15	0
No. 8	Mr Robert Seaman *do* on £200 *do*	5	0	0
No. 9	Mr Edward Plant (late Ralph) *do* on £200 *do*	5	0	0
No. 10	The Exers. of Mrs Kersey *do* on £200 *do*	5	0	0
No. 12	Mrs Lebbould *do* on £100 *do*	2	10	0
No. 14	Nich. Revett Esq (late Braham) *do* on £600 due *do*	15	0	0
	The Revd Jn. Lumkin (late N. Revett) *do* on £300 *do*	7	10	0
	Thos. Maynard Esq. (late *do*) *do* on £200 *do*	5	0	0
	Geo. Chenery Esq. (late *do*) *do* on £200 *do*	5	0	0
	Ann Burners Hutchinson (late *do*) *do* on £200 *do*	5	0	0
	Mrs Mary Lany (late *do*) *do* on £200 *do*	5	0	0
	Maria Rebecca Reilly (late *do*) *do* £200 due *do*	5	0	0
No. 15	Lady Andover & William Lygon Esq. administratrix and administrator of William Jennens Esq. deceased half a years interest on £500 *do*	12	10	0
No. 16	Richd Chaplin (late I. Ablett) *do* on £100 *do*	2	10	0
No. 19	Mr Thomas Threadkell *do* on £500 *do*	12	10	0
No. 20	Mr George Thomas Esq. *do* on £1,000 due *do*	25	0	0
No. 21	Miss Mary Gross *do* on £500 due *do*	12	10	0
		141	5	0

Allowances to the poor who have large families

Monday 13 July 1795

A Committee for the Relief of the Poor of the Hundreds of Loes and Wilford who have large families.[6]

		No. of weeks	Allow. per week	Total allow.		
Bawdsey	James Bridges has a wife & five children under the age of 12 yrs.					
	He earns 9s. wife earns 2s.	3	3s. 8d.	0	11	0
Petistree	Warner Gooch has a wife and five children[7]					
	W.G. earns 9s. his wife 2s.	3	3s. 8d.	0	11	0
	Robt. Howard has a wife and five children					
	R.H. earns 9s. his wife 2s.	3	3s. 8d.	0	11	0
	James Hervey has a wife and six children					
	J.H. earns 9s. his wife 2s.	3	4s. 6d.	0	13	6
	Isaac Potkins has a wife and 4 children					
	I.P. is himself lame can earn 7s.	3	4s. 6d.	0	13	6
	J. Kirk has a wife and 5 children					
	J.K. earns 9s. his wife 2s.	3	3s. 8d.	0	11	0
	J. Curtis has a wife and three children					
	J. Curtis earns 8s. his wife 2s.	3	2s. 0d.	0	6	0
Rendlesham	Thomas Jennings is a widower and has a nurse and 5 children					
	T.J. earns 8s. his children 2s.	3	4s. 0d.	0	12	0
Debach	John Wade has a wife and seven children					
	J. Wade earns 8s. his wife is lame	3	6s. 0d	0	18	0
	Robt. Allen blind his wife infirm					
	They have a quarterly order of 2s.	3	1s. 6s.	0	4	6
Easton	Henry Hearn has a wife and five children					
	H. Hearn earns 9s. his wife 2s.	3	3s. 8d.	0	11	0
	Robt Clover has a wife and three children					
	R.C. earns 9s. his wife 2s.	3	1s. 6d.	0	4	6
	John Ward has a wife and 3 children					
	J.W. earns 8s. his wife 2.s	3	1s. 6d.	0	4	6
	Lionel Baldry has a wife and four children					
	L.B. earns 9s. his wife 2s.	3	2s. 0d.	0	6	0
	William Baldry has a wife and 5 children					
	W.B. earns 9s. his wife 2s.	3	1s. 6d.	0	4	6
	L. Upson has a wife and 4 children					

---

[6] SROI ADA11/A/B/3/11.

[7] Under the age of 12 years omitted from this and subsequent entries.

	L.U. earns 8s. his wife 2s.	3	2s. 0d.	0	6	0
	Robt. Bayly has a wife and three children					
	R.B. earns 9s. his wife 2s.	3	1s. 6d.	0	4	6
Wickham M.	Henry Kemp has a wife and 4 children					
	H.K. earns 8s. his wife 2s.	3	2s. 0d.	0	6	0
	William Barber wife and 4 children	3	2s. 0d.	0	6	0
	Henry Beart wife and 4 children	3	2s. 0d.	0	6	0
	John Bridges wife and 3 children	3	1s. 6d.	0	4	6
	John Hurt wife and 5 children	3	3s. 8d.	0	11	0
	Harman Garrett wife and 4 children	3	2s. 0d.	0	6	0
	Edmund Kadman wife and 6 children	3	4s. 0d.	0	12	0
	Daniel Mills wife and 6 children	3	4s. 0d.	0	12	0
	John Simmons wife and 3 children	3	1s. 6d.	0	4	6
	Thos. Smith wife and 4 children	3	2s. 0d.	0	6	0
	James Hewitt wife and 3 children	3	1s. 6d.	0	4	6
	John Clow wife and 3 children	3	1s. 6d.	0	4	6
	Hannah Gray 2 children	3	2s. 0d.	0	6	0
	Thomas Sheet lame wife 1 child	3	1s. 0d.	0	3	0
	John Kemp wife 6 children	3	4s. 0d.	0	12	0
	Wm. Brereton wife 3 children	3	1s. 6d.	0	4	6
Creetingham	John Swan wife 4 children	3	2s. 0d.	0	6	0
Monewden	Richard Woods wife 6 children	3	4s. 0d.	0	12	0
Marlesford	Samuel Smith wife 4 children	3	2s. 0d.	0	6	0
	William Ely wife and 3 children	3	1s. 6d.	0	6	0
	Robert Bryns wife and 4 children	3	2s. 0d.	0	6	0
	Thomas Barrell wife and 5 children	3	3s. 8d.	0	11	0
	Robt. Jay wife and 3 children	3	1s. 6d.	0	4	6
Sutton	Edward Woods wife and 4 children	3	2s. 0d.	0	6	0
	Wm. Ablett 5 children	3	3s. 8d.	0	11	0
	Widow Long 2 children	3	1s. 0d.	0	3	0
	John Middleditch wife and 5 children	3	3s. 8d.	0	11	0
	Wm. Whinney wife and 7 children	3	6s. 9d.	0	18	0
Hacheston	James Sager wife 3 children	3	1s. 6d.	0	4	6
	James Smith wife and 4 children					
	he is allowed some corn by his master	3	1s. 0d.	0	3	0
	Thomas Button wife and 4 children					
	he is allowed some corn by his master	3	1s. 0d.	0	3	0
	John Paxton wife and 4 children					
	he is allowed wheat by his master	3	1s. 0d.	0	3	0
	Thomas Skinner wife and 3 children	3	1s. 6d.	0	4	6
	Robert Goodroom wife and 4 children	3	2s. 0d.	0	6	0
	Charles Man wife and 5 children	3	3s. 8d.	0	11	0
	Samuel Leech wife and 5 children	3	3s. 8d.	0	11	0
Shottisham	Henry Leek wife is lame and 2 children	3	1s. 0d.	0	3	0
Eyke	James Smith wife and 6 children	3	3s. 8d.	0	11	0
	James Booth wife and 5 children	3	3s. 2d.	0	9	6
	Robert [ ] wife and 3 children	3	1s. 6d.	0	4	6
	James Jeffrys wife and 3 children	3	1s. 6d.	0	4	6
	Robert Clouton wife and 4 children	3	2s. 0d.	0	6	0
	Robert Luck wife and 3 children	3	1s. 6d.	0	4	6

	Widow Pollard 3 children	3	1s. 6d.	0	4	6
Ash	Thomas Ling wife and 5 children	3	3s. 8d.	0	11	0
	William Ling wife and 5 children	3	3s. 8d.	0	11	0
	David Downing wife and 5 children	3	2s. 0d.	0	6	0
Charsfield	William Read wife and six children	3	4s. 0d.	0	12	0
	Ben Read wife and 3 children	3	1s. 6d.	0	4	6
	Charles Nun wife and 5 children	3	3s. 8d.	0	11	0
	Widow Man 3 children	3	1s. 6d.	0	4	6
	E. Durrant 4 children	3	2s. 0d.	0	6	0
	S. Fulcher wife and 4 children					
	S. Fulcher is a bricklayer	3	1s. 0d.	0	3	0
	John With wife and 3 children	3	1s. 6d.	0	4	6
	John Gelman wife and 4 children	3	2s. 0d.	0	6	0
	Widow Clements 3 children	3	2s. 0d.	0	6	0
	Abraham Garnham wife and 5 children	3	3s. 8d.	0	11	0
	Jonathan Wright wife and 5 children	3	3s. 8d.	0	11	0
	John Nun wife and 4 children	3	2s. 0d.	0	6	0
	Thomas Birch wife and 4 children	3	2s. 0d.	0	6	0
Ufford	James Reeve wife and 7 children	3	6s. 0d.	0	18	0
	John Andrews wife and 5 children	3	3s. 8d.	0	11	0
	William Upston wife and 5 children	3	3s. 8d.	0	11	0
	Robert Cockerill wife and 4 children	3	2s. 0d.	0	6	0
	Thomas Harwood wife and 3 children	3	1s. 6d.	0	4	6
	John Buckenham wife and 4 children	3	2s. 0d.	0	6	0
	L. Blackwell wife and 4 children	3	2s. 0d.	0	6	0
	The wife of Denis Buckenham with 3 child.	3	1s. 6d.	0	4	6
Hollesley	John Sawer wife and 6 children	3	4s. 0d.	0	12	0
	Widow Day with 3 children	3	2s. 0d.	0	6	0
	John Miller wife and 4 children	3	2s. 0d.	0	6	0
Dallingho	Joseph Bonet wife and 6 children	3	3s. 6d.	0	10	6
	John Wicks wife and 6 children	3	4s. 0d.	0	12	0
	Robert Giborn wife and 3 children	3	1s. 6d.	0	4	6
	Elizabeth Sawer widow	3	1s. 0d.	0	3	0
Bredfield	William Leggatt wife and 5 children	3	3s. 8d.	0	11	0
	Widow Lancaster	3	1s. 0d.	0	3	0
	Samuel Brundish wife and 5 children	3	3s. 8d.	0	11	0
	Samuel Norman wife and 5 children	3	3s. 8d.	0	11	0
	Benj. Jacob wife and 3 children	3	1s. 6d.	0	4	6
	Thomas Catchpole wife and 3 children	3	1s. 6d.	0	4	6
Hoo	James Laver wife and 6 children	3	4s. 0d.	0	12	0
		Total		37	15	6

FOURTH QUARTERLY MINUTE BOOK
17 October 1805–15 October 1812[1]

17 October 1805

Directors	Present	Guardians
Thomas Pytches Esq		Mr John Sherwood
Revd Jacob Chilton		Mr John Waller
John Syer M.D.		Mr John Woolnough
Revd. W. Browne		
Philip Dikes		
Jeremiah Wase		
Jacob Whitbread Esq.		
Revd F. Capper		
Mr William Henchman		
Revd S. Kilderbee		
Mr Thomas Waller		

Ordered that the rate for the ensuing Quarter be made in the following manner, viz. the same as last Quarter i.e. two rates, and the out allowances and bills having been examined at the previous meeting be forthwith paid by the Treasurer.

Ordered that the following children be apprenticed in their respective parishes:

Ash	Joseph Booth	13½ yrs.	to Mr Joseph Chapman of Blaxhall
Alderton	Jemima Riches	13 yrs.	to Mr John Ablitt of Alderton
Bawdsey	Sarah Hammond	14 yrs.	to Mr Gardner Utting of Bawdsey
	James Hammond	11¼ yrs.	to Mr Samuel Brewer of Alderton
Charsfield	James Clements	11¼ yrs.	to Mr Jeremiah Burch of Charsfield
Earl Soham	Sophia Spalding	12 yrs.	to Mr James Kent of Earl Soham
Hatcheston	Elizabeth Hart	12 yrs.	to Mr Thomas Walker of Hatcheston
	Samuel Skinner	11¾ yrs.	to Mr George Bond of *do*
Kettleburgh	Joseph Dobson	13¾ yrs.	to Mr John Orford of Kettleburgh
Hoo	Mary Rowe	11¼ yrs.	to Mr John Mayhew of Hoo
Wickham	Jemima Marjoram	11¾ yrs.	to Mr Robert Welton of Petistree
	Lydia Hewitt	11 yrs.	to Mr Stephen Vertue of W. Market
Boyton	Susanna Jessup	14¼ yrs.	to Mr Samuel Gross of Capel
Wickham	Charlotte Sayer	15 yrs.	to Mr John Largent of W. Market

---

[1] SROI ADA11/A/B/1/4.

Quarterly Orders
Loes Hundred

				weekly		allowed per quarter		
				s.	d.	£.	s.	d.
Ash								
Widow Wright	1s. 6d.	Widow Skinner	1s.	2	6	1	12	6
do Clarke	1s.	Henry Graystone & wife	4s.	5	0	3	5	0
do Holmes	1s. 6d.	William Crisp	1s. 6d.	3	0	1	19	0
do Bailey	1s.	Mary Ann Downing	1s.	2	0	1	6	0
John Knights	2s.	Deborah Skinner	1s. 6d.	3	6	2	5	6
Hannah Holmes	1s. 6d.	Girl Skinner	1s.	2	6	1	12	6
Hannah Kemp	1s. 6d.	Widow Robinson	1s. 6d.	3	0	1	19	0
						13	19	6
Brandeston								
Widow Barker	1s. 0d.	Mary Chaplin	1s. 6d.	2	6	1	12	6
do Brianton	1s. 6d.	Jeffrey Boon & wife	2s. 0d.	3	6	2	5	6
do Edwards	1s. 6d.	Widow Boon	1s. 6d.	3	0	1	19	0
Ann Driver	1s. 6d.	Mary Reeve	1s. 6d.	3	0	1	19	0
Mary Bradlaugh	1s. 0d.			1	0	0	13	0
						8	9	0
Butley								
Widow Buckingham	1s. 0d.	Widow Luff	1s. 0d.	2	0	1	6	0
		William Jolly	2s. 0d.	2	0	1	6	0
William Caley's wife	1s. 0d.	Mary Jordan's BB child	6d.	1	6	0	19	6
		Deborah Kettle	6d.	0	6	0	6	6
Ann Clarke	1s. 6d.	Sarah Crosby	1s. 0d.	2	6	1	12	6
Widow Arthrold	1s. 6d.	Widow Garrod	1s. 0d.	2	6	1	12	6
Sarah Mays		Widow Johnson						
(late Cook)	1s. 6d.	2 chd.	3s. 0d.	4	6	2	18	6
						10	1	6
Charsfield								
Mary Mauldon	1s. 0d.	Thos. Buckle & wife	2s. 0d.	3	0	1	19	0
Widow Mallett	0s. 6d.	John Durrant	1s. 0d.	1	6	0	19	6
do Waters	2s. 0d.	Henry Rattle	2s. 0d.	4	0	2	12	0
Sarah Gillman	2s. 0d.	James Mann	1s. 0d.	3	0	1	19	0
Sophia Mauldon	1s. 6d.	Mary Spendlove	0s. 6d.	2	0	1	6	0
Amy Wythe	1s. 6d.			1	6	0	19	6
						9	15	0
Creetingham								
Lydia Harvey	1s. 0d.	Widow Browne	1s. 0d.	2	0	1	6	0
Mary Moyse	1s. 6d.	do England	1s. 0d.	2	6	1	12	6
John Copping	1s. 6d.	Mary Cook	1s. 0d.	2	6	1	12	6
James Alexander	2s. 0d.	Pleasance Creasy	1s. 0d.	3	0	1	19	0
						6	10	0
Dallingho								
Mary Norman	1s. 0d.	Thos. Lanham & wife	1s. 0d.	2	0	1	6	0

243

Stephen Goymer	1s. 6d.	Lanham's son	1s. 0d.	2	6	1	12	6
Eliz. Carter	1s. 0d.	Mary Spall	1s. 0d.	2	0	1	6	0
Mary Goymer	3s. 0d.	Widow Cooper	2s. 6d.	5	6	3	11	6
Sarah Garnham	1s. 6d.	*do* Capon	1s. 0d.	2	6	1	12	6
Hannah Read	1s. 6d.	Jane Garnham	1s. 6d.	3	0	1	19	0
Susan Wright	1s. 0d.			1	0		13	0
						12	0	6

Earl Soham

Eliz. Gooch	1s. 0d.	Widow Lambert	1s. 0d.	2	0	1	6	0
Widow Scott	2s. 0d.	*do* Read	0s. 6d.	2	6	1	12	6
do Burrows	1s. 0d.	Joseph Kerridge	2s. 0d.	3	0	1	19	0
do Lanceter	1s. 0d.	Robt. Lanham's daug.	1s. 6d.	2	6	1	12	6
do Sawyer	1s. 0d.	Amy Kemp (Leiston)	1s. 6d.	2	6	1	12	6
Mark Pettitt & wife	3s. 0d.	Widow Cracknell	1s. 0d.	4	0	2	12	0
Widow Watling	1s. 0d.	Will Smith & wife	2s. 6d.	3	6	2	5	0
do Creasy	1s. 0d.	Sarah Potkin's BB child	1s. 0d.	2	0	1	6	0
John Sills & children	2s. 0d.			2	0	1	6	0
						15	12	0

Easton

Hannah Kerridge	1s. 0d.	Widow Cracknell	1s. 0d.	2	0	1	6	0
Sarah Alderton	1s. 6d.	Unice Levett	1s. 0d.	2	6	1	12	6
Susanna Hurren		Will. Baldrey & wife	3s. 0d.	3	0	1	19	0
Nathl. Smith	1s. 0d.	Lionel Upson	1s. 0d.	2	0	1	6	0
Steph. Spink & Wife	3s. 6d.	Samuel Crisp	1s. 0d.	4	6	2	18	6
Widow Long	1s. 0d.			1	0	0	13	0
						9	15	0

Eyke

Widow Pollard	1s. 0d.	Widow Girling	1s. 0d.	2	0	1	6	0
Henry Fiske	8s. 0d.	Mary Martin	0s. 6d.	8	6	5	10	6
Widow Gooding	1s. 0d.	Rebecca Catten	1s. 0d.	2	0	1	6	0
do Kettle	1s. 0d.			1	0	0	13	0
Ann Greystone	1s. 0d.			1	0		13	0
						9	8	6

Hacheston

Sarah Knight & 2 ch.	2s. 6d.	Ralph Cotton & wife	3s. 0d.	5	6	3	11	6
Eliz. Porter	1s. 0d.	Late S. Eagles child	1s. 0d.	2	0	1	6	0
John Scrutton	1s. 6d.	Widow Block	1s. 0d.	2	6	1	12	6
Timothy Martin	1s. 0d.	do Woods, 1 child	1s. 6d.	2	6	1	12	6
Widow Leech	1s. 0d.	Willm. Bucke	1s. 0d.	2	0	1	6	0
do Lingwood	1s. 6d.	Child Friend	1s. 0d.	2	6	1	12	6
James Garrod & wife	3s. 0d.	Mary Mann	1s. 6d.	4	6	2	18	6
Willm. Blaxhall	1s. 6d.	John Clowe	1s. 0d.	2	6	1	12	6
Eliz. Eagle	1s. 0d.	Ralph Cotton's gchild.	0s. 6d.	1	6	0	19	6
Abigail Davis	1s. 6d.			1	6	0	19	6
						17	11	0

Hoo

Name	Amt	Name	Amt	s	d	£	s	d
Widow Fryatt	2s. 0d.	Eliz. Vincent	1s. 0d.	3	0	1	19	0
Robert Hill	2s. 6d.	James Sawyer's daug.	1s. 0d.	3	6	2	5	6
Widow King	1s. 6d.			1	6	0	19	6
						5	4	0

Kettleburgh

Name	Amt	Name	Amt	s	d	£	s	d
Mary Newman	3s. 0d.	Sarah Baxter	1s. 6d.	4	6	2	18	6
Window Ringe	1s. 0d.	Widow Miller	1s. 0d.	2	0	1	6	0
do Stannard	1s. 0d.	Margt. Keer	0s. 6d.	1	6	0	19	6
Sarah Rogers	1s. 6d.	Wid. Smith & 5 Chd.	5s. 0d.	6	6	4	4	6
		Simon Nicolls	2s. 0d.	2	0	1	6	0
Robert Spalding	1s. 0d.			1	0	0	13	0
						11	7	6

Letheringham

Name	Amt	Name	Amt	s	d	£	s	d
Widow Hudson	1s. 0d.	Eliz. Adams	1s. 6d.	2	6	1	12	6
Hanah Garnham	1s. 0d.	Eliz. Markham	1s. 0d.	2	0	1	6	0
Widow Eade's child	1s. 6d.	Richd. Cuthbert	1s. 6d.	3	0	1	19	0
						4	17	6

Monewden

Name	Amt	Name	Amt	s	d	£	s	d
Ann Booth	1s. 0d.	Widow Fuller	1s. 6d.	2	6	1	12	6
John Fiske	1s. 6d.	do Jennings	1s. 0d.	2	6	1	12	6
Mary Durrant	1s. 0d.			1	0	0	13	0
						3	18	0

Marlesford

Name	Amt	Name	Amt	s	d	£	s	d
Widow King (1st)	1s. 0d.	Eliz. Flute	1s. 0d.	2	0	1	6	0
do Harvey	1s. 0d.	Widow Riches	1s. 6d.	2	6	1	12	6
Markham & wife	2s. 0d.	do Sheppard	1s. 0d.	3	0	1	19	0
Widow Burrell & 1 ch.	1s. 6d.	Eliz. Goldsmith	1s. 0d.	2	6	1	12	6
Sarah Wilson	1s. 6d.	Susan Farrer	1s. 0d.	2	6	1	12	6
Saml. Bridges' wife	2s. 0d.	Widow King (2nd)	1s. 0d.	3	0	1	19	0
Eliz. Downing	1s. 0d.	Theodosia Marjoram	0s. 6d.	1	6	0	19	6
						11	1	0

Rendlesham

Name	Amt	Name	Amt	s	d	£	s	d
Esther Smith	1s. 0d.	Widow Smith	1s. 0d.	2	0	1	6	0
Catharine Carr	1s. 0d.	Mary Howard	1s. 0d.	2	0	1	6	0
Maria Reeve & 2 ch.	3s. 0d.	Rebecca Braham for daughter	1s. 0d.	4	0	2	12	0
Widow Simpson	1s. 6d.			1	6	0	19	6
						6	3	6

Wilford Hundred
Alderton

Name	Amt	Name	Amt	s	d	£	s	d
Widow Mealing	1s. 0d.	Widow Fox	1s. 0d.	2	0	1	6	0
do Pratt	1s. 0d.	do Wright	1s. 0d.	2	0	1	6	0
do Andrews	1s. 0d.	do Sawyer (dead)		1	0	0	13	0
do Bing	1s. 0d.	do Good	1s. 0d.	2	0	1	6	0
do Leich	1s. 0d.	do Girling	1s. 0d.	2	0	1	6	0
do Jordan	1s. 0d.	do Clarke	1s. 0d.	2	0	1	6	0
do Bird	1s. 0d.	Eliz. Knights & sister	1s. 0d.	2	0	1	6	0

do Cook	2s. 0d.	John Lyon	1s. 0d.	2	0	1	6	0
do Cuthbert	1s. 0d.	Widow Cooper	1s. 0d.	2	0	1	6	0
						11	14	0

Bawdsey

Widow Moore	1s. 6d.	Robert Pooley	1s. 0d.	2	6	1	12	6
do Button	2s. 0d.	Henry Gooding	1s. 0d.	3	0	1	19	0
John Spatchett	1s. 0d.	Widow Freeman	1s. 0d.	2	0	1	6	0
Widow Browne	1s. 0d.	do Burrell	2s. 0d.	3	0	1	19	0
John Pratt's wife	2s. 6d.	Samuel Moss	2s. 0d.	4	6	2	18	6
Widow Jordan	1s. 0d.	Widow Ransby	1s. 0d.	2	0	1	6	0
						11	1	0

Boulge

Widow Rowe	1s. 6d.			1	6	0	19	6
						0	19	6

Bredfield

Widow Button	1s. 6d.	Widow Lankester Jun.	1s. 0d.	2	6	1	12	6
do Jaques	1s. 6d.	do Clarke	1s. 0d.	2	6	1	12	6
do Henley	1s. 6d.			1	6	0	19	6
Ann Dewell	1s. 0d.	do Good & 2 children	2s. 0d.	3	0	1	19	0
Sarah Marjoram	1s. 0d.	do Catchpole	1s. 0d.	2	0	1	6	0
Widow Lankester	1s. 0d.	J. Thompson & wife	2s. 6d.	3	6	2	5	6
do Wright	1s. 0d.	John Oxborne	1s. 6d.	2	6	1	12	6
do Lankester	1s. 0d.	Widow Allen	1s. 6d.	2	6	1	12	6
Eliz. Barker	1s. 0d.	Francis Adams	1s. 0d.	2	0	1	6	0
Deborah Burward	1s. 6d.	Widow Browne	1s. 0d.	2	6	1	12	6
Willm. Scapy & wife	3s. 0d.	Widow Alexander	1s. 6d.	4	6	2	18	6
James Crane & 6 child.	3s. 0d.			3	0	1	19	0
						15	16	0

Bromswell

Widow Day	1s. 6d.	Barnabas Collins child	1s. 0d.	2	0	1	6	0
do Brundle	1s. 6d.	Widow Branch	1s. 0d.	2	6	1	12	6
Temperance Downing	1s. 0d.			1	0	0	13	0
Thos. Farrow	1s. 0d.			1	0	0	13	0
						4	4	6

Boyton

Thos. Browne's wife	1s. 0d.	John Robinson's daug.	1s. 0d.	2	0	1	6	0
Widow Pettit	1s. 0d.			1	0	0	13	0
do King	1s. 0d.	Mary Lamb	1s. 0d.	2	0	1	6	0
do Ellis	1s. 0d.			1	0	0	13	0
William Minter's wife	1s. 6d.	Frs. Ashkettle	3s. 0d.	4	6	2	18	6
						6	16	6

Capel

Wid. Foreman & 2ch	1s. 0d.	M Browne for BB ch.	1s. 0d.	2	0	1	6	0
Sarah Nunn	1s. 0d.	Martha Howes	1s. 0d.	2	0	1	6	0
Mary Markham	2s. 6d.	Widow Wyard	1s. 0d.	3	6	2	5	6
						4	17	6

Debach

Sarah Gross

Hollesley

Widow Andrews	2s. 0d.	Widow Bridges	1s. 0d.	3	0	1	19	0
John Punchard	1s. 6d.	*do* King	1s. 0d.	2	6	1	12	6
Widow Elmer	1s. 0d.	Willm. Easter	1s. 6d.	2	6	1	12	6
do Fox	1s. 0d.	Widow Woods & 3 ch.	3s. 0d.	4	0	2	12	0
Mary Disbury	1s. 0d.	*do* Lamb & *do* ch.	3s. 0d.	4	0	2	12	0
Thos. Jenning's wife	1s. 0d.	A. King for BB Child	1s. 0d.	2	0	1	6	0
Widow Gibbs	1s. 0d.	John Luecock	1s. 6d.	2	6	1	12	6
Amy Johnson	1s. 6d.	Robert Walker	1s. 0d.	2	6	1	12	6
Widow Cook	1s. 6d.	Mary Baxter	1s. 6d.	3	0	1	19	0
Eliz. Hunt	1s. 0d.			1	0	0	13	0
						17	11	0

Melton

John Avis & wife	2s. 0d.	Sarah Girling	1s. 0d.	3	0	1	19	0
Widow Fuller	1s. 0d.	William Cole	2s. 0d.	3	0	1	19	0
do Cooper	1s. 0d.	Widow Kettle	1s. 6d.	2	6	1	12	6
do Lester	1s. 0d.	Sarah Farehead	1s. 0d.	2	0	1	6	0
do Clowe	3s. 0d.	Mary Button	1s. 0d.	4	0	2	12	0
John Harper	1s. 6d.	Mary Ewens	1s. 0d.	2	6	1	12	6
John Topple & wife	2s. 0d.	Widow Gall	3s. 0d.	5	0	3	5	0
Widow Cockerell	1s. 0d.	Susan Branch	1s. 0d.	2	0	1	6	0
do Flory	1s. 0d.	Edw. Durrant & wife	2s. 0d.	3	0	3	5	0
Widow Hawes	1s. 0d.	Denis Gibson & wife	2s. 0d.	3	0	3	5	0
Willm. Sawer	2s. 6d.			2	6	1	12	6
						21	2	6

Pettistree

Widow Curtis	1s. 0d.	Robert Boon	2s. 6d.	3	6	2	5	6
do Scott	1s. 0d.			1	0	0	13	0
						2	18	6

Ramsholt

Widow Osbourne	1s. 0d.	Widow Ablett	5s. 0s.	6	0	3	18	0

Sutton

Widow Mann	1s. 0d.	Widow Middleditch	1s. 0d.	2	0	1	6	0
Martha Robinson	1s. 0d.	*do* Hammond	1s. 6d.	2	6	1	12	6
John Worby's gch.	1s. 0d.	*do* Spall the younger	5s. 6d.	6	6	4	4	6
Widow Spall	1s. 0d.	*do* Flegg	1s. 6d.	2	6	1	12	6
Warner Gooch's daug.	1s. 0d.	John Precious	1s. 0d.	2	0	1	6	0
Widow Crane	1s. 0d.	Widow White	2s. 0d.	3	0	1	19	0
						12	0	6

Shottisham

Henry Leek's wife	1s. 6d.	Thos. Symonds	2s. 0d.	3	6	2	5	6
Widow Bird	4s. 0d.	Eliz. Mann	3s. 0d.	7	0	4	11	0
						6	16	6

Ufford

Widow Russell	1s. 0d.	[Joshua Brighten]		1	0	0	13	0
[Saml. King & wife]		Widow Beatty	1s. 0d	1	0	0	13	0
John Skeet & wife	2s. 0d.	do Bennett	1s. 0d.	3	0	1	19	0
Widow Able & 2 ch.	2s. 0d.	Hannah Wolton	1s. 0d.	3	0	1	19	0
Martha List	1s. 0d.	[Widow Baxter]		1	0	0	13	0
Widow Bloomfield	2s. 6d.	do Manning	1s. 0d.	3	6	2	5	6
do Brighten	1s. 6d.	Susan Powling	1s. 6d.	3	0	1	19	0
[Susan Olding]		Widow Baxter						
Wife of Rich. Booth	2s. 0d.	Widow Parkes	1s. 0d.	3	0	1	19	0
						12	0	6

Wickham

Widow Fosdike	1s. 6d.	Widow Hewitt	1s. 0d.	2	6	1	12	6
Mary Brewer	1s. 0d.	Thos. Barham	2s. 0d	3	0	1	19	0
Wid. Broome & daug.	1s. 6d.	Widow Durrant	1s. 0d.	2	6	1	12	6
do Harvey	1s. 0d.	do Holmes	1s. 0d.	2	0	1	6	0
Wife of George Care	2s. 0d.	do Plowman	1s. 0d.	3	0	1	19	0
Widow Beart	1s. 0d.	do Noy	2s. 0d.	3	0	1	19	0
Jemima Tylor	1s. 0d.	do Lever	1s. 0d.	2	0	1	6	0
Hannah Tylor	1s. 0d.	Mary Dammant	2s. 0d.	3	0	1	19	0
Widow Hart	5s. 0d.	Robt. Curtis & wife	2s. 0d.	7	0	4	11	0
do Tuffield	1s. 0d.	Widow Mully	1s. 6d.	2	6	1	12	6
Eliz Wright	1s. 0d.	Saml. Lambert	1s. 0d.	2	0	1	6	0
Widow Olding	1s. 0d.	Widow Jackson	1s. 0s.	2	0	1	6	0
Charles Murrell	1s. 0d.	Eliz Pendle	1s. 0d.	2	0	1	6	0
Widow Whistlecraft	1s. 0d.	Widow Smith	1s. 0d.	2	0	1	6	0
Susan Holder BB ch.	1s. 6d.			1	6	0	19	6
						26	0	0

10 April 1806

Directors	Present	Guardians
Mr William Henchman		Mr Edward Crisp
Mr Robert Ashford		Mr J. Stow Baldry
Revd Jacob Chilton		Mr John Waller
John Syer M.D.		Mr Benjamin Colchester
Mr Philip Dikes		Mr George Bates
Thomas Pytches Esq.		
Revd William Browne		
Revd George Turner		
Jacob Whitbread Esq.		
Mr Samuel Gross		
Mr Jeptha Waller		
Mr Thomas Simpson		
Revd Chares Brooke		
Revd Isaac Clarke		
Revd Samuel Kilderbee		

The following persons were duly elected Directors and Acting Guardians:

	Directors	Guardians
May	Revd George Turner	Mr George Bond
	Mr Jeptha Waller	Mr Benjamin Colchester
June	Edmund Jenney Esq.	Mr John Woolnough
	Mr Jeremiah Wase	Mr Thomas Garneys
July	Robert Trotman Esq.	Mr John Pitcher
	Mr William Henchman	Mr Nathaniel Gross
Aug.	Revd William Browne	Mr Samuel Brewer
	Revd Samuel Kilderbee	Mr John Sherwood
Sept.	John Syer M.D.	Mr William Kemp
	Revd Francis Capper	Mr James Page
Oct.	Mr Henry Edwards	Mr Edward Crisp
		Mr Joseph Jeaffreson
Nov.	Revd William Kett	Mr John Randall
	Mr Robert Ashford	Mr John Waller
Dec.	Mr Thomas Waller	Mr Thomas Baldwin
	Mr Philip Dikes	Mr John Jarrold
Jan.	Revd Isaac Clarke	Mr Joseph Stammers
	Revd Charles Brooke	Mr William Pitts
Feb.	Jacob Whitbread Esq.	Mr James Clubbe
	Mr Samuel Gross	Mr George Bates
Mar.	Mr Thomas Simpson	Mr Samuel Thompson
	Thomas Pytches Esq.	Mr William Orford
Apl.	Revd Jacob Chilton	Mr Thomas Warren
	Colonel White	Mr J. S. Baldry

16 October 1806

Resolved that in future the surgeons be allowed to order wine brandy or porter for sick paupers out of the House for no longer time than one week, and at the end of that time to recommend it to the Weekly committee to continue such allowance of wine brandy or porter if necessary.

9 April 1807

Directors	Present	Guardians
J. Syer M.D.		Mr Joseph Jarrold
Mr Samuel Gross		Mr John Randall
Revd William Browne		Mr John Sherwood
Mr Philip Dikes		Mr John Waller
Jacob Whitbread Esq.		Mr Thomas Baldwin
Revd Jacob Chilton		Mr Edward Crisp
Thomas Pytches Esq.		Mr George Bond
Mr Thomas Simpson		Mr George Bates
Revd Christopher Jeaffreson		
Revd George Turner		

The following persons were duly elected Directors and Acting Guardians:

	Directors	Guardians
May	Revd George Turner	Mr George Bond
	Mr Jeptha Waller	Mr Henry Edwards
June	Edmund Jenney Esq.	Mr Thomas Miller

	Mr Jeremiah Wase	Mr Thomas Garneys
July	Robert Trotman Esq.	Mr Henry Cupper
	Mr William Henchman	Mr Nathaniel Gross
Aug.	Revd William Browne	Mr Thurston Whimper
	Revd Samuel Kilderbee	Mr John Sherwood
Sept.	John Syer M.D.	Mr Thomas Kersey
	Revd. Francis Capper	Mr Joseph Hare
Oct.	Mr Henry Edwards	Mr Edward Crisp
	Mr Jonathan Abbott Studd	Mr Richard Dove
Nov.	Revd William Kett	Mr John Randall
	Mr Robert Ashford	Mr John Waller
Dec.	Mr Thomas Waller	Mr Thomas Baldwin
	Mr Philip Dikes	Mr John Jarrold
Jan.	Revd Isaac Clarke	Mr William Pitts
	Revd Charles Brooke	Mr John Button
Feb.	Jacob Whitbread Esq.	Mr James Clubbe
	Mr Samuel Gross	Mr George Bates
Mar.	Mr Thomas Simpson	Mr Benjamin Cooper
	Thomas Pytches Esq.	Mr James Aldhouse
Apl.	Revd Jacob Chilton	Mr John Gooding
	Revd Christopher Jeaffreson	Mr Robert Mabson

9 July 1807

Ordered that Mrs Johnstone be continued Governess at the salary of sixty pounds per annum, and that she engage a fit and proper person as clerk to the Directors and Acting Guardians as soon as possible, to be paid by her out of the said salary, and which said clerk shall be approved of by a Weekly or Special Committee.

7 April 1808

Directors	Present	Guardians
Jacob Whitbread Esq.		Mr John Goodwin
Revd George Turner		Mr George Bond
Revd Charles Brooke		
John Syer M.D.		
Revd William Browne		
Revd Jacob Chilton		
Mr Philip Dykes		
Mr Samuel Gross		
Revd Isaac Clarke		
Revd Samuel Kilderbee		
Revd Christopher Jeaffreson		

The following persons were duly elected Directors and Acting Guardians:

	Directors	Guardians
May	Revd George Turner	Mr George Bond
	Mr Jeptha Waller	Mr Whimper Cook
June	Edmund Jenney Esq.	Mr William Bumpstead
	Mr Jeremiah Wase	Mr Robert Vertue
July	Robert Trotman Esq.	Mr Jeremiah White
	Mr William Henchman	Mr John Catchpole
Aug.	Revd William Browne	Mr Samuel Brewer

	Revd Samuel Kilderbee	Mr John Sherwood
Sept.	John Syer M.D.	Francis Chisnall
	Revd William Aldrich	William Threadkell
Oct.	Mr Henry Edwards	Mr Edward Crisp
	Mr Jonathan Abbott Studd	Mr Henry Farrer
Nov.	Revd William Kett	Mr John Randall
	Mr Robert Ashford	Mr John Waller
Dec.	Mr Thomas Waller	Mr Thomas Baldwin
	Mr Philip Dykes	Mr John Jarrold
Jan.	Revd Isaac Clarke	Mr William Kitson
	Revd Charles Brooke	Mr John Button
Feb.	Jacob Whitbread Esq.	Mr James Clubbe
	Mr Samuel Gross	Mr George Bates
Mar.	Mr Thomas Simpson	Mr Samuel Randall
	Thomas Pytches Esq.	Mr James Aldhous
Apl.	Revd Jacob Chilton	Mr John Goodwin
	Revd Christopher Jeaffreson	Mr Andrew Blake

13 October 1808

Ordered that the sum of eleven pounds per annum be added to the salary of the Governess to enable her to pay the clerk's salary as agreed by the Committee of the day.

Resolved that R. W. Oldham be appointed Clerk to the Directors and Acting Guardians of the Incorporated Hundreds of Loes and Wilford.

Ordered that the sum of five guineas be paid to Robert Lamb of Marlesford in consideration of much sickness and lameness. That the sum of two pounds be paid to Edmund Parsons, residing in Wattisfield, having been confined with illness. That Abram Parsons and family residing in Ipswich be admitted into the House, and that St. Mayes's bill of sixteen shillings be paid for medicines to the above Ab. Parsons.

Resolved that a book be provided for the use of every Weekly Committee in which the resolutions of every Quarterly or other meeting (from the date of the year 1791) relative to the general regulations of the House and parish officers should be entered together with such other resolutions as may hereafter be approved of by any subsequent Quarterly or other meeting.

1. That in order to avoid errors in the lists of apprentices it is desired that the overseers of every parish be provided with a book to be called The Apprentice Book in which shall be entered, in separate columns, the valuation of each occupier, his name and the number of apprentices he has had ◇, and that this list be renewed every year and laid before the parish at their Easter Meeting, and then examined and signed by the churchwardens, overseers and inhabitants present. And that each book so signed be then carried to the House of Industry and checked by the clerk, and that the overseers do exhibit the book at the next Quarterly Meeting, to the Apprenticing Committee there appointed.

2. That the overseers of every parish to which apprentices are to be allotted at the Quarterly Meeting be desired not to leave the meeting till the allotment for their respective parishes has taken place in order that the Apprenticing Committee may be enabled to make any enquiries of them which they may think necessary.

3. That many bills having been brought in by the surgeons for attending paupers belonging to their respective parishes but residing out of the Hundreds, it is recommended that it be proposed to the surgeons that they shall attend such paupers as belong respectively to the parishes under their care although residing out of the Hundreds provided they are not compelled to go to a greater distance than four miles from their own residence.

4. Resolved that Mr Wood, solicitor, do state a case for the opinion of counsel whether the Directors and Acting Guardians are obliged to go back beyond the date of the last Incorporating Act (viz. in the year 1791) to ascertain the number of apprentices each person has had and other business as may be determined upon at a future meeting.

12 January 1809

Ordered and resolved that as the cowpox or vaccine inoculation has become a general practice as a substitute for the small pox, it is agreed at this meeting that in the schedule or bye law relating to apprentices after the words, "that no child be apprenticed who has not had the small pox" the following words shall be added "or cow pox or vaccine inoculation", and that these words shall stand as a bye law of this Corporation.

6 April 1809

	Directors Present	Guardians
	Revd William Browne	Mr Edward Crisp
	Thomas Pytches Esq.	Mr Jeremiah White
	Jacob Whitbread Esq.	Mr John Waller
	Revd Jacob Chilton	Mr Bond
	John Syer M.D.	Mr Goodwin
	Revd S. Kilderbee	Mr Clubbe
	Mr Henchman	
	Mr Ashford	
	Revd George Turner	
	Mr Samuel Gross	
	Revd Mr Jeaffreson	

The following persons were duly elected Directors and Acting Guardians:

	Directors	Guardians
May	Revd George Turner	Mr Thomas Walker
	Mr Jeptha Waller	Mr William Cook
June	Edmund Jenney Esq.	Mr Robert Vertue
	Mr Jeremiah Wase	Mr Samuel Kersey
July	Robert Trotman Esq.	Mr William Hambling
	Mr William Henchman	Mr Jeremiah White
Aug.	Revd William Browne	Mr Francis Ablett
	Revd Samuel Kilderbee	Mr John Sherwood
Sept.	John Syer M.D.	James Page
	Revd William Aldrich	Mr John Edwards
Oct.		Mr Edward Crisp
	Mr Jonathan Abbott Studd	Mr Richard Dove
Nov.	Revd William Kett	Mr John Cole
	Mr Robert Ashford	Mr John Waller
Dec.	Mr Thomas Waller	Mr Thomas Baldwin

	Mr Philip Dikes	Mr John Wilson
Jan.	Revd Isaac Clarke	Mr William Kitson
	Revd Charles Brooke	Mr John Crisp
Feb.	Jacob Whitbread Esq.	Mr James Clubbe
	Mr Samuel Gross	Mr George Bates
Mar.	Mr Thomas Simpson	Mr Charles Harris
	Thomas Pytches Esq.	Mr Thomas Ling
Apl.	Revd Jacob Chilton	Mr John Goodwin
	Revd Christopher Jeaffreson	Mr William Moore

6 July 1809

Ordered that the wood work about the House of Industry particularly the outside be painted.

It appearing to this Meeting that it would be highly proper and necessary that an application be made to Parliament for a new Incorporated Act. Ordered that the following advertisement be inserted in the Ipswich Journal and Bury and Norwich Post from the 15th July to the last day of publication before the meeting therein mentioned, and that the solicitor do provide printed letters with copies of the advertisement to be sent to the non-resident proprietors in the said Hundreds.

"A General Meeting of the Owners and Occupiers of lands within the Incorporated Hundreds of Loes and Wilford in the County of Suffolk, and also of the creditors of the said Corporation, is requested to be held at the Session Hall, in Woodbridge, on <8 August> in order to take into consideration the necessity of making an application to Parliament for a new Act of Incorporation".

31 July 1809

Mr Jenney being called to the chair.

It was proposed that he should submit to the meeting of Guardians and creditors to be held the 8th August next the necessity of applying to Parliament for a new Act of Incorporation, the present act being deficient in a variety of instances, particularly in not giving the present Directors and Acting Guardians power to raise sufficient money for the maintenance of the poor or for paying off any part of the principal money now due on the rates of the said Corporation.

22 August 1809 [*Committee to prepare bill*]

The several clauses of the Bill for the Amended Act were this day gone through, and the solicitor requested to write the same fair to be produced at the next meeting. And this meeting is hereby adjourned <> to be held at the House of Industry in Melton. Notice thereof to be given to the absent members of the Committee.

29 August 1809 [*Committee to prepare bill*]

The above Committee having this day met, read over, gone through and agreed upon the several clauses of the Bill for amending the said Act of the 31st Geo 3rd. The solicitor is hereby ordered to make a fair copy of the same, to be left at the House of Industry for the inspection of the Guardians of the Poor <> and he is also ordered to advertise in the Ipswich Journal that the same is so left for that purpose. And Mr John Wood, our said solicitor, is directed to have the same clauses perused and settled by Counsel and to use his best endeavour in giving such evidence and getting the same passed both Houses of Parliament as soon as he possible can.

15 March 1810 [*Committee to prepare bill*]

After reading and considering the several clauses proposed by the opposition to the said Bill, adjourned to <21 March> and ordered the solicitor to write to Mr Philpot to inform him of the said meeting that he and his friends might attend.

21 March 1810 [*Committee to prepare bill*]

Mr Philpot attended and produced the intended plan of the opposition, and after considering of the same the following advertisement was ordered to be inserted in the Ipswich Journal and the Committee adjourned to <29 March>.

Loes and Wilford Hundreds

Notice is hereby given that a General Meeting of the Owners and Occupiers of lands within the said Incorporated Hundreds will be held at the White Hart Inn in Wickham Market, on <29 March>, in order to take into consideration the necessity of inserting in the intended new Act to amend the present Act of Incorporation certain clauses for equalizing the several rates or assessments within the several parishes in the said Hundreds and for discharge of the debt.

29 March 1810

Jacob Whitbread Esq in the chair.

The first clause for equalizing the rates or assessments for the maintenance of the poor etc. being produced by the Directors and Acting Guardians upon a certain new ratio was agreed to in substance subject to the perusal and alteration of counsel on both sides.

The second clause for paying off and discharging the debt being produced by the Directors and Guardians agreeable to the old ratio of assessment was first agreed to be left to the determination of the Committee of the House of Commons, but after some further conversation and when several persons had objected it was put to the vote whether the debt should be paid off by the old ratio of assessment or according to the new ratio of assessment for the maintenance of the poor etc. And upon a division, 33 were for paying the debt off by the new ratio and 25 were for paying the debt according to the old ratio of assessment.

12 April 1810

Directors	Present	Guardians
Jacob Whitbread Esq.		Mr John Edwards
Thomas Pytches Esq.		Mr John Goodwyn
John Syer M.D.		Mr John Waller
Revd Mr Turner		Mr James Clubbe
Revd Mr Browne		
Revd Mr Kett		
Mr Thomas Waller		
Mr Henry Edwards		
Mr Jeremiah Wase		
Mr Robert Ashford		
Mr William Henchman		
Revd Jacob Chilton		

The following persons were duly elected Directors and Acting Guardians:

	Directors	Guardians
May	Revd George Turner	Mr Thomas Walker

	Mr Jeptha Waller	Mr John Button
June	Edmund Jenney Esq.	Mr John Fuller
	Mr Jeremiah Wase	Mr Samuel Kersey
July	Robert Trotman Esq.	Mr William Hambling
	Mr William Henchman	Mr Thomas Edwards
Aug.	Revd William Browne	Mr James Churchyard
	Revd Samuel Kilderbee	Mr John Largent
Sept.	John Syer M.D.	Mr Thomas Thredkell
	Revd William Aldrich	Mr Joseph Hare
Oct.	Mr Henry Edwards	Mr Edward Crisp
	Mr Jonathan Abbott Studd	Mr John Edwards
Nov.	Revd William Kett	Mr Lionel Dove
	Mr Robert Ashford	Mr John Waller
Dec.	Mr Thomas Waller	Mr Joseph Jeaffreson
	Mr Philip Dikes	Mr Thomas Wood
Jan.	Revd Isaac Clarke	Mr William Kitson
	Revd Charles Brooke	Mr John Crisp
Feb.	Jacob Whitbread Esq.	Mr James Clubbe
	Mr Samuel Gross	Mr John Ablitt
Mar.	Mr Thomas Simpson	Mr Charles Harris
	Thomas Pytches Esq.	Mr Robert Mabson
Apl.	Revd Jacob Chilton	Mr John Goodwyn
	Revd Christopher Jeaffreson	Mr William Moore

12 July 1810

Upon a question from Mr Pulham, as solicitor from the parish of Kenton, to know whether the Directors and Acting Guardians would pay the expences of the opposition to the obtaining and passing an Act of Parliament of the 50th Geo 3rd for Amending an Act of the 31st Geo 3rd <>. It was the opinion of a majority of this meeting that the Directors and Acting Guardians had no power to authorise the payment of the above from the funds of the Corporation.

Ordered that the solicitor do prepare a case for the opinion of Mr Nolan upon the non-payment of the last quarterly rate by the parish of Kenton in the Hundreds of Loes, and that when so prepared the solicitor do submit the same to the inspection of <3 named directors> previous to it being laid before Mr Nolan.

13 August 1810 [*Special meeting*]

Resolved and ordered that the yearly assessments upon each of the several and respective parishes within the said Hundreds be taken and made in the proportions following and that all decreases or increases be made upon the ratio for the ensuing ten years.

Parishes in Loes				Parishes in Wilford			
Ash	161	17	5½	Alderton	258	3	9½
Butley	107	11	3¼	Bawdsey	146	8	10
Brandeston	205	9	4	Bromeswell	54	19	9
Creetingham	187	10	10¼	Boulge	72	7	4
Charsfield	138	5	½	Bredfield	228	8	6½
Dallingho	227	19	5½	Boyton	96	1	2¼
Earl Soham	239	13	11	Capel	67	11	5¼

Easton	151	15	8¾	Debach	30	15	10¼
Eyke	108	6	1¼	Hollesley	264	16	8¼
Hacheston	275	9	4¾	Melton	230	0	0
Hoo	116	11	10¼	Petistree	135	17	2¼
Kettleburgh	171	8	1	Ramsholt	119	16	2½
Kenton	142	1	3	Sutton	280	16	10¾
Letheringham	75	11	2¾	Shottisham	91	7	½
Monewden	88	3	8¼	Ufford	138	16	6½
Marlesford	192	17	2¼	Wickham Market	336	18	3¼
Rendlesham	119	12	8		2,553	5	6
	2,710	4	6	Loes	2,710	4	6
				Total	5,263	10	0

Resolved that the proportion of each of the several parishes for paying off the debt and the interest of the debt for the first year is found to be as following which is to be assessed accordingly:

Parishes in Loes				Parishes in Wilford			
Ash	74	15	3	Alderton	43	10	6
Butley	47	10	10	Bawdsey	32	5	5
Brandeston	48	13	11	Bromeswell	20	5	6
Creetingham	58	7	2	Boulge	21	1	6
Charsfield	68	6	8	Bredfield	53	16	6
Dallingho	40	16	5	Boyton	7	7	6
Earl Soham	58	11	7	Capel	28	16	6
Easton	68	13	8	Debach	6	12	1
Eyke	37	4	11	Hollesley	67	11	3
Hacheston	52	1	4	Melton	53	11	4
Hoo	17	16	3	Petistree	46	11	5
Kettleburgh	39	2	6	Ramsholt	46	6	10
Kenton	60	12	2	Sutton	106	19	10
Letheringham	23	17	6	Shottisham	18	15	6
Monewden	11	10	1	Ufford	69	3	7
Marlesford	71	0	10	Wickham Market	79	0	0
Rendlesham	26	13	8	Wilford	701	15	3
	805	14	9	Loes	805	14	9
				Total	1,507	10	0

11 October 1810

Ordered that the assessments for the ensuing quarter be made in the following manner viz. one rate and one half of a rate, according to the ratio taken and settled as appears by the entry in this book on the 13th August 1810. And likewise an assessment for one quarter of the ratio as fixed for the payment of the debt and interest thereof, and that the out allowances and bills having been examined at the Previous Meeting be forthwith paid by the Treasurer.

12 March 1811

A meeting of the Directors and Acting Guardians of the poor within the said hundred held for the purpose of revising or repealing the present and of making new bye laws rules orders and regulations as may be deemed proper and necessary according to the powers vested in them by the several acts of Parliament of the 31st and the 50th of his present Majesty king George 3rd.

11 April 1811

Directors	Present	Guardians
Thomas Pytches Esq.		Mr John Button
Jacob Whitbread Esq.		Mr Edward Crisp
John Syer M.D.		Mr William Hambling
Revd Mr Brooke		
Revd Mr Clarke		
Mr Henry Edwards		
Revd Mr Kilderbee		
Mr Thomas Simpson		

The following persons were duly elected Directors and Acting Guardians:

	Directors	Guardians
May	Revd George Turner	Mr George Bond
	Mr Jeptha Waller	Mr John Button
June	Edmund Jenney Esq.	Mr Thomas Miller
	Mr Jeremiah Wase	Mr Thomas Garneys
July	Robert Trotman Esq.	Mr Henry Cupper
	Mr William Henchman	Mr John Wolton
Aug.	Revd William Browne	Mr James Churchyard
	Revd Samuel Kilderbee	Mr Cornelius Bedingfield
Sept.	John Syer M.D.	Mr Hodgson
	Revd William Aldrich	Mr Joseph Roe
Oct.	Mr Henry Edwards	Mr Thomas Simpson
	Mr Jonathan Abbott Studd	Mr John Edwards
Nov.	Revd William Kett	Mr Lionel Dove
	Mr Robert Ashford	Mr John Waller
Dec.	Mr Thomas Waller	Mr Joseph Jeaffreson
	Mr Philip Dikes	Mr Thomas Wood
Jan.	Revd Isaac Clarke	Mr William Kitson
	Revd Charles Brooke	Mr Edgar Smith
Feb.	Jacob Whitbread Esq.	Mr James Clubbe
	Mr Samuel Gross	Mr John Ablitt
Mar.	Mr Thomas Simpson	Mr Samuel Randall
	Thomas Pytches Esq.	Mr Robert Mabson
Apl.	Revd Jacob Chilton	Mr John Goodwyn
	Revd Christopher Jeaffreson	Mr Gardner Utting

All the present bye laws of this Corporation are hereby repealed and at this meeting are approved all the following rules orders and instructions as proper to be observed as bye laws of this Corporation for the better government and support of the poor. And they are hereby constituted bye laws agreeably to the powers granted by the incorporating Acts of Parliament.

We do accordingly direct the same to be printed, and likewise a sufficient number of copies of the amended Act of Parliament, and a copy of each to be given to every Director and Acting Guardian and to the churchwarden or overseer of every parish within the incorporated hundreds and to such other persons as are interested in the execution thereof <list of 8 directors and 1 acting guardian>.

Melton House of Industry

Rules orders and regulations for the good order and government of the House and for the comfortable provision of the poor in and out of the same

(1)

That exclusive of the Committees appointed by the Incorporating Acts, the following Committee be appointed.

A Committee of Superintendence for the repairs and general regulation of the House.

That this Committee consists of the following gentlemen:

Jacob Whitbread Esq.	Revd Mr Kett	Revd Mr Chilton
Revd Mr Brooke	Revd Mr Is Clarke	John Syer M.D.
	Mr Thomas Simpson	

And that to them be referred the direction of the education and instruction of the poor in the House; and also the appointment and superintendence of the religious duties respectively to be performed by the Chaplain, Governor, Matron, Schoolmaster and Schoolmistress. And also the provision and inspection of the cloathing necessary for the poor in the House; and all other matter relating to the internal management of the House. That this Committee be empowered to meet for the above purposes as often as they may think proper, but it is recommended to them to meet not less than twice within each quarter of a year, and that any three be sufficient to transact business and that their proceedings be entered into a book and reported at every Quarterly Meeting.

(2)

That the Weekly Committee shall meet at the House of Industry at the hour of ten in the forenoon, and to encourage the early attendance of the Overseers of the Poor, and other persons who have any business to transact with the Committee, it is hereby directed, they shall be called into the Committee Room by turns, in the order in which they come to the House. And in order that the business of the Weekly Committee may the more easily and readily be carried into effect, it is determined that one Director and Acting Guardian, who shall have been acting the preceding month, shall continue to attend the first committee day in the then next month.

(3)

That at every Quarterly Meeting the business shall begin precisely at ten o'clock in the forenoon and be concluded before dinner.

(4)

That at all the Committees, the names of those present shall be entered into the Committee Book, and at the conclusion of the business of the day, the minutes be read over, and the book signed by the members of the committee.

Allowances out of the House

(1)

That no out allowances shall be granted on account of sickness by any Weekly Committee, or by any Directors between Weekly Committees (except in cases of urgent necessity) untill the surgeon of the Corporation has visited the pauper or paupers and reported their respective cases in writing.

(2)

That no allowance be made for a midwife exceeding five shillings, and that no such allowance be granted except in extraordinary cases, such as a man having more than two children or not being in health.

(3)

That no pauper shall be relieved by a Weekly or Quarterly Committee unless an application be made for them by the Overseer, who (for the greater security) is expected to bring with him a certificate of the case signed by a Director or Acting Guardian, if either live in the parish, and if not, by the Minister, or some principal inhabitant.

(4)

That if any pauper shall apply for relief to any Committee without a parish officer, inquiry shall be made into the reason why such parish officer did not attend; and before the relief is ordered, such pauper shall be sent (if able, and the circumstances of the case will admit) to some one Director nearest to the pauper's abode with a written request that he would examine into the circumstances of the case, and order such relief as to him shall seem requisite; that such order be in writing and signed by such Director, and continue in force until the next Weekly Committee. But if such pauper be not in a situation to be sent, he or she shall be received into the House that such further inquiry may be made; and in such manner as the Committee shall think necessary or proper.

(5)

When application for relief of a pauper is made to any Committee and the Committee think it expedient to receive into the House a part of the children of such pauper, the children between the ages of five and ten years should be selected.

(6)

That when any parish officer is called upon to apply for relief for the burial of any pauper, he shall take an account of the effects (if any) of the deceased, and state the circumstances of the case to such Director or Acting Guardian as resides in or nearest to the parish where such pauper died. That such Director of Acting Guardian may order under his hand, such sum as he shall think necessary for the funeral of such pauper, and direct the parish officer to deliver such order to the next Weekly Committee, provided that not more than thirty shillings be (in any case) allowed.

(7)

That no allowance shall be granted to any parish officer for the removal of paupers to the House of Industry from their respective parish within the Incorporated Hundreds, it being the duty of such officer to attend such removals; nor any remuneration made to overseers from the Corporation for their loss of time in executing the orders of the different Committees or Quarterly Meetings, but that the parishes for which they respectively act shall pay them for such loss of time.

Overseers
(1)

That as it is the duty of every Overseer of the poor to be well acquainted with the situation, circumstances and characters of all persons who apply to them for relief, so it is when they apply for relief for any pauper, to report the same in writing to the Weekly Committee and, which they are expected to do, that the penalty for neglect of duty affixed by the 36th clause of the Incorporating Act of the 31st Geo 3rd may not be incurred.

(2)

That no poor are to be admitted into the House but who shall be carried thither on the Monday in every week (being the Committee Day) and on no other, unless in extraordinary cases, as sudden sickness, or other accidental misfortune under which circumstances such poor will be received into the House at any time, provided an order for their admission be signed by one Director upon a proper representation to him of the necessity of the case. And the Governor shall admit no person a pauper of the House unless such person be attended by one of the churchwardens or overseers of the parish to which such pauper belongs (or has been residing, if within the Hundreds). And if any doubt appears as to the settlement of such pauper, the Governor shall carry the said pauper to Woodbridge on the next sitting day, to be examined by the Magistrates there touching his or her settlement, and shall without loss of time, inform the Overseer of the parish in which the said pauper claims to be settled of the admission of the said pauper into the House, in order that they may attend the examination of the pauper before the magistrates, if they think proper, provided that if the said sitting day shall happen before sufficient notice can be given to the parish officer, the Governor shall be allowed to defer carrying the pauper to be examined until the following week.

(3)

That they (the Overseers) do not require the attendance of the Surgeon but in person, or by writing under their hand and never till they have visited the patient, and informed themselves of the necessity of the case. And that every labourer having a wife within the Incorporated Hundreds shall be considered a pauper and when requesting medical assistance shall be attended by the Surgeon, on his being requested so to do by the overseer of the parish in which such pauper resides, and that they do not require his immediately going over without knowing or judging his attendance to be immediately necessary, because such an order may prevent him visiting patients who really are in a situation that demands his utmost present care, only to do what might be deferred hours, or perhaps to the next day without any danger or inconvenience. And the poor are to be informed that all phials and pots in which medicines are sent them are to be returned to the surgeon who sent them. Surgeons are not to be called in, in midwifery cases, unless the woman midwife declares the necessity of such assistance. That it is the duty of the overseer to see that the surgeon attends in consequence of the notice sent by him, and that in every case in which it shall appear to him that the surgeon has neglected to attend, he is required to state the same to the next committee. Overseers to recommend to paupers to attend the surgeons at as early an hour in the morning as possible.

(4)

That (when any pauper by accident or sudden illness wants any pecuniary relief between one Weekly Committee and another) no overseer shall grant such relief without first applying to, and having an order in writing from a Director or Acting Guardian, specifying the sum to be allowed, which order the overseer is expected to produce to the next Weekly Committee, and then report in writing the case of the pauper. That this order, as far as it respects relief to be given, cannot extend to orders made by Justices of the Peace, but that all orders of Justices of the Peace be brought to the next Weekly Committee.

(5)

That overseers of the poor, when they remove any pauper or paupers to the House of Industry, are expected to make strict enquiry, whether such pauper or paupers have any annual or weekly allowances (not arising from any Friendly Benefit Society) and report the same in writing to the next Weekly Committee, that proper steps may be taken to have such allowances paid to the Corporation in aid of the maintenance of such pauper or paupers. And they are to deliver an inventory, signed by them, of the goods, furniture etc. of or belonging to any pauper who may be brought with his or her family into the House of Industry, either for temporary relief, or for a permanency to the first Weekly Committee after such pauper or paupers have been admitted. If it was not done at their admission, a copy of which inventory will be given to the person to whom the goods etc. belong and the said officers are required to take proper care that such goods etc. are not embezzled or injured during the paupers absence from their own dwellings. And should there not be a proper place at their late dwellings to keep the said goods etc. in a proper manner, that the same shall be brought to the House of Industry, to be there kept and taken care of, that upon the dismission from the House of such pauper or paupers, the goods etc. may be restored to them in the same condition they were left. And in case of the death of the pauper or paupers happening in the House, the goods etc. to become the property of the Directors and Acting Guardians to be disposed of as they shall think proper any of their meetings; and the parish officers are not in any case to sell or otherwise dispose of the goods etc. belonging to a pauper who shall come into the House without first having first taken the advice of the Directors and Acting Guardians at any of their meetings, such parish officers to be allowed all reasonable expences in removing such furniture etc.

(6)

That overseers of the poor when they bring any children (who are paupers) to the House of Industry, are expected to obtain certificates of the age of such children, and bring or send the same as soon as they conveniently can to the Governor of the said House.

(7)

That all paupers sent by orders of removal to any parish within the Incorporated Hundreds shall be as soon as possible conveyed to the House of Industry but if such paupers cannot be removed the same day that applications shall be made to the nearest Director for such relief or directions as may be thought proper and necessary.

(8)

That in the removal of paupers, and other incidental journies taken by overseers in virtue of their office, not less than 15 miles out from home shall be considered as a days journey – five shillings to be allowed for a single horse, ten shillings for a cart and horse, and five shillings for the overseers expences per day, with other reasonable allowances for himself and horse, in the event of his being out all night.

(9)

That when an overseer applies to any committee for relief for any pauper, he is expected to bring with him a certificate of the case signed by a Director or Acting Guardian, if one lives in the parish, if not, by the minister or some principal inhabitant.

(10)

That when application is made to any parish officer, for any allowance towards the funeral of any pauper, such officer is expected to take account of the effects (if any) of the deceased, and state the circumstances of the case to such Director or Acting Guardian as shall reside in or nearest to the parish where the pauper died.

(11)

That the overseers are expected to give in an exact copy of the poor's rate of their respective parishes, the Monday previous to every Quarterly Meeting, and likewise a correct statement of the number of apprentices each person or occupation has had since the year 1791, according to the forms delivered to them. And that such lists be renewed every quarter or every year, and laid before the parish, at the Easter meeting and then examined and signed by the churchwardens, overseers and inhabitants present and that the book so signed be taken to the House of Industry and checked by the Apprentices Book there kept , and signed by the clerk. And the overseer of every parish to which apprentices are to be allotted at the Quarterly Meeting are desired not to leave the meeting untill the allotment for their respective parishes has taken place, in order that the Apprenticing Committee may be enabled to make any inquiries of them they may think necessary, and that the overseers do give immediate notice to every person whom an apprentice shall be allotted.

(12)

That overseers are required to give notice that no allowance will be granted to any person who keeps a dog, unless such person be a shepherd, a warrener or a rat catcher.

Surgeons and Apothecaries

(1)

The surgeons and apothecaries employed by the Directors and Acting Guardians shall attend all such paupers to whose assistance they are called within their proper parishes for so long time as they shall be incapable of going to them; but they shall not be required to attend any pauper living out of the hundreds, altho' belonging to a parish within the incorporated hundreds, and that they shall supply the paupers under their care with all proper medicines and drugs of the best quality which shall be subject at any time to an examination by such person or persons as the Directors shall appoint at any of the Quarterly or other meetings. And the surgeon and apothecary of the House or his assistant, is expected to attend the weekly committee to inform them of the condition of his patients, and to answer such questions as may be necessary for them to know; and he is at all times to keep in the room fitted up for him within the House such medicines as may be deemed sufficient, in the opinion of a skilful physician to make up all common prescriptions, and that he or his assistant is to attend the House two days at least in each week, and oftener if required; and the surgeons are to attend all accidental paupers within the parishes of the Incorporated Hundreds, but are not to be called in midwifery cases, unless the woman midwife declares the necessity of such assistance. And in case of their being so called upon to attend, they shall be allowed a guinea and a half for such attendance. And the surgeons etc. are to be allowed to order wine, brandy or porter for sick persons out or in the House, which order shall be made in writing, and returned by the overseer to the next Weekly Committee; and they are expected to deliver to the Weekly Committee a written report of all out patients, stating the nature of their complaints and their situation. That the surgeon of the House is to order in writing what diet the sick are to have, and deliver it to the Governor or Matron, who are to see that it is complied with.

Apprentices

In apportioning apprentices, the following table and rules be observed:

Every person occupying per annum

	£300 who should have	6	1st 3rd 6th 10th 15th 21st
And every person occupying £250 should have		5	2nd 5th 9th 14th 20th
And do do £200 do		4	4th 8th 13th 19th
do do £150 do		3	7th 12th 18th
do do £100 do		2	11th 17th
do do £50 do		1	16th

That every person occupying under £50 and above £10; or any sum between £50 and £100 shall have one each, beginning with the highest.

That every tradesman (if judged capable) shall take one each, a male or female being appointed as best suited to the trade.

That in all cases where more than one child is to be apprenticed in any parish, the eldest child shall be first allotted and so on to the youngest.

That care be taken (if possible) that two girls be not apprenticed to the same person immediately following each other.

That no child shall be apprenticed who has not had the smallpox or cow pox or vaccine inoculation. Nor any child under the age of twelve years.

That all children who are in the House and in a fit and proper state be apprenticed at every quarter, except the Christmas Quarter, and that none be apprenticed unless they have been three months in the House of Industry previous to the quarter they are to be allotted. And notice thereof shall be given to the churchwardens or overseers of the respective parishes one month before such quarter day. And that they be sent to their respective masters or mistresses within twenty one days from such quarterly meeting properly cloathed with two suits or the master or mistress to receive the sum of two pounds at his or her option, in lieu of clothing. And they are at the same time to execute the counterpart of the indentures, in default of which, they subject themselves to the penalty of ten pounds.

That every person refusing to take an apprentice regularly allotted shall pay the penalty of ten pounds. The next person in turn to have the option of taking the child with the penalty so paid or to pay another penalty of ten pounds. The third person in turn to have the option of taking the child with the two penalties so paid, amounting to twenty pounds, or to pay a penalty of ten pounds. The fourth person in turn to take the apprentice with the said sum of twenty pounds or to pay the penalty of ten pounds, or the Directors and Acting Guardians may apprentice such child with the thirty pounds to be paid as above, to any indifferent person, whether within or out of the Incorporated Hundreds; the Directors and Acting Guardians to have the option of so apprenticing whenever the penalty amounts to or exceeds thirty pounds.

In case of any person refusing to take an apprentice or execute the indenture, or pay the penalty as aforesaid he or she is to be summoned before the magistrates to show cause why the penalty should not be levied upon him or her.

When any apprentice is to be allotted in any parish where the occupiers have had more than in the proportion of one to fifty pounds then the manner of apportioning the apprentices shall be to divide the sum of the valuation by one more than the number of apprentices such person has had for that occupation then the highest quotient will be the person to whom the apprentice shall be ordered.

When there are any children within the Incorporated Hundreds whose parents are unable to maintain them and who are by infirmity fit for particular trades only and not wanted to be employed in the House of Industry, the Directors and Acting Guardians shall be impowered to place such child or children out as apprentices, in or out of the Incorporated Hundreds, with such premium as shall be deemed proper at a General Quarterly Meeting, but that no premium be given to a certificate person out of the hundreds.

All accumulation of penalties paid for not taking apprentices shall be applied to the above purposes.

Governor and Clerk

(1)

That the Governor be directed to deliver in at every Weekly Committee a state of the number of paupers in the House, the quantities of provisions in hand, received, left and expended, together with the amount of the work done in the preceding week, according to a plan in a book provided for that purpose, which if approved, is to be signed and allowed by such Weekly Committee.

(2)

That the Governor shall enter into a book the exact account of all household goods, cloathes, linen, shoes and other things sent into the House, examine their goodness, weight, quantity and quality and make his report thereof (if deficient) to the Weekly Committee. That he shall also deliver in a general inventory of the household goods and furniture etc. of and belonging to the House etc. when required at any Quarterly Meeting.

(3)

That the Governor shall receive no provision, coals, wood or goods of any kind without a bill of the same, to be delivered with them signed by the respective tradesmen and merchants, and that he shall keep the same upon a file.

(4)

That stamped weights and scales and measures be provided for the Governor.

(5)

That the Governor shall keep a general register of all paupers now are, or here-after, may be admitted into the House, after the manner laid down in a book provided for that purpose; and that he shall report to every Weekly Committee, or any time when required, such as are well and fit to be discharged. That he shall also keep a proper register of all apprentices.

(6)

That no clothing or effects of any kind belonging to paupers dying in the House shall be disposed of by the Governor or matron without the direction of the Weekly Committee, to whom the Governor is required to deliver a true account in writing.

(7)

That no provisions or liquor shall be given away to any gentleman's servant or any other person whatever, who comes to the House.

(8)

That the Governor or Matron shall see the provisions of the House made ready in a lean wholesome manner, agreeably to the settled bill of fare, they are to prevent waste of provisions, to see them distributed in the regular portions, that no bread be cut under one day old, and that no more fires be kept in the House than are absolutely necessary.

(9)

That the Governor, upon the admission of any person into the House who is in health and not disabled by lameness, shall immediately employ said person in any work he shall think him or her best capable of performing. That he shall cause all persons to be called up by ring of bell at five in the morning in summer and seven in winter, and set all those to work who are able by six o'clock in the morning from Lady Day to Michaelmas and by eight from Michaelmas to Lady Day, and to continue until four in the afternoon from Michaelmas to Lady Day and from Lady Day to Michaelmas till six in the afternoon (meal times excepted). And if any shall refuse, or neglect to do such work as shall be allotted them, or wilfully spoil the same, or in any other way misbehave themselves, the Governor is required to exercise the authority given him by the 44th Sect. of the Incorporating Act, which together with the 45th, 46th, and 47th Sections of the Incorporating Act of 31st Geo 3rd shall be painted and hung up in the dining room and publicly read by the school-master, together with the rules for the poor to observe, the first Saturday in every month immediately after breakfast.

(10)

That persons not in health when admitted shall be received into a proper room till the surgeon can give his directions concerning them. That all children who have scalt heads, or are lousy shall have their hair cut off and then be placed in proper wards. That all the poor in the House, who can bear it, shall be washed every morning, the males under care of the Governor and the females under care of the matron. The Governor is required to pay particular attention to this order, and on no account (except ordered to the contrary by the surgeon) to have it omitted as to the children, whose hair must be kept cut close once a month.

(11)

That when any person complains of illness the Governor shall take care to stop his or her common diet until such time as the surgeon shall have examined into the case. The sick poor shall be properly attended, and during their illness they shall remain under the direction of the surgeon, upon the sick list, and if possible be lodged in separate beds. With respect to diet, during their illness they are required to obey the orders of the surgeon.

(12)

That the Governor shall go round the men and boys wards every night and see that they are in their proper beds and punish such as are noisy or in any way behave ill.

(13)

That the Governor shall reside within the House, and that neither the Matron nor himself be absent at the same time; and that neither of them be out later than ten o'clock at night except (on either occasion) by leave of the Weekly Committee.

(14)

That no person shall be admitted to visit any of the poor in the House without an order from a Director or by leave of the Governor or Matron. That no pauper be permitted to go out without the leave of a Director or Weekly Committee, or Governor or Matron, which leave shall be expressed in writing if from a Director and denote the time of return; and that all persons who offend shall be reported to the next Weekly Committee.

(15)

That the Governor may appoint and select out of the poor proper persons to do the necessary business and work of the House.

(16)

That he shall deliver a copy of the Incorporating Acts and all general standing orders to every Director and Acting Guardian; and also to the several persons concerned in the execution of them.

(17)

That he shall attend all committees, make minutes and copy the same fair into a book; write letters, and do such other business as may be required of him.

(18)

That he shall be intitled to no perquisites of any kind, but shall account for every-thing that comes into or passes through his hands.

Matron

(1)

That the Matron shall employ proper nurses from among the poor to attend the sick, and also the infant children. That she shall diligently inspect their conduct and behaviour with respect to the poor under their care. That she shall see that all the beds, furniture, wards, rooms and sick wards, and every part of the House are swept daily and kept clean, and that all the rooms be washed once a week in winter and twice in summer. The bed clothes turned down, the windows opened and the doors locked till ten o'clock every morning.

(2)

That she takes care that the women and girls wash and comb themselves every morning and evening; and that the children have their hair cut close, and their heads kept clean.

(3)

That she delivers out the soap, starch and blue by weight for washing the linen and that she sees that the washerwomen and laundresses employed do their business well, and enter into a book an account of their linen delivered, and like account when it is clean and got up. And that every poor person have a clean shirt once a week. That the beds have clean sheets once a month and that no linen be dried in any of the wards but as much abroad as may.

(4)

That the Matron distribute to the nurses, for the sick poor, and the young children such a quantity of milk, pearl barley, rice and other necessities as the surgeon shall advise, and that the common diet be stopped until they are well.

(5)

That she attends all meals with the Governor and see that all provisions are fairly and duly delivered.

(6)

That the Matron shall receive from the Governor; cloth necessary for shirts, shifts and sheets etc. and shall cut them out, taking care that they are well made; no waste committed, and when finished be placed in the store room; and that an account of all clothes and linen delivered to the poor in the House and also an account of the stock remaining on hand be given once a quarter to the Committee of Clothing, and that the old linen shall be repaired and mended every time.

(7)

That she keeps an account of the number of women and girls employed as seam-stresses, or in other work for the use of the House and of what they earn by such work and report the same to the Weekly Committee.

(8)

That she shall go round the women's and girls' wards every night and see that they are in their proper beds and punish as are noisy or in any way behave ill.

(9)

That if the nurses, or any other servants belonging to the House, should at any time be guilty of a breach of any order given to them, she shall report the same to the Weekly Committee.

(10)

That she is intitled to no perquisites of any kind, but to account for everything that passes through her hands.

The Poor in the House are required to observe the following rules.

(1)

That they shall obey the Governor and Matron in all their reasonable commands.

(2)

That they shall at all times keep themselves decent and clean, and behave themselves orderly and peaceably.

(3)

That they shall be careful and diligent at their work during the hours appointed.

(4)

That they do not pretend sickness or other excuses to avoid work.

(5)

Slothful and lazy persons who pretend ailments to excuse themselves from work shall be carefully examined; and if it appears they have made false excuses, complaint shall be made to the Weekly Committee, who shall order such punishment as they shall think proper.

(6)

That they breakfast, dine and sup (all who are able) in the dining hall and go to their respective works when summoned by ring of bell.

(7)

That they be allowed half an hour at breakfast and supper and an hour at dinner.

(8)

That they all be in bed by nine o'clock from Lady Day to Michaelmas, and by eight o'clock from Michaelmas to Lady Day and all fires and candles to be put out by the above times, except such as are necessary and in the nursery and sick wards.

(9)

That they never go out at any time without leave; and when leave is granted, they shall return against the time appointed.

(10)

That they regularly attend Divine Services on Sundays and the daily prayers after breakfast and after super.

(11)

That those who have been sick, on their recovery, do attend the first Weekly Committee to be examined by them concerning the care and attendance which they have had during their illness and to return thanks for the same.

(12)

That they presume not upon any account to beg of any person attending, or coming to visit the House.

(13)

That all persons guilty of telling lies or profane swearing shall have a label fixed upon their breasts with these words, Infamous Liar – Profane Swearer. And shall be made to stand in the middle of the hall during the time of dinner.

(14)

That all who offend against these rules shall be punished in such a manner as the Act directs.

Treasurer

(1)

That the Treasurer shall be required to return a list of the names of such parishes as neglect to pay their assessments at the time appointed in the warrant issued for that purpose, in order that the officers of such parishes may be proceeded against, and if guilty, be punished as the Act directs. This return shall be made at the second Weekly Committee after the day appointed for payment.

(2)

That no Treasurer shall be appointed at any time, unless he shall give security himself, and to other bondsmen (to be approved at a Quarterly Meeting) in the sum of £1,500.

Servants

That if any officer, nurse or servant of the House shall receive any fee or gratuity from any tradesman or from the poor or their friends, he or she shall be immediately discharged from their employment.

Tradesmen

That if any merchant, tradesman or artificer shall by himself or by any other person or persons directly or indirectly give or offer to give any sum or sums of money or anything as a reward or gratuity to any officer or servant of the House, such merchant, tradesman or artificer shall be deemed incapable of serving the House in future.

Chaplain

That the Chaplain be required to read the service of the church as set forth in the Book of Common Prayer and to preach a sermon at eleven in the morning and at two in the afternoon alternately, every Sunday and on Good Friday and Christmas Day; to baptize the children born in the House; to bury the dead, the day after notice has been given him for that purpose; to visit the sick and when desired to administer the sacrament to them; to administer the sacrament in the chapel four times in the year viz. on Easter Day or Good Friday, on Whit Sunday or Trinity Sunday at or about Michaelmas, and on Christmas Day, or the Sunday before or after; to keep a register of all baptisms and burials; to catechise the children in the chapel, on the first Sunday in every month after the second lesson, if in the afternoon, and between the prayers and the communion service if in the morning, and report to the Committee of Superintendence and Inspection any improper behaviour, neglect or omission; and also any other matter which he thinks may promote the Religious and Moral duties necessary to be observed, to the edification of the paupers and the good order and decency of the House.

School master

(1)

That the schoolmaster shall see that the boys attend the school, that he teaches them to read, and be particularly careful and diligent to instruct them in their catechism, which he is required to hear them repeat twice a week, and to report to the Governor any misbehaviour in the boys and if they came to school dirty or lousy.

(2)

That he shall read prayers morning and evening immediately before breakfast and after supper, in a proper and becoming manner. That he shall catechise the children every Sunday, and take care that all who are able to attend at those times that he shall call over the names before prayers morning and evening and report the absentees and the reason of their absence to the Governor.

School mistress

That the school mistress shall observe the same as to the girls and also teach them to sew and knit as may be directed and report to the Matron any misbehaviour and also those who come to school dirty or lousy.

Finis

17 October 1811

Resolved and ordered that in case an application is made for any allowance to any family who have not a sufficient quantity of wheat be allowed. When there are more than 3 children under 12 years of age 6d. per week shall be allowed for every child there are more than three.

Ordered that 300 forms for the Poor Rate of each parish of the Incorporated Hundreds be printed and delivered to each overseer every quarter.

Mr G. Lynn having resigned attending the out parishes usually under his care but he is to continue attending the House of Industry as usual. He having been requested to attend the out parishes until Christmas next which he has agreed to do.

The discussion relating to the surgeons having taken place the following gentlemen were appointed a Committee to meet for further discussion of the same <15 named directors>, and that any five be competent to transact business.

5 November 1811

Resolved that it is the opinion of this meeting that the several parishes shall contribute to the pay of the surgeons in proportion to their respective populations.

Resolved that for this purpose the Clerk shall previous to the Annual Meeting in April next prepare an account of the sum to be paid by each respective parish to the surgeons according to the equalized assessment upon which the Poor's Rates are now paid.

Resolved that for ensuring a more convenient and ready attendance of the poor, the parishes in the Incorporated Hundreds shall be divided into the following districts viz:

The House at £60 per annum.

Woodbridge			
Melton	1st District to be	Bredfield	4th District
Bromeswell	offered to Mr Lynn	Boulge	to be offered to
Eyke	at £36 per annum.	Debach	Mr Dyer
Rendlesham		Charsfield	at £24 per annum.
Ufford			
		Wickham	
Bawdsey		Petistree	
Alderton	2nd District	Dallingho	5th District
Ramsholt	to be offered to	Letheringham	to be offered to
Shottisham	Mr Hughes	Easton	Mr Harsant
Sutton	at £40 per annum.	Hacheston	at £48 per annum.
		Marlesford	
		Ash	

Butley	3rd District	Earl Soham	6th District
Capel	to be offered to	Brandeston	to be offered to
Boyton	Mr Ashwell	Kettleburgh	Mr Bellman
Hollesley	at £28 per annum.	Creetingham	at £42 per annum.
		Hoo Kenton	
		Monewden	

At this meeting it being represented to the Committee that the business of the Treasurer is considerably increased by the regulations of the new Act of Parliament, it was resolved that the Committee do recommend to increase the salary of the Treasurer to the sum of £30 per annum.

Resolved that this Committee do meet again to receive the answers of the surgeons on Tuesday the 19th November.

19 November 1811

Mr G. D. Lynn attended and declined to accept the attendance upon any of the out poor within the Incorporated Hundreds but to continue attending the poor in the House of Industry at the usual salary of £60 per annum.

A letter was received from Mr Bellman in which he agreed to accept the parishes upon the terms as offered at £42 per annum.

Mr Hughes attended and agreed to accept the parishes as offered at £40 per annum.

Mr Ashwell has agreed to accept the parishes offered with the addition of Rendlesham at £35 per annum.

Mr Harsant attended and has agreed to attend the poor in the several parishes of Wickham Market, Petistree, Letheringham, Easton, Hacheston, Marlesford and Ash (7) at £49 per annum.

Mr Dyer of Woodbridge has agreed to attend the following parishes at £62 per annum viz. Melton, Bromeswell, Eyke, Ufford, Bredfield, Boulge, Debach, Charsfield, Dallingho and Woodbridge (10).

The above alterations to take place at Christmas next.

Memorandum

Mr Lynn to attend the House at £60 per annum.

Melton		Wickham Mkt	
Bromeswell		Petistree	
Eyke		Letheringham	
Ufford	10 parishes	Easton	7 parishes
Bredfield	Mr Dyer	Hacheston	Mr Harsant
Boulge	at £62 pa.	Marlesford	at £49 pa.
Debach		Ash	
Dallingho			
Charsfield			
Woodbridge			

Bawdsey		Earl Soham	
Alderton	5 parishes	Brandeston	7 parishes
Ramsholt	Mr Hughes	Kettleburgh	Mr Bellman
Shottisham	at £40 pa.	Creetingham	at £42 pa.

Sutton   Monewden
                                          Kenton
                                          Hoo

Butley
Capel   5 parishes
Boyton   Mr Ashwell
Hollesley   at £35 pa.
Rendlesham

9 April 1812

Directors	Present	Guardians
Revd Mr Wm Browne		Mr Samuel Randall
Revd Mr Chilton		Mr James Clubbe
Revd Mr Turner		and
Dr Syer		Mr Samuel Gross
Mr H. Edwards		
Revd Mr Jeaffreson		
Revd Mr Kilderbee		
Revd Mr Isaac Clarke		
Mr P. Dykes		

The following persons were duly elected Directors and Acting Guardians:

	Directors	Guardians
May	Revd George Turner	Mr George Bond
	Mr Jeptha Waller	Mr James Aldhous
June	Edmund Jenney Esq.	Mr John Youngman
	Mr Jeremiah Wase	Mr Thomas Garneys
July	Robert Trotman Esq.	Mr Samuel Goater Stearn
	Mr William Henchman	Mr John Wolton
Aug.	Revd William Browne	Mr Robert Welton
	Revd Samuel Kilderbee	Mr Fenn Sheming
Sept.	John Syer M.D.	Mr Hodgson
	Revd William Aldrich	Mr Joseph Roe
Oct.	Mr Henry Edwards	Mr Thomas Simpson
	Mr Jonathan Abbott Studd	Mr Thomas Catlin
Nov.	Revd William Kett	Mr Samuel Syred
	Mr Robert Ashford	Mr John Waller
Dec.	Mr Thomas Waller	Mr James Garnham
	Mr Philip Dykes	Mr Edward Field
Jan.	Revd Isaac Clarke	Mr William Kitson
	Revd Charles Brooke	Mr Edgar Smith
Feb.	Jacob Whitbread Esq.	Mr James Clubbe
	Mr Samuel Gross	Mr Samuel Browne
Mar.	Mr Thomas Simpson	Mr John Sherwood
	Thomas Pytches Esq.	Mr Thomas Edwards
Apl.	Revd Jacob Chilton	Mr John Goodwyn
	Revd Christopher Jeaffreson	Mr Gardner Utting

15 October 1812

Ordered that Mr William Minter overseer of Shottisham be fined in the mitigated penalty of forty shillings for not paying the rate of his parish to the Treasurer in due time according to his warrant.

That William Collins the overseer of Marlesford be fined the sum of three pounds for not paying the rate of his parish to the Treasurer in due time according to his warrant.

Ordered that the Governor do apply to the Magistrates next Wednesday for a summons for Mr Kersey of Kenton to appear to shew cause why the penalty incurred for his refusing to take an apprentice as allotted at the last Quarterly Meeting should not be levied upon him.

The sixth Weekly Minute Book,
21 October 1805–29 June 1812[2]

21 October 1805

Ordered that the Overseers allow as under

Kettleburgh	clothing for Thomas Fulcher 20s., *do* for Phoebe Harvey 20s.	2	0	0
Creetingham	clothing for William Warner let to Richard Dove	1	0	0
Earl Soham	clothing for Philip Beck let to D. Trusson	1	0	0
Easton	clothing for Samuel Baldrey let to Henry Capper	1	0	0
Wickham	Mary Dammant 1s. 2 week	0	2	0
Letheringham	Mary Fisher towards clothing his son William to service to Mr S. Thompson	1	0	0
Brandeston	Mary Bradlaugh her husband in prison 1s. 6d. 2 weeks	0	3	0
Ufford	William Upson 3s. 2 weeks, funeral J. Gillingham's daughter and 2 weeks of former allowance	1	6	0
Easton	Henry Plant's wife 1s. 2 weeks, Susan Hurren 1s. 6d. 3 weeks	0	6	6
Sutton	Hannah Holby 2s. 2 weeks, Isaac Clarke 3s. 6d. 1 week in addition to former order	0	7	6
	Susan Spall 3s. 1 week	0	3	0
		8	8	0

Directors	Guardians
Jacob Chilton for the Revd. Hingeston	Edward Crisp
Henry Edwards	Joseph Jeaffreson

7 October 1806

Ordered that Susan Long, late Nurse at the Pest House, having been proved to have acted improperly towards the sick under her care, by curtailing their allowances of provisions and using bad language be dismissed from her office as Nurse and punished by being stinted 5 pence per day on the Spinning Room, placed at the bread and water table in the Hall, and have only bread and water diet for the space of one week.

12 June 1809

John Smith a pauper in the House ordered into solitary confinement for 3 days having behaved ill to, and kicked a boy in the House.

---

[2] SROI ADA11/A/B/3/6.

16 October 1809

Ordered at this meeting that in commemoration of his majesty George the Third commencing the fiftieth year of his reign on Wednesday 25th October, the paupers in the House to have plumb puddings and beef for dinner and a pint of the best beer each and to be allowed half a days holiday.

\1 December 1809

Mr Oldham will receive the bearer Robert Bailey of Hoo into the House who is quite out of employ and if the new Committee on Monday think proper the best plan would be to allow this poor fellow 2s. 6d. for 3 weeks, he might get some employment now and then and be much cheaper for the parish than keeping him in the House all winter as he was last winter.

J. Syer/[3]

9 April 1810

Ordered that the Overseers of the respective parishes do allow as under

Parish pauper resides in	Parish belonging to				
Hollesley	Hollesley	John Curtis for midwife to his wife 5s.			
	Ramsholt	John Whiting for *do* to *do* 5s.	0	10	0
Melton	Melton	John Took 7s. for 3 weeks including last week	1	1	0
	do	John Ayer's wife 1s. 6d. 5 weeks *do*	0	7	6
	Wickham	William Cole 2s. 5 weeks	0	10	0
	Ufford	John Skeet 2s. 5 weeks	0	10	0
	Bredfield	Thomas Goldsmith's wife 2s. 6d. 5 weeks	0	12	6
	Ash	William Read's wife 4s. 5 weeks	1	0	0
Kenton	Kenton	Samuel Roper 2s. 4 weeks, Sarah Moor 1s. 4 weeks	0	12	0
	do	John Baley 1s. 4 weeks, Thos. Calver's wife 2s. 4 w.	0	12	0
	do	Robert Ling 1s. 6d. 4 weeks	0	6	0
Alderton	Alderton	Carey Wade 4s. 2 w., William Dorley 3s. 2w.	0	14	0
	do	Carey Wade by Mr Pytches last week 5s. 7½d.	0	5	7½
Bromeswell	Bromeswell	Sophia Keable 1s. 3 weeks	0	3	0
Easton	Letheringham	James York 2s. 4 weeks	0	8	0
Marlesford	Marlesford	William Packard's wife for midwife 5s.	0	5	0
	do	Frances Rose 1s. 6d. 4 weeks	0	6	0
Hacheston	Hacheston	George Twitell 2s. 6d. 2 w James Gissing 1s. 4w.	0	9	0
Bredfield	Bredfield	William Jewell 2s. 4 weeks	0	8	0
	Easton	Samuel Loom's wife 3s. 4 weeks	0	12	0
Ufford	Sutton	John Gillingham 4s. 2 weeks	0	8	0
Wickham	Wickham	Wm. Burrows 2s. 3w Hannah Yallop			

---

[3] Note inserted in SROI ADA11/A/B/3/6.

		1s. 1w.	0	7	0
	Petistree	James Webber 1s. 2 weeks	0	2	0
Earl Soham	Earl Soham	Wm. Spink 2s. 6d. 2 w., John Templing for midwife 5s.	0	10	0
Petistree	Hacheston	Richard Garrett for midwife 5s.	0	5	0
Eyke	Ash	James Fitch 5s. 1 week	0	5	0
	Butley	William Roberts 3s. 1 week	0	3	0
Creetingham	Creetingham	Ann Turner ordered into the House			
Marlesford	Marlesford	Sarah Clarke discharged from the House			
	Boyton	Ann Archer *do* pd. by R.W.O.	0	3	0
	Melton	John Avis *do* pd. by *do*	0	2	0
	Creetingham	William Cuthbert *do* pd. by *do*	0	10	0
Monewden	Monewden	Samuel Lamy's wife 2s. 6d. for 2 weeks	0	5	0
	Creetingham	John Cullum *do* 6s. 4 weeks	1	4	0
Capel	Hollesley	Funeral Edmund Clodd 20s., Widow Clodd 6s. 1 w.	1	6	0
	Wickham	John Wyard 2s. 1 week	0	2	0
			15	3	7½

Directors	Guardians
Chris Jeaffreson	John Goodwyn
Jacob Chilton	Wm Moore

Miscellaneous documents 39–60 relating
to the 1810 Amendment Act

39. Resolutions passed at a general meeting convened to consider applying to Parliament for an amending act, 8 August 1809[4]

A General Meeting of the Owners and Occupiers of lands within the said Hundreds of Loes and Wilford and also the creditors of the said Corporation held at the Sessions Hall in Woodbridge in the same county ◇ for the purpose of taking into consideration the necessity of making an application to Parliament for a Bill to repeal and amend an Act passed in <1765 and 1791> and for granting further powers and provisions for carrying the same Act more effectively into execution.

Edmund Jenney Esq., Chairman.

It appearing to the Meeting that an application to Parliament for such Bill is not only unavoidable but absolutely necessary.

Resolved unanimously that an application be made for the same as soon as possible.

Resolved that the following petition be read and sealed with the Corporation Seal and forwarded (by Mr John Wood, the Solicitor) to the Members for the County of Suffolk that he do request them to present the same to the Hon'ble House of Commons.

To the Hon'ble the Commons of the United Kingdom of Great Britain and Ireland in Parliament assembled.

The humble Petition of the Guardians of the Poor within the Hundreds of Loes and Wilford in the County of Suffolk.

Sheweth,

That an Act of Parliament was passed whereby your petitioners were authorised to make certain rates or assessments for the purposes therein mentioned.

That by an Act of Parliament passed in <1791> for the enlarging the powers of the Guardians of the Poor within such Hundreds ◇ as to the assessments made for the support and maintenance of the poor whereby your petitioners were authorised to make rates to exceed in any one year the amount of double the sum then raised by virtue of their Incorporated Act.

That the money arising by the said rates and assessments made by virtue of these Acts ◇ is found wholly insufficient for the support and maintenance of the poor within the said Hundreds of Loes and Wilford and for the other purposes of the said Act. And that your petitioners have no power or authority ◇ of raising any further sum or sums of money than is or are now levied by the present rates or assessments. And that that their said Act is in other respects insufficient for the purposes thereby intended. That on account of the great increase in number of the poor and other unavoidable expences your petitioners have incurred a debt of £10,150 which debt

---

[4] SROI ADA11/A/A/1/8.

they are unable to pay nor can they support or maintain the poor or pay the interest of the money borrowed under the authority of their said Act or pay off or discharge any part of their debt alto' applied to and positively prosecuted for the payment thereof unless a power be given your petitioners to increase and advance their rates and assessments beyond what they are now empowered to do by law.

Your petitioners therefore most humbly pray that leave may be given to your Petitioners to bring in a Bill for effecting the several purposes before mentioned by such ways and means and in such manner as this Hon'ble House shall direct or think proper.

Given under the Common Seal of our Corporation at Woodbridge in the said County of Suffolk <8 August 1809>.

Resolved that the above petition be agreed to and that the same be immediately written fair on parchment and the Corporation Seal be affixed thereupon.

Resolved that no time ought to be lost in framing the intended new Act of Incorporation. That a Committee be appointed consisting of <9 names> to prepare frame and forward the Bill to Parliament for the purpose of obtaining the intended new act. That any five of them be a Committee and the Committee be open to any off the Guardians of the Poor who choose to attend.

Resolved that the first meeting of the Committee be held at the House of Industry <15 August 1809>.

Edmund Jenney   Chairman.

40. Report of a meeting convened by parishes opposed to the amending Act[5]

21 December 1809

At a Meeting of Owners and Occupiers of lands and hereditaments lying in several parishes within the incorporated Hundreds of Loes and Wilford, held at the White Hart in Wickham Market <21 December 1809>, pursuant to public advertisement. \only three parishes out of 33 which comprise the whole corporation\

This meeting having learnt \they learnt it from public advertisement\ that it is the intention of the present Directors and Acting Guardians of the Poor within the said Incorporated Hundreds, to apply at the next session of Parliament for leave to bring in a Bill, "for amending and repealing \for amending and making more effectual an act\ certain parts of an Act made and passed in <1765> and for granting some further powers and provisions for carrying the same into Execution," and a copy of such intended bill \heads of a bill as first drawn\ having been produced and read, and the meeting having taken into its serious consideration the alarming magnitude of the debt which has accumulated \debt increased only £250 since the year 1791\ upon the Hundreds since their first incorporation; the large sums which have been annually raised by the different parishes under the late and present Incorporating Acts towards the maintenance of the poor within the said hundreds; the keeping down the interest of the debt, \the interest is always regularly paid every half year\ and the support of the establishment itself; the great and injurious inequality of the

---

5   SROI ADA11/A/A/1/6. The Incorporation's draft bill retained the original parochial assessments, as calculated in 1765. Those parishes opposing the bill argued that these figures failed to reflect the current situation and they wished to recalculate the assessments. The extant copy of the report was obtained by a director of the Incorporation and then annotated by him in the margin. The annotations are shown in italics above within \ /. Certain phrases were also underlined in the original, as shown above.

assessments charged from time to time on the respective parishes; the uniform want of success which has unfortunately attended the system hitherto pursued; whether such _failure_ *what failure, why this question*\ be attributable to mismanagement, misfortune or any other cause; *not want of success but from the increase of the poor and advances in the principal necessary of life, "bread"*\ the general state of embarrassment in which the affairs of the Corporation are considered to be, and the absolute and indispensable necessity of devising and applying a remedy for these evils, adequate to their magnitude and importance:

It was unanimously resolved,

That it is the opinion of this meeting that the objects principally in view, when the hundreds were first incorporated, were to better the conditions of the poor, and to lighten to the incorporated parishes the burthen of their maintenance. *no doubt and so it has. In the rates and assessments in the adjoining parishes not incorporated are very much higher than any parish in these Hundreds*\

That to accomplish this end, and to provide for the support of the establishment, and for the several other purposes of the Incorporation, it was required that each parish should from time to time contribute towards the expense in a rateable proportion, such proportion to be in the first instance ascertained by that criterion which was thought the least fallible, namely, the averaged annual amount of the poor rate of each parish *this average was taken under the statute from returns made by each parish and in order to correct any mistake that might happen days of appeal were laid and several parishes appealed and were relieved upon which the whole assessments were finally fixed and adjusted. The legislature thought this mode the best or they would not have enacted it*\ taken for the seven years next preceding the time of the incorporation.

That although this mode of apportioning the future burthen of the contribution from each parish carried upon the face of it, and might at the time actually possess (as it was intended it should) the principle of fairness, yet it was at best speculative, and has in its subsequent operation proved in many instances injuriously erroneous: speculative, in as far as it was taking a scale of expense adapted to one particular system of management as the basis of and as applicable to another system, extremely different and perfectly novel and untried; and injuriously erroneous because in several instances the amount of the poor rates as delivered in by some of the parishes was uncommonly large, in consequence of their having had to meet extraordinary expenses incurred by unusual and unforeseen casualties, particularly the small pox, which had in some of the parishes, during the great part of the seven years alluded to, raged with great and continued virulence, and these expenses were improvidently and incorrectly admitted to form a part of the data whereon the calculation of the future burthen of these suffering parishes was to be made. *the whole proceedings are fairly entered upon the records of the incorporation together with the appeals upon the final adjustment of the assessments. How was this the case? And if it was why was it not stated so upon the appeals and how is this to be proved*\

That, however, in regard to some few of the incorporated parishes the proportion of contribution may have happened to have been but in a just ratio to the expenses actually incurred by them, yet, in others it will be found that the sums contributed in a given number of years to the fund and general purposes of the corporation have exceeded, in a quadruple degree, the whole expense they have actually occasioned to it during the same period, whist there are several parishes whose expenses have far exceeded the amount of their respective assessments, *the actual expences incurred* *by the parishes cannot be ascertained on account of divers paupers residing in one parish and belonging to another in the same Hundred and allowances are granted to the paupers therein indiscriminately as belonging to the parish in which they reside/* and which have consequently, but unjustly, been supported by the excess contribution of the less burthensome parishes.

That it is therefore evident that the data whereon the contribution to be made by each parish was calculated was erroneous, the assessments unequal, and the burthen of them, in consequence, the more grievous and unjust. *\these parishes 33 in number incorporated themselves in 1765 for the equal relief and benefit of each other and for their mutual assistance in case any dreadful disorder or unforeseen casualties should happen to any one individual parish. The proportion of the assessment was first ascertained according to the average of 7 years and since that time has again been sanctioned by Parliament. And all persons within these Hundreds who have purchased or hold estates considered this ratio as finally fixed and adjusted for in these parishes which were even considered more moderately assessed than any of the others was and is the uniform practice to state in the advertisement for sale that such estate was very moderately assessed to the poor rate and persons have not only bought and sold accordingly but have also let and hired upon the same principal, The first question generally put by a person about to purchase or hire is "How is the estate assessed to the Poor Rate"/*

That in proportion as the expenses by the corporation have unhappily occasioned a proportionate increase in the general assessment of the hundreds, the injustice and inequality of it have been the more severely felt, and call the more imperiously for redress, by the substitution of some plan by which the burthen may be more equally distributed.

That to obtain the equalisation of assessment throughout the hundreds, which is so justly desirable, the following plan appears to this meeting to be the best calculated and most effectual; viz.

The money taken out of the House for the relief of the poor belonging to each parish, but not resident in the House. *\as before stated this cannot be ascertained on account of a great deal of money allowed out of the House to paupers resident in one parish and belonging to another and such paupers would have been removed home had they not been in the corporation/*

The number of poor belonging to each parish resident in the House. *\this can be ascertained/*

The aggregate number of paupers resident in the House. *\and this also/*

The whole expense of the establishment itself, including the clothing and maintenance of the poor resident in the House (after deducting the amount of their earnings) and also the interest of money borrowed. *\and this/*

And that each of the above amounts be then averaged.

By the result of the first would be seen what has been the average receipt of each parish annually from the House for out relief, as before stated. *\this cannot as before stated/*

And by working the several other averaged amounts by the rule of proportion, it would also be seen what is the actual amount of each parish's proportion of the annual expense of the establishment.

For as the average of the aggregate number of poor resident in the House is to the average or the whole expense of the establishment, so will be the average of the number of the poor belonging to each parish to the expense which each individual parish has incurred to the corporation in respect of their poor maintained in the House.

279

The sum thus found, <u>added to the averaged annual receipt of each parish for out relief</u>, would then give the whole expense which each parish had been to the corporation, and thus a rule for its just assessment would be formed. *this cannot be done accurately*/

That a plan of this kind has, in the opinion of this meeting, a decided preference over that which has been hitherto adopted as the criterion of assessment, inasmuch as it is founded on certainty, and on facts and data actually arising out of the concern itself, and in the course of its management; whereas, on the contrary, the other had its origin in uncertainty and inequality, and has, by an experience of nearly half a century, progressively proved its own fallibility and oppressive tendency. *this cannot be founded on certainty neither ought it to be disturbed for the reasons before stated*/

That the plan now suggested has also another advantage – that, however its arithmetical accuracy may be affected in the course of time by a variation in the number of paupers and amounts of relief, or other circumstances, yet its principal will remain correct and unaltered, and fresh averages may and ought to be taken, say once in four years, according to the variations which may have occurred. This will also have the good effect of creating a degree of interest in the respective parishes as to the prosperity of the Corporation, and of inducing them to be circumspect in the applications they may make to the House for relief, and vigilant in guarding against impositions and unworthy and improper objects.

That this plan will also apply with equal accuracy in the attaining another most important and desirable object, that of liquidating the debt with which the corporation is unfortunately now weighed down, <u>by making for that purpose such addition to the assessment of each parish</u> as the Directors and Guardians may think proper, keeping, however, in view the same principle of proportion and equalization. *no further addition can be made to the assessments under the present act they are now raising as much as the law allows*/

That it appears to this meeting that the intended Bill is materially defective in many respects, and more particularly so as it contains no provision <u>for nor adverts to any other plan or principle of assessment than that which has been hitherto pursued,</u> *certainly not, as it would be more injurious to the purchases of estates in those parishes said to be under rated and would relieve the purchases of estates in those parishes said to be over rated*/ and that if it be passed into law in its present shape, the continuance of grievances of a most oppressive and injurious tendency to the <u>interests of the hundreds at large</u> *not to the Hundreds at large but to a few individuals in three parishes*/ is most seriously to be apprehended.

It was therefore unanimously resolved,

That a Petition be presented to the House, to be heard by Counsel against <u>the said Bill's passing into a law,</u> *what good will that do to prevent the bill passing into a law*/ and that the same shall be opposed in every stage of its progress through Parliament, by all lawful and constitutional means.

That Mr James Pulham, of Woodbridge, attorney-at-law, be employed to prepare such Petition, and to take the necessary steps under the direction of the Committee to be now appointed to render the opposition now resolved on effectual. *Sutton, Kenton and Marlesford the only three parishes that object to this Bill*/

And that a sum of money be raised according to the plan now proposed in the several aggrieved parishes, in order to defray the expense attending such proceedings.

It was further resolved,

That it appears to this meeting, that the present <u>accumulation of debt</u> upon the corporation amounts to the <u>enormous sum of 10,000*l* and upwards,</u> and that its remaining altogether unliquidated has been occasioned, it <u>is feared, principally by improvident expenditure, and by a want of due attention to economy in the management of the various concerns of the establishment.</u> *why such fears as the direction has been under the management of the first and best men in the Hundreds*\

That from the information which this meeting has been able to obtain, it is conceived that the present income of the corporation to be regulated by the principle of equalization on the several parishes as before suggested, would be sufficient (if properly economised and applied) to keep down <u>the interest of the debt,</u> *the interest of the debt is always invariably kept down*\ to provide for the necessary relief for the poor, and to defray the other just expenses of the corporation, if not to liquidate from time to time the principal debt itself.

That in order to accomplish <u>so desirable an object,</u> it is necessary that the accounts of the corporation should be inspected and revised, and such a system of reform in the various departments of the concern adopted as the peculiar circumstances of the case may render advisable. *what reform is necessary. If the number of poor etc. is lessened and the provisions less the debt might be very soon liquidated*\

That <8 names> be a Committee for the purpose of examining the Corporation accounts, and from taking from time to time such measures as shall be deemed by them best calculated to promote the several objects of the present meeting, and that three of such gentlemen be an efficient committee.

owner as Rector only	HENRY WILLIAMS	Rector Marlesford		
owner	WILLIAM SHULDHAM	attorney at *do*		
owner at Kenton	WILLIAM PHILPOT	Lord Huntingfield's steward		
owner	HENRY EDWARDS	farmer at Sutton		
occupier	B. COLCHESTER Jun	*do*	*do*	
owner	THOMAS WALLER	*do*	*do*	
occupier	JOHN BUTTON	*do* at	Marlesford	
occupier	WILLIAM ORFORD	*do*	*do*	occupier
	SAMUEL KERSEY	farmer at Kenton	*do*	
	THOMAS EDWARDS	*do*	Sutton	*do*
	STEPHEN BUMPSTEAD	*do*	Kenton	*do*
	WILLIAM WHIMPER COOK	*do*	Sutton	*do*
	EDGAR SMITH	*do*	*do*	owner
	ROBERT ABLITT	*do*	Marlesford	owner
	JEREMIAH WHITE	*do*	Sutton	occupier

41. Parishes opposing the Incorporation's amending Act focussed their attention on the two clauses outlined below. The document also cites their replacement clauses.[6]

A Bill is introduced into the House of Commons by the Solicitor to the Incorporated Parishes within the Hundreds of Loes and Wilford, in the county of Suffolk, to amend an Act passed in <1765>. Against some of the provisions in this Bill, several of the parishes within the Incorporated Hundreds have petitioned.

---

6   SROI ADA11/A/A/1/7.

The objectionable clauses, with those intended to be substituted, and the reasons for their substitution, are as follows:

Objectionable clauses in the Bill:

"And whereas it became necessary in some respects to amend the same, and to alter and enlarge the powers and provisions whereof."

"And whereas by the said recited Act it is enacted, that the sums to be assessed by the said Directors and Acting Guardians upon any parish <> should not exceed, in any one year, one-third of the sum which had been assessed for the relief and maintenance of the poor in any one year by virtue of an Act made in <1791>; and shall be in the same ratio and proportion as the assessments which had been levied by the said last recited Act, within the said parishes: And whereas the sums raised under and by virtue of the said provision have been found wholly insufficient for the several purposes in the said Act mentioned: be it therefore enacted, that from and immediately after the [   ] it shall and may be lawful to and for the said Directors and Acting Guardians, to assess upon every parish <> within the said Hundreds, all such sums which shall or may be necessary for the purposes of carrying the said recited Act of <1791> and this present Act, into execution: provided always, that all sums by the said Directors and Acting Guardians raised or to be raised upon such parishes respectively, under and by virtue of this Act, shall be rated and assessed upon each of them respectively in the like proportion towards each other, as the assessments made and imposed under and by virtue of the said recited Acts of 1765 and 1791 formerly were and have hitherto been made, rated, and imposed; and that nothing either in the said recited Act of <1791> nor in this Act contained, shall be construed to impower the said Directors and Acting Guardians to raise more money for the purpose of paying off and discharging in any one year a larger or greater sum of principal money already borrowed, or hereafter to be borrowed by virtue of the said Acts, or either of them, than the sum of [   ] anything therein or herein contained to the contrary notwithstanding."

Clauses intended to be submitted:

Instead of the first clause, it is intended to insert the following:

"And whereas some of the provisions of the said recited Act have been found by experience to be insufficient for the purposes thereby intended; and the annual payments rated and imposed upon the several parishes, hamlets, and places within the said Incorporated Hundreds, are very disproportionate and injurious to many of the said parishes, places, and hamlets."

Instead of the second clause, it is intended to insert the following:

"And whereas by the said recited Act it is enacted, that the sums to be assessed by the said Directors and Acting Guardians upon any parish <> should not exceed, in any one year, one-third of the sum which had been assessed for the relief and maintenance of the poor in any one year, by virtue of an Act made in <1791>; and shall be in the same ratio and proportion as the assessments which had been levied by the said last recited Act, within the said parishes: And whereas the sums raised under and by virtue of the said provision have been found not only insufficient for the purposes of the said Act, but have been unequal, disproportioned, and injurious to many of the united parishes within the said Hundreds: be it therefore enacted that from the [   ] quarter day next and immediately after the passing of this Act, it shall and may be lawful to and for the said Directors and Acting Guardians, and they are hereby directed and required, to assess upon every parish, hamlet, and place within the said Hundreds, such sum and sums of money as shall or may be necessary to be raised for the clothing, relieving, and maintaining the respective poor of such several

282

parishes, hamlets, and places respectively, and the legal and necessary expences of the establishment of the said House of Industry, and the said incorporated parishes, in the proportions and manner following, that is to say, that an average of the whole expence of the said House of Industry, including the payments for interest on money borrowed, and for out relief to paupers belonging to the said hundreds, not residing in any of the said incorporated parishes, shall be taken for the last [ ] years; and after deducting therefrom the earnings of the said paupers, together with all other profit and advantages arising from the concerns of the said corporation during that period, such amount shall be divided by the aggregate number of paupers which (on an average for the same period) shall be found to have been clothed and maintained in the said House; and each parish shall be charged such sum of money for each pauper, in proportion to the average number of paupers sent from or belonging to such parishes, hamlets, and places respectively, during that period, adding thereto the average annual amount of all sums paid by the Treasurer for the relief of the poor belonging to, or residing in, each parish respectively, not resident in the said House; and that the sums so found by the averages aforesaid being added together (making the actual amount of the expence which each parish, hamlet, and place hath respectively incurred to the Corporation, on an average for the period of the said last [ ] years), shall be the sum, rate, or assessment to be levied and raised (by quarterly payments) on each of the said parishes, hamlets, and places respectively. Provided always, that the said Directors and Acting Guardians, or the major part of them, present at any of the annual or quarterly meetings to be held, shall and may, and they are hereby empowered, authorised, and directed to increase or diminish the said rates and assessments, made and equalized as aforesaid from time to time, and as occasion may require, for and during the term of four years, at the end of which time, and every succeeding four years, they, the said Directors and Acting Guardians, are hereby empowered, authorised, and required to take fresh averages of the accounts of the said Corporation, and to make such alterations in the assessments of the said several parishes, hamlets, and places, as circumstances shall and may require, regard being had to the fair and just proportion of the expences which each parish, hamlet, and place respectively shall have incurred to the said Corporation, in manner aforesaid."

"And be it further enacted, that for the purpose of paying off and discharging the principal money already borrowed, or to be borrowed, by virtue of the said Acts, or of this Act, or either of them, it shall and may be lawful to and for the Directors and Acting Guardians, and they are hereby directed and required, to raise and levy from time to time, according to the mode of assessment prescribed in the last mentioned clause, upon every parish, hamlet, and place respectively, within the said Hundreds, not exceeding the sum of [ ] in the pound, in addition to every pound which the said parishes, hamlets, and places, shall be called upon and required to contribute respectively for the purposes aforesaid; and such additional sum, not exceeding the sum of [ ] in the pound, so to be raised aforesaid shall be for the purpose of creating a fund for paying off and discharging the principal money borrowed, or to be borrowed, by virtue of the said Acts, or this Act, or either of them, and shall be so applied by the said Directors and Acting Guardians, at such time or times, and in such manner as by any bye-laws, rules, orders, and regulations, made, or to be made for that purpose, shall be established."

The method pointed out in the Bill (which is introduced to the House) for raising the rates, is precisely the same as in the 31st of his present Majesty, the inequality and injustice whereof is pointed out in the following comparative statement, and which the foregoing clause, if introduced in the Bill, will effectually remove.

42. Letter from John Dorrington, the Incorporation's parliamentary agent, expressing the sentiments of Sir Charles Bunbury, chairman of the Commons Committee[7]

12 February 1810

Sir,

I am desired by Sir Charles Bunbury to say to you that he wishes the Committee on the Loes and Wilford Poor Bill not to sit before this day fortnight as he will not be able to attend. He has had a letter from your opponents requesting him to support their opposition but he seems, I think, inclined to your favour. As soon as the Petition against is presented I will send you a copy.

House of Commons.   John Dorrington.

43. Letter from John Dorrington, the Incorporation's parliamentary agent, updating the Incorporation regarding the opponent parishes' demands[8]

14 February 1810[9]

Sir,

Mr Ellis has just delivered to me the clauses that will satisfy his clients, and also a list of papers that they wish to be produced before the Committee. I am afraid you will not be able to resist the production of these accounts if the Committee require it. When do you mean to come to town?

House of Commons.   J. Dorrington.

44. Letter from John Dorrington, the Incorporation's parliamentary agent, updating the Incorporation on events in Parliament[10]

16 February 1810[11]

Sir,

It will depend on yourself when the Committee is to meet and the Chairman's Order could not therefore specify it. In fact there was no authority for issuing that Order but as the power is easily obtained from the House I should advise you to bring the papers and you can then object to producing them if the Committee will support you in it, which I doubt. When you are prepared let me see you, and we can then fix a day for the meeting of the Committee.

House of Commons.   J. Dorrington

The petition is not presented. I believe they wait for your answer – of course I shall not disclose your sentiments.

---

7   SROI ADA11/A/A/1/7.
8   SROI ADA11/A/A/1/7.
9   To Wood Esq., Woodbridge.
10 SROI ADA11/A/A/1/7.
11 To Wood Esq., Woodbridge.

45. Letter from T. S. Gooch, a director of the Incorporation, commenting on his efforts to delay the convening of the Commons Committee[12]

23 February 1810[13]

Dear Sir,

I had a letter from Sir Charles Bunbury yesterday telling me that the Committee on your Bill was to meet on Monday. I wrote to him to ask if it would be possible to defer the Committee till Thursday as it would be extremely inconvenient for me to attend on Monday. If I should not hear from Sir Charles Bunbury, either by tomorrows post or Sundays to tell me the Committee is deferred, I shall set off for London in order to be at my post by Monday. I must then send around to a large party of friends who were coming to me that day to put them off till another. I will get all the information in my power between this and then as to the operation of our new Bill in the Cosford Hundred.

Your Obed. Servant   T. S. Gooch

46. Brief on behalf of the petitioners for the bill[14]

Petition of the Directors and Acting Guardians of the Poor within the Incorporated Hundreds of Loes and Wilford in the county of Suffolk presented to the House of Commons the 25th day of January 1810 for leave to bring in a bill for amending an Act passed in <1765>. The said petition was received and ordered to a Committee. The Committee passed the same and a Bill was accordingly ordered to be brought in which was accordingly brought in and read and ordered to be printed and afterwards the same was printed. (*vide* copy of petition and copy of printers bill).

Case,

The Directors and Acting Guardians of the Poor within the said Hundreds, on account of the great increase of the price of corn and other commodities, have been obliged to raise their rates to the upmost limit of their present Act of Parliament and have even been obliged to go beyond that limit, being indebted to their Treasurer in about £4 or £500.

A meeting of the whole body of Guardians within the said Hundreds was convened by public advertisement, and which was held upon the Sessions Hall at Woodbridge on the 8th August last. At which meeting Mr Pulham attended as attorney for the parish of Sutton in the Hundred of Wilford and Mr Moor as attorney for the parish of Kenton in the Hundred of Loes, two parishes of thirty-three which thought themselves aggrieved by being over rated in proportion to some of the other parishes in the said Hundreds, and stated unless the parishes were equalized they should oppose the intended Bill. However it was finally determined that the Petition they produced should be sealed with the Corporation Seal and presented to the House of Commons.

A Committee was also appointed to prepare and settle the clauses of the intended Bill, and which Committee sat for several days and was open to any Director or Guardian, and Mr Pulham and Mr Moor, as attorneys for the above parishes, also attended, but the clauses they wished to be inserted were rejected by a very consid-

---

12   SROI ADA11/A/A/1/7.

13   To Wood Esq., Woodbridge.

14   SROI ADA11/A/A/1/6.

erable majority of the Committee. The several clauses so agreed upon were afterwards submitted to the perusal of Mr Nolan, and by him passed and settled on behalf of the Hundreds at large previous to going before the House of Commons.

The two opponent parishes, with the parish of Marlesford in the said Hundred of Loes, convened a meeting at Wickham Market, which was held on the 21st December 1809 and attended by about 18 persons from three parishes when certain resolutions were then entered into. (*vide* copy of same). And it was there resolved that a petition should be presented to the House to be heard by Counsel against the Bill passing into a law, and that the same should be opposed in every stage of its progress through Parliament by all lawful means.

Another meeting of the opponent parishes has since been held which was attended by about eight persons. And Mr Pulham, their solicitor, was instructed to go to London in order to oppose the intended new Bill, and he accordingly went and has employed a Mr Ellis as his Parliamentary Agent, and he has delivered a copy of the clauses that those opponent parishes wish to be inserted in the new Bill, and by which it will be observed that the intention is to take the power of relief to the paupers out of the hands of the Directors and Guardians and place the same into the hands of a set of illiterate officers, the Overseers and Churchwardens of the several parishes.

And in order to ascertain the quota of expences and assessments to be paid by each parish, a mode is to be adopted of taking an average account of the poor relieved in and out of the House belonging to each parish, and which upon all occasions be attended not only enormous labour but must inevitably be an erroneous account, and if it was not it would constantly vary every month. And if the mode be accepted the greater part of the poor would have to appear before the magistrates to swear their settlements, so many of them living in one parish and belonging to another in the same Hundreds, and constantly relieved by the Directors and Acting Guardians in the residing parish and not in the parish to which they belong. And further if those clauses should be admitted, the cruelty of the Churchwardens and Overseers would be very severely felt by the poor, for previous to their average account they would screw down the number of poor relieved by them as much as possible, for in proportion to the number of poor receiving relief in their parish so would be the proportion of their assessment. It would therefore be their interest, and no doubt they would study that to make the number of paupers receiving relief as small as possible.

It is therefore the particular desire of the Corporation to resist those clauses, not only on account of the increased trouble attending the same, but on account of the very material injury the poor may and no doubt will sustain by these clauses being inserted into the Bill. And such clauses appear to be repugnant to the general code of Poor Laws and in themselves unconstitutional.

The opponents to this Bill complain of the very great accumulation of debt, which is certainly not the case, for only £250 has been borrowed since the passing of their last Act, and as to their rates being so considerably increased they were much higher in the years 1800 and 1801 than they now are, and at that period money was obliged to be borrowed for a short time from the Directors themselves during the high price of provisions and which was not secured upon the rates of the Corporation. The sum first borrowed in the years 1765, 1766 and 1767 was £9,200 which was afterwards increased to £9,900 the debt which was due upon passing the Act <1791> since which £250 has been added to the debt, making the present debt £10,150, an accumulation of only £250 in 19 years.

The proportion of the rates under <Act of 1765> was taken upon an average of seven years previous to the passing of that Act of the amount of expences incurred by each parish in the maintenance of their poor during that period. And which average amount was delivered to the then Directors and Acting Guardians, and days of appeal were by them fixed for all parishes who themselves felt aggrieved to attend, and many did attend, were heard and the assessments finally fixed upon. It does appear that some parishes pay more in proportion than other parishes, but that was in a great measure owing to those parishes that appear to be moderately assessed having divers quantities of charity lands in their parishes whereby the expences of the maintenance of their poor by rate was proportionably small. And this quota of assessment, having been now assessed for near 50 years, if altered those parishes are stated to be moderately assessed will be very much aggrieved for there is scarcely an estate in the two Hundreds but what have been bought and sold since the establishment of this Corporation, and persons who have purchased where the estates have been moderately assessed have given more money for them than they would had they been highly assessed, and on the other hand those persons who have purchased estates in the parishes stated to be highly assessed have given less money for them than they would had done had they been moderately assessed. Therefore the purchasers in the one case would be materially benefitted and in the other case materially injured, and so it would also be in the cases of occupations only for farmers hiring of farms make that their first inquiry "how are the estates assessed to the poor rate". And which is a consideration generally noticed in advertisements, either that they are moderately assessed to the poor rate, or that estates are situated within an incorporated hundred implying that the rates paid are moderate. And so they are even in those parishes which state themselves to be over rated to what they are in the adjoining parishes not incorporated, many of which would with great pleasure be joined with this Corporation their expences being so very great. Those 33 parishes incorporated themselves in the year 1765 by way of an association for the equal benefits and advantage of each of how that in case any dreadful disorder or unforeseen calamities should happen to any one single parish the other parishes should (being so incorporated) assist such parish, as a body or number of parishes could better bear an expence of that kind than one single person or parish could do. Their quota was fixed upon passing of the first act of <1765> and all persons purchasing and selling estates within the said incorporated hundreds considered the rates to be finally fixed and bought and sold their estates accordingly and also let and hired farms under the same idea.

The number who oppose the passing of this Bill are very small, being only three parishes out of 33, which compose the Corporation. And even in those parishes there are but few persons who object to the principal of the old or new bill, and those objections are stated only as to the inequality of the rates. There appears to be only two Directors and three Acting Guardians that have joined with the opposition party, and the Corporation consist of 24 Directors and 24 Guardians. Therefore it is not to be supposed that such an inconsiderable number should have power to over throw the whole and present system of the Corporation and which, in fact, is in a flourishing state except as to the high price of bread and other food. The interest of the debt is always regularly paid every half year and also all tradesmen's bills, none ever suffered to remain unpaid beyond a quarter of a year.

The opponent parishes contend that the amount of their Poor Rate as delivered in under the first act was uncommonly large in consequence of them having had to meet extraordinary expences incurred by unusual and unforeseen casualties particularly the small pox, which they contend had for the 7 years alluded to raged with great and continued virulence, and they state that those expences were improvidently and incorrectly admitted to form a part of the data whereon the calculation of the future burthern of those parishes was to be made. How they are to prove these statements is unknown to the friends of this Bill but, even were they to prove it, what would it avail them: the time to have done that was upon their appeal to their own returns, but which not being done, their quota was fixed upon by the then sitting Directors and Guardians. These matters are all very properly and regularly entered upon the proceedings of the Corporation and which took place in the year 1768 being 42 years since.

The opponent parishes or their employers wish for a reform in the system but they cannot state on what account (except the theme of equalisation) for the business and interest of the Corporation has been duly and regularly attended to by the first and largest landowners in the Hundreds and gentlemen of the first respectability – but those reformers, at most three or four of them are men of small estates, the others are men of no state whatever within the said Hundreds.

If it had not been for the very high price of corn, food and cloathing this application to Parliament would not have been necessary, but as the expences are so much increased on that account the Corporation are compelled to go to Parliament having no power or authority to raise by the assessments sufficient for the expences of their current quarter.

The number of paupers belonging to the opponent parishes and maintained in the House the last 10 years were very considerable, with those in the parish of Sutton, one of the opponent parishes amounted in the last ten years to 93, which only taken at ¼ of them maintained in the House for that period and at only 5s. a week per head maintenance and cloathing come to the sum of   £2,990 00 0
and Sutton has received during the same period for relief of out paupers   £614 19 1
and their proportion or share towards payment of interest money, salaries etc. about   £100 00 0
                    £3,704 19 1
that parish has paid into the House for the said ten years the sum of   £3,694 01 3
leaving a balance from that parish in favour of the corporal the sum of   £10 17 10

Therefore from this statement that parish cannot be aggrieved by the assessments that has been paid by them for the last 10 years. And the other two parishes are much in the same state of proportion for that time. The same assessment as was made in 1800 (which is much greater than the one in 1809) was made upon the several parishes in these Hundreds in the year 1796 when the interest money was at only 4 per cent.

If the clauses proposed by the opponent parishes should be introduced into this Bill, the Directors will be obliged to employ an extra clerk and also a man and horse and cart constantly to send round the Hundreds to the several parishes to bring up the poor before the Magistrates to swear to their settlement. And the Directors and Acting Guardians would be obliged to set at each of their Quarterly Meetings three days at least, under the present system they do their business in the day. And should these clauses be introduced no Director of Guardian will act.

In the Hundred of Cosford in Suffolk clauses similar to those proposed by the opponent parishes were introduced in their Act of Parliament some few years over, but which it is understood cannot be proceeded upon without the utmost difficulty, and not with any degree of accuracy, and which Mr Gooch, who is a Director there and one of the Members for the county, and also on the Committee will state as he has as Director in that Hundred acted under these same clauses.

47. Proceedings of the Commons Committee, 27 February 1810[15]

At the Committee to whom the Bill for amending An Act passed in <1791> is committed.
27 Feb 1810.
Sir Charles Bunbury Bart. in the Chair.
Ordered.
That the present Acting Guardians and Directors under the above mentioned Act do on <2 March> produce and lay before the said Committee all the bye laws made for the government of the House of Industry established under the said Act. And all rates and assessments made for the relief of the poor within the said Hundreds during the last ten years. Also the annual accounts during that period passed by the Clerk or Officers of the said Corporation. Also a list or account of the number of poor admitted into the House of Industry from every parish <> within the Incorporated Hundreds during the last ten years, distinguishing their sexes, and whether they were of ages or minors and from what parishes <> they were respectively sent, and also distinguishing the number of such persons so admitted in each of those years. Also an account of the several sums of money for which every such parish <> has been annually assessed during the last ten years. Also an account of the annual amount of relief paid to paupers not resident in the said House of Industry, specifying to what parish such paupers so relieved did belong. Also an account of the money due and owing on the credit <> at the time of the passing of the said act of the thirty first year of his present majesty.
Charles Bunbury.

48. Notice for the Incorporation to produce their books of account for the Commons Committee[16]

6 March 1810[17]
Gent.
I give you notice to produce all the books of account and the bye laws relative to the incorporated hundreds of Loes and Wilford in the County of Suffolk that the same may be inspected before the Committee of the House of Commons on Wednesday the 7th day of March instantly.
    I am,
    Gent., your obedient servant.
    James Pulham.   Solicitor to the Petitioners.

49. Proceedings of the Commons Committee, 6 March 1810[18]

Committee on Loes and Wilford Poor Bill 6 March 1810.

---

15 SROI ADA11/A/A/1/6.
16 SROI ADA11/A/A/1/6.
17 SROI ADA11/A/A/1/6. To Mr John Wood Treasurer and Mr Joseph Oldham the Clerk.
18 SROI ADA11/A/A/1/6. Answers to questions are shown in *italics*.

Sir Charles Bunbury Bt. in the Chair.
Petition against received.   Counsel, Mr Warren.   Agent, Mr Ellis.

Richard Oldham, Clerk to House of Industry examined.
(printed statement shewn).
Were you present when these remarks were taken out of the book?
Yes and believe them to be correctly taken from the book.
Are always paupers, when they become chargeable within the Hundred, removed from the parish in which their settlement is?
No
Does it not often happen that a pauper, when settled in one parish, becomes chargeable in another? Do you keep a book in which you can ascertain to what parish a pauper belongs to or where he resides?
Yes, where he belongs to, when we can find out, but not to the parish where resides.
Whether paupers who are sent to that House are sworn to their settlements previous to their admittance?
Not always.
Then you cannot say correctly to which parish paupers belong?
It is always done when it can be found out, there is no pains taken.
Do you always make a point of enquiring when any pauper is brought to the house the parish he belongs to, as well as the parish where he lives?
The account is taken of the parish where he is settled.
Look at the paper delivered in containing a list of paupers for the last ten years in each parish. How long have you been clerk?
One year and a quarter.
Is that a correct copy from the book which you found in the House?
It is.
Does that paper contain a correct account of the paupers brought into the House during the time you have been clerk?
Yes.
Does it contain a correct account of the paupers belonging or settled in each parish?
Yes.
Are there not several paupers relieved out of the house?
Yes, great numbers.
Are they relieved in the parish in which they became chargeable, or in which they are settled?
In the parish they reside, no notice is taken of the parish to which they belong for out relief.
Do you know from the book when the debt of £10,000 was contracted?
No it is not in my department.
Do you know the gentlemen that have signed the petition against?
Not all of them.
Are they farmers of the land or proprietors?
Principally farmers.
Witness delivered in account of the average number of paupers maintained in the House for the last ten years, and also a paper intituled "Relief to paupers not resident in the House", and also a paper intituled "Number of paupers admitted for last ten years", and stated they were correct.
    Withdrew.

Mr John Wood delivered in an account of the money assessed upon and paid by the several parishes within the Hundreds of Loes and Wilford for 10 years from 1st January 1800 to 1st January 1810. A paper intituled "Extract of the annual receipts and disbursements for the last ten years from 1800 to 1809". A paper intituled "Money borrowed and paid, present debt £10,150".
Examined.
When was the principal part of the debt owing by this corporation incurred?
In 1776/7/8 and 9, £9,200 was borrowed for building the house, £10,150 is still owing.
[This taken down wrong, it was in 1766, 7, 8, 9].
Is not one of the objects of the Corporation in coming to Parliament to pay off the debt?
Yes, and I have been sued as Treasurer by the creditors.
Withdrew.

Mr Samuel Gross, Guardian and Director of House of Industry about 10 years, examined by Mr Warren.
Are you acquainted with the system of rating the parishes of Loes and Wilford?
Yes I am.
Have you attended to the mode of rating Marlesford, Kenton, Sutton and Charsfield?
Yes I have.
In your judgement are these parishes equally assessed with the others?
I believe not.
Have you made any observation with respect to other parishes, Sutton for instance, is Boyton and Sutton, of the same size?
No, and Sutton has more population than Boyton.
Is the quality of the land better in Boyton than Sutton?
It varies so much I cannot say.
Examined by members.
Can you say whether Sutton is 3, 4 or 5 times as large in population as Boyton?
I cannot say. I believe it is considerable more.
Look at the paper "Sutton and Boyton" can you state whether that is a fair rate for Boyton?
Certainly not.
How many parishes are there incorporated?
Thirty three.
During the ten years has the mode of assessment varied?
No.
In your judgement are they equally rated as they ought?
No they are not, the inequality is very great.
Can you instance any other parish which is very great?
I cannot one.
How do you calculate that inequality?
Upon the value of the land.
What do you suppose the value of the land in Boyton and in Sutton?
I have not made an exact valuation. I only know it from general observation.
In giving an order for relief to a poor person to whom is that order addressed?
To the Overseers of the parish in which he resides.
Do you, in that order, at all state the parish he is settled in?
No we do not.

Has any valuation been made of the parishes?
   No.
Have any of them been inclosed?
   No.
Do you not take the necessary steps in examining the man whether he belongs to the parish or not?
   When we are at all doubtful.
Do you not as a Director of these hundreds know that poor persons in and belonging to the hundred may reside in any parish they like without being removed?
   They may.
You only go to a magistrate for an order to remove a pauper in case of his not belonging to your hundreds?
   Yes.
Do you know when the proportions upon which the present rate made by the directors was settled?
   I do not know.
Was it not in 1767/8?
   I cannot speak.
Do you happen to know whether there is not a proportion of charity land in Boyton?
   There is.
Does not the profit of that land go in part to maintain the poor of that parish?
   I never heard it did.
Have you ever made any alteration in the rates in consequence of paupers greatly increased in one parish and diminished in another?
   No we never do.
Have you had any litigation with respect to the settlement of paupers within these hundreds?
   Not any to my knowledge.
Has any very material increase in the value of land in Sutton within your knowledge?
   Not any.
   [It has increased in value very considerably. A farm that sold for £2,600 about 15 or 20 years since has now sold for the sum of £11,500, the proprietor asks £22,000].
Do they remain nearly in an equal state of improvement with each other?
   Yes.
Withdrew.

Henry Edwards examined. Lives at Sutton, has been Director of House of Industry not quite a year, is acquainted with Sutton and Boyton.
Do you know of any single farms in Sutton that are assessed as much as the whole parish of Boyton?
   Yes several single and small farms, my own (Woodhall) for instance. I think I am paying twice as much   as the whole parish of Boyton. I think the valuation of Sutton and Boyton are nearly equal.
What opportunity have you had of knowing the valuation?
   As being a Director.
In what way did you make that valuation?
   I cannot say. Sutton has the greatest population, twice as much as that of Boyton. Some farms pay as much as of 120 acres of land that pay as much as the whole parish of Boyton individually, the Directors and Guardians all agree the rating very unequal.

Have the directors taken any means to remedy that?

No they have not.

Withdrew.

Mr John Button examined. Guardian of the House of Industry 8 or 9 years.

Are you acquainted with the parish of Marlesford?

Yes.

Have you made any comparisons with the rates of this parish and others?

Yes, Monewden and Hoo.

In comparison with those is it too much or too little?

Too little. I have seen the valuation as a guardian and acted upon it, have not made any observation on any other parishes but those two.

Cross examined.

You have made no survey?

Yes, Marlesford.

Have you made any survey of any other parish – can you state the rental of any one parish but your own?

I cannot state it but from the paper I have seen.

Withdrew.

William Philpot Esq. examined.

Have you had any opportunity of observing the disproportion of the rates in the parishes?

Yes.

State them?

From the examination of the extracts taken from the books it is very evident that there is a very great inequality in the assessments – the parishes of Sutton and Boyton, comparing the expences which have been respectively incurred by those parishes with the assessments of them, there is a very great disproportion. I believe from the examination of the papers and books it will be found that the parish of Boyton has incurred an expence to the Corporation of at least four times as much as they have contributed, and the parish of Sutton has over paid in a very great proportion to the expences incurred. The parish of Kenton in very considerable over rated, Marlesford the same, Charsfield the same.

Have you seen the clause proposed?

Yes, it would be an infallible rule for the assessments are made according to the plan suggested in the clause. It must be correct because it would be taken in proportion to the expence incurred in each parish and which will be ascertained from the concern itself. There can be no difficulty in acting under that clause. I averaged the parish in 6 hours.

Cross examined.

All your knowledge is taken from the books?

Yes.

Examined by Members.

The ground work of your average is to be the number of paupers maintained in the House and residing in the parish?

Yes and the relief and money paid to those parishes for paupers to or residing.

On what do you ground the division of expense to each parish?

The average number of paupers maintained in the house from the several parishes for a certain period, then the total expence of the house for maintaining those

paupers – money paid for paupers resident in parishes belonging to the several parishes but not residing in any of the incorporated parishes, together with all other expences of the establishment from which the earnings of the poor and all other advantages arising from the concern should be deducted – the average payments for out relief for poor belonging to or residing in the several parishes – then as the average aggregate number of paupers maintained in the House is to the whole expence as above so will the number of paupers from each parish respectively be to the expence incurred by that parish the sum so found added to the payment for out relief will be the expence incurred to each parish respectively to the corporation.
Do you think it possible to know correctly the number of paupers belonging to each individual parish?
   No I cannot.
Adjourned till tomorrow.

50. Proceedings of the Commons Committee, 7 March 1810[19]

Sir Charles Bunbury Bart. in the Chair.

Mr Wood examined by Mr Nolan.
Are you acquainted with the mode in which the rates are made in these hundreds?
   Yes.
Has this mode been uniformly pursued?
   Yes, ever since the establishment of the workhouse.
I believe a power of appealing against the assessments originally made under the statute of 5 Geo. III was given to each of the parishes. Was there any appeals?
   Yes, eight immediately after the establishment – Charsfield, Cretingham, Hoo, Boyton, Debach and Ufford – all the others acquiesced under the Act as then made.
Examined by Members
Have you heard of any complaints of any oppression from them?
   No.
Is Mr Kilderbee against the introduction of the new clauses?
   No.
Does Mr Kilderbee act as a Director in the Hundreds?
   Yes, and is a very active Director.
What sum is due to you now?
   £400.
Withdrew.

Mr James Pulham examined by Mr Warren.
Are you able to state why no more than four parishes have petitioned?
   On account of the expence.
Examined by Members.
Do you know that any clauses were shown to the Directors?
   There was a plan.
Was the subject the same?
   I don't know.
Do you know many of the Directors and Acting Guardians of Loes and Wilford?

---

[19] SROI ADA11/A/A/1/6. Answers to questions are shown here in italics.

Yes.

Are not these Directors and Acting Guardians composed of the most respectable and best informed yeomanry of that part of the county?

Yes.

Have these Directors and Acting Guardians had proper information laid before them of this petition?

They must have known it.

What could prevent them from petitioning?

I understand that at a meeting that four parishes by petitioning might decide as to the rest.

Is Marlesford equally rated with Kenton?

There must be a difference according to the size.

Examined Mr Nolan.

Do you know of your own knowledge that any parish has declined?

Yes, Bredfield. I only know it from private individuals.

Examined by Members

Is not Mr Jenny the principal owner in Bredfield?

Yes.

Withdrew.

Mr Warren summoned up the evidence and the tendered clauses.

Mr Nolan replied.

Adjourned till tomorrow.

50. Clauses proposed by the Incorporation to remove the opposing parishes' objections[20]

Whereas the several rates or assessments made under and by virtues of the said recited act of <1765> have been found wholly insufficient for the purposes of the said act and are in part become unequal and disproportionate. Be it therefore enacted that it shall and may be lawful to and for the said Directors and Acting Guardians of the Poor within the Incorporated Hundreds of Loes and Wilford and they or the major part of them then and there present are hereby authorised and required at their General Quarterly Meeting to be held in the month of October next after the passing of this Act, to alter and equalise the several proportions or quotas of the rates and assessments made under and by virtue of the said recited act upon the several parishes hamlets and places within the said Incorporated Hundreds, according to an average of 10 years of the expenses incidental to the supporting and maintaining the poor and other purposes of the said recited act. To be taken and drawn from the 1st day of January 1800 inclusive to the 1st day of January 1810 exclusive such average to be calculated upon the actual relief given to paupers respectively belonging to each parish and whether residing in their respective parishes or elsewhere or maintained in the House of Industry. And be it further enacted that the said Directors and Acting Guardians or the major part of them present at any of the annual or quarterly meetings appointed to be held by virtue of the said recited act shall and they are hereby empowered and are required to assess the several parishes hamlets and places within the said Hundreds in such respective sums of money (according to and

---

20 SROI ADA11/A/A/1/6.

in the proportion to be taken aforesaid) as the said Directors and Acting Guardians shall think necessary for defraying the expences attending the supporting and maintaining the poor for the current quarter of the year and for paying off any principal money under and by virtue of this act with the interest thereof to be borrowed and other expences of the said Corporation.

Provided always that nothing in the aforesaid clauses shall extend or be construed to extend to the altering of the ratio of the rates or assessments for the purpose of paying off and discharging the principal money already borrowed and due by virtue of an act passed in <1765> and of the said recited act of<1791>. But such principal money and interest shall be paid off in just proportion to the sums assessed by virtue of the said recited acts or either of them <> and that the said principal money now due shall all be paid off and discharged within [ ] years from and after the passing of this act by an equal sum yearly and in every year until such principal money shall be all paid off and discharged <>.

And the said Directors and Acting Guardians are hereby authorised and required to add to their Quarterly Assessment for the relief and maintenance of the poor and for the other purposes hereby directed to be made according to the aforesaid average or medium such sum or sums of money as shall be deemed the just proportion of each of the said several parishes <> for paying off and discharging the principal money borrowed and due by virtue of the said recited acts together with the interest thereon.

52. Richard Wood's account of the public meeting held on 29 March 1810, focussing on how, at key votes, the Incorporation was outmanoeuvred by the dissenting parishes[21]

Dear Sir,

Loes and Wilford Hundreds Poor Bill.

We this day had a public meeting of the owners and occupiers of lands within the Hundreds convened by public advertisement, at which meeting a clause was produced by the petitioners for the bill for equalizing the assessment for relief of the poor, and was agreed to in substance but subject to yours and Mr Warrens perusal and adjustment. Another clause for paying off the debt was produced by the (directors & guardians) petitioners for the bill which was also first agreed to be left to the Committee of the House of Commons to determine whether the sum should be paid off according to the new ratio of assessment or according to the old ratio. But after a great deal of talk and cabal the question over payment was put to the vote of the meeting and carried for paying off the debt according to the new ratio by a majority of 8, being 33 for it and 25 against it. But nevertheless our Gents. intend trying it before the Committee for this meeting, quite unexpectedly to these Gents., was made up by circular letters from Mr Philpot to the supposed aggrieved parishes, which was the cause of their being outnumbered. However I have prevailed upon 3 of our Gents. to come up to town again Monday, and they will get there tomorrow night. I have fixed with them for a meeting at your chambers at 11 o'clock on Saturday morning, if it meets with your convenience. Mr Kilderbee, Mr Turner, and Mr Whitbread are the three gents., and I believe Mr Jenney will be there although

---

[21] SROI ADA11/A/A/1/6. This letter is addressed to Mr Nolan.

he was not at our meeting. I expect to be at the Temple Coffee House tomorrow evening at 7 or 8 o'clock and will look in at your chambers at 9 o'clock. Should Saturday's meeting not be convenient to you I would acquaint my friends immediately of the same. In hope of seeing you soon. I am,
  Richard Wood.

53. A pamphlet circulated by the opponent parishes justifying their actions in an attempt to encourage the dissenting parishes to attend the general meeting of 29 March 1810[22]

The Directors of the affairs of the Incorporated Hundreds of Loes and Wilford, in Suffolk, having applied to Parliament for an Act to amend the Act of the 31st of his present Majesty, for the Relief of the Poor within the said Hundreds, the accounts of the Corporation have been accurately and impartially examined, and it thereby clearly appeared that 16 of the 33 incorporated parishes have, on an average of the last ten years, exceeded and been deficient in their respective just contributions to the Corporation, in the following disproportions: viz.

	Excess of just contribution for the last 10 years				Deficiencies of just contribution for the last 10 years		
	£	s.	d.		£	s.	d.
The eight parishes of				The eight parishes of			
Ash	1,077	18	6	Hacheston	1,023	15	10
Sutton	968	18	1½	Dallingho	908	18	1½
Charsfield	875	10	2½	Melton	869	10	10
Kenton	813	1	0½	Alderton	762	10	2½
Ufford	752	14	2	Boyton	761	17	8½
Easton	695	2	8½	Wickham	687	16	8
Butley	544	15	0	Bredfield	561	11	5½
Marlesford	536	16	10½	Hoo	540	15	0
The Corporation gained	6,264	16	7½	The Corporation lost	6,116	15	10

It appears by the above statement, that the first eight mentioned parishes have in the last ten years paid (besides having maintained their own poor in and out of the house), the sum of £6,264 16s. 7½d. more than their just proportion of the expenses of the corporation, while the other eight parishes have not contributed so much, by the sum of £6,116 15s. 10d. as their just proportion of the same expenses. And it appeared, by the same examination, that of the 33 incorporated parishes, 16 paid in the last 10 years £7,759 more than their fair proportions of the expenditure of the corporation, while the remaining 17 did not contribute so much by £8,625 as their just proportion of the same expenditure; hence it is evident, that without the receipt of those excesses of contribution, these deficiencies must long since have ruined the corporation. It has also been ascertained, that one farm of about £100 a year in Sutton, has annually paid in support of the corporation as much money as the parish of Boyton has contributed in the same time to the same institution; that one farm of about the same yearly value in Marlesford, has paid annually for the same purpose as much money as the whole parish of Monewden has contributed yearly in support

---

22 SROI ADA11/A/A/1/6.

of the corporation; and that the parish of Easton has paid to the corporation as much money, within seven pounds a year, as both the parishes of Monewden and Kettleburgh have contributed in the same time to the same institution. Of these unjust and extremely oppressive inequalities in the respected contributions of the incorporated parishes, the injured parishioners have complained, hoping their grievances would be redressed by the amended Act; but they were told by the Directors that the injustice could not be remedied, and that not only the future assessments must be made, but the ancient debts of the corporation, amounting to above £10,000 must be paid in the same unjust proportion. Of a different opinion, however were many gentlemen of the Committee of the House of Commons, and also the majority of a general meeting of the principal parishioners within the said Hundreds, at Wickham, who conceived, that in distributive justice, all the incorporated parishes ought to be rated and contribute in fair proportion to the necessary expenditure and the payment of the just debts of the corporation. But this arrangement, though so equitable, some of the directors (whose motives some of the deficiencies sufficiently explain), exerted all their influence to defeat, although they were convinced of the disproportions of the rates, and knew that the debts of the corporation were contracted for the general interest of all the incorporated parishes. But not one half of the parishioners of those parishes knew, when they hired their present occupations, that the corporation was at all indebted, or if it were, did they conceive that the just expenditure of the corporation could for a series of years have been so exactly equal to its revenues of £5,000 a year, that there might not have been some surplus applied in the reduction of the just debt of the institution. And less did they imagine, that they should be compelled to pay, by contributions so unequal and oppressive as the present assessments (at the rate of 9s. in the pound, and £8,000 per annum) are upon them, – debts from which they have never derived nor can derive any benefit, till the affairs of the corporation be conducted with strict economy and perfect impartiality.

Wickham Market.

54. An account of the general meeting held on 29 March 1810, including a breakdown of the voting[23]

Meeting of owners and occupiers of lands within the incorporated hundreds of Loes and Wilford to consider the propriety of introducing certain clauses for equalizing the several rates and assessments within the said parishes in the said Hundreds and for discharging the debt.

The first clause, for equalizing the rates and assessments for the maintenance of the poor being produced by the Directors and Guardians upon a certain ratio was agreed to in substance, subject to the perusal and alteration of Counsel on both sides.

The second clause, for paying off the debt produced by the said Directors and Guardians agreeable to the old assessment, was first agreed to be left to the determination of the Committee of the House of Commons, but after some further conversation, and when several persons had retired, it was put to the vote whether the debt should be paid off by the old assessment or according to the new ratio of the assessment for the maintenance of the poor. And upon a division, 33 were for paying the debt by the new ratio, and 26 were for paying the debt according to the old ratio of assessment, viz:

---

[23] SROI ADA11/A/A/1/7.

For paying the debt by the old assessment:		For paying by the new:	
1 Jacob Whitbread Esq.	19 Mr P. Dikes	1 Mr Shuldham	21 Mr William Wright
2 Revd G. Turner	20 Mr Barrow	2 Mr Philpot	22 Mr Freeman
3 Revd J. Kilderbee	21 Revd Wm Kett	3 Mr Trotman	23 Mr W. W. Cork
4 Revd W. Aldrich	22 C. J. Sharpe Esq.	4 Mr H. Edwards	24 Mr Farmer
5 Revd C. Jeaffreson	23 Mr Syred	5 Mr Thomas Waller	25 Mr Henry Marsden
6 Revd Jacob Chilton	24 Mr Wm Sherwood	6 Mr S. Gross	26 Mr Roe
7 Revd Wm Browne	25 Mr John Wood	7 Mr Jn. Waller	27 Mr Ashford
8 Dr Syer M.D.		8 Mr Edward Crisp	28 Mr D. Kemp
9 Mr Jer. Wase		9 Mr Jn. Edwards	29 Mr Dove
10 Mr Jn. Woolnough		10 Mr Kersey	30 Mr K. Welton
11 Mr N. Barthropp		11 Jn. Goodwin	31 Mr I. Threadkell
12 Mr W. Kitson		12 Mr Wm Cotton	32 Mr W. Barthropp
13 XXXXXXXXXX		13 Mr Hamblin	33 Mr W. Orford
13 Mr W. Hinchman		14 Mr Woodward	
14 Mr Js. Clubbe		15 Mr Chisnall	
15 Mr Catkin		16 Mr B. Colchester	
16 Mr W. Moor		17 Mr Henry Kenton	
17 Mr James Cooper		18 Mr Buffest	
18 Mr Lucock		19 Mr Button	
		20 Mr Randall	

55. A copy of a pre-printed letter sent by William Philpot to the dissenting parishes, encouraging their attendance and voting at the general meeting to be held on 29 March 1810[24]

To the owners and occupiers of lands within the parish of Ufford in the Hundred of Wilford.

Gentlemen,

The Directors and Acting Guardians of the Poor, within the incorporated hundreds of Loes and Wilford, having proposed to call a General Meeting of the owners and occupiers of lands within the said hundreds, on Thursday next, the 29th instant, at 10 o'clock in the forenoon, at the White Hart, in Wickham Market, in order to take into consideration the inequality of the present assessments, and also certain clauses for the more just and equal regulation of them, and for providing for the payment of the existing debt, which are proposed to be inserted in the Bill now before Parliament. It is particularly requested, that some respectable occupiers from every parish will

---

24 SROI ADA11/A/Q/2/1(6). This was a pre-printed document. The insertions in bold italic were inserted by hand on the original, as were the amounts underlined. As the owner of this document did not wish to part with the original, a copy was made by R. Oldham and sent to the directors.

make a point of attending the meeting at which a statement will be laid before them, shewing at one view, the aggregate receipts and expenditure of the Corporation for the last ten years, in respect of the maintenance of the poor, and support of the establishment, the expence which each parish has been to the Corporation, and the contribution in money made by it to defray such expence; together with the degree of excess or deficiency in which each parish has so contributed. And by which it most clearly appears that the excess of payment by 16 parishes, in the course of ten years, has amounted to the sum of £7,759 and upwards, of which the parish of Ufford has paid the sum of £752 14s. 2d. and that the deficiency of contribution of 17 parishes, for the same period, amounts to the sum of £8,625 and upwards.

This great and injurious inequality calls most imperiously for regulation, and precludes all necessity of pointing out how much it must be the interest of the owners and occupiers in the 16 aggrieved parishes to lend their aid towards correcting this very oppressive evil. For doing this, the present meeting affords them an opportunity of which, I trust, they will avail themselves.

As one individual who am in some degree interested in the question, I have felt it my duty, and have spared neither time nor trouble to investigate as accurately as I could, the accounts of the Corporation; and I have from the result of that investigation, endeavoured to form a plan, which I shall beg permission to submit to the meeting, for the more just distribution of the burthen, and a more perfect equalization of the assessments of each of the incorporated parishes, and also for the liquidating the existing debt within a given period.

I beg leave again to press the urgent and indispensable necessity of a full attendance, at the time and place proposed,

and am gentlemen,
with great respect,
your most faithful and obedient servant.

Huntingfield.   (signed)   Wm. Philpot

Dear Sir,

As Mr S. did not wish to part with the letter, I have taken an opportunity of making a copy from it, which you have on the other side, the words in pencil were written in the original and the rest part printed, except the signature which was of course written.

Hope you arrived safe with respect to Mrs W.

I remain,
yours very respectfully,
R. W. Oldham

Melton House.
30th March 1810.

NB. The letter was addressed to the Churchwarden and Overseers of the parish of Ufford, Suffolk.

56. Letter to the Commons Committee by the Incorporation arguing against the opponent's clauses, 2 April 1810[25]

The opposition to the Loes and Wilford Poor Bill have prepared a clause from the averages they have taken from the accounts of the Corporation of the sums expended

---

25 SROI ADA11/A/A/1/6.

by each parish, as well as of those poor maintained in the House belonging to each parish, and which average it is understood is to be taken every 4 years. The clerk has been instructed in part to take this average, and which he can in some measure accomplish, but not yet accurately although he is very well versed in figures. And it is also to be understood that the present clerk is not very likely to continue in such office, being there at present only until he can find a better situation. And if this intended clause of theirs could be easily worked upon, it would materially injure the present condition of the Poor and those institutions are intended to better the condition of the poor, for overseers, when applied to by a poor person for relief, would say no! You want no relief and would not apply for it because he would have to pay such relief out of his parish, or the assessment would have to be regulated by the quantum of relief given in each parish, therefore the condition of the poor would be injured, and the condition of the farmer benefitted. And the case of some of the parishes in these Hundreds (which consist of only very small farmers and many paupers) would be very materially felt by their mode being adopted. And it would inevitably make these small farmers paupers themselves. This clause of theirs being adopted would have the same effect ultimately as the clauses contained in the Cosford Hundred Act of Parliament which clauses they at first proposed to be inserted in this Act of Parliament, but which they have since abandoned.

There are in these hundreds several parishes called favourite parishes on account of what they call good natured Gentlemen living therein, and the poor flock into those parishes and do what they can to gain settlement therein, when on the contrary they flee from parishes differently situated. And if any of the very poor parishes should be visited with any sickness and heavy expences it will under this clause be the total ruin of these parishes, or at least the poor inhabitants therein. Surely it is land that ought to contribute to the maintenance of the poor, and not to raise the money from those indigent parishes as by this clause is proposed.

Their petition states four parishes as aggrieved, but there is only one person, a small farmer, signed for the parish of Charsfield. The petition is signed only by fourteen persons.

57. Additional brief on the part of the Incorporation in support of the bill[26]

In Parliament.

Loes and Wilford Hundreds Poor Bill.2 April 1810.

Additional brief on the part of the Petitioners in support of the Bill.

This Petition and Bill having gone through the Committee of the House and read a second time, a petition was presented against it by four parishes out of the 33 which compose these Hundreds. And counsel were heard before the Committee of the House, and witnesses examined on both sides. But the Committee would not then decide and adjourned the further hearing the 2nd April, and also recommended to the parties to meet in the country and for them to endeavour to meet each other by way of compromise. Upon a return into the country, a meeting of the Committee first appointed to frame the bill was held at the House of Industry. At which meeting (which composed the Gentlemen who petitioned for the bill), Mr Philpot and his friends attended, by invitation. And clauses were agreed upon in order to meet the wishes of them, the petitioning parishes, and they was directed to call a meeting of

---

26   SROI ADA11/A/A/1/6.

the owners & occupiers of lands within the said Hundreds to consider the propriety of introducing these clauses for equalizing the several rates & assessments within the several parishes in the said Hundreds and for discharging the debt. This meeting was accordingly called by public advertisement, and was held at Wickham Market within the said Hundreds, on Thursday 29 March. But previous to that, & unknown to the petitioners for the bill, Mr Philpot sent a most pressing circular letter to the 16 supposed aggrieved parishes, stating to them that they were very much aggrieved and that they had in 10 yrs. paid a large sum of money more than they ought to have paid. And requesting particularly that some of the reputable occupiers from their parishes would make a point of attending and stating that this great & injurious inequality called most imperiously for regulation and proclaimed all necessity of pointing out how much it must be the interest of the owners & occupiers in the 16 aggrieved parishes to lend their aid towards correcting such oppressive evil for doing, which the present meeting afforded them an opportunity of which he trusted they would avail themselves. And as one individual who was in some degree interested in the question he had felt it his duty ◇ to investigate as accurately as he could the accounts of the Corporation and he has from the result of such investigation endeavoured to form a plan which he should beg permission to submit to the meeting for the more just distribution of the burthen and more perfect equalization of the assessments of each of the Incorporated parishes, and also for liquidating the debt within a given period. And he also stated in this letter that the excess in assessments by 16 parishes in the course of ten years amounted to the sum of £7,759 & upwards & that the deficiency of contribution of 17 parishes for the same period amounted to the sum of £8,625 and upwards. And he concluded by begging leave again to press the urgent and indispensable necessity of a full attendance at the time and place proposed.

This was duly circulated into the 16 aggrieved parishes & not one into the other parishes and it was kept so great a secret that no one of the Gentlemen who composed the meeting for framing the bill knew of this until they came to the meeting at Wickham Market. This meeting was convened at 10 o'clock and Mr Whitbread, (in the absence of Mr Jenney, the former chairman), was called to the chair. The advertisement which called the meeting was read after which a clause was proposed & read by the Revd Mr Turner for equalizing the rates & assessments for the maintenance of the poor upon a certain ratio, and was in substance agreed to subject to the perusal & adjudctn of counsel on both sides. Another clause was also proposed & read by Mr Turner which was for paying of the debt agreeable to the old assessment and which was at first agreed by the meeting to be left to the determination of the Committee of the House of Commons. But after further conversation, and part of the meeting were gone, nothing would satisfy a part of the meeting unless this clause, or the support thereof, was put to the vote, viz. whether the debt should be paid off by the old assessment or according to the new ratio of assessment for the maintenance of the poor etc. And upon the meetings dividing, there appeared 33 for paying the debt by the new ratio, and 25 for paying the debt according to the old ratio of assessment. Upon this the meeting was dissolved, and the Gentlemen on behalf of the Bill retired to another room and the determination of several of those attending the Committee of the House of Commons. And Mr Whitbread, the chairman, Mr Kilderbee & Mr Turner are come on behalf of themselves, and the other Gentlemen composing the Committee.

It seems very singular that such a man as Mr Philpot should come into these Hundreds to oppose the principal Gents. & land owners by adopting his rule & system only, and which he positively insists upon shall be only observed. To confute

302

the principal of Mr Philpot's printed statement the following short extract from two parishes are stated and will show the fallacy of the printed one

	Annl. expence in the House	Out relief to paupers belonging only	Annual assessment	Deficiency of contribution
Hacheston	204 17 8½	36 19 11¾	190 12 0	51 5 3 ¼
		and not 102 7 7 as stated by Mr Philpot.		
				excess
Eyke	63 0 10	18 2 10	136 7 0	55 5 6
		and not 5 1 3¾ as stated by Mr Philpot.		

There was not sufficient time to get from other parishes a statement as above, but these two will sufficiently shew how erroneous Mr Philpot's printed statement must be, particularly as to relief to paupers relieved in one parish belonging to another, and also as to out relief to paupers relieved in parishes out of the Hundreds and belonging to parishes within the Hundreds.

58. John Wood's expenses in overseeing the bill through Parliament[27]

	£	s.	d.
Perusing settling & altering the Bill	3	3	0
Copies of Committee on Petition		10	
Settling report & drawing order of leave		13	4
Making copy of the Bill for the House	1	14	
Drawing brief & fair copy for the speaker		10	6
Copies of Committee on the Bill		10	
Preparing amendments for the Committee		10	
Filling up & altering Bills		16	
Copies of clauses	1	12	
Paid House fees on petition & bill	31	18	8
Committee Clerks *do*	31	2	
Housekeepers & messengers	15	8	
Doorkeepers for delivering printed bills	1	1	
Completing bills for ingrossing clerks	1	10	
Paid ingrossing fees	17	2	
For assistance to examine Inq & Proofs		12	
Printing the Bill and Act	12	12	
Correspondence	2	2	
Sending a bill to the Lord in the Chair & attedg him	2	2	
Paid House fees at the Lords	54		
Fees to yeoman usher & door keeper	5	5	
For order of committee	1	1	
Swearing witnesses		2	
Committee clerks fees	4	4	
Porters, small gratuities & other incidentals	2	10	
Solicitation fee	26	5	
	218	15	6

May 17 1810.

---

[27] SROI ADA11/A/A/1/6.

Rec'd of John Wood Esq. the sum of two hundred and eighteen pounds 15/6.

59. Letter from R. Oldham to Mr Shuldham and Mr Philpot stating that the Incorporation is not bound to pay the opposing parishes' costs[28]

29 December 1810

Sir,

I am desired to communicate to you, that in consequence of an order at the last Quarterly Meeting of the Directors & Guardians of the poor within the Hundreds of Loes and Wilford, Mr Nolan's opinion has been taken, whether the Directors & Guardians were authorized under the late Act of Parliament to pay all or any part of the expences of the opposing parishes in obtaining the same. His opinion was that the Directors & Acting Guardians were neither bound nor authorized to direct their Treasurer to pay all or any part of the expences incurred by the opposing parishes.

I am Sir,

Your obedt hble sevt,

R.W. Oldham

Melton House, 29th Dec. 1810.

Copy of the above sent to Mr Shuldham and to Mr Philpot.

R.W.O.

Mr Nolan's words are

I am of opinion that the Directors & Acting Guardians are neither bound nor authorized to direct their Treasurer to pay all or any part of the expences incurred by the opposition parishes under the circumstances stated in the case.

Copy of letter to Messrs, Shuldham and Philpot 29th Dec 1810,

60. Letter from Mr Philpot requesting the Incorporation meet the opposing parishes' legal expenses and the reply from R. Oldham on behalf of the Incorporation[29]

9 January 1811

Huntingfield, Jan 9 1811.

Sir,

When I had the honour of attending the last quarterly meeting of the Directors and Acting Guardians of the poor within the incorporated hundreds of Loes and Wilford, for the purpose of soliciting from them, on the behalf of those parishes which had petitioned against the Bill brought into Parliament last session, under the sanction of the Corporation an allowance of the expenses which such parishes had incurred in consequence of the part they had felt it incumbent upon them to take throughout the progress of that Bill, the gentlemen present expressed a wish to defer the discussion of the subject till the following meeting when they requested me to state my claim in writing, and promised that it should then be taken into consideration and determined upon. In consequence of which, Sir, I now take the liberty of addressing you.

In urging the claim in question, 'tis not at all necessary for me to enter into the causes, which gave rise to the differences of opinion that prevailed between the

---

[28] SROI ADA11/A/A/1/6.
[29] SROI ADA11/A/Q/2/1(6).

Corporation and the contending parishes, as to the propriety or justice of continuing, by the new Bill, that old principle of assessment, which had been recognized and established by the former acts; nor will I trespass so far the time of the meeting, as again to go over these grounds of opposition or rather self-defence, which the aggrieved parishes were compelled to take, in combating the re-enactment of a principle so erroneous and injurious, as that was proved to be.

The whole circumstances of the case, from its commencement to its termination, must be in the recollection of the meeting: and the result has proved the tenability of those grounds, and has also, I trust, justified with every impartial, reasoning and liberal mind, the conduct of the aggrieved parishes in maintaining them.

It, therefore, only remains for me to endeavour to impress upon the minds of the meeting, the propriety of the present application, and the reasonableness and justice, and I may add (with submission) the legal obligation, on the part of the Directors and Acting Guardians of acceding to it.

In the procuring of the new Act in its present form, it is plainly to be seen that many great expenses must have been incurred, not only by those gentlemen who, in their capacity of Directors, have the peculiar management of the affairs of the Corporation, but by those aggrieved parishes, by whose exertions the most effectual and beneficial clauses of the Act were obtained.

That the expenses which the parishes in question have thus incurred by their successful exertions for the general good of the whole incorporated hundreds, ought to be borne by such parishes exclusively, 'tis not either in justice or reason to suppose. They therefore now apply to have them allowed and reimbursed out of the general funds of the Corporation, under the sanction of the last clause but one in the Act, which in acts "That all the charges and expenses incident to and attending the obtaining and passing of the Act shall be paid by the Treasurer out of the funds of the Corporation."

On the part of the Directors, it has been urged, that it is altogether without precedent, to allow the expenses incurred by an opposing party; and that were they disposed to do it, they would not be warranted in allowing them by any clause or words of the incorporating act; and any rate which they might make on the hundreds, for raising the money, might be opposed by some or other of the parishes.

On the part of the parishes in question, I beg to contend, that they are incorrectly designated as an opposing party; for that they were labouring for the same end to which the exertions of the Directors tended, the general befit of the hundreds at large; and that the only difference between them was, as to the means by which this end was best to be accomplished; they sought not their own individual advantage, to the exclusion of the other parishes, but merely one common general benefit in which all were equally to participate.

That when the scheme of alteration was first suggested, it was submitted with all possible respect, and in the least expensive manner, to the Directors etc. of the hundreds. That when the meeting of the hundreds was called, the whole plan, which has since in a great measure adopted, was submitted to them; and that had there been at that time a sufficient confidence placed in the proposers and their plan, the opposition, which the rejection of it afterwards occasioned in Parliament, would never have existed, and consequently little or no expense, comparatively, would have been incurred. That the little encouragement they met with in their outset, they were, of necessity, driven to the more expensive, but only effectual method, of having their suggestions duly weighed, and of being adopted, if entitled to credit and confidence: that of submitting their plan and calculations to the Committee of the House, who had the charge of the Bill. The result of that Committee's deliberations has incontestably proved them to have been well grounded in their opposition; for the most material parts of their plan, indeed not merely parts, but even the detail of it, have been adopted, and now form the most prominent feature in the new incorporating act. That the several facts, which were proved by the witnesses before the Committee, brought up at a very considerable expense, could have been admitted and allowed without this formality, had the contest been conducted with more amity, and less suspicion and jealousy. It is, therefore, fairly to be contended, that as the expenses have been necessarily forced on these parishes, by the opposition and resistance of the Corporation, they have a most legitimate claim upon the funds of the Corporation, to reimburse them. The reasonableness of their suggestions, and the adoption of not only the principle but the detail of them, clearly prove that they were in the right, and consequently warrant a conclusion that the Corporation were in the wrong.

That, therefore, the parishes have a right to say, on their part, "How with propriety can the expenses of an ill grounded opposition to us, be a legitimate subject for the appropriation of the funds of the Corporation? Why should not the individuals themselves, in the individual parishes, if there were any, bear these expenses? Why are the whole hundreds to be called on to bear expense which has been improvidently incurred, and particularly why are those parishes, which were compelled to resistance, to contribute? Merely because the purse of the hundreds is in the hands of the Corporation, and the strings of it can be at will undrawn, to reimburse those expenses which the holders of it have incurred, and conceive legitimate, and shut against those individual parishes, who have contended with them; altho' the result has clearly proved that in the latter instance, the expense has been forced upon these parishes, by their opposers refusing to admit those suggestions which they were afterwards compelled by reason and conviction to adopt, as correct, rational and essential to the wellbeing of the Corporation; and in the former instance, that those of the Corporation, which all the parishes are now called upon to contribute towards, were unnecessarily and injudiciously incurred.

It cannot, therefore, be contended that the Corporation has no power to authorize the payment of the expenses in question: for it was in fact, with the Corporation itself, that the contest originated and by that contest the large expenses incurred were occasioned. If there be anything legitimate in the expenses incurred, surely the complaining parishes have the greatest right to assume distinction, for 'tis their exertions, and their expenses which have gained the most material and most beneficial part of the new Act. That desirable equalization of the burthens and contributions, which had been so long looked for and at last with so much difficulty obtained. If both parties have contributed to the same end, upon what principle of justice ought the expenses of the one to be rejected and those of the other allowed?

Besides, I beg further to contend that the clause above alluded to, is sufficiently comprehensive to justify an allowance of the expenses in question – for how would the act itself, which is in a great measure formed by, nay derives its most essential and prominent features from the suggestions of the parishes in question, have been obtained, but for their exertions? And the expenses occasioned by such exertions, are indisputable 'incident to and attended the obtaining of the act.'

I have thus endeavoured, Sir, and I trust not unsuccessfully, (certainly in the absence of every wish or intention to give the slightest offence to the meeting either collectively or individually) to shew both the reasonableness, justice and legality of the claim which the parishes in question have requested me to urge on their behalf; and with due deference to the learned counsel whose opinion has been taken, and a copy of which has been lately transmitted to me by your clerk. I beg to submit that their right to have their expenses allowed is legitimate, and ought to be recognized by the Directors and their reimbursement ordered out of the funds of the Corporation. I am further authorized to say that the parishes are ready to lay the amount of their expenses before the Directors for their taxation and correction and to accept whatever sum they in their justice shall think proper to allow.

I beg to apologise, sir, for having detained the attention of yourself and the meeting so long and have the honour to be

Sir, with all possible respect,
Your very obed^t humble servant,
Wm Philpot.

Reply:
Wickham 10 Jan. 1811.
Sir,

In answer to your letter to the chairman of the quarterly meeting of the Directors etc. of the poor within the hundreds of Loes and Wilford dated the 9th inst. I am desired to inform you they feel themselves bound to abide by the opinion of Mr Nolan as stated in my letter to you of the 29th December last, by which they are not authorized to order their Treasurer to pay any part of the expenses incurred by the opposing parishes.

I am, sir etc.   R.W. Oldham.

FIFTH QUARTERLY MINUTE BOOK
4 January 1813–9 July 1818[1]

7 January 1813

Directors	Guardians
John Syer M.D.	Mr John Waller
Revd Mr Brooke	Mr William Kitson
Revd Mr Chilton	
Mr Thomas Waller	
Mr Henry Edwards	
Mr Thomas Simpson	
Mr Jeptha Waller	
Jacob Whitbread Esq.	
Revd Mr Turner	
Revd Mr Isaac Clarke	
Revd Mr Kilderbee	
Mr Dikes	

Ordered that the assessments for the ensuing Quarter be made in the following manner viz. the same as last Quarter viz. 1½ rate. That the out allowances and bills having been examined at the previous meeting be forthwith paid by the Treasurer.

That the solicitor do defend the appeals to order of removal of the cases Framsden appellants and Brandeston respondents, and Framsden appellants and Letheringham respondents. The parish officers of Brandeston and Letheringham having received notices to that effect.

That Ann the daughter of Colin Holmes of Kettleburgh aged [ ] be apprenticed to [ ] Capon of Framlingham with a premium of thirty pounds.

That the Chaplains salary be advanced from £35 per annum to £40 per annum to take place from this day.

That the parishes formerly under the care of Mr Ashwell be placed under the care of Mr Hughes at the same salary as Mr Ashwell had.

Ordered that the following allowances be granted:

Parish residg	Parish belonging to		Weekly	Quarter		
Ash		Widow Bailey	2s. 0d.	1	6	0
	Eyke	Widow Clarke	2s. 6d.	1	12	6
		Widow Haddock	1s. 6d.	0	19	6
		Widow Holmes	2s. 6d.	1	12	6
		Widow King	1s. 6d.	0	19	6
		Widow Muttin	6s. 0d.	3	18	0
	Kettleburgh	Widow Ringe	1s. 6d.	0	19	6
		Widow Robinson	1s. 0d.	0	13	0
	Hatcheston	Widow Skinner	2s. 0d.	1	6	0

---

[1]   SROI ADA11/A/B/1/5.

Alderton	Deborah Skinner	1s. 6d.	0	19	6
	Mary Ann Downing	1s. 0d.	0	13	0
	Hannah Holmes	1s. 6d.	0	19	6
	Hannah Kemp	3s. 0d.	1	19	0
	William Ling's daughter	1s. 0d.	0	13	0
	Thomas Ling	1s. 0d.	0	13	0
	John Youngman	1s. 6d.	0	19	6
			20	3	0
Brandeston	Widow Baker	1s. 6d.	0	19	6
	do Boon sen.	2s. 6d.	1	12	6
	do Boon jun.	1s. 6d.	0	19	6
	do Brianton	3s. 0d.	1	19	0
	do Edwards	2s. 0d.	1	6	0
Earl Soham	do Spalding	1s. 6d.	0	19	6
Ash	do Wade	1s. 6d.	0	19	6
	Elizabeth Boon	1s. 6d.	0	19	6
	Joseph Harvey's child	2s. 0d.	1	6	0
	Richard Herrington's grandchild	1s. 0d.	0	13	0
	Robert Jay	3s. 0d.	1	19	0
	Eliz. Read 2 B.B. children	3s. 0d.	1	19	0
	Mary Reeve 1 do	1s. 6d.	0	19	6
	Mary Chaplin	2s. 6d.	1	12	6
	James Nunn	2s. 0d.	1	6	0
	Robert Callum	1s. 6d.	0	19	6
			20	9	6
Butley	Edward Cattermole	1s. 0d.	0	13	0
	Ann Clarke	1s. 6d.	0	19	6
	Mary Cooper	1s. 6d.	0	19	6
Sutton	[ ] Crane's child	1s. 0d.	0	13	6
	Sarah Crosby	1s. 6d.	0	19	6
	Mary Manning	1s. 0d.	0	13	0
	Sarah Scotchmer	1s. 6d.	0	19	6
Kettleburgh	Widow Smith	1s. 6d.	0	19	6
	James Warner	2s. 0d.	1	6	0
	Widow Dowsing	2s. 0d.	1	6	0
Bredfield	William Clarke	3s. 0d.	1	19	0
			11	7	6
Charsfield	Widow Atkins	3s. 0d.	1	19	0
Dallingho	do do child	1s. 6d.	0	19	6
	do Birch	1s. 0d.	0	13	0
Creetingham	do Godbold	1s. 0d.	0	13	0
	do Flory	1s. 6d	0	19	6
	Mary Brown	1s. 0d.	0	13	0
	Samuel Block	2s. 0d.	1	6	0
	James Block's wife and children	4s. 0d.	2	12	0
	Widow Buckle	3s. 0d.	1	19	0
	James Crane	2s. 6d.	1	12	6

Easton	Deborah Driver	2s. 0d.	1	6	0
	John Durrant	2s. 0d.	1	6	0
Hacheston	Sarah Gilman	2s. 0d.	1	6	0
	Abel Herring	4s. 6d.	2	18	0
Earl Soham	Hannah Long	1s. 0d.	0	13	0
	Mary Maulden	1s. 6d.	0	19	6
Kenton	Sophia Maulden	1s. 6d.	0	19	6
Monewden	Henry Rattle	2s. 0d.	1	6	0
do	Elizabeth Rattle	1s. 0d.	0	13	0
	Benjamin Read	2s. 0d.	1	6	0
	Mary Rose	1s. 0d.	0	13	0
	John Spendlove	1s. 0d.	0	13	0
Wickham	Mary Spendlove	1s. 6d.	0	19	6
	Mary Wythe	1s. 6d.	0	19	6
			29	5	0

Creetingham	Widow Barber	1s. 3d.	0	16	3
	do Brown	1s. 0d.	0	13	0
	do Harvey	1s. 6d.	0	19	6
	do Spink	1s. 6d.	0	19	6
	Mary Cook	1s. 0d.	0	13	0
	Susan Godbold	4s. 0d.	2	12	0
	Hannah Marjoram	1s. 3d.	0	16	3
	Mary Moyse	1s. 6d.	0	19	6
	William Moss	2s. 0d.	1	6	0
	Ann Nicholls	2s. 0d.	1	6	0
	John Tye and wife	1s. 0d.	0	13	0
	John Avis	2s. 0d.	1	6	0
	Samuel Peck	1s. 6d.	0	19	6
			13	19	6

Dallingho	Widow Keable	2s. 0d.	1	6	0
	do Pipe	1s. 6d.	0	19	6
	Sarah Barrell	1s. 6d.	0	19	6
Petistree	Joseph Button	2s. 0d.	1	6	0
	Robert Clarke	2s. 0d.	1	6	0
	Jane Garnham	1s. 6d.	0	19	6
	Stephen Goymer	2s. 6d.	1	12	6
	Sarah Lanham	1s. 6d.	0	19	6
Petistree	Joseph Lanham's son	1s. 6d.	0	19	6
Kettleburgh	Mary Nicholls	1s. 6d.	0	19	6
	Robert Orsborn	2s. 0d.	1	6	0
	Samuel Pulham	2s. 0d.	1	6	0
	Ann Rosier B.B. child	1s. 6d.	0	19	6
			14	19	0

Earl Soham	Widow Burrows	1s. 0d.	0	13	0
	do Cracknell	2s. 0d.	1	6	0
	do Creasy	1s. 0d.	0	13	0
Hoo	do Jennings	2s. 0d.	1	6	0

	do Lambert	1s.	0d.	0	13	0
	do Pettit	4s.	0d.	2	12	0
	do Read	1s.	0d.	0	13	0
	do Wade	3s.	0d.	1	19	0
	do Watling	1s.	0d.	0	13	0
	Edmund Barker	1s.	0d.	0	13	0
	Mary England	1s.	6d.	0	19	6
	Henry Fellingham's wife	1s.	0d.	0	13	0
Creetingham	Robert Lanham's daughter	1s.	6d.	0	19	6
	Susan Manning	1s.	6d.	0	19	6
	Sarah Potkins	1s.	0d.	0	13	0
	Mary Runicles	1s.	0d.	0	13	0
	John Sills	1s.	0d.	0	13	0
	William Smith and wife	2s.	6d.	1	12	6
	Judith Warner	1s.	0d.	0	13	0
	Martha Watling	1s.	6d.	0	19	6
	Susanna Woolnough	1s.	6d.	0	19	6
	Thomas Adams	2s.	0d.	1	6	0
				22	2	0
Easton	Widow Cady	3s.	6d.	2	5	6
Rendlesham	*do* Death	2s.	0d.	1	6	0
Brandeston	*do* Garrod	2s.	0d.	1	6	0
	do Long	2s.	0d.	1	6	0
	do Smith	2s.	0d.	1	6	0
Charsfield	Thomas Bennett	4s.	0d.	2	12	0
Wickham	Lydia Clayton	1s.	6d.	0	19	6
	John Frost	2s.	0d.	1	6	0
	Thomas Grimwood	3s.	0d.	1	19	0
	Robert Lawrence	1s.	6d.	0	19	6
Kenton	Susan Long	1s.	6d.	0	19	6
	Robert Hayward	3s.	0d.	1	19	0
	John Plant	1s.	6d.	0	19	6
	Mary Plant	1s.	0d.	0	13	0
Dallingho	Hannah Read	2s.	6d.	1	12	6
Earl Soham	Lionel Upson	1s.	0d.	0	13	0
				23	8	0
Eyke	Widow Barham	1s.	0d.	0	13	0
Hacheston	*do* Brinkley	1s.	0d.	0	13	0
Rendlesham	*do* Girling	2s.	0d.	1	6	0
	do Gooding	1s.	6d.	0	19	6
Ash	*do* Kettle	1s.	6d.	0	19	6
do	*do* King	1s.	0d.	0	13	0
	do Mossley	1s.	6d.	0	19	6
Creetingham	*do* Orsborn	1s.	0d.	0	13	0
Hacheston	*do* Sarah Clark	1s.	6d.	0	19	6
	John Howes	1s.	6d.	0	19	6
	Esther Smith	1s.	0d.	0	13	0
Bromeswell	Jane Read	1s.	0d.	0	13	0

311

do	Robert Read's wife	1s. 6d.	0	19	6
			11	1	0

Hacheston Marlesford	Widow Aldrich	2s. 0d.	1	6	0
	do Block	1s. 6d.	0	19	6
Ash	*do* Coleman	2s. 0d.	1	6	0
do	*do* Ling	2s. 0d.	1	6	0
	do Curtis	4s. 0d.	2	12	0
	do Garrard	1s. 6d.	0	19	6
Brandeston	Ralph Cotton and wife	6s. 0d.	3	18	0
Sutton	Ann Farrer B.B. child	1s. 6d.	0	19	6
	John Howard	3s. 0d.	1	19	0
	Mary Mann B.B. child	1s. 6d.	0	19	6
Letherngham	Timothy Mattin	2s. 0d.	1	6	0
	Elizabeth Orsborn	1s. 6d.	0	19	6
Marlesford	Elizabeth Porter	2s. 0d.	1	6	0
Bromeswell	Thomas Read	1s. 6d.	0	19	6
	John Scrutton	2s. 0d.	1	6	0
Wickham	Elizabeth Wright	1s. 6d.	0	19	6
Easton	Margaret Wright's child	1s. 6d.	0	19	6
	Charles Mann	1s. 0d.	0	13	0
			24	14	0

Hoo	William Dennant	3s. 0d.	1	19	0
Kenton	Robert Hill	2s. 6d.	1	12	6
do	Edward Parker	1s. 0d.	0	13	0
Brandeston	Widow King	2s. 0d.	1	6	0
Bawdsey	James Sawyer's daughter	2s. 6d.	1	12	6
			7	3	0

Kenton	Jonathan Allen's children	2s. 6d.	1	12	6
	Mary Banister	1s. 6d.	0	19	6
	Calver's child	1s. 6d.	0	19	6
	John church	8s. 0d.	5	4	0
	Widow Collin's children	3s. 0d.	1	19	0
	Widow Parker	1s. 6d.	0	19	6
	Sarah Porcher	1s. 6d.	0	19	6
	Samuel Roper's wife	1s. 6d.	0	19	6
			13	13	0

Kettleburgh Hoo	Widow Cracknell	2s. 0d.	1	6	0
	do England	1s. 6d.	0	19	6
Earl Soham	*do* Keer	1s. 6d.	0	19	6
	do Newman	3s. 0d.	1	19	0
	do Nicholls	3s. 0d.	1	19	0
	do Miller	2s. 0d.	1	6	0
	do Smith	1s. 6d.	0	19	6
Monewden	*do* Smith	2s. 0d.	1	6	0
	do Stannard	1s. 6d.	0	19	6
	Lucy Day B.B. child	1s. 6d.	0	19	6

			£	s	d
	Benj. Dove (dead 18 Jan. pd. 3 wks)	2s. 6d.	0	7	6
	John Kent	3s. 0d.	1	19	0
	Robert Spalding	1s. 6d.	0	19	6
	Widow Coats	1s. 6d.	0	19	6
			11	19	0
Letheringham	Hannah Garnham	2s. 0d.	1	6	0
	Widow Markham	1s. 6d.	0	19	6
Rendlesham	Widow Pollard	1s. 6d.	0	19	6
			2	5	0
Marlesford	Widow Burrell	1s. 6d.	0	19	6
	do Carr	1s. 6d.	0	19	6
Hacheston	*do* Claxon	1s. 0d.	0	13	0
Wickham	Samuel Bridges and wife	4s. 0d.	2	12	0
	Sarah Bickers	1s. 0d.	0	13	0
	Henry Cooper	1s. 6d.	0	19	6
	Elizabeth Downing	1s. 6d.	0	19	6
	Susan Farrer	1s. 6d.	0	19	6
	Elizabeth Goldsmith	2s. 0d.	1	6	0
	Samuel Markham	2s. 0d.	1	6	0
	Thomas Markin	2s. 0d.	1	6	0
	Sarah Paternoster	1s. 6d.	0	19	6
	Frances Rose B.B. child	1s. 6d.	0	19	6
	Ann Skeet	1s. 6d.	0	19	6
	Jacob Watling	1s. 0d.	0	13	0
			16	5	0
Monewden	Ann Boon	2s. 0d.	1	6	0
Creetingham	John Browning's wife	1s. 6d.	0	19	6
	Benjamin Curtis's wife	2s. 6d.	1	12	6
Creetingham	Sarah Cullum	1s. 6d.	0	19	6
Charsfield	William Durrant	1s. 6d.	0	19	6
	Widow Fuller	2s. 0d.	1	6	0
	Richard Woods	1s. 0d.	0	13	0
			7	16	0
Rendlesham	Ash Widow Howard	1s. 6d.	0	19	6
	do Smith	1s. 6d.	0	19	6
	Rebecca Braham	1s. 0d.	0	13	0
	William Coleman	2s. 6d.	1	12	6
	Mary Crow B.B. child	1s. 6d.	0	19	6
	Margaret Farrow	1s. 6d.	0	19	6
	Hannah Holder	1s. 6d.	0	19	6
	Martha Howes	1s. 6d.	0	19	6
	Ann Jacques	1s. 6d.	0	19	6
	John Lincoln's wife	1s. 6d.	0	19	6
	Maria Reeve 2 B.B. children	3s. 0d.	1	19	0
	Esther Smith B.B. child	1s. 0d.	0	13	0

313

	Jane Vince B.B. child	1s. 6d.	0	19	6
			13	13	0

Loes	265	2	6
Wilford	299	16	3
Total	564	18	9

Alderton	Widow Bloomfield	5s. 0d.	3	5	0
Sutton	*do* Blaxhall	1s. 0d.	0	13	0
	do Clark	1s. 6d.	0	19	6
	do Cone	1s. 6d.	0	19	6
	do Cook	1s. 0d.	0	13	0
	do Cooper	2s. 0d.	1	6	0
Bredfield	*do* Cousins	1s. 0d.	0	13	0
Ramsholt	*do* Girling 5 children	7s. 0d.	4	11	0
Boyton	*do* Girling	1s. 6d.	0	19	6
do	*do* Good	1s. 0d.	0	13	0
Bawdsey	*do* Heffer	1s. 0d.	0	13	0
do	*do* Leech	1s. 6d.	0	19	6
	do Holder	1s. 0d.	0	13	0
	do Horn	4s. 0d.	2	12	0
Wickham	*do* Johnson	2s. 0d.	1	6	0
	do Steward	1s. 6d.	0	19	6
Sutton	*do* Wright	1s. 6d.	0	19	6
	do Woolnough's child	1s. 0d.	0	13	0
	John Burrows	2s. 0d.	1	6	0
	Robert Cook	1s. 6d.	0	19	6
	John Scoggins 4 children	3s. 0d.	1	19	0
	Elizabeth Knights	1s. 0d.	0	13	0
	William Murrill	3s. 0d.	1	19	0
	Carey Wade	1s. 0d.	0	13	0
	Henry Woods	3s. 0d.	1	19	0
Sutton	Ann Woods B.B. child	1s. 0d.	0	13	0
Bawdsey	Barbara Clark	1s. 0d.	0	13	0
			34	8	6

Bawdsey Alderton	Widow Barrell	1s. 0d.	0	13	0
do	*do* Button	2s. 0d.	1	6	0
	do Freeman	1s. 0d.	0	13	0
	do Kettle	1s. 0d.	0	13	0
	do Moore	1s. 0d.	0	13	0
	do Pratt	3s. 6d.	2	5	6
	Lucy Clutterham B.B. child	0s. 6d.	0	6	6
	Henry Gooding	1s. 0d.	0	13	0
	James Hall	1s. 0d.	0	13	0
	James Peacock	1s. 6d.	0	19	6
	John Wilson's child	1s. 0d.	0	13	0
Alderton	Elizabeth Pooley	1s. 6d.	0	19	6
	Michael Stollery	2s. 6d.	1	12	6

	James Patridge's child	1s. 0d.	0	13	0
	Elizabeth Goodall	1s. 0d.	0	13	0
			13	6	6
Boulge Charsfield	James Abbott	1s. 0d.	0	13	0
	Abraham Marsh	2s. 0d.	1	6	0
	Jeremiah Marjoram	5s. 0d.	3	5	0
	Rebecca Marjoram	1s. 6d.	0	19	6
	Widow Row's child	1s. 6d.	0	19	6
	Edward Sheppard	2s. 0d.	1	6	0
			8	9	0
Boyton Alderton	Widow Brown	1s. 0d.	0	13	0
	do King	1s. 0d.	0	13	0
Rendlesham	*do* Minter	6s. 0d.	3	18	0
	do Pettitt	1s. 6d.	0	19	6
	do Long	3s. 6d.	2	5	6
Capel	Francis Ashkettle	2s. 0d.	1	6	0
do	James Chambers	2s. 6d.	1	12	6
	Miles Berry's wife	4s. 0d.	2	12	0
	Elizabeth Button	1s. 0d.	0	13	0
Alderton	William Gunnell	2s. 6d.	1	12	6
	Samuel Hart	1s. 6d.	0	19	6
	do for late Brown B.B. child	1s. 3d.	0	16	3
Sutton	Samuel Mays	3s. 0d.	1	19	0
	James Elvin	5s. 0d.	3	5	0
			23	4	9
Bredfield	Widow Allen	2s. 0d.	1	6	0
Bawdsey	*do* Brown	1s. 6d.	0	19	6
	do Button	2s. 0d.	1	6	0
	do Catchpole	1s. 0d.	0	13	0
	do Clarke	1s. 6d.	0	19	6
	do Lankester Sen.	1s. 6d.	0	19	6
	do Lankester Jun.	1s. 0d.	0	13	0
	do Thompson	3s. 0d.	1	19	0
	do Wright	8s. 0d.	5	4	0
	Francis Adams	2s. 0d.	1	6	0
	Robert Battle	2s. 0d.	1	6	0
	Hannah Dewell	1s. 0d.	0	13	0
Charsfield	William Durrant	1s. 0d.	0	13	0
	Sarah Good late Smith	1s. 6d.	0	19	6
	William Leggatt	1s. 6d.	0	19	6
Easton	Samuel Loom	2s. 0d.	1	6	0
	Margaret Marjoram	1s. 6d.	0	19	6
	Sarah Mays	1s. 0d.	0	13	0
			22	15	0
Bromeswell Sutton	Widow Branch	1s. 6d.	0	19	6
do	*do* Fuller	4s. 0d.	2	12	0

Alderton	*do* Flegg	1s. 6d.	0	19	6
Bredfield	*do* Crane	1s. 6d.	0	19	6
Hacheston	Thomas Farrow	1s. 6d.	0	19	6
	Francis Good	1s. 6d.	0	19	6
	Mary Keable	1s. 6d.	0	19	6
	Beliza Riches B.B. child	1s. 6d.	0	19	6
	Thomas Soames at Harleston	3s. 0d.	1	19	0
Sutton	Mary Stebbing	1s. 6d.	0	19	6
			12	7	0

Capel	Hollesley	Widow Clodd	6s. 0d.	3	18	0
	Boyton	*do* Jessup	2s. 6d.	1	12	6
	do	*do* Markham	2s. 0d.	1	6	0
	do	Ann Markham	1s. 0d.	0	13	0
	Butley	Hannah Cooper	1s. 6d.	0	19	6
	do	Widow Snowling	7s. 0d.	4	11	0
	Dallingho	John Wyard and wife	5s. 0d.	3	5	0
		Elizabeth Wolton	1s. 6d.	0	19	6
				17	4	6

Debach	John Crane's wife and 3 children	4s. 6d.	2	18	6
	Lydia Garnham	2s. 6d.	1	12	6
	John Kitson	2s. 6d.	1	12	6
			6	3	6

Hollesley	Alderton	Widow Creasy	0s. 6d.	0	6	6
	do	*do* Cook	1s. 0d.	0	13	0
	do	*do* Fox	1s. 0d.	0	13	0
		do Fox	7s. 6d.	4	17	6
		do Kettle	2s. 0d.	1	6	0
		do Lamb	1s. 0d.	0	13	0
		do Sawyer	3s. 0d.	1	19	0
		do Trusson	2s. 0d.	1	6	0
		do Woods	1s. 0d.	0	13	0
	Ash	*do* Wood's child	2s. 0d.	1	6	0
	Kenton	Robert Annis's daughter	1s. 0d.	0	13	0
		Mary Andrews	1s. 0d.	0	13	0
		James Battle	2s. 6d.	1	12	6
		Elizabeth Hunt	1s. 0d.	0	13	0
	Boyton	Ann Hunt	1s. 6d.	0	19	6
	do	Thomas Jennings	2s. 0d.	1	6	0
	Butley	William Kettle	1s. 0d.	0	13	0
				20	3	6

Melton	Widow Clow	2s. 0d.	1	6	0
	do Cooper	2s. 0d.	1	6	0
Sutton	*do* Flory	1s. 6d.	0	19	6
	do Sheldrake	1s. 0d.	0	13	0
	do Took	3s. 0d.	1	19	0
	do Tunmer	3s. 0d.	1	19	0

Dallingho	*do* Wright	1s. 6d.	0	19	6
	John Baines and wife	1s. 6d.	0	19	6
	Mary Clow B.B. child	1s. 0d.	0	13	0
	Crane's wife and child	1s. 0d.	0	13	0
	Sarah Denny	1s. 6d.	0	19	6
	Mary Ewers	1s. 6d.	0	19	6
	Sarah Girling	2s. 0d.	1	6	0
	Dennis Gibson	1s. 0d.	0	13	0
Bredfield	Thomas Goldsmith's wife and childn.	5s. 0d.	3	5	0
Ufford	Ann Stearn B.B child	1s. 0d.	0	13	0
	William Sawyer and wife	1s. 6d.	0	19	6
Boulge	John Topple and wife	3s. 0d.	1	19	0
	Thomas Ruth	5s. 0d.	3	5	0
	John Syres' wife	1s. 6d.	0	19	6
			26	6	6

Petistree	Widow King	1s. 6d.	0	19	6
	do Levett Sen.	1s. 6d.	0	19	6
	do Levett jun.	2s. 6d.	1	12	6
	Robert Barnard	2s. 6d.	1	12	6
	Robert Boon	2s. 6d.	1	12	6
	Sarah Boon	1s. 6d.	0	19	6
	Thomas Capon	1s. 6d.	0	19	6
	Martha Capon	1s. 6d.	0	19	6
Wickham	Martha Garnham	2s. 6d.	1	12	6
do	Susan Potkins	1s. 6d.	0	19	6
			12	7	0

Ramsholt	Elizabeth Allen	1s. 0d.	0	13	0
	Widow Ablett	3s. 0d.	1	19	0
	do Berry	3s. 0d.	1	19	0
Melton	*do* Orsborn	2s. 0d.	1	6	0
	do Whiting 7 children	7s. 0d.	4	11	0
			10	8	0

Shottisham	Widow Bird	1s. 6d.	0	19	6
Hollesley	*do* Brown	2s. 0d.	1	6	0
	do Brown at Trimley	5s. 6d.	3	11	6
	do Roper	1s. 0d.	0	13	0
	do Richardson	1s. 6d.	0	19	6
Hollesley	Henry Hunt and wife	4s. 0d.	2	12	0
	Thomas Symonds	2s. 0d.	1	6	0
			11	7	6

Sutton	Widow Boulter	2s. 0d.	1	6	0
	do Brown	1s. 6d.	0	19	6
Bawdsey	*do* Hammond	1s. 6d.	0	19	6
	do Howell	2s. 0d.	1	6	0
	do Hudson	1s. 6d.	0	19	6
Marlesford	*do* Nicholls	1s. 6d.	0	19	6

	do Spall	2s. 0d.	1	6	0
	do Steel	1s. 0d.	0	13	0
	John Austen	2s. 0d.	1	6	0
	Buckle's wife and 2 children	2s. 6d.	1	12	6
	Warner Gooch's daughter an idiot	1s. 0d.	0	13	0
	William Spall's wife	2s. 0d.	1	6	0
	Thomas Stebbings Jun.	1s. 6d.	0	19	6
			14	6	0
Ufford	Widow Amis	1s. 0d.	0	13	0
	do Andrews	1s. 6d.	0	19	6
	do Bennett	1s. 6d.	0	19	6
Ash	*do* Brightwell	1s. 6d.	0	19	6
do	*do* Hawkins	2s. 0d.	1	6	0
	do Howell	1s. 6d.	0	19	6
	do Parker	1s. 6d.	0	19	6
Shottisham	*do* Pearsons	1s. 6d.	0	19	6
	do Smith	3s. 0d.	1	19	0
	do Stimpson	3s. 0d.	1	19	0
	John Bloomfield	1s. 6d.	0	19	6
Petistree	Charles Bloomfield	5s. 0d.	3	5	0
Wickham	Samuel Buckle's wife and child	1s. 6d.	0	19	6
Melton	Jonathan Hutton	2s. 0d.	1	6	0
Bromeswell	Richard Keable	1s. 6d.	0	19	6
	Martha List	2s. 0d.	1	6.	0
	Sarah Prew	2s. 0d.	1	6	0
	John Shreeve	2s. 6d.	1	12	6
	John Skeet sen. and wife	3s. 0d.	1	19	0
	Robert Wolton	2s. 0d.	1	6	0
	Hannah Wolton	1s. 6d.	0	19	6
			27	12	6
Wickham	Widow Beart	2s. 0d.	1	6	0
	do Broom and daughter	2s. 0d.	1	6	0
	do Curtis at Snape	1s. 6d.	0	19	6
	do Fysh	1s. 6d.	0	19	6
	do Garnham	1s. 6d.	0	19	6
Hacheston	*do* Hart	5s. 0d.	3	5	0
	do Harvey	1s. 6d.	0	19	6
	do Hewett	2s. 0d.	1	6	0
Petistree	*do* Jackson	2s. 0d.	1	6	0
	do Parsons	1s. 6d.	0	19	6
	do Plant	2s. 0d.	1	6	0
	do Plowman	2s. 0d.	1	6	0
Hacheston	*do* Sparrow	2s. 0d.	1	6	0
Bawdsey	*do do* for child Holder	1s. 6d.	0	19	6
Creetingham	Ann Barnard	2s. 0d.	1	6	0
Hacheston	John Brown	1s. 0d.	0	13	0
	William Burrows	1s. 6d.	0	19	6
	Elizabeth Burrows	1s. 6d.	0	19	6

William Buckle and wife	4s. 0d.	2	12	0
Martha Curtis	1s. 6d.	0	19	6
Mary Drake's child	0s. 6d.	0	6	6
James Hewett	1s. 6d.	0	19	6
James Lambert	1s. 6d.	0	19	6
Elizabeth Pendle BB child	2s. 0d.	1	6	0
Mary Rands	1s. 6d.	0	19	6
Thomas Spink	1s. 6d.	0	19	6
Phoebe Taylor	1s. 6d.	0	19	6
Christian Taylor's BB child	1s. 6d.	0	19	6
Susan Tyler	1s. 0d.	0	13	0
William Tyler	2s. 0d.	1	6	0
Samuel Warren	1s. 6d.	0	19	6
Thomas Woolnough	1s. 6d.	0	19	6
Hannah Yallop	2s. 0d.	1	6	0
		39	6	6
Wilford		299	16	3

8 April 1813

	Directors Present	Guardians
	Jacob Whitbread Esq.	Mr John Wolton
	Mr Samuel Gross	Mr John Waller
	Mr Thomas Waller	Mr Thomas Garney
	Mr Henry Edwards	
	Mr Jeremiah Wase	
	Revd. Mr Browne	
	John Syer M.D.	
	Mr Robert Ashford	
	Revd Mr Chilton	
	Revd Mr I. Clarke	
	Edmund Jenney Esq.	
	Revd Mr Jeaffreson	
	Mr Thomas Simpson	

The following persons were duly elected Directors and Acting Guardians:

	Directors	Guardians
May	Revd George Turner	Mr Thomas Walker
	Mr Jeptha Waller	Thomas Brooks
June	Edmund Jenney Esq.	Mr William Shearing
	Mr Jeremiah Wase	John Youngman
July	Mr William Henchman	Mr John Wolton
	John Purcell Esq.	William Hambling
Aug.	Revd William Browne	Mr Fenn Sheming
	Revd Samuel Kilderbee D.D.	Robert Welton
Sept.	John Syer M.D.	Mr Francis Chisnall
	Revd William Aldrich	Thomas Kersey
Oct.	Mr Henry Edwards	Mr Thomas Simpson
	Mr J. A. Studd	Thomas Miller
Nov.	Revd William Kett	Mr John Waller
	Mr Robert Ashford	Samuel Syred
Dec.	Mr Thomas Waller	Mr Thomas Baldwin Jun.

	Mr Philip Dykes	Edward Field
Jan.	Revd Mr Isaac Clarke	Mr William Pitts
	Revd Charles Brooke	James Aldous
Feb.	Jacob Whitbread Esq.	Mr James Clubbe
	Mr Samuel Gross	Charles Cooper
Mar.	Mr Thomas Simpson	Mr John Sherwood
	Thomas Pytches Esq.	Thomas Edwards
Apl.	Revd Jacob Chilton	Mr Thomas Woodward
	Revd Christopher Jeaffreson	John Felgate

5 July 1813

It having been proposed by Dr Syer that two of the Quarterly Meetings be held at the Horse and Groom Inn Melton, it being seconded by Mr Samuel Gross and to be determined at the next Quarterly Meeting.

8 July 1813

Resolved that Mr Wood the solicitor do write to Edward Banks, of Wickham Market, for not allowing sufficient and proper cloathing to his apprentice Emily Hawkins at the time she left his service.

Ordered that Robert Austin aged 15½ yrs. be admitted into the House he be employed as a taylor or shoemaker belonging to Sutton.

The proposed alteration to the Quarterly Meetings having been proposed from the Chair, the voices of the Directors and Acting Guardians being taken upon it, there appeared 14 for the alteration and 13 against it, but by a clause in the Act of Incorporation it is provided that two thirds of the Directors and Acting Guardians present must concur in any alteration; therefore the meetings continue as usual at Wickham Market.

14 October 1813

Revd Mr Kett was proposed by the Revd Mr Brooke, seconded by Dr Syer, to be appointed Chaplain to the House of Industry (the Revd Mr Black, the late Chaplain being dead) was unanimously elected with the usual salary of forty pounds per annum.

6 January 1814

N.B. there not being a sufficient number of Directors and Guardians present to constitute a legal meeting, the assessments and warrants for collection were made by two Magistrates after the ratio of one rate and a half.

7 April 1814

Directors	Present	Guardians
Revd Mr Browne		Mr Fenn Sheming
Revd Mr Chilton		
Revd Mr Brooke		
Jacob Whitbread Esq.		
Mr Samuel Gross		
Mr John Woolnough		
Mr Jeremiah Wase		
Mr John Syer M.D.		
Mr Thomas Simpson		
Revd Dr Kilderbee		

The following persons were duly elected Directors and Acting Guardians:

	Directors	Guardians
May	Revd George Turner	Mr Thomas Walker
	Mr Jeptha Waller	Mr Thomas Brooks
June	Edmund Jenney Esq.	Mr Thomas Garneys
	Mr Jeremiah Wase	Mr John Fuller
July	John Purcell Esq.	Mr John Wolton
	Mr William Henchman	Mr Henry Capper
Aug.	Revd Mr Browne	Mr Fenn Sheming
	Revd Dr Kilderbee	Mr Robert Welton
Sept.	John Syer M.D.	Mr Francis Chisnall
	Revd Mr Aldrich	Mr Thomas Kersey
Oct.	Mr Henry Edwards	Mr Henry Farrer
	Mr J. A. Studd	Mr John Ablitt
Nov.	Mr John Woolnough	Mr John Waller
	Mr Robert Ashford	Mr William Catling
Dec.	Mr Thomas Waller	Mr Thomas Baldwin Jun.
	Mr Philip Dykes	Mr Charles Harris
Jan.	Revd Mr Isaac Clarke	Mr Peter Kersey
	Revd Mr Charles Brooke	Mr James Aldous
Feb.	Jacob Whitbread Esq.	Mr James Clubbe
	Mr Samuel Gross	Mr William Cooper
Mar.	Mr Thomas Simpson	Mr William Moore
	Thomas Pytches Esq.	Mr Jeremiah White
Apl.	Revd Jacob Chilton	Mr John Goodwin
	Revd Christopher Jeaffreson	Mr John Felgate

Ordered that the salary of the House surgeon (Mr G. B. Lynn) be increased from £60 per annum to £80. And that the thanks of this meeting be given to him for his particular attention to the sick under his care.

Ordered that Mr William Kitson, overseer of Monewden, be fined five pounds for not paying the rate of his parish to the Treasurer in due time, and for not attending at this meeting accord to summons.

14 July 1814

Ordered that the fine ordered last quarter upon Mr William Kitson be remitted upon his paying the Treasurer 1 guinea for the summons.

Ordered that five guineas be paid to Mrs Oldham, Governess of the House of Industry, as a donation for her extra trouble and attention to the sick in the House, and that 1s. per week be allowed to Nurse Gazely for her attendance upon the sick to commence from Lady Day last.

6 April 1815

Directors	Present	Guardians
Jacob Whitbread Esq.		Mr Jeremiah White
John Syer M.D.		Mr William Cooper
Revd Mr Browne		Mr James Clubbe
Mr Jeptha Waller		
Mr John Woolnough		
Mr R. Ashford		
Mr Thomas Waller		

Mr Henchman
Revd Mr Brooke
Revd Mr Turner
Mr Samuel Gross

The following persons were duly elected Directors and Acting Guardians:

	Directors	Guardians
May	Revd George Turner	Mr George Bond
	Mr Jeptha Waller	Mr Benjamin Colchester
June	Edmund Jenney Esq.	Mr Thomas Garneys
	Mr Jeremiah Wase	Mr Samuel Jeaffreson
July	John Purcell Esq.	Mr John Wolton
	Mr William Henchman	Mr S. G. Stearn
Aug.	Revd Samuel Kilderbee D.D.	Mr Edwards Crisp
	Revd William Browne	Mr Robert Welton
Sept.	John Syer M.D.	Mr Joseph Roe
	Revd William Aldrich	Mr John Randall
Oct.	Mr Henry Edwards	Mr Henry Farrer
	Mr J. A. Studd	Mr John Ablitt
Nov.	Mr John Woolnough	Mr John Waller
	Revd Charles Davy	Mr William Catling
Dec.	Mr Thomas Waller	Mr James Garrett
	Mr Philip Dykes	Mr Samuel Randall
Jan.	Revd Isaac Clarke	Mr J. D. Leach
	Revd Charles Brooke	Mr James Aldous
Feb.	Jacob Whitbread Esq.	Mr James Clubbe
	Mr Samuel Gross	Mr William Cooper
Mar.	Thomas Pytches Esq.	Mr John Largent
	Mr Thomas Simpson	Mr Jeremiah White
Apl.	Revd Jacob Chilton	Mr John Goodwin
	John Woolnough	Mr G. Utting

Ordered that the solicitor do prepare a case for Mr Nolan, the counsel, upon the clauses of the Act of Incorporation of the 31st Geo. 3rd relating to apprentice indentures, clauses 18 & 50.

12 October 1815

Resolved and ordered that R. W. Oldham be allowed 7s. 6d. from each parish of the Incorporated Hundreds for settling the churchwardens, overseers and surveyors accounts for making returns to Parliament for the last three years.

Resolved and ordered that the paupers in the House of Industry are not to be allowed to go out of the House on a Sunday unless to some specific place with a written leave of absence by the Governor or Governess, at their discretion, in manner and form following, viz:

_____ the bearer hereof has leave of absence to _____ until _____ signed _____ Governor.

Anyone disobeying this order to be punished for the first offence with abatement of diet, and for the second and further offences with abatement of diet and solitary confinement till the next committee day.

11 April 1816

Directors	Present	Guardians

Jacob Whitbread Esq.
Revd Mr Browne
Revd George Turner
John Syer M.D.
Mr Thomas Waller
Thomas Pytches Esq.
Revd Charles Davy
Mr Henchman
Revd Isaac Clarke

Mr John Goodwyn
Mr William Catling
Mr James Clubbe

The following persons were duly elected Directors and Acting Guardians:

	Directors	Guardians
May	Revd George Turner	Mr Nathaniel Barthrop Jun.
	Mr Jeptha Waller	Mr Benjamin Colchester
June	Edmund Jenney Esq.	Mr Samuel Kersey
	Mr Jeremiah Wase	Mr Samuel Jeaffreson
July	John Purcell Esq.	Mr Philp Dykes Jun.
	Mr William Henchman	Mr Peter Kersey
Aug.	Revd Samuel Kilderbee D.D.	Mr Edwards Crisp
	Revd Mr Browne	Mr Robert Welton
Sept.	John Syer M.D.	Mr Joseph Hare
	Revd. Mr Aldrich	Mr William Threadkell
Oct.	Mr Henry Edwards	Mr Thomas Simpson
	Mr J. A. Studd	Mr Samuel Brewer
Nov.	Andrew Arcedeckne Esq.	Mr John Waller
	Revd Charles Davy	Mr William Hambling
Dec.	Mr Thomas Waller	Mr Thomas Baldwin Jun.
	Mr Philip Dykes	Mr Samuel Randall
Jan.	Revd Isaac Clarke	Mr J. D. Leach
	Revd Charles Brooke	Mr John Largent
Feb.	Jacob Whitbread Esq.	Mr Isaac Clubbe
	Mr Samuel Gross	Mr William Cooper
Mar.	Thomas Pytches Esq.	Mr William Moore
	Mr Thomas Simpson	Mr Edgar Smith
Apl.	Revd Jacob Chilton	Mr John Goodwin
	Mr John Woolnough	Mr G. Utting

10 April 1817

Directors Present	Guardians
Jacob Whitbread Esq.	Mr William Hambling
John Syer M.D.	Mr James Clubbe
Revd Mr Browne	Mr J. D. Leach
Mr John Woolnough	Mr Nathaniel Barthrop Jun.
Revd Mr Davy	Mr Robert Welton
Mr Samuel Gross	
Mr Thomas Waller	
Mr Jeptha Waller	
Mr William Henchman	
Thomas Pytches Esq.	
Edmund Jenney Esq.	
Revd Mr Turner	

The following persons were duly elected Directors and Acting Guardians:

	Directors	Guardians
May	Revd George Turner	Mr Nathanial Barthrop Jun.
	Mr Jeptha Waller	Mr Thomas Edwards
June	Edmund Jenney Esq.	Mr Samuel Kersey
	Mr Jeremiah Wase	Mr Thomas Miller
July	John Purcell Esq.	Mr Philip Dykes Jun.
	Mr William Henchman	Mr Thomas Kersey
Aug.	Revd S. Kilderbee D.D.	Mr Fenn Sheming
	Revd Mr Browne	Mr Robert Welton
Sept.	John Syer M.D.	Mr Francis Chisnall
	Revd Mr Aldrich	Mr J. R. Hodgson
Oct.	Mr Henry Edwards	Mr Thomas Simpson
	Mr J. A. Studd	Mr Charles Ablitt
Nov.	Andrew Arcedeckne Esq.	Mr John Waller
	Revd Charles Davy	Mr William Hambling
Dec.	Mr Thomas Waller	Mr Thomas Baldwin Jun.
	Mr Philip Dykes Sen.	Mr Benjamin Cooper
Jan.	Revd Isaac Clarke	Mr John Wilson Sen.
	Revd Charles Brooke	Mr James Aldhous
Feb.	Jacob Whitbread Esq.	Mr James Clubbe
	Mr Samuel Gross	Mr Charles Cooper
Mar.	Thomas Pytches Esq.	Mr William Moore
	Mr Joshua Rodwell	Mr Edgar Smith
Apl.	Revd Jacob Chilton	Mr John Goodwyn
	Mr John Woolnough	Mr John Felgate

10 July 1817

Resolved that it is the opinion of this meeting that the resolutions of the Committee of the date of the 5th May last, by which a labourer with only two children is not to be considered as an object of relief, be recommended for the adoption of the present and future Weekly Committees until the arrival of harvest, or some of other change of circumstances, shall enable them to set the number of children at more than two to be maintained without assistance from the Corporation.

8 January 1818

Resolved that as great inconvenience having been found to arise from the increased number of married persons residing in the House of Industry, it is recommended to the Weekly Committee to take all such cases into consideration with a view to the discharging any of them who may be found not proper objects to be continued.

9 April 1818

Directors	Present	Guardians
Revd Mr Davy		Mr Thomas Kersey
Jacob Whitbread Esq.		Mr James Clubbe
Mr Thomas Waller		Mr Robert Welton
Mr H. Edwards		
Mr J. Woolnough		
Mr Joshua Rodwell		

Revd Mr Turner
Revd Mr Broadhurst
Dr Syer
Revd Mr Chilton
Revd Mr Brooke
Mr Henchman

The following persons were duly elected Directors and Acting Guardians:

	Directors	Guardians
May	Revd George Turner	Mr George Bond
	Mr Jeptha Waller	Mr J. D. Leach
June	Edmund Jenney Esq.	Mr William Shearing
	Revd. G. F. Tavell	Mr T. Miller
July	John Purcell Esq.	Mr T. Edwards
	Mr William Henchman	Mr T. Kersey
Aug.	Revd Mr Browne	Mr Edwards Crisp
	Revd Thomas Broadhurst	Mr Robert Welton
Sept.	John Syer M.D.	Mr F. Chisnall
	Revd Mr Aldrich	Mr J. Randall
Oct.	Mr H. Edwards	Mr H. Farrer
	Mr J. A. Studd	Mr C. Ablitt
Nov.	A. Arcedeckne Esq.	Mr J. Waller
	Revd C. Davy	Mr T. Simpson
Dec.	Mr T. Waller	Mr Edward Turner
	Mt P. Dykes	Mr B. Cooper
Jan.	Revd Isaac Clarke	Mr P. Kersey
	Revd C. Brooke	Mr J. Aldhous
Feb.	Jacob Whitbread Esq.	Mr J. Clubbe
	Mr S. Gross	Mr James Glanfield
Mar.	Thomas Pytches Esq.	Mr John Blake
	Mr J. Rodwell	Mt B. Colchester
Apl.	Revd J. Chilton	Mr J. Largent
	Mr J. Woolnough	Mr J. Felgate

9 July 1818

That notices to the following effect be sent to every parish in the Incorporated Hundreds yearly at the Michaelmas Quarter

Hundreds of Loes and Wilford

At the meeting held this day it was ordered that a calculation should be made in how much per week the maintenance of the poor in the House of Industry amounted per head, on an average of the old and young. And that an account should be taken of the number of poor maintained in the House belonging to each parish in the Hundreds. By the calculation of maintenance and other expences, it appears that the expence of each person taken upon an average is _____. Thus a man, wife and four children cost the parish to which they belong, if supported in the House of Industry _____ per week _____ per year. It was further ordered that the account of the average number of their poor for the last year should be sent to each parish with the amount of their expence for the year. The ground for this order is, the frequent practice in parishes, of getting their poor into the House of Industry when they do not know what else to do with them, and the object of it is, that parishes may see, at one view, what their expences are, and what their real interest is; they are thus called upon to consider whether they could not provide for their poor (who only want employment or temporary assistance) at a cheaper rate, than by sending those to be maintained in the House of Industry who by health are able to work, though they may occasionally want some assistance. Parishes are to consider that though they have to pay only a certain rate into the House quarterly for the maintenance of the poor, yet that rate is to be taken every ten years upon an average of their actual expence and cost of the ten foregoing years and that consequently the quarter expence they are to the House intermediately the quarter will be the amount of their next average.

The seventh Weekly Minute Book,
4 January 1813–13 June 1817[2]

4 January 1813
Ordered that the Overseers of the respective parishes do allow as follows:

Parish pauper residing in	Parish belonging to			
Eyke	Eyke Samuel Barber 4s. 4wks. William Brightwell 3s. 4wks	1	8	0
	do Jonathan Catchpole 1s. 6d. 4wks. William Miller 4s. 6d. 4wks	1	4	0
	do Jane Booth 1s. 4wks	0	4	0
	Ash James Fitch 4s. 6d. 4wks	0	18	0
	Rendlesham John Forsdick 1s. 4wks, Robert Clouting 1s. 4wks	0	8	0
	Bredfield James Smyth's wife 2s. 2wks	0	4	0
	Kettleburgh Edmund Clark for cloathing his son to service	1	0	0
	Petistree Frances Curtis aged 16 and Susan Curtis aged 14yrs to be admitted			
Butley	Capel Isaac Smith for burial of a child aged 13yrs	0	10	0
	Butley Widow Buckenham towards funeral	0	9	6
Creetingham	Creetingham John Row 15s. 2wks, Robert Nichols 1s. 2wks	1	12	0
	do John Grey 2s. 4wks, Samuel Moys 2s. 4wks	0	16	0
	do William Howard 1s. 6d. 4wks, William Clemence 1s. 6d. 4wks	0	12	0
	do Nathan Butcher 3s. 4wks, John Moss 2s. 6d. 4wks	1	2	0
Kettleburgh	Kettleburgh Colin Holmes 3s. 4wks, Amos Peck 2s. 4wks	1	0	0
	do William Walner 1s. 4wks, John Jays 2s. 4wks	0	12	0
	do Thomas Baker 1s. 4wks, William Stork 1s. 4wks	0	8	0
	do Widow Miller 1s. 4wks	0	4	0
Shottisham	Shottisham William Fox 2s. 4wks, William Lewis 2s. 4wks	0	16	0
	Sutton John Middleditch 2s. 4wks	0	8	0
	Hollesley Thomas Gooding 2s. 4wks, Henry Hunt 2s. 4wks	0	16	0
Shottisham	Samuel Moles for cloathing his son to service to			

2 SROI ADA11/A/B/3/7.

	Mr Rodwell	1	0	0
Hollesley	Hollesley Stephen Birch 2s. 4wks, John Cooper			
	2s. 4wks	0	16	0
	do John How 4s. 4wks	0	16	0
	Creetingham Wayman Bardwell and wife 1s. 6d. 4wks	0	6	0
	Sutton John Curtis 2s. 6d. 4wks	0	10	0
	Boyton Ann Hunt 1s. 6d. 4wks	0	6	0
	Rendlesham John Pretty's wife for midwife 5s. and			
	2s. 6d. 4wks	0	15	0
Alderton	Alderton Jonathan Wright 2s. 6d. 4wks,			
	James Audley 5s. 4wks	1	10	0
	do John Scoggins omitted last month 3s. 4wks	0	12	0
	do Susan Berry by Mr Pytches	0	3	0
	do James Audley *do* 20s., Iona Wright *do* 10s.	1	10	0
Kenton	Kenton James Driver 6s. 4wks, James Garnham			
	midwife 5s. and 4s. 2wks	1	17	0
	do Sarah Moore for funeral 30s., Samuel Smith			
	1s. 4wks	1	14	0
	do William Pollard 1s. 4wks, William Read's			
	wife 2s. 4wks	0	12	0
	do Sarah Goddard aged 15yrs, Susan Goddard			
	aged 12 to be admitted			
Bredfield	Bredfield Widow Allen 1s. 6d. 4wks and 1s. 6d.			
	last week	0	7	6
	do Samuel Herring for midwife 5s.	0	5	0
	Dallingho John Orsborne 1s. 6d. 4wks	0	6	0
Dallingho	Dallingho Mary Cooper for funeral	1	0	0
	Bredfield Benjamin Dowsing for cloathing to			
	service with Mr Baker	1	0	0
	Dallingho Stephen Garner 6d. 4wks, Jane Garnham			
	6d. 4wks	0	4	0
	do John Read 2s. 6d. 4wks, Maria Read 1s. 4wks	0	14	0
	do James Caton 1s. 6d. 4wks, Jeremiah Davy			
	1s. 6d. 4wks	0	12	0
	do William Brown 2s. 4wks, Jane Eade to be			
	admitted pregnant	0	8	0
	Kettleburgh Mary Nichols 6d. 4wks	0	2	0
Monewden	Monewden Samuel Siny last week 5s. and 2s. 6d. 4wks	0	15	0
	Dallingho Jonathan Adams 2s. 6d. 4 wks	0	10	0
Ufford	Marlesford West Trusson 1s. 6d. 4wks,			
	John Bloomfield 2s. 4wks	0	14	0
	Melton Thomas Lewis 2s. 2wks	0	4	0
Charsfield	Charsfield James Crane 1s. 4wks, John Durrant			
	1s. 4wks	0	8	0
	do Benjamin Reed 1s. 4wks, Robert Leech			
	2s. 6d. 4wks	0	14	0
	do Samuel Atkins 3s. 6d. 4wks, John Spendlow			
	3s. 2wks	1	0	0
	do Widow Atkins in addition to Qtly. Order			
	1s. 4wks	0	4	0

	Monewden Henry Rattle 2s. 4wks,			
	John Barker's boy 1s. 6d. 4wks	0	14	0
	do James Crowfoot 5s. 2wks	0	10	0
	Dallingho Robert Aldis 2s. 4wks	0	8	0
	Hacheston John Gilman 1s. 4wks	0	4	0
Capel	Capel John Sheldrake midwife 5s. and 3s. 6d. 2wks	0	12	0
Wickham	Wickham Samuel Botwright 1s. 4wks, Thomas			
	Olding 2s. 4wks	0	12	0
	do John Fosdick 2s. 4wks, James Beart 2s. 4wks	0	16	0
	do Samuel Harper 2s. 4wks, John Clow 3s. 2wks	0	14	0
	Rendlesham John Olding 2s. 6d. 4wks	0	10	0
	Hacheston Nathan Noy 1s. 6d. 4wks	0	6	0
	Petistree James Webber 1s. 4wks, Samuel Leech			
	1s. 4wks	0	8	0
Sutton	Sutton Isaac Clarke 2s. 4wks, James Freston			
	2s. 4wks	0	16	0
	do Samuel Foster 2s. 4wks	0	8	0
	Ramsholt Samuel Cady 2s. 4wks	0	8	0
Bromeswell	Bromeswell Samuel Ellis 1s. 6d. 4wks, Samuel			
	Holmes 2s. 6d. 2wks	0	11	0
	do William Farrow 5s. 2wks, William Cook			
	1s. 6d. 2wks	0	13	0
	Bredfield Widow Crane 1s. 4wks	0	4	0
	Alderton Widow Flegg 1s. 4wks	0	4	0
	Sutton Widow Fuller 1s. 4wks, Joseph King 2s. 4wks	0	12	0
	Ufford Edmund Taylor 1s. 4wk	0	4	0
	Bromeswell John Mills 2s. 4wks	0	8	0
	Hacheston Thomas Farrow 1s. 6d. 4wks	0	6	0
	Petistree John Bugg 1s. 4wks	0	4	0
Easton	Easton George Girdler midwife 5s. and 5s. 3wks	1	0	0
	do Robert Lawrence 1s. 6d. 3wks	0	4	6
	Hoo Robert Bailey 2s. 1wk	0	2	0
	Earl Soham Lionel Upson for cloathing his son			
	to service	1	0	0
	Easton Henry Smith *do* daughter *do*	1	0	0
	do William Hurren 5s. 4wks, John Scoulden			
	2s. 4wks	1	8	0
	do Joseph Templin 3s. 4wks, Isaac Upson			
	aged 11½ to be admitted	0	12	0
	Hoo Robert Bailey 2s. 6d. 2wks	0	5	0
Petistree	Hacheston Richard Garrett 1s. 4wks	0	4	0
	Brandeston Allen Cotton 2s. 4wks	0	8	0
Rendlesham	Rendlesham William Friend's son 2s. 4wks,			
	William Boon 4s. 4wks	1	4	0
	do Samuel Simpson 1s. 6d. 4wks, Jeremiah			
	Scopes 1s. 4wks	0	10	0
	do Robert Markham 1s. 6d. 4wks, Margaret			
	Farrow 2s. 4wks	0	14	0
	do Margaret Denny 10s. 4wks	2	0	0
Marlesford	Marlesford Samuel Maskin 2s. 4wks for porter			

329

	1s. 11d.	0	9	11
	do Samuel Brooks 3s. 4wks, Thomas Skeet 1s. 4wks	0	16	0
	do Daniel Clow 5s. 4wks	1	0	0
	do William Last for cloathing his son George to service	1	0	0
	Charsfield John Colthorp 1s. 4wks and 5s. by Dr Kilderbee	0	9	0
Ash	Ash Widow Mattin 2s. 4wks, John West 3s. 4wks	1	0	0
	do Nathaniel Self 7s. 2wks, and 5s. by Dr Kilderbee	0	19	0
	do Robert Battle 1s. 4wks, Widow King 6d. 4wks	0	6	0
	do John Ling's wife 2s. 4wks	0	8	0
	Butley Robert Crisp 3s. 1 wk	0	3	0
Hacheston	Hacheston William Butcher 1s. 6d. 4 wks	0	6	0
	Creetingham Thomas Turner 1s. 4wks	0	4	0
Melton	Melton Widow Abbott 3s. 4wks, Widow Clow 1s. 4wks	0	16	0
	do Widow Cooper 6d. 4wks, Sarah Girling 6d. 4wks	0	4	0
	do Samuel Pipe 5s. 4wks, Sarah Fearhead 1s. 4wks	1	4	0
	Brandeston George Collins 3s. 4wks	0	12	0
	Sutton Widow Knappet 6s. 4wks	1	4	0
	Ash John Porter's wife 1s. 6d. 4wks	0	6	0
	Boulge John Topple 2s. 4wk	0	8	0
Hoo	Hoo William Smith 2s. 4wks, Joseph Jordan 1s. 4wks	0	12	0
	do James Brianton 1s. 4wks, John Woolnough 6s. 1wks	0	10	0
Bawdsey	Melton Richard Whiting 1s. 4wks	0	4	0
	Alderton John Garnmage 2s. 4wks and 3s. last week	0	11	0
	Ramsholt John Pipe 2s. 4wks	0	8	0
Earl Soham	Earl Soham John Burch 6s. 1 wk, Webb's wife 1s. and 7 past wks	0	14	0
	do Widow Sawyer for funeral 20s.	1	0	0
	do John Burch 3s. 4wks, William Alexander 4s. 4wks	1	8	0
	do William Spink 4s. 4wks, William Paxman 5s. for this Qtr.	0	16	0
	Melton John Pizzey 2s. 4wks	0	8	0
Brandeston	Brandeston Bartholomew Barker 1s. 4wks, Edmund Moore 2s. 4wks	0	12	0
	do William Moore for cloathing to service to Mr R. Adams	1	0	0
	do Thomas Brianton 2s. 4wks, Thomas Scotchmer 3s. 4wks	1	0	0
	do Thomas Driver 1s. 4wks, John Allwin 1s. 4wks	0	8	0
	Ash William Wade 4s. 4wks	0	16	0
	Letheringham William Rogers 1s. 4wks	0	4	0
	Creetingham Robert Cathcart 2s. 4wks	0	8	0

Monewden Simon Glasscock 4s. 2wks   0   8   0

                                                       80   1   5

Ordered that the Treasurer do pay the Governor two hundred pounds
for the use of the poor in the House.   200   0   0

Directors	present	Guardians
Francis Clarke		Edward Field
Thomas Waller		William Kitson
Charles Brooke		

The eighth Weekly Minute Book,
7 July 1817–30 September 1820[3]

7 July 1817

Ordered that the Overseers of the respective parishes do allow as follows:

Parish pauper residing in	Parish belonging to				
Sutton	Sutton Widow Ambrose past week 4s.				
		Richard Banks *do* 4s.	0	8	0
	do	Samuel Forster *do* 8s., Elisha Gunn 12s.	1	0	0
	do	James Friston *do* 8s., James Clow for midwife 5s.	0	13	0
	do	James Crisp for mutton by order Mr Hughes 7s.	0	7	0
	Melton John Pizzey 9s. 6d. and 1s. 6d. for 4 wks		0	15	6
	Sutton Isaac Clark 2s. 6d. 4, Samuel Forster 4s. 4		1	6	0
	do	Edward Clodd 2s. 6d. 4, John Crisp 9s. 4	2	6	0
	do	John Copping 3s. 4, Richard Banks 1s. 4	0	16	0
	do	James Friston 5s. 4	1	0	0
	Kenton William Larter 3s. 4		0	12	0
	Ramsholt Samuel Cady 2s. 6d. 4		0	10	0
Bredfield	Bredfield James Fulcher not allowed				
	William Goldsmith 4s. 4		0	16	0
	do	Samuel Hurren 3s. 4, Hannah Dewell 2s. 4	1	0	0
	do	Sarah Lankaster 1s. 4wks, Thomas Catchpole 7s. 4	1	12	0
	do	William Dewell 7s. 4 wks, John Good 2s. 4 *do* for porter 1s. 9d.	1	17	9
	do	Sam. Richardson 2s. 4wk. Th. Goldsmith 1s. 6d. 4	0	14	0
	do	Abram Addison 1s. 6d. 4wks, Mary Hailes 1s. 6d. 4	0	12	0
	Boulge Thomas Glandfield 7s. 4		1	8	0
	Dallingho George Marjoram 6s. 4		1	4	0
	Charsfield Jonathan Denny 4s. 4		0	16	0
	Brandeston James Crane for porter by Mr Dyer 1s. 9d.		0	1	9
Ufford	Melton John Cook for funeral of daughter 25s.		1	5	0
	do	Thomas Lewis 4s. 4, John Cook 2s. 4	1	4	0
	Ufford William Archer 4s. 4, John Wix 3s. 4		1	8	0
	do	Samuel Wise 5s. 4, Robert Lenney 5s. 4	2	0	0
	do	John Croft 3s. 4, James Manning 3s. 4	1	4	0

---

[3]   SROI ADA11/A/B/3/8.

	do Thomas Ox 3s. 4	0	12	0
	Wickham Elijah Cook 7s. 4	1	8	0
	Dallingho C. Keeble 1s. 4	0	4	0
	Petistree Abraham Harvey 11s. 2, J. Curtis 5s. 1	1	7	0
	Ash Samuel Buckles 7s. 4, William Read 3s. 4	2	0	0
	do Robert Brightwell for funeral 25s.	1	5	0
	Kettleburgh Martha Lord 1s. 4	0	4	0
	Debach Elizabeth Orsborn 1s. 6d. 4	0	6	0
	Kenton Widow Goddard 5s. 4	1	0	0
Bromewell	Bromswell Wm. Cook 6s. 4, Wm. Farrow 6s. 6d. 4			
	James Haws 5s. 4	3	10	0
	do Jonas Lion 5s. 4 Jonth. Keable 3s. 6d. 4			
	Sam. Burrows 3s. 4	2	6	0
	do John Riches 3s. 6. 4, Samuel Ellis 2s. 4	1	2	0
	Sutton Joseph King 6s. 4, Widow Fuller 6d. 4	1	6	0
	do Widow Branch 6d. 4, Henry Lines 7s. 4	1	10	0
	do Mary Stebbings 6s. 4	1	4	0
	Eyke Samuel Adams 3s. 4, John Mills 2s. 4	1	0	0
	Capel Jane Clow 1s. 4	0	4	0
Alderton	Alderton John Batten past week 9s., Robert Wiskin			
	do 10s	0	19	0
	do Robert Wilson 6s., J. Simmonds 4s.			
	Samuel Lanham 15s.	1	5	0
	Ramsholt William Wade 10s. for past weeks	0	10	0
	Sutton John Girling 16s. 9d. *do*	0	16	9
	Hollesly George Dunn for mutton 1s. 9d.	0	1	9
	Alderton John Scoggings 6s. 4, Widow Blomfield			
	2s. 4	1	12	0
	do William Mann 3s. 4, Joseph Buck 5s. 4	1	12	0
	do William Gunnell 5s. 6d. 4, George Gray 3s. 4	1	14	0
	do Casey Wade 2s. 4, Thomas Hubbard 2s. 4	0	16	0
	do William Knights 2s. 4, William Hudson 2s. 4	0	16	0
	do Robert Wilson 2s. 4, Widow Cooper 1s. 4	0	12	0
	do Robert Dewell 1s. 4	0	4	0
	Ramsholt Widow Girling 4s. 4	0	16	0
	Alderton John Boon 1s. 6d. 4	0	6	0
	Brandeston William Wright 1s. 4	0	4	0
	Bawdsey Widow Leech 6d. 4	0	2	0
	Hollesley Elizabeth Hollery 2s. 6d. 4	0	10	0
	Sutton John Girling 4s. 4	0	16	0
	Shottisham Elizabeth Bird 2s. 4, Elizabeth Cooper			
	1s. 4	0	12	0
Brandeston	Cretingham Pricilla Wright last week 2s.	0	2	0
	Marlesford Widow Clarke *do* 2s.	0	2	0
	Brandeston Daniel Doole *do* 4s. and 6s. 4	1	8	0
	do Allan Cotton 8s. 4, B. Barker 1s. 4	1	16	0
	do Thomas Bradlaugh 6s. 4, Thomas Brianton 7s. 4	2	12	0
	do Joshua Allen 7s. 4, Jonathan Scotchmer 10s. 4	3	8	0
	do Edward Moore 4s. 4, James Taylor 3s. 4	1	8	0
	do James Nunn 4s. 4, James Aldhous 2s. 4	1	4	0

do	Robert Brown 7s. 4, Ann Martins 3s. 4	2	0	0
do	Samuel Smith 2s. 6d. 4, Robert Callum			
	for funeral 25s.	1	15	0
	Earl Soham John Jennings 6s. 4	1	4	0
Earl Soham	Earl Soham Widow Warner past weeks 1s. 6d.			
	William Spink *do* 17s.	0	18	6
do	Thomas Cook *do* 9s., Nath. Edwards 7s.			
	George Potter 13s.	1	9	0
do	Jonathan Cattermole *do* 3s., John Aldrich 13s.	0	16	0
do	Robert Harvey 5s. 4, Abraham Spalding 3s. 4	1	12	0
do	William Spink 5s. 4, William Moss 4s. 4	1	16	0
do	George Broom 6s. 4, Widow Keer 3s. 4	1	16	0
do	William Spalding 3s. 4, Jonah Cattermole 3s. 4	1	4	0
do	Charles Smith 3s. 4, Benjamin Flory 2s. 4	1	0	0
do	George Rivers for a truss 10s. 6d.			
	Edward Barker 1s. 4	0	14	6
do	Widow Long 4s. 4, Susan Manning 6d. 4	0	18	0
do	John Mann 5s. 4, Emanuel Hall 3s. 4	1	12	0
do	Stephen Allen 3s. 4, William Chapman 3s. 4	1	4	0
do	James Jennings 6s. 4, John Spink 5s. 4	2	4	0
do	John Aldrich 8s. 1, Nathaniel Edwards 2s. 2	0	12	0
do	Isaac Cook 4s. 4 in addition to Qtrly order	0	16	0
	Monewden Philip Bury 8s. 4	1	12	0
	Brandeston Edward Scutton 4s. 4	0	16	0
	Cretingham John Howlett 5s. 4	1	0	0
	Earl Soham Thomas Potter 1s. 4	0	4	0
Kettleburgh	Kettleburgh John Jaye 11s. 4, Amos Peck 8s. 4	3	16	0
do	Colin Holmes 8s. 4, John Orsborn 3s. 6d. 4	2	6	0
do	Edward Salter 8s. 4, William Walner 3s. 6d. 4	2	6	0
do	George Creasy 3s. 6d. 4, Joseph Peck 1s. 4	2	18	0
do	William Starks 3s. 6d. 4, Robert Maulden 8s. 4	2	6	0
do	James Mayhew 7s. 4, John Smith 6s. 4	2	12	0
do	Samuel Bloomfield 5s. 6d. 4, Widow Wakely			
	1s. 4	1	6	0
do	Widow Coats 1s. 4, Widow England 1s. 4	0	8	0
do	Mary Nicholls 1s. 4, James Wakely 1s. 4	0	8	0
do	Mary Gooding 2s. 4. Mary Pemberton 1s. 6d. 4	0	14	0
do	Matilda Ramsey 1s. 6d. 4			
	Colin Holmes' daughter 1s. 4	0	10	0
do	Sarah Jordan 1s. 4, Groom 7s. 4	1	12	0
do	William Leeder 3s. 6d. 4, William Hall 9s. 4	2	10	0
	Easton Susan Smith 1s. 4	0	4	0
	Alderton James Turner 6s. 4	1	4	0
	Marlesford Thomas Nicholls 3s. 6d. 4	0	14	0
Shottisham	Sutton John Middleditch past wks 4s.			
	John Linstead 11s 9d.	0	15	9
	Hacheston Henry Leak 7s. 9d. and 6s. 2wk	0	19	9
	Hollesley Widow Trusson 1s. 9d. and 3s. 6d. 2wk	0	8	9
do	Widow Gooding 7s. 6d. 4 Mary Andrews 1s. 1	1	11	0
	Dallingho Charles Woolnough 4s. 4	0	16	0

		£	s	d
	Sutton John Middleditch 4s. 4	0	16	0
	Shottisham Elizabeth Symonds 1s. 4, William Daines 2s. 6d. 4	0	14	0
Monewden	Monewden Richard Woods 1s. 4, James Crowfoot 6s. 4	1	8	0
	do Thomas Birch 2s. 4, Honor Smith 6d. 4	0	10	0
	Cretingham William Creasy 1s. 6d. 4	0	6	0
	Dallingho Jonathan Adams 4s. 4	0	16	0
Dallingho	Dallingho William Browne ill by Order Revd. Mr Browne 21s. 9d.	1	1	9
	do Jereh. Davy 8s. 4, Willm. Caton 7s. 4 Jas. Caton 7s. 6d. 4	4	10	0
	do Widow Ford 8s. 1, Widow Aldous 6s. 4 John Read 1s. 4	1	16	0
	do Maria Sawyer 1s. 6d. 4, Jas. Buckles 1s. 4 Jas. Runnacles 1s. 4	2	8	0
	do Samuel Pulham 8s. 4, Henry Runnacles 4s. 4	2	8	0
	do Robert Blois 4s. 4, John Wix 3s. 2	1	2	0
	do William Browne 10s. 2	1	0	0
	Earl Soham Frederick Debenham 5s. 4	1	0	0
	Bredfield Reuben Dowsing 5s. 4	1	0	0
Bawdsey	Hatcheston Thomas Jarvis past week 12s. and 4s. 4wks	1	8	0
	Ramsholt Elizabeth Bridges *do* 6s. 6d.	0	6	6
	Bawdsey Thomas Garrod 3s. 6d. 4, John Cook 3s. 6d. 4	1	8	0
	do Robert Dunn 5s. 2	0	10	0
	Alderton John Garnmage 5s. 4, Richard Francis 5s. 4	2	0	0
Hoo	Hoo John Nunn past week 5s. and 2s. 4wks	0	13	0
	Bawdsey James Sawyer for burial of his daughter 30s.	1	10	0
	Dallingho Jabez. Leech 6s. 4	1	4	0
	Hoo David Nunn 7s. 4, James Balls 6s. 4 John Nunn 5s. 4	3	12	0
	do Elizabeth Curtis 1s. 6d. 2	0	3	0
Wickham	Wickham Mary Rands 6d. 4, Sarah Smith 1s. 4	0	6	0
	do Henry Starling 3s. 4, Henry Chamberlain 5s. 4	1	12	0
	do Henry Kemp 4s. 4, John Clow 4s. 4	1	12	0
	do James Spink 2s. 4, John Palmer 6s. 4	1	12	0
	do James Flory 4s. 4, James Beart 3s. 6d. 4	1	10	0
	do Samuel Harper 4s. 4, John Culpeck 6s. 4	2	0	0
	do Sarah Kemp 1s. 6d. 4, Widow Kerridge 4s. 4	1	2	0
	do Samuel Cotton 3s. 6d. 4, James Block 8s. 4	2	6	0
	Hacheston Mary Brown 6d. 4, Widow Hart 2s. 4	0	10	0
	do Thomas Sheldrake 8s. 4	1	12	0
	Petistree James Webber 4s. 4, John Denton 2s.	1	4	0
	Rendlesham John Olding 3s. 4	0	12	0
	Ash Thomas Howard 8s. 4	1	12	0
	Ufford Samuel King 3s. 4	0	12	0
Easton	Easton Joseph Cady 8s. 1, Hannah Read 3s. 6d. 1	0	11	6
	do Mary Scutt at Norwich 24s.	1	4	0

	Letheringham Thomas Nicholls for wine 3s.	0	3	0
Letheringham	Charsfield Joseph Leech 4s. 4	0	16	0
	Letheringham William Rogers 7s. 4, Joseph Rawling 7s. 4	2	16	0
do	William Cattermole 6s.4, Thomas Nicholls 5s. 4	2	4	0
do	John Peck 6s. 4, Edward Battle 6s. 4	2	8	0
do	James York 6s. 4, William Howard 5s. 4	2	4	0
do	John Smith 6s. 4, John Redgrave 7s. 4	2	12	0
Ash	Ash Isaac Gibbs 7s. 4, Chris. Baldrey 2s. 6d. 4	1	18	0
do	John West 6s. 4, William Cracknell 2s. 6d. 4	1	14	0
do	George May 5s. 4, Thomas Lanham 6s. 4	2	4	0
do	William Wade 4s. 4, Nathaniel Barham 2s. 6d. 4	1	6	0
do	Isaac Ling 2s. 6d. 4, John Youngman 3s. 6d. 4	1	4	0
do	James Knights 2s. 6d. 4, Philip Kerridge 2s. 6d. 4	1	0	0
do	Robert Battle 6s. 4, Thomas Downing 7s. 4	2	12	0
do	Nathaniel Self 2s. 6d. 4, James Fitch 10s. 4	2	10	0
do	Widow Baily 1s. 4, Widow Mattin 2s. 4	0	12	0
	Brandeston James Naunton's wife's child 2s. 4	0	8	0
	Charsfield Martha King 2s. 4	0	8	0
	Rendlesham James Chilvers 3s. 6d. 4	0	14	0
	Alderton William Skinner 2s. 6d. 4	0	10	0
Capel	Capel John Levett 11s. 4, John King 5s. 4	3	4	0
do	Francis Pollard 2s. 6d. 4, Widow Lyon 1s. 6d. 4	0	16	0
do	John Precious 1s. 6d. 4, Isaac Naunton 2s. 4	0	14	0
	Bredfield John Kirk 5s. 4	1	0	0
Debach	Debach Stephen Colthorpe 3s. 4, John Kitson 3s. 4	1	4	0
do	Henry Curtis 4s. 4, William Fairweather 2s. 4	1	4	0
do	William Robertson 2s. 6d. 4, John Newby 1s. 6d. 4	0	16	0
do	Robert Crane 1s. 6d. 4	0	6	0
	Boulge John Quinton 5s. 4	1	0	0
Hollesley	Hollesley Elizabeth Andrews for mutton 3s. 6d. and 3s. and 3s. 4w	0	18	6
do	Mary Baker 1s. 6d., Mary Warnet porter 3s. 6d.	0	5	0
do	John Spalding for cloathing his son to service 20s.	1	0	0
do	John Brown 10s. 2, James Middleditch 2s. 6d. 4	1	10	0
	Capel John Kemp 2s. 6d 4, and wife ill 2s. 6d. 4	1	0	0
	Rendlesham John Pretty 18s. 6d. 4	3	14	0
Marlesford	Marlesford Robert Rouse past week 17s. 6d., Henry Cooper 3s.	1	0	6
do	Robert Mattin 10s., Jon. Packard 9s., Jon. Blaxall 2s.	1	1	0
do	John Meadows 5s. 4, John Birt 7s. 4	2	8	0
do	Henry Cooper 3s. 6d. 4, Daniel Smith			

		£	s	d
	3s. 6d. 4	1	8	0
	do John Jordan 7s. 4, Thomas Knights 5s. 4	2	8	0
	do William King 3s. 6d. 4, Robert Mattin 3s. 6d. 4	1	8	0
	do Richard Blois 2s. 4, Francis Clow 7s. 4	1	16	0
	do William Last 5s. 4, Frances Betts 1s. 4	1	4	0
	do James Woodley 3s. 6d. 4, Joseph Adams 1s. 4	0	18	0
	do John Packard 9s. 2, Robert Rouse 3s. 6d. 4	1	12	0
	Melton John Chenery 5s. 4	1	0	0
	Wickham Sarah Crane 1s. 4	0	4	0
Cretingham	Cretingham William Lockwood for midwife 5s.	0	5	0
	do Daniel Salter 6s. 6d. 4, William Runacles 12s. 6d. 4	3	16	0
	do John Moss 8s. 4, Samuel Moyse 16s. 4	4	16	0
	do Jonathan Row 4s. 4 Nathan Butcher 8s. 4	2	8	0
	do Anthony List 4s. 4, Widow Gray 10s.4	2	16	0
	do Widow Orsborn 2s. 6d. 4, Joseph Rands 2s. 6d. 4	1	0	0
	do Thomas Clements 4s. 4, William Howard 8s. 4	2	8	0
	do James Garnham 7s. 4, Thomas Pepper 5s. 6d. 4	2	10	0
	do James Spall 7s. 4, Thomas Robinson 4s. 4	2	4	0
	do Abraham Simpson 5s. 6d. 4 William Clements 5s. 6d. 4	2	4	0
	do William Last 11s. 4, Abraham Orsborn 4s. 4	3	0	0
	do Widow Coppen 2s. 4, William How 8s. 4	2	0	0
	Ash James Durrant 12s. 6d. 4	2	10	0
Petistree	Petistree Widow King 1s. 4, Robert Barnard 1s. 4	0	8	0
	do Ann Brundish 6d. 4, Martha Capon 6d. 4	0	4	0
	do Thomas Capon 1s. 4, John Bragg 4s. 6d. 4	1	2	0
	do James Brown 3s. 6d. 4, Charles Gibbs 3s. 6d. 4	1	8	0
	do Abraham Cooper 6s. 4	1	4	0
	Wickham Isaac Potkins 1s. 4, William Thompson 2s. 4	0	12	0
	do Martha Garnham not allowed			
	Boyton Samuel Scott 4s. 4wk	0	16	0
Eyke	Eyke Stannard for porter 6s. and 6s. 4 wks	1	10	0
	do William Miller 6s. 4, Henry Woodward 5s. 4	2	4	0
	do Widow Fuller 8s. 4, Samuel Barber 2s. 4	2	0	0
	do Widow Clouting 1s. 6d. 4, Lucy Worledge 2s. 4	0	14	0
	do James Birch 6s. 4, William Fisk 2s. 6d. 4	1	14	0
	do William King 3s. 4, William Clark 3s. 4	1	4	0
	Melton William Gowing 2s. 6d. 4	0	10	0
	Rendlesham James Crisp 3s. 4, Abraham Smith 4s. 4	1	8	0
	Ufford William Clow 3s. 4	0	12	0
	Bromewsell John Luffer 5s. 4	1	0	0
Hacheston	Hacheston Thomas Cable 6s. 6d. 4, Robert Button			

337

	6s. 4	2	10	4
do	John Garrod 5s. 4, Nathan Noy 4s. 4	1	16	0
do	William Butcher 9s. 4, George Turtle 6s. 6d. 4	3	2	0
do	Thomas Skinner 6s. 4, Edmund Page 5s. 4	2	4	0
do	Robert Orsborn 6s. 6d. 4, Richard Nicholls 2s. 4	1	14	0
do	William Mayhew 9s. 4, Henry Towndrow 4s. 4	2	12	0
do	Thomas Head 9s. 4, D. Howard 6s. 6d. 4	3	2	0
do	James Copping 4s. 4, John Gilman 4s. 4	1	12	0
do	William Mowser 4s. 4, James Gissing 4s. 4	1	12	0
do	Robert Death 4s. 4, James Price 9s. 4	2	12	0
do	Widow Curtis 4s. 4, Richard Garrett 4s. 4	1	12	0
	Marlesford John Mills 5s. 4, Widow Aldrich 6d. 4	1	2	0
	Letheringham Mary Mattin 1s. 4, Thomas Mattin 3s. 4	0	16	0
	Cretingham Thomas Turner 2s. 6d. 4	0	10	0
	Wickham John Scopes 1s. 4, Widow Damant 6d. 4	0	6	0
do	Widow Sayer 6d. 4	0	2	0
Ash	Widow Ling 1s. 4	0	4	0
Rendlesham	Rendlesham Thomas Rout 2s. 4, Crispen King 5s. 6d. 4	1	10	0
do	John Horn 5s. 6d. 4, John Mays 5s. 6d. 4	2	4	0
do	George Scopes 5s. 6d. 4, James Ling 7s. 6d. 4	2	12	0
do	Thomas Jennings 4s. 6d. 4 William Tibbenham 4s. 6d. 4	1	16	0
do	James Fearhead 4s. 6d. 4, William Chenery 4s. 4	1	14	0
do	Sarah Pipe 1s. 6d. 4, Sam Simpson 4s. 6d. 4	1	4	0
do	Noah Benham 4s. 6d 4, Thomas Ward 4s. 6d. 4	1	16	0
do	Lucy Clutterham 1s. 4, William Boon 2s. 4	0	12	0
	Eyke John Markham 4s. 6d. 4	0	18	0
	Wickham Michael Mayhew 4s. 6d. 4	0	18	0
	Ufford William Bayley 4s. 6d. 4	0	18	0
Kenton	Kenton Samuel Smith 3s. 4, Stephen Clark 2s. 4	1	0	0
do	Thomas Surry 3s. 4, Robert Amis 3s. 4	1	4	0
do	Thomas Reynolds 2s. 6d. 4, Edward Allard 7s. 4	1	18	0
do	William Elliott 3s. 4, James Garnham 1s. 6d. 4	0	18	0
do	Edward Paine 1s. 4, Robert Plant 2s. 6d. 4	1	6	0
do	Edmund Parker 2s. 6d. 4, William Garnham 1s. 4	0	14	0
Butley	Butley Thomas Hazelwood past week 10s.	0	10	0
do	Thomas Caley 5s. 4, Takeley Caley 2s. 4	1	8	0
do	John Levis 2s. 4, Isaac Smith 5s. 4	1	8	0
do	Isaac Fox 2s. 6d. 4, James Crosley 2s. 6d. 4	1	0	0
	Charsfield Charles Ward 3s. 4	0	12	0
	Bredfield Jane Clark 2s. 4	0	8	0

	Hollesley Sarah Brightwell 1s. 4	0	4	0
	Capel James Smith 4s. 4	0	16	0
	Rendlesham Samuel Riches 7s. 4	1	8	0
Melton	Melton John Sawyer 2s. 6d. 4, Richard Whiting 5s. 4	1	10	0
	do John Crane 4s. 6d. 4, Robert Jay 2s. 6d. 4	1	8	0
	do Simon Read 4s. 4, William Lester 10s. 4	2	16	0
	do William Hutton ill 20s.	1	0	0
	Bromeswell Daniel Bardwell 4s. 4	0	16	0
	Ufford Thomas Barnard 3s. 4, Mary Taylor 2s. 4	1	0	0
	Eyke Richard Booth's wife 3s. 4	0	12	0
	Ash Matthew Denton 4s. 4	0	16	0
Boyton	Boyton Charity for porter 3s. 6d.	0	3	6
	Bawdsey William Beecraft 2s. 1 wk	0	2	0
Charsfield	Charsfield Widow Atkins past week 3s., Samuel Atkins 2s.	0	5	0
	do Widow Maulden 1s., Jonthn. Nunn 10s. William Brooks 16s.	1	7	0
	do Jonathan Nunn 10s. 1, James Mann 1s. 4	0	14	0
	do Benjamin Read 2s. 4, John Marjoram 7s. 6d. 2	1	3	0
	do John Parker 12s. 1, Samuel Atkins 5s. 2	1	2	0
	do William Brooks 6s. 1, Benjamin Flory 7s. 4	1	14	0
	do Isaac Flory 2s. 4, John Colthorpe 5s, 4	1	8	0
	do Zachery Fisk 2s. 4	0	8	0
	Brandeston James Kerridge 3s. 4	0	12	0
	Hollesley Elizabeth Grayston 2s. 4	0	8	0
Wickham	Wickham Mary Hopson and child to be discharged and 3s. 2wks	0	6	0
		378	2	0

Directors   Guardians
H. Edwards for Mr Henchman   Thomas Kersey
C. Brooke for Mr Purcell   P. Dykes Jun.

18 May 1818

At the above meeting ◇ the following poor persons being settled inhabitants in the parish of Hollesley, namely

William Stannard	Stephen Birch	Jonathan Cook
Robert Hubbard	Edward Persons	John Howard
John Turner	John Butcher	Richard Creasy
John Prew	William Lucock	John Mays
Francis Andrews	William Richardson	William Lock
William Jarvis	James Cook	James Elvin
Timothy Riches	John Birch	James Middleditch
James Stannard	Henry Grayston	James Middleditch Jun.
James Jolly	Thomas Pannifer	William Branch
William Brett	John How	Stephen Smith
Robert Hadman	William Smith	William Easter
Samuel Jolly	John Knights	and John Cooper

Apply for relief and say that they are able and willing to be employed in any service or work at the usual rates and prices payable within these Hundreds, but that the persons following trades or occupying lands within the same have neglected to employ them and further, that they have each and every of them applied to Mr Samuel Jeaffreson, one of the Overseers of the Poor of the said parish of Hollesley, in order to be employed in some service or work, but that he, the said Overseer, hath not procured for them or any of them such service or work within seven days of such application so made as aforesaid. In consequence of the above application the Committee do hereby order the Governor forthwith to make complaint to a Justice of the Peace for this County, in order that the Overseers of the Poor of Hollesley may be summoned and such other proceedings had as are directed by the 25th Section of the Incorporating Act of the 31st of Geo. 3rd. And the Committee do further direct the Overseers of the Poor of the said parish of Hollesley to relieve the above named poor persons inhabitants of the said parish for the time during which they have been unemployed according to such rate of relief as the poor of the said parish have been lately accustomed to receive by the direction and recommendation of the Bench of Justices at Woodbridge.

George Turner   J. D. Leach
Jeptha Waller   George Bond

Extract from the Fourth Treasurer's Account Book, 1817–26[4]

Lady Quarter 1817

Dr

To one quarter rate being two rates and a quarter for general purposes as appears by the assessment.	2,960	14	4½	2,960	14	4½	
To cash received of the Governor for wool spinning	24	19	11				
To cash received of *do* for bastardy	55	16	6				
To cash received of *do* for maintenance	4	7	0				
To cash received of *do* for Hides	32	4	0				
To cash received of *do* for tallow	29	7	6				
To cash received of *do* for farm	5	0	0	151	14	11	
				3,112	9	3½	

Cr

1817

By balance brought forward from last book due to the Treasurer		145	5	9½			
By interest on *do* for one Quarter		1	16	3	147	2	0½
Jan. 30	By cash paid the Governor as per order	100	0	0			
Feb. 11	By cash paid *do* as per order	100	0	0			
24	By cash paid *do* as per order	100	0	0			
March 6	By cash paid *do* as per order	100	0	0			
17	By cash paid *do* as per order	100	0	0			
April 1	By cash paid *do* as per order	200	0	0			
7	By cash paid *do* as per order	100	0	0	800	0	0

Out allowances paid as under:

Loes Hundred				Wilford Hundred			
Ash	72	3	0	Alderton	103	4	6
Brandeston	94	4	0	Bawdsey	36	5	0
Butley	28	10	0	Boulge	18	18	0
Charsfield	103	5	0	Boyton	36	2	6
Creetingham	106	19	9	Bredfield	74	5	3
Dallingho	66	4	5	Bromeswell	60	14	3
Earl Soham	99	10	3	Capel	45	4	9
Easton	47	17	0	Debach	21	12	0
Eyke	71	18	9	Hollesly	61	17	1
Hacheston	75	5	0	Melton	110	3	9
Hoo	35	18	0	Petistree	24	1	3

---

4   SROI ADA11/A/C/1/1/4 fourth Treasurer's Account Book.

Kenton	42	2	6	Ramsholt	14	19	0
Kettleburgh	84	1	0	Shottisham	36	6	3
Letheringham	32	15	0	Sutton	47	5	6
Marlesford	92	5	0	Ufford	102	14	9
Monewden	19	7	6	Wickham M	136	7	7
Rendlesham	58	15	9		930	1	5
	1,131	1	11	Loes	1,131	1	11
					2,061	3	4

Repairs

No. 1	Robert Allen glaziers	17	2	6
No. 2	James Baxter whitesmith	7	3	5
No. 3	Corn. Collett bricks	32	10	0
No. 4	Alex Rufus Marsden bricks	20	13	6
No. 5	Benj. Dove bricklayer	7	8	3
No. 6	Oliver Pells carpenter	7	13	1
No. 7	Henry Collins millwright	2	15	9
No. 8	Charles Beard cooper	5	2	3
No. 9	Robert Smith stonemason	1	19	10

92 8 7

Surgeons

No. 1	Robert Dyer surgeon salary	15	10	0
No. 2	Hugh David Hughes *do*	20	6	6
No. 3	Thomas Harsant *do*	44	9	6
No. 5	R. Bellman *do*	18	10	0

98 16 0

Miscellaneous bills

No. 1	The Revd Kett chaplain salary	10	0	0
No. 2	Robert Bennington coals			
	do lime	64	18	0
No. 3	John Banyard tea etc.	5	12	2
No. 4	William Braggs drapery	20	12	7
No. 5	William Chaplin sundries	95	15	2
No. 6	John Edwards leather	54	19	6
No. 7	John Gross & Co. grocery	22	16	7
No. 8	William Haken potash	1	1	0
No. 9	Hannah Hubbard carting bricks	17	8	6
No. 10	Robert Jacobs earthenware	1	19	4
No. 11	Edward Keeble salt	15	4	0
No. 12	Isaac Last hemp cloth	20	3	0
No. 13	Nath. Licence *do*	29	4	4
No. 14	James Leggatt hosiery	24	0	0
No. 15	Sarah Loder stationary	7	10	10
No. 16	William Lockwood malt	55	4	0
No. 17	William Morley earthenware	2	17	8
No. 18	R. W. Oldham salary	18	10	0
	Ordered by Q. Meeting gratuity	10	10	0
No. 19	William Pattison drapery	34	16	3
No. 20	A. Pottle grinding	4	1	3
No. 21	Frances Sillett leather breeches	15	7	0
No. 22	William West hemp cloth	12	4	0

No. 23	Thomas Sheming brazier	1	15	3
No. 24	Stephen Oxborrow butcher	9	2	1
No. 25	John Stow oatmeal	7	5	0
No. 26	John Wood solicitor bills	33	15	10
	do Treasurers salary etc .	7	17	8
	do	1	1	0

605	19	0

Balance due to the Treasurer.

692	10	8

SIXTH QUARTERLY MINUTE BOOK
15 October 1818–14 August 1820[1]

15 October 1818

Directors	Present	Guardians
Jacob Whitbread Esq.		Mr Thomas Kersey
Revd Mr Davy		Mr Edward Crisp
Revd Mr Broadhurst		Mr H. Farrer
Mr John Woolnough		Mr George Bond
Mr Henry Edwards		
Mr Joshua Rodwell		
Revd Mr Tavell		
Revd Mr Brooke		
John Syer M.D.		

Ordered that the Assessments for the ensuing Quarter be made as before, that is after the ratio of one rate and half rate for the general purposes of the Act of Incorporation. The Assessment for the Debt of Interest as before.

Ordered that the following out allowances be granted

Loes Hundred		Quarterly Order 12 weeks	allowance per week		sum for Quarter		
Parish pauper resides in	Parish pauper belonging to	Name					
Ash		Widow Bailey	3s.	6d.	2	2	0
		do Barber	2s.	6d.	1	10	0
		do Ling for child	1s.	6d.	0	18	0
		do Ling	4s.	0d.	2	8	0
	Kettleburgh	*do* Ringe	3s.	6d.	2	2	0
		do Robinson	1s.	0d.	0	12	0
	Hatcheston	*do* Abi. Skinner	3s.	0d.	1	16	0
	Alderton	*do* Deb. Skinner	1s.	6d.	0	18	0
		do Wade	3s.	0d.	1	16	0
		Wife of Rich. Underwood & Child	3s.	0d.	1	16	0
		Widow Howard	3s.	6d.	2	2	0
					18	0	0

---

[1] SROI ADA11/A/B/1/6.

344

Brandeston		Widow Baker	3s.	0d.	1 16 0	
		do Boon	2s.	6d.	1 10 0	
		do Cullin	3s.	0d.	1 16 0	
		do Nunn	8s.	0d.	4 16 0	
	Earl Soham	*do* Spalding	1s.	6d.	0 18 0	
		do Wade	2s.	0d.	1 4 0	
		Eliz. Boon	2s.	6d.	1 10 0	
		Cooper Bradlaugh	2s.	6d.	1 10 0	
		Mary Chapman	2s.	0d.	1 4 0	
		Joseph Harvey's child	2s.	6d.	1 10 0	
		Richd Harrington's gch.	3s.	0d.	1 16 0	
		Mark Noble & wife	4s.	0d.	2 8 0	
		Eliz. Read B.B. Child	1s.	6d.	0 18 0	
		Ann Martin	3s.	0d.	<u>1 16 0</u>	
					24 12 0	
Butley		Edward Cattermole	1s.	0d.	0 12 0	
	Bredfield	Widow Clark	6s.	0d.	3 12 0	
	Kettleburgh	Widow Smith	2s.	0d.	1 4 0	
	Sutton	*do* Jarvis for Crane's child	1s.	6d.	0 18 0	
		Robt. Pemberton	1s.	6d.	0 18 0	
		Sarah Scotchmer	1s.	0d.	0 12 0	
	Capel	Widow Mary Smith	1s.	6d.	<u>0 18 0</u>	
					8 14 0	
Charsfield		Widow Atkins	4s.	0d.	2 8 0	
		do Burch	2s.	6d.	1 10 0	
		do Maulden	2s.	6d.	1 10 0	
	Kettleburgh	*do* Parker	2s.	0d.	1 4 0	
		do Payne	2s.	6d.	1 10 0	
		do Wythe's children	4s.	0d.	2 8 0	
		James Abbott	6s.	0d.	3 12 0	
		Jas Block's wife & children	8s.	0d.	4 16 0	
		John Bradstreet	6s.	0d.	3 12 0	
		Jane Branch	2s.	0d.	1 4 0	
	Easton	Deb. Driver widow	2s.	0d.	1 4 0	
		Mary Maulden	2s.	0d.	1 4 0	
		Wm. Reed	1s.	0d.	0 12 0	
		Mary Rose B.B. child	1s.	0d.	0 12 0	
		Jonth. Sad for Robt. Creasy	0s.	6d.	<u>0 6 0</u>	
					27 12 0	
Creetingham		Widow Brown	1s.	6d.	0 18 0	
		do Copping	2s.	6d.	1 10 0	
		do Harvey	2s.	0d.	1 4 0	
		do Moss	3s.	0d.	1 16 0	
		do Osborn	2s.	0d.	1 4 0	
		John Avis	2s.	0d.	1 4 0	
		Susan Godbold	3s.	0d.	1 16 0	
		Mary Moyse	1s.	6d.	0 18 0	

	Willm. Moss	2s.	0d.	1	4	0
	Ann Nicholls	2s.	0d.	1	4	0
	Eliz Oxborrow B.B. Child	2s.	0d.	1	4	0
	John Scotchmer	1s.	6d.	0	18	0
	John Tye	2s.	0d.	1	4	0
	Robert Cudham	2s.	0d.	1	4	0
	Sarah Brunwin	5s.	0d.	3	0	0
	Robt. Nicholls	2s.	0d.	1	4	0
	Wm. Creasy	2s.	0d.	1	4	0
				22	16	0
Dallingho	Widow Aldous	4s.	0d.	2	8	0
	do Ford	6s.	0d.	3	12	0
	do Wyatt	2s.	0d.	1	4	0
Kenton	Do Keer	2s.	6d.	1	10	0
	Robt. Clark	3s.	0d.	1	16	0
	Robt. Osborn	2s.	0d.	1	4	0
	Ann Rosier's B.B. child	1s.	6d.	0	18	0
	Charity Woolnough	2s.	6d.	1	10	0
				14	2	0
Earl Soham	Widow Harvey	1s.	6d.	0	18	0
	do Keer	3s.	0d.	1	16	0
	do Long	2s.	0d.	1	4	0
	do Read	2s.	0d.	1	4	0
	do Wade	3s.	0d.	1	16	0
	do Warner	2s.	6d.	1	10	0
	Benj. Alexander	2s.	0d.	1	4	0
	Edmd. Barker	2s.	0d.	1	4	0
	Jas. Bournefield's wife	1s.	6d.	0	18	0
	Charles Fellingham	1s.	0d.	0	12	0
	Robt. Lanham	2s.	0d.	1	4	0
Cretingham	Mary Lanham	2s.	0d.	1	4	0
Kenton	Mary Lancetors B.B. child	2s.	0d.	1	4	0
	Susan Manning *do*	1s.	6d.	0	18	0
	Maria Nesling *do*	1s.	9d.	1	1	0
	James Pryke at Holbrook	4s.	0d.	2	8	0
	Mary Rimacles	1s.	0d.	0	12	0
	Wm. Smith & wife	2s.	0d.	1	4	0
	Robt. Spink & *do*	5s.	0d.	3	0	0
	Robt. Moss & *do*	4s.	0d.	2	8	0
	Wm. Paxman & *do* blind	4s.	0d.	2	8	0
	Sus. Woolnough B.B. child	1s.	6d.	0	18	0
				30	15	0
Easton	Widow Cady	2s.	0d.	1	4	0
Rendlesham	*do* Death	2s.	0d.	1	4	0
	do Hayward	2s.	6d.	1	10	0
Petistree	*do* Perriman	2s.	0d.	1	4	0
	do Smith	1s.	6d.	0	18	0

		George Dorling	4s.	0d.	2	8	0
Charsfield		Thos. Bennett	6s.	0d.	3	12	0
		John Block	2s.	0d.	1	4	0
		Rebecca Brooks	2s.	0d.	1	4	0
		John Capon	2s.	6d.	1	10	0
		Hannah Coats B.B. child	2s.	0d.	1	4	0
		Mary Eades	2s.	6d.	1	10	0
Kettleburgh		Lucy Flegg B.B. Child	1s.	6d.	0	18	0
		John French	2s.	6d.	1	10	0
		Thos. Grimwood	6s.	0d.	3	12	0
		Robt. Lawrence	2s.	6d.	1	10	0
Hacheston		Jemmima Page B.B. child	3s.	6d.	2	2	0
		Emma Tricker B.B. child	2s.	0d.	1	4	0
Earl Soham		Lionel Upson	2s.	0d.	1	4	0
		Emma Yeldow	2s.	0d.	1	4	0
					30	12	0

Eyke		Widow Barham	1s.	4d.	0	18	0
		do Brightwell	4s.	0d	2	8	0
		do Clouting	2s.	0d.	1	4	0
	Bredfield	do Catchpole	1s.	6d.	0	18	0
	Ash	do Kettle	2s.	6d.	1	10	0
	do	do King	2s.	0d.	1	4	0
		do Fuller	3s.	0d.	1	16	0
		do Mossley	3s.	0d.	1	16	0
		Peggy Barber	1s.	0d.	0	12	0
		Jane Booth	1s.	0d.	0	12	0
	Sutton	Martha Howes	2s.	6d.	1	10	0
	Marlesford	Mary Martin	2s.	6d.	1	10	0
		John Luff's idiot child	1s.	6d.	0	18	0
		Eliz. Topple B.B. ch.	1s.	0d.	0	12	0
		Lucy Worledge B.B. Child	2s.	0d.	1	4	0
		Robt. Riches	2s.	6d.	1	10	0
					19	7	0

Hacheston	Marlesford	Widow Aldridge	3s.	6d.	2	2	0
		do Block	2s.	0d.	1	4	0
		do Curtis	3s.	0d.	1	16	0
	Wickham	do Damant	1s.	6d.	0	18	0
	Kettleburgh	do Flick	1s.	0d.	0	12	0
		do Garrard	2s.	0d.	1	4	0
	Ash	do Ling	2s.	6d.	1	10	0
	Wickham	do Sayer	2s.	0d.	1	4	0
		do Smith	4s.	0d.	2	8	0
		Lydia Aldridge	2s.	0d.	1	4	0
	Sutton	Ann Farrer's B.B. child	1s.	6d.	0	18	0
		Sarah Gilman	2s.	0d.	1	4	0
	Marlesford	Mary Hatcher's B.B. Child	1s.	6d.	0	18	0
		John Howard	3s.	0d.	1	16	0
	Brandeston	Mary Mills	1s.	6d.	0	18	0

Letheringham	Timothy Mattin	2s.	6d.	1	10	0	
Do	Thos. Mattin	1s.	6d.	0	18	0	
Marlesford	Eliz. Porter	3s.	0d.	1	16	0	
Wickham	John Scopes	4s.	0d.	2	8	0	
	John Scrutton	4s.	0d.	2	8	0	
Cretingham	Thos. Turner	8s.	0d.	4	16	0	
				35	8	0	

Hoo	Robt. Bailey's wife	1s.	6d.	0	18	0	
Cretingham	Willm. Branton	4s.	0d.	2	8	0	
	John Gibb's wife	1s.	0d.	0	12	0	
	Susan Studd 2 B.B. children	4s.	0d.	2	8	0	
	Susan Studd *do* at Rushmere	3s.	0d.	1	16	0	
	Mary Marjoram at Harleston	1s.	6d.	0	18	0	
				9	0	0	

Kenton	John Church blind	10s.	6d.	6	6	0	
	Stephen Clarke	4s.	0d.	2	8	0	
	Robt. Hill & wife	5s.	0d.	3	0	0	
	Widow Parker	2s.	6d.	1	10	0	
	Sarah Porcher	1s.	0d.	0	12	0	
	Sarah Roper	2s.	6d.	1	10	0	
	James Stammers	2s.	0d.	1	4	0	
	Widow Collins	2s.	6d.	1	10	0	
				18	0	0	

Kettleburgh	Widow England	2s.	0d.	1	4	0	
	do Kent	2s.	0d.	1	4	0	
	do Newman	3s.	6d.	2	2	0	
	do Nicholls	3s.	6d.	2	2	0	
Monewden	*do* Smith	2s.	0d.	1	4	0	
	Jane Smith	2s.	0d.	1	4	0	
	Robt. Spalding	2s.	0d.	1	4	0	
	C. Sculthorpe B.B. child	1s.	6d.	0	18	0	
Alderton	James Turner	3s.	0d.	1	16	0	
	Eliz. Crowfoot	1s.	6d.	0	18	0	
	Colin Holmes' daught.	1s.	0d.	0	12	0	
				15	12	0	

Letheringham	Widow Markham	2s 6d	1	10	0	
Kenton	*do* Long	3s 0d	1	16	0	
Rendlesham	*do* Pollard	2s 6d	1	10	0	
			2	16	0	

Marlesford	Widow Burrell	2s.	0d.	1	4	0	
	do Cave	2s.	0d.	1	4	0	
	do Maskin	3s.	0d.	1	16	0	
	do of Thos. Maskin	2s.	0d.	1	4	0	
	Sarah Bickers	3s.	0d.	1	16	0	
Wickham	Saml. Bridges	6s.	0d.	3	12	0	

		Nathl. Cockerill	3s.	0d.	1	16	0
		Henry Cooper	3s.	6d.	2	2	0
		Elizabeth Goldsmith	2s.	6d.	1	10	0
		Saml. Markham	2s.	0d.	1	4	0
		John Pells	2s.	6d.	1	10	0
		Ann Skeet	2s.	0d.	1	4	0
		Eliz. Smith	1s.	0d.	0	12	0
					20	14	0
Monewden	Cretingham	Sarah Culliams daught.	2s.	0d.	1	4	0
	Butley	Widow Dowsing	3s.	0d.	1	16	0
		N. Hazlewood a B.B. Child	2s.	0d.	1	4	0
		Henry Rattle	5s.	0d.	3	0	0
		Willm. Smith (7 wks)	3s.	0d.	1	1	0
		Richd. Woods	3s.	0d.	1	16	0
		George Woods	1s.	6d.	0	18	0
					11	14	0
Rendlesham		Widow Banthorp	2s.	0d.	1	4	0
	Monewden	*do* Boon	3s.	0d.	1	16	0
		do Coleman	2s.	0d.	1	4	0
		do Lock	4s.	0d.	2	8	0
	Bredfield	*do* May	2s.	6d.	1	10	0
		Rebecca Barham	1s.	6d.	0	18	0
		W. Chenery	1s.	0d.	0	12	0
		Mary Crow's B.B. child	1s.	6d.	0	18	0
		Charlotte Fearhead's B.B. c.	1s.	6d.	0	18	0
		Ann Jacques *do*	1s.	6d.	0	18	0
		Hannah Holder's *do*	1s.	6d.	0	18	0
		John Lincoln's wife	1s.	0d.	0	12	0
	Earl Soham	Hannah Orams	1s.	0d.	0	12	0
		Thos. Rout	2s.	6d.	1	10	0
					15	18	0
					327	12	0

Wilford Hundred

Alderton		Widow Alexander	4s.	6d.	2	14	0
		do Bloomfield	6s.	0d.	3	12	0
		do Barnard	1s.	6d.	0	18	0
	Cretingham	*do* Bardwell	1s.	6d.	0	18	0
	Sutton	*do* Blaxhall	2s.	0d.	1	4	0
		do Clark	2s.	0d.	1	4	0
		do Cooper	2s.	0d.	1	4	0
	Ramsholt	*do* Girling	6s.	0d.	3	12	0
	Boyton	*do* Good	2s.	0d.	1	4	0
	Bawdsey	*do* Heffer	2s.	0d.	1	4	0
		do Holder	1s.	6d.	0	18	0
		do Horn	2s.	0d.	1	4	0
	Wickham	*do* Johnson	1s.	0d.	0	12	0
		do Smith's children	6s.	0d.	3	12	0

	do Steward	1s.	6d.	0	18	0
Hollesly	*do* Thurston	1s.	6d.	0	18	0
Sutton	*do* Wright	2s.	0d.	1	4	0
Hollelsy	*do* Woods	2s.	0d.	1	4	0
	do Woolnough's child	1s.	0d.	0	12	0
	Mary Aldis	2s.	0d.	1	4	0
Bawdsey	Widow Batten	2s.	0d.	1	4	0
	do 1 child	1s.	0d.	0	12	0
Shottisham	Eliz. Cooper	1s.	6d.	0	18	0
Holleelsy	George Dunn	4s.	0d.	2	8	0
	Eliz. Emmonds B.B. child	1s.	0d.	0	12	0
	Eliz. Girling	1s.	6d.	0	18	0
	Thos. Hubbard	2s.	0d.	1	4	0
Boyton	Ann Hunt	1s.	6d.	0	18	0
	Mary Knights	1s.	6d.	0	18	0
	Iona Lawrence	2s.	0d.	1	4	0
	Wm. Murrill	2s.	6d.	1	10	0
	Robt. Pooley's wife	1s.	6d.	0	18	0
	Casey Wade's daught.	1s.	6d.	0	18	0
	Henry Woods	2s.	0d.	1	16	0
Sutton	Ann Woods B.B. child	1s.	0d.	0	12	0
				46	0	0
Bawdsey						
	Widow Backhouse	2s.	6d.	1	4	0
Sutton	*do* Hunt	1s.	6d.	0	18	0
	do King	1s.	6d.	0	18	0
	do Moor	1s.	0d.	0	12	0
	do Pratt's child	2s.	6d.	1	10	0
Melton	*do* Sheldrake	1s.	6d.	0	18	0
	John Burrows	1s.	6d.	0	18	0
	Mary Burrows B.B. child	2s.	0d.	1	16	0
	Lucy Clutterham's B.B. child	1s.	6d.	0	18	0
	Mary Flower	1s.	6d.	0	18	0
	Elizth. Goodall	2s.	0d.	1	16	0
	James Hall	1s.	0d.	0	12	0
				12	0	0
Boulge						
	Jeremiah Marjoram & wife	4s.	0d.	2	8	0
	C. Read 2 B.B. ch.	3s.	0d.	1	16	0
	Rachel Brookman	2s.	0d.	1	4	0
				2	8	0
Boyton						
	Widow King	3s.	0d.	1	16	0
	do Pettitt	2s.	6d.	1	10	0
	do Long	2s.	6d.	1	10	0
	do Button	5s.	0d.	3	0	0
Bawdsey	Wm. Beecraft	2s.	6d.	1	10	0
Kettleburgh	Edw. Brown	4s.	6d.	2	14	0
	Martha Ellis B.B. child	2s.	6d.	1	10	0
	Saml. Hart	2s.	6d.	1	10	0

Ash		*do* for late Brown's B.B. child	2s.	0d.	1	4	0
					18	12	0
Bredfield		Widow Allen	2s.	6d.	1	10	0
	Ufford	*do* Andrews	2s.	6d.	1	10	0
	Bawdsey	*do* Brown	2s.	6d.	1	10	0
	Cretingham	*do* Godbold	1s.	6d.	0	18	0
		do Fox	1s.	6d.	0	18	0
		do Lankester	2s.	6d.	1	10	0
		do Wright	4s.	0d.	2	8	0
		Robt. Battle	5s.	0d.	3	0	0
		Mary Hailer's B.B. child	1s.	6d.	0	18	0
		Thos. Hendley's wife & child	2s.	6d.	1	10	0
	Easton	Saml. Loom	5s.	0d.	3	0	0
		Margt. Marjoram	1s.	6d.	0	18	0
		Hanah Richardson's B.B. child	1s.	6d.	0	18	0
		Susan Fitch	1s.	0d.	0	12	0
					21	0	0
Bromeswell		Widow Dawson late Coleman	2s.	0d.	1	4	0
	Sutton	*do* Branch	2s.	0d.	1	4	0
	do	*do* Fuller	3s.	0d.	1	16	0
	Alderton	*do* Flegg	3s.	0d.	1	16	0
		Willm. Cook	5s.	0d.	3	0	0
		Francis Good	4s.	0d.	2	8	0
		Beliza Riches B.B. child	1s.	6d.	0	18	0
	Marlseford	Frances Rose *do*	1s.	6d.	0	18	0
	Sutton	Mary Stebbings & 4 child.	5s.	0d.	3	0	0
					17	8	0
Capel		Robt. Penn's wife	1s.	6d.	0	18	0
		Widow Frost	2s.	0d.	1	4	0
	Hollesly	*do* Collins	6s.	0d.	3	12	0
	Boyton	*do* Markham	2s.	6d.	1	10	0
	Rendlesham	*do* Minter	3s.	0d.	1	16	0
		do Snowling's children	4s.	0d.	2	8	0
		do Wolton	2s.	0d.	1	4	0
					12	12	0
Debach		Widow Crane & 4 children	6s.	0d.	3	12	0
		Lydia Garnham	2s.	0d.	1	4	0
		John Kitson	3s.	0d.	1	16	0
		Wm. Robinson	1s.	6d.	0	18	0
					7	10	0
Hollesly		Widow Andrew	2s.	0d.	1	4	0
		do Clodd	1s.	6d.	0	18	0
		do Crick	7s.	6d.	4	10	0
	Alderton	*do* Creasy	2s.	0d.	1	4	0
	Do	*do* Fox sen.	2s.	0d.	1	4	0

	Do	*do* Fox jun.	6s.	0d.	3 12 0
		do Skipper	1s.	6d.	0 18 0
		James Battle	8s.	0d.	4 16 0
		Wm Cheverson's 2 ch.	5s.	0d.	3 0 0
		Thos. Curtis	2s.	6d.	1 10 0
		Mary Cooper's B.B. child	2s.	0d.	1 4 0
	Dallingho	Thos. Thornton's wife	3s.	0d.	1 16 0
		Mary Branch B.B. child	2s.	6d.	1 10 0
					27 6 0
Melton	Sutton	Widow Flory	2s.	0d.	1 4 0
	do	*do* Knappet	6s.	0d.	3 12 0
	Alderton	*do* Lambert	1s.	6d.	0 18 0
		do Ruth's children	8s.	0d.	4 16 0
		do Sawyer	2s.	0d.	1 4 0
		do Story	1s.	6d.	0 18 0
		do Tonk	4s.	6d.	2 14 0
		do Chilton	4s.	6d.	2 14 0
		Crane's wife & child	1s.	0d.	0 12 0
	Ash	Matthew Denton	6s.	0d.	3 12 0
		Mary Ewens	2s.	0d.	1 4 0
		Sarah Girling	3s.	0d.	1 16 0
		George Goldsmith Sen .	3s.	6d.	2 2 0
		Haken's 5 orphaned children	10s.	0d.	6 0 0
		John Harper	2s.	0d.	1 4 0
	Bawdsey	Wm. Hammond B.B. child	1s.	6d.	0 18 0
		Robt. Jay 2 idiot children	2s.	6d.	1 10 0
		Jemima Prentice	1s.	6d.	0 18 0
	Ufford	Martha Skeet	1s.	6d.	0 18 0
	Pettistree	Henry Turner & wife	6s.	0d.	3 12 0
	Boulge	Eliz. Wilson	1s.	6d.	0 18 0
					43 4 0
Petistree		Widow King	2s.	6d.	1 10 0
		Widow Levett	2s.	0d.	1 4 0
		Robt. Barnard	4s.	0d.	2 8 0
		Joseph Button	4s.	0d.	2 8 0
		Thos. Capon	3s.	6d.	2 2 0
		Ann Chandler	0s.	6d.	0 6 0
	Wickham	Susan Potkin's B.B. child	1s.	6d.	0 18 0
					10 16 0
Ramsholt		Widow Ablett	2s.	0d.	1 4 0
	Alderton	*do* Berry's child	2s.	6d.	1 10 0
	Melton	Orsborn	2s.	0d.	1 4 0
		Eliz. Allen B.B. child	2s.	0d.	1 4 0
		Thomas Lewis's daught.	1s.	6d.	0 18 0
		do Whiting	2s.	0d.	1 4 0
	Capel	Smith's child	1s.	0d.	0 12 0
					7 16 0

Shottisham		Widow Bird	1s.	6d.	0 18 0
		do Brown	2s.	6d.	1 10 0
		do Roper	2s.	6d.	1 10 0
	Hollesly	*do* Hunt's child	1s.	6d.	0 18 0
	Do	Mary Andrew's B.B. child	2s.	0d.	1 4 0
		Wm. Daynes	3s.	0d.	1 16 0
		Eliz. Symonds	1s.	0d.	0 12 0
		Eliz. Bird B.B. child	1s.	6d.	0 18 0
		Mary Harvey *do*	1s.	6d.	0 18 0
					10 4 0
Sutton		Widow Ambrose	1s.	6d.	0 18 0
		do Boulter	3s.	0d.	1 16 0
	Bawdsey	*do* Hammond	1s.	6d.	0 18 0
		do Howell	2s.	0d.	1 4 0
		do Hudson	2s.	0d.	1 4 0
		do Lovis	1s.	6d.	0 18 0
		do Spall	3s.	0d.	1 16 0
		do Steel	1s.	0d.	0 12 0
		James Burrows	2s.	0d.	1 4 0
		Eliz. Button B.B. child	2s.	0d.	1 4 0
		Warner Gooch's idiot daugh.	1s.	0d.	0 12 0
		Henry King	6s.	0d.	3 12 0
		Wm. Law's wife	1s.	6d.	0 18 0
		Mary Middleditch's B.B. child	2s.	0d.	1 4 0
		Ann Mullinger's B.B. child	2s.	6d.	1 10 0
					22 16 0
Ufford		Widow Amis	1s.	6d.	0 18 0
		do Bennett	2s.	0d.	1 4 0
	Ash	*do* Brightwell	1s.	0d.	0 12 0
	Wickham	*do* Catton	1s.	0d.	0 12 0
	Melton	*do* Hutton	3s.	0d.	1 16 0
		do Partick	2s.	0d.	1 4 0
		do Parker	2s.	6d.	1 10 0
		do Stimpson	3s.	0d.	1 16 0
	Petistree	Charles Blomfield	1s.	0d.	0 12 0
		Middleton Cracknell	5s.	0d.	3 0 0
	Petistree	Robt. Glanfield	4s.	0d.	2 8 0
	Kenton	Widow Goddard	2s.	0d.	1 4 0
	Do	Mary Goddard's B.B. child	2s.	0d.	1 4 0
		Saml. Harland's wife	1s.	6d.	0 18 0
	Bromeswell	Richard Keeble	2s.	0d.	1 4 0
	Do	Frances Farrow	2s.	0d.	1 4 0
	Dallingho	Catherine Keeble	1s.	6d.	0 18 0
		Martha List	2s.	6d.	1 10 0
	Kettleburgh	Martha Lord	1s.	0d.	0 12 0
	Debach	Eliz Orsborn	2s.	0d.	1 4 0
		Sarah Prew	2s.	6d.	1 10 0
		Hugh Read	2s.	0d.	1 4 0

	John Shreeve	5s.	0d.	3	0	0
	John Skeet	3s.	0d.	1	16	0
	Wm. Upson	4s.	0d.	2	8	0
	Robt. Wolton	5s.	0d.	3	0	0
				38	8	0

Wickham		Widow Brown at					
		Framlingham	2s.	6d.	1	10	0
	Marlesford	Widow Berry	2s.	6d.	1	10	0
		do Cotton	1s.	6d.	0	18	0
		do Curtis	1s.	6d.	0	18	0
		do Fish	3s.	0d.	1	16	0
		do Garnham	1s.	6d.	0	18	0
	Dallingo	*do* Good	1s.	6d.	0	18	0
	Hacheston	*do* Hart	2s.	0d.	1	4	0
		do Harvey	2s.	0d.	1	4	0
		do Hewitt	2s.	6d.	1	10	0
		do Kerridge	1s.	6d.	0	18	0
		do Plant	2s.	6d.	1	10	0
		do Plowman	2s.	6d.	1	10	0
	Ufford	*do* Sayer	2s.	0d.	1	4	0
	Hollesly	*do* Skinner	1s.	6d.	0	18	0
	Hatcheston	John Brown's daught.	1s.	0d.	0	12	0
		Wm. Burrows	1s.	6d.	0	18	0
		Wm. Buck	5s.	0d.	3	0	0
	Earl Soham	Jacob Cook	6s.	0d.	3	12	0
		Martha Curtis	1s.	6d.	0	18	0
		Harman Garrett	1s.	0d.	0	12	0
		James Hewett	2s.	0d.	1	4	0
	Petistree	Robt. Howard	3s.	0d.	1	16	0
		Henry Kenton's daugh.	1s.	0d.	0	12	0
		Thos. Partridge	6s.	0d.	3	12	0
	Earl Soham	Thos. Potter	2s.	0d.	1	4	0
		Mary Rands	2s.	6d.	1	10	0
		Saml. Sayer	2s.	0d.	1	4	0
	Hatcheston	Thos. Spink	4s.	6d.	2	14	0
		Christine Taylor's B.B. child	1s.	6d.	0	18	0
		Susan Tyler	2s.	6d.	1	10	0
		Robt. Tuffield	2s.	0d.	1	4	0
		Thos. Woolnough	3s.	0d.	1	16	0
		Sarah Wright	2s.	0d.	1	4	0
	Hachestson	John Lanham	4s.	0d.	2	8	0
	do	Barbara Turpin	2s.	6d.	1	10	0
	Easton	Samuel Hearn's wife	1s.	6d.	0	18	0
	do	John Scutt	3s.	6d.	2	2	0
					56	8	0
		Wilford			357	8	0
		Loes			327	12	0
		Total			685	0	0

Ordered that the following children be apprenticed as under:

Parishes	Names	Ages	To whom apprenticed	Remarks
Alderton	Charlotte Francis	13	Mr John Bird	paid penalty
Ash	Eliza Downing	14½	Jacob Whitbread Esq.	paid penalty
do	Hannah Downing	13	Mr John Goodwyn	£10 taken
Brandeston	Robert Boon	14	Mr Thos. Baldwin Jun.	taken
Cretingham	Mary Cook	13½	Mr Henry Ashford	paid penalty
Dallingho	Mary Ann Adams	13	Mr Jos. Bugg of Debach	£10 paid penalty
Earl Soham	William Webb	12	Mr James Kent	paid penalty
Eyke	William Worledge	14½	Mr John Culham	£20 deferred
Hacheston	Elizabeth Holder	12½	Mr Jonth. Paternoster	£10 paid penalty
Hoo	Mary Cracknell	13	Mr James Catchpole of Letheringham	£10 taken
Hollesley	Robert Rust	12	Revd Wm. Bolton	paid penalty
do	Henry Grayston	12	Mr Robert Barthrop	paid penalty
Melton	Sophia Lester	14	Mr Benj. Cooper of Bredfield	taken
Monewden	Mark Wade	12½	Mr Thos. Catchpole	paid penalty
W Market	Mary Ann Block	13	Mr John Threadkell	£10 taken

Ordered: That Mr Wm. Pitts of Monewden has leave to assign his apprentices Eliza Bloss and Wm. Berry to Mr Wm. Kitson of Monewden aforesaid.

And that Henry Kent of Kettleburgh has leave to assign his apprentice Joseph Peck to Wm. Green of Kettleburgh, blacksmith.

That George Branch, a poor lad in the House of Industry belonging to Hollesly, be apprenticed to John Ransby of Bawdsey, cordwainer, with a premium of fifteen pounds, for three years.

That Daniel Kerridge a poor lad belonging to Wickham be apprenticed to Henry Motram of Heveningham for 4 years with a premium of five pounds.

7 January 1819

Resolved unanimously that after attentive consideration that the grounds alleged by Mr Dyer for the augmentation of the salaries of the surgeons attending the different divisions did not appear sufficient to justify any such augmentation for the present. Resolved that at the next Quarterly Meeting it be taken into further consideration the propriety of taking the parish of Rendlesham from Mr Hughes's attendance and added to Mr Harsant's on account of better local arrangement.

8 April 1819

Directors	present	Guardians
Thomas Pytches Esq.		Mr Thomas Kersey
John Syer M.D.		Mr Edward Crisp
Mr H. Edwards		Mr James Clubbe
Mr Joshua Rodwell		
Mr Thomas Waller		
Mr W. Henchman		
Revd Mr Chilton		
Revd Mr Is. Clarke		
Revd Mr Davy		

The following persons were duly elected Directors and Acting Guardians

	Directors	Guardians
May	Revd George Turner	Mr George Bond
	Mr Jeptha Waller	Mr J. D. Leach
June	Edmund Jenny Esq.	Mr Samuel Kersey
	Revd G. F. Tavell	Mr S. Jeaffreson
July	John Purcell Esq.	Mr Edgar Smith
	Mr W. Henchman	Mr Philip Dykes
Aug.	Revd Mr Browne	Mr Edward Crisp
	Revd. T. Broadhurst	Mr John Walton
Sept.	John Syer M.D.	Mr Joseph Roe
	Revd Mr Aldrich	Mr J. R. Hodgson
Oct.	Mr Henry Edwards	Mr H. Farrer
	Mr J. A. Studd	Mr S. Brewer
Nov.	Andrew Arcedeckne Esq.	Mr Thomas Catlin
	Revd Chas. Davy	Mr T. Simpson
Dec.	Mr Thomas Waller	Mr Edward Turner
	Mr Philip Dykes	Mr Samuel Randall
Jan.	Revd Isaac Clarke	Mr Thomas Kersey
	Revd Chas Brooke	Mr John Button
Feb.	Jacob Whitbread Esq.	Mr James Clubbe
	Mr Samuel Gross	Mr James Glanfield
Mar.	Thomas Pytches Esq.	Mr John Blake
	Mr Joshua Rodwell	Mr B. Colchester

On account of the great inconvenience of holding the previous meetings at the House of Industry on the Monday before the Quarterly Meeting (the committee meetings being also held on those days). It was resolved that it be taken into consideration at the next Quarterly Meeting whether it may not be proper that the previous meetings should for the future be holden on the Thursday before the Quarterly Meetings.

8 July 1819

In reference to the resolution as to the time of holding the previous meeting. It is now resolved that the previous meetings be henceforth held on the Tuesday preceding the Quarterly Meeting, and that the amount of out allowances in the overseers' books be examined by the Directors on the first Monday of each month in order that the attendance of the overseers at the Previous Meetings may not be required. And that the Governor does give notice to every Director of the above resolution.

14 October 1819

Ordered that the surgeons of the Corporation be particularly required at the proper seasons to vaccinate all paupers within the incorporated parishes who have not been already vaccinated.

6 April 1820

Directors	present	Guardians
Revd Mr Davy		Mr P. Dykes
Revd Mr Brooke		Mr J. R. Hodgson
Revd Mr Groome		

Revd Mr Chilton
Mr John Woolnough
Mr Samuel Gross
Dr Syer
Jacob Whitbread Esq.

The following persons were duly elected Directors and Acting Guardians <>

	Directors	Guardians
May	Revd George Turner	Mr Nathaniel Barthrop Jun.
	Mr Jeptha Waller	Mr Edward Field
June	Edmund Jenny Esq.	Mr Thomas Garneys
	Revd G. F. Tavel	Mr Samuel Jeaffreson
July	John FitzGerald Esq.	Mr Edgar Smith
	Revd J. H. Groome	Mr Philip Dykes Jun.
Aug.	Revd Wm. Browne	Mr Fenn Sheming
	Revd Thos. Broadhurst	Mr John Wolton
Sept.	John Syer M.D.	Mr Joseph Roe
	Revd. Wm. Aldrich	Mr Charles Jackson
Oct.	Mr Henry Edwards	Mr William Hambling
	Mr J. A. Studd	Mr Edmund Plant
Nov.	Andrew Arcedeckne Esq.	Mr Thos. Catlin
	Revd Chas Davy	Mr Thos. Simpson
Dec.	Mr Thos. Waller	Mr George Largent
	Mr Philip Dykes	Mr Benj. Cooper
Jan.	Revd Isaac Clarke	Mr Thos. Kersey
	Revd Chas Brooke	Mr John Button
Feb.	Jacob Whitbread Esq.	Mr Jas. Clubbe
	Mr Samuel Gross	Mr T. F. Josslyn
Mar.	Thomas Pytches Esq.	Mr John Thredkell
	Mr Joshua Rodwell	Mr T. W. Baldwin
Apl.	Revd Jacob Chilton	Mr John Goodwyn
	Mr John Woolnough	Mr G. Utting

That as Mr Dyer has tended his resignation as medical attendant for the paupers in certain parishes within the Incorporated Hundreds, the said resignation is received. And that all or any five directors be a committee to meet to consult upon the best means of having the paupers attended by a medical practitioner. And that the Governor do give notice to the Directors accordingly.

24 April 1820 [*Medical care committee*]

The above directors having met for the purpose of consulting upon the best means of having the paupers in certain parishes within the Incorporated Hundreds attended by a medical practitioner do resolve that an advertisement as follows be inserted for 2 weeks in the two Ipswich papers. And a meeting of the Directors and Acting Guardians be held at the House of Industry on <9 May> for the purpose mentioned in the advertisement.

To surgeons etc.

A meeting of the Directors and Acting Guardians of the poor within the Hundreds of Loes and Wilford will be held at the House of Industry in Melton on Tuesday, the 9th May at 11 o'clock in the forenoon in order to receive offers from any medical gentlemen to attend the poor within the following parishes viz. Bredfield, Boulge, Bromeswell, Charsfield, Dallingho, Debach, Eyke, Melton, Ufford and Woodbridge. Any further particulars may be had by application to the Governor of the said House.

9 May 1820 [*Medical care committee*]

No offer was made to this meeting to take the medical attendance of the parishes agreeable to the foregoing advertisement, but an arrangement was entered into with Mr Lynn and Mr Harsant (who were present) with the former to take the parishes of Woodbridge, Melton, Bredfield and Boulge from Midsummer to Michaelmas next for the salaries now paid for those parishes, the latter to take the parishes of Charsfield, Dallingho, and Debach for the same time at the present salaries also.

A letter having been received from Mr Hughes offering to take the parishes of Bromeswell and Eyke and also any two or three other parishes, in case his so doing should be any accommodation to the Corporation until a final arrangement shall be made. The clerk was directed to write to Mr Hughes to request his taking the parishes of Bromeswell, Eyke and Ufford from Midsummer to Michaelmas next on the present terms.

A letter was also received from Mr Weeding of Alderton offering to take the parishes of Melton, Bromeswell, Ufford and Eyke or any part of them, but this offer was declined on account of the distance of his residence from the parishes.

Resolved that this meeting do recommend to the next Quarterly Meeting to increase the salaries of the out surgeons about 10 per cent upon the present payments.

6 July 1820

Ordered that the following advertisement be inserted in the Ipswich Journal and Suffolk Chronicle 3 weeks, viz. 15th 22nd 29th July.

To surgeons

A vacancy having occurred in the medical department of the Incorporated Hundreds of Loes and Wilford, in the attendance upon the House of Industry and the district comprehending the following parishes viz. Bredfield, Boulge, Bromeswell, Charsfield, Dallingho, Debach, Eyke, Melton, Ufford & Woodbridge. Notice is hereby given that a meeting of Directors and Acting Guardians will be held on <14 August> in order to receive offers from any medical gentlemen who will undertake the same conjointly at Michaelmas next. Further particulars may be had by applying to the Governor at the said House by letter, post-paid.

14 August 1820 [*Medical care committee*]

At this meeting proposals for attending the poor in the House of Industry conjointly with the parishes advertised were received from the following gentlemen viz. Mr Hamilton of Ipswich, Mr Gissing of Woodbridge, Mr Steggall of Elmswell, Mr Chandler of Grundisburgh, and Mr Hughes of Shottisham.

But it being stated to the meeting that Mr Lynn was desirous of retaining the attendance on the House and that he was willing to take the care of the poor residing in Woodbridge without any addition to his present salary, and that Mr Bloomfield was ready to take the care of the nine remaining parishes at the sum of sixty five pounds per annum. It was decided that Mr Lynn should be continued as House surgeon at the present salary of eighty pounds per annum including the attendance of the poor residing in Woodbridge. And that Mr Bloomfield should attend the parishes of Bredfield, Boulge, Bromeswell, Charsfield, Dallingho, Debach, Eyke, Melton and Ufford at the salary of sixty five pounds per annum.

It was also resolved that the salaries of the other surgeons viz. Mr Harsant, Mr Hughes and Mr Bellman should be advanced at the rate of one pound for each parish per annum, from Michaelmas next, at which time all the above alterations are to take place.

Mr Lynn	£80 per annum
Mr Blomfield	£65
Mr Hughes	£85
Mr Harsant	£56
Mr Bellman	£49
	£335

26 October 1818

Ordered that the Overseers of the respective parishes do allow as follows:

Debach	Debach	Henry Curtis 2s. 1 week, John Kitson in addition 1s.	0	3	0
Ufford	Ufford	Elizabeth Hearn 1s. 1 week	0	1	0
	Melton	Thomas Lewis 1s. 2w including last week	0	2	0
Hatcheston	Hatcheston	Daniel Hayward 1s. 6d. 1w William Mayhew 1s. 6d. 1w	0	3	0
	do	Alice Fisk for clothing to service at Yoxford	1	0	0
Petistree	Petistree	Wm. King in addn. to Qtr. Order 6d. 4w Thos. Capon 6d. 4w	0	4	0
Dallingho	Dallingho	Jer. Davy 6s. 1w, Widow Aldhous in addn. Qtr. Order 1s. 1w	0	7	0
Hoo	Hoo	Susan Page 2s. 6d. 1w, David Nunn 1s. 6d. 1 w	0	4	0
	Letheringham	John Smith 1s. 6d. 1w and 2s. last week	0	3	6
Boyton	Boyton	Saml. Charity 4s. 4 w, Wm. Middleditch 1s. 6d. 4w	1	2	0
	do	Robert Walker 6s. 4w including past week	1	4	0
	Bawdsey	Wm. Beecraft 3s. 4w in addition to Qtr. Order	0	12	0
	Capel	James Chambers 3s. 4 weeks	0	12	0
Bromeswell	Bromswell	John Riches 5s. 1 w, John Keable 10s. 1 w	0	15	0
	Sutton	Henry Lines 12s. 1w, Mary Stebbings 1s. 1w	0	13	0
Hollesley	Hollesley	Oct 19th John Birch 10s., Thos. Curtis 5s., Robt. Hubbard 6s.	1	1	0
	do	do Wm. Lucock 6s., Wm Jarvis 2s.	0	8	0
	Capel	do the wife of Andrew Williams 9s	0	9	0
	Alderton	do Benjamin Bobbitt 15s. 1 w	0	15	0
	do	do Oct 26th do do 15s. 1 w	0	15	0
	Ramsholt	do Isaac Scott 7s. 1 w	0	7	0
	Hollesly	John Birch 10s. 1w, Thos. Curtis 5s. 1w	0	15	0
	do	Chas. Warner 10s. 1w, Thos. Knights			

---

2   SROI ADA11/A/B/3/8.

		8s. 1w.	0	18	0
do		John Butcher 9s. 1w, Francis Andrews 10s. 1w	0	19	0
do		Jeptha Roper 2s 1w.	0	2	0
do		the following persons apply for relief or work have had no employment for more than 7 days, have applied to the Overseer Charles Walker and Richard Clarke single men			
Eyke	Eyke	James Larters wife and child to be discharged.			
			13	14	6

Directors   Guardians
Henry Edwards   Chas. Ablitt
J. A. Studd

SEVENTH QUARTERLY MINUTE BOOK
12 October 1820–12 October 1826[1]

12 October 1820

Directors	Present	Guardians
Revd Mr Brooke	Revd Mr Broadhurst	Mr Hambling
Revd Mr Chilton	Jacob Whitbread Esq.	Mr Wolton
Mr Rodwell		Mr Woolnough
Mr J. Waller		Mr S. Gross
Mr Dykes		

Ordered that the following children be apprentices as under

Parishes	Names	Ages	to whom apprenticed	remarks
Ash	John Mays	14	Mr William Blomfield	£10 taken
do	James Mays	12½	Mr John Goodwyn	paid penalty
Charsfield	James Wythe	13½	Mr S. Lenny	£10 taken
Creetingham	Thomas Turner	14	Mr Henry Farrer	£10 taken
Dallingho	Jeremiah Orsborn	13¼	Mr John Wilson Jun.	£10 taken
Hatcheston	John Orsborn	13¾	Mr George Bond	£10 taken
Hollesley	William Mays	12½	Revd William Bolton	£20 taken
Kettleburgh	James Starks	13	Mr John Grout	taken
Melton	Henry Took	13	Mr Henry Rout	£10 taken
Rendlesham	Mary Horn	13	Lord Rendlesham	paid penalty
Ufford	Emma Reeve	14	Mr Stephen Oxborrow	£10 taken
do	Samuel Wix	12	Mr Edward Turner	taken
Wickham Mkt	Mary Hewett	12	Mrs Sarah Blake	taken

The Revd Mr Davy, having this day tendered his resignation as a Director on account of his leaving the neighbourhood, the same is hereby received. The vacancy occasioned by this resignation to be filled up at the meeting in April next.

Resolved that this meeting do adjourn to <31 October> for the purpose of hearing and determining appeals, if any, to the accounts for the past 10 years, and to make a rate for the ensuing quarter according to the new ratio, the same to be advertised in the Ipswich papers.

Ordered that the following Out Allowances be granted for this Quarter:

Parish pauper Resides in	Parish belonging to	Names	sum per week s. d.	allowed per Quarter £ s. d.
Ash		Widow Barber	2s. 0d.	1 6 0
		do Downing	7s. 6d.	4 17 6

---

[1] SROI ADA11/A/B/1/7.

	do Howard	4s.	0d.	2 12 0
	do Ling and child	4s.	0d.	2 12 0
	do Newson	2s.	0d.	1 6 0
	do Robinson	1s.	0d.	0 13 0
Kettleburgh	*do* Ringe	3s.	6d.	2 5 6
Hatcheston	*do* Abi. Skinner	3s.	0d.	1 19 0
Alderton	*do* Deb. Skinner	1s.	6d.	0 19 6
	Richd Underwood's wife's child	2s.	0d.	1 6 0
	Ling aged about 9yrs	2s.	0d.	1 6 0
				21 2 6
Brandeston	Widow Baker	2s.	6d.	1 12 6
	do Boon	3s.	0d.	1 19 0
	do Cullum	3s.	0d.	1 19 0
	do Nunn	7s.	0d.	4 11 0
	Ann Calver	2s.	6d.	1 12 6
	Mary Chapman	2s.	0d.	1 6 0
	Joseph Harvey's child	2s.	6d.	1 12 6
	Rd Herrington's child	3s.	0d.	1 19 0
	Ann Martin	4s.	0d.	2 12 0
	Mark Noble	4s.	0d.	2 12 0
	Eliz. Read's B.B. child	1s.	0d.	0 13 0
	Widow Selby	3s.	0d.	1 19 0
				24 7 6
Butley	Edward Cattermole	1s.	6d.	0 19 6
	Robert Pemberton (dead)	2s.	0d	0 2 0
	Widow Hazelwood	1s.	6d.	0 19 6
Bredfield	*do* Clark	5s.	0d.	3 5 0
Kettleburgh	*do* Smith	2s.	0d.	1 6 0
Capel	*do* Mary Smith	2s.	0d.	1 6 0
				7 18 0
Charsfield	Widow Atkins	5s.	6d.	3 11 6
	do Buck	2s.	6d.	1 12 6
Easton	*do* Driver	2s.	0d.	1 6 0
	do Fisk	6s.	6d.	4 4 6
	do Mauldon	2s.	6d.	1 12 6
Kettleburgh	*do* Parker	2s.	6d.	1 12 6
	James Ablett	7s.	0d.	4 11 0
	Jas. Block's wife and child	7s.	0d.	4 11 0
	John Bradstreet	5s.	0d.	3 5 0
	Jane Branch	2s.	6d.	1 12 6
	Jas. Fulcher	1s.	6d.	0 19 6
	Mary Mauldon	2s.	0d.	1 6 0
	Sarah Read	2s.	0d.	1 6 0
	Robert Creasy	0s.	6d.	0 6 6
	Amy Wythe	2s.	0d.	1 6 0
				33 3 0

Creetingham		Widow Capper	5s.	0d.	3	5 0
		do Harvey	2s.	0d	1	6 0
		do Moss at				
		Burton on Trent	3s.	0d.	1	19 0
		do Orsborn	2s.	6d.	1	12 6
		Robert Cudbear	2s.	0d.	1	6 0
		Mary Lanham	2s.	0d.	1	6 0
		Mary Moyses	1s.	6d.	0	19 6
		William Moss	2s.	0d.	1	6 0
		Robert Nicholls	2s.	0d.	1	6 0
		Ann Nicholls	1s.	6d.	0	19 6
		Eliz. Oxborrow's				
		B.B. child	1s.	6d.	0	19 6
		John Scotchmer	2s.	0d.	1	6 0
		John Tye	2s.	0d.	1	6 0
					18	17 0
Dallingho		Widow Aldous	5s.	0d.	3	5 0
	Earl Soham	*do* Debenham	2s.	0d.	1	6 0
		do Ford	5s.	6d.	3	11 6
	Kenton	*do* Keer	2s.	6d.	1	12 6
		do Read	5s.	0d.	3	5 0
		do Wright	2s.	0d.	1	6 0
		do Wyard or Wyatt	1s.	0d.	0	13 0
		Robert Clark	5s.	0d.	3	5 0
		Ann Rosiers B.B. child	1s.	0d.	0	13 0
		John Rummacles	1s.	0d.	0	13 0
		Charity Woolnough	2s.	0d.	1	6 0
		Eliz. Wyatt or Wyard	1s.	0d.	0	13 0
					21	9 0
Earl Soham		Widow Hall	2s.	0d.	1	6 0
		do Harvey	1s.	6d.	0	19 6
		do Keer	4s.	0d.	2	12 0
		do Long (dead)	3s.	0d.	1	1 0
	Monewden	*do* Smith	1s.	0d.	0	13 0
		do Wade	1s.	6d.	0	19 6
		do Warner	2s.	6d.	1	12 6
		Benj. Alexander	2s.	0d.	1	6 0
		Edmund Barker	3s.	0d.	1	19 0
		James Bromefield	1s.	6d.	0	19 6
		Sarah Eade	2s.	0d.	1	6 0
		Robert Lanham	3s.	0d.	1	19 0
	Kenton	Mary Lanceker's B.B. child	2s.	0d.	1	6 0
		Susan Manning's *do*	1s.	6d.	0	19 6
		Maria Nesling's *do*	1s.	9d.	1	2 9
		William Moss and wife	3s.	0d.	1	19 0
		William Paxman and wife	5s.	0d.	3	5 0
		James Pryke	4s.	0d.	2	12 0
		Mary Runacles	1s.	6d.	0	19 6

					£ s d
		Robert Spink	5s.	0d.	3 5 0
		Susan Woolnough's B.B. child	1s.	6d.	0 19 6
					33 1 3
Easton		Widow Capon	3s.	0d.	1 6 0
	Charsfield	do Bennett	2s.	6d.	1 12 6
	Rendlesham	do Death (dead)	2s.	6d.	0 10 0
		do Hayward	2s.	6d.	1 12 6
	Petistree	do Persimon	2s.	6d.	1 12 6
		do Smith	2s.	0d.	1 6 0
		Robert Brooks	2s.	0d.	1 6 0
		Hannah Coat's B.B. child	2s.	0d.	1 6 0
		John French	2s.	6d.	1 12 6
		Thomas Grimwood	6s.	0d.	3 18 0
		Mary Neve	2s.	6d.	1 12 6
	Hatcheston	Jemima Page's B.B. child	2s.	6d.	1 12 6
		John Scutt	2s.	6d.	1 12 6
		Emma Tricker's B.B. child	1s.	6d.	0 19 6
		Emma Yeldon	2s.	6d.	1 12 6
					23 11 6
Eyke		Widow Barham	1s.	6d.	0 19 6
		do Brightwell	2s.	0d.	1 6 0
		do Clouting	1s.	6d.	0 19 6
	Ash	do King	2s.	0d.	1 6 0
		do Mossley	4s.	0d.	2 12 0
		Margaret Barber	1s.	0d.	0 13 0
		Jane Booth	1s.	0d.	0 13 0
	Sutton	Martha Howse	3s.	0d	1 19 0
	Bromeswell	John Luffe's idiot ch.	1s.	6d.	0 19 6
		John Stannard	3s.	0d.	1 19 0
		Eliz Topple B.B. child	1s.	6d.	0 19 6
		Lucy Worledge's B.B. child	2s.	0d.	1 6 0
	Rendlesham	James Jeffries	5s.	0d.	3 5 0
					18 17 0
Hatcheston	Marlesford	Widow Aldridge	3s.	6d.	2 5 6
		do Curtis	3s.	6d.	2 5 6
	Wickham	do Damant	1s.	6d.	0 19 6
	Kettleburgh	do Flick	1s.	0d.	0 13 0
		do Garrod	3s.	6d.	2 5 6
	Wickham	do Sayer	2s.	0d.	1 6 0
		do Smith	4s.	0d.	2 12 0
	Marlesford	Lydia Aldrdge	2s.	0d.	1 6 0
	Sutton	Ann Farrer's B.B. child	1s.	6d.	0 19 6
		Sarah Gilman	2s.	0d.	1 6 0
	Marlesford	Mary Hatcher's B.B. child	2s.	0d.	1 6 0
		George Kettle	5s.	0d.	3 5 0
	Brandeston	Mary Mills	1s.	6d.	0 19 6

Letheringham	Timothy Mattow	2s.	6d.	1	12	6
Letheringham	Thomas Mattow	6s.	6d.	4	4	6
Marlesford	Eliz Porter	3s.	0d.	1	19	0
Wickham	John Scopes	4s.	0d.	2	12	0
	John Scrutton	7s.	0d.	4	11	0
Cretingham	Thomas Turner	7s.	0d.	4	11	0
Hollesley	Eliz. Grayston	2s.	0d.	<u>1</u>	<u>6</u>	<u>0</u>
				42	5	0

Hoo	Robert Bailey & wife	1s.	6d.	0	19	6
Cretingham	Wm. Brainton	5s.	0d.	3	5	0
	John Gibbs' wife	1s.	0d.	0	13	0
	Mary Marjoram's B.B. child	1s.	0d.	0	13	0
	Susan Studd at Rushmere 2 B.B.	2s.	0d.	1	6	0
	Susan Studd at Raisfield 2 B.B.	2s.	0d.	<u>1</u>	<u>6</u>	<u>0</u>
				7	2	6

Kenton	Widow Collins	1s.	6d.	0	19	6
	do Parker	3s.	0d.	1	19	0
	do Pollard	5s.	0d.	3	5	0
	do Porcher	2s.	6d.	1	12	6
	do Roper	2s.	6d.	1	12	6
	John Church blind	10s.	6d.	6	16	6
	Stephen Clark	8s.	0d.	5	4	0
	Robert Hill	5s.	0d.	3	5	0
	James Stammers	1s.	6d.	0	19	6
	Mary Thompson	1s.	0d.	<u>0</u>	<u>13</u>	<u>0</u>
				26	6	6

Kettleburgh	Widow England	2s.	3d.	1	9	3
	do Kent	3s.	0d.	1	19	0
	do Newman	3s.	6d.	2	5	6
	do Jane Smith	2s.	0d.	1	6	0
	Eliz Crowfoot	1s.	6d.	0	19	6
	Colin Holmes' daught	1s.	0d.	0	13	0
	C. Sculthorpe 2 B.B. child.	3s.	0d.	1	19	0
Alderton	James and Fanny Turner	7s.	6d.	<u>4</u>	<u>17</u>	<u>6</u>
				15	8	9

Letheringham	Widow Markham	2s.	6d.	1	12	6
Kenton	*do* Long	3s.	0d.	1	19	0
Hollesley	Hannah Disberry BB child	1s.	6d.	<u>0</u>	<u>19</u>	<u>6</u>
				4	11	0

Marlesford	Widow Burrell	2s.	0d.	1	6	0
Wickham	*do* Bridges	3s.	0d.	1	19	0
	do Cave	2s.	0d.	1	6	0

	do Martin	2s.	0d.	1	6	0
	Sarah Bickers	3s.	0d.	1	19	0
	Robt Boynes	2s.	0d.	1	6	0
	Nathl. Cockerill	3s.	0d.	1	19	0
	Henry Cooper	3s.	6d.	2	5	6
	Saml. Markham	2s.	0d.	1	6	0
	John Pells	2s.	6d.	1	12	6
	Ann Skeet	2s.	0d.	1	6	0
	Eliz Smith	2s.	0d.	1	6	0
	Jacob Watling blind and Child	6s.	6d.	4	4	6
				23	1	6

Monewden		Sarah Brown	2s.	6d.	1	12	0
	Creetingham	Sarah Cullum	2s.	0d.	1	6	0
		H. Hazelwood a B.B. child	2s.	0d.	1	6	0
		Henry Rattle	4s.	0d.	2	12	0
		Rich Woods	4s.	0d.	2	12	0
		George Woods	1s.	6d.	0	19	6
		Widow Wade	2s.	0d.	1	6	0
					11	14	0

Rendlesham		Widow Barthorp	2s.	0d.	1	6	0
		do Coleman	2s.	0d.	1	6	0
		do Lock's child	1s.	6d.	0	19	0
	Bredfield	*do* Mays	2s.	6d.	1	12	6
		Rebecca Barham	1s.	6d.	0	19	0
		Charlotte Fearhead's B.B. child	1s.	6d.	0	19	0
		Hannah Holden's *do*	1s.	6d.	0	19	0
		John Lincoln's wife	1s.	0d.	0	13	0
	Earl Soham	Hannah Orams	1s.	6d.	0	19	0
		Thomas Rout	2s.	6d.	1	12	6
					11	7	6
	Total Loes				345	3	6

Alderton		Widow Alexander	2s.	6d.	1	12	6
		do Baxter's child	1s.	6d.	0	19	6
		do Barnard	1s.	6d.	0	19	6
		do Bloomfield	4s.	0d.	2	12	0
	Sutton	*do* Blaxall	2s.	0d.	1	6	0
	Shottisham	*do* Bigsby	1s.	6d.	0	19	6
		do Button	1s.	6d.	0	19	6
	Bawdsey	*do do* for a child	1s.	0d.	0	13	0
		do Cooper	2s.	0d.	1	6	0
	Ramsholt	*do* Girling	6s.	0d.	3	18	0
	Boyton	*do* Good	2s.	0d.	1	6	0
	Bawdsey	*do* Heffer	2s.	0d.	1	6	0
		do Holden	1s.	6d.	0	19	6
		do Horn	2s.	0d.	1	6	0

Wickham	*do* Johnson	2s.	0d.	1	6	0
	do Smith's children (3)	2s.	0d.	1	6	0
	do Steward	1s.	6d.	0	19	6
Hollesley	*do* Thurston	1s.	6d.	0	19	6
Hollesley	*do* Woods	2s.	0d.	1	6	0
Sutton	*do* Wright	2s.	0d.	1	6	0
	Mary Aldis	1s.	6d.	0	19	6
Boyton	Joseph Baxter	2s.	0d.	1	6	0
Shottisham	Eliz. Cooper	1s.	6d.	0	19	6
Hollesley	George Dunn	2s.	6d.	1	12	6
	Eliz. Girling	1s.	6d.	0	19	6
	Thos. Hubbard	1s.	6d.	0	19	6
Boyton	Ann Hunt's B.B. child	1s.	6d.	0	19	6
	Mary Knights	2s.	6d.	1	12	6
	Jonathan Lawrence	2s.	0d.	1	6	0
	Wm. Murrell	2s.	6d.	1	12	6
	Robt. Pooley's wife	1s.	6d.	0	19	6
Hollesley	Eliz. Slotlery	2s.	0d.	1	6	0
	Casey Wade's daught.	1s.	6d.	0	19	0
	Henry Woods blind	3s.	0d.	1	19	0
				44	17	0

Bawdsey	Widow Brockhouses	2s.	6d.	1	12	6
	do Hubbard	1s.	6d.	0	19	6
Sutton	*do* Hunt	1s.	6d.	0	19	6
	do King	1s.	6d.	0	19	6
	do Moor	1s.	6d.	0	19	6
	do Pratt's child	3s.	6d.	2	5	6
Melton	*do* Sheldrake	1s.	6d.	0	19	6
	Mary Burrow's B.B. child	2s.	0d.	1	6	0
	Lucy Clutterham's *do*	1s.	6d.	0	19	6
	Eliz. Goodall	1s.	6d.	0	19	6
	Mary Flower	1s.	6d.	0	19	6
				13	0	0

Boulge	Jeremiah Marjorem and wife	4s.	0d.	2	12	0
	C. Read 2 B.B. child.	4s.	0d.			
	do omitted last Q.	1s.	0d.	3	5	0
	James Harmen	5s.	0d.	3	5	0
				7	2	0

Boyton	Widow Bullow	2s.	6d.	1	12	6
	do Hunt	2s.	0d.	1	6	0
	do Jessup	2s.	0d.	1	6	0
	do King	2s.	6d.	1	12	6
	do Pettitt	3s.	0d.	1	19	6
	William Beecraft	7s.	0d.	4	11	0
Kettleburgh	Edward Brown	4s.	0d.	2	12	0
	Saml. Charity	4s.	0d.	2	12	0
	Martha Ellis' B.B. child	2s.	0d.	1	6	0

		Saml. Hart	2s.	6d.	1 12 6
Ash		*do* for late Brown's			
		B.B. child	1s.	6d.	0 19 6
					21 9 0
Bredfield		Widow Allen	3s.	0d.	1 19 0
	Ufford	*do* Andrews	3s.	0d.	1 19 0
	Bawdsey	*do* Brown	2s.	6d.	1 12 6
	Cretingham	*do* Godbold	1s.	6d.	0 19 6
		do Fox	1s.	6d.	0 19 6
		do Lankester	3s.	0d.	1 19 0
		do Wright	3s.	6d.	2 5 6
		Robt. Battle	5s.	0d.	3 5 0
		Susan Fitch	1s.	0d.	0 13 0
		Mary Hailes' B.B. child	0s.	6d.	0 6 6
		Thos. Hendley's wife	1s.	6d.	0 19 6
	Easton	Saml. Loom	5s.	0d.	3 5 0
		Mary Marjerom	1s.	6d.	0 19 6
		Hannah Richardson's			
		B.B. child	1s.	6d.	0 19 6
					22 2 0
Bromeswell	Sutton	Widow Branch	2s.	6d.	1 12 6
	Sutton	*do* Fuller	3s.	0d.	1 19 0
	Melton	*do* May's child	2s.	0d.	1 6 0
		do Good	2s.	6d.	1 12 6
		William Cook	5s.	0d.	3 5 0
		John Mills	2s.	0d.	1 6 0
		Charlotte Leek's B.B. child	1s.	6d.	0 19 0
		Beliza Riches's' *do*	1s.	6d.	0 19 0
	Marlesford	Frances Rose's *do*	1s.	6d.	0 19 0
	Sutton	Ann Mullinger's *do*	1s.	6d.	0 19 6
	do	Stebbing's child	6s.	0d.	3 18 0
					18 17 0
Debach		John Crane's 2 child.	3s.	0d.	1 19 0
		Lydia Garnham	2s.	0d.	1 6 0
		John Kitson	5s.	0d.	3 5 0
		Wm. Robinson	2s.	6d.	1 12 6
					8 2 6
Hollesley		Widow Andrews	2s.	0d.	1 6 0
		do Clodd	1s.	6d.	0 19 6
		do Crick	6s.	6d.	4 4 6
		do Cooper	3s.	0d.	1 19 0
		do Gooding	3s.	0d.	1 19 0
	Alderton	*do* Creasy	2s.	0d.	1 6 0
	do	*do* Fox sen.	2s.	0d.	1 6 0
	Do	*do* Fox jun.	6s.	0d.	3 18 0
		do Skipper			

Ramsholt	Frances Andrews' B.B. child	1s.	6d.	0 19 6
	Mary Branch and *do*	2s.	6d.	1 12 6
	James Battle	8s.	0d.	5 4 0
	Wm. Cheversons child	2s.	6d.	1 12 6
	Mary Cooper 2 B.B. child	4s.	0d.	2 12 0
Capel	John Kemp and wife	4s.	0d.	2 12 0
				31 10 6

Melton		Widow Chilton	4s.	6d.	2 18 6
		do Day	1s.	6d.	0 19 6
	Cretingham	*do* Bardwell	1s.	6d.	0 19 6
	Ash	*do* Denton and 4 ch.	8s.	0d.	5 4 0
	Sutton	*do* Flory	2s.	0d.	1 6 0
	do	*do* Knappet	6s.	0d.	3 18 0
	do	*do* Ruth's orphan children (3)	6s.	0d.	3 18 0
		do Sawyer	2s.	0d.	1 6 0
		do Took	4s.	6d.	2 18 6
		do Whiting	12s.	0d.	7 16 0
	Rendlesham	*do* Woods	1s.	6d.	0 19 6
		John Harper	2s.	0d.	1 6 0
		Mary Ewens	3s.	0d.	1 19 0
		Thos. Hatton's 4 orphan children	10s.	0d.	6 10 0
	Bawdsey	Wm. Hammond a B.B. child	1s.	6d.	0 19 6
		James Holder's child	1s.	6d.	0 19 6
		Robt. Jay 2 idiot ch.	2s.	6d.	1 12 6
		Jemima Prentice's 2 B.B. child.	1s.	6d.	0 19 6
	Petistree	Henry Turner & wife	8s.	0d.	5 4 0
	Boulge	Eliz. Wilson	1s.	6d.	0 19 6
					52 13 0

Petistree		Widow King	3s.	0d.	1 19 0
		do Levett	2s.	0d.	1 6 0
		Robert Barnard	4s.	0d.	2 12 0
		Jos. Button	6s.	0d.	3 18 0
		Thos. Capon	4s.	0d.	2 12 0
		Ann Chandler	0s.	6d.	0 6 6
		Charity Lambert	4s.	0d.	2 12 0
	Wickham	Susan Potkin's B.B.	1s.	6d.	0 19 6
		Margaret Rose's *do*	1s.	6d.	0 19 6
					17 4 6

Ramsholt	Alderton	Widow Berry's child	2s.	6d.	1 12 6
	Melton	*do* Orsborn	2s.	0d.	1 6 0
		Eliz. Allen's B.B. ch.	1s.	0d.	0 13 0
		Thos. Lewis's daught.	1s.	6d.	0 19 6
	Capel	Smith's child	1s.	0d.	0 13 0
		Widow Orsborn and daught.	3s.	0d.	1 19 0
					7 3 0

Shottisham		Widow Bird	1s.	6d.	0	19 6
		do Brown	2s.	0d.	1	6 0
		do Gilbert's 2 ch.	3s.	0d.	1	19 0
		do Roper	2s.	6d.	1	12 6
	Hollesley	*do* Hunt's child	1s.	6d.	0	19 6
		do Steward	2s.	0d.	1	6 0
		Eliz. Bird's B.B. ch.	1s.	6d.	0	19 6
		Mary Harvey's *do*	1s.	6d.	0	19 6
		Wm. Daynes	1s.	6d.	0	19 6
		Eliz. Symonds	1s.	0d.	<u>0 13 0</u>	
					11	14 0
Sutton		Widow Ambrose	1s.	0d.	0	13 0
		do Howell	2s.	0d.	1	6 0
		do Lewis	1s.	6d.	0	19 6
		do Steel	1s.	0d.	0	13 0
		Jas. Burrows	2s.	0d.	1	6 0
		John Curtis	2s.	6d.	1	12 6
		Eliz. Driver's B.B. ch.	1s.	6d.	0	19 6
		Eliz. Button's *do*	2s.	0d.	1	6 0
		Warner Gooch's idiot daug.	1s.	0d.	0	13 0
		Henry King	6s.	0d.	3	18 0
		William Laws's wife	1s.	0d.	0	13 0
		Mary Middleditch's B.B. ch.	2s.	0d.	1	6 0
	Ramsholt	Martha Whiting	2s.	0d.	<u>1 6 0</u>	
					16	11 6
Ufford		Widow Amos	1s.	6d.	0	19 6
		do Bennett	2s.	0d.	1	6 0
	Ash	*do* Brightwell	1s.	6d.	0	19 6
	Wickham	*do* Cotton	1s.	0d.	0	13 0
	Kenton	*do* Goddard	2s.	0d.	1	6 0
		do Harvey	2s.	0d.	1	6 0
	Melton	*do* Hattow	3s.	0d.	1	19 0
		do Paitrick	2s.	0d.	1	6 0
		do Parker	2s.	6d.	1	12 6
		do Stimpson	3s.	0d.	1	19 0
		William Archer	4s.	0d.	2	12 0
		Midleton Cracknell	5s.	0d.	3	5 0
		John Croft	4s.	0d.	2	12 0
	Petistree	Robt. Glanfield	4s.	0d.	2	12 0
		Saml. Harland's wife	2s.	0d.	1	6 0
	Bromeswell	Frances Farrow	2s.	0d.	1	6 0
	Dallingho	Catherine Keeble	1s.	6d.	0	19 0
		Martha List	3s.	0d.	1	19 0
	Kettleburgh	Martha Lord	1s.	0d.	0	13 0
	Petistree	Joseph Mallett	5s.	0d.	3	5 0
	Debach	Eliz. Orsborn	2s.	0d.	1	6 0
		Sarah Prew	2s.	6d.	1	12 6
		Hugh Reed	2s.	0d.	1	6 0

371

	Eliz. Read lame	2s.	6d.	1	12	6
	John Skeet	5s.	0d.	3	5	0
	William Upson	2s.	6d.	1	12	6
	Robt. Wolton	5s.	0d.	3	5	0
	Martha Skeet	1s.	6d.	0	19	6
Sutton	John Gillingham	10s.	0d.	6	10	0
				55	5	0

Wickham M		Widow Broom	2s.	6d.	1	12	6
		do Buck	3s.	0d.	1	19	0
	Ash	*do* Betts	2s.	6d.	1	12	6
		do Cotton	2s.	0d.	1	6	0
		do Curtis	2s.	6d.	1	12	6
		do Garnham	2s.	0d.	1	6	0
		do Garrett	1s.	6d.	0	19	6
	Dallingho	*do* Good	1s.	6d.	0	19	6
	Hatcheston	*do* Hart	2s.	0d.	1	6	0
		do Harvey	2s.	0d.	1	6	0
		do Howell	3s.	0d.	1	19	0
	Hatcheston	*do* Holmes	2s.	0d.	1	6	0
		do Kerridge	1s.	0d	0	13	0
		do Pearsons	2s.	6d.	1	12	6
		do Plant	2s.	6d.	1	12	6
		do Plowman	2s.	6d.	1	12	6
		do Rands	2s.	6d.	1	12	6
	Ufford	*do* Sayer	2s.	0d.	1	6	0
	Hollesley	*do* Skinner	1s.	6d.	0	19	6
		do Tyler	2s.	6d.	1	12	6
		do Walne	2s.	0d.	1	6	0
	Hacheston	Mary Brown	1s.	6d.	0	19	6
	Brandeston	Eliz. Boon	3s.	0d.	1	19	0
		Willm. Burrows	1s.	6d.	0	19	6
	Earl Soham	Jacob Cook	6s.	0d.	3	18	0
		Martha Curtis	2s.	0d.	1	6	0
	Easton	Saml. Hearn	2s.	6d.	1	12	6
		James Hewell	2s.	0d.	1	6	0
		Henry Kemp	1s.	0d.	0	13	0
	Hatcheston	John Lanham	3s.	6d.	2	5	6
	Earl Soham	Thos. Potter (dead)	3s.	0d.	0	12	0
		Samuel Sayers	2s.	0d.	1	6	0
	Hatcheston	Thos. Spink	4s.	0d.	2	12	0
		James Spink	5s.	0d.	3	5	0
		Christ. Taylor's B.B.	1s.	6d.	0	19	6
		Robt. Tuffield	2s.	0d.	1	6	0
		Thos. Woolnough	3s.	0d.	1	19	0
		Total			56	11	0

Wilford	397	3	0
Loes	345	3	6
Total	742	6	6

31 October 1820

Resolved and ordered that the yearly assessments upon each of the several and respective parishes within the said hundreds to be taken and made in the proportions following, and that all decreases or increases be made upon this ratio for the ensuing ten years.

Loes				Wilford			
Ash	357			Alderton	432	6	
Brandeston	378	6		Bawdsey	198	10	8
Butley	144	2	8	Boulge	124	4	
Charsfield	263	2		Boyton	179		
Creetingham	361	18		Bredfield	321	10	
Dallingho	380	8		Bromeswell	111	14	
Earl Soham	358	14		Capel	161	10	
Easton	268	10		Debach	69	10	
Eyke	192			Hollesly	426	16	
Hacheston	277	6		Melton	381	12	
Hoo	154			Petistree	138	8	
Kenton	290	10		Ramsholt	168		
Kettleburgh	323	12		Shottisham	126	10	8
Letheringham	141	10		Sutton	449	8	
Marlesford	323	10		Ufford	405	12	
Monewden	178	2		Wickham Market	527	2	
	4,618	12	8		4,221	13	4
					4,618	12	8
					8,840	6	

Upon the motion of the Revd Mr Brooke, it was unanimously resolved that the thanks of this meeting be given to those gentlemen composing the committee <6 named directors> for the arrangement and settlement of the accounts before mentioned, for their particular attention and trouble therein.

11 January 1821

Resolved that, it having been represented to this meeting, indictments have been brought by the parish officers of Kettleburgh against Robert Scase of Kettleburgh, bricklayer, for resistance to the parish officers in the execution of a distress warrant for the poor rates, and also against Felgate of the same parish, thatcher, for securing his goods after they were distrained. And it appearing to this meeting, to be for the general benefit of the Incorporation that the punishment of persons obstructing the execution of the laws should be made as public and exemplary as possible. This meeting doth, therefore, order that the prosecution of the said Robert Scase and Felgate be carried on by the solicitor of the Corporation, at the expense of the said Corporation.

Resolved that upon comparison of the expenditure of the House of Industry at Melton with that of some of the similar institutions in this county, that it is expedient to appoint a committee for the purpose of making further enquiry upon the subject, and making a report thereupon. That the following gentlemen be appointed for the said committee viz. <7 named directors>, and that the Committee be open to any other or others of the Directors and Guardians belonging to the establishment. And that the committee do hold their first meeting <13 March>.

13 March 1821 [*Committee investigating Melton's expenditure*]

A Meeting of the Directors and Acting Guardians of the poor agreeably to the resolutions entered into at the last Quarterly Meeting held at Wickham Market, for a committee therein named to enquire into the outgoings and expenditure of the Melton House compared with those of the Bulcamp House and other similar institutions. <7 directors and 10 acting guardians>.

Resolved that from an inspection of the amount expended in the several articles of maintenance during the period of one year from January 1820 to January 1821. That the governor is requested to prepare a detailed statement of the amount for that period, including such articles as are enumerated under the head of food and washing, in a former statement of the average of 10 years. Resolved also, that from a difference of a comparative statement of the expence of cloathing in Melton House and Bulcamp House, it is expedient that an inquiry be instituted into that department of the establishment, and that <3 names> be requested to inspect the Bulcamp House, and to enquire into the particulars of the articles connected therewith. Resolved also that the subject of firing be referred to the next meeting of the committee to be held <10 April>.

10 April 1821 [*Committee investigating Melton's expenditure*]

The committee resumed their enquires to ascertain the comparative difference in the expence of cloathing and various other articles in Melton House of Industry with similar institutions. They have limited their enquiring generally to the expenditure of the last year ending in December 1820, and have founded their report accordingly, and that Mr Pytches is requested to deliver the same at the next Quarterly Meeting.

The Committee having proceeded to an enquiry into a detail of the articles connected with the indoor consumption for one year from January 1820 to January 1821, have chiefly confined the comparative expenditure of similar establishments to the same period of time and have agreed to the following report:

The Committee consider it necessary to prepare a statement of the comparative ratio of expenditure of this with other establishments of a similar kind, that a more correct opinion may be formed of the regulations by which the government of this House is regulated.

The Committee are of opinion that some alterations may be adopted which would improve the present system, and tend to remove, in some degree, the responsibility which in so large an establishment must necessarily fall upon the Governor. Viz., that beef for the use of the House shall be served by contract, and upon a committee day shall be delivered between the hours of ten and one o'clock, subject to the inspection of the committee.

That coals shall be delivered at a time specified by advertisement, nine months consumption be contracted for at the midsummer Quarterly Meeting in every year.

The Committee also having examined carefully into the causes which have produced so heavy a charge in the department of drapery and other clothing, suggest the necessity of using the utmost discrimination in giving clothes and linen to those paupers who are leaving the House for their respective parishes, and they also submit some further regulations respecting the mode of sending out apprentices, in the following manner:

That no child be bound out from the House of Industry unless such child has been resident within the House at least six months immediately preceding the date of indenture, and immediately after the allotment that the Governor be directed to employ the children, according to the best means the House may afford, in such offices and services as they may be required to perform during their apprenticeship.

And the committee also, having found some salutary regulations for the better management of these institutions embodied in the bye laws of other corporations, beg leave to suggest some amendment in those by which the business of this corporation is considered.

On the conclusion of this report, the committee are desirous of bearing testimony to the readiness with which the Governor has furnished every information which has been required of him relative to this enquiry.

12 April 1821

Directors	present	Guardians
Revd Mr Groome	Revd Mr Broadhurst	Mr Thomas Kersey
Revd Mr Chilton	John Syer M.D.	Mr Catlin
Thos. Pytches Esq.	Mr Rodwell	Mr Wolton
Mr Woolnough	Mr H. Edwards	Mr Josselyn
Mr Thos. Waller	Mr S. Gross	Mr N. Barthrop
Mr Dykes	Revd Mr Is. Clarke	Mr Jos. Clubbe

The following persons were duly elected Directors and Acting Guardians

	Directors	Guardians
May	Revd George Turner	Mr N. Barthrop
	Mr Jeptha Waller	Mr J. D. Leach
June	Edmund Jenney Esq.	Mr Thos. Garneys
	Revd G. F. Tavell	Mr S. Jeaffreson
July	John FitzGerald	Mr B. Colchester
	Revd J. H. Groome	Mr R. Welton
Aug.	Revd Wm. Browne	Mr F. Sheming
	Revd T. Broadhurst	Mr Jas. Glanfield
Sept.	John Syer M.D.	Mr Jos. Hare
	Revd Mr Aldrich	Mr Wm. Cooper
Oct.	Mr H. Edwards	Mr W. Hambling
	Mr J. A. Studd	Mr Edmund Plant
Nov.	Andrew Arcedeckne Esq.	Mr E. Turner
	Mr Rich. Brooke	Mr Simpson
Dec.	Mr Thos. Waller	Mr T. Miller
	Mr P. Dykes	Mr B. Cooper
Jan.	Revd Is. Clarke	Mr T. Kersey
	Revd C. Brooke	Mr James Aldhous
Feb.	Mr S. Gross	Mr Jas. Clubbe
		Mr J. F. Josselyn
Mar.	Thos. Pytches Esq.	Mr S. Clark
	Mr Rodwell	Mr H. Farrer
Apl.	Revd Mr Chilton	Mr J. Goodwyn
	Mr Woolnough	Mr J. Felgate

Resolved that the report of the committee to make enquiry into the expenditure of the indoor establishment be now received and approved, and that the following regulations be adopted as resulting therefrom.

That in future, beef be contracted for quarterly, and the time of delivery to be specified in the advertisement.

That not less than nine months consumption of coals be contracted for at the July Quarterly Meeting in every year, and that the delivery of them shall be completed previous to the ensuing Michaelmas quarter. And that the governor is required to apportion the consumption of coals to each ward as, in his discretion, he shall think necessary, and to recommend economy in every department.

Resolved that the following alterations and amendments be made in the bye laws of this establishment.

1st under the head of apprentices. The period of allotting be confined to the Lady and Michaelmas quarters only, and that six months residence in the House be required previous to such allotment. And that every person refusing to take an apprentice regularly allotted shall pay the penalty of ten pounds. The next person in turn to have the option of taking the child with eight pounds, or to pay a penalty of ten pounds. The third person, in turn, to have the option of taking the child with fifteen pounds, or to pay a penalty of ten pounds. The fourth person, in turn, to take the apprentice with twenty pounds, or to pay a penalty of ten pounds, or the Directors and Acting Guardians may apprentice such child according to the present regulation.

That all persons coming into the House having a pension shall pay half of it towards their maintenance and support.

11 October 1821

Resolved that the Building Committee be requested to inspect the apartments of the House for the purpose of ascertaining the facility afforded to classify and keep separate the females who are removed to the House for confinement with bastard children, and that they do report thereon at the next Quarterly Meeting.

10 January 1822

Resolved that in consequence of wool not being able to be had for the employment of the paupers in the House of Industry in the usual manner, the Governor is now ordered to procure a quantity of combed wool, of a coarse description, to be spun and made into yarn, and to be knit into stockings for the use of the House. And likewise, to procure a quantity of hemp tow to be spun, and afterwards wove into cloth for the use of the House. In order to do this, he is to procure a loom and a twisting machine, and a proper number of tow wheels, and to engage a proper man as a weaver, and to superintend that department.

11 April 1822

Directors	Present	Guardians
Thos. Pytches Esq.	Revd Mr Is. Clarke	Mr J. F. Josselyn
Revd Mr Browne	Mr R. Brook	Mr Thos. Kersey
Revd Mr Chilton	Mr John Woolnough	Mr John Goodwyn
John Syer M.D.		Mr Clubbe
Revd Mr Groome		Mr H. Farrer
Mr Joshua Rodwell		
Revd Mr Broadhurst		
Mr H. Edwards		
Mr N. Bart		

The following persons were duly elected Directors and Acting Guardians

	Directors	Guardians
May	Revd George Turner	Mr George Bond

	Mr Jeptha Waller	Mr J. R. Hodgson
June	Edmund Jenney Esq.	Mr Thomas Garneys
	Revd G. F. Tavell	Mr Thomas Waller
July	John FitzGerald Esq.	Mr John Hillen
	Revd J. H. Groome	Mr R. Welton
Aug.	Revd Wm. Browne	Mr E. Adams
	Revd T. Broadhurst	Mr James Glanfield
Sept.	John Syer M.D.	Mr W. Walker
	Revd Wm. Aldrich	Mr S. Syred
Oct.	Mr Thos. Waller	Mr W. Hambling
	Mr J. A. Studd	Mr Edmund Plant
Nov.	A. Arcedeckne Esq.	Mr E. Turner (Ufford)
	Mr Richard Brook	Mr James Last
Dec.	Mr H. Edwards	Mr Thomas Miller
	Mr P. Dykes	Mr George Cooper
Jan.	Revd Is. Clarke	Mr William Threadkell
	Revd C. Brooke	Mr James Aldhous
Feb.	Mr Samuel Gross	Mr James Clubbe
	Mr N. Barthropp	Mr Edgar Smith
Mar.	Thomas Pytches Esq.	Mr S. Clark
	Mr Rodwell	Mr H. Farrer
Apl.	Revd Mr Chilton	Mr John Lewin
	Mr Woolnough	Mr John Felgate

Resolved that from the heavy charges incurred in the attendance upon the paupers who are not resident within the incorporated hundreds, it is ordered that no bills for medical attendance to such persons be allowed in future.

10 April 1823

Directors	Present	Guardians
Mr Rodwell	Mr H. Edwards	Mr Plant
Revd Mr Browne	Mr T. Waller	Mr Thos. Waller Jun.
Revd Mr Aldrich	Mr Dykes	Mr Wm. Hambling
Revd Mr Brooke	Mr Jeptha Waller	Mr Felgate
Revd Mr Chilton	Revd Mr Is. Clarke	Mr Thomas Miller
Mr Woolnough	Thomas Pytches Esq.	Mr J. R Hodgson
Mr S. Gross		Revd Mr Groome
Mr R. Brooke		
Mr N. Barthropp		

The following persons were duly elected Directors and Acting Guardians

	Directors	Guardians
May	Revd Mr Turner	Mr Thomas Walker
	Mr Jeptha Waller	Mr J. R. Hodgson
June	Edmund Jenney Esq.	Mr Thomas Waller Jun.
	Revd G. F. Tavell	Mr D. Taylor
July	John FitzGerald Esq.	Mr J. Hillen
	Revd J. H. Groome	Mr S. C. Gross
Aug.	Revd Wm. Browne	Mr E. Adams
	Revd Thomas Broadhurst	Mr Thomas Cole
Sept.	Revd Mr Aldrich	Mr W. Walker
		Mr P. Dykes

Oct.	Mr Thomas Waller	Mr Wm. Hambling
	Mr J. A. Studd	Mr Edmund Plant
Nov.	A. Arcedeckne Esq.	Mr T. Catlin
	Mr R. Brook	Mr James Last
Dec.	Mr H. Edwards	Mr T. Miller
	Mr P. Dykes	Mr T. Grimwood
Jan.	Revd Is. Clarke	Mr John Button
	Revd C. Brooke	Mr Abraham Watkins
Feb.	Mr N. Barthropp	Mr J. Clubbe
	Mr S. Gross	Mr Thomas Hersey
Mar.	Thomas Pytches Esq.	Mr J. Goodwyn
	Mr J. Rodwell	Mr H. Farrer
Apl.	Revd Mr Chilton	Mr J. Lewin
	Mr J. Woolnough	Mr G. Utting

Resolved that the evil arising from the want of separate apartments for women who are removed to the House of Industry for confinement with bastard children being very much increased, and the remedy contemplated having been abandoned, and a plan subsequently suggested as practicable for carrying this desirable measure into effect, the Committee appointed for the enquiry into the eligibility of the last plan suggested have procured an estimate of the probable expences of the one now under consideration, and find it would not exceed one third of that required for the completion of the former. It is further resolved that Mr S. Gross of Petistree be added to the usual committee of inspection, and that it be referred to them to carry the last suggested plan into effect in the manner they deem most proper, for which purposes they will meet <24 April>.

Resolved that it is the opinion of this meeting that the corporation would derive considerable advantages by contracting for the supply of flour and meal for the use of the House of Industry, and that the subject be taken into further consideration.

Resolved that the applications for allowances to the paupers residing in the towns of Ipswich and Woodbridge be considered by the Weekly Committee the second Monday in every month, and that the applicants be desired to attend accordingly.

16 October 1823

Resolved that it is deemed expedient to revise, amend and add to the bye laws, rules, orders and regulations of this incorporation, and to have a number printed for the use of the Directors etc., for which purpose the following gentlemen be appointed a committee and to meet on <13 November> <12 named directors>.

13 November 1823 [*Committee to revise the bye laws*]

The above business was gone into but not thoroughly finished, therefore resolved that the meeting be adjourned to <27 November>.

27 November 1823 [*Committee to revise the bye laws*]

The Committee having examined the bye laws, and compared them with the present state of the exigencies of this Incorporation, and with the laws and regulations of other similar establishments, recommend the following to be adopted for the good order and management of this Incorporation.

8 January 1824

<12 named directors and 6 acting guardians>

Rules, orders and regulations for the good order and government of the House and for the comfortable provision of the poor in and out of the same.[2]

8 April 1824

Directors		Guardians
Revd George Turner		
Revd Wm. Browne	Revd C. Brooke	Mr Hodgson
Revd C. Henley	Revd C. G. Watson	Mr T. Kersey
Mr S. Gross	Mr T. Waller	Mr T. Waller Jun.
Mr H. Edwards	Mr N. Barthropp	Mr J. Lewin
Mr R. Brook	Revd Mr Chilton	Mr J. Goodwyn
Revd Mr Tavell	Mr J. Rodwell	Mr J. Button
Mr Dykes		Mr H. Farrer
		Mr Wm. Hambling
		Mr Thomas Cole

The following persons were duly elected Directors and Acting Guardians

		Directors	Guardians
May	3rd	Revd George Turner	Mr G. Utting
		Mr John Woolnough	Mr G. Bond
	17th	Revd G. Turner	Mr G. Bond
		Mr Jeptha Waller	Mr J. R. Hodgson
June	7th	Mr Jeptha Waller	Mr J. R. Hodgson
		Edmund Jenney Esq.	Mr John Page
	21st	Edmund Jenney Esq.	Mr John Page
		Revd G. F. Tavel	Mr T. Waller
July	5th	Revd G. F. Tavel	Mr T. Waller
		John FitzGerald Esq.	Mr J. Button
	19th	John FitzGerald Esq.	Mr J. Button
		Revd J. H. Groome	Mr S. C. Gross
Aug.	2nd	Revd J. H. Groome	Mr S. C. Gross
		Revd Wm. Browne	Mr E. Adams
	16th	Revd Wm. Browne	Mr E. Adams
		Revd T. Broadhurst	Mr E. Turner
Sep.	6th	Revd T. Broadhurst	Mr E. Turner
		Revd C. Henley	Mr J. May
	20th	Revd C. Henley	Mr J. May
		Revd W. Aldrich	Mr P. Dykes
Oct.	4th	Revd W. Aldrich	Mr P. Dykes
		Mr Thos. Waller	Mr S. G. Stearn
	18th	Mr Thos. Waller	Mr S. G. Stearn
		Mr J. A. Studd	Mr Plant
Nov.	1st	Mr J. A. Studd	Mr Plant
		A. Arcedeckne Esq.	Mr J. Glanfield
	15th	A. Arcedeckne Esq.	Mr J. Glanfield
		Mr R. Brooke	Mr T. Catlin
Dec.	6th	Mr R. Brook	Mr T. Catlin
		Mr H. Edwards	Mr Jeremiah Wase

---

2   These bye laws were virtually identical to those enacted in 1810. See page 258.

	20th	Mr H. Edwards	Mr Jeremiah Wase
		Mr P. Dykes	Mr T. Grimwood
Jan.	3rd	Mr P. Dykes	Mr T. Grimwood
		Revd Mr Brooke	Mr William Wolton
	17th	Revd Mr Brooke	Mr William Wolton
		Revd Mr Is. Clarke	Mr Barret
Feb.	7th	Revd Mr Is. Clarke	Mr Barret
		Mr N. Barthropp	Mr Clubbe
	21st	Mr N. Barthropp	Mr Clubbe
		Mr S. Gross	Mr Edward Cole
Mar.	7th	Mr S. Gross	Mr Edward Cole
		Revd C. G. Watson	Mr J. Goodwyn
	21st	Revd C. G. Watson	Mr J. Goodwyn
		Mr Rodwell	Mr Charles Cordy
Apl.	4th	Mr Rodwell	Mr Charles Cordy
		Revd J. Chilton	Mr John Lewin
	18th	Revd J. Chilton	Mr John Lewin
		Mr J. Woolnough	Mr G. Utting

Resolved that it appears to this meeting that it would be highly proper and necessary that an application be made to Parliament for an amended act of Parliament to enable the Directors to alter the time of taking the average of the accounts of this Incorporation. And that a special meeting of the Directors and Acting Guardians be held at the House of Industry on <17 May> for the purpose of preparing certain resolutions to be submitted to a general meeting of the Guardians of the poor within the said Incorporated hundreds, to be held at the said House of Industry, on Monday the 21 day of June next, to be convened by public advertisement. The Committee <9 named directors>.

17 May 1824 [*Special meeting*]

Resolved 1st that it is the opinion of this meeting that it is highly expedient that the accounts of the expenditure of this Incorporation be in future divided into two classes viz. permanent and fluctuating.

Resolved 2nd that the permanent class shall include the following heads of expenditure viz.

1st class. Buildings and repairs.	Rent, taxes, tithes and insurance.
Household furniture and repairs of *do.*	Working utensils and repairs of *do.*
Salaries and wages of officers, including occasional gratuities.	Salaries of surgeons.
Law expences.	Expences of Governor's journals.
Stationery and stamps.	Money borrowed on bonds of incorporation.
	The interest thereof.

2nd class viz. fluctuating expences.
All expences not included under the foregoing heads.

Resolved 3rd that the rate at which the respective parishes shall be assessed to both the permanent and fluctuating expences of this Incorporation for the first time under the proposed amendment of the Incorporating Act, shall be fixed by an average of the expenditure of such parishes for the five years preceding Michaelmas 1825.

Resolved 4th that from and after Michaelmas 1825, the average upon the fluctuating expences of this Incorporation shall be taken annually.

Resolved 5th that from and after Michaelmas 1825, the permanent expences of this Incorporation shall be borne by the respective parishes according to the average to be taken at Michaelmas 1825, and shall not be subject to any future variation.

Resolved 6th that a select committee consisting of the following gentlemen, viz. <5 named directors>, be appointed to meet <24 May>, to examine the last Acts of Parliament and suggest such alterations as may be deemed advisable to adopt in the ensuing application to Parliament. And that Mr Wood, the solicitor to the Corporation, be requested to attend this meeting.

Resolved 7th That the following advertisement be inserted in the Ipswich papers three weeks viz. 5th, 12th, and 19th June.

Loes and Wilford Hundreds

A General Meeting of the owners and occupiers of lands within the incorporated hundreds of Loes and Wilford in the county of Suffolk, is requested to be holden at the House of Industry, in Melton, on Monday the 21st day of June, at 11 o'clock in the forenoon, in order to take into consideration the plan or plans to be submitted to them for the purpose of making an application to Parliament to enable the Directors etc. to alter the time or times of taking the averages of the accounts of the Corporation, as fixed by the 6th and 7th clauses of the last amended act of Incorporation.

24 May 1824 [*Special meeting*]

At a special meeting of the Directors and Acting Guardians for the purpose of taking into consideration the plan to be submitted to the General Meeting of the Guardians within the said Hundreds to be held <21 June>, for applying to Parliament for an amended act of Parliament, to enable the Directors and Acting Guardians to alter the time in taking the averages of the accounts of the Corporation and for other purposes.

It was proposed that the chairman should submit to the meeting of Guardians to be held the 21st June next, the necessity of applying to Parliament for an amended act of Parliament to enable the Directors and Acting Guardians to alter the time in taking the averages of the accounts of the Corporation for regulating the several assessments to be made within the said Hundreds and for other purposes.

Resolved

1st that it is the opinion of this Committee that the fifth clause of the Act of the 55th Geo 3rd c. 137 be adopted in the intended amended Act of Parliament.[3]

2nd that the 25th clause of Incorporated Act of the 31st Geo 3rd be amended by the omission of the words "within seven days".

3rd that the 36th clause of the Incorporated Act of the 31st Geo 3rd be amended in summoning the churchwardens and overseers to appear at the next Quarterly,

---

[3] This act was entitled 'An Act to prevent Poor Persons in the Workhouse from embezzling certain property for their use; to alter and amend so much of an Act of the 36th year of his present Majesty as retrains Justices of the Peace from ordering relief to poor persons in certain cases for a longer period of one month at a time; and for other purposes their mentioned, relating to the Poor'. The fifth clause related to the penalties that could be inflicted on those supplying a workhouse with 'any goods, materials or provisions'.

Weekly or other meeting, such summons to be served four days at least previous to his time of appearance, and that the fine inflicted by the said clause be increased from the sum of five pounds to the sum of ten pounds, as the maximum of the same.

4th that Mr Wood, the solicitor, do prepare a petition for Parliament founded upon the foregoing resolutions of this day, and of the 17th to be submitted to this committee previous to the 21st June next.

14 June 1824 [*Special meeting*]

The draft of the petition to Parliament was produced by Mr Wood, and read over by the above Committee and approved by them, and ordered to be written out fair and produced to the General Meeting to be held according to advertisement the 21st June inst.

21 June 1824

A General Meeting of the owners and occupiers of lands within the Incorporated Hundreds of Loes and Wilford in the county of Suffolk, held at the House of Industry in the parish of Melton within the said Hundred of Wilford, on the twenty first day of June <1824>, pursuant to public advertisement to take into consideration the plan or plans to be submitted to this meeting for the purpose of making an application to Parliament to enable the Directors and Acting Guardians to alter the time or times of taking the averages of the accounts of the said Corporation, as fixed by the sixth and seventh clauses of last amended act of the 50th year of his late majesty's reign.

Edmund Jenney Esq., in the chair.

It appearing the unanimous opinion of this meeting that an application to Parliament for such purpose is absolutely necessary.

Resolved that an application be made for the same forthwith.

Resolved that the following petition be agreed to.

To the Honourable the House of Commons of the United Kingdom of Great Britain and Ireland in Parliament assembled. The humble petition of the Guardians of the poor within the Hundreds of Loes and Wilford in the county of Suffolk.

Sheweth,

That an Act of Parliament was passed in <1792>. And that another act was passed in <1810>, wherein and whereby divers provisions and regulations for the management of the poor within the said Hundreds were enacted, which since the passing of the said last mentioned act have been found very beneficial to the said Hundreds, and would be attended with still greater utility if the powers therein given were further extended and enlarged and certain defects in the said last mentioned act amended.

That by several clauses in the last mentioned act, provision was made to take averages of expences of the said Hundreds every ten years, in manner therein particularly stated. That your petitioners have acted upon this provision, and have twice taken averages of such expences in the manner therein directed.

That by extending this provision, and thereby allowing your petitioners to take the average every year in lieu of every ten years, a much greater benefit would accrue to the said Hundreds and the expences annually incurred be very considerably diminished.

That the several acts under which the said Hundreds are regulated are in other respects insufficient for the purposes thereby intended, and that further powers and amendments are considered as expedient and necessary by the Directors and Acting Guardians of the poor within the said Hundreds.

Your petitioners therefore most humbly pray that leave may be given to your petitioners to bring in a bill for effecting the several purposes herein before mentioned by such ways and means and in such manner as this Honourable House shall in its wisdom direct or think proper.

Given under the common seal of our corporation at Melton, in the said county of Suffolk, <21 June 1824>.

Resolved that the petition now read be fairly written upon parchment, and sealed with the common seal of the said Corporation, and that Messrs Wood and Son, the solicitors, do forward the same to the Members of the county of Suffolk with a request they will present the same to the Honourable the House of Commons.

Resolved that a committee be appointed, consisting of <10 names> to prepare and forward the Bill to Parliament for the purpose of obtaining the intended new Act of Parliament. That any five of them be a Committee, and that the said committee be open to any of the Guardians who choose to attend.

Resolved that the first meeting of the said Committee be held <16 August>.

Resolved unanimously that the thanks of this meeting be presented to the chairman for his attention to the business of the day.

R. W. Oldham, clerk to the Directors etc.

16 August 1824 [*Committee to draft a new bill*]

The resolutions passed at the three several former meetings were read over, and also the draft of the bill for the intended new act of Parliament, which said draft of bill was fully approved of and Messrs Wood and Son ordered to forward the same to Parliament in common cause.[4]

7 April 1825

Directors present	Guardians
Revd George Turner	Mr John Lewin
Revd Groome	Mr S. C. Gross
Revd G. F. Tavel	Mr Jonathan Goodwyn
Revd C. Henley	
Revd C. G. Watson	
Revd C. Brooke	
Mr Rodwell	Mr S. Gross
Mr J. Waller	Mr N. Barthropp
Mr Dykes	

The following persons were duly elected Directors and Acting Guardians:

	Directors	Guardians
May 2nd and 9th	Revd Mr Turner	Mr G. Utting
	Mr John Woolnough	Mr John Willis
16th, 23rd, 30th	Revd Mr Turner	Mr John Willis

---

4   No further reference is made in the Quarterly Minute Book either to the proposed bill or to the subsequent process of disincorporation.

	Mr Jeptha Waller	Mr Thomas Hersey
June 6th and 13th	Mr Jeptha Waller	Mr Thomas Hersey
	Edmund Jenney Esq.	Mr E. Barker
20th and 27th	Edmund Jenney Esq.	Mr E. Barker
	Revd G. F. Tavel	Mt Thomas Waller
July 4th and 11th	Revd G. F. Tavel	Mr Thomas Waller
	John FitzGerald Esq.	Mr John Largent
18th and 25th	John FitzGerald Esq.	Mr John Largent
	Revd J. H. Groome	Mr S. C. Gross
Aug. 1st and 8th	Revd J. H. Groome	Mr S. C. Gross
	Revd Mr Browne	Mr F. Sheming
15th, 22nd and 29th	Revd Mr Browne	Mr F. Sheming
	Revd T. Broadhurst	Mr E. Turner
Sept. 5th and 12th	Revd T. Broadhurst	Mr E. Turner
	Revd C. Henley	Mr J. Chapman
19th and 26th	Revd C. Henley	Mr J. Chapman
	Revd Mr Aldrich	Mr S. Clark
Oct. 3rd and 10th	Revd Mr Aldrich	Mr S. Clark
	Mr T. Waller	Mr S. G. Stearn
17th, 24th and 31st	Mr T. Waller	Mr S. G. Stearn
	Mr J. A. Studd	Mr C. Baldrey
Nov. 7th and 14th	Mr J. A. Studd	Mr C. Baldrey
	A. Arcedeckne Esq.	Mr J. Glanfield
21st and 28th	A. Arcedeckne Esq.	Mr J. Glanfield
	Mr R. Brook	Mr Catlin
Dec. 5th and 12th	Mr R. Brook	Mr Catlin
	Mr H. Edwards	Mr Jackson
19th and 26th	Mr H. Edwards	Mr Jackson
	Mr P. Dykes	Mr John Trott
Jan. 2nd and 9th	Mr P. Dykes	Mr John Trott
	Revd C. Brooke	Mr W. Wolton
16th, 23rd and 30th	Revd C. Brooke	Mr W. Wolton
	Revd Is. Clarke	Mr Brevet
Feb. 6th and 13th	Revd Is. Clarke	Mr Brevet
	Mr N. Barthropp	Mr Clubbe
20th and 27th	Mr N. Barthropp	Mr Clubbe
	Mr S. Gross	Mr E. Cole
Mar. 6th and 13th	Mr S. Gross	Mr E. Cole
	Revd C. G. Watson	Mr William Walker
20th and 27th	Revd C. G. Watson	Mr William Walker
	Mr Rodwell	Mr C. Cordy
Apl. 3rd and 10th	Mr Rodwell	Mr C. Cordy
	Revd J. Chilton	Mr John Threadkell
17th and 24th	Revd J. Chilton	Mr John Threadkell
	Mr Woolnough	Mr G. Utting

Resolved, that in order to assimilate the diet of the paupers who are the inmates of this establishment to that of other establishments in this county, a meat dinner be henceforth provided for them two days in every week. And that the bill of fare now produced by the Governor be hereafter adopted as follows:

Sunday (dinners) seed cake, Monday dumplings, Tuesday meat, Wednesday peas soup or bread and cheese, Thursday suet puddings, Friday meat, Saturday peas soup with 4oz. of bread.

Breakfast and supper as usual.

13 October 1825

Resolved that it is the opinion of this meeting that the Governor be directed to look out for a proper person to take the care of the paupers confined in the lunatic asylum of the House of Industry.

6 April 1826

Directors	Present	Guardians
Revd Mr Groome		Mr S. C. Gross
Revd Mr Browne		Mr Largent
Revd Mr Chilton		Mr Cordy
Mr R. Brook		Mr Baldrey
Mr Dykes		Mr Jackson
Mr N. Barthropp		Mr W. Walker
Mr Rodwell		Mr John Threadkell
Revd Mr Broadhurst		
Mr Thomas Waller		
Revd Mr Watson		
Mr H. Edwards		
Mr Jeptha Waller		
Revd Mr Tavel		

The following persons were duly elected Directors and Acting Guardians

	Directors	Guardians
May 1st and 8th	Revd G. Turner	Mr G. Utting
	Mr J. Woolnough	Mr John Willis
15th, 22nd and 29th	Revd G. Turner	Mr John Willis
	Mr Jeptha Waller	Mr Thomas Kersey
June 5th and 12th	Mr Jeptha Waller	Mr Thomas Kersey
	Edmund Jenney Esq.	Mr D. Taylor
19th and 26th	Edmund Jenney Esq.	Mr D. Taylor
	Revd G. F. Tavel	Mr T. Waller
July 3rd and 10th	Revd G. F. Tavel	Mr T. Waller
		Mr George Largent
17th, 24th and 31st	Revd J. H. Groome	Mr George Largent
Aug. 7th and 14th	Revd J. H. Groome	Mr S. C. Gross
	Revd Mr Browne	Mr S. C. Gross
21st and 28th	Revd Mr Browne	Mr Edward Crisp
	Revd T. Broadhurst	Mr Edward Crisp
Sept. 4th and 11th	Revd T. Broadhurst	Mr S. Armstrong
	Revd C. Henley	Mr S. Armstrong
18th and 25th	Revd C. Henley	Mr J. Chapman
	Revd Mr Aldrich	Mr J. Chapman
Oct. 2nd and 9th	Revd Mr Aldrich	Mr P. Dykes
	Mr Thomas Waller	Mr P. Dykes
		Mr W. Hambling

6 July 1826

That about thirty feather beds, bedheads, blanket, sheets and coverlids be sold by auction on Monday 17 July.

12 October 1826

It appearing to this meeting that a balance will remain in the hands of the Treasurer after all just and legal claims upon the Corporation shall be duly paid. It is ordered that, after such balances shall have been scrutinized by the Finance Committee and submitted to the magistrates of the division at the next general Quarter Sessions to be holden at Woodbridge, shall be paid over by the Treasurer into the hands of the Trustees, (or to whom they shall appoint), appointed by the late act for disincorporating the hundreds of Loes and Wilford.

At this last Quarterly Meeting of the Directors and Acting Guardians of the poor within the said Hundreds of Loes and Wilford, it is resolved.

1st that the sincere thanks of this meeting be given to the Revd Mr Kett, the chaplain of the Incorporation, and also to John Wood Esq., the Treasurer, for their long and faithful service.

2nd that the sincere thanks of this meeting be also given to Mr Lynn, the House surgeon, and to Messrs Harsant, Bellman, Hughes and Bloomfield, the district surgeons, for their attention to their respective duties.

That a year's gratuity be also paid to the Governor, Mr R. W. Oldham with the thanks of this meeting for his services.

That a copy of these resolutions be inserted in the two Ipswich papers.

The ninth Weekly Minute Book,
2 October 1820–3 April 1824[5]

2 October 1820

A Weekly Committee of the Directors and Acting Guardians of the Poor within the said Hundreds held at the House of Industry the 2 October 1824.

Ordered that the Overseers of the respective parishes do allow as follows:

Creetingham	Creetingham	Widow Gray 5s. 5 William Runacre 4s. 5	2	5	0
	do	William Butcher 1s. 6d. 5 John Moss 1s. 5	0	12	6
	do	Widow Harvey 3s. 6d. 5 Widow Coppen 3s. 6d. 5	1	15	0
	do	Robert Jaye 3s. 5 William Clements 2s. 5	1	5	0
	do	Thomas Clements 1s. 5 James Spall 1s. 5	0	10	0
	do	Mary Lanham 1s. 6d. 5 Mary Last 5s. 5	1	12	6
Debach	Debach	William Fairweather's wife 2s. 5 John Crane 5s. 2	1	0	0
Shottisham	Shottisham	Elizabeth Bird 1s. 6d. 5 William Fox 10s. 1	1	0	0
	Sutton	John Webber 9s. 5	2	5	0
	Hollesly	Henry Andrews 2s. 5	0	10	0
Ufford	Ufford	Robert Lemey 2s. 5 John Skeet 4s. 6d. 5	1	12	6
	do	John Upson 1s. 6d. 5 Thomas Head 5s. 5	1	12	6
	do	John Skeet Sen. 1s. 5 Stephen Blomfield 5s. 5	1	10	0
	do	John Wix's wife 1s. 6d. 5 Hugh Read 4s. 5	1	7	6
	do	Charles Crow 8s. 5	2	0	0
	Petistree	Abraham Harvey 7s. 5 Jeff Curtis 6s. 5	3	5	0
	Ash	Samuel Buckles and lad 3s. 5 William Read 10s. 1	1	5	0
	Debach	Elizabeth Orsborn's lads 6d. 5	0	2	6
	Sutton	John Gillingham 10s. 1	0	10	0
	Dallingho	John Orsborn 8s. 5	2	0	0
	Wickham	Mary Cook 1s. 6d. 3	0	4	6
Wickham	Wickham	Edward Cadman midwife 5s.			

---

5   SROI ADA11/A/B/3/9.

		James Block 1s. 4	0	9	0
	do	Michael Mayhew 2s. 5 Benj. Churchyard 3s. 6d. 5	1	7	6
	do	Thomas Partridge 2s. 1 Nicholas Felgate 3s. 5	0	17	0
	Petistree	John Webber 1s. 6d. 5	0	7	6
	Eyke	Henry Chilby 2s. 6d. 2	0	5	0
	Hacheston	Sarah Brown 1s. 1	0	1	0
Hoo	Hoo	Widow Balls 11s. 5 David Nunn 2s. 5	3	5	0
	do	Francis Fitch 1s. 5 Robert Bailey 2s. 5	0	15	0
	Letheringham	John Smith 2s. 6d. 5	0	12	6
Monewden	Monewden	Widow Crowfoot 10s. 5 Nathaniel Wade 3s. 6d. 5	3	7	6
	do	Daniel Erling's 6 children referred to Qtly. Meeting			
Rendlesham	Rendlesham	John Horn 1s. 5 Jeremiah Scopes 1s. 5	0	10	0
	do	John Mays midwife 5s. and 1s. 5 James Chilvers midwife 5s.	0	15	0
	do	Thomas Jennings 1s. 5 William Tibbenham 1s. 5	0	10	0
	do	Samuel Simpson 1s. 5	0	5	0
Petistree	Petistree	Samuel Eagle 8s. 1	0	8	0
Capel	Capel	John King 2s. 5 Isaac Naunton 8s. 5	2	10	0
	do	Thomas Lyons 8s. 5 Robert Topple 6s. 5	3	10	0
	do	William Wyard 9s. 6d. 2	0	19	0
	Butley	Robert Mays 2s. 5	0	10	0
Butley	Butley	Thomas Caley 1s. 6d. 5 Toakly Caley 1s. 5	0	12	6
	do	James Crosby 3s. 5 John Lewis 2s. 5	1	5	0
	do	John Markham 1s. 5 Nathaniel Mills 1s. 6d. 5	0	12	6
	do	Robert Pemberton 2s. 6d. 5 Isaac Smith 8s. 2	1	8	6
	Charsfield	Charles Ward 2s. 5	0	10	0
	Ufford	Peter Brundle 15s. 5	3	15	0
Alderton	Alderton	Corey Wade 2s. 5 Francis Kettle 5s. 5	1	15	0
	do	Joseph Boon 3s. 5 Widow Wilson 5s. 5	2	0	0
	do	Widow Howard 4s. 5 Sparrow's child 1s. 5	1	5	0
	do	Widow Baxter 1s. 6d. 5 Widow Cooper 1s. 1	0	8	6
	Hollesley	George Dunn 1s. 6d. 5	0	7	6
	Boyton	Widow Good 1s. 1	0	1	0
Eyke	Eyke	Philip Smith 2s. 6d. 2 William Cotton 1s. 6d. 5	0	12	6
	do	John Stannard 3s. 5 Mary Jennings 1s. 5	1	0	0
	do	John Foreman 1s. 6d. 2 Henry Clark 2s. 6d 5	0	15	6

	Hatcheston	John Jackson 2s. 6d. 5	0	12	6
	Rendlesham	James Jeffries 4s. 1 and 20s. extra	1	4	0
	Hollesley	Widow Brightwell 1s. 5	0	5	0
	Melton	William Gowing 5s. 1	0	5	0
Earl Soham	Earl Soham	Widow Spink 7s. 6d 5 George Potter 4s. 5	2	17	6
	do	Widow Barker 4s. 5 Widow Edwards 2s. 5	1	10	0
	do	John Mann 4s. 2 Robert Broom for cloathing 20s.	1	8	0
	Monewden	Philip Berry 3s. 5	0	15	0
Brandeston	Brandeston	Allen Cotton 3s. 5 Frederick Scotchmer 3s. 5	1	10	0
	do	James Taylor 5s. 5 Charles Barker for cloathing 20s.	2	5	0
	Kettleburgh	Widow Driver 5s. 5	1	5	0
Melton	Melton	John Chenery 1s. 6d. 5 Thomas Wiffew 1s. 6d. 5	0	15	0
	do	Widow Storer 4s. 2	0	8	0
	Sutton	Widow Flory 2s. 5 Widow Knappet 2s. 5	1	0	0
	Alderton	John Nunn 4s. 5	1	0	0
	Eyke	Richard Booth's wife 1s. 6d. 5	0	7	6
Ash	Ash	Thomas Lanham 1s. 6d. 5 Robert Battle 1s. 6d. 5	0	15	0
	do	James Fitch 3s. 6d. 2 Isaac Gibbs 3s. 5	1	12	0
	do	James Knights 1s. 6d. 5 Thomas Howard 2s. 5	0	17	6
	do	John Youngman 1s. 6d. 5 Nathl. Barham 1s. 6d. 5	0	15	0
	do	Widow Ling 1s. 6d. 5 and her daughter 1s. 6d. 5	0	15	0
	do	Philip Kerridge 1s. 6d. 5	0	7	6
	Charsfield	Martha King 2s. 5	0	10	0
	Brandeston	James Naunton's wife's child 1s. 6d. 5	0	7	6
Bawdsey	Bawdsey	Thomas Demey 2s. 5 Thomas Garrod 2s. 5	1	0	0
	do	William Shilcop 8s. 3 Jane King 2s. 5	1	14	0
	do	Robert Tillett 3s. 6d. 3	0	10	6
	Alderton	Jane Mark 5s. 5 John Garmnage 6s. 1	1	11	0
Charsfield	Charsfield	Samuel Read 1s. 1 Joseph Leach 3s. 5	0	16	0
	do	Benjamin Atlkins 2s. 2	0	4	0
Kettleburgh	Kettleburgh	Samuel Blomfield 2s. 5 William Hall 3s. 5	1	5	0
	do	Matilda Ramsey 6d. 5 Edward			

389

		Clark 1s. 5	0	7	6
	do	Edward Salter 2s. 5 John Smyth 1s. 5	0	15	0
	do	George Creasy 1s. 5 Robert Malden 1s. 5	0	10	0
	do	William Leader 1s. 5 Colin Holmes 1s. 5	0	10	0
	do	Amos Peck 1s. 5	0	5	0
Easton	Easton	William Hurren 3s. 5 Francis Wood 3s. 5	1	10	0
	do	Joseph Templing 3s. 5 James Wix 2s. 5	1	5	0
	do	James Callum 2s. 5 John Knights 2s 5	1	0	0
	do	Joseph Cudbard 2s. 5 George Dorling 6s. 5	2	0	0
Sutton	Sutton	John Crisp 2s. 6d. 5	0	12	6
Hollesley	Hollesley	John Turner 2s. 5 Thomas Hubbard 4s. 5	1	10	0
	do	John Lamb 6s. 6d. 5 Robert Hubbard 10s. 2	2	12	6
	do	William Lock 1s. 6d. 5	0	7	6
	do	Sarah Brightwell's child 1s. 6d. 5 Wid. Andrews 2s. 5	0	17	6
	Dallingho	Henry Runnacles 10s. 5	2	10	0
	Rendlesham	John Pretty 4s. 5	1	0	0
Hacheston	Hacheston	James Cuthbert 7s. 5 Wid. Beecraft 1s. 6d. 5	2	2	6
	do	John Skinner 3s. 5 Wiliam Nicolls 2s. 5	1	5	0
	do	Richard Garrett 1s. 5 and his boy 2s. 6d. 5			
		Richard Paternoster 3s. 5	1	12	6
	Kettleburgh	Widow Flick 1s. 5	0	5	0
	Wickham	Widow Damant 3s. 5	0	15	0
	Letheringham	Mary Malton 1s. 5	0	5	0
Rendlesham	Rendlesham	Charles Orsborn 2s. 6d. 2	0	5	0
Dallingho	Dallingho	Jeremiah Davy 3s. 5 James Catow 1s. 6d. 2	0	18	0
	do	Samuel Pulham 1s. 2 and boy 1s. 6d. 5	0	18	0
	do	Robert Spall 1s. 6d. 5	0	7	6
Hollesley	Hollesley	The following persons apply for work or relief the Governor is ordered to make informations James Mann, Edward Friars (single) Samuel Jolly (single) and James Knights (single)			
Letheringham	Letheringham	Samuel Newson 2s. 5	0	10	0
	Hollesley	Hannah Disbery 1s. 6d. 1	0	1	6

Bromeswell	Bromeswell	Samuel Burrows 1s. 6d 5 Joseph Lion 1s. 6d. 5	0	15	0
	do	William Cook 1s. 1	0	1	0
	Sutton	Joseph King 1s. 6d. 5 Widow Branch 6d. 5	0	10	0
	do	Widow Fuller 1s. 5	0	5	0
	Dallingho	James Hinchlow 3s. 5	0	15	0
	Bromeswell	John Mills 5s. 2	0	10	0
Marlesford	Marlesford	Francis Betts 1s. 6d. 5 John Jordan 1s. 6d. 5	0	15	0
	do	John Birt 2s. 5 Francis Clow 1s. 6d. 5	0	17	6
	do	William Last 1s. 5 Robert Rouse 1s. 6d. 5	0	12	6
	do	Robert Jay 6s. 2	0	12	0
Wickham		Widow Bridges 1s. 5	0	5	0
Bredfield	Bredfield	Joseph Chapman 3s. 2 Samuel Richardson 1s. 5	0	11	0
	do	Samuel Norman 2s. 5 James Fulcher 10s. 5	3	0	0
	do	Robert Battle 1s. 5 John Button 3s. 5	1	0	0
	do	Hannah Dewell 1s. 6d. 5 Sarah Baldry 1s. 5	0	12	6
	do	William Goldsmith 2s. 5 James Cudhard 8s. 2	1	6	0
	do	John Good 8s. 2	0	16	0
	Monewden	Ann Birch 1s. 6d. 5	0	7	6
	Alderton	William Creasy 3s. 6d. 5	0	17	6
Boulge	Boulge	Joseph Sparrow ill 8s. 1	0	8	0
		Total	138	18	0

Directors   Guardians
Jonathan Abbott Studd   Edmund Plant
Samuel Gross for Mr Edward   Joseph Roe
                                William Hambling

The tenth Weekly Minute Book, 10 April 1824–12 October 1826[6]

Parish belonging to as under	Paupers Names and parishes Residing in Campsey Ash	No. of	5th Ap.	12th	19th	26th	Total		
Ash	Robert Battle	4	2				0	8	0
do	James Fitch	4	2				0	8	0
do	Isaac Gibbs	4	2				0	8	0
do	James Knights	4	2				0	8	0
do	John Youngman	4	2						
	do extra	2			1		0	10	0
do	Philip Kerridge	4	1				0	4	0
do	Samuel West	4	2						
	do extra	2			1		0	10	0
do	Mary Downing	4	1 6				0	6	0
do	James Fitch in addition to former								
	Order for a funeral		2 6				0	2	6
do	Mary Baldry	4	1 6				0	6	0
Brandeston	James Naughton's wife's child	4	1				0	4	0
Ash	Thomas Howard ill	1				5	0	5	0
	Brandeston								
Brandeston	Allen Cotton	4	11	2	2	2	0	17	0
	Samuel Meers	4	4				0	16	0
	Samuel Loads	4	2 6				0	10	0
	Elizabeth Boon	4	0 6				0	2	0
	Samuel Meer's daughter	4	2 6				0	10	0
	John Bedingfield	4	10				2	0	0
Monewden	Simon Glascott	4	1				0	4	0
Brandeston	Bradlaugh ill	1		1			0	1	0
do	John Meadows ill	3		9			1	7	0
	Widow Boon	3		1 6			0	4	6
	B. Barker	1			8		0	8	0
	Butley								
Butley	James Crosby	4	4				0	16	0
do	John Crosby	4	1				0	4	0
	Thomas Caley	4	2				0	8	0

6   SROI ADA11/A/B/3/10.

Parish	Name								£	s	d
	Toakly Caley	4	1						0	4	0
	John Lewis	4	1						0	4	0
	John Markham's daughter	1	2	6					0	2	6
	James Riches	4	1						0	4	0
	Isaiah Fox	2	7						0	14	0
Charsfield	Charles Ward	4	2	6					0	10	0
Ufford	Peter Brundle	4	7	6					1	10	0
Butley	Nathaniel Mills	1					2	6	0	2	6
	Charsfield										
Charsfield	Joseph Leech	4	2						0	8	0
Do	Jona Nunn	4	1						0	4	0
	William Mullinger	4	1						0	4	0
	John Colthorp	4	1						0	4	0
	John Mann	4	1						0	4	0
	Widow Fletcher	4	7	6					1	10	0
	Jonathan Nunn	4	5						1	0	0
	Mary Curtis	4	1	6					0	6	0
	Isaac Flory	4	9						1	16	0
	Samuel Atkins	1	1	6					0	1	6
Boyton	Mary Lewis	4	2						0	8	0
Letheringham	William Rogers	3	8		6	6			1	0	0
do	William Cattermole	2				1			0	2	0
Dallingho	Maria King	4	1	6					0	6	0
do	Harriot King	4	1						0	4	0
Charsfield	H. Collins midwife				5				0	5	0
do	Samuel Atkins wife ill	3			1	6			0	4	6
do	Is. Flory for mutton						3	9	0	3	9
	Creetingham										
Creetingham	Robert Jay ill	4	15						3	0	0
do	Samuel Fisk	4	2						0	8	0
	John Moss	4	1						0	4	0
	Thomas Clements	4	1						0	4	0
	Widow Rummacres	4	12						2	8	0
	Widow Gray's child	4	1						0	4	0
	Samuel Moyse	4	1	6					0	6	0
	William Hawes	4	1	6					0	6	0
	William Avis	4	1	6					0	6	0
	Nathaniel Butcher's child	4	1						0	4	0
	Abraham Emerson ill	4	10						2	0	0
	E. Moyse's wife ill	2	3						0	6	0
	Widow Orsborn	4	2						0	8	0
	F. Simonds	1					5	6	0	5	6
	Dallingho										
Dallingho	Robert Spall 7 ch.	4	3						0	12	0
	Jeremiah Davy 7 ch.	4	2	6					0	10	0
	James Caton 6 ch.	4	2						0	8	0

Parish	Name							£	s	d
	Samuel Pulham 6, wife ill	4	3					0	12	0
	W. Caton 5	4	1					0	4	0
	W. Scarce 9	4	3					0	12	0
	Ann Hinchlow	4	3					0	12	0
	Joseph Wayman's lame boy	4	2					0	8	0
Petistree	Samuel Smith lame	4	2					0	8	0
	Earl Soham									
Earl Soham	Widow Spink	4	2					0	8	0
	Widow Spalding	4	5					1	0	0
	Widow Barker	4	2	6				0	10	0
	Charles Eames	4	2					0	8	0
	William Spalding	4	6					1	4	0
	John Mann	4	8	8		12	12	2	0	0
	John Templing	4	2	2		1 6	1 6	0	7	6
	William Chapman's wife ill	2	1					0	2	0
	Edmund Barker to be discharged and allowed					2 6	2 6	0	5	0
Eyke	Sarah Spalding and B. Child	4	3					0	12	0
Monewden	Mary Glassen ill	4	1	6				0	6	0
Brandeston	James Edwards ill	1					5	0	5	0
Earl Soham	Richard Gooch ill	3			7			1	1	0
do	John Watson	1					2	0	2	0
	Easton									
Easton	William Hurren	4	1					0	4	0
do	Francis Wood	4	2					0	8	0
	Joseph Templing	4	1					0	4	0
	Samuel Cullem	4	1					0	4	0
	Robert Adam	4	1					0	4	0
	Joseph Cudbard	4	1					0	4	0
	Elizabeth Page	4	1	6				0	6	0
	Widow Dorling	4	0	6				0	2	0
	George Smyth's wife	4	0	6				0	2	0
	Thomas Grimwood	4	1	6				0	6	0
	Sarah Abbott	4	1					0	4	0
	Widow Smith	4	0	6				0	2	0
Charsfield	Widow Bennett	4	1					0	4	0
Earl Soham	L. Upson	2			7 6	3 6		0	11	0
	Eyke									
Eyke	Anthony King	4	3					0	12	0
	William Clark	4	4					0	16	0
	William Pannifer	4	1					0	4	0
	Jane Booth	4	1	6				0	6	0
	John Stannard	4	1	6				0	6	0
	John Smith	4	2					0	8	0

										£	s	d
	Sarah Smith	4	1							0	4	0
	John Masterson	4	1							0	4	0
	Charles Francis	1	1	6						0	1	6
	Samuel Barber's son lame	3	1	6						0	4	6
	Joseph Barber ill	1							6	0	6	0
	William Minter's daughter	2	1	6						0	3	0
Bromeswell	Robert Leech	4	4							0	16	0
Hacheston	John Jackson ill	2			4					0	8	0
Melton	William Gowing	2	4							0	8	0
Wickham	William Wright's wife ill	2			1					0	2	0
	Hacheston											
Hacheston	Samuel Woods	4	1	6						0	6	0
do	Sanders Green	4	8							1	12	0
	John Porter	4	2							0	8	0
	Robert Orsborn	4	1							0	4	0
	James Copping	4	1							0	4	0
	Daniel Howard	4	2							0	8	0
	William Mayhew	4	1							0	4	0
	John Smith	4	1							0	4	0
	Widow Gissing	4	2	6						0	10	0
	Nathan Noy	4	1							0	4	0
	Q. Page	4	1	6						0	6	0
	Ann Birt	1				2				0	2	0
	Ann Gissing ill	4	2							0	8	0
	do error last month									0	4	0
Sutton	Ann Farmer	4	1	6						0	6	0
Cretingham	Thomas Turner	4	1							0	4	0
	Hoo											
Hoo	David Nunn	4	2							0	8	0
	John Nunn	4	2							0	8	0
	Stephen Alexander	4	4							0	16	0
	John Gibbs	4	1	6						0	6	0
	James Studd	4	1	6						0	6	0
	John King	4	4							0	16	0
	Widow Balls	4	1							0	4	0
	Francis Fitch's wife	4	1	6						0	6	0
	Samuel Branton	2	6							0	12	0
	Benjamin Harvey's wife ill	2	2							0	4	0
	Daniel Smith ill	1	7							0	7	0
Letheringham	John Smith's wife ill 8 ch.	4	4							0	16	0
do	Michael Hawes	2				1	6			0	3	0
	James Rawling	2				1	6			0	3	0
Bawdsey	James Sawyer lame	4	4							0	16	0
	Kenton											
Kenton	Robert Ling	2	1							0	2	0

395

Place	Name						£	s	d
do	Robert Plant	4	9				1	16	0
	Widow Pollard	4	2				0	8	0
	Samuel Smith	4	1				0	4	0
	Sarah Calver	2	1				0	2	0
	Samuel Page	4	3	6			0	16	0
	Thomas Bannister	2	1	6			0	3	0
	David Church illness	4	5	5	10	10	1	10	0
	Thomas Calver's wife ill	4	2	2	1	1	0	6	0
	William Page ill	2	5				0	10	0
	John Church	2			1		0	2	0
	James Sheldrake's wife B.C.	2	5				0	10	0
	Kettleburgh								
Kettleburgh	William Hall	4	5	6			1	2	0
	William Leader	4	4	6			0	18	0
	Mayhew's 3 ch.	4	3	6			0	14	0
	Richard Sculthorp	4	5				1	0	0
	Edward Clark's wife	4	1				0	4	0
	Benjamin Synd not allowed								
	Matilda Ramsey	4	2				0	8	0
	Sarah Jordan	4	0	6			0	2	0
	Sarah Clark	4	0	6			0	2	0
	Mary Leech	4	0	6			0	2	0
	Rachel Colthorpe	4	0	6			0	2	0
	John Orsborn's wife	4	1				0	4	0
	O. Hatcher's wife ill	4	2				0	8	0
	John Jay 5 ch.	4	1				0	4	0
	Widow Kent	4	0	3			0	1	0
	William Leader	4	1				0	4	0
	John Smyth	4	3				0	12	0
	Mary Sykes	4	1	6			0	6	0
	Mary Wakely	4	1				0	4	0
	Emma Wakeley	4	1	6			0	6	0
	John Herring	4	6	6			1	6	0
	John Driver	4	2				0	8	0
	Mary Cousins	4	0	6			0	2	0
	George Creasy	4	2				0	8	0
	John Clark	4	6	6			1	6	0
	Samuel Davy	4	10				2	0	0
	Henry Smith	2	12				1	4	0
	John Smith	4	2				0	8	0
Alderton	Fanny Turner	4	0	6			0	2	0
Kettleburgh	Henry Kent	2	6				0	12	0
	Benjamin Syred	4	1				0	4	0
	John Peck	2	5				0	10	0
	William Nicholl's wife funeral	1	2	1	10		1	12	0
	Henry Smith	2			10		1	0	0
	John Jay midwife etc.					10	0	10	0

Parish	Name						£	s	d
	Thomas Mortimer	2			5	6		0	11	0
	O. Hatcher's wife ill midwife						10	0	10	0
	John Herring	2			2	6		0	5	0
	John Baldry midwife						5	0	5	0
	Letheringham									
Letheringham	Samuel Newson	4	3					0	12	0
	Edward Cuthbert	4	1					0	4	0
	Thomas Nicholls ill	4	8					1	12	0
	Marlesford									
Marlesford	J. Beart	4	1					0	4	0
	Robert Rouse	4	1					0	4	0
	Thomas Nicholls	4	1					0	4	0
	John Aldred	4	1					0	4	0
	James Wordley	4	1					0	4	0
	George Pizzey	2	2					0	4	0
	Thomas Hill	2	5					0	10	0
	Monewden									
Monewden	Samuel Copping and 2 ch	4	4					0	16	0
	Widow Crowfoot	4	6					0	16	0
	Sarah Collins	4	2					0	8	0
	Philip Berry's wife	4	5					1	0	0
	Martha Durrant	4	1	6				0	6	0
	Ann Woods	4	1	6				0	6	0
	Peggy Wade	4	1	6				0	6	0
	Elizabeth Nunn	4	1					0	4	0
	John Leggatt	4	4					0	16	0
	William Syth	4	1					0	4	0
	John Brianton ill	2					3	0	6	0
	Rendlesham									
Rendlesham	John Mays	4	2					0	8	0
	do very ill	3					9	1	7	0
	Jeremiah Scopes	4	1					0	4	0
	Thomas Ward	4	1					0	4	0
	James Chilvers	4	2					0	8	0
	Robert Kerridge lame	1	5					0	5	0
	Thomas Rout for wife's funeral							1	10	0
	Alderton									
Alderton	Francis Kettle	4	5					1	0	0
do	Widow Wilson	4	4	6				0	18	0
	Widow Alexander	4	4					0	16	0
	Robert Wisken	4	2					0	8	0
	Widow Knights	4	6	6				1	6	0
	Lewin Blaxall	4	2	6						
	do extra	1					5	0	15	0

Place	Item							£	s	d
	John Fayett funeral							1	0	0
	Carey Wade	4	5					1	0	0
	Widow Blaxhall	4	4	6				0	18	0
Hollesley	George Dunn	4	4					0	16	0
Bawdsey	Shelcott's family	4	6	6				1	6	0
Alderton	Joseph Murrell	2	6					0	12	0
	Ab. Sweeney ill	3			5			0	15	0
	William Smith ill	1				5		0	5	0
	Knight's mutton						5	0	5	0
	Mary Aldous in addition to Qtly relief					1		0	1	0
	Bawdsey									
Alderton	John Gamnage's family 6 ch.	4	12					2	8	0
Bawdsey	Widow Demney	4	6					1	4	0
do	Letty Spatchett and B. Ch.	4	2	6				0	10	0
	Widow Blaxhall and child	4	2	6				0	10	0
	Margaret Mealing	4	1					0	4	0
	William Davies 5 ch.	4	1					0	4	0
	John Hunt ill	4	5							
	and mutton						3 3	1	3	3
	Mary Ann Smith	3				1 6		0	4	6
	Robert Horn	4	3					0	12	0
	Boulge									
Boulge	Joseph Sparrow ill	4	7					1	8	0
	Boyton									
Boyton	Francis Ashkettle	4	5	6				1	2	0
	William Middleditch	4	11					2	4	0
	James Elvin	4	4					0	16	0
	Mary Debenham	4	7	6						
	do for burial of child		15	0				2	5	0
	Thomas Richardson	4	2					0	8	0
	James Burndle	2	5	6				0	11	0
	John Disberry	4	1					0	4	0
	James Markham in London ill	1	0	0 pd by Governor						
Bredfield	James Fulcher	4	7	6				1	10	0
	Samuel Richardson	4	2					0	8	0
	Samuel Norman	4	6					1	4	0
	John Button	4	5					1	0	0
	William Goldsmith	4	4					0	16	0
	Benjamin Garnham	4	1					0	4	0
	Thomas Catchpole	4	10					2	0	0
	William Brown	4	2	6				0	10	0
	John Crane	4	1					0	4	0
	Harriet Reed	4	2					0	8	0

Parish	Name										£	s	d
	James Archer	4	8								1	12	0
	James Clow	1							2		0	2	0
	Robert Marjoram	4	1								0	4	0
	John Good	3			1						0	3	0
	James Smith	1							1		0	1	0
	Sarah Lankester and Widow Lankester	1							2		0	2	0
Alderton	William Creasy	4	2	6							0	10	0
Boulge	Thomas Glanfield	4	7								1	8	0
Melton	Isaac Allen	1			5						0	5	0
do	Susan Wright	1							1	6	0	1	6
	Bromeswell												
Bromeswell	Jonas Lion	4	2	6							0	10	0
	Samuel Burrows	4	1	6							0	6	0
	James Burrows	4	0	6							0	2	0
	William Farrow ill	4	7								1	8	0
	John Farrow	4	1								0	4	0
	James Sheming	4	1								0	4	0
Eyke	Samuel Adams daughter	4	1	6							0	6	0
Sutton	Widow Fuller	4	0	6							0	2	0
	Capel												
Capel	Isaac Naunton	4	3								0	12	0
do	John King	4	1										
	do ill	3				7					1	5	0
	Thomas Lion	4	3								0	12	0
Boyton	John Chambers wife's midwife		10								0	10	0
Bredfield	John Kirk	4	2								0	8	0
	Debach												
Debach	James Pooley ill	1			5						0	5	0
	Stephen Colthorpe	4	1								0	4	0
	Hollesley												
Hollesley	John Elvin 5 ch	4	1								0	4	0
do	Mary Keeble's B.B. ch.	4	2	6	2	6	2	0	2	0	0	9	0
	Widow Dorley and 2 ch.	4	5								1	0	0
	William Sharman 7 ch.	4	3								0	12	0
	Samuel Hoby	2			8						0	16	0
	Widow Andrews very ill	4	1								0	4	0
	John Lamb	4	2	6							0	10	0
Eyke	Lucy Taylor	4	1	6							0	6	0
Hollesley	James Lucock midwife						5				0	5	0
do	Widow Andrews for funeral							1	5	0	1	5	0
	Melton												
Melton	John Sawyer 6 ch.	4	2								0	8	0
do	John Chenery 5 ch.	4	1								0	4	0

Parish	Name						£	s	d
	Thomas Wiffen 5 ch.	4	1				0	4	0
	William Smith ill	4	3				0	12	0
	John Barker's wife ill	4	2				0	8	0
	James Silver ill 5 ch.	2			5		0	10	0
	Robert Goodwin ill by Mr Studd						0	12	0
	Thomas Haker's children ill d *do*						0	4	0
	Petistree								
Petistree	James Brown	4	10						
	do porter					1 9	2	1	9
	John Bugg	4	1				0	4	0
	James Harvey	4	1				0	4	0
	Joseph Potter	1			6		0	6	0
	Ramsholt								
Ramsholt	James Lewis ill	4	5				1	0	0
	Samuel Foster's wife ill	4	5 6				1	2	0
	James Haye's wife ill	4	6				1	4	0
	Shottisham								
Shottisham	John Blomfield	4	2				0	8	0
do	Sophia Bird	4	3						
	do mutton					3 3	0	15	3
	William Daynes	4	4						
	do mutton					3 3	0	19	3
Sutton	John Webber ill	4	2 6				0	10	0
	Sutton								
Sutton	John Jacob's wife ill	4	7						
	do midwife				5		1	13	0
do	Samuel Forster's wife ill	4	2				0	8	0
	James Cook lame	4	6	7	8	7	1	8	0
	John Copping ill	1	6				0	6	0
	John Sheppard ill porter						0	7	0
	James Calver ill	1			5		0	5	0
Melton	Howard Crane ill	4	2 6				0	10	0
	Ufford								
Ufford	John Skeet	4	2 6						
	do lame extra	4	1				0	14	0
do	Thomas Head	4	3				0	12	0
	Widow Wix	4	7 6				1	10	0
	William Gross	4	2				0	8	0
	Thomas Robinson	4	6				1	4	0
	Widow Folkard	4	2 6				0	10	0
	Robert Lemmey	4	1				0	4	0
	Samuel Wix	4	1				0	4	0
	Samuel Davis	4	1				0	4	0
	Thomas Ox 12th instant ordered in Woodbridge	1	2 6				0	2	6

Parish	Name							£	s	d
	Lucy Stollery	4	1	6				0	6	0
Petistree	Jeffry Curtis ill	4	5					1	0	0
do	Charles Gibbs	4	1					0	4	0
Ash	Samuel Buckles 6 ch.	4	1					0	4	0
Sutton	William Ramsey ill	4	5					1	0	0
Melton	Mary Trusson	4	0	6				0	2	0
Wickham	John Buckingham	4	5		5	5	4	0	19	0
Ufford	John Smith midwife and nurse						10	0	10	0
do	James Wolton do						10	0	10	0
	Wickham Market									
Wickham	Thomas Walker 5 ch.	4	2					0	8	0
do	Lionel Baldrey	4	1	6				0	6	0
	Ann Buckenham	4	0	6				0	2	0
	Sarah Crane	4	0	6				0	2	0
	B. Stannard	1	1					0	1	0
	Mary and William Etheredge	4	3	6				0	14	0
	Samuel Clayton	4	1					0	4	0
	Samuel Cotton 5 ch.	4	1					0	4	0
	John Middleton lame	4	5					1	0	0
	Elizabeth Wright	4	1					0	4	0
	John Palmer 5 ch.	4	1					0	4	0
Petistree	Samuel Eagle 5 ch.	4	1	6				0	6	0
Hollesley	Widow Skinner	4	1					0	4	0
Wickham	Henry Baldrey midwife					5		0	5	0
do	James Hewett towards funeral						10	0	10	0
	Thomas Walker ill	1					5	0	5	0
	Thomas Finch porter etc.							0	3	6
	Total							195	2	9

Ordered that the Treasurer pays the Governor one hundred pounds on account.

Directors   Guardians

Jacob Chilton   John Lewin   John Woolnough.

Miscellaneous documents 61–88
associated with Disincorporation

**61. The Incorporation initially proposed another amending Act.
This letter, from R. Oldham, suggests clauses to be adopted from
Stow's recent amending Act.[7]**

11 August 1824

Dear Sir,

I have looked over the Stow Act, and the resolutions of the meeting here, and have enclosed for you a draft of the heads of the clauses wanted, as far as my information or judgement go, if it will be of any service to you – I think some kind of account must be drawn out similar to the Stow Accounts, in order to show the inequalities complained of to a Committee of the House of Commons or upon presenting the petition.

I am yours etc.,   R. W. Oldham

**62. Letter from J. Dorrington offering his services to the Incorporation
as their parliamentary agent[8]**

17 August 1824

Gentlemen,

I have received your favour and am happy to renew my acquaintance with you. The Standing Orders now require that notices should be inserted three times in the newspapers in August, Sept., Oct., or November, affixed for three successive Sundays on the church door of all the parishes, and on the Sessions House Door at the Michaelmas Quarter Sessions – your bill being to amend makes no difference in giving the notices. In parishes where there is no church, it will be sufficient to affix the notice on the door of the church where the inhabitants of such parishes attend divine service. When the service is performed once a fortnight, you should affix it so that it may be on the door for three Sundays when divine service is performed.

I will send to town about the act you want.

I am Gent., your very obed. servant,   J. Dorrington   Chatham, Kent.

---

7   SROI ADA11/A/A/1/8. 5 Geo. 4 c. 18, 'An Act for altering and enlarging the powers of two acts of his later Majesty for the better relief and employment of the poor within the Hundred of Stow, in the County of Suffolk'.

8   SROI ADA11/A/A/1/8.

63. Notice of the Incorporation's intention to apply for an amending act[9]

14 October 1824

Hundreds of Loes and Wilford, in the County of Suffolk

Notice is hereby given to all persons whom it may concern, that application will be made to Parliament in the ensuing session, for leave to bring in a Bill for altering, amending, and enlarging the powers and provisions of two several Acts of Parliament, <1792 and 1810>, and in the said Bill provision is intended to be made for enabling and empowering the Directors and Acting Guardians, acting under the authority of the first mentioned Act, to alter and vary the period of taking the averages directed by the last mentioned Act, by taking the same annually, as they shall deem proper, and from the time of first taking such last mentioned averages, to take fresh and new averages annually, and also to make such alterations in the assessments upon the several parishes, hamlets and places within the said Hundreds of Loes and Wilford, as on any taking of such new averages shall appear just and necessary, and for other purposes therein mentioned.

By order.   Wood and Son, solicitors.

64. Announcement of a general meeting to be held on 26 October 1824[10]

Loes and Wilford Hundreds

A General Meeting of the owners and occupiers of lands within the Incorporated Hundreds of Loes and Wilford, in the county of Suffolk, is requested to be holden at the White Hart, Wickham Market, on Tuesday the 26th day of October at eleven o'clock in the forenoon, to take into consideration the general management of the poor of the said hundreds, and other objects relating thereto.

Rendlesham	John Fitz-Gerald
Andrew Arcedeckne	J. W. Sheppard
W. A. Shuldham	Edmund Jenney

William Woods Page exec. of the late Jacob Whitbread Esq.

65. Resolutions passed at the general meeting of 26 October 1824, where the possibility of disincorporation is raised publicly for the first time[11]

1st Resolution proposed by Lord Rendlesham and seconded by Mr Page.

That considering the great sum to which the maintenance of the poor amounts in the said hundreds annually, it appears to this meeting most desirable that a committee should be appointed to consider the best means of reducing every unnecessary expense in providing for the poor in the thirty-three incorporated parishes in the said Hundreds.

2nd Resolution proposed by Lord Rendlesham and seconded by the Revd George Turner.

That the committee shall consist of the following noblemen and gentlemen, being proprietors or occupiers of lands, or acting for such proprietors, within the said

---

9   SROI ADA11/A/A/1/8.
10 SROI ADA11/A/A/1/10.
11 SROI ADA11/A/A/1/10.

Hundreds, and Directors and Acting Guardians of the Melton House of Industry, chosen by shew of hands, and that they proceed forthwith to the dispatch of the duties imposed upon them, viz:

The Rt. Hon. Lord Rendlesham	Mr Richard Brook
John FitzGerald Esq.	Mr Thomas Waller
Andrew Arcedeckne Esq.	Mr Joshua Rodwell
John W. Sheppard Esq.	Mr Samuel Gross
Edmund Jenney Esq.	Mr Philip Dykes
William A. Shuldham Esq.	Mr Nath. Barthropp
William Woods Page Esq.	James Wenn Gent.
Revd William Bolton	Mr Robert Barthorp
Revd George Turner	Mr Thomas Brooke
Revd Charles Brooke	Mr James Clubbe
Revd William Browne	Mr Thomas Catlin
Revd John H. Groome	Mr Edmund Plant
Revd G. F. Tavel	Mr Samuel Turner
Revd Jacob Chilton	Mr Edward S. Crisp
Revd T. Broadhurst	Mr John Lewin
Mr John Woolnough	Mr John Button
Mr Henry Edwards	Mr John Hodgson

That seven form a quorum, and that the chairman have a casting vote when necessary.

3rd Resolution proposed by Lord Rendlesham, seconded by Mr W. Shuldham.

That it be recommended to such Committee to ascertain whether any material alteration can be made in the present system of maintaining the poor, with a view to lessen the very heavy expenses attendant on the house of Industry at Melton; and whether the existence of the said House does, or does not, materially and unnecessarily increase the expense of maintaining the poor of the incorporated parishes, without adequate beneficial result.

That the said Committee shall, for this purpose, have access to all books and accounts at the Melton House of Industry, and the power of examining witnesses, so as to enable them to gain every information on the subject, and report the result of the enquiries to a future general meeting, to be called by their chairman whenever they think proper.

4th Resolution proposed by Lord Rendlesham, seconded by Mr Jenney.

That the bill which has already been adopted by the general meeting, at the House of Industry, shall be laid before the Committee, in order that they may suggest such alterations or amendments therein, as may be thought necessary.

5th Resolution proposed by Lord Rendlesham, seconded by the Revd J. H. Groome.

That the Committee shall meet on Tuesday 2nd November next, at the House of Industry, at eleven o'clock, for the dispatch of business, and continue to meet on every succeeding Tuesday, at the same time and place, as long as necessary.

6th Resolution proposed by Lord Rendlesham, and seconded by Mr Dykes.

That these resolutions be published in the Ipswich papers.

7th Resolution proposed by Lord Rendlesham, seconded by Mr Arcedeckne.

That the cordial thanks of this meeting be offered to the High Sheriff for his kindness in taking the chair, and for the very able manner in which he has conducted the business of the day.

66. Resolutions proposing a review of the Incorporation's accounts, and the findings of Mr Lewin's investigations which were unfavourable towards the Incorporation[12]

2 November 1824
Resolutions

Resolved – that this Committee shall go into the accounts of the Corporation for the last 24 years, and that such accounts shall be forthwith produced to the Committee.

Resolved – that the accounts of the first two periods of 10 years, each having been made up, Mr Lewin of Wickham Market, and Mr Pizey of Woodbridge, be employed to assist Mr Oldham, the Governor, to make out the last four years accounts of the Corporation for the use of the Committee, and that the same be laid before them at their next meeting.

Edmund Jenney, Chairman.

The accounts of the corporation for the last 24 years, as extracted from the books by Mr Oldham, assisted by Mr Lewin and Mr Pizey, and referred to in the foregoing resolution, are as follows:

General Average statement of 24 years' expenditure from Michaelmas 1800 to Michaelmas 1824.

	£	s.	d.
Total expenditure for 10 years Michaelmas 1800 to Michaelmas 1810	52,685	12	0
out relief	20,208	2	0
indoor paupers (275)	32,477	10	0
	52,685	12	0
Yearly average	5,268	11	2
Total expenditure for 10 years Michaelmas 1810 to Michaelmas 1820	93,268	10	11
out relief	51,908	6	8
indoor paupers (260)	37,466	9	0
law expenses, earnings of paupers etc. deducted from General Fund, as agreed at the time	3,893	15	3
	93,268	10	11
Yearly average	9,326	17	1
Total expenditure for 10 years Michaelmas 1820 to Michaelmas 1824	40,035	8	11
out relief	23,916	19	6
indoor paupers (260)	15,036	16	2
law expenses, earnings of paupers etc deducted from General Fund,	1,081	13	3
	40,035	8	11
Yearly average	10,008	17	3

---

[12] SROI ADA11/A/A/1/10.

67. Resolutions ordering the circulation of Mr Lewin's financial statements[13]

9 November 1824

Resolved that the accounts of the Corporation for the last 24 years were produced and inspected by this committee, in pursuance of the resolution of the last meeting.

Resolved that the document or statement produced by Mr Lewin, be copied, and that one copy thereof be transmitted by the solicitors to each member of the committee, previous to the next meeting.

Edmund Jenney, Chairman.

68. Resolutions ordering the circulation of the Revd J. H. Groome's financial statements based on his inspection of the Incorporation's accounts, his findings being favourable towards the Incorporation[14]

16 November 1824

1st Resolution – That the document or statement produced by the Revd Mr Groome be copied, and that one copy thereof be transmitted by the solicitors to each member of the committee, previous to the next meeting.

2nd Resolution – That a return be made of the number of paupers belonging to each parish, and of the amount of their maintenance, both in and out of the House, for the last year, including the average of the quarterly allowances, and that the same be transmitted to each member of the committee.

Edmund Jenney, Chairman.

The statement of the Revd Mr Groome, referred to in the resolution first above mentioned, is as follows:

Melton House of Industry with the Hundreds of Loes and Wilford

Dr			Cr
Cash by rates and incidentals for 24 years	£201,556	Out-allowances including out surgeons for 24 years	£96,032
		Law expenses for 24 years averaged at £10 per year for each parish	£7,920
		Balance carried forward	£97, 934
	£201,556		£201,556
Balance brought forward	£97,334	Cost of maintenance of poor for 24 years	£45,385
Produce of land for 24 years	£3,868	Cost of 33 workhouses for 24 years averaged at £50 each	£39,600
		Extra expenses, over and above the sum taken for maintenance, owing to sickness, casualties, small pox, vaccination etc. averaged at £10 per annum for	

---

13 SROI ADA11/A/A/1/10.
14 SROI ADA11/A/A/1/10.

	24 years	£7,920
	Balance carried forward	£8,897
£101,802		£101,802

From the foregoing statement, there is *prima facie*, a balance of £8,897 which appears to have been expended by the Corporation, more than would have been expended in the 24 years had the parishes remained distinct and separate; but it is the opinion of many gentlemen, that a much larger addition would have been made to their expenditure than is here assumed, leaving a balance in favour of the incorporation.

It ought to be observed, that in this statement, and in the one submitted to the Committee the previous week, a great deal is hypothetical. The items of apprentices, overseers' expenses, interest on money, and extra out allowances, are not noticed in this statement because, as it is contended, the three former items of expense would have been incurred whether the parishes had been incorporated or not. The last item is omitted, because of the supposition upon which it is calculated, appears wholly unsupported by fact. On the other hand, in the credit side of the previous statement, the only items that appear are the out allowances, and the bare cost of maintenance (i.e.) food. In this statement it is contended, that expenses, nearly equal to that which the House at Melton has cost, would have been incurred in law expenses, maintenance and government of 33 work houses, and extra expenses, had there been no incorporation. The conclusion is, that instead of £95,271 having been expended more than would have been requisite or necessary had there been no incorporation that probably a larger sum than the house has actually expended, would have been called for.

69. Resolutions concerning the adjustments to be made to the financial reports offered by Mr Lewin and the Revd Groome[15]

23 November 1824

1st Resolution – That the Revd Mr Groome, having, at the suggestion of the Committee, consented to withdraw his statement as hypothetical, and consequently incapable of proof before the Committee, the following parts of Mr Lewin's statement, being of the same description, be expunged, viz.

	£	s.	d.
The interest upon the debt of £10,150 paid off	5,075	0	0
The interest upon £9,200 costs of erecting the House	1,840	0	0
The attendance of overseers	2,376	0	0
Out-allowances	14,000	0	0
	23,291	0	0

and in lieu of the sum of £12,720 charged for the apprentices, there be substituted such a sum as shall be found from the books of the Corporation to have been actually paid as fines for refusal to take apprentices, viz. the sum of £5,000, and that the sum of £45,385 14s. 8d. on the credit side of the account, be also struck out.

---

15 SROI ADA11/A/A/1/10.

2nd Resolution – That it is the opinion of this Committee, that the financial department of this Incorporation has hitherto been so conducted, as not to answer the purposes for which it was instituted.

3rd Resolution – That the Committee do proceed to take into their consideration, whether by any modification, under the bill in contemplation, and by exterior and interior management, this incorporation can be made to answer the purposes for which it was instituted.

4th Resolution – That the solicitors do produce the proposed bill at the next meeting of the committee.

Edmund Jenney, Chairman.

70. Resolutions stating that the proposed bill for an amendment act would fail to address the financial issues that had been identified[16]

30 November 1824

1st Resolution – That the proposed bill was produced by the solicitors, and read by the chairman, and afterwards debated clause by clause, and the expenses of the out surgeons and law expences, be expunged from the first class or division of expences, and be added to, and incorporated with, the second class or division of expences in the said proposed bill, in case the said bill should be proceeded with.

2nd Resolution – That it is the opinion of this Committee that the proposed bill does not appear calculated to make such reductions in the expenses of the establishment of the Melton House of Industry, as is the object of the bill to obtain.

Edmund Jenney, Chairman.

71. Resolutions for convening a general meeting to debate the possibility of disincorporation[17]

7 December 1824

1st Resolution – That the report prepared since the last meeting was read by the chairman, and that the statement now read by Mr Lewin, should become part thereof, and be added thereto.

2nd Resolution – That the said report be laid before a General Meeting, and that it be left to the wisdom of such meeting to decide whether a further committee should be appointed to substitute a bill in lieu of the one rejected, or apply to parliament for a bill to disincorporate the hundreds.

3rd Resolution – That a General Meeting of the owners and occupiers, or acting for owners and occupiers, within the said hundreds, be convened at the White Hart Inn, in Wickham Market, upon the last Tuesday in January, at eleven o'clock in the forenoon – and that such meeting be advertized in both Ipswich papers for three successive weeks preceding such meeting.

Edmund Jenney, Chairman.

---

16 SROI ADA11/A/A/1/10.
17 SROI ADA11/A/A/1/10.

72. Resolutions concerning the recording of vestry meetings that were to be held in all thirty-three parishes so as to ascertain the depth of support for disincorporation[18]

10 February 1825

1st – Resolved that Messrs. Wood and Son be appointed solicitors to the bill intended to be introduced into Parliament. And that they do forthwith make application to every parish in this the Incorporated Hundreds to hold vestry meetings, in order to ascertain whether they will consent and agree to pay, out of their parochial funds, such proportion of the expences incurred, or to be incurred, by the bill before mentioned, whether the same be passed into a law or not as shall be demanded of them by this Committee, and that such application be made by a circular letter to be addressed to the churchwardens and overseers of each parish.

2nd – Resolved that as soon as answers be obtained from every parish the solicitors do request a second meeting of this committee by giving ten days' notice to each member previous to such meeting.

73. Letter from Wood & Son outlining the procedure the parishes were to adopt for reporting the vestry meetings[19]

16 February 1825
GENTLEMEN

At the first meeting of the committee appointed to frame a bill for repealing the acts relative to the Incorporation of the Hundreds of Loes and Wilford, holden at the White Hart Inn, Wickham Market, on Thursday the 10th instant, after a discussion upon the subject of raising a fund in order to forward the object of the committee, it was:

Resolved – "That Messrs Wood and Son be appointed solicitors to the bill intended to be introduced into Parliament, and they do forthwith make application to every parish within the Incorporated Hundreds, to hold vestry meetings, in order to ascertain whether they will consent and agree to pay out of their parochial funds such proportion of the expences incurred by the bill before mentioned, whether the same be passed into a law or not as shall be demanded of them by this committee; and that such application be made by a circular letter, to be addressed to the churchwardens and overseers of each parish".

In obedience to the above resolution, we make this application to you, and as it is desirable that the several vestry meetings be held in a legal form, and proper entries made in your parish book of the proceedings of such meeting, we annex the necessary forms and other instructions for your guidance; and we are desired to request that after your vestry meeting shall have been holden in your parish, you will cause a duplicate of the proceedings of such meeting, signed by the several persons attending the same, to be forwarded to our office for the information of the committee, on or before the sixteenth day of March next ensuing.

We are, Gentlemen,
        Your most obedient servants,   Wood and Son.

---

[18] SROI ADA11/A/A/1/14.
[19] SROI ADA11/A/A/1/13.

To,

The Church Wardens and Overseers of the Poor of the parish of **Kettleburgh**[20]

Instructions for holding vestry meetings

In case your parish be not provided with a book for the express purpose of entering proceedings of vestry meetings, you are required forthwith to provide such a book wherein all proceedings of vestry meetings are to be entered.

Three days at least previous to you holding the vestry meeting, as mentioned on the other side, a notice in the following form must be published in your parish church, on some Sunday during or immediately after divine service, and a copy of such notice must be affixed on the principal door of your church, viz:

"Notice is hereby given that a meeting of the inhabitants of this parish in vestry, is appointed to be holden at *Kettleburgh* on *Friday* the *11th* day of *March inst.* at *10* o'clock in the *fore* noon, for the purpose of considering and determining whether it will be advisable to assent and agree to pay out of the public parochial funds of this parish, such proportion of the expenses incurred, or to be incurred, by a committee appointed to frame a bill for repealing the acts relating to the incorporated Hundreds of Loes and Wilford, whether the same be passed into a law or not, as shall be demanded of this parish by such a committee".

The meeting being thus convened, the rector, vicar, or curate, if present, must take the chair, if not, then a chairman shall be nominated and appointed by plurality of votes to be ascertained as after mentioned, who shall preside; and being thus chosen, he shall in case of equality of votes (in addition to such vote or votes he may have by the regulation after mentioned) have the casting vote at the meeting. The regulation of votes in vestry are as follows:

Every inhabitant present who shall in the last poor rate have been assessed at any sum less than £50, shall be entitled to give one vote.

And every inhabitant present, who shall have been assessed in such rate £50 or upwards shall be entitled to give one vote or every £25 upon his assessment, so that no inhabitant shall be entitled to give more than six votes.

In case two or more inhabitants shall be jointly rated, each of them are entitled to vote according to the proportion borne by him of the joint charge; and in case one only of the persons jointly rated shall attend, he shall be entitled to vote in respect of the whole joint charge.

Persons, who shall have become inhabitants, or liable to be rated since the making of the last rate, are entitled to vote in respect of the property for which they shall be liable to be rated; and persons rated in the poor rates, though not resident in or inhabitant thereof, and clerks and agents of corporations are also entitled to vote in vestry, according to the value of the premises rated.

No person, who shall have neglected or refused to pay any poor rate due, shall be entitled to vote or be present in any vestry, until he shall have paid the same.

The question being put and voted agreeable to the above regulation, you are then to make an entry in your parish book of the proceedings of such meeting in the following form, varying the same as occasion may require. And the chairman of the meeting and such other inhabitants as aforesaid, present, as shall think proper, shall sign their names at the foot of such entry.

---

[20] Example of the pre-printed form which was issued to each parish. In this example the details for the parish of Kettleburgh have been entered by hand.

"At a vestry meeting of the inhabitants of the parish of _____ holden in pursuance of the above written notice at _____ in the said parish on _____ the _____ day of _____ one thousand eight hundred and twenty five, at _____ o'clock in the _____ noon, for the purpose of considering and determining whether it would be advisable to assent and agree to pay out of the funds of this parish, such proportion of the expenses incurred or to be incurred by a committee appointed to frame a bill for repealing the Acts relating to the Incorporated Hundreds of Loes and Wilford, whether the same be passed into a law or not, as shall be demanded of this parish by such a committee. The object of the said meeting having been discussed, the question was put by the chairman, and the votes were found to be as follows:–

VOTES

Assenting thereto
Dissenting therefrom _____
Majority in favour (or against) the motion (as the case may be) _____

It is therefore
'Resolved – that our parish of _____ do (or, do not) consent and agree to pay out of the public parochial funds of the said parish, such proportion of the expenses incurred by the said committee, touching or concerning the said bill, whether the same shall be passed into law or not, as shall be demanded by the said committee'.

74. Summary of the returns received from the parishes following the vestry meetings[21]

Parish	Assenting	Dissenting	Majority Assenting	Majority Dissenting
Ash	30	0	30	
Brandeston	18	1	17	
Butley	19	0	19	
Charsfield	24	0	24	
Creetingham	21	0	21	
Dallingho	20	6	14	
Earl Soham	8	17		9
Easton	5	13		8
Eyke	7	2	5	
Hacheston	21	0	21	
Hoo	8	0	8	
Kenton	34	0	34	
Kettleburgh	10	28		18
Letheringham	7	0	7	
Marlesford	38	1	37	
Monewden	18	0	18	
Rendlesham	19	0	19	

Parishes	Assenting	Dissenting	Majority Assenting	Majority Dissenting
Alderton	19	18	1	
Bawdsey	28	0	28	
Boulge	10	1	9	
Boyton	17	0	17	
Bredfield	16	11	5	
Bromeswell	15	0	15	
Capel	12	0	12	
Debach	4	5		1
Hollesly	27	0	27	
Melton	19	12	7	
Petistree	35	0	35	
Ramsholt	0	24		24
Shottisham	6	0	6	
Sutton	28	0	28	
Ufford	10	28		18
W Mkt	33	0	33	

---

[21] SROI ADA11/A/A/1/13.

411

75. Pamphlet issued to outline the reasons for the bill for disincorporation[22]

Loes and Wilford Hundreds in the County of Suffolk
Points for consideration and reasons in favour of the Bill for Disincorporating these Hundreds
Loes and Wilford Hundreds.
The following points are submitted for consideration:

That the most industrious and best characters as labourers in the Hundreds, are perfectly content with 12s. per week, if they have a wife and four children to maintain: thus, six individuals are provided for with 12s. per week, of £31 4s. per year: but if any misfortune happen to the man, and he be sent with his family, into the Melton House, they would cost £1 18s. 10½d. per week, or £101 1s. 6d. per year.

Now, if £31 4s. be sufficient, when the man *did labour*, why should they cost £101 1s. 6d. when he *did not labour?*

It may be said, that 12s. *are not enough*; but we have thousands of living proofs that sum is sufficient; as we submit, that the labourers of these Hundreds will be found, on inspection, in as comfortable condition *as any peasantry* in the kingdom.

There being now in the House no more than an average of six paupers (two men, two women, and two children) to each parish, but little difficulty will arise in providing for them in their respective parishes.

Finally, it must be remembered, that money paid in the form of wages for work is more gratefully received, and more economically expended, than that given in compulsory relief, and does not interfere with or injure the market of free labour; whereas the relief enforced by local acts of Parliament is so burthensome to the contributors, that they are less willing to give employment, and less able to pay wages to honest and independent industry.

76. Committee to oversee the disincorporation: Resolutions to prepare the draft petition following the returns from the vestry meetings[23]

25 July 1825
1st Resolved – Upon the production of the returns from every parish within the Incorporated Hundreds of Loes and Wilford, by which it appears a great majority of the parishes have consented and agreed to pay a proportion of the expences incurred or to be incurred in obtaining an act to repeal all the acts relative to the incorporation of the said Hundreds now in existence. That the solicitors do proceed in the regular way to comply with the Standing Orders of the House of Commons by giving the necessary notices in order to obtain such act.

2nd Resolved – That the solicitors do previously to the next meeting prepare the draft of petition upon which the bill is to be passed and introduced into the House of Commons.

3rd resolved – That the next meeting of the committee be held at the same place on Thursday the 25th August inst.

---

22 SROI ADA11/A/A/1/18.
23 SROI ADA11/A/A/1/14.

77. Committee to oversee the disincorporation: Resolutions for the drafting of a bill of disincorporation[24]

25 August 1825

1st Resolved. That the draft notice and petition produced and read at this meeting be adopted and that the solicitors do lay both drafts before their parliamentary clerk to be finally settled before the same are acted upon. And that after the said draft be so settled the solicitors do comply with the standing orders of the House of Commons.

2nd Resolved. That the solicitors do proceed to prepare the draft bill to be presented to the House of Commons should the petition be received, and that in such bill the whole of the members of this committee be named as trustees to carry the provisions thereof into effect, and that a clause be therein contained to enable the said trustees to dispose of, by public auction, the real and personal property now belonging to the said Incorporated Hundreds, and to collect and receive all money due to them and that, after paying the expences of the said act and other expences attending the same, such trustees be therein empowered to make a distribution of the residue of the proceeds of such sale and disposition in proportion to the original payment made by each parish towards discharging the debt and interest of the said incorporated hundreds.

78. Warranty from the Incorporation to Messrs Wood and Son to cover any liability for the costs incurred with disincorporation[25]

We whose names are hereunto subscribed do hereby individually and collectively undertake to hold ourselves responsible to Messrs Wood and Son, solicitors of Woodbridge, for all costs charges and expences incurred by the committees sitting at Melton House and Wickham Market upon an inquiry into the management of the Incorporated Hundreds of Loes and Wilford, and the propriety of disincorporating the same. And also for all such costs charges and expences as the second committee shall hereafter incur in causing our petition to be presented to Parliament for a bill to disincorporate the said Hundreds, and all subsequent proceedings to be had thereupon whether the said bill shall be passed into a law or not.

Dated August 25th 1825.

Rendlesham   Andrew Arcedeckne   W. A. Shuldham

79. Public notice of the application to be made to Parliament for disincorporation[26]

Hundreds of Loes and Wilford in the County of Suffolk

Notice is hereby given that application will be made to Parliament, in the ensuing Sessions, for leave to bring in a Bill for repealing two several Acts of Parliament, <1792 and 1810>, by the repeal of which said Acts, the Corporation constituted under the authority of the said first mentioned Act, by the name of and called "Guardians of the Poor within the Hundreds of Loes and Wilford, in the county of

---

[24] SROI ADA11/A/A/1/14.
[25] SROI ADA11/A/A/1/14.
[26] SROI ADA11/A/A/1/8.

Suffolk" will be dissolved. And in the said Bill, provisions are intended to be made for selling and conveying the present workhouse, and all other the messuages, lands, tenements, hereditaments and real estate, and for selling and disposing of the goods and chattels, and all other personal property whatsoever respectively, now vested in, or held by, or in trust for the said Corporation, and for distributing and dividing the proceeds of such sale or sales among the several parishes within the said Hundreds, and for other purpose relative thereto.

Dated this first day of September 1825.

By Order, Wood and Son, solicitors.

80. Committee to oversee the disincorporation: Resolutions for presenting the draft bill for perusal by William Harrison Esq., King's Counsel[27]

19 September 1825

1st resolved – that the draft bill now produced and read by the solicitors is approved, and that the same be immediately laid before William Harrison Esq., the King's Counsel, to be settled and approved by him, and that he be retained to support the said Bill in Parliament.

2nd resolved – that one of the solicitors do forthwith proceed to London for the purpose of having a personal interview with Mr Harrison for the purpose of explaining the intentions and views of this Committee.

81. Opinion of Mr Harrison on the bill for disincorporation[28]

This bill has been most carefully and accurately drawn. I have therefore after going through it twice with great attention, no other alteration than the very few I have made in the preamble to suggest. I have stated my reasons for objecting to the introducing the glebe clauses in the first instance, and I think it probable that they will be introduced better under cover of a petition against the bill than in any other form, or at least by parties appearing to require their introduction as arising out of the effects and operation of the bill if they are not inserted. I have explained to Mr Wood of my reason for having detained the draft so much longer than I had promised.

W. Harrison.

82. Committee to oversee the disincorporation: Draft petition in support of the bill following amendments made by William Harrison Esq., King's Counsel[29]

10 October 1825

Resolved that the draft petition, as altered by Mr Harrison (before whom the same was laid to be settled), and now read with his marginal notes be adopted and returned to him as final grounds of instructions for him upon which to settle the draft bill.

---

27 SROI ADA11/A/A/1/14.
28 SROI ADA11/A/A/1/14.
29 SROI ADA11/A/A/1/14.

To the honourable, the House of Commons of the United Kingdom of Great Britain and Ireland in Parliament assembled.

The humble petition of the several owners and occupiers of land tenements and hereditaments within the Hundreds of Loes and Wilford, in the county of Suffolk, whose names are hereunto subscribed.

Sheweth,

That an act of parliament was passed in <1765>. That by virtue of the said act a large house of industry and other buildings were erected at a very considerable expence and great numbers of poor persons were from time to time received into and maintained in the said House.

That another act of parliament was passed in <1792> whereby the first mentioned act was repealed, and various other provisions enacted in lieu thereof.

That another act was passed in <1810> whereby divers provisions and regulations for the management and employment of the poor within the said hundreds were enacted, which have occasioned a great and unequal burthen on the several parishes composing the incorporation.

That inconvenience and increase of expence in the management of the poor have arisen from the said establishment, without any adequate beneficial results either to the poor themselves or to the greater number of the parishes composing the incorporation.

That it has therefore become expedient that the said acts of parliament, herein before mentioned, should be repealed and that the said corporation should be dissolved.

That upon the dissolution of the said incorporation, it will be necessary that certain powers should be given to sell and convey the land purchased under the authority of the said first mentioned act, and the House of Industry, and other buildings thereupon erected, to sell and dispose of the goods and chattels, and other personal property whatsoever respectively now vested in or held by or in trust for the said corporation, and to distribute, and divide the proceed of such sale or sales among the several parishes within the said hundreds all which cannot be done without the aid and authority of Parliament.

83. Committee to oversee the disincorporation: Evidence to be offered in support of the bill[30]

5 December 1825

At the fourth meeting of this committee the draft bill was produced and read by the solicitors and approved of by the committee, and the same was directed to be laid before counsel to be settled and approved by him. At the 5th meeting of the committee, the draft petition as altered by counsel was read and adopted, and the same was directed to be returned to him as final grounds of instruction upon which to settle the draft bill. At the sixth and last meeting of the committee the draft bill as settled by counsel as read and adopted. A copy of which bill accompanies this brief.

Having set forth in consecutive order the whole proceeding of the different general meetings of the owners and occupiers of the said Hundreds, and of the two committees appointed by them, we shall proceed to state in support of the bill, the case which we have to submit to the committee of the House of Commons. Such

---

30 SROI ADA11/A/B/3/11.

is founded and built upon the presented report and documentary evidence, as it is conceived will carry conviction of its truth and solidity to every unprejudiced mind.

Before going further into this case, it may perhaps be necessary to apprise counsel that a select committee of the House of Commons was appointed some years since to consider of the poor laws, and to report their observations thereon from time to time to the house. It will be seen by several very able reports that the investigation instituted was such as to embrace every topic connected with or affecting the interest of the poor. Of course, justifications such as that which it is our object to remove were not overlooked by them in their research, and they have from the general evidence elicited from the witnesses examined before them, reported an opinion decidedly in favour of workhouses, and consider them a general benefit to the poor, but they have not merely confined themselves to this opinion, they have thoroughly recommended incorporation all over the kingdom.

Reasons for dissolving the Incorporated Hundreds of Loes and Wilford in the County of Suffolk.

The original act of Incorporation, <1765> shows by the preamble that it was passed for the following reasons:

For the general reception and more effectual relief of the aged, infirm, and diseased poor.

There are a much greater number of the aged and infirm within the Hundreds, who maintain themselves with more comfort at home, in their own cottages, as out paupers, with about one-third of the money they would have cost in the House.

This is one proof that the experiment has not answered the purpose.

For the education of poor children, in religion and industry.

The number of fines, at £10 each, paid by the occupiers, rather than take strong healthy boys and girls, at twelve or thirteen years of age as apprentices, although requiring their services, show that so many of both sexes come out of the House of Industry such bad characters. This is another proof that the experiment has not answered the purpose.

For the better employment of the able and industrious.

The greater proportion of the inmates of this house are the profligate and idle, who are so fond of being there, that it is the greatest difficulty imaginable to drive them out: and then they have all manner of excuses and schemes to get in again.

For the correction and punishment of the profligate and idle.

Instead of correction and punishment, the indulgences they meet with in this house act as a reward, and actually induce many of those, who were previously able and industrious, to become profligate and idle. This is the third proof that the experiment has not answered the purpose.

That they might be made to contribute to the support and relief of each other.

Though there have been many able bodied men, strong women, and healthy children in this House during the last four years, their average earnings do not amount to a half-penny per head per week. This is a fourth proof that the experiment has not answered the purpose.

And not be that heavy and grievous burthen to the community they had hitherto been.

This burthen, instead of decreasing, has increased to an enormous extent; so much so, that these profligate and idle have cost the hundreds more than twice the amount the most industrious families could obtain, or obtain by their hard labour. This is a fifth proof that the experiment has not answered the purpose.

In fact, time and experience have proved very clearly, that this system has nourished, promoted and increased every evil it was intended to remedy.

With respect to the preamble, and enactments of <1792 and 1810> which are the acts under authority of which the incorporation exists at this day; and which are chiefly financial.

See the Report of the Melton House Committee, generally, and particularly page 14, where it is shown that 565 aged and infirm persons (who are the subject of quarterly orders), cost 1s. 10d. per head per week. See also page 16, where it is shown that 271 paupers, which is the average number maintained in that house, have cost 6s. 5¾d. per head per week, on the average of the last twenty-four years. Certainly more than thrice the cost of the *outdoor poor*.

Evidence divided into two heads.

1st Inequality.

That the first ground of complaint has not been removed by any of the above mentioned acts appears by a reference to the printed report of the committee of inquiry at Melton House which includes a period of 24 years, from 1800 to 1824.

On reference to the said report, to pages 4 and 5, including a period from 1800 to 1810 we find the following cases of inequality:

Alderton paid in	£1,502	drew out	£2,644
Ufford paid in	£2,388	drew out	£1,405
Difference	£886		£1,239

Thus it appears that Alderton has taken advantage of Ufford to the amount of £2,125.

Again,

Hatcheston paid in	£1,797	drew out	£2,758
Ash paid in	£2,570	drew out	£1,605
	£779		£1,153

Thus it appears that Hatcheston has taken the advantage of Ash to the amount of £1,932.

These, and other similar inequalities, gave rise to the application to parliament, and the act passed in 1810 to remedy them. However that act failed to do so for on reference to the said report, at pages 6 and 7, including a period of 10 years from 1810 to 1820 we find the following:

Ufford paid in	£2,334	drew out	£4,055
Hacheston paid in	£4,634	drew out	£2,772
Difference	£2,300		£1,283

Thus it appears that Ufford has taken advantage of Hatcheston to the amount of £3,583.

Again,

Ash paid in	£2,721	drew out	£3,569
Petistree paid in	£2,284	drew out	£1,384
Difference	£437		£2,185

Thus it appears Ash has taken an advantage of Petistree to the amount of £1,748.

At the end of the last mentioned period a fresh average was taken, as required by the act of 1810, which was intended and expected to equalise these inequalities for the future. But on the contrary, we found during the period of four years 1820 to 1824 – see pages 18 and 19 of the printed report – the following cases of inequality:

Kettleburgh paid in	£1,415	drew out	£1,827

Wickham paid in	£2,306	drew out	£1,897
Difference	£891		£67

Thus it appears that Kettleburgh has taken advantage of Wickham to the amount of £824.

Again,

Alderton paid in	£1,891	drew out	£2,145
Hollesly paid in	£1,867	drew out	£1,214
Difference	£24		£931

Thus it appears that Alderton has taken advantage of Hollesly to the amount of £907.

From the foregoing cases it therefore clearly results that during the period of 14 years from the time of passing the last act of parliament for the remedy of inequalities, such as those set forth above, those inequalities, so far from having been prevented have actually been nearly doubled, as will be seen by the two following extreme cases – first, in page 4 of the report, being £2,125 and, second, in page 6, being the sum of £3,583.

Moreover, with respect to the proposed scheme of annual averages as intended to be carried into effect by a new act of parliament, it may easily be shewn from the proceeding tables given in the report, that such scheme would like all the rest which have been hitherto tried, prove ineffectual to remedy the inequalities which have been constantly found to exist from the commencement of the corporation. Thus, at page 22, the concluding one of the printed report it appears that during the last mentioned period of 4 years:

Brandeston had an average of 22 paupers in the house and Debach ¼ (or one pauper for 3 months per annum).

If Brandeston send only 2 paupers to the house under the proposed annual average

bill they would pay permanent	2s.	£114	8s.	0d.
Fluctuating	4s.	£20	16s.	0d.
Total expence under that bill		£135	4s.	0d.

Again if Debach send 10 paupers they would pay,

Permanent expence	2s.	£1	6s.	0d.
Fluctuating	4s.	£104	0s.	0d.
		£105	6s.	0d.

Thus, the paupers from Brandeston would cost that parish £67 12s. per head per annum, or £1 6s. per head per week.

And the paupers from Debach would cost that parish only £10 10s. 7d. per head per annum, or £0 4s. 0½d. per head per week.

Thus it is manifest that whether the establishment be conducted under the acts now in force, or that proposed to be substituted for them, inequalities of the description above set forth would still exist.

2nd Increase of Expence

That the other evil complained of viz., increase of expence of the establishment at Melton has not been amended by the act of 1810 appears by reference to page 10 of the printed report.

The annual expence of the corporation during the period

from 1800 to 1810 was	£5,268	11s.	2d.
Again from 1810 to 1820 the annual expence was	£9,326	17s.	1d.
Lastly from 1820 to 1824 the annual expence was	£10,008	17s.	3d.

Thus it appears that the annual expence of the incorporation has very nearly doubled in the period of 14 years from 1810 to 1824.

Again, to show that, on a dissolution of the corporation, the poor can be maintained in greater comfort (as their preference of that mode of relief amply testifies) in their respective parishes at a cost far less than they occasion to the establishment, a reference to the printed report, at page 14, will suffice to show. We there find that 565 out door paupers, on quarterly orders, cost the establishment £2,704 18s. 9d., being an average of 1s. 10d. per head per week. The report (see page 16) shews that 271 persons were maintained in the house at the expence of £109,646 12s. 5d., or 6s. 5¾d. per week per head for the last 24 years.

Again on reference to the said report, at page 14, the following four cases may be selected as calculated to shew the same result:

Ash had	9	paupers in the house who cost	£116
Hatcheston	15		£193
Alderton	12		£161
Shottisham	_3_		_£38_
	39		£508

Ash had	22½	paupers out of the house who cost	£113
Hatcheston	30		£105
Alderton	35		£160
Shottisham	10¾		_£36_
	98¼		£474

Thus it appears that 98¼ out door paupers cost £34 less money than 39 paupers in the house, or in round numbers it may be stated that 40 of paupers within the house cost more than 100 out of the house, without taking into the account sundry other items of expence not included in the return given of the indoor expenditure at page 14 of the report.

This last result will appear still more clearly elucidated by the following concise statement founded on cases which actually happened.

One of the incorporated parishes, Creetingham, had a pauper belonging to them (having a wife and ten children) who was ill a long time and cost the parish 14s. per week per annum, which included a medical bill of £8, amounted to £36 8s. This same pauper, if sent into the house with his wife and children and maintained therein for the same period, would have cost £202 3s. being in excess of £165 15s., which latter sum was actually saved to the parish by keeping him and the family out of the house.

Another parish, Letheringham, on the contrary sent a man his wife and 3 children all in good health into the house, because they were considered a nuisance (which be it observed has been no uncommon reason for sending able bodied persons into the house). This man and his family cost during the year £84 4s. 7d. Now if the parish had allowed this man 10s. per week, with which he would have been well satisfied, his maintained for the year would have amounted to no more than £26.

Objections to intended bill answered.

It is objected, by those who support the system of incorporated hundreds, that these houses form a convenient receptacle for those able bodied men and women and their families who cannot procure for themselves separate dwellings in the parish to which they belong, and accordingly, on this pretext, a great number of able bodied persons and their families have been at various times received into the Melton House.

Now it is contended by those who combat the above mentioned system, that it is neither the literal nor implied meaning of any of the acts of parliament under authority, of which the affairs of the said house are administered, that able bodied persons of either sex should be admitted as paupers who as being able and often even willing to work, and actually wanting nothing but a habitation, are not within the legal definition of paupers, or standing in need of parochial relief, such persons requiring of their overseer only work wages and thereby the means of procuring habitation for themselves. But besides the alleged illegality of the practice, a very great moral evil has moreover resulted from the admission of able bodied persons into the house and the following case shows:

Case of Edward Salter (aged 45) a pauper from Kettleburgh sent into Melton House of Industry, 14 March 1821, having no dwelling, with his wife Rachel (aged 42) and 5 children, Hannah, Mary, Naomi, Lucy and Eliza from the ages of 1 to 12.

This Edward Salter and his wife, after being shut up in the house 3 years and 5 months in perfect health, went out at his own request on the 10th Aug 1824 to harvest work, and left all their 5 children in the house. They had not been out long before the man went to live with another woman, and his wife Rachel Salter went to live with another man, and had a child by him. Thus the whole family of 5 children were deserted by their parents who both went to live in open adultery.

But granting even that the embarrassment of want of sufficient habitation may exist in a few, and very few only, of the incorporated parishes, on the dissolution of the house and granting even that that the annually increasing population of the kingdom renders it probable that this embarrassment may in turn extend to those other parishes of the incorporation which do not at this day labour under.

It is contended first, that such persons may be placed as inmates in cottages occupied by other families whether they be single or married, or if there be any objection to placing the latter class of persons at all events, one or two additional cottages maybe erected to an expence such would not exceed one half of one year's contribution to the said house, which sum, if the financial calculations comprised in the report are correct, might be saved on the same year, especially when it is remembered that the portion due to each parish upon the sale of the property of the incorporation would more than suffice for that purpose.

Finally, it is contended that no evil has been pointed out by the objectors as justifying the longer duration of the said incorporation such has not been provided for by the act of 43 of Eliz., under the dominion of which the majority of the parishes are now desirous to return, when equitably constituted and fairly administered, and to prove that the above mentioned objection is entirely removed by the said act the following extract will suffice. <There follows an extract from 43 Eliz.>.

To produce the books of accounts of the incorporation for the last 24 years, and to prove that the accounts or statement as set forth in pages 4, 5. 6 7 8, 9 10, 11, 12 and 14 of the printed report are true extracts or statements from such books call,
 Mr R. W. Oldham, the Governor of the Melton House of Industry.

To prove that the acts of parliament herein before referred to have failed to correct the abuses which they were intended to remedy and to reduce the expences. That the proposed act for annual averages would also fail to correct the inequalities existing between the several parishes, and that no act would be of any avail in checking the profuse and unnecessary system of expenditure. The inequality of contribution, as particularly set forth in pages 15, 16, and 17 of this brief. The increase of expence, as detailed on page 18. That the average expence of outdoor paupers was only 1s. 10d. per head per week, while that of indoor paupers was 6s. 5¾d. per head per week for the last 24 years, see also page 18. And further, that (calculating in round numbers) 100 outdoor paupers might be maintained for less money than 40 in door paupers, as set forth on page 18 and 19, particularly the two cases of Creetingham and Letheringham, as also set forth in page 19, and the principal facts of the case and evidence as set forth on the foregoing brief and bill call Mr John Lewin.

If counsel should require any further information or explanation upon any of the accounts or statements set forth, or the points called in support of the Bill, Mr Wood will be very happy in attending upon you at any time.

84. Broadsheet offering reasons in favour of disincorporation, issued during 1825 with no precise date[31]

REASONS

For dissolving the Incorporation of the Hundreds of Loes and Wilford, in the County of Suffolk, consisting of thirty three parishes.

In the year 1765, (sixty years ago), a majority of the owners and occupiers within these Hundreds, obtained an Act of Parliament, to enable them to try the experiment of incorporation; they tried it twenty five years, and it failed.

They then obtained a *second* Act, and the improvements thereby introduced were tried for twenty years – which also failed.

They then obtained a *third* Act, under which a system of averages was introduced, and tried for fifteen years – but this system also failed.

Thus, in a period of sixty years, three experiments have been tried under the incorporation system, and each has altogether failed. In fact, time and experience have proved, that this system of incorporation, instead of benefitting the poor and decreasing the expences, has promoted and increased every evil it was intended to remedy; therefore a very large majority* of the principal owners and occupiers within these Hundreds, are convinced that they have no other remedy but a dissolution of the incorporation, and a return to the original plan of parochial management.

Not one, nor all, of the *three experiments*, produced any benefit to the poor but the expences were thereby increased more than sixty thousand pounds!!!

*Nineteen parishes assented to dissolve, without one dissenting voice.

One parish *only* dissented, without an assenting voice.

Total assenting parishes, 28.   Dissenting, 5 – majority, 23.

This majority of 23 parishes had 493 assenting votes to 5 dissenting.

The Hundreds are computed to contain about 40,000 acres of land.

Owners of about 30,000 acres, and occupiers of about the same number of acres, have signed the petition to dissolve.

A majority of the Directors and Acting Guardians themselves have signed the petition.

---

[31] SROI ADA11/A/A/1/14.

85. Committee to oversee the disincorporation: Further resolutions concerning the passage of the bill for disincorporation[32]

5 December 1825

1st Resolved. That the draft bill as settled and approved by Mr Harrison and now read over to this committee be adopted.

2nd Resolved. That the solicitors do obtain a fair copy of the resolutions passed at the General Meeting <25 January 1825>, the signature of John FitzGerald Esquire, the chairman, it being necessary to produce those resolutions before the Committee of the House of Commons.

3rd Resolved. That the solicitors do insert an advertisement in both Ipswich papers on Saturday next, that the petition to Parliament lies at their office for signature and that the bill (founded upon that petition) after being settled and approved by counsel has been adopted by the Committee.

4th resolved. That such petition when signed be intrusted to the Members for the County of Suffolk to be presented by them to the House of Commons and that they be requested to approve it.

86. List of persons who have signed the petition against the bill, no date[33]

Edmund Jenney Esq., Director
Charles Brooke, Clerk, Director
Joshua Rodwell, Clerk, *do*
Cuthbert Henley, Clerk, *do*
Joseph Hare, farmer
Jon. Abbott Studd, Gent. Director
Charles S. Sharpe, Clerk
Chris. G. Watson, Clerk, Director
J. Ayton, Esq.
James Clubbe, Gent.
Thomas Broadhurst, Clerk, Director
William Aldrich, Clerk, *do*
John Allen Esq.

87. Brief on behalf of the petitioners for the bill[34]

House of Commons Sessions 1826.

Bill for disincorporating the Hundreds of Loes and Wilford in the county of Suffolk.

Brief on behalf of the petitioners for the bill.

In <1765> An Act of Parliament was passed intitled <title> by virtue of which act a large house of Industry and other buildings were erected in the parish of Melton within the Hundreds of Wilford at a very considerable expense and great numbers of poor persons were received into and maintained in the said House and under this act the Incorporation was managed and conducted for a period of 25 years.

---

32 SROI ADA11/A/A/1/14.
33 SROI ADA11/A/A/1/17. Unlike 1810, there are no papers extant offering details as to the opponents' reasons.
34 SROI ADA11/A/A/1/12.

In consequence of the money authorised to be raised by virtue of that Act not being sufficient to defray the expence of maintaining the poor of the said Hundreds, and that Act being in many other respects defective and ineffectual, the same was, in <1792>, repealed and a new act intituled <title> passed in lieu thereof, and under this last mentioned act the incorporation was managed and conducted for a period of 20 years, and at the expiration of the 45 years a debt of £10,150 was found due from the Incorporation.

To pay off which debt and to amend, alter and enlarge the powers and provisions of the last mentioned act, another act was passed in <1810> intituled <title>. Under the 7th sec. of which act, the Directors and Acting Guardians were required to take an account of the whole expences of the Incorporation as well as the paupers clothed and maintained in the House, as of all sums paid by the Treasurer for relief granted to poor persons resident out of the house for the 10 years immediately preceding the passing of that act, and to divide the average amount thereof by the average aggregate number of paupers which during the same period should have been clothed and maintained in the said House, and the amount so found should be considered the expense which each parish had annually incurred to the incorporation during the said period of 10 years, and should be the rate or assessment to be annually levied and raised by quarterly payments on each of the parishes within the said Hundreds during the 10 years there next following for all expences of the establishment, except the sums thereby directed to be raised for payment of the debt then due together with the annual interest thereof.

By the following section the directors and acting guardians were authorized and required, at the end of 10 years next ensuing the October quarterly meeting after the passing of the said act, and of every succeeding ten years in like manner, to take fresh and new averages in the proportions aforesaid and to make such alterations in the assessments of the said parishes as on the taking such new averages should appear necessary.

At the end of the first ten years, viz. at the October Quarterly Meeting 1820, a new rate or assessment was made in compliance of the directions of the foregoing enactments.

By a subsequent section of the last mentioned act, the Directors and Acting Guardians were requested yearly and every year until the whole of the principal money borrowed under the former acts and the interest then due or thereafter to become due thereon should be discharged, to make a distinct rate or assessment to pay off and discharge the interest then due and accruing due upon the said debt, and also the sum of £1,000 part of the principal thereof, and the several parishes were thereby directed to be assessed towards payment thereof in the same manner as the rates and assessments made and imposed under and by virtue of the former acts thereof been made and imposed.

Under the authority of this and the next following clauses of the now reciting act, the whole of the principal sum of £10,150 and the interest thereby accruing thereof, were in the course of 10 years fully paid off and discharged, and there is now no debt whatsoever for money borrowed at interest due and owing from the Incorporated Hundreds.

Since the act of <1792> the business of this Incorporation has been conducted by 24 Directors who have perpetual succession (the first 24 having been nominated by that Act) and 24 guardians or occupiers, annually elected at the April quarterly meeting by the 24 directors and 24 acting guardians of the preceding year.

The 48 persons so appointed or elected, constitute this corporation to 4 of whom (viz. two directors and two acting guardians) is allotted one month out of the 12, and they meet every Monday during such month at the House of Industry at Melton for the purpose of managing the business of the Incorporation and granting allowances to poor persons belonging to the several parishes within the Incorporated Hundreds but not residing in the House of Industry. These payments, called out allowances, are made under written orders from the weekly committee to the several persons there so mentioned. A meeting is held a few days previously to every quarterly meeting where these several out allowances, as well as the several tradesmen's bills, are examined and allowed, and the Treasurer directed to pay the amount at the following quarterly meeting.

At the several quarterly meetings held by the whole body of the Directors and Guardians, a rate is made for the following quarter. Quarterly orders for relief are granted, and contracts entered into according to tenders made for supplying the house of industry with the staple commodities of life for the succeeding quarter. The rates made upon the several parishes are raised or demanded at every quarterly meeting according to the expenses incurred to the incorporation during the previous quarter, and are paid to the Treasurer by the overseers of the respective parishes in obedience to a warrant directed to them under the common seal of the corporation.

The treasurer's accounts are annually examined by a Committee of Directors appointed for that purpose, and subsequently produced at the quarter sessions and examined and allowed by the court.

The foregoing is an outline of the plan by which the management of the corporation has been carried on for 60 years, and experience has proved it to be in every respect radically bad and cannot proceed further without some amended act.

In consequence of many owners and occupiers within these hundreds being dissatisfied as well as alarmed at the increasing expences of the corporation, on the 9th, 16th and 23rd days of October 1824, a notice was published in one of the provincial papers to convene a general meeting of the owners and occupiers of lands within the hundreds for the purpose of taking into consideration the general management of the poor of the said hundreds. In consequence of this notice a meeting was held at Wickham Market where, after taking into consideration the great sum to which the maintenance of the poor amounted in the said hundreds annually, it appeared to the meeting most desirable that a committee should be appointed to consider the best means of reducing every unnecessary expence in providing for the poor in the 33 incorporated parishes in the said hundreds.

A committee accordingly appointed consisting of 34 gents. being the principal proprietors or occupiers of lands, or acting for such proprietors, within the said hundreds, and directors and acting guardians of the Melton house of industry. And the meeting recommended to such committee to ascertain whether any material alteration could be made in the present system of managing the poor with a view to lessen the very heavy expences attendant on the House of Industry at Melton, and whether the existence of the said house did or did not materially and unnecessarily increase the expence of managing the poor of the incorporated parishes without adequate beneficial result. The committee were for this purpose to have free access to all books of account at the Melton house of industry, and the power of examining witnesses so as to enable them to gain every information on the subject and report the result of their inquiries to a future general meeting, to be called by the chairman whenever they thought proper. A bill for amending the several acts here before mentioned, and which had been adopted by the general meeting of the Directors and

Guardians at the house of industry, was directed to be laid before the committee in order that they might suggest such alterations or amendments therein as might be thought necessary. It was also proposed that the committees should meet on Tues 2nd Nov., at the House of Industry, for the dispatch of business and continue to meet on every succeeding Tuesday as long as necessary.

The committee so appointed held six meetings viz. Nov. 2nd, 9th, 16th, 23rd, and 30th, and Dec. 7th at the time and place above mentioned, and at such meetings they went into and examined the accounts of the corporation for the last 24 years.

At one of the meetings the committee were presented with a return of the number of paupers belonging to each parish, and the amount of their maintenance, both in and out of the house, for the preceding year including the average of the quarterly allowances – this account was transmitted to each committee.

And after examining the several accounts produced and returns made, the committee resolved that the financial department of the incorporation had hitherto so conducted as not to answer the purposes for which it was instituted. The committee therefore proceeded to take into their consideration whether by any modification under the bill then under contemplation, and by exterior and interior management, the incorporation could be made to answer the purposes for which it was instituted. The solicitor therefore produced the proposed bill, which was read by the chairman of the committee, and after debating the bill clause by clause the final opinion of the committee on the same was that it did not appear calculated to make such reductions in the expences of the establishment of the Melton house of industry as was the object of the bill to obtain.

In consequence of this resolution the intended bill for amending the former acts was abandoned as being insufficient although the best that could be passed.

Thus it will be observed that this committee, after six meetings and entering into a minute and careful investigation of the different accounts of the corporation for the preceding 24 years which were produced for their consideration, and after debating and considering the proposed bill which was introduced with a view of correcting existing defects and abuses and checking the extravagant system of expenditure, finally determined from the view that they had taken of the entire management of the incorporation, that the financial department was so conducted as to render the anticipated benefit of incorporation utterly abortive. And that no measure which could be introduced for its management would tend to diminish these evils.

The result of the five meetings of the committee were drawn up in the form of a report embracing all the documents produced and made during the discussion and at the 6th and last meeting held on the 7th Dec. 1824, such report after being read by the chairman was directed to be laid before a general meeting of the hundreds to be held on the last Tuesday in January 1825. 100 copies were printed, with 2 copies sent to each parish and one copy to each member of the committee.

We have forborne to make any reference to certain hypothetical statements of different gentlemen <> but have confined ourselves merely to the accounts of the corporation kept by the governor of the Melton House. But we beg leave to call the particular attention of counsel to the considered statement of Mr Lewin, at page 16, whereby it appears that during the period of 24 years the indoor expences of the Melton House have amounted to the enormous sum of £109,646 12s. 5d. for the 271 paupers, who have cost on an average during that time 6s. 5¾d. per head per week.

425

Another general meeting of the owners and occupiers of lands within the incorporated hundreds was held on the 25th of January 1825, at Wickham Market, in pursuance of the resolution of the weekly committee on the 7th Dec., and public advertisement, to consider the report of the committee appointed at the before mentioned general meeting of the said Hundreds. And it was resolved by the meeting, from an examination of such report, that the principle which had hitherto governed the administration of the finances of the incorporated hundreds of Loes and Wilford had occasioned a great and unequal burthern of contribution on the several parishes comprising the incorporation. And from practical experience, it appeared to them, that no adequate beneficial result had in any manner had occurred, either to the parishes or to the poor, from the profuse expenditure of public money which during the last 24 years had taken place within the said incorporated hundreds. That therefore any modification under the bill then in contemplation, or any alteration in the exterior or interior management of the pecuniary and domestic affairs of the poor house at Melton, would fail to correct and prevent those abuses which had hitherto foiled the enlarged provisions of repeated acts of parliament. And that it would be expedient to return to the old English system of parochial economy with regard to the poor, as enacted by the 43 of Eliz., as amended and facilitated by several more modern and efficacious acts of the legislature. And it is therefore the final opinion of the said meeting that application should be made to parliament as soon as might be according to the standing orders of the house of commons for an act to repeal the said several acts of incorporation with such clauses and provisions therein as related to the sale or dispossession of the lands and buildings as committee to be appointed should deem meet.

The committee appointed for the above purpose consisted of the following gentlemen

Lord Rendlesham

Andrew Arcedeckne	W. Shuldham	Edmund Jenney
William Woods Page	Revd Jon. Hindes Groome	Revd G. F. Tavel
Mr James Wenn	Mr John Lewin	

88. An account of fees paid and expences incurred in obtaining the Act of Disincorporation[35]

By Dorrington and Son. House of Commons.
Session 1826.

	£	s.	d.
Perusing settling and altering the Bill	4	4	
Copies of Committee on the Petition		10	
Settling Report and Drawing order of leave	1	10	
Copy of Bill for the House	6	12	
Drawing Brief and fair copy for the Speaker	1	1	
Copies of Committee on the Bill		10	
Preparing Amendments for the Committee	1	1	
Filling up and altering Bills	1	12	
Copies of Clauses	3	18	
Completing Bills for Ingrossing Clerks and Printers	2	16	

---

35 SROI ADA11/A/A/1/17.

Paid	House Fees	29	18	8
"	Committee Clerk's fees	22	1	8
"	Housekeepers and Messengers fees	3	11	
"	Fees in the Private Bill Office and Attends	8	18	8
"	Ingrossing Fees	28	19	6
"	doorkeepers for delivering printed bill	1	1	
"	for examination of Ingrossment and Proofs	3	16	
"	for printing the bill and Act	25	4	
Correspondence		2	2	
Sending a Bill to the Lord in the Chair and attg him		2	2	
Paid	House fees at the Lords	54		
"	Fees to yeoman usher and doorkeepers	5	5	
"	For Order of Committee	1	1	
"	for swearing witnesses and Delivering bills		16	6
"	Committee clerk's fees	4	4	
"	porters small gratuities and other incidents	3	5	
Solicitation Fee		26	5	0
		246	5	0
Paid King's printer for 50 copies of the Act.		3	2	6
		249	7	6

Paid 9th March 1826.

427

POST-DISINCORPORATION DOCUMENTS

Trustees' documents 89–120 for the disposal of the Incorporation's assets

89. Letters to Lord Rendlesham and Mr Lewin from the Incorporation's solicitors, Wood & Son, concerning the timing of the first Trustees' Meeting[1]

5 May 1826 [*To Lord Rendlesham*]
My Lord,

Having this morning received a letter from Mr Lewin, stating that your Lordship, Mr Arcedeckne and Mr Shuldham have fixed Thursday the 18th May instant, to hold a meeting of the Committee, and trusting us to apprise the other members of such intended meeting. We beg to remind your Lordship that the Act of Parliament has put an end to the powers of the Committee which was appointed solely to frame the Bill. The Act takes effect from the 16th day of October next, on which day, the Trustees are thereby directed to hold their first meeting.

Wood & Son.

[*To Mr Lewin*]   Sir,

In consequence of your letter received this morning, we have written to Lord Rendlesham, Mr Arcedeckne and Mr Shuldham to remind them that the Act of Parliament has put an end to the powers of the Committee, which was appointed solely to frame the Bill, and that the Act does not take effect until the 16th October next, and that the Trustees are thereby directed to hold their first meeting on that day, which perhaps you were not aware of. We have not, therefore, at present informed your co-trustees of any intended meeting, which we humbly think cannot yet be legally held.

Mr Lewin.   Wood & Son.

6 May 1826[2] [*Lord Rendlesham's reply to Wood & Son's letter*]
Gentlemen,

In answer to your letter received this morning. The meeting wished for by Mr Arcedeckne, Mr Shuldham and myself is of the old committee which framed the Bill. It appeared to us a duty we owe to the General Meeting of the Hundreds to publish some statement of what has been done, and an official notice of the Bill having been passed into law. At present the only notice I believe they have had has been from hearsay, and a full statement from us would possibly prevent any mistake arising on the 16th October from any one or more of the parishes not having removed all their paupers from the House of Industry by that day on the plea of ignorance.

I trust this will explain our wishes, and that one of you will be good enough to attend the meeting to carry such resolutions as may be agreed upon into effect, giving, as soon as possible, the necessary requisition to all the members of the Bill Committee to attend at Wickham on Thursday the 18th instant at 12 o'clock.

---

[1]   SROI ADA11/A/A/1/22.
[2]   SROI ADA11/A/A/1.

I am, gentlemen,
Your obedient, humble servant, Rendlesham.

8 May 1826[3] [*Letter from Wood & Son in reply to Rendlesham's letter, above*]
My Lord,
In reply to your Lordships letter of the 6th instant, and to assure your Lordship
that other notice beside hearsay has been given. We beg to inform your Lordship
that on the 6th April last, a printed copy of the Act was delivered to the overseers of
every parish within the Hundreds, a copy has been given to nearly all the Directors
and Guardians, and we do not believe there is one occupier of any consequence
within the hundreds but who will know the intent and meaning of the Act.

If, after this explanation, your Lordship still wish for the meeting on the 18th we,
of course, are quite ready to summon the other members of the Committee, and to
attend such meeting. But, as we entertain a doubt as to the legality of any meeting,
other than the Committee of Trustees, before the 16th of October, we feel it our
bounden duty to inform your Lordship of such doubt, as we can have no objection
to the meeting in question, and your Lordship will therefore have the goodness to
give us your directions accordingly waiting the receipt thereof.

Wood & Son.

90. Letter to Wood & Son, from Robert Cana and George Thompson, soliciting the right to act as auctioneers for the disposal of Melton House[4]

10 October 1826
Sir,
We respectfully beg leave to address you, as one of the Trustees appointed by
the Act of Parliament for disincorporating the Hundreds of Loes and Wilford, as to
the sale of the workhouse lands and premises at Melton.

It has been intimated to us that the former is to be offered in several lots. Should
this be determined upon, we venture to suggest that the assistance of a competent
surveyor will be requisite to make plans and sections of the various buildings, ascertaining the quantities of material and value of each lot, similar to the mode adopted
at the sale of the barracks in the towns of Ipswich, Norwich, and Harwich, which
were arranged and sold under our immediate direction.

If 25 years' experience in a pretty full practice as auctioneers and surveyors
should be a recommendation, or in your opinion, have qualified us for the business
by giving any advantage over numerous competitors.

We respectfully and earnestly solicit your patronage in the appointment of the
sale, hoping that our attention and exertions will prove satisfactory to you and to all
the parties in the produce of the property.

Should we be honoured with your confidence, allow us to add we shall separately
attend to each branch of the business: the planning, dividing and estimating by
George Thompson, the selling by Robert Cana, at the usual and customary commission of one and a quarter to four per cent in proportion to the amount sold.

We are sir, your obedient servants,
R. Cana & George Thompson.

---

3   SROI ADA11/A/A/1/22.
4   SROI ADA11/A/A/1/22.

91. Letter to Wood & Son from J. Lewin questioning the venue for the first Trustees' Meeting. In the attachment Lewin also solicits the right to act as auctioneer for the disposal of Melton House.[5]

13 October 1826

Gentlemen,

In page 18 of the Act of Parliament you will find the Trustees are bound to meet at Melton House, or within 5 miles of it, and I have arranged with Mr Shuldham and several of the Trustees to meet at the White Hart, Wickham Market on that day, and hope you will make the arrangement with all the Trustees accordingly. As we held our Committee meeting there to frame the Act, and it will be more convenient for the major part of the Trustees, particularly for those who attended most of the business so far as it has proceeded.

I am Gentlemen, very truly yours,

John Lewin.

[*Attachment*]

We the undersigned, being interested in the House property, are perfectly satisfied with the judgement and ability and integrity of John Lewin, and consider his being appointed auctioneer for the sale and disposal of that property will give general satisfaction to a very great majority of the parties concerned. [*60 signatures follow*]

92. Letter to Wood & Son from the Revd George Tavel offering apologies for not attending the first Trustees' Meeting[6]

14 October 1826

Dear Sirs,

I have received your summons to attend the meeting of Trustees for the disposal of the Melton House property on Monday next at Wickham Market. I should have made a point of attending were I not still confined at home by an inward complaint which prevents any exertion of motion etc. I shall thank you therefore to convey my apologies to the gentlemen assembled for my absence from them.

I remain etc.,   G. F. Tavel

93. First Trustees' Meeting, 16 October 1826[7]

Under the authority of the said Act, John Wood and John Wood the younger, both of Woodbridge in the county of Suffolk, were appointed joint clerks to the said Trustees, and were directed to produce, at the next General Meeting, securities for their faithful execution of their office, to the amount of £6,000.

And under the like authority, Richard Wood Oldham, the late governor of the said House of Industry, was appointed Superintendent of the said House and of all the property therein contained, at the wage or salary of 2 guineas a week. He was directed to select 3 or 4 able bodied men, and 2 effective women, to assist him in the execution of his office, such men and women not being previously paupers in

---

5   SROI ADA11/A/A/1/22.
6   SROI ADA11/A/A/1/22.
7   SROI ADA11/A/A/1/22.

the said House of Industry, at such weekly salary or wages as he shall be able to obtain them.

It was resolved that the said House of Industry should be cleared of the paupers now therein as soon as it can be conveniently done. And in order to carry the same into effect, that the form of the order for the removal of all paupers now in the House to their respective parishes be adopted, and that our clerk do procure a sufficient number of copies to be printed and signed by two of the said Trustees as soon as the same can be completed.

At this meeting a letter signed R. Cana and George Thompson, to be employed in the sale of the property was received. The consideration of the application therein contained was deferred until the next General Meeting, as was a similar application by J. Lewin.

The clerks were directed to draw a case for the opinion of a civil lawyer as to the ecclesiastical restrictions upon the purchase of the burial ground attached to the said House of Industry, and to lay the draft of such a case before some subsequent meeting of the Trustees for their perusal and approval.

At this meeting, a letter from the Revd George Frederick Tavel, one of the Trustees appointed by the said Act, stating his absence from this meeting to be occasioned by sickness, such absence is allowed by the Trustees present.

At this meeting, Andrew Arcedeckne and Edmund Jenney, two of those appointed by the said Act, being absent from home and unavoidably prevented from attending, the absence therefore of these gents is allowed by the Trustees present.

At this meeting, the said Richard Wood Oldham is directed to prepare, and produce to the next adjourned meeting, a new fair and correct inventory of all the personal chattels and effects now in or at the said House, and the buildings, and lands thereto belonging.

The Treasurer of the late incorporated hundreds is directed to produce his accounts at the next General meeting.

[Attachment. An example of the paperwork to be circulated to the parishes]

To Mr Richard Wood Oldham, our Superintendent, and to the Churchwardens and Overseers of the poor of the parish of _____, in the Hundred of _____, in the county of Suffolk.

For as much as it appears unto us _____ whose names are here unto subscribed and set, being two of the Trustees named and appointed, in and by an Act of Parliament, made and passed in the seventh year of his present Majesty's reign, intitled <Act's title>. From an examination of the books lately kept by the Directors and Acting Guardians of the Incorporated Hundreds of Loes and Wilford, that:

[A B Labourer & _____ his wife and C & D & E & F & G their children] were received into the House of Industry, at Melton, belonging to the said Incorporated Hundreds, from your parish of _____.

We are, therefore, by virtue of the said Act, to require you, the said Richard Wood Oldham to remove or send the said _____ from the said House of Industry to the said parish of _____, and to deliver them with this order, or a true copy thereof, to the Churchwardens and Overseers of the Poor of the said parish of _____ who are hereby required to receive and provide for them according to law.

Given under our hands, this _____ day of _____ One Thousand Eight Hundred and Twenty Six.

William Wood Page & John Hindes Groome.

94. Draft case for legal opinion on the disposal of ecclesiastical lands[8]

Case,

Under and by virtue of <Act's title and date>, the Directors and Acting Guardians, elected and chosen in the manner prescribed by the said Act, were authorized and empowered to enter into contract, or contracts, for the absolute purchase, in fee simple, of any quantity of land for the use of the said Guardians and their successors not exceeding 50 acres, with or without buildings thereon, lying in such part or parts of the said Hundreds which they might think most fit and convenient for the situation of an House, or Houses, for the reception and employment of the poor, and such other buildings as the said Directors should deem necessary for executing the purposes of the said act.

The Directors and Acting Guardians, to be elected and chosen as aforesaid, were also authorized and empowered to appoint a clergyman of the Church of England to instruct the poor persons maintained in the said House in the principles of the Christian religion, and the children in the church catechism, and also to baptize the children, visit the sick, bury the dead, and perform other offices of his function in the said House.

In compliance with such authority, and to fulfil the charge and duty imposed on them by the said act, the Directors and Acting Guardians entered into a contract for the purchase of 30 acres of land, or thereabouts, situated in the parish of Melton, in the county of Suffolk. And the same was accordingly conveyed to them, and upon the lands so purchased, a very large and commodious House of Industry was built for the reception of the poor, the centre of which was appropriated to a chapel, wherein divine service has, ever since the erection of the House, been performed every Sunday by a clergyman of the Church of England appointed by the Directors as Chaplain to the said Hundreds. And a sufficient quantity of the land so purchased, as aforesaid, was set apart for the burial of such persons who might happen to die in the said House of Industry whilst under the management of the Guardians and Directors of the poor. And a register of such burials, as well as of all children baptized in the House, has been regularly kept by the Chaplain. This burial ground, as well as the Chapel, were solemnly consecrated by the Bishop of the Diocese, and cannot as such, we presume, be desecrated without violating the Ecclesiastical Law.

Two other acts were subsequently passed to remedy certain defects in each preceding act, and for extending and enlarging the powers and provisions therein.

By an Act passed in <1826> the before mentioned Acts were repealed, and the said Hundreds disincorporated. By the same Act, certain Trustees were appointed to carry it into effect. And all lands, tenements and hereditaments which were, by the said therein recited acts, vested in the Corporation, and also all lands, tenements and hereditaments which had since been purchased or taken in, or were in any manner then held by any person or persons in trust for or for the use of the said Corporation, either in fee or for any life or lives, or any term or terms of years, and all erections and buildings which there were erected and built thereon, together with the rights belonging thereto, be fully and absolutely vested in the said Trustees by the said Act, constituted and appointed, and the favours and favour of them and the heirs of such favour for such and the like estates, tenements and hereditaments, and to such

---

8   SROI ADA11/A/A/1/20.

and the like effects in law to all intents and purposes of the same were previously vested in or held or passed by or in trust for the said Guardians.

And the said Trustees were authorized and empowered at any time, or times within 12 months from and after the passing of that Act, when they in their discretion should think proper, to make sale and absolutely dispose of all, or any part or parts, of the said workhouse and buildings thereunto belonging, and of the site or sites thereof and the ground thereunto belonging, and also all, or any part or part of any other buildings, lands, tenements and hereditaments which did or should belong to, or which previously to the passing of that Act were vested in or held by or in trust for the said Corporation constituted by the therein recited Acts, or which had been theretofore purchased by the said Corporation out of the money raised for the relief of the poor under their care and management, or the rents and profits whereof had been thereunto applied towards the relief and maintenance of such poor subjects to such encumbrances as might affect the same. And the Trustees, under and by virtue of that Act, either altogether and in one lot, or by parcels and in several lots, and either by public auction or private contract, for the best price as could be obtained for the same, and by indenture or indentures under their hands and seals, to grant and convey the same by way of absolute sale, in fee simple or for such estate and interest as they, the said Trustees, should have thereunto to the person or persons who should agree, to become the purchaser or purchasers thereof and his her and their heirs and assignees.

It is to be observed that no distinct notice is taken in the foregoing act of the Chapel and burial ground attached to it, but the whole real and personal estate which was by the repealed Acts vested in the Directors and Acting Guardians for the benefit of the hundreds has been by the late act divested from them and the same is now vested in the Trustees to such and the like effect in law to all intents and purposes as the same were previously vested in or held or possessed by or entrusted by the said Guardians. This being the case the Trustees are apprehensive that they have not competent authority, by the said act, to convey the consecrated burial ground and chapel to a purchaser free from all ecclesiastical restrictions, and therefore request your opinion upon the following points hereafter.

95. List of paupers resident in the House of Industry, 16 October 1826[9]

Ash	John Baldrey, Edward Woods	2
Brandeston	Martha Flatt, Ann Rands, William Crane	
	Hannah, Elizabeth, Mary Ann, James and Caroline Collins	
	Naomi Coates	9
Butley	Amelia Nunn	1
Creetingham	Hannah Lanham, John Brunning, wife and 2 children	5
Eyke	Mary and Thomas Fisk, Henry Chilly and wife	
	Ann Larter and 2 children, Mary Booth and 2 children	10
Hacheston	Charlotte Clow, Wm Pallant & Mary Gooderham	
	Richard Garrett, Charles Barker	5
Letheringham	James York, wife and 3 children, Geo. Smith	
	Ann Rogers and 2 children	9

---

[9]   Individual sheets for each of the 17 parishes are located at SROI ADA11/A/Q/2/1(2) and SROI ADA11/A/A/1/22.

Marlesford	John Bird, Peter Aldred	2
Monewden	Elizabeth Vincent, Elizabeth Rattle and child	
	Thomas Collins, Elizabeth Bloss and child not	
	able to be removed	6
Boyton	Ann Cook, Elizabeth Button	2
Bredfield	Elizabeth Welham, Elizabeth Hurran, Mary Lockwood	
	Honor Girling	4
Hollesly	Barbara Hunt, Henry Grayston	2
Melton	John Burrows, Robert Goodwyn, wife and 4 children	7
Petistree	Esther Fricker and child (cannot yet be removed)	2
Ramsholt	Robert Thurston, wife and 3 children, Emma Thurston	
	Jacob Dowsing wife and 2 children, James Parker	
	Mary Forster and 3 children, Mary Wayman	
	James Bacon and Isaac Scott	18
Ufford	Ann Barrell, Sarah Mills and 2 children	
	Catherine Harland, John Rye and wife	
	Esther Blomfield & 3 children	11
Easton	Mary Tuffield and child	2
		97

96. Letter received by Wood & Son, from Robert Cana, reiterating his request to act as auctioneer[10]

21 October 1826

Sir,

Since I had the honour of addressing you on the 10th instant, requesting to be employed as auctioneer upon the sale of the House of Industry at Melton, I have been informed of solicitations being made by one of the Trustees to be appointed auctioneer, and that his pretentions are to be supported by signatures obtained in public markets etc. Concluding this to be the fact, I am induced to submit to you the enclosed letter which I received from the Inspector General of the Barrack Department, which I hope you will think a sufficient testimonial of my competency to undertake the business I now solicit.

I have the honour to remain sir your obedient servant.

R. Cana.   Woodbridge.

97. Adjourned First Trustees' Meeting[11]

23 October 1826

The proceedings of the original meeting were read over. Mr Oldham produced the report together with the new inventory he was, at the original meeting, directed to make.

Mr Oldham is directed to return to the parishes heretofore composing the Incorporated Hundreds of Loes and Wilford, all indentures of apprenticeship, orders of removal, and orders of filiation, taking receipts from the overseers of the different parishes for the same.

---

10 SROI ADA11/A/A/1/22.
11 SROI ADA11/A/A/1/22.

The clerks are directed to insert an advertisement in both the Ipswich papers on Saturday next, the 28th October instant, desiring all persons having demands upon the late Incorporation, forthwith, to send in accounts of the same to the clerks of the Trustees.

It is ordered that all the personal chattels and effects contained in the inventory produced at this meeting by Mr Oldham, and now the property of the Trustees, shall be sold by auction without any reservation whatever, and that Mr John Lewin shall be employed in such sale upon the usual charges for commission, and such auction to take place with all convenient despatch.

It is further ordered that in case the house and buildings, with the land thereto belonging, should be sold by public auction by Robert Cana of Woodbridge, in the same county, who shall be employed as surveyor and auctioneer (but in case the property shall be sold by private contract, that George Thompson of Woodbridge shall be appointed to survey measure and value the house and buildings. He shall be appointed as surveyor at a commission of 2 per cent upon the value of the buildings, and at the sum of three guineas for the valuation of the lands) at the following charges for commission: if sold at any sum less than £4,000, 4 per cent; if for £4,000 and less than £6,000, 3.5 per cent; if £6,000 and less than £10,000, 3 per cent; to include all charges for adverts and other incidental expenses. But in case the whole property shall be sold by private contract, he shall be appointed surveyor at a commission of 2 per cent upon the value of the buildings, and be paid the sum of three guineas for a valuation of the land.

The clerks are directed to advertise, for two weeks in the four county papers, the real property to be sold by auction early in the month of January next unless an acceptable offer be previously made by private contract, and that offer to purchase the property will be received at their office in Woodbridge.

98. Second Trustees' Meeting[12]

23 October 1826

Messrs. Wood & Son, who at the first General Meeting of the said Trustees were appointed their clerks, produced at this meeting a bond of indemnity in the sum of £6,000 for the faithful execution of such offices, and the said bond was deposited in the hands of Mr James Wenn, one of the Trustees.

Messrs. Thompson & Cana produced a proper plan of all the buildings, divided into proper sections, standing upon the lands now the property of the Trustees, and a valuation of the same with the lands. The clerks are therefore directed to retain possession of the same.

Mr Barton, the Clerk of the Peace for the County of Suffolk, having applied for the referral of the whole property on behalf of the County for the purpose of converting the same into a lunatic asylum. This meeting adheres to the former resolution of waiting until the first day of December, instant, to receive tenders according to public advertisement. Mr Barton is allowed the loan of the plan of the buildings to be returned by him to the clerks within 7 days.

The clerks are directed to cause an advertisement to be inserted in two London daily papers, The Morning Herald and Courier, once every week until the 1st of December.

---

12 SROI ADA11/A/A/1/22.

All future meetings are appointed to be held at the White Hart Inn, Wickham Market.

The treasurer of the late Incorporated Hundreds of Loes and Wilford produced his accounts, as directed by the last meeting, and a balance of £280 13s. 1d. appearing to remain in his hands. He is directed to pay over the same to the clerks of the Trustees, who are directed to have the possession of the late treasurer's books, vouchers and other papers.

The consideration of the case as to the burying ground drawn by the solicitors for the opinion of counsel is deferred until the next General Meeting.

Edmund Jenney Esq., one of the Trustees appointed by the said Act, being absent and unavoidably prevented from attending this meeting. His absences allowed by the Trustees attending.

99. Woods' bond of indemnity for £6,000 to act as clerk for the Incorporation[13]

Know all men by these presents that we John Wood of Melton in the county of Suffolk gentleman, John Wood the younger of Woodbridge in the said county, gentleman, attorneys and solicitors and co-partners, and Thomas Brooke of Melton, aforesaid, esquire, are held and firmly bound to Andrew Arcedeckne, William Abraham Shuldham, Edmund Jenney and William Woods Page esquires, the Reverend John Hindes Groome and the Reverend George Frederick Tavel, clerks, James Wenn gentleman, John Lewin and Edwards Crisp, farmers, Trustees duly nominated and appointed under and by virtue of an Act of Parliament, in the sum of six thousand pounds of lawful money current in Great Britain, to be paid to the said Trustees, or some or one of, for which payment to be well and faithfully made. We jointly and severally bind ourselves, our and each of our heirs, executors and administrators, firmly by these presents, sealed with our seals dates this <6 November 1826>.

Whereas the said Trustees are by the said Act of Parliament, herein before recited, or referred to authorise and impowered respectively from time to time, if they should think fit and proper for the purposes of the said Act, to nominate and appoint a clerk or clerks, and to take, if they should think it necessary, such security or securities for the faithful execution of such office as they, the said Trustees, should from time to time think fit. And whereas at the first General Meeting of the Trustees, under or by virtue of the Act of Parliament here before recited or referred to, held at the House of Industry at Melton aforesaid, on the sixteenth day of October now last past, the above bounden John Wood and John Wood the younger were duly nominated and appointed joint clerks to the said Trustees of the said recited Act, and they were directed to produce at the next General Meeting security for the faithful execution of the duties of the said office of clerks to the said Trustees in a bond of indemnity to the amount of six thousand pounds. And whereas upon the application and request of the said John Wood and John Wood the younger, the said Thomas Brooke hath consented and agreed to enter into the above written bond or obligation, with such condition for making the same void as hereunder mentioned.

Know the condition of the above written bond or obligation is such that if the said John Wood and John Wood the younger do and shall during such time as they

---

13 SROI ADA11/A/A/1/20.

shall continue in the office of clerks to the said Trustees under the Act of Parliament hereinbefore referred to, keep a true and faithful account in writing of all and every the goods, chattels, sum and sums of money debts, demands, rents and effects whatsoever which shall be paid to them or otherwise come into their hands as such clerks, as aforesaid, and of all other monies and property which they shall receive, or with which they may be entrusted as such clerks aforesaid. And do and shall when, thereunto requested, by the above named Andrew Arcedeckne, William Abraham Shuldham, Edmund Jenney, William Woods Page, John Hindes Groome, George Frederick Tavel, James Wenn, John Lewin, and Edwards Crisp, or the survivors or survivor of them, or the Trustees or Trustee for the time being of the said Act of Parliament, well and truly render or cause to be rendered to such present or future Trustees or Trustee, or to such other person or persons as such Trustees or Trustee for the time being shall appoint to receive the same, true and faithful account of all monies, and other property books, writings, and transactions whatsoever which they, the said John Wood and John Wood the younger, shall have received or been entrusted with as such clerks as aforesaid. And do and shall whenever thereunto so requested, as aforesaid, pay over and deliver up to the present, or any future Trustees or Trustee of the said Act of Parliament, or to such person or persons as they shall appoint, all and every the monies, books, property, writings, accounts and things whatsoever of or in any wise relating or belonging to the said Trustees appointed under the said Act, which shall for the time being be in the hands custody, power or possession of the said John Wood and John Wood the younger, or which the said John Wood or John Wood the younger shall be liable to pay, deliver up, and account for. And also do and shall during such time as aforesaid in every other respect faithfully perform and discharge all the duties of or belonging to the said office or situation of clerks to the said Trustees, appointed or to be appointed under or by virtue of the Act of Parliament, hereinbefore referred to. Then and in such case the above written bond or obligation shall be void, otherwise the same shall remain in full force and virtue.

Sealed and delivered by the said John Wood, John Wood the younger, and Thomas Brooke in the presence of William Rudall, Clerk to Messrs. Wood and Son, solicitors, Woodbridge.

100. Details of the advertisement to be placed for the sale of Melton House[14]

26 October 1826

To be sold by Auction by Robert Cana, early in the month of January next (unless an acceptable offer be previously made by private contract), the House of Industry at Melton, the Pest House (detached), and all other the buildings, gardens, and lands thereto belonging containing by survey 30a. 0r. 34y., nearly the whole, of which is rich old pasture, late the property of the Directors and Guardians of the Incorporated Hundreds of Loes and Wilford, and now of the Trustees appointed by the Act of Parliament for dissolving the Incorporation.

The whole property is freehold, and situated in the parish of Melton. Offers to purchase by private contract, post-paid, sealed up, and indorsed, "Tenders for Melton House" will be received on or before the first of December next, at the

---

14 SROI ADA11/A/A/1/22.

offices of Messrs Wood and Son, solicitors, Woodbridge, clerks to the Trustees, where further particulars may be had and a plan of the property seen.

101. An inventory and valuation of the house fixtures and fittings, and other articles at Melton House, compiled on 30 October 1826 by Robert Cana[15]

30 October 1826

Brewhouse. 550 gallon copper with pipe and back furnace, bricks and lids etc. as fixed; lead work pump; lead liquor pipe from the pump into the copper. Square liquor stand, 15 feet long, 5 feet 10 inches wide, 1 foot deep, 2½inch deal iron bolted through. Square mash tun, 8 feet by 6½ feet, 3 feet 3 inches deep; *do* cooler, 12 feet by 10 feet 7 inches deep, square work under back 9 feet 6 inches by 5 feet, 2 feet deep, 2½ inch deal bolted through. 2 square coolers, 8½ feet by 4½ feet and 5 feet deep. One *do,* 5 feet by 4 feet, 2 feet 2 inch deep. 3 cask pullies; 2 step ladders; 4 work troughs; hop basket; 2 rakes; 3 rudders.

Cellar. 100 feet double ale stallage. Bottle rack.

Bed room no. 1. Front to closet door, 2 splines, 12 hat pegs, bell as fixed.

No. 2. Splines and hat pegs.

No. 3. Small bath stove; front to closet 8 feet by 4 feet. Wash hand and shelf.

Store room. Deal counter, 8 feet by 3 feet with 9 drawers complete. *do,* 5 feet with 9 drawers. *do* 9½ feet with 3 drawers and 2 partitions to *do,* and boarded in front. 2 shelves, 16 feet 9 inches by 1 foot 9 inches with 11 partitions in *do.* All the shelving round the room containing 109 feet.

Store room No. 2. Dresser, 9 feet by 1 foot 10 inches, *do* 8½ feet by 1 foot 6 inches and boards in front. Partition shelf and shelves over door.

Entrance. Shoe closet and wash hand closet etc. as fixed, 9 feet by 5 feet. Hat spline; 2 *do* pins.

Committee Room. 36 inch bath stove fitted up with stone plinths etc. Book cupboard, 9 feet by 8 inches complete. Green baize door, 7 feet by 3 feet, spring door. Bell as fixed.

Counting House. Deal desk. Shelf over *do.* Wind stove and fire board. 2 book cupboards. 2 book cupboards by the side of the fireplace fitted up complete. 2 letter splines.

Surgery. 5 drawer counter, 11 feet 4 inches by 2 feet 4 inches. Desk at end of *do,* 3 shelves over *do.* Nest of 22 drawers; *do* 24 drawers. 5 shelves; 2 mortar posts. Wind stove. 4 hat pins. 2 seats at the door.

Dairy. 9 feet dresser shelf. *do* hand *do.* Bell at the door.

Wash House. Copper with turned copper cock etc. as fixed. Furnace etc. 36 gallon copper. Lids and furnace etc. Fixed. 20 feet run inch shelving. Deal dresser, as fixed.

Laundry. 2 drawer dresser etc., fixed 11 feet by 2 feet 6 inches. *do* at the end, 8 feet by 2 feet 6 inches. 2 *do* under the window, 13 feet.

Kitchen. Coal range as fixed, with iron back etc. Smoak jack; cooking copper as fixed. 6 drawer deal dresser, 21 feet long by 1 foot 11 inches. Candlestick cupboard with 3 shelves. *do* a pepper mill. Cupboard, front 8 feet by 5 feet. Door to *do* with batons and 3 shelves. Saucepan dresser and shelf, 2 shelves above *do* 14 feet. Towel roller, spit racks and a chimney shelf.

---

[15] SROI ADA11/A/A/1/30. See Plate 7 for the final page of Robert Cana's valuation of Melton House, 4 November 1826.

Summary of Valuation

The house and Offices together with the Outbuildings. Walling, Pumps & Drains as per Plans are estimated at the Sum of Three Thousand Eight hundred and forty Six Pounds and two Shillings — — — — — — } £. s. 3846. 2.

The Brewing Copper, Plant and house fixtures at the Sum of One hundred and Seventy one Pounds, ten Shillings and sixpence — — } 171. 10.

The Twenty Nine Acres and Thirty four perches of Land at the Sum of Two Thousand two hundred and Sixty Eight Pounds — — — — — } 2268. 0.

£ 6285. 12.

By us

R. Cana

George Thompson

Woodbridge
11th Nov. 1826

Plate 7. Summary of valuation made by R. Cana and George Thompson, 1826

Scullery. 3 iron boilers as fixed, with iron furnaces, brick work etc. Stone sink, 12 feet by 2 feet. Oak curb and brickwork to *do*. Dresser under the window; lath cupboard, 4 shelves, 35 feet run.

Bake office. Deal kneading chest, 12 feet by 2 feet 6 inches in the top, 1 foot 8 inches deep. Salt chest; dresser and shelf over *do*. Iron oven door and furnace.

Bread room. Dresser, 30 feet run, *do* 8 feet and 2 bread knives. 8 shelves, 60 feet. Cupboard front. Towel roller.

Larder. Stout dresser, 14 feet run. Canvas meal safe. Lath partition, 8 feet by 7 feet 9 inches and shelf. *do* same size. Stout dresser, 7 feet by 2 feet. Shelf, 9 feet 1½ inches; 2 hanging *do,* 16 feet.

Chapel. The large bell as fixed.

Little wash house in the men's yard. Small copper as fixed.

In the several rooms 24 small cast iron grates.

Hospital. 10 wind stoves. 35 feet run shelving. Washing copper as fixed. Irons, bricks and lids.

Valued at £171 10s. 6d.

4th November 1826.

Quantity of land by survey is 30 acres 0 rods 34 perches

26. 2. 9   in eight inclosures including the kitchen garden.

 2. 2. 30   site of buildings and drift.

29. 0. 39

 0. 3. 35   burying ground – not valued.

The whole is freehold, subject to an annual land tax of £4 8s. 0d.

Estimated value for the 29 acres 0 rods 39 perches is £80.[16]

per annum 30 years' purchase is   £2,400

deduct 30 years purchase of land tax   £132

Estimated value   £2,268

Estimated at a higher rate than a farm of greater extent. The meadows are the richest in the neighbourhood, and long esteemed for their wonderful productive quality, and there is in the nature of the grass produced, as we are informed, a more than common nutritious quality that raises cattle faster and supports a greater stock than other lands of the same contents.

The enclosures are well proportioned to the quantity of land; divided by handsome lipped fences, planted with useful and ornamental trees and shrubs.

To the adjoining proprietors this property is of considerable interest and certainly possesses many local advantages.

The whole estate is situated in a most eligible and beautiful spot for the erection of a gentleman's seat, and as the buildings are now on a good scale this might be done by alterations at no great expense; enlarged entrances may be had from the fine roads contiguous to it, and it might, by management of the present well-arranged fences and trees by a little planting, be rendered as interesting a situation as any in the county, both as it respects the natural situation itself and the extensive and almost unbounded prospects it commands over very fine scenery. It would afford plenty of game as it nearly adjoins pheasant reserves.

---

16 This figure excludes the burying ground, which was not valued.

Summary of valuation

The House and offices together with the outbuildings, walling, pumps and drains as plans are estimated at the sum of three thousand eight hundred and forty six pounds and two shillings.	3,846	2	0
The brewing copper, plant and House fixtures at the sum of one hundred and seventy one pounds, ten shillings and six pence.	171	10	6
The twenty nine acres and thirty four perches of land at the sum of two thousand two hundred and sixty eight pounds.	2,268	0	0
	6,285	12	6

By us, R. Cana and George Thompson, Woodbridge, 4th November 1826

102. R. Cana's charges for his work undertaken on behalf of the Trustees[17]

4 November 1826

To the Trustees appointed by an Act of Parliament for Disincorporating the Hundreds of Loes and Wilford, Suffolk.

To Robert Cana, Dr.

1826 Nov. 4

Making survey, plans and valuation of the late House of Industry at Melton and buildings, with fixtures therein, being a commission at 2 per cent upon the sum of £4,017 12s. 6d., the amount of such valuation as per agreement with the Trustees:

£80 7s. 0d.

Making valuation of land other part of the same property £3 3s. 0d.

£83 10s. 0d.

Received May 4th 1827, of the said Trustees by the payment of Messrs Wood and Son, their Treasurers, of the above sum of eighty-three pounds and 10 shillings.

R. Cana.

103. Third Trustees' Meeting[18]

4 December 1826

A deputation of County Magistrates, with the consent and approbation of this meeting, being in attendance.

Our chairman and the chairman of such deputation met together, and the result of their conference was that the deputation of County Magistrates refused to make any tender or offer for the property, but requested to know what the Trustees were willing to accept.

After debating the request of that deputation, it was resolved to ask them for the sum of £10,000 on the following terms:

"The Trustees for the sale of Melton House, offer the whole premises and land and fixtures as now standing, at the sum of £10,000. At the same time, they are willing to entertain today, any counter proposition on the part of the magistrates deputed by the county. Unless a satisfactory arrangement takes place this morning,

---

17 SROI ADA11 A/A/1/30.
18 SROI ADA11/A/A/1/22.

the property according to the terms of original advertisement, be put up to public auction in the month of January".

Signed on behalf of the meeting, Andrew Arcedeckne, Chairman, Wickham Market, Dec. 4th 1826.

A second meeting of the two chairmen consequently took place. The result of which was an offer of £6,500 was made by the county deputation, which being rejected by this meeting, Mr Arcedeckne, the chairman, was requested, and did ask, the sum of £8,000 as the lowest price that would be accepted for the whole property. And Ambrose Harbord Steward Esq., the chairman of the Magistrates, afterwards attended this meeting, and accepted the property, including all fixtures, at the last mentioned sum of £8,000, and an agreement for the sale thereof was entered into between the said parties.

It is ordered that the clerks do deliver over to the Magistrates the book of plans and sections of the said House of Industry.

Edmund Jenney esq., and the Revd George Frederick Tavel, clerk, are excused their attendance at this meeting on the plea of ill health, and on other reasonable excuses.

104. Letter received by the trustees from R. W. Oldham requesting their recommendation for a position at the pauper lunatics asylum[19]

4 December 1826

Gentlemen,

Understanding it has been agreed upon to have an establishment for pauper lunatics in this county, and that there is a great probability of the Melton House being taken for such purpose. I humbly beg leave to request you will have the goodness to recommend me, and to give your interest on my behalf, upon offering myself as master and clerk, or superintendent in concert with, or under the direction of the medical attendant of such establishment. My services in the public situation I have filled for more than eighteen years, I trust, will be some recommendation, as well as my being known to most of the magistrates and gentlemen in this part of the county. Soliciting your goodness and protection,

I remain, gentlemen,

Your most obedient, humble servant,   R. W. Oldham

105. Agreement between the trustees and the Suffolk magistracy for the purchase of Melton House[20]

An agreement made and concluded the fourth day of December 1826, between Andrew Arcedeckne Esq., on behalf of himself and the other Trustees appointed by an Act of Parliament made and passed in <1826> whose names are hereunto subscribed of the one part, and Ambrose Harbord Steward Esq., Thomas Quayle Esq., Thomas Burch Western Esq., Henry Bence Bence Esq., and Edward Moor Esq., on behalf of themselves and the rest of his Majesty's Justices of the Peace, acting in and for the said county of Suffolk of the other part.

---

19 SROI ADA11/A/A/1/22.
20 SROI ADA11/A/A/1/23.

The said Trustees whose names are hereunto subscribed, do hereby agree in virtue of the powers vested in them, and in Edmund Jenney Esq. and the Revd George Frederick Tavel, to sell to the said Justices, acting in and for the said county, all and every the messuages, lands, tenements at, therewith, belonging and attached thereto, at or for the price or sum of eight thousand pounds.

And that the said messuages, lands, tenements, and hereditaments shall be conveyed to the said Justices, or to whom they shall appoint, free from all encumbrances whatsoever, except land tax, on or before, the twenty second day of March now next ensuing, and that a good title to the same shall be made by and at the costs and charges of the said Justices.

The said Justices, parties hereto on such behalf as aforesaid, hereby agree to pay to the said Trustees, the said sum of eight thousand pounds, the aforesaid purchase money on or before the said twenty second day of March, and in case the purchase be not completed on that day, the purchases shall pay interest at four per cent per annum from that day until payment of the purchase money. The conveyances to be executed by the said Justices to be at the expense of the said Justices.

And it is further agreed that the possession of all the said premises shall be delivered to the Justices on the first day of January next, on which day possession shall be accepted by them. In witness whereof, the said parties to these presents have hereunto set their names this day and year first above written.

Andrew Arcedeckne	William Shuldham	William Woods Page
John Hindes Groome	J. A. Wenn	John Lewin
Edward Crisp	A. H. Steward	J. Burch Western
Henry Bence Bence	E. Moor	
Witness, John Wood Jn.,	and J. Barton.	

106. Fourth Trustees' Meeting[21]

5 February 1827

The minutes of the last meeting having been read over, the solicitors reported that they had prepared and delivered abstracts to the title deeds to the solicitor to the County Magistrates, and such abstracts had since been examined and assigned with the title deed.

That a bill of John Loder's, amounting to the sum of £15 14s. 10d., produced to the meeting for printing reports and other documents, be paid by the Treasurers.

Mr Lewin, the auctioneer employed to sell the personal property at the House of Industry at Melton, do before the next meeting pay to the Treasurers the net proceeds of such sale. That Mr Lewin do also produce the accounts of that sale at the next meeting.

107. Adjourned Fourth Trustees' Meeting[22]

12 February 1827

At this meeting the clerk reported that Mr Lewin had not paid to them, as Trustees, the net proceeds of the sale of the personal effects at the House of Industry, Melton, sold by him by auction by order of the Trustees. But, that on being requested

---

[21] SROI ADA11/A/A/1/22.
[22] SROI ADA11/A/A/1/22.

to pay the same, he tendered a balance of £42 5s. 0d., and an account of charges for services considered by him to have been performed to the amount of £630 0s. 6d. touching the procuring the Act of Disincorporation, in addition to his commission, on the before mentioned sale and charges for printing and advertisements.

After a long discussion upon Mr Lewin's bill, which was read over and a difference of opinion having arisen. Mr Lewin personally declared his readiness to accept such a sum of money as the Trustees might think proper of his bill of £630 0s. 6d. And the meeting, having taken the same into consideration, do not think themselves justified in allowing the charges in that bill relating to 2nd November 1826, amounting to the sum of £254 8s. 6d., but having taken the subsequent charges, amounting to the sum of £375 12s. 0d. into consideration, do allow him the sum of £300 in discharge of the same.

I, John Lewin, of Wickham Market, in the county of Suffolk auctioneer hereby consent and agree to accept, in discharge of my bill for £630 0s. 6d., such a sum of money as the Trustees this day present think proper to allow.

Mr Lewin refused to sign the above

That the solicitors two bills, amounting both to the sum of £863 8s. 2d., be reduced to the sum of £790 10s. 10d., and that they as Treasurers be allowed to retain that sum out of the first monies which come to their hands.

108. John Lewin's disputed account[23]

The Trustees of the Melton House property To John Lewin.
1824

May. Attended a meeting at Melton House, when it was proposed that a draft bill should be prepared and framed to submit to some future general meeting – to amend and improve the system by annual averages. And much discussion arose in dividing the expenses under the heads or classes. And after they were divided it was declared that one part of the expenses were to be fluctuating and the other permanent – and it was resolved that a General Meeting should be held on the 21st June 1824 to take the same into consideration. 0 0 0

Attending several times at Melton House and taking copies of sundry items from the books to prove that these permanent expenses amounted to near £1,600 the last year, and that the average of the last three years was near £1,400 a year. Showed these to many persons largely interested, and who were astonished, and all agreed that these expenses would provide for all the poor that had been in the House the last three years if they were out. And they begged that I would see the principals in the different parishes and appraise them of it, as they all supposed that the whole was to be in yearly averages. This surprised many and they begged that I would attend the General Meeting, introduce and explain their ideas of disincorporating, as they all agreed that £2,000 might be saved by disincorporating without lessening the comforts of the deserving poor. Attending at the different parishes

---

23 SROI ADA11/A/A/1/30. See Plate 8, page 445, for details of the sale catalogue for Tuesday 14 November 1826. The auction of the house's goods was held over nine days – 2, 7, 9, 14, 16, 21, 23 and 30 November and 7 December.

Melton House
OF INDUSTRY.

To be Sold by Auction,

BY

JOHN LEWIN,

On Tuesday, November 14, 1826,

UPON THE PREMISES.

LOT			LOT			LOT		
1	PAIL, hod, and keeler		43	2 long forms		85	Iron bedstead	
2	Ditto		44	Child's crib		86	Feather bed	
3	Ditto		45	Ditto		87	Ditto	
4	Pail, dustpan, and 2 chamber utensils		46	Ditto with Bed		88	Ditto	
5	Ditto		47	Pair blue curtains		89	Ditto	
6	Ditto		48	Ditto		90	Ditto	
7	Ditto		49	Ditto		91	Blanket and coverlet	
8	Ditto		50	Iron bedstead		92	Ditto	
9	Ditto		51	Ditto		93	Ditto	
10	Iron bedstead		52	Ditto		94	Ditto	
11	Ditto		53	Smaller ditto		95	Ditto	
12	Ditto		54	Ditto		96	2 pair sheets	
13	Smaller ditto		55	Ditto		97	2 ditto	
14	Ditto		56	Ditto with boards		98	1 ditto, bed, and bolster case	
15	Ditto		57	Ditto		99	2 straw beds and bolster cases	
16	Ditto with boards		58	Wood ditto		100	2 ditto	
17	Ditto		59	Ditto		101	2 ditto	
18	Wood ditto		60	Feather bed		102	Deal table, form, and 2 stools	
19	Ditto		61	Ditto		103	Ditto	
20	Feather bed		62	Ditto		104	Ditto	
21	Ditto		63	Ditto		105	Very large dining table	
22	Ditto		64	Ditto		106	Ditto	
23	Ditto		65	Blanket and coverlet		107	Barrel beer cask	
24	Ditto		66	Ditto		108	Ditto	
25	Blanket and coverlet		67	Ditto		109	Ditto	
26	Ditto		68	Ditto		110	Ditto	
27	Ditto		69	Ditto		111	Ditto	
28	Ditto		70	2 pair sheets		112	Ditto	
29	Ditto		71	2 ditto		113	Ditto	
30	2 pair sheets		72	2 straw beds and 2 bolster cases		114	Ditto	
31	2 ditto		73	2 ditto		115	Ditto	
32	2 ditto		74	2 ditto		116	Ditto	
33	Pair stays and 2 shifts		75	2 ditto		117	Hogshead ditto	
34	Ditto		76	10 yards of linsey-woolsey		118	Ditto	
35	Ditto		77	10 ditto		119	Ditto	
36	Deal table, form, 2 stools		78	5 ditto		120	Ditto	
37	Ditto		79	5 ditto		121	Ditto	
38	Ditto		80	5 ditto		122	Ditto	
39	Very large dining table		81	Iron bedstead		123	Perfect ale stalling, 10 tin cans and pails, in lots	
40	Ditto		82	Ditto		124	Sundries	
41	2 long forms		83	Ditto		125	Ditto	
42	2 ditto		84	Ditto				

*** *Sale to begin at Ten o'clock.*

J. LODER, PRINTER AND BOOKSELLER, WOODBRIDGE.

Plate 8. Items to be sold by auction, at Melton House of Industry by John Lewin, 1826

according to 20 days 21/- per day.	21	0	0
Chaise hire and expenses on only 100 miles at 1s. 6d.	7	10	0
Messengers, postage and stationary.	10	6	

June 21st. Attending General Meeting when I made a proposition on
the part of 6 parishes in writing, and a majority of the parishes then
present personally, to appoint a committee to investigate if it was
expedient or not to disincorporate. This meeting recommended another
to be called, but as no meeting was called, I attended the Quarterly
Meeting, 8th July, when the Directors and Guardians then present wished
me to write to, and wait on, all the principal landed proprietors and state
my reasons for wishing such meeting to be called.   0   0   0

July 12th. Drawing long statement of reasoning on all the points, showing
that the institution has not met any of the intended purposes, injuring
the morals, and destroying the comforts of the poor and increasing
the expences more than £50,000 the last 24 years. 20 days at 21/-.   21   0   0

July 30th. Searching for, and obtaining, different documents to prove
and substantiate the reasoning and calculations. 16 days at 21/-.   16 16   0

Two clerks copying, casting, multiplying, dividing and proving. 12 days at 21/- each.	25	4	0
Chaise hire and sundry expenses in travelling 150 miles at 1/6 per mile.	11	5	0
Messengers, postage and stationary.	2	7	6

Writing Earl of Rochford, Lord Rendlesham, Mr FitzGerald, and many
other landed proprietors for their opinions and also for advice and
instructions for further proceedings. 3 days.   3   3   0

According to such advice and instructions received – drew up a form
addressed to the principal landed proprietors of the hundreds and the
directors of Melton House for the several parishes in order that the
principal parishioners might sign to show their sentiments on the question.

Attending many persons interested for approval of the same. 2 days.	2	2	0
Messengers, postage, stationary etc.	0	10	6

August.   Attending the principal occupiers in the different parishes and
explaining the purpose of these documents. And a very great majority sign
in 32 of the parishes to say that they consider the whole establishment

was useless and unnecessary. 20 days at 21/-.	21	0	0
Two clerks copying and calculating. 8 days each.	16	16	0
Chaise hire and sundry expenses. Travelling 150 miles at 1/6 per mile.	11	5	0

Attending Lord Rendlesham with the reasons and remarks, and the above
documents signed by the principal occupiers in the 32 parishes, and many
other documents. And went through the whole from beginning to end with
his Lordship and his solicitor who sifted and examined the matter very
closely, and then said he should meet his lordship's tenants the next day,
and would enquire further into the business and wished me to attend him
again after seeing them.   3   3   0

Attending Lord Rendlesham and his solicitor who then said upon enquiry
he found every one of his Lordships tenants to a man were my friends and
consider everything I had shewn perfectly correct and true. Therefore, they
felt anxious to go more fully into the business and we again went through
the whole from beginning to end discussing every point and, at his Lordships
request, I left all my papers for three days at Rendlesham. Working very
hard at this business before I went, and after I came home, full 20 hours

this day.		4	4	0

Attending Lord Rendlesham again, and received very full instructions
how to proceed further in the matter, one part of which was to attend
and submit the same to Mr Shuldham, and if he approve what was done,
then to attend Mr Arcedeckne, Mr Sheppard, Mr Page, Mr FitzGerald,
Mr Jenney and other principal landed proprietors.   3   3   0

Chaise hire and expenses. 18 miles at 1/6.   1   7   0

Sept. Attending Mr Shuldham who examined and approved the same and
also Mr Arcedeckne and Mr Sheppard. 3 days.   3   3   0

Attending Mr Jenney, Mr FitzGerald and several others on the business.
3 days.   3   3   0

Attending Mr Page several different times, and many others too numerous to
mention in many parts of the Hundreds. 5 days.   5   5   0

Chaise hire and expenses more than 100 miles at 1/6.   7   10   0

Messengers, postage, stationary etc.   1   5   0

Oct. 1st. Attending Lord Rendlesham, the High Sheriff (Mr FitzGerald)
Mr Arcedeckne, Mr Sheppard, Mr Shuldham, Mr Jenney, Mr Page and
many other principal landed proprietors for the purpose of submitting
the requisition for their sanction and signatures, and fixing a day most
convenient for the principals to attend the meeting. 8 days.   8   8   0

Chaise hire and travelling expenses. 150 miles at 1/6.   11   5   0

10th. Attending the same parties, and also attending and writing to many
Others, and assisting in drawing, altering and correcting the resolutions
intended to be submitted at the General Meeting to be held 26th October.
6 days.   6   6   0

Oct. 3rd. After these were arranged and settled, attended all the different
parishes submitting and explaining the intent and meaning of the different
resolutions, and shewing the necessity for the principals in the different
parishes to attend the General Meeting, and also explaining many other
parts of the business. 10 days.   10   10   0

Two clerks. Copying many resolutions for movers and seconders, and
calculating many different statements and documents which many of the
parties largely interested wished to have done in order that the matter
might be more generally explained and understood. 6 days each.   12   12   0

Chaise hire and expenses. 150 miles at 1/6.   11   5   0

Messengers, postage, stationary and other expenses.   1   10   0

26th. Attending General Meeting accordingly (see report of investigating
committee).   0   0   0

Nov. 2nd. Attending first committee meeting.   0   0   0

Received orders and instructions to attend to the accounts. Instructing
and assisting Mr Oldham and Mr Pizey to make out the last 4 years
accounts of the whole expenditure of all the different parishes, and
considering myself answerable for any inaccuracy. Examined and
investigated the whole 24 years accounts, and proved them correct
principally by documents before in my possession. Having pledged
myself to produce the whole account, and Mr Wood the Treasurer
being in London and not being able to get at his last 4 years accounts
of the receipts, I made a calculation of what Mr W. should have received
and produced it at the next meeting when Mr W. had returned from
London and produced his, which was near £40,000 and there was but

three pence difference, and that was six half pence which bankers
never take into account. Six very long days from 16 to 18 to 20 hours
per day at 63/-, including all chaise hire and other expenses.   18 18 0
Two clerks to assist me in copying, casting, multiplying, dividing and
proving. 6 days at 21/- each.   12 12 0
Sitting up nearly all night, with two clerks to assist me, in making a
general statement of the whole 24 years accounts which were only
finished on the evening of the 8th.   5 5 0
Messengers, postage and stationary.   0 10 6
Nov. 9th. Attending committee meeting.   0 0 0
Nov. 9th. Received instructions to attend to several different parts of the
accounts and, among others, one that would shew what the parishes had
paid and what they ought to have paid which did shew that some had
taken enormous advantages of others. And also taking abstracts to
shew inequalities and cases of injustices which amount to some thousands.
6 long days at 63/- per day.   18 18 0
Two clerks to assist me. 4 days each at 21/-.   8 8 0
Messengers and stationary.   0 10 6
Nov. 16th. Attending committee meeting.   0 0 0
Received instructions to attend to different parts of the accounts, and to
make several statements for different members of the committee and,
among others, to shew what the paupers cost in the House and what they
cost out the last year for all the different parishes. And these were the
cause of producing the 2nd resolution on the 23rd Nov. 6 days at 63/-
per day.   18 18 0
Two clerks the same time at 21/- each per day.   12 12 0
Messengers, stationary etc.   0 12 0
Nov. 23rd. Attending committee meeting.   0 0 0
In consequence of the 3rd and 4th resolutions, received instructions from
different members of the committee to prepare and get ready all the
different statements that were considered necessary to meet the different
points of the bill then prepared to submit to Parliament, as the Directors
had declared at the Public Meeting that they could not proceed any further
without an amended act. These statements, so prepared, did prove that bill
would fail as the others had done and, after a great and long discussion,
produced the 2nd resolution on the 30th Nov. 6 days at 63/- per day.   18 18 0
Two clerks to assist me in copying and calculating. 3 days each at 21/-.   6 6 0
Messengers, postage and stationary.   0 10 6
Nov. 30th. Attending committee meeting.   0 0 0
Received orders and instructions to prepare several statements and
memorandums and, among others, one that would explain from the
inequalities that had happened in what manner they might happen again,
and also upon what terms parishes might be allowed to withdraw from
the establishment in order that they might form part of the report.
Drawing them from the accounts of the different parishes accordingly,
and attending Mr Shuldham and Mr Page several days at Mr Wood's
office to assist in making the report. 4 days at 63/- per day.   12 12 0
Two clerks to assist in making these statements. 1 day each at 21/- per day.   2 2 0
Messengers, postage etc.   0 2 6
Dec. 7th. Attending committee meeting.   0 0 0

1825 Jan. Attending many parties interested, and explaining the different
statements in the printed report, and also attending Lord Rendlesham,
Mr Shuldham, Mr Bolton and many others and assisting in framing
resolutions ready for General Meeting on 25th January 1825. 7 days at
63/- per day.   22   1   0
One clerk copying 4 sets of resolutions for movers and seconders.
3 days at 21/- per day.   3   3   0
Messengers, postage and stationary.   0   7   0
25th. Attending General Meeting.   0   0   0
Feb. 10th. Attending first committee meeting.   0   0   0
Attending many parishes at the request of the principals, and writing in
reply to many others who wrote me to know what the circulars meant,
which Messrs Wood had sent them, as they all considered that the question
was decided, and a report having been circulated, that those who signed
were to pay for the act, and those who did not sign were not to pay any
part of the expense. Some were afraid to sign, and I was sent for by many
parishes to explain and satisfy the parties. 20 days at 21/- per day. 21   0   0
Chaise hire and travelling expenses. 50 miles at 1/6.   3 15   0
March. Calling at Messrs. Woods office and finding many of the circulars
not returned. Attended and wrote to the different parishes and found,
on the return of the whole, that a very great majority had signed assenting
to pay for the act in 28 of the parishes out of the 33, and only 5 dissenting.   2   2   0
July 5th. Attending second committee meeting.   0   0   0
Aug. 25th *do* third *do do*   0   0   0
Sept. 19th *do* fourth *do do*   0   0   0
Oct. 10th *do* fifth *do do*   0   0   0
Dec. 5th *do* sixth *do do*   0   0   0
1826 Jan. 2nd In consequence of many gentlemen, yeoman and farmers
having declared that they would not go to Messrs Woods to sign the
petition, because they wished it to be carried all round to the different
parishes, I took a copy and attended most of the principal parishioners
in all the different parishes and, in 20 days, obtained 260 signatures and
prevailed on 16 to go and sign at Messrs Woods who only obtained 12
in the whole beside the 16 I sent. 20 days at 21/-.   21   0   0
Chaise hire and expenses on 200 miles at 1/6.   15   0   0
Messengers, postages and parchment.   1   5   0
Jan. 24th. Drawing statement of facts and reasons for dissolving the
Incorporation, and some points for consideration, and drawing a short
statement of facts and reasons, and attending Lord Rendlesham, Mr
Arcedeckne, and Mr Shuldham several times to submit these documents
for correction and approval before they were printed to hand to Members
of Parliament.   3   3   0
Chaise hire and expenses. 26 miles at 1/6.   1 19   0
Feb. 6th. Attending Mr Shuldham and Mr Arcedeckne at Messrs Woods
office, and Lord Rendlesham at Rendlesham, several days previous to going
to London, and making the necessary arrangements accordingly, and received
full instructions for presenting the petition and forwarding the bill for the
1st and 2nd reading in the House of Commons, and received a packet of
letters from Lord Rendlesham introducing me to many different members
of Parliament. 4 days.   4   4   0

449

Chaise hire and expenses. 30 miles at 1/6.	2	5	0
Feb. 15th. Seven days in London at 84/- per day.	29	8	0
Coach hire and expenses in London.	4	2	0
Coach hire to and from London.	3	4	0
Other travelling expenses on the road.	1	2	0

16th and 17th. Attending Lord Rendlesham and Mr Shuldham and explaining to them very fully the manner in which the business had so far proceeded. 2 days. 2 2 0

21st and 23rd. Attending Lord Rendlesham and his solicitor, and received very full instructions for further proceedings, and a packet of letters introducing me to several members of the House of Lords. And his Lordship desired me to apply to his solicitor, if I considered his advice necessary, when I was in London. This I found of very great service in the absence of Mr Wood. 2 days. 2 2 0

March 15th. 19 days in London forwarding the bill through both Houses of Parliament, at 84/- per day. 79 16 0

Coach hire, postage and messengers and tavern expenses for the 19 days. 10 7 0

Coach hire to and from London. 3 5 0

Other travelling expenses. 1 5 0

Attending Lord Rendlesham and Mr Shuldham several times when they wished to call another meeting to give the parishes formal notice of what was done. Wrote Mr Arcedeckne accordingly, to know when he would be in the country, in order that the meeting might be fixed for when most convenient for him to attend, but instead of holding a meeting Messrs Wood were instructed to send a copy of the act of Parliament into every parish which was considered sufficient. 0 0 0

Oct. 16th. Attending first meeting as a Trustee. 0 0 0

1827 Feb. Attending every other meeting of the Trustees from that date up to the present. 0 0 0

630 0 6

If it should be considered that I have set too high a value upon my time in this matter I hope the following will be taken into consideration also at the same time.

That although I am not in the same affluent circumstances that most of the other trustees are, with whom I have the honour to act in this business, yet, I trust, I am not to be considered as a common mechanic to work for 5/- per day and board myself.

The expenses of carrying on my own business directly and indirectly are more than £1,000 a year, and without my personal attention and exertion, a great portion of these expenses must be paid out of my capital, and I now declare that I have suffered very seriously in this way (much more than the amount of this account) during the time I have been attending to this business besides making myself some powerful enemies. But I found that no person in the Hundreds had paid the attention to it that I had or made themselves sufficiently master of the subject to meet the question.

£525 Every person concerned must be aware that I could have charged £500 more days than I have, and perhaps half these within the period of the date of this account which I have a legal right to do by the Act of Parliament, as a part of the previous proceedings – the act would never have been passed. This at 1 guinea per day is £525.

£75 Travelling at least 1,000 miles more than I have charged in this account at 1/6 per mile.

£600 These acts of Parliament must be very expensive. Mr Wood's bill for the last act was above £700, and Mr Pulham's £690. Thus it cost the Hundreds £1,400, and when I saw Mr Wood pay between £300 and £400 of hard cash for fees and other expenses, and I know his bill must be heavy, something like what it is. It has been said that there was no opposition to this bill, but I contend all the difference is that our opposition was in the country and theirs in London. They brought most serious burthens on the Hundreds. And we have taken them off and I will venture to assent that no solicitor would have done what I have for less than 12 or £1,400 thus saving the Hundreds at least £600. And in this way upon the old fashioned adage of a penny saved is a penny earned I contend I make the Hundreds a present of this £1,200 beside saving them for the future from 2 to £3,000 a year!!!

£1,200   £630 0 6

This account will shew that I have not made any charge since I became a Trustee.

I hope it will be perfectly understood that in making out this account I have never lost sight of the proposition of the trustees at the last meeting, of making one a handsome gratuity in addition to this for my personal exertions, which they all then agreed I was intitled to for such services as I could not and have not charged in this account. The act (pages 12 and 13) directs and empowers the Trustees to give gratuities to clerks, officers and other persons who may have been appointed to certain services in any wise relating to this business, and I fully expect a handsome gratuity accordingly, for not only the services in saving £1,200 aforesaid, and the 2 or £3,000 a year in future, but in getting rid of (in the opinion of a very great majority of all classes of the Hundreds) one of the worst dens of infamy and profligacy, and in short in every point of view the heaviest burden and the greatest nuisance the Hundreds ever had to complain of.

1826

Brought forward amount of this account		630	0	6
Advertisements in Ipswich Journal		2	13	2
do in Suffolk Chronicle		2	15	0
Mr Loder's bill for printing		8	11	6
Commission		36	2	4
Balance carried forward		42	5	0
		722	7	6

Nov. 2nd produce of	1st days auction as per catalogue	97	0	2
7th	2nd days do	80	1	10
9th	3rd days do	229	17	0
14th	4th days do	53	10	2
16th	5th days do	47	0	3
21st	6th days do	43	2	2
23rd	7th days do	43	9	6
30th	8th days do	60	13	8
Dec. 7th	9th days do	67	12	9
		722	7	6

Advertisements in Ipswich Journal for 1st General Meeting if not paid by Messrs Woods			
do for Suffolk Chronicle			
Brought forward amount of this account	630	0	6
Not taken in this account the first			
Part before 2nd Nov. 1824	254	8	6

Deduct from the other part	75 12. 0.	330	0	6
Amount allowed only from 2nd Nov. 1824		300	0	0
Advertisements in Ipswich Journal		2	13	2
Chronicle		2	15	0
Printing		8	11	6
Commission		36	2	4
Balance		372	5	6
		722	7	6

109. R. Oldham's closing account with the Incorporation[24]

12 February 1827

Trustees of Loes and Wilford.   Dr. to R. W. Oldham

17th–21st Oct. 1826	Expenses sending paupers to Hollesly, Boyton, Butley, Ash, Marlesford, Hacheston, Monewden, Brandeston, Letheringham & Creetingham including toll gate.	0	17	6
	Paid man looking after lunatics 4 days.	0	2	0
	2 men weeks work & 10s. each. 1 woman 3 days 3s.	1	3	0
23rd	Soap and potash as per bill.	0	12	0
28th	Job to pump as per bill.	0	6	0
	3 men and 2 women weeks wages.	1	11	0
4th Nov.	do do do	1	11	0
9th	Poor rate 6/3. Surveyors rate 3/9.	0	10	0
	Medicine for a cow as per bill.	0	6	0
11th	Men and woman weeks wages.	1	11	0
	Expenses sending paupers to Petistree, Monewden & Easton.	0	4	6
18th	Men and womans weeks wages.	1	11	0
20th	Turning up muck for sale.	0	2	0
25th	Men and woman weeks wages.	1	11	0
29th	Men taking down bedsteads for sale.	0	2	6
2nd Dec.	Men and woman weeks wages.	1	11	0
9th	do do do	1	11	0
16th	1 man and woman weeks wages.	0	12	0
23rd	do do do	0	12	0
30th	do do do	0	12	0
	Qtrs. Land tax due Xmas.	1	2	0
	Hire of furniture as per bill.	0	18	0
		18	18	6

Cr. by cash for grass feed.	6. 0. 0			
do for butter sold	1. 7. 0	7	7	0
		11	11	6

To salary from 16 Oct.–31st Dec.				
11 wks at 2gns.		23	2	0
		34	13	6

Allowed Feb. 12 1827.

---

[24] SROI ADA11/A/A/1/30.

110. Fifth Trustees' Meeting[25]

19 April 1827

At this meeting, William Abraham Shuldham, William Woods Page esquires, Revd John Hindes Groome, and Mr John Lewin, are appointed as a Committee to meet at the late House of Industry at Melton, on Saturday next, and examine the books, papers, and vouchers now in the said House. And that any two of those gentlemen shall be considered sufficient for that purpose, who shall report the result of their examination to the next meeting.

Application having been made to the meeting, on behalf of several parishes within the said Hundreds of Loes and Wilford, for a return of certain sums of money which were from time to time received by the Directors and Acting Guardians to indemnify certain putative fathers against all future claims for bastard children, and not wholly expended on the maintenance of such bastard children. The Trustees, upon reference to the Act, considered they had no power to make a return of any such unexpended money.

The Treasurers are directed to pay Mr Robert Cana the sum of £80 7s. 0d. for his survey, plans and valuation of the late House of Industry buildings and fixtures, and the further sum of three guineas for his valuation of the land, as by his agreement and take his receipt of these sums.

The Treasurers are also ordered to pay to Mr Richard Wood Oldham the sum of fifteen pounds, to defray all the fees and expences of receiving two bodies from the Chapel at Melton House of Industry to the churchyard belonging to the parish of Melton.

That Andrew Arcedeckne and Edmund Jenney esquires, and the Revd George Frederick Tavel, be severally cancelled from their attendance at these meetings on account of their absence from the neighbourhood.

That the next meeting of the Trustees be held on Thursday the third day of May instant, at which meeting the Treasurers are ordered to produce all accounts up to that period.

That the advertisement for all creditors to deliver their accounts before the next meeting, now produced and approved, be inserted for two weeks in both the Ipswich papers:

> The Trustees appointed <by Act of Parliament> do hereby give notice that all persons having any demands upon or against the said Directors and Guardians or the said Trustees, do deliver an account of the same to us on or before the 1st of May next, when the accounts of the said Trustees will be closed, and all demands not then received will be excluded from payment. Wood and Son, Treasurers to the said Trustees.

111. An account of the money received from the parishes concerning illegitimate children from October 1820 to October 1826[26]

Parishes	Sum Rec'd	Sum expended	Difference	
	£	£	£	
Butley	30	19 10s.	10 10s.	Mill's child

---

25 SROI ADA11/A/A/1/22.
26 SROI ADA11/A/A/2/3.

Capel	30	20	16s.	9	4s.	Williams' child
Creetingham	40	25	7s.	14	13s.	Peck's 2 child
Hatcheston	30	23	9s.	6	11s.	Barham's child
do	20	11	14s.	8	6s.	Bevet's child
Melton	20	13	0s.	7	0s.	Amis's child
Kettleburgh	30	7	16s.	22	4s.	Baker's child
do	22	10s.	9	9s.	13	1s.	Rackham's child
Shottisham	30	12	8s.	17	12s.	E. Bird's child
Rendlesham	30	28	0s.	2	0s.	Clouting's child
	282 10s.	171	9s.	111	1s.	
	171 9s.					
	111 1s.					

112. R. Oldham's expenses for removing two bodies from the Incorporation's chapel into Melton churchyard[27]

21 April 1827

Received April 21 1827, of Messrs Wood and Son, the Treasurers to the Trustees appointed by <Act of Parliament>, the sum of fifteen pounds, being a sum ordered at the last meeting of the Trustees held on the 19th instant, to be paid to me to defray all fees and expenses to be incurred in removing two bodies from the chapel into Melton churchyard.   R. W. Oldham. £15.

113. Sixth Trustees' Meeting[28]

3 May 1827

The said William Abraham Shuldham, William Woods Page, and John Hindes Groome reported to this meeting that they did, pursuant to an order made at the last meeting, meet at Melton House on 21st day of April last, and examined all the books, papers, vouchers and documents left there necessary or important to the Hundreds. The Treasurer to procure proper chests to be made for the preservation of such books and vouchers. And a schedule of such books having been then made. It is now ordered that such schedule be printed and copies thereof sent to each parish within said Hundreds of Loes and Wilford.

It is further ordered that all owners and occupiers of lands, and all rated inhabitants of any of the parishes included in the late Incorporated Hundreds of Loes and Wilford, be allowed to search and inspect any of the books in the custody of the Clerk to the Trustees upon paying them 2s. 6d. for each search and examination.

Mr William Bilby's bill for making two chests to contain the several books and vouchers, before mentioned, amounted to £2 16s. was allowed, and the Treasurers are directed to pay him that sum.

The solicitors third bill, amounting to £101 14s. 3d., having been examined, is allowed by this meeting, and the Treasurers are directed to retain that amount of the cash now in their hands.

---

27 SROI ADA11/A/A/1/30. No further information is provided concerning the two bodies. As the house had been emptied of inmates, it is to be assumed that the bodies had been delivered to the chapel for burial in the Incorporation's burial ground which was now no longer possible, hence their transportation to the parish churchyard in Melton.

28 SROI ADA11/A/A/1/22.

It appearing that the expences of the Trustees since they began amount to £47 4s. 11d., which sum is allowed by this meeting.

The next and final meeting of the Trustees be held at the same place on Monday 24th day of September next, for the purposes of distributing and paying the balance in the hands of the trustees.

It is referred to Mr John Wood the elder and Mr John Lewin to settle the scale of division of the sum of £7,568 14s. 3d., the balance in the hands of the Trustees according to section 13 of the said Act.

That an advertisement to the form or effect produced by Mr Shuldham be inserted for two weeks in both the Ipswich papers, after the scale of division is settled, and completed by Mr Wood and Mr Lewin.

114. Messrs Wood and Son's bill for legal services[29]

The Trustees appointed by an Act of Parliament for disincorporating the Hundreds of Loes and Wilford.   To Messrs Wood and Son.

1826

May 5th On receiving letter from Mr Lewin stating that himself and others named as Trustees in an act for disposing of the property lately vested in the Guardians of Loes and Wilford Hundreds had fixed to meet on the 18th instant, writing Mr Lewin in reply, that the above act will not take effect till the 10th October, and that any meeting of the Trustees previous to that time would be illegal.   0   5   0

Writing to Lord Rendlesham, Mr Arcedeckne and Mr Shuldham the like effect.   0   15   0

May 8th On receiving a letter from Lord Rendlesham still wishing for a meeting of the Trustees for the purpose of giving publicity to the act, writing in reply that a print of the act had been delivered to the overseers of every parish in the Hundreds and to all the directors and acting guardians.   0   5   0

Oct. 4th Attending upon Mr Lewin, receiving of him the sum of £191 13s. 4d. being the balance of his accounts of proceeds of auction at Melton House on the 17th July, and giving him memorandum of receipt for same.   0   6   8

12th Attending upon the Revd Mr Groome, one of the Trustees, as to the meeting of the trustees on the 16th inst., when as he thought there would not be sufficient number of trustees present to form a meeting. Receiving instructions to write to the remaining 8 trustees and request their attendance on that day.   0   6   8

Writing letters to other trustees accordingly, informing them that the first meeting would be at Melton House.   1   8   0

13th On receiving letter from Mr Lewin, requesting to have the first meeting at the White Hart Inn, Wickham Market, perusing the act of parliament and ascertaining that the same must be held at Melton House unless another place is appointed by five of the trustees.   0   6   8

---

29 SROI ADA11/A/A/1/30.

Writing Mr Lewin in reply referring him to the clause, and giving him an opinion upon the subject.	0	5	0
14th Paid inserting resolutions of the last Quarterly Meeting in the Ipswich Journal.	0	9	10
The like in the Suffolk Chronicle.	0	9	10
Attending upon printer with a copy of this act, printed by the King's Printer, instructing him to prepare a proper book in which to enter the proceedings of the committee, and to bind up copy of act therewith	0	3	4
paid him for such book and binding.	0	3	0
15th Attending upon Mr Page, one of the trustees, who was abroad during the progress of the act through parliament, explaining several clauses, particularly as to the place of the meeting and the correspondence that had taken place thereon, consulting and advising as to the proceedings of the meeting tomorrow, which he promised to attend.	0	6	8
16th Attending the first meeting of the trustees at Melton House, debating upon the proceedings under the act, drawing resolutions and orders and making fair copy thereof in the book provided for that purpose.	2	2	0
Drawing special orders of removal of the paupers from Melton House to their respective parishes, as directed by the meeting.	0	6	8
Fair copy thereof for printer.	0	3	4
Attending therewith instructing him to print 60 copies.	0	3	4
Paid him printing same .	0	9	0
17th Filling up 17 pair of orders for removal of paupers accordingly, including 97 paupers, and attending upon Mr Groome and Mr Page, two of the Trustees, and also Justices of the county where they signed the above orders at 4/- per pair, being the usual Justice clerks fees.	3	8	0
Drawing case for the opinion of counsel as to the sale and conveyance of the burial ground and chapel, for the opinion of counsel, as directed at the first meeting and fair copy, eight sheets.	2	13	4
Writing to Mr Jenney, Mr Tavel and Mr Arcedeckne informing them of the next meeting of the trustees at the White Hart, Wickham Market on the 23rd inst., they having been absent at the last meeting.	0	10	6
23rd Journey to Wickham Market, and attending the first adjourned meeting of the trustees, drawing minutes of proceedings and entering same.	2	2	0
Chaise hire and expenses.	0	11	0
Writing Mr Jenney, one of the trustees absent at the last meeting, informing him the next meeting would be held on 6th November next at 12 o'clock.	0	3	6
24th Drawing advertisement, agreeable to the resolutions at the last meeting, for all claims upon the Directors and Guardians and also the Trustees etc. to be sent in immediately.	0	7	0
Two fair copies thereof for the printers of the two Ipswich papers.	0	7	0
Writing them therewith for insertion one week each.	0	7	0
Paid insertions in the Ipswich Journal and paper.	0	8	6
The same in the Suffolk Chronicle and paper.	0	8	10
26th Drawing advertisements of sale by auction of the Melton House and land early in the month of June unless previously disposed of by private contract.	0	7	0
Four fair copies thereof for the four county papers agreeably to the resolutions of the last meeting.	0	14	0

	£	s	d
Letters to printers of the four papers therewith for insertion two weeks each.	0	14	0
Paid insertion in the Ipswich Journal two weeks and one paper.	1	2	6
Likewise in Suffolk Chronicle and paper.	1	2	10
Likewise in Bury Post and paper.	1	2	9
Likewise in Bury Gazette and paper.	1	2	8
Attending upon Mr Jenney, explaining to him the proceedings which had taken place at the several meetings of the trustees, and consulting as to the future proceedings of the trustees.	0	6	8
Nov. 3rd Drawing bond from Messrs Wood and Son (and Thomas Brooke Esq. as their surety) to the trustees in £6,000 for the due execution of their office as clerks to the Justices.	1	0	0
Ingrossing same.	0	10	0
Stamp and paper.	1	15	6
Attending executing such bond, and also clerks attendance upon Mr Brooke, attesting his executing of same .	0	13	4
6th Mr Wood Jun., journey to Wickham Market attending the second general meeting of the trustees, producing the above bond and draft case, drawing out resolutions of the meeting, and entering same etc.	2	2	0
Mr Woods journey to Wickham Market, as the late Treasurer of the Hundreds, to produce his book of account to the present meeting, as directed by the last.	2	2	0
Chaise hire and expenses for both.	0	10	6
7th Attending at Mr Thompson's house several times before he could be met with, in order to ascertain the exact area of the property in order to state same in the following advertisements.	0	6	8
Drawing advertisement for sale of Melton Hose etc. by private contract for insertion in the Courier and Morning Herald papers once a week till 1st December agreeably to the resolutions of the last meeting.	0	7	0
Two fair copies thereof.	0	7	0
Third fair copy, in large text, to be placed up at the auction chart.	0	5	0
Writing agents with the above, giving him full directions as to inserting the advertisements and to procure and send us the newspapers containing them.	0	3	6
Agents writing into the country acknowledging receipt of advertisements.	0	3	6
Agents attending at the auction chart placing notice there.	0	6	8
Paid for same.	0	7	0
Agents attendance at the Courier office with advertisements and giving instructions for insertion as above.	0	13	4
The like attendance at the Herald office.	0	13	4
7th Paid for insertion 4 weeks in Courier and paper.	2	16	4
Paid for insertion 4 weeks in Herald and paper.	2	16	4
Making copy valuation of fixtures for Mr Lewin as directed by the last meeting that he might proceed to sell all the personal in the House except the fixtures by auction.	0	10	0
8th Attending Mr Lewin, delivering him same.	0	3	4
29th Agents writing to Messrs Barton as to price etc. in reply to their letter.	0	5	0
Dec. 1st Attending Mr Arcedeckne, consulting as to the proceedings of the next meeting which he promised to attend and informing him of the hour of meeting.	0	3	4

2nd Attending several times upon Mr Cana, the auctioneer, as to the sale
of the House and land, and recommending him to attend the meeting
to be held on the 4th inst. 0 6 8
4th Journey to Wickham Market, and attending the 3rd general meeting
of the trustees. Writing proposal to a deputation of the county magistrates
for sale of these premises, which after several meetings of the chairman
of the trustees and the magistrates, a contract was concluded between
them at £8,000 for the whole premises including fixtures etc. 2 2 0
Pursuing the draft agreement prepared by Mr Barton making alterations
therein, a fair copy thereof, and attending the signatures of the trustees
and the magistrates. 1 1 0
Chaise hire and expenses. 0 12 0
15th Attending upon Mr Cana informing him of the above contract and
that there would in consequence be no further occasion for his services. . 0 3 4
20th Attending upon Mr Oldham as to payments of the Land Tax for this
property which we instructed him to pay the property being still vested
in the Trustees. 0 3 4
1827
Jan. 3rd Writing Mr Barton that the abstract of title would be ready to be
delivered to him at the next sessions, and that the deeds would be at our
office so that he might examine same with the abstract before he left
Woodbridge. 0 5 0
Drawing abstract of title, 15 brief sheets. 5 0 0
Fair copy of same. 2 10 0
8th On receiving letter from Mr Barton at Beccles, requesting us to forward
him this abstract of title and print of the disincorporating act, writing him
therewith and thereon. 0 5 0
24th Attending upon Mr Barton, examining and comparing abstract of
title with the deeds and acts of Parliament. 1 1 0
Feb. 5th Journey to Wickham Market, attending the 4th general meeting
of the trustees drawing resolutions and entering same. 2 2 0
Chaise hire and expenses. 0 11 6
Attending upon Mr Loder, paying him £15 16s. 11d., the amount of his
bill upon the trustees and taking receipt for same. 0 3 4
12th Journey to Wickham Market, attending the adjourned 4th general
meeting of the trustees, drawing resolutions and entering same and
attending generally to the business of the day. 2 2 0
Chaise hire and expenses. 0 10 6
Making copy of minutes of the last meeting as directed by the trustees. .. 0 5 0
Writing Mr Lewin therewith. 0 3 6
March 1st Attending upon A. H. Steward Esq., who wished for a plan of
these premises, which was said to be in our possession, but finding on
reference to the papers, found it was not. Attending upon Johnson the
surveyor procuring a rough sketch. 0 10 0
Several attendances upon Major Moor and also upon Mr Charles Moor,
agent to the Suffolk office, as to the injury done by the fire at Melton House,
and producing the policy of insurance to them for inspection. 0 13 4
11th On receiving letter from Mr Barton, as to the course of this property.
Writing him in answer requesting him to forward the draft conveyance
to us forthwith and objecting to the trustees covenanting for further

assurance.	0	5	0
On receiving abstract of title with counsels opinion, and observations upon the title, perusing abstract and answering same.	0	16	8
Copy of opinion and observations of counsel and our answers to keep.	0	5	0
15th On receiving this draft conveyance from Mr Barton, pursuing same on behalf of the trustees, and making many alterations therein, and 7 skins.	1	15	0
Making copy release to keep as solicitors to the trustees.	2	2	6
Writing Mr Barton returning him draft approved by us.	0	5	0
21st Examining ingrossment of this conveyance with draft previous to the same being executed by the trustees, 7 skins.	1	3	4
Attending upon Mr Crisp, Mr Page and Mr Lewin, attesting their execution of this conveyance.	1	0	0
Drawing authority pointed out by the act from the trustees to ourselves to receive the purchase money of the county upon tendering the conveyance duly executed.	0	7	0
March 21st Fair copy thereof for signature of the trustees attending Mr Crisp, Mr Page and Mr Lewin.	0	3	6
Signing same.	0	10	0
22nd Journey to Ipswich and attending upon Mr Wenn, attesting his execution of this conveyance, and signing the above authority.	1	1	0
Horse hire and expenses.	0	12	6
Journey to Earl Soham, attending upon the Revd Mr Groome attesting his execution of this conveyance, and signing the above authority. Thence to Marlesford and attending upon Mr Shuldham, thereupon the like purpose.	2	2	0
Chaise hire and expenses.	0	14	0
These conveyances being of too much importance to risk by the coach, attending upon Revd Mr Barlow at his house at Burgh, therewith he having promised to take the same to town for us.	0	13	4
25th Writing our agents that these deeds were sent up by Mr Barlow requesting they would call upon him at No. 4, Old Square, Lincolns Inn for same and attend upon Mr Arcedeckne and Revd Mr Tavel therewith for execution.	0	5	0
Agents attending upon Mr Barlow at Lincolns Inn for deeds accordingly.	0	6	8
26th Agents attending upon Mr Arcedeckne at Grosvenor Square and attesting his execution of this conveyance, and signing the authority.	0	13	4
Also attending upon Revd G. F. Tavel at North Audley Street, and attesting his execution of the conveyance and signing the authority.	0	13	4
Paid coach hire.	0	2	6
Writing our agents herein, and to know if these deeds were yet executed.	0	5	0
30th Agents attending upon Mr Barlow, delivering him these deeds for him to bring back in the country.	0	6	8
Writing into the country that the deeds were forwarded as above.	0	5	0
April 3rd Attending several times this day upon Mr Barton as to the settlement of this purchase when he promised to write us tomorrow thereon.	0	6	8
4th Journey to Hasketon for the purpose of having this conveyance executed by Mr Jenney, but he being from home writing him a note requesting he would call at our office.	0	13	4
5th Writing Messrs Barton, proposing to meet one of them at Ipswich			

on the 4th inst. or Saturday next, to deliver to them this conveyance executed by the trustees and receive purchase money, and requesting an answer.	0	5	0

on the 4th inst. or Saturday next, to deliver to them this conveyance
executed by the trustees and receive purchase money, and requesting
an answer.   0 5 0
9th Attending upon Mr Jenney at our office, attesting his execution of
this conveyance and signing the authority.   0 10 0
On receiving letter from Mr Barton, proposing to meet on Saturday
next at Needham Market, writing him that he should have the meeting
desired.   0 5 0
14th On receiving letter from Mr Barton that he wished to have the
meeting at Ipswich today. Journey there for that purpose attending
him, delivering up prior deeds and the present conveyance, calculating
interest and receiving same and purchase money making together
£8,007 etc.   2 2 0
Chaise hire and expenses.   0 15 6
19th Journey to Wickham Market, attending the 5th general meeting of
the trustees, drawing minutes and resolutions, and entering same.   2 2 0
Chaise hire and expenses.   0 10 0
April 19th Drawing advertisement for all claims upon the trustees to
be delivered to us by 1st May next, agreeably to resolution at last meeting. 0 7 0
Two fair copies thereof for the printers of the Ipswich papers.   0 7 0
Writing them therewith for insertion two weeks in each paper.   0 7 0
Paid insertion in Journal.   0 17 4
Paid insertion in Chronicle.   0 18 8
Attending upon Mr Cana for the purpose of paying him £80 7s. 0d.
as ordered at the last meeting, but he refused to accept same for the
present.   0 3 4
21st Journey to Melton House and attending upon Mr Groome, Mr
Shuldham and Mr Page, going over the books of accounts and papers,
making a list of such of the former as were to be preserved, and fair
copy thereof, which was signed by the above gentlemen – and all the
bills and receipts etc were burnt.   2 2 0
Attending upon Mr Oldham two different times paying him the several
sums of £34 13s. 6d. and £15 allowed by the trustees and writing receipts
for the same upon stamp.   0 6 8
Drawing account of receipts and disbursements of the trustees since
passing of the act for their perusal and inspection at the last meeting. 0 7 0
Paid for book to enter such account in   .   0 2 0
Fair entry thereof.   0 3 6
May 3rd Journey to Wickham Market, attending the 6th general meeting
of the trustees, drawing minutes and resolutions, and entering same and
attending generally to the business of the day.   2 2 0
Chaise hire and expenses.   0 11 0
Postage of letters, porterage and carriage of parcels up to this day. 1 5 0
Paid stamping agreements between the trustees and the county magistrates
for sale of Melton House.   1 0 0
Attending at the stamp office, Somerset House for that purpose.   0 6 8
                                                                                                          101 14 3

115. Final accounts of Messrs Wood & Son[30]

Dr.

1826		£	s.	d.
Nov. 7	To cash received of the Treasurer of the late Incorporated Hundreds of Loes & Wilford the balance of his accounts as examined by the Directors and all overseen by the Sessions.	280	13	1
1827				
Feb. 14	To cash of Mr John Lewin, amount of the gross proceeds arising from the sale of the fixtures and effects at Melton House of Industry.	722	7	6
Apl. 14	To cash of Messrs Barton, the purchasers money of the real estate.	8,000	0	0
	To interest thereon at 4 per cent per annum from the 6th inst. as agreed by the vendors.	7	0	0
	Cash.	15	9	0
		9,010	0	7

Cr.

1827		£	s.	d.
Feb. 5	By cash paid Mr Loder his bill for printing reports and other documents as per bill & receipt.	15	14	10
Feb. 14	By cash paid Mr R. W. Oldham his salary, bill and balance of accounts as by his receipt.	34	13	6
	By cash allowed Mr Lewin for advertisements in Ipswich Journal.	2	13	2
	By cash allowed Mr Lewin for advertisements in Suffolk Courier.	2	15	0
	Mr Loders bill for printing.	8	11	6
	By cash paid.	36	2	4
	By cash John Lewin allowed him at the Meeting of the Trustees on the 12th inst. as per receipts for that sum.	300	0	0
	By cash allowed the Treasurers their bill previous to the application for the act of Parliament.	67	6	0
	By cash allowed the Treasurers their bill for soliciting the act of Parliament.	473	17	4
	By cash paid to Messrs Dorrington parliamentary agent.	249	7	6
	By cash paid Mr Robert Cana for his valuation upon sum of £4,017 12s. 6d. the amount of the value of the buildings at 2 per cent as per agreement.	80	7	0
	By cash paid Robert Cana for valuation of land.	3	3	0
Ap. 21	By cash paid Mr R. W. Oldham fees and expences for removing bodies from the Chapel into Melton			

---

30 SROI ADA11/A/A/1/9.

		£	s.	d.
	Church .	15	0	0
May 3	By cash paid Mr William Bilby for chests to preserve the books belonging to the late Directors and Trustees.	2	16	0
	By cash allowed the solicitors their bill for carrying the terms of the Act into execution.	101	14	3
	By expences of the Trustees.	47	4	11
	Balance in hand to be distributed amongst the 33 parishes.	7,568	14	3
		9,010	0	7

116. Division of the final balance in the treasurer's hands between the incorporated parishes[31]

7 May 1827

Loes and Wilford Hundred.

   A division of the sum of £7,568 17s. 2d. (the net balance in the Treasurers hands) among the several parishes comprised in the late Incorporated Hundreds of Loes and Wilford calculated upon the first annual assessments made for paying off and discharging the debt and interest of the said Incorporated Hundreds according to the direction of the late Act of Parliament for disincorporating the same.

Parishes	amount to be paid to each parish			Parishes	amount to be paid to each parish		
Loes Hundred				Wilford Hundred			
	£	s.	d.		£	s.	d.
Ash	373	7	4	Alderton	218	10	7
Brandeston	244	9	10	Bawdsey	162	0	6
Butley	238	13	11	Boulge	105	16	3
Charsfield	343	1	9	Boyton	37	0	7
Creetingham	293	0	1	Bredfield	270	4	11
Dallingho	204	19	1	Bromeswell	101	15	11
Earl Soham	294	2	4	Capel Saint Andrew	144	14	6
Easton	344	16	11	Debach	33	3	2
Eyke	187	0	1	Hollesly	339	4	4
Hacheston	261	8	4	Melton	268	18	11
Hoo	89	8	8	Petistree	233	16	5
Kenton	304	6	1	Ramsholt	232	13	5
Kettleburgh	196	8	9	Shottisham	94	5	4
Letheringham	119	17	5	Sutton	537	3	9
Marlesford	356	13	9	Ufford	347	6	9
Monewden	57	5	2	Wickham Market	396	12	11
Rendlesham	133	19	5		3,523	8	3
	4,045	8	11				
	3,523	8	3				
	7,568	17	2				

---

[31] SROI ADA11/A/A/1/20.

The above division arranged made and settled by us the undersigned on the 7th day of May 1827.

John Wood.   John Lewin.

117. Seventh Trustees' Meeting[32]

24 May 1827

The Trustees, having met pursuant to public advertisement, paid to the Church-wardens and Overseers of the Poor of the several parishes who attended this meeting, the several sums of money proved to be due to their respective parishes. And to the Churchwardens and the Overseers of the Poor of those several parishes who did not attend this meeting the Treasurer was directed to pay when and as soon as they had executed the necessary papers.

The Treasurers accounts having been this day examined and allowed were signed by the Trustees present.

118. Final accounts presented by trustees[33]

The Trustees appointed in and by an Act of Parliament made and passed in the 7th year of his present Majesty's reign hereby give notice that the following is a true and just statement or account of all sum and sums of money received paid and disbursed by them by virtue of the said act.

Dr   Messrs. Wood and Sons, Treasurers in account with the said Trustees   Cr

1826	£ s. d.		£ s. d.
Nov. 7	To cash of the Treasurer of the late Incorporated Hundreds of Loes and Wilford. The balance of his accounts examined by the Directors and allowed by the Sessions. 280 13 1	By Solicitors bill for the application to Parliament. 67 6 0 By Will. Loder's bill for printing reports and other documents. 15 14 10	
1827		March 1 1827 By Parliamentary agents bill for passing act through both Houses. 249 7 6	
Feb. 14	To cash of Mr John Lewin amount of the gross proceeds arising from the sale of furniture and effects at Melton House. 722 7 6	Feb. 14th By solicitors bill for obtaining Act. 473 17 4	
Apl. 14	To cash of the county magistrates purchase money for the house buildings and lands. 8,000 0 0 To interest thereon at 4% from the 6th instant. 7 0 0	By Mr Oldhams salary bill and balance of account. 34 13 6 By Mr John Lewins charges for advertisement, printing and commission upon the sale of furniture and effects of Melton House. 50 2 0 By cash allowed Mr John Lewin	

---

[32] SROI ADA11/A/A/1/22.
[33] SROI ADA11/A/A/1/26.

in discharge of his bill for
journeys to London and
elsewhere and for his trouble
during the progress of the bill
through Parliament.   300   0   0
May 3
By solicitors bill for carrying the
trusts of the Act into execution
up to this day.   101 14   3
May 4
For Robert Cana's commission
for survey plans and valuation
of the property prior to it being
offered for sale.   83 10   0
By expenses of the trustees
from the commencement of the
Act and solicitors last bill for
completing accounts dividing the
balance advertisements
thereof.   47   2   0
By balance to be divided among the
several disincorporated parishes.
                          7,568 17   2
                          9,010   0   7

9,010   0   7

And the said Trustees do hereby further give notice that they have directed their Treasurer to attend at the White Hart Inn, Wickham Market, on Monday the 24th day of September next, at 10 o'clock in the morning, to pay the above balance of £7,568 17s. 2d. to the Churchwardens and Overseers, for the time being, of the several late incorporated parishes in the following shares and proportions.

And notice is hereby also given that any persons thinking themselves aggrieved by any matter or thing done in pursuance of the said Acts, may appeal to the Justices of the Peace at any General Quarter Sessions of the Peace to be holden within the County of Suffolk within four calendar months from the date hereof, in the manner prescribed by and upon complying with the provisions of the said Act.

And lastly notice is hereby given that in case there shall be no appeal, as aforesaid, the clerk to the said Trustees will attend at the White Hart Inn, Wickham Market on Monday the 24th September next at 10 o'clock, to pay the above mentioned shares to the said Churchwardens and Overseers, when and where all those persons are hereby required to attend to receive and give discharge for the same.

Signed Wood and Sons.

119. Record of the final payments to parishes[34]

24 September 1827

Second Schedule being a list of the parishes comprised in the said late Incorporated Hundreds of Loes and Wilford, with a statement or account shewing the several sums paid to the Churchwardens and Overseers of the said several parishes.

				Churchwarden	Overseer
Loes Hundred					
Ash	373	7	4	John Goodwyn	George Whincopp
Brandeston	244	9	10	James Garnham	Thomas Baldwin
Butley	238	13	11	Thomas Catlin	
Charsfield	343	1	9	Jonathan Robert Hodgson	
Creetingham	293	0	1	Charles Corey	
Dallingho	204	19	1	Thomas Cole	
Earl Soham	294	2	4	George Scotchmer	
Easton	344	16	11	William Hambling	
Eyke	187	0	1	Thomas Waller Jun.	
Hacheston	261	8	4	George Bond	Nathaniel Barthropp
Hoo	89	8	8	William Cutting	
Kenton	304	6	1	John Page	John Clarke
Kettleburgh	196	8	9	James Page	
Letheringham	119	17	5	James Catchpole	
Marlesford	36	13	9	John Button	George Largent
Monewden	57	15	2	Abraham Watkins	
Rendlesham	133	19	5	Fenn Sheming	
Wilford Hundred					
Alderton	218	10	7	Samuel Gross	
Bawdsey	162	0	6	Gardiner Utting	
Boulge	103	16	3	Joseph Smith	
Boyton	37	0	7	Nathaniel Bennington	
Bredfield	270	4	11	Thomas Grimwood	
Bromeswell	101	15	11	John Gross	
Capel	144	14	6	Edmund Plant	
Debach	33	3	2	John Payne	
Hollesly	339	4	4	Jeptha Waller	Billy Smith
Melton	268	18	11	Jonathan A. Studd	Samuel Armstrong
Petistree	233	16	5	Philip Dykes	
Ramsholt	232	13	5	John May	
Shottisham	94	5	4	William Wright	
Sutton	537	3	9	Henry Edwards	Henry Archer
Ufford	347	6	9	William Wright	Edward Jarman
Wickham	396	12	11	Philip Dykes	John Lewin

---

34 SROI ADA11/A/A/1/26.

120. Closing trustees' accounts[35]

24 September 1827

The following sums paid out of pocket

1st advert, 2 weeks in Ipswich Journal.	6	6	4
do Suffolk Chronicle.	6	6	4
Loders Bill for printing schedules etc.	2	0	6
Advert of last meeting in Ipswich Journal.	0	9	4
do Suffolk Chronicle.	0	9	4
Fees to counsel and clerk settling & release.	3	5	6
Stamps and parchment for release.	7	8	6
	26	5	10
Tavern bills as above.	7	7	0
Total cash paid.	33	12	10

Law bill.	49	2	6
Trustees expenses.	7	7	0
	56	9	6
N.B. Loss by Wood & Son.	9	7	6
Cash retained, Sept. 24 1827.	47	2	0

35 SROI ADA11/A/A/1/30.

BIBLIOGRAPHY

UNPUBLISHED SOURCES

British Library of Political and Economic Science, London
Webbs' Collection
Volumes 230–4, Suffolk Poor Law Records
Miscellaneous Collection 195, Papers relating to Loes and Wilford Incorporation

Suffolk Record Office, Ipswich
ADA10 Carlford and Colneis Incorporation
ADA10/A/B/1/1   Carlford and Colneis Quarterly Minutes, 1756–85

ADA11 Loes and Wilford Incorporation
ADA11/A/A/1/1   Bundle containing various Acts
ADA11/A/A/1/2   Book containing Acts and Rules and Orders of Melton House
ADA11/A/A/1/3   Incorporation Act of 1791
ADA11/A/A/1/4   Bundle of printed copies of bill and Act for disincorporation
ADA11/A/A/1/5   Bundle of Acts for disincorporation
ADA11/A/A/1/6   Papers connected with the amending Acts
ADA11/A/A/1/7   Bill of 1791 amendment Act
ADA11/A/A/1/8   Bundle containing incorporation and disincorporation papers
ADA11/A/A/1/9   Resolutions and minutes of owners and occupiers, 1824–26
ADA11/A/A/1/10   Minutes of General Meeting, 1825
ADA11/A/A/1/11   Notice of application to repeal Incorporation
ADA11/A/A/1/12   Draft petition for disincorporation
ADA11/A/A/1/13   Copy of the petition to the Commons for disincorporation
ADA11/A/A/1/14   Resolutions of select committee, 1825
ADA11/A/A/1/15   Resolutions of select committee, 1825
ADA11/A/A/1/16   Papers relating to the disincorporation
ADA11/A/A/1/17   Bill for disincorporation and related papers
ADA11/A/A/1/18   Bundles of papers linked to reasons for disincorporation
ADA11/A/A/1/19   Papers relating to disincorporation
ADA11/A/A/1/20   Papers relating to disincorporation
ADA11/A/A/1/21   Act of disincorporation
ADA11/A/A/1/22   Minutes of Trustees' meetings
ADA11/A/A/1/23   Papers linked to disposal of Melton House
ADA11/A/A/1/24   Abstract of title to lands in Melton and Ufford
ADA11/A/A/1/25   Copy of conveyance of Melton House from Trustees
ADA11/A/A/1/26   Drafts of release from Churchwardens to the Trustees
ADA11/A/A/1/27   Release of Churchwardens to the Trustees
ADA11/A/A/1/28   Release to Trustees
ADA11/A/A/1/29   Accounts of the Trustees
ADA11/A/A/1/30   Accounts relating to the Act of Disincorporation
ADA11/A/A/1/31   Account Book of Messrs Wood and Son, Treasurers

ADA11/A/A/1/32   Schedule of Books and Papers held, 1827
ADA11/A/A/1/33   Papers associated with various Acts of Incorporation
ADA11/A/A/2/1   Rules and Orders, various dates
ADA11/A/A/2/2   List of Guardians, 1807–26
ADA11/A/B/1/1   Quarterly Meeting Minutes, 1765–84
ADA11/A/B/1/2   Quarterly Meeting Minutes, 1784–91
ADA11/A/B/1/3   Quarterly Meeting Minutes, 1795–1805
ADA11/A/B/1/4   Quarterly Meeting Minutes, 1805–12
ADA11/A/B/1/5   Quarterly Meeting Minutes, 1813–18
ADA11/A/B/1/6   Quarterly Meeting Minutes, 1818–20
ADA11/A/B/1/7   Quarterly Meeting Minutes, 1820–26
ADA11/A/B/2/1   Draft Quarterly Meeting Minutes, 1765
ADA11/A/B/2/2   Draft Quarterly Meeting Minutes, 1768–69
ADA11/A/B/2/3   Draft Quarterly Meeting Minutes, 1769–75
ADA11/A/B/2/4   Draft Quarterly Meeting Minutes, 1776–85
ADA11/A/B/2/5   Draft Quarterly Meeting Minutes, 1785–95
ADA11/A/B/3/1   Weekly Meeting Minutes, 1768–74
ADA11/A/B/3/2   Weekly Meeting Minutes, 1774–80
ADA11/A/B/3/3   Weekly Meeting Minutes, 1780–90
ADA11/A/B/3/4   Weekly Meeting Minutes, 1790–98
ADA11/A/B/3/5   Weekly Meeting Minutes, 1798–1804
ADA11/A/B/3/6   Weekly Meeting Minutes, 1804–12
ADA11/A/B/3/7   Weekly Meeting Minutes, 1812–17
ADA11/A/B/3/8   Weekly Meeting Minutes, 1817–20
ADA11/A/B/3/9   Weekly Meeting Minutes, 1820–24
ADA11/A/B/3/10   Weekly Meeting Minutes, 1824–26
ADA11/A/C/1/1   Treasurer's Accounts, 1781–91
ADA11/A/C/1/2   Treasurer's Accounts, 1792–1802
ADA11/A/C/1/3   Treasurer's Accounts, 1803–16
ADA11/A/C/1/4   Treasurer's Accounts, 1817–20
ADA11/A/C/3/1   Extracts from Treasurer's Accounts, 1800–10
ADA11/A/C/6/1   Proportions of Debt and Interest among the constituent parishes
ADA11/A/C/7/1   Clerk's accounts with Directors and Guardians, 1791
ADA11/A/C/7/2   Clerk's accounts with Directors and Guardians, 1796
ADA11/A/G/1/1   Draft account of out allowances, 1795
ADA11/A/G/2/1   Out Relief, 1810–20
ADA11/A/G/2/2   Out Relief, 1820–26
ADA11/A/H/1/1   Bundles of papers and vouchers for supplies to House, 1766–89
ADA11/A/K/1/1   Register of Loan Agreements, 1774–90
ADA11/A/K/2/1   Register of Securities, 1791–1801
ADA11/A/L/1/1   Register of Apprentices, 1811–20
ADA11/A/L/1/2   Register of Apprentice, 1820–26
ADA11/A/P/1/1   Register of Bastardy Orders, 1758–1826
ADA11/A/Q/1/1   Miscellaneous correspondence, 1775–1810
ADA11/A/Q/2/1   Bundles of miscellaneous papers, 1766–1826
ADA11/A/Q/2/1/1   Extracts from Treasurer's Accounts, 1780–1826
ADA11/A/Q/2/1/2   Schedule of Title deeds relating to Melton House
ADA11/A/Q/2/1/3   Orders for removal of paupers to parishes, 1826
ADA11/A/Q/2/1/4   Bond to perform articles of agreement, 1766
ADA11/A/Q/2/1/5   Memorial from Directors, 1782

ADA11/A/Q/2/1/6   Correspondence over assessment disputes, 1810–11
ADA11/A/Q/2/1/7   Report of Committee of 1791
ADA11/B/1/1   Treasurer's Account Book, 1766–92
ADA11/B/1/2   Treasurer's Account Book, 1811–20
ADA11/C/B/1/1   Admissions and discharges, 1768–80
ADA11/C/B/1/2   Account Book of Admissions and discharges, 1781–91
ADA11/C/B/1/3   Account Book of Admissions and discharges, 1790–1820
ADA11/C/B/3/1   Quarterly Account of Admissions and discharges, 1780–86
ADA11/C/B/5/1   Register of Baptisms and Burials, 1768–95
ADA11/C/B/5/2   Register of Baptisms and Burials, 1796–1826
ADA11/C/D/1/1   Accounts of Rope Manufactory, 1817–26
ADA11/C/D/3/1   Bills and vouchers for 1795 and 1806

ID407 St Audry's Hospital
ID407/D/1   Isaac Johnson's draft plan of Melton House and grounds, September 1825
ID407/D/3   Plans of St Audry's Hospital, April 1879
ID407/D/18   Isaac Johnson's finished plan of Melton House and grounds, September 1825

PRINTED WORKS

Blatchly, J., *Isaac Johnson of Woodbridge: Georgian Surveyor and Artist* (Dorchester, 2014)

Boyer, G., *An Economic History of the English Poor Law, 1750–1850* (Cambridge, 1990)

Brundage, A., *The Making of the New Poor Law 1832–39* (London, 1978)

Charlesworth, L., *Welfare's Forgotten Past: A Socio-Legal History of the Poor Law* (London, 2010)

Clarke, G., *The History and Description of Ipswich* (London, 1830)

Cowherd, R., *Political Economists and the English Poor Laws* (Athens, 1977)

Crabbe, G., *The Life and Poetical Works of the Rev George Crabbe by his Son* (London, 1866)

Digby, A., *Pauper Palaces* (London, 1978)

Eden, F. M., *The State of the Poor* (London, 1797)

Fearn, H., 'The Apprenticing of Pauper Children in the Incorporated Hundreds of Suffolk', *PSIA*, 26 (1953), pp. 85–97

Fearn, H., 'The Financing of the Poor Law Incorporation for the Hundreds of Colneis and Carlford in the County of Suffolk, 1758–1820', *PSIA*, 27 (1956), pp. 96–111

Fiske, J., *The Oakes Diaries: Business, Politics and the Family in Bury St Edmunds, 1778–1827*, Suffolk Records Society Volumes 32 and 33 (Woodbridge, 1990–91)

Healey, J., *The First Century of Welfare* (Woodbridge, 2014)

Himmelfarb, G., *The Idea of Poverty: England in the Early Industrial Age* (London, 1984)

Hoppit, J., *Britain's Political Economies: Parliament and Economic Life, 1660–1800* (Cambridge, 2017)

Kidd, J., 'Historians or Polemicists? How the Webbs wrote their History of the English Poor Laws', *Economic History Review*, XL (1987), pp. 400–17

King, S., *Poverty and Welfare in England 1700–1850: A Regional Perspective* (Manchester, 2000)

King, S., and Tomkins, A., *The Poor in England 1700–1850: An Economy of Make-shifts* (Manchester, 2003)

Lees, L., *The Solidarities of Strangers: The English Poor Laws and the People, 1700–1948* (Cambridge, 1998)

Lloyd-Prichard, M., 'Early Days of the Wangford Hundred Workhouse', *PSIA*, 30 (1965), pp. 351–65

Marshall, D., *The English Poor Law in the Eighteenth Century* (London, reprinted 1969)

Marshall, J., *The Old Poor Law 1795–1834* (London, 1968)

Muskett, P., 'A Picturesque Little Rebellion? The Suffolk Workhouses in 1765', *Bulletin for the Society for the Study of Labour History* (1980), pp. 28–30

Muskett, P., *Riotous Assemblies: Popular Disturbances in East Anglia, 1740–1822* (Ely, 1984)

Poynter, J., *Society and Pauperism* (London, 1968)

Ruggles, T., *The History of the Poor Laws* (London, 1793–94)

Shaw, J., 'The Financing and Construction of the East Anglian Houses of Industry', *PSIAH*, 37 (1992), pp. 351–65

Snell, K., *Annals of the Labouring Poor: Social Change and Agrarian England 1660–1900* (Cambridge, 1985)

Snell, K., *Parish and Belonging: Community, Identity and Welfare in England and Wales 1700–1950* (Cambridge, 2006)

Stone, L., *The Past and Present Revisited* (London, 1987)

Thompson, S., 'Population Growth and Corporations of the Poor, 1660–1841', in Briggs, C. (ed.), *Population, Welfare and Economic Change in Britain 1290–1834* (Woodbridge, 2014), pp. 227–48

Tomkins, A., *The Experience of Urban Poverty: Parish, Charity and Credit* (Manchester, 2006)

Twisleton, E., *Report on Local Acts*, Ninth Annual Report of the Poor Law Commissioners (London, 1843)

Webb, S. and B., *Statutory Authorities for Special Purposes* (London, 1922)

Webb, S. and B., *English Poor Law History: Part 1 The Old Poor Law* (London, 1927)

Young, A., *General View of the Agriculture of Suffolk* (London, 1804)

UNPUBLISHED WORKS

Hitchcock, T., 'The English Workhouse: A Study in Institutional Poor Relief, 1696–1750', unpublished D.Phil., University of Oxford, 1985

Shaw, J., 'The Development of the Local Poor Law Acts 1696–1833, with particular reference to the Incorporated Hundreds of East Anglia', unpublished PhD thesis, University of East Anglia, 1989

INDEX OF PEOPLE AND PLACES

All places are in Suffolk unless otherwise shown in brackets. Place names have been given in their modern form. Page references for the Incorporation's parishes do not reference out-relief. Individuals offered relief in the following quarterly or weekly relief lists have not been indexed: pp. 243–8, 308–19, 327–39, 344–54, 362–72, and 387–401.

INDEX OF SUBJECTS

THE SUFFOLK RECORDS SOCIETY

For over sixty years, the Suffolk Records Society has added to the knowledge of Suffolk's history by issuing an annual volume of previously unpublished manuscripts, each throwing light on some new aspect of the history of the county.

Covering 700 years and embracing letters, diaries, maps, accounts and other archives, many of them previously little known or neglected, these books have together made a major contribution to historical studies.

At the heart of this achievement lie the Society's members, all of whom share a passion for Suffolk and its history and whose support, subscriptions and donations make possible the opening up of the landscape of historical research in the area.

In exchange for this tangible support, members receive a new volume each year at a considerable saving on the retail price at which the books are then offered for sale. Members are also welcomed to the launch of the new volume, held each year in a different and appropriate setting within the county and giving them a chance to meet and listen to some of the leading historians in their fields talking about their latest work.

For anyone with a love of history, a desire to build a library on Suffolk themes at modest cost and a wish to see historical research continue to thrive and bring new sources to the public eye in decades to come, a subscription to the Suffolk Records Society is the ideal way to make a contribution and join the company of those who give Suffolk history a future.

THE CHARTERS SERIES

To supplement the annual volumes and serve the need of medieval historians, the Charters Series was launched in 1979 with the challenge of publishing the transcribed texts of all the surviving monastic charters for the county. Since then, twenty volumes have been published as an occasional series, the latest in 2018.

The Charter Series is financed by a separate annual subscription leading to receipt of each volume on publication.

CURRENT PROJECTS

Volumes approved by the Council of the Society for future publication include *The Crown Pleas of the Suffolk Eyre of 1240,* edited by Eric Gallagher, *The Woodbridge Troop of the Suffolk Yeomanry, 1794–1818,* edited by Margaret Thomas, *Monks Eleigh Manorial Documents,* edited by Vivienne Aldous, and *The Records of Medieval Newmarket,* edited by James Davis and Joanne Sear; and in the Charters Series, *The Charters of the Priory of St Peter and St Paul, Ipswich,* the second of two volumes edited by David Allen, *Bury St Edmunds Town Charters,* edited by Vivien Brown, and *Rumburgh Priory Charters,* edited by Nicholas Karn. The order in which these and other volumes appear in print will depend on the dates of completion of editorial work.

MEMBERSHIP

Membership enquiries should be addressed to Mrs Tanya Christian, 8 Orchid Way, Needham Market, IP6 8JQ; e-mail: membership@suffolkrecordssociety.com.

The Suffolk Records Society is a registered charity, No. 1084279.